Goldmine

price guide to alternative records

Tim Neely

Published by

**krause
publications**

700 E. State Street • Iola, WI 54990-0001
Telephone: 715/445-2214

Please call or write for our free catalog of music publications. Our toll-free number to place
an order or obtain a free catalog is 800-258-0929 or please use our regular business telephone
715-445-2214 for editorial comment and further information.

Library of Congress Catalog Number: 96-76694
ISBN: 0-87341-463-2
Printed in the United States of America

Table of Contents

On the Cover...
The three sleeves on the front cover reflect the mainstream, the fringe and the evolution of "alternative music." From left, the unusual gold, silver and bronze audiophile pressing of *Synchronicity* by The Police; the U.S. picture sleeve for the Sex Pistols' only stateside 45, "Pretty Vacant"; the LP cover for Liz Phair's *Exile in Guyville*. All three are from the author's collection.

Acknowledgments

A book like this is never the work of one person, although only one person's name is on the cover. I'd like to thank all those who helped with discographies, pricing and encouragement as the process went along. Fortunately, I heard from more people who said "It's about time!" than those who said "Why are you doing this?" So, in alphabetical order, thank you:

Mark Akiyama, Panama City Beach, Fla.
John Beasley, Augusta, Mich.
Steve Bertram, Peekskill, N.Y.
Sean Brady, Eltham, London, England
Rupert Burton, Greensboro, N.C.
Ron DePeter, Tallahassee, Fla.
Jim Gibson, Croton Falls, N.Y.
John Hagelston, Rhino Records,
    Los Angeles, Calif.
Ethan Hennessey, Portland, Ore.
Greg Langston, Kensington, Calif.
Heather Mann, Larchmont, N.Y.
Anthony Musiala, Minty Fresh Records,
    Chicago, Ill.
Steven Rovner, Springfield, N.J.
Anthony Rubbo, Kennesaw, Ga.
Mike "Metal Mike" Saunders,
    Hayward, Calif.

SST Records, Lawndale, Calif.
Chelsea Starr, Bomp! Records,
    Burbank, Calif.
Malcolm Tent, TPOS Productions,
    Danbury, Conn.
Karen Thomas, Mobile Fidelity Sound
Labs, Sebastopol, Calif.
Tom Timony, T.E.C. Tones,
    Hoboken, N.J.
Dan Trager, Sub Pop Records,
    Seattle, Wash.
Vinyl Vendors, Los Angeles, Calif.
Billy Visconti, Huntsville, Ala.
Brian Ware, Oviedo, Fla.
Greg Werckman, Alternative Tentacles
    Records, San Francisco, Calif.
Robbie White, Wheaton, Md.
Clive Young, New York, N.Y.

Also, I'd like to thank:
Greg Loescher, publisher of *Goldmine,* for his guidance and help;
Jeff Tamarkin, former editor of *Goldmine,* for his enthusiasm when the idea for an alternative price guide first came up at a brainstorming meeting in September 1995;
Bonni Miller, *Goldmine* managing editor;
Pat Klug, head of the Krause Publications book department, for understanding the merits of the project;
Ross Hubbard and Kara Gunderson, KP's photographers, for a job well done on the illustrations;
Phil LaFranka of the KP art department for his cover;
various staff members of WSND-AM 640 (now known as WVFI), the campus radio station at the University of Notre Dame, who first interested me in some of the music now considered "alternative" in my days as a DJ there (1981-82);
and finally, to all the radio stations that routinely talk over the beginnings and endings of songs. Had not a Philadelphia station done that in 1973, I might have never started collecting records; I might still be taping songs off the radio.
Last but far from least, I want to thank my sisters, Sue, Mary, Eileen and Nancy, for putting up with my collecting for many years; my brother Chris (1963-1985), who had to share a bedroom with both me and my ever-expanding collection in the 1970s; and my parents, William and Judith Neely, for everything. I love you all.

Foreword

by Greg Loescher, *Goldmine* Publisher

Over the past five years, we at Goldmine have noticed the collectible music market-place increasingly expand its scope to include more modern artists. While collectible recordings for hobby stalwarts such as the Beatles, Elvis, the Beach Boys, Kiss, Prince, David Bowie, Frank Sinatra, the Rolling Stones and other collecting icons continue to command high prices, prices for recordings of many bands of the past 20 years have climbed very fast.

One example has been the meteoric rise in collecting circles of Tori Amos, whose recording output is still very small --and very recent. In general, prices for collectibles and antiques tend to rise over a long period of time, many decades in most cases. People "relive" their youth 20 or 30 years after it by picking up things they used to have as a youngster, usually at prices many times the original retail price. Going back to the Tori Amos reference, her material was selling at the $100 range in *Goldmine* ads short-ly after its release. Are today's young people reliving their youths at a quicker pace than previous generations? Or has record collecting become yet another area that "in-vestors" have entered into for quick gains? Only time will tell.

The material in this book has basically *not* been included in previous hobby price guides, whether they be published by *Goldmine* or other publishers. Long-time collec-tors (which include those who compiled earlier record price guides) and dealers tend to focus on the "Golden Age" of popular music collecting: the '50s and '60s. Over the past decade, there have been many new collectors entering the hobby; collectors who did not grow up during those early years of rock 'n' roll. These collectors, which ob-viously include those of you who purchased this book, may have an interest in music from those "roots" eras, but their passion is for the music they grew up with -- collect-ible recordings from the past 20 years.

This is *Goldmine*'s first attempt at documenting the rapidly collectible area of newer music. We have had many requests to publish a price guide for this era of music. As with all new price guides, as Tim Neely, our new *Goldmine* book editor points out in the subsequent pages, there will undoubtedly be prices that collectors and dealers dis-agree on, listings that may be lacking in completeness, or recording artists that should either be included or excluded.

As a publisher, I ask that you be kind to our author. I know what goes into the accu-mulation of data and the production of these price guides. Tim has put in an incredible number of hours compiling the data and made plenty of phone calls to gather as much information as possible. I also know that he struggles inside hoping that all who pur-chase this book are happy with it. The fact that we have identified over 12,000 records by nearly 1,000 artists to place in this book in its first edition is a monumental feat.

The book provides collectors and the hobby *for the first time* pricing and checklists for recordings of the artists you grew up with and collect. We hope you do take time to let us know how we can improve on this edition, as there will definitely be a second edition somewhere down the turnpike. Until then, enjoy and use this book to help you in your collecting and researching efforts.

Greg Loescher
Publisher
June 26, 1996

Introduction:

Why We Need This Book

This book ventures into mostly uncharted waters.

Plenty of guides exist to help you decide which records of the past 20 years, broadly defined as "alternative," are worth buying, based on their musical merits. From *The Trouser Press Record Guide* to the *Spin Alternative Record Guide,* references like that have been around for over 15 years.

But except for volumes limited to one artist, this is the first book that tries to tell you what those early punk singles and new wave albums might actually be worth monetarily, in the collector's market.

Before we go any further, a reminder: **This book is only a guide.** It will give you an indication of what these records can be worth to the right buyer. But to take the values here as gospel would be wrong. The nature of publishing is such that some of the values may already be outdated by the time you read this. So consider that in any transactions.

Why an Alternative Price Guide?

When I began this project, I got mixed feedback. One dealer even tried to discourage me from continuing.

Why, you might ask. Two reasons, both of which this book should help cure: Ignorance and volatility.

The average person on the street has probably heard by now about certain Elvis (Presley, not Costello) records and the Beatles' infamous "butcher cover" as hot collectibles. But they may not know about "Cough Cool," the first single by the Misfits; "Baltimore," the first 45 by an unknown singer named Ellen Amos (later to change her name to Tori Amos); or the picture sleeve to "House We Used to Live In" by the Smithereens, which accompanied a never-released 45 and never actually was used on any promos of the 45. All of these fetch hundreds of dollars in the alternative market (assuming you could find one; these are rarely, if ever, offered for sale).

Many people assume that a record that's only a few years old can't be worth much. Most of the time, that's true. But not always. This book should help people know the difference so they don't get taken.

Also, the alternative market in the past has been notoriously volatile. As bands' popularity ebbs and flows; as certain styles and sounds gain or lose favor; so goes the alternative market. At one point, anything with the Sub Pop label was highly collectible; now, only those bands that became prominent (Nirvana, Mudhoney, Soundgarden, etc.) and many early Singles Club 45s have risen in value, while the rest have either leveled off or plummeted. Actually having a readily available book on current (or at least 1995-96) prices for alternative records should help end the yo-yo syndrome.

So, based on the positive reaction I've received from most collectors and dealers, this is a sorely-needed volume. Because most previous price guide compilers seem to lose interest in music about the time the Beatles broke up, they can't possibly imagine how a band or performer from the 1970s, 1980s or 1990s might actually have records that fetch well over $100! And because of that, they assume that most 1970s, 1980s and 1990s music is worthless.

But no music is worthless. (Well, Michael Bolton's ridiculous version of "When a Man Loves a Woman" might be, but that's merely my opinion, and it's not in here, anyway.) True, there are many more inexpensive records from recent years than from the 1950s and 1960s. But in time, that will change. As groups such as Depeche Mode and Erasure, to name two examples, become more sought-after, collectors will discover just how difficult it is to find some of their early American singles, especially stock copies, in any condition, much less Mint or Near Mint!

In general, people collect the music they grow up with. Today's music fans in their teens, 20s and 30s didn't listen to doo-wop, rockabilly, British Invasion or garage/psychedelic (unless they had access to oldies radio, and even then, most of the highly collectible genres except Motown get scant airplay at best). And as more people in younger age groups get more disposable income, they are going to try to find the music they liked as kids.

Who's In Here?

Using the word "alternative" rather than, say, "punk" or "new wave" or even "modern rock," in the title allows a lot of latitude as to who we've included.

This, of course, has led to some grousing. Some of the contributors to the book, and some who were asked to but didn't, want to define "alternative" very narrowly -- basically, to encompass only those performers who never recorded for a major label, or never sold a lot of records, or never got any airplay to speak of. If I defined it that narrowly, you'd have a high percentage of valuable records, but a very skinny book. And the average collector probably wouldn't have a prayer of finding the listed records.

I started talking to one potential contributor about such performers as INXS, Madonna and Split Enz, all of whom you'll find listed in here, and he said, "I don't consider them alternative." Plenty of other people probably don't, either. But certainly, at the time they broke here, they were definitely different than what was played on the radio and what sold in most record stores. That comes as close as anything else to defining "alternative" to me.

I'm less interested in how popular someone became; I'm more interested in where they began. The Hooters, for example, became very mainstream rockers, but in their pre-Columbian days, they were a white-boy ska band heavily influenced by the 2-Tone scene. Even Hootie and the Blowfish, the band alterna-rockers seem to love to hate, took six months to break big after their first major-label album came out; before they began to sell gazillions of CDs, their music was common on "modern rock" radio. And then there's U2 and R.E.M.; to omit them because they're popular and on major labels would be a joke.

Obviously, not every artist of the past 20 or so years qualifies as "alternative." Certainly, I've included some that you might not define as outside the mainstream. Also, I probably have omitted some who belong. That's what second editions are for. I doubt I'd delete listings from one edition to the next, unless I've inadvertently included a record or sleeve that doesn't really exist, but I certainly can add things.

When I was in doubt, I consulted other books and my contributors, some of whom made convincing arguments in favor of certain acts. However, while the previously mentioned *Spin* guide was a help, I couldn't in good conscience consider Kiss, AC/DC, Abba, Black Sabbath, Cheap Trick and most disco music "alternative." So you won't find them here. (All those performers will be in my *Goldmine Price Guide to 45 RPM Records,* available at fine bookstores everywhere.) Nor could I include alternative "heroes" such as Johnny Cash and Tony Bennett. I did make an exception for Neil Young, though. He did, after all, record with Pearl Jam.

So who is in here? Probably everyone you'd expect, from indie-label titans such as the Misfits, Fugazi and Minor Threat to the ultra-popular MTV stars such as Duran Duran, Eurythmics and Culture Club. And there are plenty that you wouldn't expect, too.

For by using the term "alternative," I could go beyond what a so-called "modern rock" station might play.

You'll find most of the significant early rappers and hip-hoppers in here, plus many of the more interesting and inventive current ones. The May 24, 1996 issue of *Goldmine* contained a brief history of rap and hip-hop with six artists pictured on the cover. All six of them are in here -- Public Enemy, Salt-N-Pepa, Beastie Boys, Grandmaster Flash, Run-D.M.C. and L.L. Cool J. (Research is still ongoing in hip-hop, however; feel free to help with incomplete or missing listings if that's a specialty of yours.)

Also in here are some country performers, all of whom, despite having the occasional hit (and even Number One hits) on the *Billboard* country chart, remain decidedly outside the mainstream.

We also have listed some performers who are utterly unclassifiable; I'll let you try if you dare.

Finally, we've opted to include some early influences. These are artists who released records before the mid-1970s, yet played a significant role in what transpired during the early (and later) years of alternative music. Examples include the Velvet Underground, Frank Zappa, David Bowie, Brian Eno, Roxy Music and The Searchers. (The Searchers? Yes, the "Needles and Pin-za" guys recorded two wonderful new-wavish albums in the early 1980s that got rave reviews and college radio airplay, but, alas, didn't sell a lick. So we've chosen to include their entire American catalog. Listen to the Searchers, and you can hear the roots of 1980s jangly guitar rock.)

Who's *Not* In Here?

Obviously, Michael Bolton isn't. Nor are Whitney Houston, Celine Dion, Barry Manilow, Boyz II Men ... well, you probably figured they wouldn't be in an alternative record price guide anyway, right?

But we've also not included some truly "alternative" performers. As the size of the book began to increase, we had to make some decisions as to whom to include. In general, we looked at collectibility and popularity in judging who to include. So some fringe bands that only seasoned collectors have heard of are not here, especially if their records don't seem to command a premium in the collector's market. Nonetheless, you'll probably find some glaring omissions.

We also, for now, excluded a lot of current bands that have yet to show either commercial or artistic staying power. When the second edition comes along, we'll take another look at those we left out and consider adding them. Your help in the decision-making process, of course, will be appreciated.

What's In Here?

Basically, once we decided who to include, we compiled as complete a discography as possible for each artist. When applicable, you'll find a performer's 45s, EPs, 12-inch singles, and albums, both stock and promo (when applicable).

You'll also find picture sleeves listed separately for all 45s and 7-inch EPs. If a sleeve isn't listed, we are unaware of its existence, and in some cases where we're certain, we even stated outright that no sleeve exists on American pressings, even if other guides have listed them before. Two obvious examples are "Roxanne" by the Police and "Little Red Corvette" by Prince -- neither has a U.S. picture sleeve.

We also list any known variations -- in color of vinyl, in style of sleeve, in label design or color, in release number -- even if we know of no variation in value because of the difference.

With releases on independent labels, we list, where known, how many copies of a particular item were pressed. That should give you some indication of just how rare something is.

We have decided, in this first edition, to focus on **American releases on vinyl records.** Therefore, with a few exceptions, no imports or non-vinyl releases are documented.

Where Are the Imports?

Yes, we recognize that many non-U.S. pressings, especially those that never came out here, are highly sought after.

Some of them fetch very good money on the collector's market. As examples, just try to find any early Sex Pistols 45 on British A&M or EMI or any other label that canned them, or Elvis Costello's "I Can't Stand Up for Falling Down" on 2-Tone, which was withdrawn before release (but some got out anyway; former *Goldmine* editor Jeff Tamarkin got his copy for *free* at an Elvis show in New York in 1980).

And some bands didn't even get released here before breaking up. To collect the Soft Boys or Crass, you have to collect British imports, because their material wasn't issued here until much later (if at all). The same with Billy Idol's early band, Generation X; while Gen X's albums came out here on Chrysalis, their 45s evidently didn't.

Finally, in the 1990s, with the disappearance of vinyl as a mass-market item here in the States, many bands' only vinyl releases have been in Europe. Thus many of the "New Britpop" bands have no listings at all, or very few (Oasis has one listing, for the American 45 of "Wonderwall"). And more established acts will have long gaps in their discographies. The Cure, for example, went six years between U.S. vinyl LPs for *Mixed Up* (1990) and *Wild Mood Swings* (1996). And as of this writing, they haven't had a U.S. 45 since 1990.

Again, we recognize that many of these imports have strong demand from U.S. collectors. But we thought it was much more important at this time to document American releases before it became impossible to do. Even in the future, we will not document every foreign pressing. We may consider those of importance (those with no U.S. counterpart or are unusually rare) as worthy of inclusion. (Actually, a couple of them have snuck in here already -- no prizes for finding them, though.) But we will need the help of those of you who already have knowledge, or collections, of these vital imports.

And Where Are the CDs?

Later in the book, we discuss compact discs more -- what generally is collectible and what will be collectible, in our estimation. But once again, we felt it was more important to document vinyl releases.

Alternative music has never totally abandoned vinyl, especially independent labels. In fact, some of those labels, rather than discontinuing records, have discontinued releasing pre-recorded cassettes!

We recognize that CDs already are part of the collections of most alternative music buffs. But with only a handful of exceptions, they have no more value than what you might get for them from your local used CD dealer. Those exceptions are detailed in our brief rundown on compact discs.

Again, as interest warrants, we are not averse to including important non-vinyl (or out-of-print) CDs in future editions.

Selling Your Collection

You've got some records worth $100 or more that are listed in here? Good! Now try to get that for them.

Yes, you recognize the problem. Take your used records to a dealer, and you're likely to get only a fraction of the prices listed here. That is for several reasons.

One, this guide reflects what these records sell for in the collector's market. That implies that a dealer who specializes in alternative or recent music has offered, and usually received, these prices.

However, dealers, in order to remain dealers, have to make a profit, so they won't buy at these prices unless they need something for their own collections.

When it comes to selling your records to a dealer, at most you'll get 50 percent of book value, and more likely you'll get about 25 percent (what we list in here as the Very Good value) for a Near Mint record. If that sounds like a ripoff, well, consider the costs a dealer has to cover through sales: Rent, employees, shipping, postage, utilities, phone service (business lines cost more than residential lines), taxes, and many other sundry items, not to mention the costs of maintaining and obtaining inventory. With all that, you can see why a dealer can't buy at the same prices he or she sells!

To get prices close to what this book suggests, the best way is to sell directly to the consumer -- in essence, to become a dealer yourself, albeit temporarily. (Many dealers became dealers by starting with their own collections and finding they enjoyed the selling.)

The best way is to place an advertisement in *Goldmine* magazine. *Goldmine,* published every other week, is the world's largest marketplace for collectible music of all eras. The magazine has advertising salespeople who will help you in putting together your ad for maximum impact.

To see what *Goldmine* is about, pick up a copy. *Goldmine* magazine is available at Tower Records and a couple other major music chains; Barnes & Noble, Borders and other larger booksellers; and many independent music shops. If you still can't find a copy, call 1-800-258-0929.

Yes, there are other magazines that are "for record and CD collectors," but none has the circulation of *Goldmine* -- and when selling, you want the largest number of people to know you're selling!

Using This Book

Here's an edited sample of the listings for Husker Du, which we'll use to illustrate what it all means.

Husker Du
Highly influential Minneapolis indie-rock legends of the 1980s. Also see **Mould, Bob.**

Vinyl Albums

New Alliance 007		Land Speed Record	1982	6.25	12.50	25.00
New Alliance 007		Land Speed Record	1982	3.00	6.00	12.00

Second pressing, "Marketed by SST" on cover

Reflex #D		Everything Falls Apart	1982	10.00	20.00	40.00
SST 020	EP	Metal Circus	1983	2.00	4.00	8.00
SST 027	(2)	Zen Arcade	1984	3.75	7.50	15.00
SST PSST E27	DJ	Eight Miles High/6 from Zen Arcade	1984	7.50	15.00	30.00

Promo sampler, etched design on side 1, sticker cover

SST 031		New Day Rising	1985	2.50	5.00	10.00
SST 055		Flip Your Wig	1985	2.50	5.00	10.00
SST 195		Land Speed Record	198?	2.50	5.00	10.00

Reissue of New Alliance 007

SST 908	10	Metal Circus	199?	2.00	4.00	8.00
SST 915	10	Eight Miles High/Makes No Sense at All	199?	2.00	4.00	8.00
Warner Bros. WBMS-145	DJ	The Warehouse Interview	1987	6.25	12.50	25.00

Promo only, part of the Warner Bros. Music Show series

Warner Bros. PRO-A-2719DJ		Warehouse: Songs and Stories	1987	2.00	4.00	8.00

Promo-only four-song sampler

Warner Bros. 25385		Candy Apple Grey	1986	3.00	6.00	12.00
Warner Bros. 25544	(2)	Warehouse: Songs and Stories	1987	3.00	6.00	12.00

45s

New Alliance 010		In a Free Land/What Do I Want/M.I.C.	1982	7.50	15.00	30.00
New Alliance 010	PS	In a Free Land/What Do I Want/M.I.C.	1982	7.50	15.00	30.00

We underline the name of the artist.

On the next line, in italics, there is a brief introduction to the artist (what kind of music they play, where they are from, etc.) Any cross-references to solo members or other related artists are in **bold.**

We then list all the performer's known records, albums first, followed by seven-inch EPs, 45s, 12-inch singles and the occasional 10-inch single. In some cases, we guessed when to call a 12-inch record an EP or a single. If it had more than one version of the same song, or the same song on both sides, it usually was called a 12-inch single. If it had multiple songs, with none really sticking out as a track to emphasize, then we called it an EP. Of course, there are exceptions.

Within the types of records, they are listed in alphabetical order by label, then in numerical order within each label. (In general, alphabetical prefixes are ignored for sorting purposes.) This, we hope, is less confusing to the neophyte collector than listing all the records chronologically. Listing records in the order of release is fine for a straight discography, but for a collector's guide, we think listing them alphabetically will make it easier to use.

You'll notice that for some entries, there are some symbols in the column to the left of the title. These are as follows:

DJ	any promotional record (whether meant for disc jockeys or not)
EP	extended play (for listings under vinyl albums)
M	mono (for records released in both mono and stereo)
PD	picture disc
PS	picture sleeve (for 45s and 7-inch EPs)
Q	quadraphonic
S	stereo (for records released in both mono and stereo)
10	10-inch records (for listings under vinyl albums)
(x)	where x is a number: the number of records that comes with that set

Where we know, we list the year of release to the right of the title. We need help replacing the "?" indicators with numbers (hint, hint).

Then we list values in three grades: Very Good, Very Good Plus, and Near Mint. In almost all cases, these follow a 1:2:4 ratio. In other words, the VG price is half of the VG+ price, which is half of the NM price. This is generally the way we notice prices set among the nation's used record dealers. There are exceptions on occasion.

If no value is listed in either the VG or VG+ column, that means in that grade it is valued under $2.

If no value is listed in any of the three grades, we have reason to suspect the record doesn't exist. Or, with singles of the 1990s, we replace a value with the designation "Cassette only" or "May be cassette-only." Cassette singles have yet to show any value in the collector's market, with only the most exceptional exception. Any information to help us discern the existence of these "blank-value" records will be appreciated.

When necessary, a line of italic type will appear under some listings. These further define the record. These notes will mention such things as colored vinyl, different label credits, reissue information, the occasional non-American release, and the like.

Finally, in a work of this size, we will make mistakes. Feel free to point them out, and point out anything we may have missed. See the section "How You Can Help" for more information.

How Values Are Determined

The values listed in here are not the work of one person. Numerous dealers, catalogs and advertisements were surveyed to determine the prices we list for the records in this book.

Even more true in alternative collecting than in other genres is the regional variations in values for certain artists. And you can't explain all of it away by citing the different costs of living in different cities.

Two examples:

Records by the Minneapolis performers in here (other than Prince, who has almost always recorded for a major label) tend to fetch significantly more in the Twin Cities area than elsewhere, especially the early ones.

In the Philadelphia area, records by The A's, a pop group from the late 1970s to early 1980s, tend to go for double or even triple what is listed in here. In other parts of the country, their records are often in the bargain bins.

And also, because of the largely undocumented (until now) nature of alternative record collecting, sometimes the same record has been listed at widely different prices even by dealers with national markets. Several of these are noted in the text; in those cases, rather than throwing out the high and the low, we took an average.

In general, regardless what this book says, a record is "worth" what an eager buyer will pay a willing seller. Or is that what a willing buyer will pay an eager seller? Well, you get the idea.

Worthless 45s?

As we began to compile prices, we found a habit that is definitely peculiar to alternative collectors and one I don't think we completely solved in this book.

Certain collectors, especially those of indie-label 45s, have to have the entire package. To these people, if the picture sleeve is missing from a record, the record is worthless, regardless of its musical merit or importance.

That position does have a certain logic to it. After all, that's the way most people treat LP purchases -- the cover has to be there (assuming it had one). And because most indie-label 45s had picture sleeves for their entire press run, if the sleeve is missing, part of the record is, too.

But at the same time, to put so much value on the picture sleeve devalues the music -- and after all, the music is what got us into record collecting in the first place, isn't it?

So in pricing indie records with picture sleeves, I could not in good conscience give that much value to the sleeve and denigrate the record. After all, if 1,000 copies of a 45 with sleeve were pressed, the record is just as rare as the sleeve! What we've done here is, in general, split the difference. Half of the value of these 45s go to the record, half to the sleeve.

(In keeping with *Goldmine* price guide tradition, we list the records and sleeves separately. That way, you know that if no sleeve is listed, it doesn't have one, or we don't yet know about it.)

Of course, there are many cases where a sleeve still is listed with a higher value than the record. Most of these are major label releases, or certain indie label items such as those by Pere Ubu on Hearthan Records, where it is known with a reasonable degree of certainty that more non-sleeved 45s than sleeved 45s exist for a title. Other examples include a record pressed on black vinyl after a colored-vinyl first pressing. Both have the same sleeve in most cases, so on average, the sleeve is worth more than the record on black vinyl but less than the record on colored vinyl.

Any further suggestions on this problem will be looked at carefully in future editions of this price guide.

Minimum Values

Finally, as of press time, at least a few hundred, and perhaps over 1,000, of the records contained in the book were still in print!

Because you can still walk into an independent record store and find these, theoretically they don't have a collector's value yet. But they will, and we wanted to put some sort of price next to these.

We've set some minimum Near Mint values for items, based on the selling price of current material. And if these values seem high, remember that these are for Near Mint, non-cut-outs, and you see items in that condition a lot less often than you might think.

$2 for 45s that came with picture sleeves;

$2 for picture sleeves that came with the above 45s;

$3 for 45s not issued with picture sleeves;

$5-$6 for 12-inch singles;

$8-$10 for LPs.

For more on what Near Mint is, see "Grading Your Records."

Grading Your Records

Basically, it's as true in collecting alternative records as it is with any other genre: **Condition is (almost) everything!**

If an item is unusually rare, it may be acceptable in any condition, as you might never see it again. But even with those items with a three- and four-figure value, the better condition a record (and sleeve), the more money it will fetch.

The grading system established by *Goldmine* magazine many years ago, with the occasional refinement, has become the most widely accepted in record collecting.

Visual or Play Grading?

In an ideal world, every record would be played before it is graded. But the time involved makes it impractical for most dealers, and anyway, it's rare that you get a chance to hear a record before you buy through the mail. Some advertisers play-grade everything and say so. But unless otherwise noted, records are visually graded.

How to Grade

Look at everything about a record -- its playing surface, its label, its edges -- under a strong light. Then, based on your overall impression, give it a grade based on the following criteria:

Mint (M): Absolutely perfect in every way -- certainly never played, possibly even still sealed. (More on still sealed under "Other considerations.") Should be used sparingly as a grade, if at all.

Near Mint (NM or M-): A nearly perfect record. Many dealers won't give a grade higher than this, implying (perhaps correctly) that no record is ever truly perfect.

The record should show no obvious signs of wear. A 45 RPM or EP sleeve should have no more than the most minor defects, such as almost invisible ring wear or other signs of slight handling.

An LP jacket should have no creases, folds, seam splits or any other noticeable similar defect. No cut-out holes, either. And of course, the same should be true of any other inserts, such as posters, lyric sleeves and the like.

Basically, an LP in Near Mint condition looks as if you just got it home from a new record store and removed the shrink wrap.

Near Mint is the highest price listed in this price guide. Anything that exceeds this, in the opinion of both buyer and seller, is worth significantly more than the highest value in here.

Very Good Plus (VG+): Generally worth 50 percent of the Near Mint value.

A Very Good Plus record will show some signs that it was played and otherwise handled by a previous owner who took good care of it.

Record surfaces may show some slight signs of wear and may have slight scuffs or very light scratches that don't affect one's listening experience. Slight warps that do not affect the sound are OK.

The label may have some ring wear or discoloration, but it should be barely noticeable. The center hole will not have been misshapen by repeated play.

Picture sleeves and LP inner sleeves will have some slight ring wear, lightly turned-up corners, or a slight seam split. An LP jacket may have slight signs of wear also and may be marred by a cut-out hole, indentation or corner indicating it was taken out of print and sold at a discount. (Jackets with cut-out markings can never be considered Mint or Near Mint!)

In general, if not for a couple minor things wrong with it, this would be Near Mint. All but the most mint-crazy collectors will find a Very Good Plus record highly acceptable.

Very Good (VG): Generally worth 25 percent of the Near Mint value.

Many of the defects found in a VG+ record will be more pronounced in a VG disc.

Surface noise will be evident upon playing, especially in soft passages and during a song's intro and fade, but will not overpower the music otherwise. Groove wear will start to be noticeable, as will light scratches (deep enough to feel with a fingernail) that will affect the sound.

Labels may be marred by writing, or have tape or stickers (or their residue) attached. The same will be true of picture sleeves or LP covers. However, it will not have all of these problems at the same time, only two or three of them.

Very Good is the lowest value we list in here. This, *not* the Near Mint price, should be your guide when determining how much a record is worth, as a dealer will rarely pay you more than 25 percent of its Near Mint value. (He/she has to make a profit, after all.)

Good (G), Good Plus (G+): Generally worth 10-15 percent of the Near Mint value.

Good does not mean Bad! A record in Good or Good Plus condition can be put onto a turntable and will play through without skipping. But it will have significant surface noise and scratches and visible groove wear (on a styrene record, the groove will be starting to turn white).

A jacket or sleeve will have seam splits, especially at the bottom or on the spine. Tape, writing, ring wear or other defects will start to overwhelm the object.

If it's a common item, you'll probably find another copy in better shape eventually. Pass it up. But if it's something you have been seeking for years, and the price is right, get it... but keep looking to upgrade.

Poor (P), Fair (F): Generally worth 0-5 percent of the Near Mint price.

The record is cracked, badly warped, and won't play through without skipping or repeating. The picture sleeve is water damaged, split on all three seams and heavily marred by wear and/or writing. The LP jacket barely keeps the LP inside it. Inner sleeves are fully seam split, crinkled, and written upon.

Except for impossibly rare records otherwise unattainable, records in this condition should be bought or sold for no more than a few cents each.

Other considerations

Most dealers give a separate grade to the record and its sleeve or cover. In an ad, a record's grade is listed first, followed by that of the sleeve or jacket, unless otherwise stated.

With **Still Sealed (SS)** records, let the buyer beware, unless it's a U.S. pressing from the last 10-15 years or so. It's too easy to re-seal one. Yes, some legitimately never-opened LPs from the 1960s still exist. But if you're looking for a specific pressing, the only way you can know for sure is to open the record. Also, European imports are not factory-sealed, so if you see them advertised as sealed, someone other than the manufacturer sealed them.

Bibliography

While this book is loaded with information never before put in one place, other previously published sources were vital in compiling it. They include:

Books

Clee, Ken. *The Directory of American 45 RPM Records.* 4 volumes. Philadelphia, Pa., Stack-O-Wax, 1985-95.

Cox, Perry, and Joe Lindsay. *Official Price Guide to The Beatles Records and Memorabilia, First Edition.* New York, House of Collectibles, 1995.

George, B. and Martha DeFoe, eds. *International Discography Of The New Wave, Volume 1982-83.* New York, One Ten Records/ Omnibus Press, 1982.

Heggeness, Fred. *Goldmine Promo Record & CD Price Guide.* Iola, Wis., Krause Publications, 1995.

Osborne, Jerry. *Rock & Roll Record Albums Price Guide, 5th Edition.* Phoenix, Ariz., O'Sullivan-Woodside, 1983.

Robbins, Ira, ed. *The Trouser Press Record Guide, 4th Edition.* New York, Collier, 1991.

Romanowski, Patricia, and Holly George-Warren, eds. *The New Rolling Stone Encyclopedia of Rock & Roll.* New York, Fireside Books, 1995.

Umphred, Neal. *Rock & Roll Record Albums Price Guide, 1985-86 Edition.* Phoenix, Ariz., O'Sullivan-Woodside, 1985.

Umphred, Neal. *Goldmine Rock 'n Roll 45 RPM Record Price Guide, 3rd Edition.* Iola, Wis., Krause Publications, 1994.

Umphred, Neal. *Goldmine Price Guide to Collectible Record Albums, Third Edition.* Iola, Wis., Krause Publications, 1993.

Umphred, Neal. *Goldmine Price Guide to Collectible Record Albums, Fourth Edition.* Iola, Wis., Krause Publications, 1994.

Uncle Willie. *Uncle Willie's Highly Opinionated Guide to The Residents.* San Francisco, Calif., The Cryptic Corporation/Ralp America, 1993.

Weisband, Eric, with Craig Marks, eds. *Spin Alternative Record Guide.* New York, Vintage, 1995.

Whitburn, Joel. *Pop Annual 1955-1994.* Menominee Falls, Wis., Record Research, Inc., 1995.

Whitburn, Joel. *Rock Tracks.* Menominee Falls, Wis., Record Research, Inc., 1995.

Whitburn, Joel. *Billboard Top Pop Singles 1955-1990.* Menominee Falls, Wis., Record Research, Inc., 1991.

Periodicals

Billboard, various issues, 1995-96.

CMJ New Music Report, various issues, 1995-96.

Discoveries, various issues, 1988-96.

Goldmine, various issues, 1980-96.

Pulse!, various issues, 1988-96.

Schwann Spectrum (published under various names over the years), various issues, 1981-96.

CD-ROMs

CD International World Reference Guide, Popular Music Edition. Milwaukie, Ore., CDI Publishing, 1995.

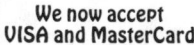

Most Valuable Alternative Records

As if to prove that, indeed, there can be some serious rarity and value in collecting (mostly) recent records, here are the 100 or so most valuable items (based on Near Mint value) listed in this book.

We cut it off at the 100th most valuable; since there was a multiple-way tie at $150, we included 113 entries.

Yes, many of these are early Velvet Underground and Frank Zappa/Mothers of Invention records. That reflects the strong demand for these discs among all collectors, not just alternative music collectors. And also you'll see Yoko Ono mentioned a few times. That is because of her collectibility among those who seek Beatles-related material, a group of collectors second only to Elvis fans in number and fanaticism.

Even without these anomalies, there are plenty of listings by punk, new wave and alternative artists. In fact, the most recent listing on here is from 1989!

In the below list, we do not discriminate between singles and albums. As opposed to the main text, however, we do combine the record and sleeve value of those indie-label singles released with both.

Most of the items listed below have explanations as to why they are worth so much, and how to tell them apart from regular issues when they are special.

These are arranged in decreasing order of value. Within each dollar amount, those with the same value are listed alphabetically by artist.

Remember, these are based on Near Mint values -- in other words, nearly perfect examples. Lesser grades will decrease the values significantly.

A couple notes: "45 PS" means only the picture sleeve; "45 w/PS" means both the record and the sleeve.

Artist	Title		Label, Number	Year

$5,000 (1)

Velvet Underground, The — All Tomorrow's Parties/ — 45 PS — Verve 10427 — 1966
I'll Be Your Mirror

Only one known copy, it sold for $4,000 Near Mint in 1992. The owner has turned down much higher offers to sell.

$4,000 (2)

Bowie, David — Diamond Dogs — LP — RCA Victor APL1-0576 — 1974

Original copies have cover with dog's genitals clearly visible. Almost all were destroyed prior to release. Normal copies, with the genitals airbrushed out, sell for $8-$20 Near Mint, depending on whether it's an original or reissue.

$3,000 (3)

Prince — The Black Album — LP (2) — Paisley Park 25677DJ — 1987

Entire album on two 12-inch records that play at 45 RPM. The value of this has gone down in the last year or so because of the legitimate release of the album and because Prince's collectibility has declined slightly.

$2,000 (4-6)

Ono, Yoko/John Lennon — Double Fantasy — LP — Nautilus NR-47 — 1982

Half-speed master; alternate experimental cover with yellow and red added to black and white front. Only one copy is known.

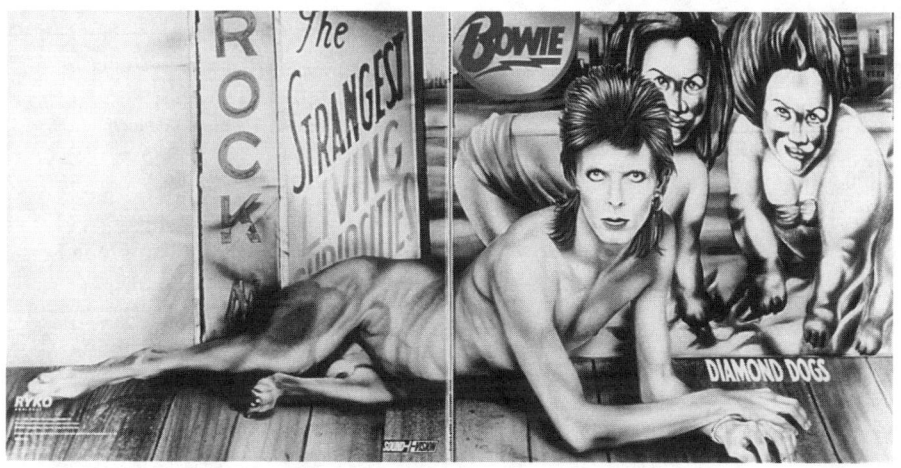

No, this isn't the No. 2 listing on our Most Valuable Alternative Records chart. But this Ryko reissue from 1990, worth about $20 in Near Mint condition, restored the original cover illustration to David Bowie's *Diamond Dogs.* Look closely to the left of the center bar and you'll see the "anatomical correctness" of the male Bowiedog. Almost all of the RCA releases have that area shaded so that the genitals are invisible. Those that aren't can easily fetch $4,000 in Near Mint condition!

Artist	Title		Label, Number	Year

Prince   The Black Album   LP   Paisley Park 25677   1987
Withdrawn prior to release, though a few copies escaped. Numerous counterfeits exist on other labels and colored vinyl. There are also promo vinyl versions from 1994, but they have different numbers and are worth nowhere near this price.

Shaggs, The   Philosophy of the World   LP   Third World 3001   1969
Legendary do-it-yourself album by three New Hampshire sisters; so bad it's good, but only 1,000 copies of the original were made.

$1,500 (7)

Residents, The   The Third Reich 'N' Roll LP   Ralph RR 1075   1976
Numbered box set on marbled vinyl, silk-screened cover and lithographs inside.

$1,000 (8-9)

Police, The   Ghost in the Machine   LP DJ   A&M SP-3730   1981
Special prototype picture disc that lights up when placed on a turntable. Truly bizarre.

Young, Neil   Ode to the Wind   LP DJ   Reprise MSK 2266   1978
Test pressing; plain white jacket with inserts. Title changed to "Comes A Time" for commercial release.

$800 (10)

Ono, Yoko   Greenfield Morning/   45 DJ   Apple GM/OYB-1   1971
                        Open Your Box
Exactly six copies were made for the personal use of Yoko Ono.

$750 (11-13)

Ono, Yoko   Give Peace a Chance/   45   Apple/Americom 1809P/M-435 1969
                        Remember Love
Four-inch flexi-disc designed to be sold in vending machines. Several other Apple titles exist, and all are extremely rare.

Yoakam, Dwight   Guitars, Cadillacs, Etc.   LP EP   Oak OR 2356   1984
The first indie-label release by this country star, it's almost impossible to find. Maybe 2,000 were sold.

Zappa, Frank   Lather   LP (4) DJ   Columbia (no #)   1977
Test pressing only, made during dispute with Warner Bros.; parts of this LP appear on three later albums -- Orchestral Favorites, Sleep Dirt and Studio Tan. With Rykodisc now owning the Zappa catalog, a legitimate release of this could happen someday.

$600 (14-15)

Bowie, David   Time/The Prettiest Star   45 PS   RCA Victor APBO-0001   1973
The record itself adds only about $4 more to the value.

Residents, The   Santa Dog: Fire/   45 w/PS   Ralph RR 1272   1972
                        Aircraft Damage;

                        Lightning/Explosion
The odd San Francisco-based group's first release, this was two 45s with a signed, intentionally misnumbered sleeve.

$565 (16)

Danzig, Glenn   Who Killed Marilyn?/   45 w/PS   Plan 9 PL 1015   1981
                        Spook City USA
Most of the value is in the record, made of black and purple swirl vinyl and only 25 of which were pressed.

$500 (17-24)

Amos, Ellen   Baltimore/   45   MEA 5290   1980
                        Walking with You
An early vanity project, this ode to her hometown was pressed in very small quantities. Ellen Amos changed her name to Tori Amos.

Bowie, David   Can't Stop Thinking   45   Warner Bros. 5815   1966
                      About Me/And I Say
                      to Myself
As "David Bowie and the Lower Third," this was his first single release in the U.S.

Artist	Title		Label, Number	Year
Fear	I Love Livin' in the City/ Now Your Dead	45 w/PS	Criminal Records (no #)	1978

Classic, and almost impossible to find, early punk single.

Minor Threat	Out of Step	LP DJ	Dischord 10	1983

Test pressing of 50; black silkscreen cover with sheep logo; paste-on back cover; blank labels; plain innersleeve with rubber stamp. Regular stock copies of this Washington, D.C. hardcore band's LP range from $20-$50 Near Mint.

Necros	Sex Drive/Police Brutality// Better Never Than Late/ Caste System	EP w/PS	Touch N Go 001	1981

The first release on prominent indie label Touch N Go.

Prince	Paisley Park/ She's Always In My Hair	45 PS	Paisley Park 29052	1985

Picture sleeve for a single that was never released, not even as a promo.

Smithereens, The	House We Used to Live In/Only a Memory	45 PS	Capitol/Enigma 44174	1988

Was supposed to accompany this single's commercial release (promos don't have picture sleeves); when that was canceled, a handful of the sleeves escaped. One is known in the hands of a collector; the Smithereens' archives hold another 75 to 100, and those aren't for sale at this time. Value is estimated and may be much lower or much higher, depending on whether any other copies got out or whether the band sells or distributes its stash. No sales have been documented.

Young, Neil	Decade	LP (3) DJ	Reprise 3RS 2257	1977

Test pressing; the song "Campaigner" contains an extra verse deleted from the final version.

$400 (25-28)

Bowie, David	Fashion/It's No Game/ Teenage Wildlife	45 DJ	RCA JE-12087	1980

Unusual 7-inch promo that was used as a sampler from the LP Scary Monsters.

Velvet Underground, The	All Tomorrow's Parties/ I'll Be Your Mirror	45	Verve 10427	1966

Stock copy of the seminal punk band's first single.

Zappa, Frank	Zappa in New York	LP (2) DJ	DiscReet 2D 2290	1978

Test pressing with "Punky's Whips," which was deleted from all regular promo and commercial copies.

Zappa, Frank	Freak Out!	LP (2) M	Verve V-5005-2	1966

White label promo.

$350 (29-30)

Misfits, The	Evilive	EP (3)	Plan 9 PL 1019	1982

33 sets of 3, each with individual sleeves of the three band members, available through the Fiend Club, the band's fan club.

Pagans, The	Six & Change/Six & Change	45 w/PS	Neck 002	1977

250 copies were made of this punk classic.

$300 (31-49)

Halo of Flies	Rubber Room/ Thoughts in a Booth/ 3 More Quarters	45 w/PS	Amphetamine Reptile (1)	1985

First single by this Minneapolis noise-punk group and the first on the highly collectible label Amphetamine Reptile.

Misfits, The	Cough Cool/She	45 w/PS	Blank 101	1977

Their first single, 500 copies were pressed. Thousands more exist on bootlegs.

Residents, The	Beyond the Valley of A Day in the Life/Flying	45 w/PS	Ralph RR 0577	1977

Also known as "The Residents Meet the Beatles and The Beatles Meet the Residents," it's sought after by both Beatles and Residents collectors, because it actually (illegally) samples Beatles music.

Residents, The	Satisfaction/Loser Is Congruent to Weed	45 w/PS	Ralph RR 0776	1976

The Residents take on the Stones' classic, and the Residents win.

Artist	Title		Label, Number	Year
Velvet Underground, The	Who Loves the Sun/Oh, Sweet Nothin'	45	Cotillion 44107	1971

Stock copies of this, the last single for the Velvets while they were together.

Velvet Underground, The	What Goes On/Jesus	45	MGM 14057	1969

This is for a stock copy, but no one in the know has ever seen one.

Velvet Underground, The	All Tomorrow's Parties/ I'll Be Your Mirror	45 DJ	Verve 10427	1966

Promo copy of the Velvets' classic debut single.

Velvet Underground, The	Femme Fatale/ Sunday Morning	45	Verve 10466	1966

Stock copy of this classic, covered often by alternative bands.

Velvet Underground, The	White Light/White Heat// I Heard Her Call My Name	45 DJ	Verve 10560	1967

Promo copies evidently have a different B-side than stock copies, which is why the promo and stock versions are worth the same.

Velvet Underground, The	White Light/White Heat// Here She Comes Now	45	Verve 10560	1967

Stock copies with a new B-side.

Velvet Underground, The	The Velvet Underground and Nico	LP M	Verve V-5008	1967

Version 1 of this all-time classic album has a peel-off banana peel and a photo of the band framed by a male torso. Most copies have some sort of damage to the banana; this price is for a cover with the sticker fully intact. (Deduct 50% if banana sticker is gone, less if parts of it are missing.)

Velvet Underground, The	The Velvet Underground and Nico	LP M	Verve V-5008	1967

Version 2 of this album is like Version 1, but the photo of the torso is obscured by a sticker. Again, this value is for copies with both stickers intact. (Deduct 50% if stickers have been removed, less if parts are missing.)

Velvet Underground, The	White Light/White Heat	LP M/DJ	Verve V-5046	1967

White label promo.

Vomit Pigs, The	Take One	EP w/PS	Bad Wrecors (# unknown)	1979

Dallas punk band's outrageously scarce four-song EP.

Young, Neil	Everyone Knows This Is Nowhere/ The Emperor of Wyoming	45 DJ	Reprise 0819	1969

This is the rare promo-only version with an alternate acoustic take of the A-side, unavailable anywhere else. Trail-off vinyl will not have the indicator "RE-1" in it.

Young, Neil	Southern Pacific/ Motor City	12	Reprise 49895	1982

Picture disc, triangle-shaped, the rarest of four variations of this unusual single release.

Zappa, Frank	Absolutely Free	LP M	Verve V-5013	1967

White label promo.

Zappa, Frank	We're Only In It for the Money	LP M	Verve V-5045	1968

White label promo.

Zappa, Frank	Freak Out!	LP (2) S	Verve V6-5005-2	1966

Yellow label promo.

$265 (50)

Mighty Joe Young	(There'll Be Other Girls) Hoss/Chump	45 w/PS	Powerhaus MJ 004	1989

Only 25 copies of this single came with picture sleeves. The record alone goes for about $15 Near Mint.

$260 (51)

Misfits, The	Horror Business/Teenagers from Mars/Children in Heat	45 w/PS	Plan 9 PL 1009	1979

Only 25 copies were pressed on black vinyl.

Artist	Title		Label, Number		Year

$250 (52-55)

Artist	Title		Label, Number		Year
Misfits, The	Bullet/We Are 138/ Attitude/Hollywood Babylon	45 w/PS	Plan 9 PL 1001		1978

Oddly, this is a reissue of this single. Exactly 2,000 were pressed on red vinyl with a new back cover that states "Better Dead in Red."

Velvet Underground, The	The Velvet Underground	LP DJ	MGM SE-4617		1969

Yellow label promo

Velvet Underground, The	White Light/White Heat	LP S/DJ	Verve V6-5046		1967

Yellow label promo

Zappa, Frank	Zappa in New York	LP (2)	DiscReet 2D 2290		1978

Stock copy with "Punky's Whips" erroneously listed on jacket. None of these actually play the missing song, however.

$240 (56)

Sonic Youth	Making the Nature Scene/ I Killed Christgau with My Big Fuckin' Dick	45 w/PS	Forced Exposure	001	1984

Special multi-color sleeve with live band shot on rear; only released with test pressings (25 made)

$225 (57)

Misfits, The	Bullet/We Are 138/ Attitude/Hollywood Babylon	45 w/PS	Plan 9 PL 1001		1978

8,000 on black vinyl with gatefold and lyric sheet

$200 (58-80)

Danzig, Glenn	Who Killed Marilyn?/ Spook City USA	45 w/PS	Plan 9 PL 1015		1981

Purple vinyl (500 made) version of solo single by ex-Misfits leader.

Gears, The	Let's Go to the Beach/ Hard Rock/ Don't Be Afraid to Pogo	45 w/PS	Four Speed (# unknown)		1979

Los Angeles band's classic (only?) single.

Halo of Flies	Snapping Back Roscoe Bottles: DDT Fin 13-PCP/ Can't Touch Her	45 w/PS	Amphetamine Reptile SCALE 2		1985

Their second single.

Injections, The	Prison Walls/Lies	45	Radio Active 04		1980

Not issued with picture sleeve. A legendary punk record.

Mudhoney	Touch Me I'm Sick/ Sweet Young Thing	45	Sub Pop 18		1988

Any of accidental purple, red, yellow or blueish vinyl pressings of this, their first single. This version was not issued with a picture sleeve. Black and brown vinyl versions are worth less.

Queers, The	Grow Up	LP	Shakin' Street 010		198?

Only 100-150 copies exist of a planned pressing of 500. Others were destroyed at the plant because the band couldn't pay for them.

Residents, The	Meet the Residents	LP	Ralph RR 0274		1974

A classic rarity. The first version of this took the original LP cover of "Meet the Beatles" and altered the Fab Four's faces. "First Edition" is on the back cover. This cover was later restored, but the catalog number is much different.

Too Much Joy	Green Eggs and Crack	LP	Stonegarden SGN-901		1987

This band's rare debut.

Velvet Underground, The	What Goes On/Jesus	45 DJ	MGM 14057		1969

Promo copy of the only single from their MGM self-titled LP.

Velvet Underground, The	Femme Fatale/ Sunday Morning	45 DJ	Verve 10466		1966

Promo of this classic.

Artist	Title		Label, Number	Year
Velvet Underground, The	The Velvet Underground and Nico	LP M	Verve V-5008	1967

Version 3 of this cover has the peel-off banana peel, but the torso is airbrushed off the cover. Again, the value assumes the banana peel is intact. (Deduct 50% if banana sticker has been removed, less for partial removal.)

Velvet Underground, The	The Velvet Underground and Nico	LP S	Verve V6-5008	1967

Stereo version 1: With a peel-off banana peel and a photo of the band framed by a male torso. Most copies have some sort of damage to the banana; this price is for a cover with the sticker fully intact. (Deduct 50% if banana sticker is gone, less if parts of it are missing.)

Velvet Underground, The	The Velvet Underground and Nico	LP S	Verve V6-5008	1967

Stereo version 2 is like Version 1, but the photo of the torso is obscured by a sticker. Again, this value is for copies with both stickers intact. (Deduct 50% if stickers have been removed, less if parts are missing.)

Young, Neil	Southern Pacific/ Motor City	12	Reprise 49895	1982

Green vinyl, triangle-shaped; the second-rarest version of this odd single.

Young, Neil	Time Fades Away	LP	Reprise MS 2151	1973

With a cardboard inner sleeve, withdrawn after the earliest pressing. Paper inner sleeve versions are worth maybe $10 Near Mint.

Zappa, Frank	How Could I Be Such a Fool/Help I'm a Rock (3rd Movement: It Can't Happen Here)	45	Verve 10418	1966

Stock copies of the Mothers of Invention's first single.

Zappa, Frank	Who Are the Brain Police/ Trouble Comin' Every Day	45	Verve 10458	1966

Stock copies of the Mothers of Invention's second single, but this is not known to exist.

Zappa, Frank	Why Don't You Do Me Right/Big Leg Emma	45	Verve 10513	1967

The Mothers of Invention's third single; stock copy.

Zappa, Frank	Mother People/ Lonely Little Girl	45	Verve 10570	1967

The Mothers of Invention's fourth single (if at first you don't succeed...); stock copy.

Zappa, Frank	Freak Out!	LP (2) M	Verve V-5005-2	1966

With cover version 1, which has a blurb on the inside gatefold on how to get a map of "freak-out hot spots" in L.A.

Zappa, Frank	We're Only In It for the Money	LP S	Verve V6-5045	1968

This bizarre second edition, after the mono version had been deleted from print, features a censored version: the songs "Who Needs the Peace Corps?" and "Let's Make the Water Turn Black" have lines altered or deleted.

Zappa, Frank	Cruising with Ruben and the Jets	LP	Verve V6-5055	1968

Yellow label promo

Zappa, Frank	Lumpy Gravy	LP	Verve V6-8741	1968

Yellow label promo

$175 (81)

Pere Ubu	Final Solution/ Cloud 149	45 w/PS	Hearthan HR-102	1976

Only the first 600 of this seminal Cleveland band's second single were issued with a picture sleeve.

$165 (82)

Next, The	Make It Quick	EP w/PS	Sharp (# unknown)	1979

This rare punk single came with a wrap-around poster that served as a picture sleeve. The back (white side) of the poster was the side visible. This value is for those few copies of the poster that had "The Next -- Make It Quick" stamped on the white side.

Artist	Title		Label, Number	Year

$160 (83-84)

Misfits, The — Horror Business/Teenagers 45 w/PS — Plan 9 PL 1009 — 1979
from Mars/Children in Heat
Yellow vinyl version, with insert.

Queers, The — The Queers — EP — Doheny (no #) — 1982
$40 of this value is for a handwritten sleeve. Otherwise, this was not issued with a proper picture cover.

$150 (85-113)

Bowie, David — David Bowie — LP S — Deram DES 18003 — 1967
Stereo version of his first American album.

Eat, The — Communist Radio/ — 45 w/PS — Giggling Hitler (# unknown) — 1979
Catholic Love (Live)
Classic punk single from a Miami band.

Huns, The — Busy Kids/Glad He's Dead 45 w/PS — God 001 — 1979
Austin, Texas punk band made one single, then broke up. But what a single!

Next, The — Make It Quick — EP w/PS — Sharp (# unknown) — 1979
Same as the $165 version above, except this one does not have the stamp on the white side of the sleeve.

Nirvana — Love Buzz/Big Cheese — 45 w/PS — Sub Pop 23 — 1988
The grunge-rockers' first single and #1 in the Sub Pop Singles Club, this was a hand-numbered edition of 1,000.

Ono, Yoko — Two Virgins -- — LP — Apple T-5001 — 1968
Unfinished Music No. 1
Legendary album of noises and whatever, with John Lennon and Yoko naked on the cover. This price includes a brown bag used to shield the cover from Middle America.

Ono, Yoko — Two Virgins -- — LP — Apple T-5001 — 1968
Unfinished Music No. 1
Same as above, except this one has a die-cut bag, through which the lovers' faces are visible. This is not to be confused with the 1985 legitimate reissue of this album.

Pere Ubu — 30 Seconds Over Tokyo/ — 45 w/PS — Hearthan HR-101 — 1975
Heart of Darkness
The band's first single, and only the first 1,000 were issued with a picture sleeve.

Queers, The — Kicked Out of the Weeblos EP — Doheny (no #) — 1983
Another burst of madness from this punk band -- heck, it even spelled "Webelos" wrong! Again, this was not issued with a proper picture sleeve; $30 of the value is for a handwritten sleeve accompanying some copies of this record.

R.E.M. — Radio Free Europe/ — 45 w/PS — Hib-Tone HT-0001 — 1981
Sitting Still
Legendary band's legendary first single. This is for the first pressing, with no address for Hib-Tone Records on the label.

Reed, Lou — Blue Mask — LP DJ — Direct Disk — 1982
This was going to be an audiophile reissue, but it was shelved. It only exists on test pressings.

Reed, Lou — Metal Machine Music — LP (2) Q — RCA Victor APD2-1101 — 1975
This legendarily bad album full of weird noises actually was released in quadraphonic sound (don't ask why). The stereo version just missed the cut by a few dollars.

Residents, The — Babyfingers — EP w/PS — Ralph RR 0377 — 1979
Another early 7-inch release by the eyeball men.

Shit Dogs — Present the History — EP w/PS — Pangolin Prod. (# unknown) — 1980
of Cheese
Punk band from Baton Rouge, Louisiana on their first 7-inch release.

Soundgarden — Screaming Life — LP EP — Sub Pop 12 — 1987
This is for one of the first 500 copies, which were pressed on orange vinyl.

Spacemen 3 — Transparent Radiation/ — 45 w/PS — Forced Exposure 017 — 1989
Honey
Full-color pasted-on art on sleeve; this only accompanied the test pressing, of which 25 were made.

Artist	**Title**	**Label, Number**	**Year**

Various artists   Dope Guns 'N' Fucking   EP w/PS   Amphetamine Reptile Scale 12   198?
in the Streets, Vol. 1
Artists on the first of this periodic 7-inch EP series include three highly collectible bands: Mudhoney, Halo of Flies and the U-Men. This is for the first pressing, 250 copies on red vinyl.

Various artists   First Decade   LP (3) DJ   WEA 10   1981
A three-record set of which only 1,000 were pressed. It pays tribute to the 10th anniversary of the WEA (Warner-Elektra-Atlantic) conglomerate. It contains tracks by Neil Young, Prince, and many others.

Velvet Underground, The   The Velvet Underground   LP S   Verve V6-5008   1967
and Nico
The stereo version 3 of this cover has the peel-off banana peel, but the torso is airbrushed off the cover. Again, the value assumes the banana peel is intact. (Deduct 50% if banana sticker has been removed, less for partial removal.)

Young, Neil   Neil Young   LP   Reprise RS 6317   1968
The first pressing of his first solo album did not have his name on the front cover. It also had a brown and orange "Reprise/W7" label, reflecting the Warner Bros.-7 Arts merger of the late 1960s that eventually fell apart.

Zappa, Frank   The Worst of the Mothers   LP   MGM SE-4754   1971
A post-Verve greatest hits collection. This is for the yellow label promo.

Zappa, Frank   Jelly Roll Gum Drop/   45   Verve 10632   1968
Deseri
Released under the name "Ruben & The Jets," this is for a stock copy with the above B-side.

Zappa, Frank   Jelly Roll Gum Drop/   45   Verve 10632   1968
Any Way the Wind Blows
Released under the name "Ruben & The Jets," this is for a stock copy with the above B-side.

Zappa, Frank   Freak Out!   LP (2) M   Verve V-5005-2   1966
This is for a mono version with a revised cover. It has no blurb inside its gatefold on getting a map of "freak-out hot spots"

Zappa, Frank   Absolutely Free   LP M   Verve V-5013   1967
Mono version of The Mothers of Invention's second album.

Zappa, Frank   We're Only In It   LP M   Verve V-5045   1968
for the Money
Mono version of the Mothers of Invention's third album, with a sheet of cut-outs a la "Sgt. Pepper's Lonely Hearts Club Band."

Zappa, Frank   Mothermania --   LP   Verve V6-5068   1969
The Best of the Mothers
Yellow label promo version of the only compilation of Mothers material on Verve or MGM that FZ helped put together.

Zappa, Frank   The XXXX of the Mothers   LP   Verve V6-5074   1969
Yellow label promo of this unauthorized, but legal, compilation.

Zero Boys   Livin' in the 80's   EP w/PS   Z-Disk (# unknown)   1980
Indianapolis punk classic; this value is an average because the prices for this ranged between $50 and $250.

So What's Alternative, Anyway?

"Alternative" is a good catch-word, because it can be defined in so many ways. Originally it meant an option other than the norm, and certainly the earliest records listed in here fit that definition.

But over the years, as "alternative" became less a lifestyle and more a marketing ploy, the word has become as broad or as narrow as you wish to define it. Today a mainstream radio format is called Triple A, or "Adult Album Alternative," which shows just how much the original sense of the word has been perverted.

Nonetheless, most of what is in the book started out as something other than the popular sound of the day. In some cases, bands became "alternative" after they had stopped making the Top 40.

The following is not meant as a detailed history of "alternative" music. Entire books and lengthy magazine articles have been written on the history of punk and new wave, any of which will go far beyond the following broad overview.

Early Influences

By a strict dictionary definition of "alternative," Elvis Presley on Sun Records would have fit. Of course, he evolved into the very cliché of the excesses of stardom, as he died overweight, drug-addicted and having released very few worthwhile records in his last five years.

When one talks about influences on the 1970s to 1990s bands whose records are listed here, the place to start is The Velvet Underground. The New York band was notoriously unpopular during its late-1960s heyday, but its refusal to compromise for mainstream success was noted by many of the later bands that achieved success on their own terms.

Among other "ahead of their time" performers who recorded before the mid-1970s, echoes of whom can be heard in many later performers, were the MC5, David Bowie, The New York Dolls, Frank Zappa and the Mothers of Invention, and Brian Eno and Roxy Music.

Although outside the scope of this book, another influence on early punk/new wave were those countless 1960s "garage" groups and homegrown psychedelic bands. They showed that you didn't have to record for a major conglomerate to make worthwhile music. Some of their records were made in pressings of 100 or less on self-created labels. Early alternative rockers often took the same do-it-yourself approach to their early records (and some still do to this day, even with major-label offers). To find out more about these garage and psych bands, we recommend the *Goldmine Price Guide to Collectible Record Albums, Fifth Edition,* by Neal Umphred (Krause Publications, 1996).

Finally, there's the peculiar case of Neil Young. He's become known as the "Godfather of Grunge" because of his influence on the Seattle music scene of the mid- to late-1980s. (For more evidence, get a copy of the album *Rust Never Sleeps* and listen to "Hey Hey, My My [Into the Black].") But it's impossible to pigeonhole him, which also is a trait of many later artists. He's recorded acoustic ballads, country, electronic music, hard rock, feedback, you name it, and remains one of the most unpredictable artists of our time. Everyone else who recorded in the 1960s, as Young did, has become, for all intents and purposes, an oldies act.

In the Beginning...

Like a wildfire, the music we've come to know as "punk" or "new wave" seemed to spring out of many places at once.

In New York, a whole scene of decidedly uncommercial music sprung up among the wastelands of mid-1970s AM and FM radio. Much of this activity was centered around a club called CBGB's, which was every bit as important to new wave as Liverpool's Cavern Club was to British beat music. Among the first to make waves, either by signing with record labels or putting out their own ditties, were Patti Smith, The Ramones, Talking Heads, Television and the remnants of the ahead-of-their-time New York Dolls.

In London and elsewhere in England, the Sex Pistols defined what became known as "punk rock." To quote someone else's album title from the era, the sound was "young, loud and snotty." And while the Pistols were the most notorious of the British new bands, they weren't the most popular or the best. But, spearheaded by their Svengali, Malcolm McLaren, they got the most publicity and symbolized everything that was both wrong and right with the new music.

From the Clash, who became internationally known, to Crass and the Soft Boys, who basically didn't, the British scene produced something for almost everyone, from guitar to synthesizer rock to dance music.

Meanwhile, back in the States, a vibrant underground scene was happening in, of all unlikely places, Cleveland, Ohio and vicinity. The number of influential and interesting new-wave performers from that area is mind-boggling: a sampling includes Pere Ubu, Devo, Tin Huey, The Waitresses, and Chrissie Hynde of The Pretenders, who had to go to England to find her band.

Los Angeles and the rest of the West Coast wasn't immune to the new music, either. From the weird Residents to the bizarre Germs to the ahead-of-their-time Runaways, there was plenty to excite from there, too.

But no one was buying it -- almost literally.

While most of the 1970s punk and new wave bands can be seen as important and vital in retrospect, few of their records sold. Such seminal recordings as "Gloria" (Patti Smith's version), "Blitzkrieg Bop," "Watching the Detectives," "The Modern Dance" and "Anarchy in the U.K." were flops here in the United States. Those handful that were big here were seen as either novelties ("Pop Muzik" by M) or the triumph of hype over talent (*Get The Knack*).

Most of this music's audience came from college radio stations, which, unfettered by big-name consultants force-feeding the same pap upon an unsuspecting public, were willing to experiment. (At many colleges, this is still true today.) For a long time, these interesting yet non-mainstream sounds emanating from literally all over the world threatened to become the private domain of the stations left of 92.1 on the FM dial.

And Then Came MTV

Music Television, or MTV, basically changed everything.

The very first "music video" aired on the cable channel on August 1, 1981 was a new-wave song, the Buggles' "Video Killed the Radio Star." And for the next year and a half or so, MTV was almost exclusively dedicated to the new music.

There was a practical reason for this: Mainstream American "dinosaur" or "corporate rock" bands didn't make videos. When a new album came out, the time-tested method of promotion was touring and other personal appearances. When it came time for television, it was usually "American Bandstand" or the newer "Solid Gold," where you lip-synched one or two current hits, or "Saturday Night Live," where you actually performed live. ("SNL," though, was usually much hipper than the typical network TV show when it came to musical guests.)

British performers, meanwhile, had been making videos, or "promotional film clips" as they were originally known, since the days of the Beatles. They were a simple and relatively inexpensive way to appear on all the variety shows without having to take the time out to actually show up.

So, to fill 24 hours of programming with music, MTV looked overseas. And it found some rather interesting sights and sounds, almost none of which coincided with what was on the American pop charts, at least not in the top 40, anyway.

The first two significant "MTV hits," songs that became big charters because of airplay on the channel, were "Tainted Love" by Soft Cell and "Don't You Want Me" by Human League. Both were British synthesizer bands. And more followed... "Hungry Like the Wolf." "Do You Really Want to Hurt Me." "Sweet Dreams (Are Made of This)." "She Blinded Me with Science." And even the decidedly non-alternative Def Leppard with "Photograph." The media began to talk about the Second British Invasion, as 1983 became a big year for these British bands formerly buried on college radio.

American record companies and performers fought back, making 1984 one of the great years ever for popular singles, right up there with 1965, the year after the first "British Invasion." But the music that used to be "alternative" wasn't any more. What to do?

Indie Rock Rules

From the earliest days of the new music, do-it-yourself (or D.I.Y.) records were a staple. Sometimes they were meant to attract the attention of a larger label. Most of the time they were one-and-done deals.

But several of the vanity projects evolved into full-fledged independent labels, with numerous artists and regular release schedules. Only on occasion were they interested in mass consumption or radio airplay. They were able to get their product to the fans the old-fashioned way: by word of mouth and live performances.

Several of the more notable American indie labels:

SST. It was founded by the California band Black Flag as an outlet for their music, usually in seven-inch single form. Over time, SST began to sign other artists. In the alterna-rock circles of the mid-1980s, probably the best known of these was Minneapolis-based Husker Du. But SST also had the Minutemen, the Descendants and Sonic Youth among its artists. It probably was the most important of the 1980s indie labels, and it's still around today.

Twin/Tone. Formed in Minneapolis as an outlet for the many unsigned punk and new wave bands in the Twin Cities, Twin/Tone also became home for several important artists. The Suicide Commandos did a live album for the label in 1979. But the two most enduring Twin/Tone artists were the Replacements, who usually get uttered in the same breath as Husker Du when talking about mid-1980s non-mainstream music, and Soul Asylum.

Amphetamine Reptile. This began as the vanity project of a way-out-there band called Halo of Flies, also in Minneapolis. The label's early records are highly collectible, especially the "Dope Guns 'N' Fucking in the Street" series of 7-inch EP compilations.

Other formerly truly independent labels, such as I.R.S. and Slash, opted to expand their reach by forging distribution links with majors. But in many ways, indie rock in the 1980s was like the entire punk/new wave scene of the 1970s -- important in retrospect, ignored at the time. From 1982-86, only the barest minimum of indie-label releases made the upper reaches of the important music charts, and only Joan Jett and the Blackhearts on Boardwalk, bubblegum impresario Neil Bogart's last label, resembled true so-called "indie rock."

Walk This Way

Much of the alternative music discussed so far was alternatives to white music. But a post-Motown, post-Stax/Volt, post-Philly Soul malaise had hit black music as well.

The "alternative" was a series of rhymes, often boastful in nature, chanted over a usually pre-recorded instrumental track that became known as "rap" or "hip-hop." Rap is a direct descendent of Jamaican "toasting," or recitations over instrumental records known as "dubs." (A reasonably accessible example of "toasting" is on UB40's wonderful "Red Red Wine.")

Much like jazz, the earliest rap never made it to record. And also like jazz's Original Dixieland Jazz Band, the first important rap record was not done by street musicians but by a studio group, the Sugar Hill Gang. "Rapper's Delight" was a big seller, though very difficult to find on an original pressing today. In addition to establishing the viability of this new form of recorded music, it helped to make the 12-inch single the preferred method of getting new music to the inner cities. Even today, the 12-inch single is the main medium for spreading the popularity of new dance-club hits.

But until 1986, rap was the more or less private domain of inner-city blacks and white denizens of the club scene. Sure, Blondie had co-opted the form in its number-one hit "Rapture," but performers like Grandmaster Flash and the Furious Five, Afrika Bambaataa, Kurtis Blow and Planet Patrol were little-known outside the dance clubs.

Then came Run-D.M.C.'s merger of rap and lite metal with its remake of "Walk This Way," the old Aerosmith song. The rap duo was even shrewd enough to use Steve Tyler and Joe Perry of Aerosmith both in the song and on the video. And mainstream America was re-introduced in a big way to hip-hop. (It also was re-introduced to Aerosmith, which had all but disappeared since the late 1970s.)

Well, elements of hip-hop ended up everywhere, from fashion to McDonald's commercials. But the most innovative stuff usually stayed outside the mainstream. It also tended to polarize the public; mainstream radio stations even today are known to publicize themselves as "no rap!" as if it's more irritating than the latest goopy ballad by some pseudo-diva. And right-wing (and sometimes centrist) politicians find rap, especially its mostly Los Angeles outgrowth, "gangsta rap," a convenient scapegoat for the ills in inner-city society, when it's more a reflection than a cause of those problems.

Alt-Rock Goes Global

Meanwhile, two of college rock's biggest darlings finally broke into the mainstream to stay in 1987.

In the early part of the year, U2 released the single "With or Without You" and the album *The Joshua Tree.* Each escaped the largely cult audience the band had had before and hit number one on all the mainstream charts. Later in the year, the Athens, Georgia cult favorites R.E.M. had its first top-10 pop single with "The One I Love." Both songs, in their own way, were as mainstream radio-friendly as anything they'd ever done before. But in neither case had the band lost its artistic integrity.

In the ensuing years, both bands have become among the most popular of any type. Yet, at the same time, they haven't succumbed to the "Fat Elvis" syndrome. Many critics would argue that *Achtung Baby* and *Zooropa,* U2's two albums of the 1990s, are their finest. And you can make an argument for *Automatic for the People* and *Monster* as among R.E.M.'s best. (Many would argue, and we won't disagree, that *Murmur,* R.E.M.s' first full-length LP, was the most important alternative album. Its stature is such that it's been given the audiophile treatment by Mobile Fidelity Sound Labs.)

Both U2 and R.E.M. proved that yes, a formerly outside the mainstream group could enter the mainstream, yet continue to make music that appealed to the college crowd.

It also caused the more commercially oriented radio stations to notice this "alternative" music. Enough radio stations had adapted a so-called "modern rock" format by 1988 that *Billboard,* which tends to react to rather than start trends, began a "Modern Rock Tracks" top 40 chart.

A fairly typical (and common) example of the Sub Pop Singles Club, the February 1991 edition by the Velvet Monkeys on black vinyl. The record (early ones were colored vinyl, later ones of the same title were black) came in a generic white sleeve inside a fold-open picture sleeve. Inside the sleeve, attached to the top, was a come-on to join the club. Only in retrospect were the Singles Club discs numbered other than by the regular issue number Sub Pop gave them.

Smells Like Seattle

In the mid-to late 1980s, some interesting sounds were starting to come out of the Pacific Northwest.

Actually, the northwest corner of the United States has always had some interesting sounds, from the Ventures and the Fleetwoods to Paul Revere and the Raiders and the Kingsmen. But much of the new excitement revolved around two record labels, C/Z and Sub Pop. And it became the next "in" sound for the college radio crowd.

Even more peculiarly, Sub Pop's primary mode of spreading its music was via an old-fashioned method -- the 7-inch 45 rpm single. It began what it called the "Singles Club," where, for a yearly membership fee, the company would send you, once a month or so, a new 45 of new music unavailable anywhere else. Usually this was on colored vinyl as well, and all were extremely limited editions -- the most copies pressed of any Singles Club 45 was 7,000. And once those were gone, they were gone. If you joined the club at number 12, you could not get 1 through 11 through Sub Pop.

Perhaps not coincidentally, the band that was on the first Singles Club 45 became Seattle's biggest export -- Nirvana.

On the strength of one album, several singles and its live act, Nirvana ended up on DGC Records, one of David Geffen's labels, distributed by the MCA conglomerate. The first album on the major label, *Nevermind,* and the first single, "Smells Like Teen Spirit," caught a nation by surprise. The album hit number one, and the single -- one of the great singles of any era -- spent about two months in the top 10. Record executives flocked to the Seattle area to see what else they could find. The combination of this noisy, loud yet melodic music and the styles that surrounded it became known as "grunge."

Some went major-label before Nirvana, some after, but several of the top Pacific Northwest bands left their indie-rock roots. Soundgarden, Mudhoney and Pearl Jam (by way of Mother Love Bone, which might have broken big a year before Nirvana had not its lead singer OD'd) were chief among them.

Smells Like Nostalgia

It was also about this time -- the early 1990s -- that the alt-rock crowd was beginning to embrace musicians and singers that had little or nothing to do with grunge or indie-rock or synth-pop or punk or anything else current. Those who got the biggest career boost out of this curious nostalgia were Tony Bennett, Johnny Cash, Neil Young and Esquivel.

The last of these had recorded cheesy instrumentals that earlier would be considered one step removed from elevator music but now were known by the catchy "space-age bachelor pad music." One of the "new music" groups, Combustible Edison, made its name by doing new tunes in the 1950s-style instrumental mode.

As this is being written, the squarest of square 1950s teen idols, Pat Boone, was about to release an album of his versions of heavy-metal tunes, from "Enter Sandman" to "Symphony of Destruction" to "Stairway to Heaven."

Continuing with nostalgia, many of the "new music" bands embraced vinyl, as in records, in a way their predecessors in the spotlight had not. Many of the "alternative" bands actually release their new full-length albums on records a week or two before the more commercial CD and cassette are released. The popularity of some of those who insist on vinyl may have saved the record from total extinction.

Not all this nostalgia is good or innocent: While many new bands are clean, others have taken to hard drugs unlike any generation since the late 1960s.

And Today

So-called "alternative" music has gone so mainstream that you might think that nothing is out there anymore.

But think again.

Pick up a copy of the *CMJ New Music Report* sometime and check out the college radio charts. Even today, despite the bands that would have been relegated to the university scene a decade ago that have reached a mass audience, the charts are loaded with music that doesn't get heard by the masses.

Some of it, like the early punk singles, will never get heard beyond a limited, cult audience. Some of it, too, may become the Next Big Thing.

There are indie labels out there, such as Epitaph and Tim/Kerr and K, that are as eagerly scanned for new releases as their predecessors were (and still are: Sub Pop never went away, it just has a slightly lower profile now, and alas, its Singles Club was ended in 1993).

And as the music scene becomes more and more fragmented and compartmentalized, some will never quite fit in the mainstream, much as the early punks didn't and the early new wavers didn't and the 1980s indie-rock titans didn't.

There will always be "alternative music." Trying to define it, though, will become more and more difficult. Just what is alternative? I don't think there's a good answer. Maybe it's a paraphrase of what used to be said about obscenity -- "I know it when I hear it."

A Few Words on Compact Discs

As we noted in the Introduction, this price guide contains records only (and a few titles that we list so that we can tell you that records don't exist for them).

That doesn't mean that compact discs for many of the artists contained here aren't collectible. In many cases, they are.

Those that have collector value fall into several broad categories:

Promo CDs

Most of the collectible compact discs are those that were not meant for the general public. They were issued to radio stations or retail stores as promotional items. And as often happens when there's a profit motive involved, many of these have filtered to collector's shops and mail-order ads.

In order from most to least desirable, promo CDs fall roughly into the following categories:

• **Radio shows.** These are concerts, retrospectives, and other programming, usually as part of an ongoing series such as the King Biscuit Flower Hour. Very few of these are pressed, and then only on a contract basis to those radio stations that have purchased the right to play them.

• **Otherwise unavailable material.** This can include unusual mixes of hit songs, including dance remixes; live versions and concerts put out by a band's record label; and sometimes, seasonal songs.

• **Promo-only compilations.** In advance of an artist's new release, or as a sampler from a box set, labels will collect significant tracks from a performer's past and issue them as a promo item. In many cases, these artists don't have a retrospective on the market at all; in others, these compilations are more eclectic and inspired than standard "best of" or "greatest hits" collections.

• **Special versions of regular releases.** Often, record labels will issue a performer's new release in different packaging to radio stations than it will to the general public. This can be in any kind of format that is other than the standard jewel box with insert. Or it can be a special "picture disc" CD with otherwise standard packaging. Whatever way, it can't be found in a regular retail store in that format.

• **CD singles.** Some promo CD singles go for $3-$4; these usually have one song, no photo insert, and are by less collectible artists. But even the one-track, no-insert promo can have siginificant value if from an artist among the most collectible. Sometimes, there is an added premium for single-track promos that were not released to the general public as singles (for example, "God Part 2" by U2).

More information on the values of many of these promos can be found in the *Goldmine Promo Record & CD Price Guide* by Fred Heggeness (Krause, 1995; available through your bookstore or by calling 1-800-258-0929).

Out-of-Print CDs

Many commercially released compact discs, more than you might realize, are no longer available. Usually, there's a good reason why (for example, no one bought it or people stopped buying it).

Far more common, though, are CDs that have gone out of print because of a transfer of rights from one record label to another. The collector's market has only begun to pick up on many of these. Among the more prominent are the David Bowie compact discs on the RCA label. They were available very briefly before they were pulled from the market, as Bowie himself owns the rights to his masters and hadn't permitted RCA to re-release his 1972-82 catalog. Compared to the generally well-regarded reissues on Rykodisc, the RCAs sound pretty bad, though, so some have stayed away.

That points out a problem with out-of-print CDs: Most often, they are replaced with a version that sounds markedly better than the deleted copies. Some CD collectors are like record collectors in that they search out these originals, regardless what they sound like. Others want the best-sounding CD and don't want anything to do with the earlier editions. It's possible that neither side will "win" the hobby, but that both will coexist. A result of this may be that early CD pressings may never reach a value that truly reflects their rarity.

Another more recent source of out-of-print CDs is commercially released CD singles. Only in the last couple years have they become a vital part of the singles market, although they've been around since 1987. (Frank Zappa, ever the pioneer, had one of the first American CD singles with "Peaches En Regalia.") Just as with 45s, most CD singles eventually will go out of print. Stock CD singles are a good bet as a future collectible.

Import CDs

Finally, there are the compact discs exclusively released outside the United States. The most common of these are CD singles and full-length releases with bonus tracks.

Many of the CD singles have otherwise unavailable tracks, photos or inserts and have become highly sought after. Sometimes, their popularity forces American record companies' hands: The high prices that dealers were getting for certain British imports actually spurred Pearl Jam to release exact duplicates (other than the catalog numbers) of its imports here in the States in 1995.

Japan often releases full-length compact discs with bonus tracks such as non-album B-sides, demo versions, or other outtakes. This is done to help spur the domestic recording industry there; U.S. imports, because of the lower manufacturing costs here, are often less expensive in Japan than Japanese pressings! Therefore, extra tracks are added in hopes that Japanese consumers will buy the homegrown rather than the imported product. Some of these songs never make it across the Pacific except on these sought-after imports.

We can't end our discussion of import CDs without mentioning live so-called "import" CDs. Often coming from (or purported to be coming from) countries with more lax copyright laws, these are often high-quality live recordings of collectible artists. But in the eyes of the authorities here, these are bootlegs; numerous busts have been made both at Customs and among suppliers here, and sometimes record shows have been raided as well.

We can't deny that many important and interesting performances are documented on these quasi-legal CDs. But we also can't deny that selling the stuff is illegal and can be subject to federal anti-piracy statutes. These so-called "imports" will never knowingly be given a value in a *Goldmine* price guide such as this one.

A Final Word on CDs

Should interest be high enough, we'll consider adding compact discs to future editions of the *Goldmine Price Guide to Alternative Records*. (We'll change the book's title accordingly if we do so.) Your comments are welcome on the subject. See the section "How You Can Help" for more information.

How You Can Help

Our goal in the *Goldmine Price Guide to Alternative Records* is to be as complete as possible. Within a particular artist's listing, we did not intentionally omit anything (U.S. releases). But we'll admit that some artists' discographies are more complete than others. If something is missing, either we didn't know about it, could not confirm it, found out about it after our deadline, or lost it in the shuffle.

If you feel a listing is missing or band information is wrong, **please help us out!** I'm not a know-it-all; I'll gladly accept additions to the listings, and I'll listen to suggestions as to who belongs in the second edition who didn't make the first.

Better yet, if you have discographical or value-related information, I'd like to see that, too.

Everyone who makes a suggestion that makes the next edition will be acknowledged, unless you don't want to be. I am:

Tim Neely
Book Editor, Goldmine
700 E. State Street
Iola, WI 54990
(715) 445-2214, ext. 782

If you write, enclose a daytime phone number where I can call in case I have any questions.

I also can be reached via fax at (715) 445-4087, but I prefer that you write or call before faxing me any large contributions.

Label, Number		Title	Year	VG	VG+	NM

A

A's, The
Philadelphia-area new wavish pop band. Their records often sell for 2-3 times the below prices in their hometown.

Vinyl Albums

Label, Number		Title	Year	VG	VG+	NM
Arista AB 4238		The A's	1979	2.50	5.00	10.00
Arista AL 9554		A Woman's Got the Power	1981	2.50	5.00	10.00
Arista CP 705	10	The A's E.P.	1979	3.00	6.00	12.00
Red vinyl with three songs from their first album						

45s

Label, Number		Title	Year	VG	VG+	NM
Arista 0452		After Last Night/				
		Teenage Jerk Off	1979		2.00	4.00
Arista 0472		Parasite/Words	1979		2.00	4.00
Arista 0609		A Woman's Got the Power/ Heart of America				
			1981		2.00	4.00

a-ha
Synth-pop band from Norway.

Vinyl Albums

Label, Number		Title	Year	VG	VG+	NM
Warner Bros. 25300		Hunting High and Low	1985	2.50	5.00	10.00
Warner Bros. 25501		Scoundrel Days	1986	2.50	5.00	10.00
Warner Bros. 25733		Stay On These Roads	1988	2.50	5.00	10.00
Warner Bros. R 114779		Hunting High and Low	1985	3.00	6.00	12.00
RCA Music Service edition						
Warner Bros. R 163775		Scoundrel Days	1986	3.00	6.00	12.00
RCA Music Service edition						
Warner Bros. R 184019		Stay On These Roads	1988	3.00	6.00	12.00
BMG Direct Marketing edition						

45s

Label, Number		Title	Year	VG	VG+	NM
Parc 07056		Shy Boys/Love Is the Winner	1987			3.00
Reprise 28684		Hunting High and Low/				
		And You Tell Me (Demo Version)				
			1986			3.00
Warner Bros. 21999		Take On Me/The Sun Always Shines on T.V.				
			198?			3.00
"Back to Back Hits" reissue						
Warner Bros. 27886		Stay on These Roads/You'll End Up Crying				
			1988			3.00
Warner Bros. 28305		The Living Daylights/(instrumental)				
			1987			3.00
Warner Bros. 28500		Cry Wolf/Maybe Maybe	1987			3.00
Warner Bros. 28594		I've Been Losing You/				
		This Alone Is Love	1986			3.00
Warner Bros. 28846		The Sun Always Shines on T.V./Driftwood				
			1985			3.00
Warner Bros. 28846	PS	The Sun Always Shines on T.V./Driftwood				
			1985			3.00
Warner Bros. 29011		Take On Me/Love Is Reason	1985			3.00
Warner Bros. 29011	PS	Take On Me/Love Is Reason	1985			3.00
Warner Bros. 29011	PS	Take On Me/Love Is Reason	1985	2.00	4.00	8.00
Promo-only comic book gatefold sleeve						

12-Inch Singles

Label, Number		Title	Year	VG	VG+	NM
Reprise 20410		The Sun Always Shines on T.V./(Instrumental)/Driftwood				
			1985	2.00	4.00	8.00

The first album by The A's, a Philadelphia pop/new-wave band, is not particularly sought after -- except in Philadelphia, where it fetches from 2-3 times what it does elsewhere.

ABC was a British band that gained an American audience thanks to MTV and kept it for most of the 1980s with some very radio-friendly ear candy. The band's first single in America, which had this somewhat tough sleeve to find, was "The Look of Love (Part One)."

Label, Number		Title	Year	VG	VG+	NM
Reprise 20478		Hunting High and Low (Remix)/Train of Thought/				
		And You Tell Me	1986	2.00	4.00	8.00
Warner Bros. PRO-A-2291	DJ	Take On Me (4:46)/ Take On Me (3:46)				
			1985	2.00	4.00	8.00
Warner Bros. PRO-A-2370	DJ	Train of Thought (same on both sides)				
			1985	2.00	4.00	8.00
Warner Bros. 20610		Cry Wolf (2 versions)/ Maybe Maybe				
			1986		3.00	6.00

ABC

British New Wave group, led by Martin Fry.

Vinyl Albums

Label, Number	Title	Year	VG	VG+	NM
Mercury SRM-1-4059	The Lexicon of Love	1982	2.50	5.00	10.00
Mercury R 143756	Alphabet City	1987	3.00	6.00	12.00
BMG Direct Marketing edition					
Mercury 814 661-1	Beauty Stab	1984	2.50	5.00	10.00
Mercury 822 890-1	The Lexicon of Love	1984	2.00	4.00	8.00
Reissue					
Mercury 824 904-1	How to Be a Zillionaire	1985	2.50	5.00	10.00
Mercury 832 391-1	Alphabet City	1987	2.50	5.00	10.00
Mercury 838 646-1	Up	1989	2.50	5.00	10.00

45s

Label, Number		Title	Year	VG	VG+	NM
Collectables 4262		The Look of Love/Poison Arrow199?				3.00
Reissue						
Collectables 4846		When Smokey Sings/Be Near Me				
			199?			3.00
Reissue						
Mercury 76168		The Look of Love (Part One)/Theme from Mantrap				
			1982			3.00
Mercury 76168	PS	The Look of Love (Part One)/Theme from Mantrap				
			1982		2.00	4.00
Mercury 810 340-7		Poison Arrow/Tears Are Not Enough				
			1983			3.00
Mercury 810 340-7	PS	Poison Arrow/Tears Are Not Enough				
		1983		2.00		4.00
Mercury 814 631-7		That Was Then But This Is Now/Vertigo				
			1983			3.00
Mercury 814 631-7	PS	That Was Then But This Is Now/Vertigo				
			1983		2.00	4.00
Mercury 814 876-7		The Look of Love (Part One)/Poison Arrow				
			1983			3.00
Reissue						
Mercury 870 102-7		King Without a Crown/The Look of Love				
			1988			3.00
Mercury 880 626-7		Be Near Me/A To Z	1985			3.00
Mercury 880 626-7	PS	Be Near Me/A To Z	1985			3.00
Mercury 884 382-7		(How to Be a) Millionaire/Tower of London				
			1985			3.00
Mercury 884 382-7	PS	(How to Be a) Millionaire/Tower of London				
			1985			3.00
Mercury 884 714-7		Vanity Kills	1986			3.00
Mercury 888 604-7		When Smokey Sings/Chicago	1987			3.00
Mercury 888 604-7	PS	When Smokey Sings/Chicago	1987			3.00
Mercury 888 783-7		The Night You Murdered Love/Minneapolis				
			1987			3.00
Mercury 888 783-7	PS	The Night You Murdered Love/Minneapolis				
			1987			3.00

12-Inch Singles

Label, Number	Title	Year	VG	VG+	NM
MCA 54055	Say It (5 versions)	1991	2.00	4.00	8.00

Label, Number		Title	Year	VG	VG+	NM
Mercury PRO 371	DJ	Be Near Me (same on both sides)				
			1985	2.00	4.00	8.00
Mercury PRO 397	DJ	How to Be a Zillionaire (4 versions)				
			1985	2.00	4.00	8.00
Mercury 811 329-1		Poison Arrow/Theme from Mantrap (2 mixes)				
			1983	2.00	4.00	8.00
Mercury 870 102-1		King Without a Crown (2 versions) + 3 live tracks				
			1988	2.50	5.00	10.00
Mercury 876 397-1		The Real Thing (3 mixes)	1989	2.00	4.00	8.00
Mercury 884 052-1		Be Near Me (2 mixes)/What's Your Destination				
			1985	2.00	4.00	8.00
Mercury 884 382-1		How to Be a Zillionaire (2 mixes)/Town of London				
			1985	2.00	4.00	8.00
Mercury 884 714-7		Vanity Kills/ABC Megamix	1986	2.00	4.00	8.00
Mercury 888 726-1		When Smokey Sings (4 versions)/Chicago Part 1 & Part 2				
			1987	2.00	4.00	8.00
Mercury 888 894-1		The Night You Murdered Love (4 versions)/Minneapolis				
			1987	2.00	4.00	8.00

Adam and the Ants

*British new-wave group, led by **Adam Ant**.*

Vinyl Albums						
Epic AE 1331	DJ	Adam and the Ants	1981	2.50	5.00	10.00
Five-song promo-only sampler						
Epic NJE 37033		Kings of the Wild Frontier	1981	3.00	6.00	12.00
Epic PE 37033		Kings of the Wild Frontier	1985	2.00	4.00	8.00
Budget-line reissue						
Epic ARE 37615		Prince Charming	1981	2.50	5.00	10.00
Epic PE 37615		Prince Charming	1984	2.00	4.00	8.00
Budget-line reissue						
Epic FE 38698		Dirk Wears White Sox	1983	2.50	5.00	10.00
First U.S. issue of U.K. debut						
Epic PE 38698		Dirk Wears White Sox	1984	2.00	4.00	8.00
Budget-line reissue						
45s						
Epic AE7 1236	DJ	Stand and Deliver/Beat My Guest				
			1981			3.00
Epic AE7 1236	PS	Stand and Deliver/Beat My Guest				
			1981			3.00
Epic 02042		Antmusic/Don't Be Square (Be There)				
			1981		2.00	4.00
12-Inch Singles						
Epic AS 973	DJ	Los Rancheros/Physical	1980	3.00	6.00	12.00
Epic 01061		Antmusic/Don't Be Square (Be There)				
			1981	3.75	7.50	15.00
Epic 02193		Stand and Deliver/Beat My Guest	1981	2.50	5.00	10.00

Adamski

12-Inch Singles						
MCA 18443	DJ	Killer (2 versions)	1990	2.00	4.00	8.00
MCA 24015		N-R-G/Viva City/I Love Technology/Love and Life				
			1990		3.00	6.00
MCA 24049		Killer (2 versions)	1990		3.00	6.00
Featuring Seal						
MCA 53961		The Space Jungle (3 versions)	1990	2.00	4.00	8.00
MCA 54000		Flashback Jack (4 versions)	1991		3.00	6.00

Label, Number		Title	Year	VG	VG+	NM

Adorable

45s

Label, Number		Title	Year	VG	VG+	NM
SBK 50444		Sunshine Smile/Pilot	1993		2.00	4.00
Clear vinyl						
SBK 50444	PS	Sunshine Smile/Pilot	1993		2.00	4.00

Afghan Whigs

Vinyl Albums

Label, Number		Title	Year	VG	VG+	NM
Sub Pop 60		Up In It	1990	6.25	12.50	25.00
First pressings have orange vinyl and a different sleeve than the black vinyl version						
Sub Pop 60		Up In It	1990	2.50	5.00	10.00
Sub Pop 130		Congregation	1992	5.00	10.00	20.00
Import only; made in Germany (no U.S. vinyl)						
Sub Pop 238		Gentlemen	1993	2.50	5.00	10.00

45s

Label, Number		Title	Year	VG	VG+	NM
Sub Pop 32		I Am the Sticks/White Trash Party				
			1989	5.00	10.00	20.00
Sub Pop 32	PS	I Am the Sticks/White Trash Party				
			1989	5.00	10.00	20.00
#6 in Sub Pop Singles Club series						
Sub Pop 84		Sister Brother/Hey Cuz	1990	2.50	5.00	10.00
First 2,000 on red vinyl						
Sub Pop 84		Sister Brother/Hey Cuz	1990	2.50	5.00	10.00
Sub Pop 84	PS	Sister Brother/Hey Cuz	1990	2.50	5.00	
Sub Pop 142		Conjure Me/My World Is Empty	1992	2.50	5.00	10.00
Lavender vinyl						
Sub Pop 142		Conjure Me/My World Is Empty	1992	2.50	5.00	10.00
White vinyl						
Sub Pop 142	PS	Conjure Me/My World Is Empty	1992	2.50	5.00	10.00

Afrika Corps

Vinyl Albums

Label, Number	Title	Year	VG	VG+	NM
Iron Cross/Dacoit (# unknown)	Music to Kill By	1977	15.00	30.00	60.00
Kleen Kut/Limp (# unknown)	Hello World!	1978	5.00	10.00	20.00
As "The Korps"; blue vinyl					

After The Fire

Vinyl Albums

Label, Number		Title	Year	VG	VG+	NM
Epic FE 38282		ATF	1983	3.00	6.00	12.00

45s

Label, Number	Title	Year	VG	VG+	NM
Epic 03559	Der Kommissar/Dancing in the Shadows				
		1983			3.00
Epic 03908	Dancing in the Shadows/Starflight				
		1983			3.00
Epic 50712	Joy/One Rule for You	1979		2.50	5.00

12-Inch Singles

Label, Number		Title	Year	VG	VG+	NM
Epic 03490		Der Kommissar (4:53)/Der Kommissar (5:43)				
			1983	2.00	4.00	8.00
Epic 03950		Dancing in the Shadows (Long)/Dancing in the Shadows (Short)				
			1983		3.00	6.00
Epic AE 1678	DJ	Dancing in the Shadows/One Rule for You				
			1983	2.00	4.00	8.00

Label, Number		Title	Year	VG	VG+	NM

Alarm, The

British rockers.

Vinyl Albums

Label, Number		Title	Year	VG	VG+	NM
I.R.S. 5666		Strength	1985	2.50	5.00	10.00
I.R.S. 39108		Electric Folklore Live	1988	2.50	5.00	10.00
I.R.S. 42061		Eye of the Hurricane	1987	2.50	5.00	10.00
I.R.S. SP 70504	EP	The Alarm	1984	3.50	7.00	14.00
I.R.S. SP 70608		Declaration	1984	2.50	5.00	10.00
I.R.S. 82018		Change	1989	2.50	5.00	10.00

45s

Label, Number		Title	Year	VG	VG+	NM
I.R.S. (# unknown)	DJ	Unsafe Building/Rain	1989	2.00	4.00	8.00
"I.R.S. Final Vinyl" promo release; B-side by Water Walk; numbered sleeve						
I.R.S. 9922		The Stand/Reason 41	1983		2.00	4.00
I.R.S. 9922	PS	The Stand/Reason 41	1983	2.50	5.00	10.00
I.R.S. 9924		Sixty-Eight Guns/Pavilion Steps	1984		2.00	4.00
I.R.S. 9924	PS	Sixty-Eight Guns/Pavilion Steps	1984		2.00	4.00
I.R.S. 9929		The Deceiver/Second Generation	1984		2.00	4.00
I.R.S. 52736		Strength/Majority	1985			3.00
I.R.S. 52736	PS	Strength/Majority	1985			3.00
I.R.S. 52792		Spirit of '76/Reason 36	1986			3.00
I.R.S. 52792	PS	Spirit of '76/Reason 36	1986			3.00
I.R.S. 52828		Absolute Reality/Room at the Top	1986			3.00
I.R.S. 52828	PS	Absolute Reality/Room at the Top	1986		2.00	4.00
I.R.S. 53219		Rain in the Summertime/Rose Beyond the Wall	1987			3.00
I.R.S. 53219	PS	Rain in the Summertime/Rose Beyond the Wall	1987			3.00
I.R.S. 53259		Presence of Love/My Land, Your Land	1988			3.00
I.R.S. 53259	PS	Presence of Love/My Land, Your Land	1988			3.00
I.R.S. 73002		Sold Me Down the River	1989		2.50	5.00
I.R.S. 73002	PS	Sold Me Down the River	1989		2.50	5.00

12-Inch Singles

Label, Number		Title	Year	VG	VG+	NM
I.R.S. 4986	DJ	Strength (edit) (same on both sides)	1985	2.00	4.00	8.00
I.R.S. L33-8927	DJ	Sold Me Down the River/Black Sun/How the Mighty Fall	1989		3.00	6.00
I.R.S. L33-17043	DJ	Strength (edit)/Strength (album version)	1985	2.50	5.00	10.00
I.R.S. L33-17068	DJ	Strength (edit)/Strength (extended)	1985	2.00	4.00	8.00
I.R.S. L33-17080	DJ	Spirit of '76 (edit)/Spirit of '76 (AOR edit)	1985	2.50	5.00	10.00
I.R.S. L33-17108	DJ	Absolute Reality/Majority/Reason 36	1986	3.00	6.00	12.00
I.R.S. L33-17406	DJ	Rain in the Summertime (edit) (same on both sides)	1987		3.50	7.00
I.R.S. L33-17474	DJ	Presence of Love (same on both sides)	1987		3.00	6.00
I.R.S. 23811		Rain in the Summertime (3 mixes)	1987		3.00	6.00
I.R.S. 70971	DJ	Sixty Eight Guns (same on both sides)	1984	2.00	4.00	8.00
I.R.S. 70975	DJ	The Deceiver/Howling Wind	1984	2.50	5.00	10.00

Label, Number			Title	Year	VG	VG+	NM
I.R.S. 74002			Sold Me Down the River/Black Sun/How the Mighty Fall				
				1989	2.50	5.00	10.00

Alice In Chains
Heavy metal/alternative band from Seattle.

Vinyl Albums
Columbia CAS 2192	DJ		We Die Young	1990	5.00	10.00	20.00
Five-song promo-only EP from the Facelift LP							
Columbia C2 57804	(2)		Jar of Flies/Sap	1994	5.00	10.00	20.00
Two cassette/CD EP releases in one vinyl package							
Columbia C2 67248	(2)		Alice in Chains	1995	3.75	7.50	15.00

45s
(Columbia) CS7-04013	DJ		Bleed the Freak/Put You Down	1991	6.25	12.50	25.00
White label with no label name							
Columbia 73851			Man in the Box/Sea of Sorrow/Bleed the Freak/Sunshine				
				1991		Cassette only	
Columbia 74820			Angry Chair/Brother	1993		Cassette only	
Columbia 78176			Grind/Nutshell	1995		2.00	4.00
Deleted on day of issue							

12-Inch Singles
Columbia CAS 2095	DJ		We Die Young/It Ain't Like That/Killing Yourself				
				1990	3.00	6.00	12.00

Allin, GG

Vinyl Albums
		Title	Year	VG	VG+	NM
Black & Blue (# unknown)		Always Was, Is and Always Shall Be				
			1985	11.25	22.50	45.00
Blood (# unknown)		Eat My Fuc	198?	12.50	25.00	50.00
Hand-decorated plain cover						
Homestead (# unknown)		You Give Love a Bad Name	1987	3.00	6.00	12.00
Orange (# unknown)		Always Was, Is and Always Shall Be				
			1980	25.00	50.00	100.00

Alphaville

Vinyl Albums
		Title	Year	VG	VG+	NM
Atlantic 80186		Forever Young	198?	2.50	5.00	10.00
Atlantic 81667		Adventures in Utopia	1986	2.50	5.00	10.00
Atlantic 81904		The Singles Collection	1988	2.50	5.00	10.00
Atlantic 81943		The Breathtaking Blue	1989	2.50	5.00	10.00

45s
		Title	Year	VG	VG+	NM
Atlantic 84974		Big in Japan/Forever Young	198?			3.00
"Oldies Series" reissue						
Atlantic 88914		Romeos	1989		2.00	4.00
Atlantic 89013		Forever Young/Lies	1988			3.00
Atlantic 89013	PS	Forever Young/Lies	1988			3.00
Atlantic 89292		Red Rose/Next Generation	1987			3.00
Atlantic 89292	PS	Red Rose/Next Generation	1987			3.00
Atlantic 89415		Dance with Me/The Nelson Highrise Sector 2: The Mirror				
			1986			3.00
Atlantic 89415	PS	Dance with Me/The Nelson Highrise Sector 2: The Mirror				
			1986			3.00
Atlantic 89553		The Jet Set/Golden Feeling	1985			3.00
Atlantic 89578		Forever Young/Lies	1985		2.00	4.00
This version not issued with picture sleeve in U.S.						
Atlantic 89665		Big in Japan/Seeds	1984			3.00
Atlantic 89665	PS	Big in Japan/Seeds	1984			3.00

Label, Number		Title	Year	VG	VG+	NM
12-Inch Singles						
Atlantic 842	DJ	The Jet Set (2 versions)	1985	2.50	5.00	10.00
Atlantic 1005	DJ	Red Rose (Remix) (same on both sides)				
			1986		2.50	5.00
Atlantic 1318	DJ	Romeos (4 mixes)	1989	2.00	4.00	8.00
Atlantic 1456	DJ	The Mysteries of Love (3 versions)				
			1989		2.50	5.00
Atlantic 2682	DJ	Romeos (edit)/Romeos (LP)	1989	2.00	4.00	8.00
Atlantic 86729		Red Rose (2 versions)/Next Generation				
			1986	2.50	5.00	10.00
Atlantic 86806		Dance with Me (8:14)/Nelson Highrise Sector 2				
			1986	2.50	5.00	10.00
Atlantic 86947		Big in Japan (3 mixes)	1984	2.50	5.00	10.00

Altered Images

Label, Number		Title	Year	VG	VG+	NM
Vinyl Albums						
Portrait FR 37738		Happy Birthday	1982	3.00	6.00	12.00
Portrait ARR 38110		Pinky Blue	1982	3.00	6.00	12.00
Portrait BFR 38585		Bite	1983	3.00	6.00	12.00
45s						
Portrait 02661		Happy Birthday/So We Go Whispering				
			1982			3.00
Portrait 03841		Don't Talk to Me About Love/Last Goodbye				
			1983			3.00
Portrait 03841	PS	Don't Talk to Me About Love/Last Goodbye				
			1983			3.00
12-Inch Singles						
Portrait AS 1417	DJ	Happy Birthday (long & short)/I Could Be Happy (long & short)				
			1982	2.00	4.00	8.00
Portrait 02840		I Could Be Happy/Insects Disco Pop Stars				
			1982		3.00	6.00
Portrait 03923		Don't Talk to Me About Love/Last Goodbye				
			1983		2.50	5.00

American Music Club

Label, Number	Title	Year	VG	VG+	NM
Vinyl Albums					
Alias A015	Everclear	1991	3.00	6.00	12.00
Frontier 4612-1-L	Engine	1987	3.00	6.00	12.00
Frontier 4619-1-L	California	1988	3.00	6.00	12.00
Reprise 45721	San Francisco	1994	2.50	5.00	10.00

Amos, Tori

Baltimore-area singer-songwriter who first became popular in England.

Label, Number		Title	Year	VG	VG+	NM
Vinyl Albums						
Atlantic 82567		Under the Pink	1995	3.00	6.00	12.00
Limited edition on pink vinyl						
Atlantic 82862	(2)	Boys for Pele	1996	2.50	5.00	10.00
Clear vinyl						
45s						
MEA 5290		Baltimore/Walking with You	1980	125.00	250.00	500.00
Released under her real name, Ellen Amos						

Label, Number		Title	Year	VG	VG+	NM

Amphetamine Reptile

7-Inch Extended Play Singles

Sub Pop 140		Smells Like Smoked Sausages	1992	5.00	10.00	20.00
Four songs on two 7-inch singles; one disc is clear pink, the other solid pink, Value is for both singles together						
Sub Pop 140	PS	Smells Like Smoked Sausages	1992	2.50	5.00	10.00
#40 and #41 in Sub Pop Singles Club series						

Anderson, Laurie

Vinyl Albums

Warner Bros. WBMS-134-2	(2) DJ	Home of the Brave Interview	1986	7.50	15.00	30.00
Part of the Warner Bros. Music Show series						
Warner Bros. PRO-A-2229	DJ	Selections from United States Live				
			1984	3.00	6.00	12.00
Warner Bros. BSK 3674		Big Science	1982	2.50	5.00	10.00
Warner Bros. 25077		Mister Heartbreak	1984	2.50	5.00	10.00
Warner Bros. 25077	DJ	Mister Heartbreak	1984	3.00	6.00	12.00
Quiex II audiophile pressing						
Warner Bros. 25192	(5)	The United States Live	1984	7.50	15.00	30.00
Boxed set						
Warner Bros. 25400		Home of the Brave (Soundtrack)	1986	2.50	5.00	10.00
Warner Bros. 25900		Strange Angels	1989	3.00	6.00	12.00

45s

One Ten (# unknown)		O Superman/Walk the Dog	1981	2.50	5.00	10.00
One Ten (# unknown)	PS	O Superman/Walk the Dog	1981	2.50	5.00	10.00
Warner Bros. 19961		Baby Doll/The Dream Before	1990			
Cassette only						
Warner Bros. 28677		White Lily/Language Is a Virus	1986			3.00
Warner Bros. 49876		O Superman/Walk the Dog	1981		2.50	5.00
7-inch 33 1/3 RPM record						
Warner Bros. 49876	PS	O Superman/Walk the Dog	1981		2.50	5.00
Includes sleeve and lyric sheet						

12-Inch Singles

Warner Bros. PRO-A-2123	DJ	Excellent Birds/Sharkey's Day/Sharkey's Night + 1				
			1984		3.00	6.00
Warner Bros. PRO-A-2465	DJ	Language Is a Virus (same on both sides)				
			1986		3.50	7.00
Warner Bros. PRO-A-7508	DJ	In Our Sleep (3 versions)/Poison (3 versions)				
			1995	2.50	5.00	10.00
Warner Bros. 49888		O Superman/Walk the Dog	1981		3.50	7.00

Angry Samoans
Irreverent hardcore band alternately based in Arkansas and California, led by "Metal Mike" Saunders.

Vinyl Albums

Bad Trip (# unknown)		Back from Samoa	1982	7.50	15.00	30.00
Bad Trip 001	EP	Different World/Unhinged + 4	1986	6.25	12.50	25.00
Bad Trip 002		The Mistaken	1987	6.25	12.50	25.00
As "The Mistaken"; 1,000 copies made						
Bad Trip 201	EP	Inside My Brain	1981	3.75	7.50	15.00
Bad Trip 201	EP	Inside My Brain	1981	7.50	15.00	30.00
Original with heavy gray cardboard cover						
PVC 6915		Yesterday Started Tomorrow	1987	3.75	7.50	15.00
PVC 8955		Inside My Brain	1987	2.50	5.00	10.00
Reissue						

7-Inch Extended Play Singles

Homophobic HOMO-02		Stupid Jerk/Time to Fuck/The Todd Killings//				
		They Saved Hitler's Cock	1982		3.00	6.00
As "The Queer Pills"						

An unusual promo-only 45 from Alice in Chains issued in 1990, it has no label name (though by the type style it's obviously a Columbia product) and was not issued with a picture sleeve. It already fetches up to $25.

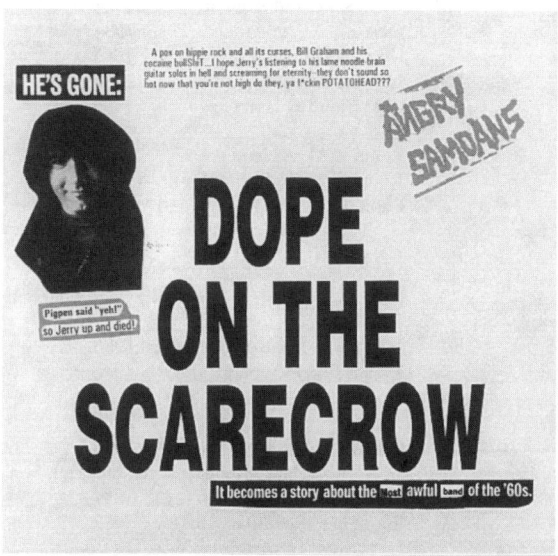

Angry Samoans was an often patently offensive band, but sometimes was right on the money. This little-known 1996 45 of "Dope on the Scarecrow" (approximately 900 were pressed) was a takeoff on the John Mellencamp song "Rain on the Scarecrow," and paid tribute to the passing of Jerry Garcia. Oddly, though, it was written and recorded in 1987, eight years before the Head Deadhead died!

Label, Number		Title	Year	VG	VG+	NM
Homophobic HOMO-02	PS	Stupid Jerk/Time to Fuck/The Todd Killings//				
		They Saved Hitler's Cock	1982	2.25	4.50	9.00
As "The Queer Pills" without "Angry Samoans" rubber-stamped on it						
Homophobic HOMO-02	PS	Stupid Jerk/Time to Fuck/The Todd Killings//				
		They Saved Hitler's Cock	1982		3.00	6.00
As "The Queer Pills" with "Angry Samoans" rubber-stamp						

45s

Bad Trip 019		Dope on the Scarecrow/Heroin	1995			3.00
Bad Trip 019	PS	Dope on the Scarecrow/Heroin	1995			3.00
A "tribute" (?) to dead Dead-man Jerry Garcia, written and recorded in 1987! 900 copies were pressed.						

Animotion

American synth-pop group with a pretty fluid lineup.

Vinyl Albums

Casablanca 826 691-1		Strange Behavior	1986	2.50	5.00	10.00
Mercury 822 580-1		Animotion	1984	2.50	5.00	10.00
Polydor 837 314-1		Animotion	1989	3.00	6.00	12.00
Featuring "Room to Move"						

45s

Casablanca 884 433-7		I Engineer/The Essence	1986			3.00
Casablanca 884 433-7	PS	I Engineer/The Essence	1986			3.00
Casablanca 884 729-7		I Want You/(B-side unknown)	1986			3.00
Casablanca 884 916-7		Strange Behavior/One Step Ahead				
			1986			3.00
Collectables 4855		Obsession/Room to Move	199?			3.00
Reissue						
Mercury 880 266-7		Obsession/Turn Around	1984			3.00
Mercury 880 266-7	PS	Obsession/Turn Around	1984			3.00
Mercury 880 737-7		Let Him Go/Holding You	1985			3.00
Mercury 880 737-7	PS	Let Him Go/Holding You	1985			3.00
Mercury 884 659-7		Obsession/Let Him Go	1986			3.00
Reissue						
Polydor 871 418-7		Room to Move/Send It Over	1989			2.00
Polydor 871 418-7	PS	Room to Move/Send It Over	1989			2.00
Polydor 889 054-7		Calling It Love/The Way Into Your Heart				
			1989			2.00
Polydor 889 054-7	PS	Calling It Love/The Way Into Your Heart				
			1989			2.00

12-Inch Singles

Casablanca PRO 403	DJ	I Engineer (same on both sides)	1986		3.50	7.00
Casablanca 884 729-1		I Want You (3 versions)	1986		3.50	7.00
Mercury PRO 353	DJ	Obsession (7")/Let Him Go (Dub)				
			1984	2.50	5.00	10.00
Mercury PRO 361		Let Him Go (dub) (dub mix)	1984	2.00	4.00	8.00
Mercury 880 266-1		Obsession (Dance Remix)/Obsession (Dub Mix)				
			1984		3.50	7.00
Polydor 871 519-1		Room to Move (5 versions)	1989		3.00	6.00

Ant, Adam

Also see Adam and the Ants.

Vinyl Albums

Epic FE 38370		Friend or Foe	1982	2.50	5.00	10.00
Epic FE 39108		Strip	1984	2.50	5.00	10.00
Epic BFE 40159		Vive Le Rock	1985	2.50	5.00	10.00
MCA 6315		Manners & Physique	1989	2.50	5.00	10.00

Label, Number		Title	Year	VG	VG+	NM
45s						
Capitol S7-18393		Wonderful/Goes Around	1995		2.00	4.00
Epic 03367		Goody Two Shoes/Crackpot History				
			1982		2.00	4.00
Epic 03529		Goody Two Shoes	1983		2.50	5.00
One-sided budget release						
Epic 03688		Desperate But Not Serious/Place in the Country	1983	2.00	4.00	
Epic 03762		Desperate But Not Serious	1983		2.50	5.00
One-sided budget release						
Epic 04337		Strip/Yours Yours Yours	1984			3.00
Epic 04337	PS	Strip/Yours Yours Yours	1984			3.00
Epic 04461		Puss 'N Boots/Kiss the Drummer	1984			3.00
Epic 05538		Goody Two Shoes/Crackpot History				
			1984			3.00
"Golden Oldies" reissue						
Epic 05574		Vive Le Rock/Greta X	1985			3.00
MCA 53679		Room at the Top/Bruce Lee	1989			3.00
MCA 79042		Rough Stuff/Bright Lights Black Leather				
			1990			3.00
12-Inch Singles						
Epic AE 1556	DJ	Hello I Love You/Desperate But Not Serious/Goody Two Shoes				
			1982	2.50	5.00	10.00
Epic AE 1593	DJ	Friend or Foe/Desperate But Not Serious				
			1983	2.50	5.00	10.00
Epic 05261		Vive Le Rock (2 mixes)/Greta X	1985		3.00	6.00
MCA 18436	DJ	Rough Stuff (4 mixes)	1990		3.00	6.00
MCA 18466	DJ	Rough Stuff (alternative mix)/Rough Stuff (alternative dub)				
			1990		3.50	7.00
MCA 24035		Rough Stuff (extended)/Rough Stuff (dub)				
			1990		3.00	6.00

Anti Nowhere League

Label, Number		Title	Year	VG	VG+	NM
Vinyl Albums						
GWR 1238		The Perfect Crime	1987	3.75	7.50	15.00
WXYZ COPE 4		We Are ... The League	1982	3.75	7.50	15.00
WXYZ FEP 1301	EP	I Hate...People	1982	3.50	7.00	14.00

Anti-Seen

Label, Number		Title	Year	VG	VG+	NM
Vinyl Albums						
Bona Fide/Chopper (# unknown)		Honor Among Thieves	1987	2.50	5.00	10.00
Repo (# unknown)		The Raw Shit	1986	2.50	5.00	10.00
Pink vinyl						
7-Inch Extended Play Singles						
Ajax 003		Blood of Freaks	1988	3.00	6.25	12.50
Red vinyl; 300 made						
Ajax 003		Blood of Freaks	1988		3.75	7.50
Black vinyl						
Ajax 003	PS	Blood of Freaks	1988	3.00	6.25	12.50
Poster sleeve; 300 made						
Ajax 003	PS	Blood of Freaks	1988		3.75	7.50
Regular sleeve						
Death Train 001		Drastic	1985	7.50	15.00	30.00
First pressing, with wrong address crossed out on labels						
Death Train 001		Drastic	1985	5.00	10.00	20.00
Second pressing, with corrected address on labels						
Death Train 001	PS	Drastic	1985	7.50	15.00	30.00
Death Train 002		N.C. Royalty	1986	2.50	5.00	10.00
Death Train 002	PS	N.C. Royalty	1986	5.00	10.00	20.00
Blue/green sleeve with lyrics						

Label, Number		Title	Year	VG	VG+	NM
Death Train 002	PS	N.C. Royalty	1986	3.75	7.50	15.00
Orange sleeve with lyrics						
Death Train 002	PS	N.C. Royalty	1986	2.50	5.00	10.00
White sleeve, no lyrics						
TPOS Productions 038		WXCI Live Radio Broadcast	1989		3.75	7.50
TPOS Productions 038	PS	WXCI Live Radio Broadcast	1989		3.75	7.50
45s						
Ajax 007		Two Headed Dog/Cause I Love You				
			1990		2.50	5.00
Blue vinyl (all copies)						
Ajax 007	PS	Two Headed Dog/Cause I Love You				
			1990		2.50	5.00
Sub Pop 174		We Got This Far (Without You)/(We Will Not) Remember				
			1992		3.75	7.50
Clear magenta vinyl						
Sub Pop 174	PS	We Got This Far (Without You)/(We Will Not) Remember				
			1992		3.75	7.50
#49 in Sub Pop Singles Club series						

Arcadia

*Side project by **Duran Duran** members Simon Le Bon, Nick Rhodes and Roger Taylor.*

Vinyl Albums						
Capitol SV-12428		So Red the Rose	1985	2.50	5.00	10.00
Capitol R 134433		So Red the Rose	1985	3.00	6.00	12.00
RCA Music Service edition						
45s						
Atlantic 89370		Say the Word/(Instrumental)	1986		2.00	4.00
Atlantic 89370	PS	Say the Word/(Instrumental)	1986		2.00	4.00
Capitol 5501		Election Day/She's Moody and Grey; She's Mean and She's Restless				
			1985		3.00	
A-side: Guest vocal by Grace Jones						
Capitol 5501	PS	Election Day/She's Moody and Grey; She's Mean and She's Restless				
			1985			3.00
Capitol 5542		Goodbye Is Forever/Missing	1985			3.00
Capitol 5542	PS	Goodbye Is Forever/Missing	1985		2.00	4.00
Capitol 5570		The Flame/Flame Game	1986			3.00
Capitol 5570	PS	The Flame/Flame Game	1986	2.50	5.00	
12-Inch Singles						
Capitol 15209		Election Day (2 versions)/She's Moody and Grey, She's Mean and She's Restless	1985	2.50	5.00	10.00
Capitol 15218		Goodbye Is Forever (3 mixes)/Missing				
			1986	2.50	5.00	10.00

Archer, Tasmin

45s						
SBK S7-17397		Sleeping Satellite/Lords of the New Church				
			1993			3.00

Arrested Development

Hip-hop group with lead rapper Speech and female vocals by Dionne Farris.

Vinyl Albums						
Chrysalis F1-21929		3 Years, 5 Months, & 2 Days in the Life of..				
			1992	2.50	5.00	10.00
Chrysalis F1-29274	(2)	Zingalamaduni	1994	3.00	6.00	12.00
45s						
Chrysalis S7-17321		Natural/Fishin' for Religion	1993			3.00

Label, Number		Title	Year	VG	VG+	NM
Chrysalis S7-17931		Ease My Mind/Shell	1994			3.00
Chrysalis S7-18087		United Front/Southern Fried Funk				
			1994			3.00
Chrysalis S7-56800		Mr. Wendal/Revolution	1993		2.00	4.00
Chrysalis S7-57882		Tennessee/People Everyday	1992	2.00	4.00	

Art Bears
With Fred Frith

Vinyl Albums

Ralph RR 7905		Winter Songs	1979	4.00	8.00	16.00

45s

Ralph RR 7904		Rats & Monkeys/Collapse	1979		2.00	4.00
Ralph RR 7904	PS	Rats & Monkeys/Collapse	1979		2.00	4.00

Art of Noise
*British techno-popsters who had worked with **ABC** and **Frankie Goes to Hollywood**, among others.*

Vinyl Albums

China R 100848		The Best of The Art of Noise	1988	3.00	6.00	12.00
BMG Music Service edition						
China 837 367-1		The Best of The Art of Noise	1988	2.50	5.00	10.00
China 839 404-1		Below the Waste	1989	4.00	8.00	16.00
Chrysalis BFV 41528		In Visible Silence	1986	3.00	6.00	12.00
Chrysalis FV 41567		Re'works of Art of Noise	1986	3.00	6.00	12.00
Chrysalis R 143956		In No Sense? Nonsense	1987	3.50	7.00	14.00
BMG Direct Marketing edition						
Island 90137		Art of Noise	1984	3.00	6.00	12.00
Island 90179		(Who's Afraid of?) The Art of Noise!				
			1985	3.00	6.00	12.00
Island 842 473-1		(Who's Afraid of?) The Art of Noise!				
			1990	2.50	5.00	10.00
Reissue of Island 90179						

45s

China 42932		Legs/Hoops and Mallets	1985			3.00
China 42932	PS	Legs/Hoops and Mallets	1985			3.00
China 42986		Peter Gunn/Something Always Happens				
			1986			3.00
A-side: With Duane Eddy						
China 42986	PS	Peter Gunn/Something Always Happens				
			1986			3.00
China 43002		Paranoimia/Why Me	1986			3.00
A-side: With Max Headroom						
China 43002	PS	Paranoimia/Why Me	1986			3.00
China 43055		Legacy/Opus III	1986			3.00
China 43055	PS	Legacy/Opus III	1986			3.00
China 871 038-7		Kiss/E.F.L.	1989			3.00
A-side: With Tom Jones						
China 871 038-7	PS	Kiss/E.F.L.	1989			3.00
Island 94999		Close (To the Edit)/Beat Box	1986		2.00	4.00
Gold label "Revival of the Fittest" series						
Island 99561		Moments in Love/A Time for Fear (Who's Afraid)				
			1986		2.00	4.00
Label credit: Trevor Horn/Paul Morley/Art of Noise						
Island 99754		Close (To the Edit)/(B-side unknown)				
			1984		2.00	4.00
Island 99754	PS	Close (To the Edit)/(B-side unknown)				
			1984		2.00	4.00
Island 99782		Beat Box/Woman in Love	1984		2.00	4.00

Label, Number		Title	Year	VG	VG+	NM
12-Inch Singles						
China VAS 2327	DJ	Peter Gunn (Long)/Peter Gunn (Short)				
			1986		3.00	6.00
With Duane Eddy						
China VAS 2841	DJ	E.F.L./One Earth/Ode to Don Juan/A Day at the Races				
			1987		3.00	6.00
China 871 039-1		Kiss (3 mixes)	1988		3.50	7.00
With Tom Jones						
China 871 957-1		Paranoimia '89 (4 versions)	1989	2.00	4.00	8.00
Chrysalis 43135		Dragnet (3 mixes)/Action Art	1987		3.00	6.00
Island 744	DJ	Close (to the Edit) (2 versions)/Beatbox (Diversion 1)				
			1984		3.50	7.00
Island 96839		Moments in Love (2 versions)/Beat Box/Love Beat				
			1984	2.00	4.00	8.00
Polydor 873 305-1		Yebol (3 mixes)	1989	2.00	4.00	8.00

Artists United Against Apartheid

*Benefit group to raise money to fight apartheid in South Africa. A far more eclectic group of musicians than either **Band Aid** or **USA For Africa**.*

Vinyl Albums						
Manhattan SPRO-9538	DJ	Voices of Sun City	1985	8.75	17.50	35.00
Promo album of interviews with participants						
Manhattan ST-53019		Sun City	1985	3.00	6.00	12.00
Includes solo tracks by Bono, Peter Gabriel...						
45s						
Manhattan 50017		Sun City/Not So Far Away (Dub)	1985			3.00
Manhattan 50017		Sun City/Not So Far Away (Dub)	1985			3.00
Manhattan 50026		Let Me See Your I.D. (Street Mix)/Let Me See Your I.D. (Album Mix)	1986		2.00	4.00
12-Inch Singles						
Manhattan 56013		Sun City (9:37)/Not So Far Away (Dub)				
			1985		3.00	6.00
Manhattan 56015		Let Me See Your I.D. (3 versions)				
			1985		3.00	6.00
Manhattan SPRO 9544/5	DJ	Sun City (Rock Version)/Silver and Gold				
			1985	2.50	5.00	10.00
B-side is a Bono song, later recorded by U2						

Ash

45s						
Generator G-26		Petrol/Punk Boy	1995			3.00
Yellow vinyl, small center hole						
Generator G-26	PS	Petrol/Punk Boy	1995			3.00

August Sons

Vinyl Albums						
Eyes in the Woods (# unknown)EP		I Am Not a Vampire	1989	8.75	17.50	35.00

Avengers

Vinyl Albums						
CD Presents 007		Avengers	1983	3.75	7.50	15.00
CD Presents 007		Avengers	1983	5.00	10.00	20.00
Red vinyl						
Go 005		Avengers	1983	30.00	60.00	120.00
White Noise 002	EP	Avengers	1978	5.00	10.00	20.00

Label, Number		Title	Year	VG	VG+	NM
45s						
CD Presents 006		Paint It Black/Thin White Line	1983		2.00	4.00
Red vinyl						
CD Presents 006	PS	Paint It Black/Thin White Line	1983		2.00	4.00
Dangerhouse SFD 400		We Are the One/I Believe in Me/Car Crash				
			1977	4.50	9.00	18.00
Black vinyl						
Dangerhouse SFD 400		We Are the One/I Believe in Me/Car Crash				
			1977	3.75	7.50	15.00
Red vinyl						
Dangerhouse SFD 400	PS	We Are the One/I Believe in Me/Car Crash				
			1977	4.50	9.00	18.00
Crucifix cover						
Dangerhouse SFD 400	PS	We Are the One/I Believe in Me/Car Crash				
			1977	3.75	7.50	15.00
Target cover						

Aztec Camera

Label, Number		Title	Year	VG	VG+	NM
Vinyl Albums						
Sire 23899		High Land, Hard Rain	1983	3.00	6.00	12.00
Sire 25183		Knife	1984	3.00	6.00	12.00
Sire 25285	10	Backwards and Forwards	1985	3.00	6.00	12.00
Ten-inch record in a 12-inch cover						
Sire 25646		Love	1987	2.50	5.00	10.00
Sire 26211		Stray	1990	2.50	5.00	10.00
45s						
Sire 27819		Somewhere in My Heart/Everybody Is a Number One				
			1988			3.00
Sire 27819	PS	Somewhere in My Heart/Everybody Is a Number One				
			1988		2.00	4.00
Sire 28155		Deep and Wide and Tall/Bad Education				
			1987			3.00
Sire 28155	PS	Deep and Wide and Tall/Bad Education				
			1987		2.00	4.00
Sire 29153		All I Need Is Everything/Jump	1984		2.00	4.00
Sire 29269		Oblivious/Queen's Tattoos	1984		2.00	4.00
Sire 29541		Lost Outside the Tunnel/Oblivious	1983		2.00	4.00
12-Inch Singles						
Sire PRO-A-2848	DJ	Deep and Wide and Tall/Deep and Wide and Tall (Edit)				
			1987	2.00	4.00	8.00
Sire PRO-A-3160	DJ	Somewhere in My Heart (2 versions)/Roddy Frame Interview				
			1988	2.00	4.00	8.00
Sire PRO-A-3232	DJ	Somewhere in My Heart (Alternate Mix)/Somewhere in My Heart				
			1988	2.00	4.00	8.00
		(Remix)				
Sire PRO-A-4517	DJ	Good Morning Britain (6 versions)				
			1990	2.00	4.00	8.00

B

B-52's, The

*Georgia-based new wave band with Kate Pierson and **Fred Schneider**.*

Label, Number	Title	Year	VG	VG+	NM
Vinyl Albums					
Reprise 25854	Cosmic Thing	1989	3.00	6.00	12.00
Warner Bros. BSK 3355	The B-52's	1979	2.50	5.00	10.00
Warner Bros. BSK 3471	Wild Planet	1980	3.00	6.00	12.00
Originals have red custom labels (deduct 33% for later pressings)					

Label, Number		Title	Year	VG	VG+	NM
Warner Bros. MINI 3596	EP	Party Mix	1981	3.00	6.00	12.00
Warner Bros. MINI 3641	EP	Mesopotamia	1982	2.00	4.00	8.00
Warner Bros. 23819		Whammy!	1983	2.50	5.00	10.00
Warner Bros. 25504		Bouncing Off the Satellites	1986	2.50	5.00	10.00
Warner Bros. R 154582		Bouncing Off the Satellites	1986	3.00	6.00	12.00
RCA Music Service edition						

45s

Label, Number		Title	Year	VG	VG+	NM
DB 52		Rock Lobster/52 Girls	1978	6.25	12.50	25.00
DB 52	PS	Rock Lobster/52 Girls	1978	6.25	12.50	25.00
MCA 54839		(Meet) The Flintstones (Fred's Edit)/ (Meet) The Flintstones (Barney's Edit)	1994		2.00	4.00
By "The BC-52's" -- The B-52's alter ego in The Flintstones, the live-action movie						
Reprise 18763		Revolution Earth	1993			*Cassette only*
Reprise 18776		Tell It Like It T-I-S	1993			*Cassette only*
Reprise 18895		Good Stuff/Deadbeat Club	1993			3.00
Reissue						
Reprise 18896		Good Stuff/Bad Influence	1992		2.00	4.00
Reprise 19430		Love Shack/Roam	199?			3.00
Reissue						
Reprise 19938		Deadbeat Club/Planet Claire (Live)	1990			3.00
Reprise 22667		Roam/Bushfire	1990			3.00
Reprise 22817		Love Shack/Channel Z	1989			3.00
Reprise 22817	PS	Love Shack/Channel Z	1989			3.00
Warner Bros. GWB 0416		Rock Lobster/Private Idaho	198?			3.00
Back to Back Hits reissue						
Warner Bros. 28561		Summer of Love/Housework	1986			3.00
Warner Bros. 28561	PS	Summer of Love/Housework	1986			3.00
Warner Bros. 29561		Song for a Future Generation/Treason	1983			3.00
Warner Bros. 29561	PS	Song for a Future Generation/Treason	1983			3.00
Warner Bros. 29579		Legal Tender/Moon 83	1983			3.00
Warner Bros. 29971		Mesopotamia/Throw That Beat in the Garbage Can	1982			3.00
Warner Bros. 49173		Rock Lobster/6060-842	1980		2.00	4.00
Warner Bros. 49173	PS	Rock Lobster/6060-842	1980		3.00	6.00
Warner Bros. 49212		Planet Claire/There's a Moon in the Sky (Called the Moon)	1980		2.00	4.00
Warner Bros. 49212	PS	Planet Claire/There's a Moon in the Sky (Called the Moon)	1980		3.00	6.00
Warner Bros. 49537		Private Idaho/Party Out of Bounds	1980		2.00	4.00
Warner Bros. 49537	PS	Private Idaho/Party Out of Bounds	1980		3.00	6.00
Warner Bros. 49717		Lava/Quiche Lorraine	1981		2.00	4.00
Warner Bros. 50064		Deep Sleep/Nip It in the Bud	1982		2.00	4.00

12-Inch Singles

Label, Number		Title	Year	VG	VG+	NM
Reprise PRO-A-5852	DJ	Revolution Earth (4 versions)	1992	2.00	4.00	8.00
Reprise 21441		Roam (3 versions)/Bushfire	1989		3.50	7.00
Reprise 40561		Good Stuff (3 versions)/Bad Influence	1992	2.00	4.00	8.00
Reprise 40594		Tell It Like It T-I-S (5 versions)/The World's Green Laughter	1992		3.00	6.00
Reprise 40642		Revolution Earth (3 versions)/Is That You Mo-Dean	1992		3.00	6.00
Warner Bros. PRO-A-890	DJ	Private Idaho/Party Out of Bounds (Instrumental)	1979	3.00	6.00	12.00
Warner Bros. PRO-A-927	DJ	Give Me Back My Man/Strobe Light	1980	3.00	6.00	12.00
Warner Bros. PRO-A-1016	DJ	Mesopotamia/Deep Sleep/Cake	1982	3.00	6.00	12.00

Label, Number		Title	Year	VG	VG+	NM
Warner Bros. PRO-A-2045	DJ	Legal Tender/Whammy Kiss/Future Generation				
			1983	2.50	5.00	10.00
Warner Bros. 20509		Summer of Love (3 versions)	1986	2.00	4.00	8.00

Babes in Toyland

Minneapolis-based all-female rock band.

Vinyl Albums

Reprise 45868		Nemesisters	1995	2.50	5.00	10.00
Twin/Tone TTR 89183		Machine	1989	2.50	5.00	10.00

45s

Reprise 17819		We Are Family/Memory	1995	3.00		
Sub Pop 66		House/Arriba	1990	10.00	20.00	40.00
Gold vinyl pressing of 2,000						
Sub Pop 66		House/Arriba	1990	2.50	5.00	10.00
Black vinyl pressing of 1,500						
Sub Pop 66	PS	House/Arriba	1990	2.50	5.00	10.00
#19 in Sub Pop Singles Club series						
Treehouse 017		Dust Cake Boy/Spit to See the Shine				
			1989	6.25	12.50	25.00
Black vinyl						
Treehouse 017		Dust Cake Boy/Spit to See the Shine				
			1989	12.50	25.00	50.00
Green vinyl						
Treehouse 017	PS	Dust Cake Boy/Spit to See the Shine				
			1989	6.25	12.50	25.00

Baby Grand

*Philadelphia-area band with Rob Hyman and Eric Bazilian, later of **The Hooters**.*

Vinyl Albums

Arista AL 4148		Baby Grand	1977	5.00	10.00	20.00

45s

Arista 0293		Bring Me Your Broken Heart/Lady of My Dreams				
			1977		2.50	5.00
Arista 0312		Never Enough/Lady of My Dreams				
			1978		2.50	5.00
Arista 0374		Walk Away Renee/Much Too Much				
			1978		2.50	5.00
Arista 0394	DJ	All Night Long (same on both sides)				
			1979		2.50	5.00
May be promo only						

Backbeat Band

Band members: Greg Dulli, Don Fleming, Thurston Moore, Mike Mills, Dave Grohl.

Vinyl Albums

Virgin SPRO-14124	DJ	Backbeat (Original Soundtrack)	1994	3.75	7.50	15.00
Green vinyl in plastic sleeve						

45s

Dry Hump 010		Money/Dizzy Miss Lizzy	1994		2.50	5.00
Dry Hump 010	PS	Money/Dizzy Miss Lizzy	1994		2.50	5.00
With insert advertising other Dry Hump releases						
Virgin S7-17912		Money/Dizzy Miss Lizzy//He's Wearing My Bathrobe				
			1994		2.00	4.00
As "Backbeat"						

Label, Number		Title	Year	VG	VG+	NM

Bad Brains

Vinyl Albums

Label, Number		Title	Year	VG	VG+	NM
Bad Brains 003	EP	I and I Survive/Destroy Babylon	1983	5.00	10.00	20.00
Caroline CAROL-1375		Quickness	1989	2.50	5.00	10.00
Caroline CAROL-1613		Rock for Light	1990	2.50	5.00	10.00
Reissue of PVC 8917 with three bonus tracks						
Caroline CAROL-1617		The Youth Are Getting Restless	1990	2.50	5.00	10.00
Important 003	EP	I and I Survive/Destroy Babylon	1983	3.75	7.50	15.00
Maverick 45882		God of Love	1995	2.50	5.00	10.00
PVC 8917		Rock for Light	1983	5.00	10.00	20.00
SST 065		I Against I	1986	2.50	5.00	10.00
SST 160		Live	1988	2.50	5.00	10.00
SST 228	10	Spirit Electricity	1991	2.00	4.00	8.00

45s

Label, Number		Title	Year	VG	VG+	NM
Bad Brains 001		Pay to Cum/Stay Close to Me	1980	2.50	5.00	10.00
Bad Brains 001	PS	Pay to Cum/Stay Close to Me	1980	2.50	5.00	10.00
With lyric insert						
Caroline (# unknown)		Pay to Cum/At the Movies	1990			2.50
Caroline (# unknown)	PS	Pay to Cum/At the Movies	1990			2.50

Bad Manners

British ska band.

Vinyl Albums

Label, Number	Title	Year	VG	VG+	NM
MCA 5218	Bad Manners	1981	3.75	7.50	15.00
MCA 5415	Klass	1983	3.00	6.00	12.00
Portrait BFR 40070	Mental Notes	1985	3.00	6.00	12.00

45s

Label, Number	Title	Year	VG	VG+	NM
Portrait 04602	My Girl Lollipop (My Boy Lollipop)/Falling Out of Love				
		1984		2.00	4.00
Portrait 05725	What the Papers Say/Louie Louie				
		1985		2.00	4.00

12-Inch Singles

Label, Number	Title	Year	VG	VG+	NM
Portrait 05009	My Girl Lollipop (3 remixes)	1984	2.50	5.00	10.00
Portrait 05020	That'll Do Nicely (2 versions)/Exodus				
		1984	2.50	5.00	10.00
Portrait 05343	Bang the Drum All Day (3 versions)/Saturday Night				
		1985	2.00	4.00	8.00

Bad Religion

California punk group. Ex-member Brett Gurevitz owns Epitaph Records.

Vinyl Albums

Label, Number	Title	Year	VG	VG+	NM
Atlantic 82870	The Gray Race	1996	2.50	5.00	10.00
Epitaph EPI-BRLP-1	How Could Hell Be Any Worse?	1982	7.50	15.00	30.00
Epitaph 86404	No Control	1988	3.00	6.00	12.00
Epitaph 86407	How Could Hell Be Any Worse?	1989	3.00	6.00	12.00
Reissue of Epitaph BRLP-1					
Epitaph 86409	Against the Grain	1990	3.00	6.00	12.00
Epitaph 86416	Generator	1992	3.00	6.00	12.00
Epitaph 86420	Recipe for Hate	1993	2.50	5.00	10.00

7-Inch Extended Play Singles

Label, Number		Title	Year	VG	VG+	NM
Epitaph 1072		Bad Religion	1981	12.50	25.00	50.00
Epitaph 1072	PS	Bad Religion	1981	12.50	25.00	50.00

45s

Label, Number	Title	Year	VG	VG+	NM
Sympathy For The Record Industry 158	Atomic Garden	1991		2.00	4.00

Label, Number		Title	Year	VG	VG+	NM
Sympathy For The Record Industry 158	PS	Atomic Garden	1991		2.00	4.00
Sympathy For The Record Industry 232		American Jesus/?	199?			2.00
Sympathy For The Record Industry 232	PS	American Jesus/?	199?			2.00
Sympathy For The Record Industry 326		Stranger Than Fiction/?	1994			2.00
Sympathy For The Record Industry 326	PS	Stranger Than Fiction/?	1994			2.00
Unplayable 87079		Punk Rock Song//The Universal Cynic/The Dodo	1996			2.50
Gray marbled vinyl, small hole						
Unplayable 87079	PS	Punk Rock Song//The Universal Cynic/The Dodo	1996			2.50

Baltimora

Real name: Jimmy McShane, from Northern Ireland. Synth-pop one-hit wonder.

Vinyl Albums

Manhattan ST-53026		Living in the Background	1986	2.50	5.00	10.00

45s

Manhattan 50018		Tarzan Boy/Tarzan Boy (Dub)	1985			3.00
Manhattan 50018	PS	Tarzan Boy/Tarzan Boy (Dub)	1985	2.50	5.00	10.00
Picture sleeve is scarce						
Manhattan 50029		Chinese Restaurant/Living in the Background	1986			3.00
SBK S7-17320		Tarzan Boy/Rockin' Over the Beat	1993		2.00	4.00
B-side by Technotronic; colored vinyl						

12-Inch Singles

Manhattan SPRO 9636/7	DJ	Living in the Background (3 versions)	1985		3.00	6.00
Manhattan 56011		Tarzan Boy (3 versions)	1985	3.00	6.00	12.00

Bambaataa, Afrika, and the Soul Sonic Force

Hip-hop/funk group from New York, led by Afrika Bambaataa. The below also includes records without the Soul Sonic Force credited.

Vinyl Albums

Tommy Boy TBLP-1007		Planet Rock -- The Album	1986	3.00	6.00	12.00
Tommy Boy TBLP-1052	EP	Don't Stop...Planet Rock (The Remix EP)	1992	2.50	5.00	10.00

45s

Capitol 44163	DJ	Reckless (same on both sides)	1988			3.00
With UB40						
Capitol 44163	PS	Reckless (same on both sides)	1988			3.00
With UB40						
Tommy Boy 823		Planet Rock/(Instrumental)	1982	2.00	4.00	8.00

12-Inch Singles

Capitol 15379		Reckless (2 mixes)/Mind, Body & Soul (3 mixes)	198?		3.00	6.00
With UB40						
Capitol 15385		Shout It Out (3 versions)/Tell Me When You Need It Again	1988		2.50	5.00
EMI 56241		Power Boy Power (4 versions)	1991	2.00	4.00	8.00
Tommy Boy 821		Jazzy Sensation (3 versions)	1983	2.50	5.00	10.00
Tommy Boy 823		Planet Rock/Planet Rock (instrumental)	1983	2.50	5.00	10.00

Label, Number		Title	Year	VG	VG+	NM
Tommy Boy 870		Funk You (4 versions)	1985		3.00	6.00
Tommy Boy 879		Bambaataa's Theme/Tension	1986		3.00	6.00
York 786		Inside Looking Out (6 versions)	1989	2.00	4.00	8.00
Green vinyl						

Bananarama

British girl group. Member Siobhan Fabey later joined Shakespear's Sister.

Vinyl Albums

London R 100616		The Greatest Hits Collection	1988	3.50	7.00	14.00
BMG Direct Marketing edition						
London R 150257		Wow!	1987	3.50	7.00	14.00
BMG Direct Marketing edition						
London 810 102-1		Deep Sea Skiving	1983	3.00	6.00	12.00
London 820 036-1		Bananarama	1984	3.00	6.00	12.00
London 828 013-1		True Confessions	1986	3.00	6.00	12.00
London 828 061-1		Wow!	1987	3.00	6.00	12.00
London 828 158-1		The Greatest Hits Collection	1988	3.00	6.00	12.00

45s

Collectables 4263		Cruel Summer/Shy Boy	199?			3.00
Reissue						
Collectables 4264		I Heard a Rumour/I Can't Help It	199?			3.00
Reissue						
Collectables 4265		Venus/More Than Physical	199?			3.00
Reissue						
London LD 201		He Was Really Saying Something/Give Us Back Our Cheap Fares				
			1982		2.00	4.00
London 810 112-7		Shy Boy (Don't It Make You Feel Good)/Give Us Back Our Cheap Fares				
			1983		2.00	4.00
London 810 112-7	PS	Shy Boy (Don't It Make You Feel Good)/Give Us Back Our Cheap Fares				
			1983		2.00	4.00
London 810 115-7		Na Na Hey Hey Kiss Him Goodbye/Tell Tale Signs				
			1983		2.00	4.00
London 810 127-7		Cruel Summer/Cruel Dub	1984		2.00	4.00
London 820 033-7		Robert De Niro's Waiting/Push	1984		2.00	4.00
London 820 033-7	PS	Robert De Niro's Waiting/Push	1984		2.00	4.00
London 882 019-7		The Wild Life/The State I'm In	1984			3.00
London 882 019-7	PS	The Wild Life/The State I'm In	1984			3.00
London 886 056-7		Venus/White Train	1986			3.00
London 886 056-7	PS	Venus/White Train	1986			3.00
London 886 080-7		More Than Physical/Scarlett	1986			3.00
London 886 080-7	PS	More Than Physical/Scarlett	1986			3.00
London 886 119-7		Trick of the Night/Cut Above the Rest				
			1986			3.00
London 886 165-7		I Heard a Rumour/Clean Cut Boy				
			1987			3.00
London 886 165-7	PS	I Heard a Rumour/Clean Cut Boy				
			1987			3.00
London 886 212-7		I Can't Help It/Mr. Sleaze	1987			3.00
London 886 212-7	PS	I Can't Help It/Mr. Sleaze	1987			3.00
London 886 255-7		Love in the First Degree/Ecstacy	1988			3.00
London 886 255-7	PS	Love in the First Degree/Ecstacy	1988			3.00
London 886 342-7		Love, Truth and Honesty/Strike It Rich				
			1988			3.00
London 886 400-7		Nathan Jones/Once in a Lifetime	1989			3.00
London 886 492-7		Help/Lananeeneenoonoo	1989			3.00

12-Inch Singles

London LLD 101		He Was Really Sayin' Something/Ail a Mwana				
			1982	3.00	6.00	12.00
London PRO 221	DJ	(He Was) Really Sayin' Somethin' (same on both sides)				
			1982	2.50	5.00	10.00

Label, Number		Title	Year	VG	VG+	NM
London PRO 240	DJ	Na Na Hey Hey (Kiss Him Goodbye) (2 versions)				
			1983	2.00	4.00	8.00
London 810 291-1		Cruel Summer/Cairo/Summer Dub				
			1984	3.00	6.00	12.00
London 869 439-1		Long Train Running (2 mixes)/Outta Sight				
			1991	2.00	4.00	8.00
London 869 547-1		Tripping On Your Love (6 versions)				
			1991		3.50	7.00
London 886 056-1		Venus (extended)/Venus (dub)/White Train				
			1986		3.00	6.00
London 886 080-1		More Than Physical (3 versions)	1986	2.00	4.00	8.00
London 886 088-1		Venus (4 mixes)	1986	2.00	4.00	8.00
London 886 119-1		A Trick of the Night (3 mixes)	1986	2.00	4.00	8.00
London 886 188-1		I Heard a Rumour (4 mixes)/Clean Cut Boy				
			1987	2.00	4.00	8.00
London 886 212-1		I Can't Help It (2 versions)/Mr. Sleaze (2 versions)				
			1987	2.00	4.00	8.00
London 886 395-1		Love, Truth and Honesty (3 versions)/Strike It Rich (Club Mix)				
			1988		3.00	6.00
London 886 481-1		Nathan Jones (3 mixes)/Once in a Lifetime				
			1988	2.50	5.00	10.00

Band Aid

*The first of a wave of all-star charity groups. Led by **Bob Geldof**. Also in the group were **Boy George, Sting, George Michael, Bono of U2, Midge Ure,** and a whole bunch of others, including **Bananarama** and American R&B stars Kool and the Gang. Because of controversy over the use in America of the registered trademark Band-Aid, their record has been unavailable here since 1985.*

45s

Columbia 04749		Do They Know It's Christmas?/Feed the World				
			1984		2.50	5.00
Columbia 04749	PS	Do They Know It's Christmas?/Feed the World				
			1984		2.50	5.00

12-Inch Singles

Columbia 05157		Do They Know It's Christmas? (2 versions)/Feed the World				
			1984	3.75	7.50	15.00

Bangles

California girl group. Featuring Susannah Hoffs on most of their hits.

Vinyl Albums

Columbia CAS 2270	DJ	Interchords	1986	5.00	10.00	20.00
Promo-only interview album						
Columbia BFC 39220		All Over the Place	1984	3.00	6.00	12.00
Columbia BFC 40039		Different Light	1986	3.00	6.00	12.00
Columbia FC 40039		Different Light	1986	2.00	4.00	8.00
Reissue with new prefix; "02" added to bar code on back cover						
Columbia OC 44056		Everything	1988	2.50	5.00	10.00
Faulty Products FEP 1302	EP	Bangles	1982	3.75	7.50	15.00
I.R.S. SP-70506	EP	Bangles	1983	3.00	6.00	12.00
Reissue of Faulty Products EP						

45s

Columbia 04479		Hero Takes a Fall/Where Were You When I Needed You				
			1984			3.00
Columbia 04479	PS	Hero Takes a Fall/Where Were You When I Needed You				
			1984		3.00	6.00
Columbia 04634		Going Down to Liverpool/Dover Beach				
			1984		2.00	4.00

Backbeat Band was an all-star alternative quintet that recorded covers of well-known Beatles remakes for use in the movie *Backbeat.* The above picture sleeve came with a 45 on the indie label Dry Hump, which licensed the rights to do this single from Virgin America.

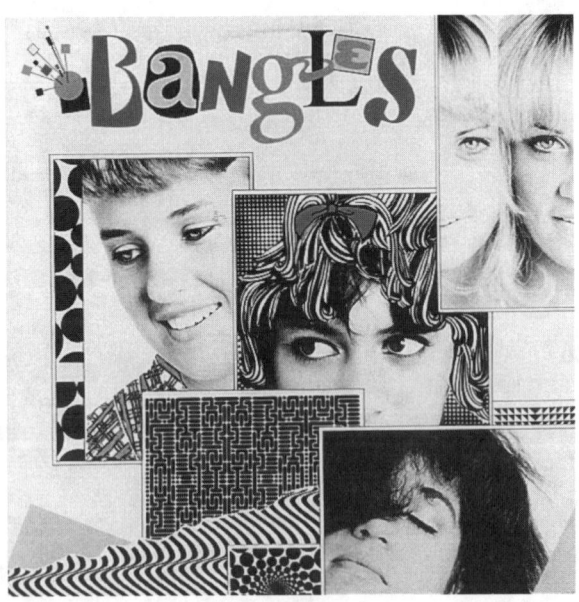

The first Bangles 12-inch EP on Faulty Products came out in 1983. It was later re-issued on I.R.S. Other than this, most American Bangles product is relatively common and inexpensive. (This doesn't include the one single they recorded under the name The Bangs.)

Label, Number		Title	Year	VG	VG+	NM
Columbia 04770		Hero Takes a Fall (Remix)/Tell Me				
			1985	2.50	5.00	10.00
Columbia 04770	PS	Hero Takes a Fall (Remix)/Tell Me				
			1985	2.50	5.00	10.00
Columbia 05757		Manic Monday/In a Different Light				
			1986			3.00
A-side written by Prince under pseudonym "Christopher"						
Columbia 05757	PS	Manic Monday/In a Different Light				
			1986			3.00
Columbia 05886		If She Knew What She Wants/Not Like You				
			1986			3.00
Columbia 05886	PS	If She Knew What She Wants/Not Like You				
			1986			3.00
Columbia 06257		Walk Like an Egyptian/Angels Don't Fall in Love				
			1986			3.00
No picture sleeve issued in U.S.						
Columbia 06674		Walking Down Your Street/Let It Go				
			1987			3.00
Columbia 06674	PS	Walking Down Your Street/Let It Go				
			1987			3.00
Columbia 08090		In Your Room/Bell Jar	1988			3.00
Columbia 08090	PS	In Your Room/Bell Jar	1988			3.00
Columbia 08385		Manic Monday/Hazy Shade of Winter				
			1988			3.00
Gray label "Golden Oldies" reissue						
Columbia 08386		Walk Like an Egyptian/Walking Down Your Street				
			1988			3.00
Gray label "Golden Oldies" reissue						
Columbia 68533		Eternal Flame/What I Meant to Say				
			1989			3.00
Columbia 68744		Be With You/Let It Go	1989			3.00
Columbia 73791		Eternal Flame/What I Meant to Say				
			1991			3.00
Reissue						
Def Jam 07630		Hazy Shade of Winter/She's Lost You				
			1987			3.00
Def Jam 07630	PS	Hazy Shade of Winter/She's Lost You				
			1987			3.00
B-side by Joan Jett and the Blackhearts						

12-Inch Singles

Label, Number		Title	Year	VG	VG+	NM
Columbia AS 1883	DJ	Hero Takes a Fall (same on both sides)				
			1984	3.00	6.00	12.00
Columbia AS 1939	DJ	Going Down to Liverpool (same on both sides)				
			1984	3.00	6.00	12.00
Columbia CAS 2249	DJ	Manic Monday (same on both sides)				
			1986	3.00	6.00	12.00
Columbia CAS 2334	DJ	If She Knew What She Wants (same on both sides)				
			1986	2.50	5.00	10.00
Columbia CAS 2453	DJ	Walk Like an Egyptian (same on both sides)				
			1986	2.00	4.00	8.00
Columbia 05935		Walk Like an Egyptian (3 versions)				
			1986		3.00	6.00
Columbia 06760		Walking Down Your Street (3 versions)				
			1986		3.00	6.00
Columbia 08170		In Your Room (4 versions)	1988		3.00	6.00
Def Jam CAS 2857	DJ	Hazy Shade of Winter (with intro)/Hazy Shade of Winter				
		(without intro)	1987	2.00	4.00	8.00
Def Jam 07540		Hazy Shade of Winter (4 versions)				
			1987	2.00	4.00	8.00
Faulty Products DJ 1000	DJ	The Real World (same on both sides)				
			1983	3.75	7.50	15.00

Label, Number		Title	Year	VG	VG+	NM

Bangs, The
Early incarnation of the Bangles.

45s
Downkiddie 001		Getting Out of Hand/Call On Me				
			1981	12.50	25.00	50.00
Yellow label (original)						
Downkiddie 001		Getting Out of Hand/Call On Me				
			1981	10.00	20.00	40.00
Blue label						
Downkiddie 001	PS	Getting Out of Hand/Call On Me				
			1981	15.00	30.00	60.00

Barbusters, The
*See **Jett, Joan, and the Blackhearts***

Barlow, Lou

45s
Sub Pop 251		I Am Not Mocking You/Survival/Helpless Heartbreak/ + 1				
			1993	2.50	5.00	10.00
Pink vinyl						
Sub Pop 251	PS	I Am Not Mocking You/Survival/Helpless Heartbreak/ + 1				
			1993	2.50	5.00	10.00
#62 (and last) in Sub Pop Singles Club series						

Base, Rob, and D.J. E-Z Rock
Hip-hop duo.

Vinyl Albums
Profile PRO-1267		It Takes Two	1988	3.50	7.00	14.00
Profile PRO-1285		The Incredible Base	1989	3.00	6.00	12.00
Rob Base solo						

45s
Profile 5186		It Takes Two/(Instrumental)	1988		2.00	4.00
Profile 5247		Joy and Pain/(B-side unknown)	1989			3.00
Profile 5247	PS	Joy and Pain/(B-side unknown)	1989			3.00

12-Inch Singles
Profile 7239		Get On the Dance Floor (4 versions)/Keep It Going Now				
		(Hardcore Remix)	1988		3.50	7.00
Profile 7292		Get Up and Have a Good Time (3 mixes)/Turn It Out				
		(2 mixes)	1990		3.00	6.00
Rob Base solo						

Basil, Toni
Los Angeles vocalist, dancer and choreographer who made her first single in 1967 at the age of 17.

Vinyl Albums
		Title	Year	VG	VG+	NM
Chrysalis CHR 1410		Word of Mouth	1982	3.00	6.00	12.00
Chrysalis FV 41410		Word of Mouth	1983	2.50	5.00	10.00
Reissue						
Chrysalis PV 41410		Word of Mouth	1986	2.00	4.00	8.00
Reissue with new prefix						
Chrysalis FV 41449		Toni Basil	1983	2.50	5.00	10.00
Chrysalis PV 41449		Toni Basil	1986	2.00	4.00	8.00
Reissue with new prefix						

45s
A&M 791		Breakaway/I'm 28	1966	2.50	5.00	10.00

Label, Number		Title	Year	VG	VG+	NM
Chrysalis 2638		Mickey/Thief on the Loose	1982			3.00
Chrysalis 2638	PS	Mickey/Thief on the Loose	1982			3.00
Chrysalis 2665		Mickey (Spanish)/Thief on the Loose				
			1982		2.00	4.00
Chrysalis 2665	PS	Mickey (Spanish)/Thief on the Loose				
			1982		2.00	4.00
Chrysalis 03537		Shoppin' from A to Z/Time After Time				
			1983			3.00
Chrysalis 03537	PS	Shoppin' from A to Z/Time After Time				
			1983			3.00
Chrysalis 03539		Mickey/Thief on the Loose	1983			3.00
Reissue						
Chrysalis 42711		Street Beat/(B-side unknown)	1983			3.00
Chrysalis 42753		Over My Head/Best Performance				
			1983			3.00
Chrysalis 42753	PS	Over My Head/Best Performance				
			1983			3.00

12-Inch Singles

Label, Number		Title	Year	VG	VG+	NM
Chrysalis 42708		Street Beat (Club Mix)/Street Beat (Dub)				
			1983		3.00	6.00
Chrysalis AS 1615	DJ	Nobody/Rock On	1983		3.00	6.00

Bastards, The

Vinyl Albums

Label, Number		Title	Year	VG	VG+	NM
Treehouse 016		Monticallo	1989	6.25	12.50	25.00

45s

Label, Number		Title	Year	VG	VG+	NM
Treehouse 011		Who Cares/Shit for Brains	1988	15.00	30.00	60.00
First 100 on green vinyl (numbered)						
Treehouse 011		Who Cares/Shit for Brains	1988	8.75	17.50	35.00
Second 100 on black vinyl (numbered)						
Treehouse 011		Who Cares/Shit for Brains	1988	3.75	7.50	15.00
Yellow label, 800 made						
Treehouse 011		Who Cares/Shit for Brains	1988	2.50	5.00	10.00
White label, 700 made						
Treehouse 011	PS	Who Cares/Shit for Brains	1988	10.00	20.00	40.00
Accompanies either of the first two pressings, linoleum block print						
Treehouse 011	PS	Who Cares/Shit for Brains	1988	3.75	7.50	15.00
Yellow or green sleeve (each the same value)						
Treehouse 011	PS	Who Cares/Shit for Brains	1988	2.50	5.00	10.00
Mostly pink covers for final 700						
Treehouse 014		Frank/Loser	1988	7.50	15.00	30.00
Burgundy vinyl (200 made)						
Treehouse 014		Frank/Loser	1988	2.50	5.00	10.00
Black vinyl (800 made)						
Treehouse 014	PS	Frank/Loser	1988	2.50	5.00	10.00
Treehouse 018		Neighbor/Motor City Kid	1989	5.00	10.00	20.00
Blue vinyl						
Treehouse 018		Neighbor/Motor City Kid	1989	3.00	6.25	12.50
Black vinyl, yellow label						
Treehouse 018		Neighbor/Motor City Kid	1989		3.75	7.50
Black vinyl, white label						
Treehouse 018	PS	Neighbor/Motor City Kid	1989	5.00	10.00	20.00
Blue cover (accompanies blue vinyl version)						
Treehouse 018	PS	Neighbor/Motor City Kid	1989		3.75	7.50
Yellow cover (accompanies both black-vinyl versions)						

Label, Number		Title	Year	VG	VG+	NM

Bators, Stiv
Ex-Dead Boys.

Vinyl Albums

Bomp! 4015		Disconnected	1980	2.50	5.00	10.00

45s

Bomp! 124		It's Cold Outside/The Last Year	1979	2.50	5.00	10.00
Bomp! 124	PS	It's Cold Outside/The Last Year	1979	2.50	5.00	10.00
Bomp! 128		Not That Way Anymore/Circumstantial Evidence				
			1979	2.00	4.00	8.00
Bomp! 128	PS	Not That Way Anymore/Circumstantial Evidence				
			1979	2.00	4.00	8.00
Bomp! X-128	DJ	Not That Way Anymore/Circumstantial Evidence				
			1979	3.75	7.50	15.00

12-Inch Singles

Bomp! BEP-1202		Too Much to Dream/Make Up Your Mind				
			1980	5.00	10.00	20.00

Bauhaus
*British cult goth-synth band. Members branched into many other projects, most notably **Love and Rockets**.*

Vinyl Albums

A&M SP 4918		The Sky's Gone Out	1982	5.00	10.00	20.00
A&M SP-4953		Burning from the Inside	1983	5.00	10.00	20.00
RCA 9804-1-R	(2)	Swing the Heartache/The BBC Sessions				
			1989	5.00	10.00	20.00

45s

A&M 2524		Ziggy Stardust/Lagartija-Nick/Third Uncle				
			1983	6.25	12.50	25.00
A&M 2524	PS	Ziggy Stardust/Lagartija-Nick/Third Uncle				
			1983	6.25	12.50	25.00

BC-52's, The
See B-52's, The

Bears, The

Vinyl Albums

I.R.S. 42011		The Bears	1987	3.00	6.00	12.00
I.R.S. 42139		Rise and Shine	1988	2.50	5.00	10.00

45s

I.R.S. 53197		Trust (Mix 106)/Save Me	1987			3.00
I.R.S. 53197	PS	Trust (Mix 106)/Save Me	1987			3.00

Beastie Boys
New York bad-boy punk/hip-hop/alternative group, impossible to pigeonhole and incredibly prolific.

Vinyl Albums

Capitol C1-28599		Ill Communication	1994	2.50	5.00	10.00
Capitol SPRO 79461	(2) DJ	Hip Hop Sampler	1994	12.50	25.00	50.00
Promo-only compilation of remixes and things						
Capitol C1-91743		Paul's Boutique	1989	2.50	5.00	10.00
Single gatefold edition						
Capitol C1-92844		Paul's Boutique	1989	3.75	7.50	15.00
Multi-gatefold edition (number on record is the same as single gatefold edition)						
Capitol C1-98938	(2)	Check Your Head	1992	3.00	6.00	12.00
Def Jam BFC 40238		Licensed to Ill	1986	3.75	7.50	15.00

Label, Number		Title	Year	VG	VG+	NM
Def Jam FC 40238		Licensed to Ill	1986	2.50	5.00	10.00
Second pressing, with "02" added to bar code on back cover						
Grand Royal GR 003		Some Old Bullshit	1994	2.50	5.00	10.00
Grand Royal GR 013		The In Sound from Way Out!	1996	3.75	7.50	15.00
Limited edition of 5,000; recorded in 1994						
Grand Royal GR 018	EP	Root Down	1995		3.00	6.00
Grand Royal GR 026	EP	Aglio E Olio	1995		3.00	6.00
Rat Cage 026	EP	Cookypuss	1983	8.00	16.00	32.00

7-Inch Extended Play Singles

Label, Number		Title	Year	VG	VG+	NM
Rat Cage MOTR 21		Polly Wog Stew	1982	5.00	10.00	20.00
Rat Cage MOTR 21	PS	Polly Wog Stew	1982	5.00	10.00	20.00

45s

Label, Number		Title	Year	VG	VG+	NM
Capitol S7-18042		Get It Together/Futterman's Rule	1994			3.00
Capitol S7-18125		Sure Shot (Clean Version)/Sabotage (Clean Version)	1994			3.00
Capitol S7-18578		Root Down/Ricky's Theme	1995			3.00
Capitol 44402		Hey Ladies	1989		*May be cassette only*	
Capitol 44454		Hey Ladies/Shake Your Rump	1989		2.00	4.00
Capitol 44472		Shadrach/And What You Give Is What You Get	1989		2.50	5.00
Def Jam 05683		She's On It/Slow and Low	1985		2.50	5.00
Def Jam 05683	PS	She's On It/Slow and Low	1985		2.50	5.00
Def Jam 05864		Hold It Now, Hit It/Hold It Now, Hit It (Acapella)	1986		3.00	6.00
Def Jam 06341		Paul Revere/It's the New Style	1986		3.00	6.00
Def Jam 06595		(You Gotta) Fight for Your Right (To Party!)/Paul Revere	1987		3.00	6.00
Def Jam 06675		She's Crafty/No Sleep Till Brooklyn	1987		2.00	4.00
Def Jam 07020		Brass Monkey/Posse in Effect	1987		2.00	4.00
Def Jam 08388		(You Gotta) Fight for Your Right (To Party!)/She's On It	1988			3.00
"Golden Oldies" reissue						

12-Inch Singles

Label, Number		Title	Year	VG	VG+	NM
Capitol 15483		Shake Your Rump/Hey Ladies/33% God/Dis Yourself in 89	1989	2.00	4.00	8.00
Capitol 58171		Get It Together/(Instrumental)	1994	2.50	5.00	10.00
Capitol 58185		Get It Together (5 versions)/Resolution Time/Sabotage/ Dope Little Song	1994		3.50	7.00
Capitol SPRO 79226	DJ	Professor Booty (same on both sides)	1992	3.00	6.00	12.00
Capitol SPRO 79269/70	DJ	Get It Together (8 versions)	1994	3.00	6.00	12.00
Capitol SPRO 79412	DJ	Sure Shot (10 versions)	1994	3.75	7.50	15.00

Beat Farmers

Vinyl Albums

Label, Number		Title	Year	VG	VG+	NM
Curb 17381	EP	Home of Country Dick	1987	6.25	12.50	25.00
Promo only with four non-LP songs						
MCA 5759		Van Go	1986	3.00	6.00	12.00
MCA 6296		Poor and Famous	1989	2.50	5.00	10.00
Rhino RNOR-021		Bugger Stones	1981	3.50	7.00	14.00
Rhino RNLP-853		Tales of the New West	1985	3.00	6.00	12.00

45s

Label, Number		Title	Year	VG	VG+	NM
MCA 53115		Make It Last/Big Big Man	1987			3.00

12-Inch Singles

Label, Number		Title	Year	VG	VG+	NM
Curb/MCA 17401	DJ	Hollywood Hills (same on both sides)	1987		3.00	6.00

Label, Number		Title	Year	VG	VG+	NM
MCA 17127	DJ	Riverside (same on both sides)	1986		3.50	7.00
MCA 17356	DJ	Dark Light (same on both sides)	1987		3.00	6.00
MCA 17457	DJ	Key to the World/Make It Last	1987		2.50	5.00
MCA 17788	DJ	Deceiver (same on both sides)	1986		2.50	5.00
MCA 17906	DJ	The Girl I Almost Married (same on both sides)				
			1989		3.50	7.00

Beat Happening

Vinyl Albums

Sub Pop 98		Dreamy	1991	2.50	5.00	10.00
Sub Pop 167		You Turn Me On	1992	2.50	5.00	10.00

45s

Sub Pop 74		Red Head Walking/Secret Picnic Spot				
			1990		2.00	4.00
Sub Pop 74		Red Head Walking/Secret Picnic Spot				
			1990	2.00	4.00	8.00
First 2,000 on red vinyl						
Sub Pop 74	PS	Red Head Walking/Secret Picnic Spot				
			1990		2.00	4.00
Sub Pop 2000		Nancy Sin/Left Behind	1992	3.00	6.00	12.00
No picture sleeve; bonus in Sub Pop Singles Club series						

Beat Rodeo

45s

Coyote 005		What's the Matter/Mimi	1983		3.00	6.00
Coyote 005	PS	What's the Matter/Mimi	1983		3.00	6.00
I.R.S. 52918		Everything I'm Not/It Could Happen Here				
			1986			3.00

12-Inch Singles

I.R.S. 17241	DJ	New Love (same on both sides)	198?	2.00	4.00	8.00

Beat, The

*Not to be confused with **The English Beat**, this is an American power-pop outfit led by Paul Collins.*

Vinyl Albums

Columbia ARC 36794		The Kids Are the Same	1982	2.50	5.00	10.00
Columbia JC 36195		The Beat	1979	3.00	6.00	12.00
Passport 5002	EP	To Beat or Not to Beat	1983	2.00	4.00	8.00

45s

Columbia 02833		Met Her Yesterday/On the Highway				
			1982	2.00	4.00	8.00
As "The Paul Collins Beat"						
Columbia 11161		Let Me Into Your Life/Walking Out on Love				
			1979	2.00	4.00	8.00
Columbia 11211		Don't Wait Up for Me/Working Too Hard				
			1980	2.00	4.00	8.00

Beautiful South, The

12-Inch Singles

Elektra ED 5444	DJ	You Keep It All In (Single Version) (same on both sides)				
			1990		2.50	5.00

Label, Number		Title	Year	VG	VG+	NM

Beavis & Butt-head

MTV's heh-heh-heh video commentators.

12-Inch Singles

Geffen 4594		(2) DJ Come to Butt-head (9 versions) 1993		3.75	7.50	15.00

Beck

Singer/rapper/songwriter/guitarist from L.A. by way of Kansas City.

Vinyl Albums

Bongload 13		Mellow Gold	1993	3.00	6.00	12.00
Fingerpaint 02	10	A Western Harvest Field by Moonlight	1992	5.00	10.00	20.00
With fingerpainting insert						
K 28		One Foot in the Grave	1994	2.50	5.00	10.00

45s

Bongload 11		Steve Threw Up/Mutherfucker	1994		3.00	6.00
Bongload 11	PS	Steve Threw Up/Mutherfucker	1994		3.00	6.00
DGC 19270		Loser/Alcohol	1994		3.00	6.00
K (# unknown)		It's All in Your Mind/ + 2	1994		2.00	4.00
K (# unknown)	PS	It's All in Your Mind/ + 2	1994		2.00	4.00

12-Inch Singles

Bongload 5		Loser/Steal My Body Home	1993		3.00	6.00
DGC 4629	DJ	Loser (same on both sides)	1993	2.50	5.00	10.00

Belew, Adrian

Vinyl Albums

Atlantic 81959		Mr. Music Head	1989	2.50	5.00	10.00
Atlantic 82099		Young Lions	1990	2.50	5.00	10.00
Island 90108		Twang Bar King	1983	2.50	5.00	10.00
Island ILPS 9751		Lone Rhino	1982	3.00	6.00	12.00

45s

Atlantic 88904		Oh Daddy/Peaceable Kingdom	1989			3.00
Atlantic 88904	PS	Oh Daddy/Peaceable Kingdom	1989			3.00

12-Inch Singles

Atlantic 3324	DJ	I Am What I Am/Men in Helicopters/Young Lions	1990		3.00	6.00

Belle Stars, The

English female band, originally known as The Bodysnatchers, a ska band.

45s

Capitol 44343		Iko Iko/Las Vegas	1989		2.00	4.00
B-side by Hans Zimmer						
Warner Bros. 29672		Sign of the Times/Madness	1983		3.00	6.00

12-Inch Singles

Capitol 15475		Iko Iko (3 versions)	1989	2.00	4.00	8.00
MCA 23632		World Domination/Just a Minute/Rock Me to the Top	1986	2.50	5.00	10.00
MCA 23671		World Domination (2 versions)	1986		3.00	6.00
Stiff TEES-12-06		Slick Trick/Hiawatha/Miss World	1981	2.00	4.00	8.00
Warner Bros. 29657		Sign of the Times/Madness	1983	2.00	4.00	8.00

Label, Number		Title	Year	VG	VG+	NM

Belly
With Tanya Donelly, ex-__Throwing Muses__ and __The Breeders__.

Vinyl Albums
Sire 45833		King	1995	3.00	6.00	12.00

45s
Sire 17938		Now They'll Sleep/Silverfish	1995			3.00
Sire 18358		Gepetto/Slow Dog	1993			3.00
Sire 18580		Feed the Tree/Star	1993		2.00	4.00

Berlin
Los Angeles band whose best-known member was lead singer Terri Nunn.

Vinyl Albums
Enigma 3	EP	Pleasure Victim	1982	6.25	12.50	25.00
Geffen GHS 2036	EP	Pleasure Victim	1982	3.00	6.00	12.00
Geffen GHS 4025		Love Life	1984	2.50	5.00	10.00
Geffen GHS 24121		Count Three and Pray	1986	2.50	5.00	10.00
Geffen GHS 24187		Best of Berlin 1979-1988	1988	2.50	5.00	10.00
Geffen R 100731		Best of Berlin 1979-1988	1988	3.00	6.00	12.00
BMG Direct Marketing edition						
Geffen R 153624		Count Three and Pray	1986	3.00	6.00	12.00
RCA Music Service edition						

45s
Columbia 05903		Take My Breath Away/Radio Radio				
			1986			3.00
B-side by Georgio Moroder						
Columbia 05903	PS	Take My Breath Away/Radio Radio				
			1986			3.00
Columbia 68719		Take My Breath Away/Top Gun Anthem				
			1989			3.00
"Golden Oldies" reissue; B-side by Harold Faltermeyer						
Geffen 28486		You Don't Know/Trash	1987			3.00
Geffen 28486	PS	You Don't Know/Trash	1987			3.00
Geffen 28563		Hideaway/Light the Flames	1986			3.00
Geffen 28563	PS	Hideaway/Light the Flames	1986			3.00
Geffen 29051		No More Words/Crazy for You	1985			3.00
B-side by Madonna						
Geffen 29192		Dancing in Berlin/Pictures of You				
			1984			3.00
Geffen 29283		Now It's My Turn/Lost in a Crowd				
			1984			3.00
Geffen 29283	PS	Now It's My Turn/Lost in a Crowd				
			1984			3.00
Geffen 29360		No More Words/Rumor of Love				
			1984		2.00	4.00
Geffen 29360	PS	No More Words/Rumor of Love	1984		2.00	4.00
Geffen 29504		Masquerade/Live Sex	1983		2.00	4.00
Geffen 29504	PS	Masquerade/Live Sex	1983		2.00	4.00
Geffen 29638		The Metro/World of Smiles	1983		2.00	4.00
Geffen 29638	PS	The Metro/World of Smiles	1983		2.00	4.00
Geffen 29747		Sex (I'm a ...)/Tell Me Why	1983		2.00	4.00
Geffen 29747	PS	Sex (I'm a ...)/Tell Me Why	1983	2.00	4.00	8.00
I.R.S. 9015		Matter of Time/French Reggae	1980		3.75	7.50
I.R.S. 9015	PS	Matter of Time/French Reggae	1980		3.75	7.50
M.A.O. F-4		The Metro/Tell Me Why	1981	3.00	6.25	12.50
M.A.O. F-4	PS	The Metro/Tell Me Why	1981	3.00	6.25	12.50
Zone H ZOH-001		Matter of Time/Overload	1980	3.00	6.25	12.50
Zone H ZOH-001	PS	Matter of Time/Overload	1980	3.00	6.25	12.50

Label, Number		Title	Year	VG	VG+	NM
12-Inch Singles						
Geffen PRO-A-2004	DJ	Sex (I'm A...)/(Instrumental)	1982	4.00	8.00	16.00
Geffen PRO-A-2121	DJ	Touch/Now It's My Turn/In My Dreams/No More Words				
			1984	2.00	4.00	8.00
Geffen PRO-A-2147	DJ	Now It's My Turn/Now It's My Turn (edit remix)				
			1984		3.00	6.00
Geffen PRO-A-2572	DJ	Like Flames/Like Flames (7" Version)				
			1986	2.00	4.00	8.00
Geffen PRO-A-2632	DJ	Pink and Velvet (same on both sides)				
			1986	2.00	4.00	8.00
Geffen PRO-A-2686	DJ	You Don't Know (Edit)/You Don't Know (LP Version)				
			1986		2.50	5.00
Geffen 20195		No More Words/Dancing in Berlin	1984	2.00	4.00	8.00

Bewitched

Label, Number		Title	Year	VG	VG+	NM
45s						
Sub Pop 199		Hey White Homey/Troll Doll	1993		2.50	5.00
Clear orange vinyl						
Sub Pop 199	PS	Hey White Homey/Troll Doll	1993		2.50	5.00
#52 in Sub Pop Singles Club series						

Big Audio Dynamite

*British band formed by Mick Jones after he was booted from **The Clash.***

Label, Number		Title	Year	VG	VG+	NM
Vinyl Albums						
Columbia BFC 40220		This Is Big Audio Dynamite	1985	2.50	5.00	10.00
Columbia BFC 40445		No. 10 Upping Street	1986	3.00	6.00	12.00
Columbia BFC 40705		No. 10 Upping Street	1986	2.50	5.00	10.00
Reissue with extra track, "Bad Rock City"						
Columbia FC 44074		Tighten Up Vol. 88	1988	2.50	5.00	10.00
Columbia FC 45212		Megatop Phoenix	1989	2.50	5.00	10.00
Columbia C 46147		The Globe	1991	3.00	6.00	12.00
Radioactive 11280	(2)	F-Punk	1995	3.50	7.00	14.00
45s						
Columbia 05841		Medicine Show/This Is Big Audio Dynamite				
			1986			3.00
Columbia 05841	PS	Medicine Show/This Is Big Audio Dynamite				
			1986			3.00
Columbia 05841	PS	Medicine Show/This Is Big Audio Dynamite				
			1986		2.50	5.00
"Demonstration -- Not for Sale" on back						
Columbia 06053		E=MC2/Party	1986			3.00
Columbia 06053	PS	E=MC2/Party	1986			3.00
Columbia 06364		C'Mon Every Beatbox (Edit)/Bad Rock City				
			1986			3.00
Columbia 06364	PS	C'Mon Every Beatbox (Edit)/Badrock City				
			1986			3.00
Columbia 06708		C'mon Every Beatbox (same on both sides)				
			1987			3.00
Columbia 06708	PS	C'mon Every Beatbox (same on both sides)				
			1987			3.00
"Demonstration -- Not for Sale" on back						
Columbia 07955		Just Play Music/Much Worse	1988			3.00
Columbia 07955	PS	Just Play Music/Much Worse	1988			3.00
Columbia 08094		The Other 99/What Happened to Eddie				
			1988			3.00
Columbia 73043		Attached/In Full Effect	1989			3.00
Columbia 73987		Rush/City Lights	1991			*Cassette only*
($7.50 NM for UK 45 with picture sleeve)						

Label, Number		Title	Year	VG	VG+	NM
Columbia 74149		The Globe (Single Edit)/Rush (New York City Club Mix)				
			1992			*Cassette only*
($6 NM for UK 45 with picture sleeve)						
WTG 73241		Free (Theme from Flashback)/The Bottom Line				
			1990			*Cassette only*

12-Inch Singles

Label, Number		Title	Year	VG	VG+	NM
Columbia CAS 01739	DJ	James Brown (3 mixes)/If I Were John Carpenter				
			1989	2.50	5.00	10.00
Columbia CAS 01899	DJ	Contact (3 versions)/Who Beats/In Full Effect				
			1989	2.00	4.00	8.00
Columbia CAS 2252	DJ	The Bottom Line (Single Version)/The Bottom Line (LP Version)				
			1985	2.00	4.00	8.00
Columbia CAS 2301	DJ	Medicine Show (London Mix)/Medicine Show (N.Y. Mix)				
			1985	2.00	4.00	8.00
Columbia CAS 2361	DJ	E=MC2 (3 mixes)	1985		3.00	6.00
Columbia CAS 2520	DJ	C'mon Every Beatbox/C'mon Every Beatbox (Edit)				
			1986		3.00	6.00
Columbia CAS 2601	DJ	V-13 (same on both sides)	1986		3.00	6.00
Columbia CAS 2647	DJ	Bad Rock City/Bad Rock City (Edit)				
			1986		3.00	6.00
Columbia CAS 2697	DJ	Hollywood Boulevard (Club Mix) (same on both sides)				
			1987		3.00	6.00
Columbia CAS 4044	DJ	Rushdance/Rush (instrumental & LP)/City Lights				
			1991	2.00	4.00	8.00
Columbia 05324		The Bottom Line/BAD	1985	2.00	4.00	8.00
Columbia 05359		Medicine Show (2 mixes)/This Is Big Audio Dynamite				
			1986	2.00	4.00	8.00
Columbia 05909		E=MC2/Party	1985		3.00	6.00
Columbia 05963		C'Mon Every Beatbox (Extended)/Badrock City/Beatboxes at Dawn				
			1986		3.00	6.00
Columbia CAS 6553	DJ	Looking for a Song (4 versions)	1994	2.00	4.00	8.00
Columbia 06780		V-13/Hollywood Blvd. (Club Mix)/Hollywood Blvd. (Dub)				
			1986		3.00	6.00
Columbia 07851		Just Play Music/Much Worse	1988		3.00	6.00
Columbia 08133	DJ	The Other 99 (Extended) (same on both sides)				
			1988		3.00	6.00
Columbia 74134		Rushdance/Rush (Club Instr.)//Rush (Album Version)/City Lights				
			1991	2.00	4.00	8.00
Columbia 74180		The Globe (5 versions)/Rush (12" Mix)				
			1992	2.00	4.00	8.00
Def Jam 05324		The Bottom Line/B.A.D.	1985	2.00	4.00	8.00
WTG 73159		Free (2 versions)/Bottom Line (2 versions)				
			1990	2.00	4.00	8.00

Big Boys

Vinyl Albums

Label, Number		Title	Year	VG	VG+	NM
Enigma 1128		Lullabies Help the Brain Grow	1984	3.75	7.50	15.00
Moment 001		Fun, Fun, Fun	1982	8.75	17.50	35.00
Moment 002		Lullabys Help the Brain Grow	1983	8.75	17.50	35.00
Radical RRR 80351		Recorded Live at Raul's	1980	15.00	30.00	60.00
One side features the Big Boys; the other side, the Dicks						
Unseen Hand 727-3		Wreck Collection	1988	3.00	6.00	12.00
Wasted Talent 3405		Industry Standard	1981	8.75	17.50	35.00

7-Inch Extended Play Singles

Label, Number		Title	Year	VG	VG+	NM
Big Boys BB 42480		Frat Cars/Heartbeat//Movies/Mutant Rock				
			1980	5.00	10.00	20.00
Big Boys BB 42480	PS	Frat Cars/Heartbeat//Movies/Mutant Rock				
			1980	5.00	10.00	20.00

Label, Number		Title	Year	VG	VG+	NM

Big Chief

45s

Label, Number		Title	Year	VG	VG+	NM
Big Chief MD 777		Brake Torque/Superstupid	1989	6.25	12.50	25.00
Purple vinyl						
Big Chief MD 777		Brake Torque/Superstupid	1989	3.75	7.50	15.00
Green vinyl						
Big Chief MD 777	PS	Brake Torque/Superstupid	1989	3.75	7.50	15.00
Sub Pop 53		Blowout Kit/Chrome Helmet	1990	5.00	10.00	20.00
White vinyl pressing of 1,500						
Sub Pop 53		Blowout Kit/Chrome Helmet	1990		2.50	5.00
Black vinyl pressing of 1,500						
Sub Pop 53	PS	Blowout Kit/Chrome Helmet	1990		2.50	5.00
#17 in Sub Pop Singles Club series						

Big Country

Scottish rock band -- and even though their music sounds like it, there are no bagpipes!

Vinyl Albums

Label, Number		Title	Year	VG	VG+	NM
Mercury 812 870-1		The Crossing	1983	2.50	5.00	10.00
Mercury 818 835-1		Wonderland	1984	2.50	5.00	10.00
Mercury 822 831-1		Steeltown	1984	2.50	5.00	10.00
Mercury 826 844-1		The Seer	1986	2.50	5.00	10.00
Reprise 25787		Peace in Our Time	1988	2.50	5.00	10.00

45s

Label, Number		Title	Year	VG	VG+	NM
Collectables 4856		In a Big Country/Breakout	199?		1.50	3.00
Reissue; B-side by Swing Out Sister						
Mercury 811 450-7		Fields of Fire/Angle Park	1983			3.00
Mercury 811 450-7	PS	Fields of Fire/Angle Park	1983		3.50	7.00
Fold-out poster sleeve						
Mercury 814 467-7		In a Big Country/All of Us	1983			3.00
Mercury 814 467-7	PS	In a Big Country/All of Us	1983		2.50	5.00
Scarce sleeve in some areas of the U.S.						
Mercury 818 834-7		Wonderland/Lost Patrol	1984			3.00
Mercury 880 412-7		Where the Rose Is Sown/Prairie Rose	1984			3.00
Mercury 880 412-7	PS	Where the Rose Is Sown/Prairie Rose	1984			3.00
Mercury 880 542-7		Winter Sky/Just a Shadow	1985			3.00
Reprise 27737		King of Emotion/The Travellers	1988			3.00
Reprise 27737	PS	King of Emotion/The Travellers	1988			3.00

12-Inch Singles

Label, Number		Title	Year	VG	VG+	NM
Mercury 884 645-1		Look Away (Outlaw Mix)/Restless Natives (16:40) 1986		3.00	6.00	12.00
Mercury 888 028-1		One Great Thing/Look Away (Outlaw Mix) + 1 1986			3.50	7.00
Mercury PRO 239	DJ	Fields of Fire/Fields of Fire (7" Version) 1984			3.00	6.00
Mercury PRO 324-1	DJ	Where the Rose... (same on both sides) 1984		2.00	4.00	8.00
Mercury PRO 333	DJ	Just a Shadow (Long)/Just a Shadow (Short) 1984			3.00	6.00
Mercury PRO 341	DJ	East of Eden (same on both sides) 1984			3.00	6.00
Mercury PRO 414	DJ	Look Away (same on both sides) 1986			3.00	6.00
Mercury PRO 442	DJ	One Great Thing (same on both sides) 1986			3.00	6.00

Label, Number		Title	Year	VG	VG+	NM

Big Damn Crazyweight

45s

Sub Pop 173		Might As Well/Off That Cow	1992		2.50	5.00
Clear gold vinyl						
Sub Pop 173	PS	Might As Well/Off That Cow	1992		2.50	5.00
#48 in Sub Pop Singles Club series						

Bikini Kill

All-girl band from Washington state featuring Kathleen Hanna.

Vinyl Albums

Kill Rock Stars 218		Pussy Whipped	1993	2.50	5.00	10.00

Bizarros, The

Their name kinda says it all.

Vinyl Albums

Mercury SRM-1-3776		The Bizarros	1979	4.00	8.00	16.00

45s

Clone 000		Lady Dobonette/I Bizarro//Without Reason/Nova	1976		3.75	7.50
Clone 000	PS	Lady Dobonette/I Bizarro//Without Reason/Nova	1976		3.75	7.50
Reissue of Gorilla release						
Clone 003		Laser Boys/It Hurts Janey//New Order	197?	2.50	5.00	10.00
Gorilla NR-7639		Lady Dobonette/I Bizarro//Without Reason/Nova	1976	3.00	6.00	12.00
Plays at 33 1/3 rpm						
Gorilla NR-7639	PS	Lady Dobonette/I Bizarro//Without Reason/Nova	1976	3.00	6.00	12.00

Black Crowes, The

Atlanta rock band.

Vinyl Albums

American 43000		Amorica	1994	3.00	6.00	12.00
All copies of the vinyl LP retained the "butt" background that was censored on most cassette and CD copies						
Def American 24278		Shake Your Money Maker	1990	2.50	5.00	10.00

45s

Def American 18803		Thorn in My Pride/Sting Me	1992			3.00
Def American 18877		Remedy/Darling of the Underground Press	1992		2.00	4.00
Non-LP B-side						
Def American 18887		She Talks to Angels/Hard to Handle	1993			3.00
Reissue						
Def American 19245		Hard to Handle/Waitin' Guilty	1991			3.00
Def American 19403		She Talks to Angels/She Talks to Angels (Live Video Version)	1991			3.00
Def American 19668		Hard to Handle/Jealous Again	1991			*May be cassette-only*
Def American 19697		Jealous Again/Thick 'N' Thin	1990			*May be cassette-only*

Black Flag

Seminal punk band from the West Coast. Their SST Records was one of the top indie labels of the 1980s.

Vinyl Albums

SST 003	EP	Jealous Again	1980	2.00	4.00	8.00

Label, Number		Title	Year	VG	VG+	NM
SST 007		Damaged	1981	2.50	5.00	10.00
SST 015	(2)	Everything Went Black	1982	3.75	7.50	15.00
SST 021		The First Four Years	1983	3.00	6.00	12.00
SST 023		My War	1984	3.00	6.00	12.00
SST 026		Family Man	1984	3.00	6.00	12.00
SST 029		Slip It In	1984	3.00	6.00	12.00
SST 035		Loose Nut	1985	3.00	6.00	12.00
SST 037	EP	The Process of Weeding Out	1985	2.00	4.00	8.00
SST 045		In My Head	1985	3.00	6.00	12.00
SST 060		Who's Got the 10 1/2?	1986	3.00	6.00	12.00
SST 081	EP	Annihilate This Week	1986	2.00	4.00	8.00
SST 166		Wasted Again	1987	3.00	6.00	12.00
SST 226	EP	I Can See You	1989	3.00	6.00	12.00
SST 907	10	Jealous Again	199?		3.00	6.00
10-inch reissue						
SST 924	10	The Process of Weeding Out	199?		3.00	6.00
10-inch reissue						
SST/Unicorn 9502		Damaged	1981	3.75	7.50	15.00

45s

Label, Number		Title	Year	VG	VG+	NM
Alternative Tentacles VIRUS 9		Six Pack/I've Heard It Before/American Waste				
			1981	2.50	5.00	10.00
Alternative Tentacles VIRUS 9	PS	Six Pack/I've Heard It Before/American Waste				
			1981	2.50	5.00	10.00
Manufactured in U.S. for export to the U.K.						
Posh Boy 13		Louie Louie/Damaged 1	1981	2.50	5.00	10.00
Posh Boy 13	PS	Louie Louie/Damaged 1	1981	2.50	5.00	10.00
SST 001		Nervous Breakdown//Fix Me/I've Had It/Wasted				
			1978	2.50	5.00	10.00
First pressing on red labels						
SST 001		Nervous Breakdown//Fix Me/I've Had It/Wasted				
			1978			2.00
Current pressing on blue labels; still in print as of 1995						
SST 001	PS	Nervous Breakdown//Fix Me/I've Had It/Wasted				
			1978	2.50	5.00	10.00
First sleeve: black and white, brick wall background						
SST 001	PS	Nervous Breakdown//Fix Me/I've Had It/Wasted				
			1978		2.50	5.00
Second sleeve: Red print						
SST 001	PS	Nervous Breakdown//Fix Me/I've Had It/Wasted				
			1978			2.00
With bar code on back; blue printing; still in print as of 1995						
SST 005		Six Pack/I've Heard It Before/American Waste				
			1981		2.00	4.00
SST 005	PS	Six Pack/I've Heard It Before/American Waste				
			1981		2.00	4.00
SST 012		TV Party/I've Got to Run/My Rules				
			1981		2.00	4.00
SST 012	PS	TV Party/I've Got to Run/My Rules				
			1981		2.00	4.00
SST 175		Louie Louie/Damaged 1	1981		2.00	4.00
SST 175	PS	Louie Louie/Damaged 1	1981		2.00	4.00
Reissue of Posh Boy single						
SST/Unicorn BOGUS 001		Thirsty and Miserable/Life of Pain (Live)				
			1981	7.50	15.00	30.00
Promo-only giveaway item						
SST/Unicorn 95006	DJ	TV Party (same on both sides)	1981	4.00	8.00	16.00
Promo only						

Until it came out on compact disc in the early 1990s, *Party Mix!,* a remix EP of early B-52's tracks, was quite difficult to find.

Black Flag was one of the kings of West Coast independent-label punk in the late 1970s and early 1980s. "Nervous Breakdown" was the band's first single, on SST 001. Almost two decades later, it's still available from SST! (Newer picture sleeves have a bar code on the back, and originals do not.)

Label, Number		Title	Year	VG	VG+	NM

Black 47

*American group of former Ireland residents. One member was formerly with **Dexys Midnight Runners.***

45s

SBK S7-17396		Maria's Wedding/Funky Ceili	1993		2.00	4.00

Black Randy and the Metrosquad

Vinyl Albums

Dangerhouse PCP 725		"Pass the Dust, I Think I'm Bowie"				
			1980	10.00	20.00	40.00

7-Inch Extended Play Singles

Dangerhouse IDI 722		Idi Amin	1978	5.50	11.25	22.50
Green vinyl						
Dangerhouse IDI 722		Idi Amin	1978	3.00	6.25	12.50
Dangerhouse IDI 722	PS	Idi Amin	1978	3.00	6.25	12.50

45s

Dangerhouse MO 721		Trouble at the Cup/Loner with a Boner				
			1977	3.00	6.25	12.50
Dangerhouse MO 721	PS	Trouble at the Cup/Loner with a Boner				
			1977	3.00	6.25	12.50
Dangerhouse KY 724		I Slept in an Arcade/Give it Up or Turnit a Loose				
			1979	3.00	6.25	12.50
Dangerhouse KY 724	PS	I Slept in an Arcade/Give it Up or Turnit a Loose				
			1979	3.00	6.25	12.50

Blake Babies

*With **Juliana Hatfield**.*

Vinyl Albums

Chewbud 001		Nicely, Nicely	1987	10.00	20.00	40.00

Blasters, The

Los Angeles roots-rock band.

Vinyl Albums

Rollin' Rock 021		American Music	1980	7.50	15.00	30.00
Slash 109		The Blasters	1981	4.00	8.00	16.00
Slash BKS 3680		The Blasters	1982	3.00	6.00	12.00
With blue labels						
Slash 23735	EP	Over There: Live at the Venue, London				
			1982	2.50	5.00	10.00
Slash 23818		Non Fiction	1983	2.50	5.00	10.00
Slash 25093		Hard Line	1985	2.50	5.00	10.00
Warner Bros. WBMS-130	DJ	The Warner Bros, Music Show	1985	3.50	7.00	14.00
One side: The Blasters; the other side: The Smiths						

45s

MCA 52378		Blue Shadows/I Can Dream About You				
			1984			3.00
B-side by Dan Hartman						
MCA 52378	PS	Blue Shadows/I Can Dream About You				
			1984			3.00
B-side by Dan Hartman						
Slash 110		I'm Shakin'/No Other Girl	1981			3.00
Slash 110	PS	I'm Shakin'/No Other Girl	1981			3.00
Slash 29055		Colored Lights/Help You Dream	1985			3.00
Slash 29055	PS	Colored Lights/Help You Dream	1985			3.00
Slash 29566		Leaving/Red Rose	1983			3.00
Slash 29678		Barefoot Rock/Bus Station	1983			3.00

Label, Number		Title	Year	VG	VG+	NM
Slash 29678	PS	Barefoot Rock/Bus Station	1983			3.00
Slash 29975		So Long Baby Goodbye/Border Radio				
			1982			3.00
Slash 29975	PS	So Long Baby Goodbye/Border Radio				
			1982			3.00
Slash 50047		I'm Shakin'/No Other Girl	1982			3.00
Slash 50047	PS	I'm Shakin'/No Other Girl	1982			3.00
12-Inch Singles						
Slash PRO-A-2017	DJ	Barefoot Rock/Fool's Paradise/Long White Cadillac				
			1983	3.00	6.00	12.00
Slash PRO-A-2259	DJ	Colored Lights/Dark Night	1985	2.00	4.00	8.00

Blind Melon

Alterna-rockers with lead singer Shannon Hoon, who died of an overdose in 1995.

Label, Number		Title	Year	VG	VG+	NM
Vinyl Albums						
Capitol 28732		Soup	1995	2.50	5.00	10.00
45s						
Capitol 7PRO-79???	DJ	Tones of Home (B-side blank)	1993		2.00	4.00
Capitol 7PRO-79???	PS	Tones of Home (B-side blank)	1993		2.00	4.00
Capitol S7-17590		No Rain/Tones of Home	1993		2.00	4.00
Gold vinyl						
Capitol S7-17713		Change/I Wonder	1994			3.00
Capitol S7-18726		Galaxie/Toes Across the Floor	1995			3.00

Blondie

*New York new-wave group with **Debbie Harry**. Also into rap music and the whole New York scene.*

Label, Number		Title	Year	VG	VG+	NM
Vinyl Albums						
Chrysalis CHS 24 PDJ	DJ	At Home with Debbie Harry and Chris Stein				
			1981	12.50	25.00	50.00
Open-end interview with script						
Chrysalis CHR 1165		Blondie	1977	3.00	6.00	12.00
Reissue of Private Stock album						
Chrysalis CHR 1166		Plastic Letters	1977	3.00	6.00	12.00
Chrysalis CHR 1192		Parallel Lines	1978	3.75	7.50	15.00
First pressing, with short "Heart of Glass" as fourth song on side 2						
Chrysalis CHR 1192		Parallel Lines	1979	2.50	5.00	10.00
Second pressing, with longer "Heart of Glass (Disco Version)" as fourth song on side 2						
Chrysalis CHE 1225		Eat to the Beat	1979	2.50	5.00	10.00
Chrysalis CHE 1290		Autoamerican	1980	2.50	5.00	10.00
Chrysalis CHR 1384		The Hunter	1982	2.00	4.00	8.00
Chrysalis CHS 1337		The Best of Blondie	1981	2.50	5.00	10.00
Chrysalis CHP 5001	PD	Parallel Lines	1979	6.25	12.50	25.00
Picture disc						
Chrysalis F1 21658	(2)	Once More Into the Bleach	1989	3.75	7.50	15.00
Remixes of Blondie and Debbie Harry tracks						
Chrysalis F1 32748	(2)	The Remix Project: Remixed, Remade, Remodeled				
			1995	3.75	7.50	15.00
Chrysalis PV 41165		Blondie	1983	2.00	4.00	8.00
Reissue						
Chrysalis PV 41166		Plastic Letters	1983	2.00	4.00	8.00
Reissue						
Chrysalis FV 41192		Parallel Lines	1983	2.00	4.00	8.00
Reissue						
Chrysalis PV 41192		Parallel Lines	1986	2.00	4.00	8.00
Reissue						
Chrysalis PV 41225		Eat to the Beat	1983	2.00	4.00	8.00
Reissue						
Chrysalis PV 41290		Autoamerican	1983	2.00	4.00	8.00
Reissue						

Debbie Harry of Blondie was one of the more recognizable faces of 1970s New York new wave music. This is probably the rarest Blondie picture sleeve, as "Heart of Glass" far outsold the number of sleeves that were made.

Blue Angel recorded one album on Polydor that might have disappeared, except that its lead singer was Cyndi Lauper! Highly sought-after during the peak of Lauper's popularity, it's tough to find even now.

Label, Number		Title	Year	VG	VG+	NM
Chrysalis FV 41337		The Best of Blondie	1983	2.00	4.00	8.00
Reissue						
Chrysalis PV 41337		The Best of Blondie	1986	2.00	4.00	8.00
Reissue						
Chrysalis PV 41384		The Hunter	1983	2.00	4.00	8.00
Reissue						
Chrysalis R 200816	(2)	Once More into the Bleach	1988	4.50	9.00	18.00
BMG Music Service edition						
Mobile Fidelity 1-050		Parallel Lines	1980	7.50	15.00	30.00
Original Master Recording						
Private Stock PS-2023		Blondie	1976	6.25	12.50	25.00

45s

Label, Number		Title	Year	VG	VG+	NM
Chrysalis 2220		Denis/I'm On E	1977		2.50	5.00
Chrysalis 2251		I'm Gonna Love You Too/Just Go Away 1978			2.50	5.00
Chrysalis 2271		Hanging on the Telephone/Fade Away and Radiate 1978			2.50	5.00
Chrysalis 2271	PS	Hanging on the Telephone/Fade Away and Radiate 1978			2.50	5.00
Chrysalis 2295		Heart of Glass/11:59	1979		2.00	4.00
Chrysalis 2295	PS	Heart of Glass/11:59	1979		2.00	4.00
Chrysalis 2336		One Way or Another/Just Go Away 1979			2.00	4.00
Chrysalis 2379		Dreaming/The Hardest Part	1979		2.00	4.00
Chrysalis 2408		The Hardest Part/Sound Asleep	1980		2.00	4.00
Chrysalis 2408	PS	The Hardest Part/Sound Asleep	1980		2.00	4.00
Chrysalis 2410		Atomic/Die Young Stay Pretty	1980		2.00	4.00
Chrysalis 2410	PS	Atomic/Die Young Stay Pretty	1980		2.00	4.00
Chrysalis 2414		Call Me/Call Me (instrumental)	1980			3.00
Chrysalis 2414	PS	Call Me/Call Me (instrumental)	1980		2.50	5.00
Photo of Richard Gere on sleeve.						
Chrysalis 2414	PS	Call Me/Call Me (instrumental)	1980			3.00
Photo of Deborah Harry on sleeve.						
Chrysalis 2465		The Tide Is High/Suzy and Jeffrey 1980				3.00
Chrysalis 2465	PS	The Tide Is High/Suzy and Jeffrey 1980				3.00
Chrysalis 2485		Rapture/Walk Like Me	1981			3.00
Chrysalis 2485	PS	Rapture/Walk Like Me	1981			3.00
Chrysalis 2603		Island of Lost Souls/Dragonfly	1982			3.00
Chrysalis 2603	PS	Island of Lost Souls/Dragonfly	1982			3.00
Chrysalis S7-18303		Rapture/One Way or Another	1995			3.00
Chrysalis S7-18304		Heart of Glass/Call Me	1995			3.00
Chrysalis S7-18396		Atomic/Atomic (Diddy Remix)	1995			3.00
Chrysalis S7-18848		Union City Blue (Diddy's Remix Edit)/Union City Blue 1995				3.00
Chrysalis 42944		Heart of Glass/Hanging on the Telephone 1985				3.00
Silver label reissue						
Chrysalis 42945		One Way or Another/Dreaming	1985			3.00
Silver label reissue						
Chrysalis 42946		Call Me/Atomic	1985			3.00
Silver label reissue						
Private Stock 45097		X Offender/In the Sun	1976	7.50	15.00	30.00
Private Stock 45097	DJ	X Offender (mono)/X Offender (stereo) 1976		2.50	5.00	10.00
Private Stock 45141		In the Flesh/Man Overboard	1977	5.00	10.00	20.00
Private Stock 45141	DJ	In the Flesh (mono/stereo)	1977	2.50	5.00	10.00

12-Inch Singles

Label, Number		Title	Year	VG	VG+	NM
Chrysalis CHS-12-2217		(I'm Always Touched By Your) Presence, Dear/Poets 1978		3.00	6.00	12.00

Label, Number		Title	Year	VG	VG+	NM
		Problem/Detroit 442				
Chrysalis CHS-12-2275		Heart of Glass (Disco Version)/(instrumental)				
			1979	2.50	5.00	10.00
Chrysalis 58277	(2)	Rapture (9 mixes)	1994	2.50	5.00	10.00
Two-record set of old and new mixes						
Polydor PRO-124	DJ	Call Me (Remix Extended Version)/Night Drive (instrumental)				
			1980	5.00	10.00	20.00
Salsoul SG 341		Call Me (Spanish)/(Instrumental)				
			1980	7.50	15.00	30.00

Blow Monkeys

British pop-rock band.

Vinyl Albums

RCA (# unknown)		She Was Only a Grocer's Daughter				
			1987	2.50	5.00	10.00
RCA NFL1-8065		Animal Magic	1986	2.50	5.00	10.00

45s

RCA 5138-7-R		It Doesn't Have to Be This Way/Ask for More				
			1987			3.00
RCA 5138-7-R	PS	It Doesn't Have to Be This Way/Ask for More				
			1987			3.00
RCA PB-14325		Digging Your Scene (U.K. Mix)/(U.S. Mix)				
			1986			3.00
Not issued with picture sleeve in U.S.						
RCA PB-14423		Wicked Ways/Walking the Blue Beat				
			1986			3.00

12-Inch Singles

RCA 5775		Sweet Murder (3 versions)	1985		3.00	6.00
RCA 6281		It Doesn't Have to Be This Way (2 mixes)/Ask For More				
			1987	2.00	4.00	8.00
RCA 8527		Forbidden Fruit/My America/Sweet Murder/Kill the Pig/Wild				
			198?	2.00	4.00	8.00
		Flower/Atomic Lullaby				
RCA JR-14326	DJ	Digging Your Scene (LP Version) (same on both sides)				
			1986	2.00	4.00	8.00
RCA JW-14426	DJ	Wicked Ways/Walking the Blue Beat/The Man from Russia/				
		It's	1985	2.50	5.00	10.00
		Not Unusual (Live)				
RCA PB-14424		Wicked Ways (Extended)/Walking the Blue Beat//				
		Wicked Ways	1986	2.00	4.00	8.00
		(Instrumental) (Wicked It)				
RCA PW-14327		Digging Your Scene (Edited Mix)/(LP Version) (Dub Cosmic)				
			1986	2.00	4.00	8.00

Blue Angel

*New York new wave band with **Cyndi Lauper** on lead vocals.*

Vinyl Albums

Polydor PD1-6300		Blue Angel	1980	5.00	10.00	20.00

45s

Polydor 2149		I Had a Love/Take a Chance	1980	2.50	5.00	10.00

Blues Traveler

New York blues-rock band.

45s

A&M 31458 1174 7		Hook/Run-Around	1995			3.00

Label, Number		Title	Year	VG	VG+	NM

BoDeans

Rock band from Waukesha, Wisconsin.

Vinyl Albums

Label, Number		Title	Year	VG	VG+	NM
Slash 25629		Outside Looking In	1987	2.50	5.00	10.00
Slash 25876		Home	1989	3.00	6.00	12.00
Slash R 153192		Outside Looking In	1987	3.00	6.00	12.00
BMG Direct Marketing edition						

45s

Label, Number		Title	Year	VG	VG+	NM
Reprise 28179		Only Love/Stella	1987			3.00
Reprise 28179	PS	Only Love/Stella	1987			3.00
Sire 28549		She's a Runaway/Still the Night	1986			3.00
Slash 17674		Closer to Free (Studio Album Version)/				
		Closer to Free (Live Album Version)				
			1996			3.00
Slash 28102		Dreams/Ooh	1988			3.00
Slash 28102	PS	Dreams/Ooh	1988			3.00
Slash 28682		Fadeaway/Try and Try	1986			3.00

12-Inch Singles

Label, Number		Title	Year	VG	VG+	NM
Reprise PRO-A-2557		Angels (same on both sides)	1986	2.00	4.00	8.00
Reprise PRO-A-2913	DJ	Say About Love (same on both sides)				
			1987		3.00	6.00
Slash PRO-A-2950	DJ	Dreams (same on both sides)	1987		3.00	6.00

Body Count

*Heavy metal/punk band featuring rapper **Ice-T**.*

12-Inch Singles

Label, Number		Title	Year	VG	VG+	NM
Sire PRO-A-5680	DJ	The Winner Loses/Fly By/Escape from the Killing Fields				
			1991		3.50	7.00

Boney M

German pop group concocted by Frank Farian, who foisted upon us Milli Vanilli (no, they're not listed in here).

Vinyl Albums

Label, Number		Title	Year	VG	VG+	NM
Atlantic SD 19145		Love for Sale	1978	3.50	7.00	14.00

45s

Label, Number		Title	Year	VG	VG+	NM
Atco 7063		Daddy Cool/Lovin' or Leavin'	1976		2.00	4.00
Atco 7080		Sunny/New York City	1978		2.00	4.00
Atlantic 3422		Ma Baker/A Woman Can Change a Man				
			1977		2.00	4.00
Sire 1027		Rivers of Babylon/Brown Girl in the Ring				
			1978		2.50	5.00
Sire 1036		Mary's Boy Child-Oh My Lord/Dancing in the Street				
			1978		2.50	5.00
Sire 1038		Dancing in the Street/Never Change Lovers in the Middle of				
		the Night	1979		2.00	4.00
Sire 1049		He Was Steppenwolf/Rasputin	1979		2.00	4.00

12-Inch Singles

Label, Number		Title	Year	VG	VG+	NM
Atco DSKO 84		Daddy Cool (same on both sides)				
			1976	2.50	5.00	10.00
Atlantic DSKO ??		Ma Baker (same on both sides)	1977	2.50	5.00	10.00
Carrere 05134		Kalimba De Luna (9:15)/Kalimba De Luna (8:40)				
			1984	2.00	4.00	8.00
Sire 1040		Dancing in the Street/Never Change Lovers in the Middle of				
		the Night	1979	2.50	5.00	10.00

Label, Number		Title	Year	VG	VG+	NM

Bonzo Goes To Washington
Jerry Harrison (Talking Heads) and Bootsy Collins

12-Inch Singles

Sleeping Bag SLX-666-13		5 Minutes (3 mixes)	1984	3.00	6.00	12.00

Boomtown Rats, The
*British new-wave group fronted by **Bob Geldof**.*

Vinyl Albums

Columbia JC 35750		A Tonic for the Troops	1979	2.50	5.00	10.00
Columbia JC 36248		The Fine Art of Surfacing	1979	2.50	5.00	10.00
Columbia JC 37062		Mondo Bongo	1981	3.00	6.00	12.00
With poster						
Columbia 5C 38097	EP	The Boomtown Rats	1982	2.00	4.00	8.00
Columbia PC 38591	EP	Ratrospective	1983	2.50	5.00	10.00
Columbia PC 39335		In the Long Grass	1985	2.50	5.00	10.00
Mercury SRM-1-1188		The Boomtown Rats	1977	3.00	6.00	12.00

45s

Columbia 03386		Never in a Million Years/Charmed Lives				
			1982			3.00
Columbia 04892		Rain/An Icicle in the Sun	1985			3.00
Columbia 05590		Drag Me Down/Hard Times	1985			3.00
Columbia 10960		Rat Trap/Do the Rat	1979		2.00	4.00
Columbia 11117		I Don't Like Mondays/It's All the Rage				
			1979		2.50	5.00
Columbia 11248		Someone's Looking at You/I Don't Like Mondays (Live)				
			1980		2.00	4.00
Columbia 60512		Up All Night/Another Piece of Bread				
			1981			3.00

12-Inch Singles

Columbia AS 544	DJ	Rat Trap/Joey's on the Street	1979	3.75	7.50	15.00
Columbia AS 920	DJ	Up All Night/Mood Mambo/Banana Republic				
			1981		3.50	7.00
Columbia AS 1565	DJ	Skin on Skin/Talking in Code	1982		3.50	7.00
Columbia CAS 2170	DJ	Drag Me Down (same on both sides)				
			1984		3.00	6.00

Bourgeois Tagg

45s

Island 99331		Waiting for the World to Turn/Coma				
			1988			3.00
Island 99372		Cry Like a Baby/15 Minutes in the Sun				
			1988			3.00
Island 99409		I Don't Mind at All/Pencil & Paper				
			1987			3.00
Island 99521		The Perfect Life/Electric Train	1986			3.00
Island 99558		Mutual Surrender (What a Wonderful World)/The Move Up				
			1986			3.00

12-Inch Singles

Island 2098	DJ	I Don't Mind at All (same on both sides)				
			1987		2.50	5.00

Label, Number		Title	Year	VG	VG+	NM

Bow Wow Wow

British new-wave group assembled by Malcolm McLaren. Lead singer was Annabella Lwin; others were ex-Adam and the Ants.

Vinyl Albums

Label, Number		Title	Year	VG	VG+	NM
Harvest SK-12234		12 Original Recordings	1982	3.75	7.50	15.00
RCA Victor AFL1-4147		See Jungle, See Jungle! Go Join Your Gang, Yeah!				
			1981	3.00	6.00	12.00
		City All Over, Go Ape Crazy				
RCA DJL1-4193	DJ	RCA Radio Special	1981	6.25	12.50	25.00
RCA Victor CPL1-4314	EP	The Last of the Mohicans	1982	3.00	6.00	12.00
RCA Victor AFL1-4375		I Want Candy	1982	3.00	6.00	12.00
RCA Victor AFL1-4570		When the Going Gets Tough, the Tough Get Going				
			1983	2.50	5.00	10.00

45s

Label, Number		Title	Year	VG	VG+	NM
RCA PB-12338		Chihuahua/Golly! Golly! Go Buddy!	1981		2.00	4.00
RCA PB-13060		Orang-Outang/Mickey, Put It Down				
			1982		2.00	4.00
RCA PB-13060	PS	Orang-Outang/Mickey, Put It Down				
			1982		2.00	4.00
RCA PB-13204		I Want Candy/Elimination Dancing				
			1982			3.00
RCA PB-13204	PS	I Want Candy/Elimination Dancing				
			1982			3.00
RCA PB-13291		Baby, Oh No/Cowboy (Remix Version)				
			1982			3.00
RCA PB-13467		Do You Wanna Hold Me?/What's the Time (Hey Buddy)				
			1983		2.00	4.00
RCA PB-13595		Love, Peace and Harmony/I Want Candy				
			1983		2.00	4.00
Studio 54	DJ	The Mile High Club/C-30. C-60, C-90, Go!				
			1981	5.00	10.00	20.00

Promo for show

12-Inch Singles

Label, Number		Title	Year	VG	VG+	NM
RCA PD-12323		Chihuahua/Sinner, Sinner, Sinner				
			1981	4.00	8.00	16.00
RCA PD-12339		Chihuahua/Golly! Golly! Go Buddy!				
			1981	3.00	6.00	12.00
RCA PB-13231		I Want Candy/Elimination Dancing				
			1982	3.00	6.00	12.00
RCA PB-13306		Baby, Oh No (Dance Version)/Cowboy				
			1982	2.00	4.00	8.00
RCA JD-13535	DJ	Do You Wanna Hold Me? (Long)/(Short)				
			1983	4.00	8.00	16.00
RCA PW-13540		Do You Wanna Hold Me?/What's the Time (Hey Buddy)				
			1983			*Unreleased*

Bowie, David

A musical chameleon. Also see **Queen and David Bowie; Tin Machine.**

Vinyl Albums

Label, Number		Title	Year	VG	VG+	NM
Deram DE 16003	M	David Bowie	1967	25.00	50.00	100.00
Deram DES 18003	S	David Bowie	1967	37.50	75.00	150.00
EMI America SPRO 9960/9961	(2) DJ	Let's Talk	1983	6.25	12.50	25.00
Promo-only interview album						
EMI America SO-17093		Let's Dance	1983	2.50	5.00	10.00
EMI America SJ-17138		Tonight	1984	2.50	5.00	10.00
EMI America PJ-17267		Never Let Me Down	1987	2.50	5.00	10.00
EMI America SPRO-79112/3	DJ	Never Let Me Down: The Interview				
			1987	6.25	12.50	25.00

Label, Number		Title	Year	VG	VG+	NM
EMI America R 153730		Let's Dance	1983	3.00	6.00	12.00
RCA Music Service edition						
EMI America R 174212		Never Let Me Down	1987	3.00	6.00	12.00
BMG Direct Marketing edition						
London 50007		Starting Point	1977	3.00	6.00	12.00
London PS 628/629	(2)	Images 1966-1967	1973	12.50	25.00	50.00
Original pressings have dark blue and silver labels. Later pressings, if any, are worth at least 50% less.						
Mercury SR 61246		Man of Words, Man of Music	1969	25.00	50.00	100.00
Mercury SR 61325		The Man Who Sold the World	1970	12.50	25.00	50.00
An often-counterfeited album; originals have matrix numbers stamped in the trail-off area.						
Mobile Fidelity 1-064		The Rise and Fall of Ziggy Stardust and the Spiders from Mars				
			1983	12.50	25.00	50.00
Original Master Recording						
Mobile Fidelity 1-083		Let's Dance	1983	7.50	15.00	30.00
Original Master Recording						
RCA Red Seal ARL1-2743		Peter and the Wolf	1978	5.00	10.00	20.00
With the Philadelphia Orchestra conducted by Eugene Ormandy; green vinyl						
RCA Red Seal ARL1-2743		Peter and the Wolf	1978	5.00	10.00	20.00
With the Philadelphia Orchestra conducted by Eugene Ormandy; black vinyl						
RCA Victor 9503/9504	DJ	David Bowie Special	1976			
This album has been listed elsewhere, but we can't confirm its existence. The numbering doesn't even make sense.						
RCA Victor APL1-0291		Pin Ups	1973	5.00	10.00	20.00
RCA Victor AFL1-0291		Pin Ups	1978	2.50	5.00	10.00
Reissue						
RCA Victor APL1-0576		Diamond Dogs	1974	1,000.00	2,000.00	4,000.00
Original copies have cover with dog's genitals clearly visible. Almost all were destroyed prior to release.						
RCA Victor APL1-0576		Diamond Dogs	1974	5.00	10.00	20.00
Standard issue, with dog's genitals airbrushed						
RCA Victor APL1-0998		Young Americans	1975	3.00	6.00	12.00
At time of release, available with either orange or tan label						
RCA Victor APL1-0998		Young Americans	1976	2.50	5.00	10.00
Black label						
RCA Victor AQK1-0998		Young Americans	1984	2.50	5.00	10.00
Reissue						
RCA Victor APL1-1327		Station to Station	1976	3.00	6.00	12.00
Originals have a brown label						
RCA Victor APL1-1327		Station to Station	1976	2.50	5.00	10.00
Black label						
RCA Victor AQK1-1327		Station to Station	1984	2.50	5.00	10.00
Reissue						
RCA Victor APL1-1732		Changesonebowie	1976			
With alternate version of "John, I'm Only Dancing." Possibly identifiable without playing, but we're not sure how.						
And it may not even exist at all.						
RCA Victor APL1-1732		Changesonebowie	1976	2.50	5.00	10.00
With common take of "John, I'm Only Dancing"						
RCA Victor AFL1-1732		Changesonebowie	1978	2.50	5.00	10.00
Reissue						
RCA Victor AQL1-1732		Changesonebowie	1984	2.50	5.00	10.00
Reissue						
RCA Victor APL1-2030		Low	1977	2.50	5.00	10.00
RCA Victor AFL1-2522		"Heroes"	1977	2.50	5.00	10.00
RCA Victor DJL1-2697	DJ	Bowie Now	1978	18.75	37.50	75.00
RCA Victor CPL2-2913	(2)	Stage	1978	5.00	10.00	20.00
RCA Victor DJL1-3016	DJ	An Evening with David Bowie	1978	12.50	25.00	50.00
Live concert for "Superstars Radio Network"						
RCA Victor AQL1-3254		Lodger	1979	2.50	5.00	10.00
RCA Victor DJL1-3545	DJ	1980 All Clear	1980	5.00	10.00	20.00
RCA Victor AQL1-3647		Scary Monsters	1980	2.50	5.00	10.00
RCA Victor DJL1-3829	DJ	Special Radio Series, Volume 1	1980	6.25	12.50	25.00
RCA Victor AYL1-3839		Diamond Dogs	1980	2.00	4.00	8.00
Reissue						
RCA Victor DJL1-3840	DJ	Scary Monsters Interview	1980	5.00	10.00	20.00

Label, Number	Title	Year	VG	VG+	NM
RCA Victor AYL1-3843	The Rise and Fall of Ziggy Stardust and the Spiders from Mars				
		1980	2.00	4.00	8.00
Reissue					
RCA Victor AYL1-3844	Hunky Dory	1980	2.00	4.00	8.00
Reissue					
RCA Victor AYL1-3856	Low	1980	2.00	4.00	8.00
Reissue					
RCA Victor AYL1-3857	"Heroes"	1980	2.00	4.00	8.00
Reissue					
RCA Victor AYL1-3890	Aladdin Sane	1980	2.00	4.00	8.00
Reissue					
RCA Victor AFL1-4202	Changestwobowie	1981	2.50	5.00	10.00
RCA Victor AYL1-4234	Lodger	1981	2.00	4.00	8.00
Reissue					
RCA Victor CPL1-4346	David Bowie in Berthold Brecht's Baal				
		1982	2.50	5.00	10.00
RCA Victor LSP-4623	Hunky Dory	1972	5.00	10.00	20.00
RCA Victor AYL1-4653	Pin Ups	1982	2.00	4.00	8.00
Reissue					
RCA Victor LSP-4702	The Rise and Fall of Ziggy Stardust and the Spiders from Mars				
		1972	5.00	10.00	20.00
RCA Victor AFL1-4702	The Rise and Fall of Ziggy Stardust and the Spiders from Mars				
		1977	2.50	5.00	10.00
Reissue					
RCA Victor AFL1-4792	Golden Years	1983	2.50	5.00	10.00
RCA Victor LSP-4813	Space Oddity	1973	5.00	10.00	20.00
Reissue of Mercury SR-61246; add 1/3 if bonus poster is enclosed					
RCA Victor LSP-4816	The Man Who Sold the World	1973	5.00	10.00	20.00
Reissue of Mercury SR-61325; add 1/3 if bonus poster is enclosed					
RCA Victor AFL1-4852	Aladdin Sane	1977	2.50	5.00	10.00
Reissue					
RCA Victor CPL2-4862	(2) DJ Ziggy Stardust, The Motion Picture				
		1983	12.50	25.00	50.00
Promo version on clear vinyl					
RCA Victor CPL2-4862	(2) Ziggy Stardust, The Motion Picture				
		1983	5.00	10.00	20.00
RCA Victor AFL1-4919	Fame and Fashion	1984	2.50	5.00	10.00
Reissue					
RCA Victor LSP-4852	Aladdin Sane	1973	5.00	10.00	20.00
Orange label is original (deduct 50% for tan labels)					
Ryko Analogue LSD-4702 DJ	The Rise and Fall of Ziggy Stardust and the Spiders from Mars				
		1990	25.00	50.00	100.00
Special promo-only package with both the LP and CD versions					
Ryko Analogue RALP 0120/1/2					
	(6) Sound + Vision	1989	25.00	50.00	100.00
Six-LP box set on clear vinyl with three gatefold cardboard inner sleeves					
Ryko Analogue RALP 0131 (2)	Space Oddity	1990	5.00	10.00	20.00
Clear vinyl with "Limited Edition" obi					
Ryko Analogue RALP 0132 (2)	The Man Who Sold the World	1990	5.00	10.00	20.00
Clear vinyl with "Limited Edition" obi					
Ryko Analogue RALP 0133 (2)	Hunky Dory	1990	5.00	10.00	20.00
Clear vinyl with "Limited Edition" obi					
Ryko Analogue RALP 0134 (2)	The Rise and Fall of Ziggy Stardust and the Spiders from Mars				
		1990	5.00	10.00	20.00
Clear vinyl with "Limited Edition" obi					
Ryko Analogue RALP 0135	Aladdin Sane	1990	5.00	10.00	20.00
Clear vinyl with "Limited Edition" obi					
Ryko Analogue RALP 0136	Pin Ups	1990	5.00	10.00	20.00
Clear vinyl with "Limited Edition" obi					
Ryko Analogue RALP 0137	Diamond Dogs	1990	5.00	10.00	20.00
Clear vinyl with "Limited Edition" obi; genitals on dog are restored					
Ryko Analogue RALP 0138/9 (2)	David Live	1990	5.00	10.00	20.00
Ryko Analogue RALP 0171 (2)	Changesbowie	1990	5.00	10.00	20.00
Clear vinyl with "Limited Edition" obi					

Label, Number		Title	Year	VG	VG+	NM
7-Inch Extended Play Singles						
RCA Victor 45-103	DJ	David Bowie	1972	5.00	10.00	20.00
RCA Victor 45-103	PS	David Bowie	1972	5.00	10.00	20.00
45s						
Backstreet 52024		Cat People/Paul's Theme	1982			3.00
B-side by Georgio Moroder						
Backstreet 52024	PS	Cat People/Paul's Theme	1982			3.00
Deram 85009		Rubber Band/There Is a Happy Land				
			1967	12.50	25.00	50.00
Deram 85016		Love You Till Tuesday/Did You Ever Have a Dream				
			1967	12.50	25.00	50.00
EMI America 8158		Let's Dance/Cat People (Putting Out Fire)				
			1983			3.00
EMI America 8158	PS	Let's Dance/Cat People (Putting Out Fire)				
			1983			3.00
EMI America 8165		China Girl/Shake It	1983			3.00
EMI America 8165	PS	China Girl/Shake It	1983		2.50	5.00
EMI America 8177		Modern Love/Modern Love (Live)				
			1983			3.00
EMI America 8177	PS	Modern Love/Modern Love (Live)				
			1983			3.00
EMI America 8190		Without You/Criminal Law	1984			3.00
EMI America 8190	PS	Without You/Criminal Law	1984			3.00
EMI America 8231		Blue Jean/Dancin' with the Big Boys				
			1984	2.00	4.00	8.00
First pressing on blue vinyl						
EMI America 8231		Blue Jean/Dancin' with the Big Boys				
			1984			2.00
EMI America 8231	PS	Blue Jean/Dancin' with the Big Boys				
			1984			2.00
Both colors of vinyl have the same picture sleeve						
EMI America 8246		Tonight/Tumble and Twirl	1984			3.00
EMI America 8246	PS	Tonight/Tumble and Twirl	1984			3.00
EMI America 8271		Loving the Alien/Don't Look Down				
			1985			3.00
EMI America 8271	PS	Loving the Alien/Don't Look Down				
			1985		2.50	5.00
Fold-out poster sleeve						
EMI America 8308		Absolute Beginners/(B-side unknown)				
			1986			3.00
EMI America 8308	PS	Absolute Beginners/(B-side unknown)				
			1986			3.00
EMI America 8323		Underground/(instrumental)	1986			3.00
EMI America 8323	PS	Underground/(instrumental)	1986			3.00
EMI America 8380		Day In Day Out/Day In Day Out	1987			3.00
EMI America 8380	PS	Day In Day Out/Day In Day Out	1987			3.00
EMI America 43020		Time Will Crawl/Time Will Crawl				
			1987			3.00
EMI America 43020	PS	Time Will Crawl/Time Will Crawl				
			1987	2.50	5.00	10.00
Easily Bowie's scarcest EMI picture sleeve						
EMI America 43031		Never Let Me Down/Never Let Me Down				
			1987			3.00
EMI America 43031	PS	Never Let Me Down/Never Let Me Down				
			1987			3.00
London 20079		The Laughing Gnome/The Gospel According to Tony Day				
			1973	12.50	25.00	50.00
Mercury 72949		Space Oddity/Wild-Eyed Boy from Freecloud				
			1969	12.50	25.00	50.00
Mercury 73075		Memory of a Free Festival Part 1/Part 2				
			1970	25.00	50.00	100.00

Label, Number		Title	Year	VG	VG+	NM
Mercury 73173	DJ	All the Madmen (mono/stereo)	1971	25.00	50.00	100.00
May be promo only						
RCA PB-10664		TVC 15/We Are the Dead	1976		2.50	5.00
RCA PB-10736		Stay/Word on a Wing	1976		2.50	5.00
RCA PB-10905		Sound and Vision/A New Career in a New Town				
			1977		2.50	5.00
RCA GB-10938		Fame/Golden Years	1977			3.00
Gold Standard Series issue						
RCA PB-11017		Be My Wife/The Speed of Life	1977		2.50	5.00
RCA PB-11121		Heroes/V-2 Schneider	1977		2.50	5.00
RCA PB-11190		Beauty and the Beast/Sense of Doubt				
			1978		2.50	5.00
RCA PB-11585		Boys Keep Swinging/Fantastic Voyage				
			1979		2.50	5.00
RCA PB-11661		D.J./Fantastic Voyage	1979		2.50	5.00
RCA PB-11724		Look Back in Anger/Repetition	1979		2.50	5.00
RCA PB-11887		John I'm Only Dancing 1972/Golden Years				
			1980		2.50	5.00
RCA PB-12078		Ashes to Ashes/It's No Game	1980		2.50	5.00
RCA PB-12078	PS	Ashes to Ashes/It's No Game	1980		2.50	5.00
RCA JH-12078	PS	Ashes to Ashes/It's No Game	1980	3.75	7.50	15.00
Promo-only sleeve of Bowie holding a shoe and looking down at it						
RCA JE-12087	DJ	Fashion/It's No Game/Teenage Wildlife				
			1980	100.00	200.00	400.00
RCA PB-12134		Fashion/Scream Like a Baby	1980		2.50	5.00
RCA PB-12134	PS	Fashion/Scream Like a Baby	1980		2.50	5.00
RCA PB-13660		White Light-White Heat/Cracked Actor				
			1983		2.50	5.00
RCA PB-13769		1984/TVC 15	1984		2.50	5.00
RCA Victor APBO-0001		Time/The Prettiest Star	1973		3.00	6.00
RCA Victor APBO-0001	PS	Time/The Prettiest Star	1973	150.00	300.00	600.00
RCA Victor APBO-0028		Let's Spend the Night Together/Lady Grinning Soul				
			1973		3.00	6.00
RCA Victor APBO-0160		Sorrow/Amsterdam	1973		3.00	6.00
RCA Victor APBO-0287		Rebel Rebel/Lady Grinning Soul	1974	2.50	5.00	10.00
All copies contain an alternate mix of "Rebel Rebel"						
RCA Victor APBO-0293		Diamond Dogs/Holy Holy	1974	2.50	5.00	10.00
Part of U.S. numbering system, but released only outside the U.S.						
RCA Victor 74-0605		Changes/Andy Warhol	1971	2.50	5.00	10.00
Orange label (original)						
RCA Victor 74-0605		Changes/Andy Warhol	1974		3.00	6.00
Tan or gray label						
RCA Victor 74-0719		Starman/Suffragette City	1972		3.00	6.00
RCA Victor 74-0719	PS	Starman/Suffragette City	1972	7.50	15.00	30.00
RCA Victor 74-0838		The Jean Genie/Hang On to Yourself				
			1972		3.00	6.00
RCA Victor 74-0876		Space Oddity/The Man Who Sold the World				
			1973		3.00	6.00
RCA Victor 74-0876	PS	Space Oddity/The Man Who Sold the World				
			1973	5.00	10.00	20.00
RCA Victor PB-10026		1984/Queen Bitch	1974		3.00	6.00
RCA Victor PB-10105		Rock and Roll with Me/Panic in Detroit				
			1974		3.00	6.00
RCA Victor PB-10152		Young Americans/Knock on Wood				
			1975		3.00	6.00
RCA Victor PB-10320		Fame/Right	1975		3.00	6.00
John Lennon co-wrote and appears on A-side						
RCA Victor PB-10441		Golden Years/Can You Hear Me				
			1975		3.00	6.00
RCA Victor GB-10468		Changes/Andy Warhol	1975		2.00	4.00
Gold Standard Series issue						

Label, Number		Title	Year	VG	VG+	NM
RCA Victor GB-10469		Young Americans/Knock on Wood				
			1975		2.00	4.00
Gold Standard Series issue						
RCA Victor GB-10470		Space Oddity/The Man Who Sold the World				
			1975		2.00	4.00
Gold Standard Series issue						
Warner Bros. 5815		Can't Stop Thinking About Me/And I Say to Myself				
			1966	125.00	250.00	500.00
As "David Bowie and the Lower Third"						

12-Inch Singles

Label, Number		Title	Year	VG	VG+	NM
Backstreet L33-1759	DJ	Cat People (Putting Out Fire) (same on both sides)				
			1982	3.75	7.50	15.00
EMI SPRO-04532	DJ	Fame 90 (4 mixes)	1990	3.75	7.50	15.00
EMI 56163		Fame 90 (5 versions, including Queen Latifah mix)				
			1990	2.00	4.00	8.00
EMI 93492		Fame 90 (5 mixes)	1990		3.00	6.00
EMI America 7805		Let's Dance/Cat People (Putting Out Fire)				
			1983	2.50	5.00	10.00
EMI America 7809		China Girl/Shake It	1983	2.50	5.00	10.00
EMI America 7811		Modern Love/Modern Love (Live)				
			1983	2.50	5.00	10.00
EMI America 7838		Blue Jean/Dancing with the Big Boys				
			1984	2.50	5.00	10.00
EMI America 7846		Tonight (2 versions)/Tumble and Twirl				
			1984	2.50	5.00	10.00
EMI America 7858		Loving the Alien (2 versions)/Don't Look Down				
			1985	3.00	6.00	12.00
With gatefold sleeve and poster						
EMI America SPRO-9222	DJ	Blue Jean/Dancing with the Big Boys				
			1984	3.75	7.50	15.00
EMI America SPRO-9295	DJ	Tonight (same on both sides)	1984	3.75	7.50	15.00
EMI America SPRO-9670	DJ	Underground (Long)/Underground (Short)				
			1986	3.00	6.00	12.00
EMI America SPRO-9904	DJ	Let's Dance (same on both sides)				
			1983	3.00	6.00	12.00
EMI America SPRO-9952	DJ	China Girl (Long)/Shake It (Long)				
			1983	3.75	7.50	15.00
EMI America SPRO-9985	DJ	Day In Day Out (same on both sides)				
			1987	2.50	5.00	10.00
EMI America SPRO-9996	DJ	Day In Day Out (4 versions)	1987	3.75	7.50	15.00
EMI America 19205		Absolute Beginners (Full Length)/Absolute Beginners (Dub)				
			1986	2.50	5.00	10.00
EMI America 19210		Underground (3 versions)	1986	2.00	4.00	8.00
EMI America 19217		Magic Dance (2 versions)/Within You				
			1986	2.00	4.00	8.00
EMI America 19234		Day In Day Out (2 versions)/Julie				
			1987	2.50	5.00	10.00
EMI America 19239		Day In Day Out (3 versions)	1984	3.75	7.50	15.00
EMI America 19247		Time Will Crawl (2 versions)/Girls (2 versions)				
			1987	2.50	5.00	10.00
EMI America 19255		Never Let Me Down (5 versions)/87 and Cry				
			1987	2.50	5.00	10.00
EMI America SPRO-79090	DJ	Never Let Me Down (same on both sides)				
			1987	3.00	6.00	12.00
RCA DJL1-3255	DJ	Star/What in the World/Breaking Glass				
			1978	6.25	12.50	25.00
White vinyl promo						
RCA DJL1-3795	DJ	Space Oddity/Ashes to Ashes (2 versions)				
			1980	7.50	15.00	30.00
With set of stamps						

Label, Number		Title	Year	VG	VG+	NM
RCA DJL1-3795	DJ	Space Oddity/Ashes to Ashes (2 versions)				
			1980	5.00	10.00	20.00
Without stamps						
RCA JD-11151		Heroes (Unedited)/Heroes (Edited)				
			1977	6.25	12.50	25.00
RCA PC-11204	DJ	Beauty and the Beast/Fame	1978	7.50	15.00	30.00
RCA JD-11306	DJ	Peter and the Wolf (Part 1)/Peter and the Wolf (Part 2)				
			1978	7.50	15.00	30.00
RCA PB-11886		John I'm Only Dancing (Again) 1975/Golden Years				
			1980	5.00	10.00	20.00
RCA JD-12079		Ashes to Ashes/Fashion	1980			*Unreleased*
RCA JD-12140	DJ	Fashion (long)/Fashion (short)	1981	3.00	6.00	12.00
RCA PD-12145		Fashion/Scream Like a Baby	1980	3.00	6.00	12.00
RCA PB-12249		Up the Hills Backwards/Crystal Japan				
			1981	5.00	10.00	20.00
RCA PB-13770		1984/TVC 15	1984	2.00	4.00	8.00
Savage 50039	DJ	Jump They Say (5 versions)/Pallas Athena				
			1993	3.75	7.50	15.00
Savage 50042		Jump They Say (5 versions)/Pallas Athena				
			1993	2.00	4.00	8.00
Savage 50045	DJ	Black Tie White Noise (7 versions)				
			1993	3.75	7.50	15.00

Bowie, David, and 808 State

12-Inch Singles

Tommy Boy 510		Sound and Vision (4 versions)	1991	3.75	7.50	15.00

Bowie, David, and Mick Jagger

Recorded specifically for the Live Aid benefit concert.

45s

EMI America 8288		Dancing in the Street/(instrumental)				
			1985			3.00
EMI America 8288	PS	Dancing in the Street/(instrumental)				
			1985			3.00

12-Inch Singles

EMI America 19200		Dancing in the Street (3 versions)				
			1985	2.50	5.00	10.00

Bowie, David/Bing Crosby

Unlikely coupling was taken from the soundtrack of Bing Crosby's final Christmas-season TV special, recorded in 1976.

45s

RCA PH-13400		Peace on Earth-Little Drummer Boy/Fantastic Voyage				
			1982		2.50	5.00
B-side by David Bowie solo						
RCA PH-13400	PS	Peace on Earth-Little Drummer Boy/Fantastic Voyage				
			1982	2.50	5.00	10.00

Bowie, David/Pat Metheny Group

Another unlikely coupling, this time for the movie The Falcon and the Snowman.

45s

EMI America 8251		This Is Not America/(Instrumental)				
			1984			3.00
EMI America 8251	PS	This Is Not America/(Instrumental)				
			1984			3.00

Label, Number		Title	Year	VG	VG+	NM
12-Inch Singles						
EMI America SPRO-9310		This Is Not America (same on both sides)				
			1985	3.75	7.50	15.00

Boy George

Formerly of Culture Club.

Label, Number		Title	Year	VG	VG+	NM
Vinyl Albums						
Virgin 90617		Sold	1987	2.50	5.00	10.00
Virgin 91022		High Hat	1989	2.50	5.00	10.00
Virgin R 100843		High Hat	1989	3.00	6.00	12.00
BMG Direct Marketing edition						
Virgin R 153255		Sold	1987	3.00	6.00	12.00
BMG Direct Marketing edition						
45s						
SBK S7-56996		The Crying Game/Stand By Your Man				
			1993		2.00	4.00
Red vinyl; B-side by Lyle Lovett						
SBK S7-56996		The Crying Game/Stand By Your Man				
			1993			3.00
Black vinyl; B-side by Lyle Lovett						
Virgin S7-17709		Everything I Own/Miss Me Blind	1994			3.00
B-side by "Boy George and Culture Club"						
Virgin S7-18735		Funtime/Same Thing in Reverse	1995			3.00
Virgin 99159		Whisper/Leave in Love	1989			3.00
Virgin 99200		You Found Another Guy/I Go Where I Go				
			1989			2.00
Virgin 99200	PS	You Found Another Guy/I Go Where I Go				
			1989			2.00
Virgin 99272		Don't Take My Mind on a Trip/Girlfriend				
			1988			3.00
Virgin 99390		Live My Life (The Mix)/Live My Life (Soul Remix)				
			1987			3.00
Virgin 99445		Everything I Own/Use Me	1987			3.00
Virgin 99445	PS	Everything I Own/Use Me	1987		2.50	5.00
Sleeve may be promo only						
12-Inch Singles						
Virgin 1052	DJ	Everything I Own (3 versions)/Use Me				
			1987		3.50	7.00
Virgin 1116	DJ	Live My Life (4 versions)	1988		3.50	7.00
Virgin 1292	DJ	Don't Take My Mind on a Trip (4 versions)/Girlfriend				
			1989	2.00	4.00	8.00
Virgin 1353	DJ	You've Found Another Guy (3 versions)/I Go Where I Go				
			1989		3.00	6.00
Virgin 2994	DJ	Whisper (Edit)/Whisper (LP version)				
			1989		3.00	6.00
Virgin 96545		You've Found Another Guy (3 versions)/I Go Where I Go				
			1989	2.50	5.00	10.00
Virgin 96577		Don't Take My Mind on a Trip (4 versions)/Girlfriend				
			1989		3.50	7.00
Virgin 96728		Live My Life (4 versions)	1988		3.00	6.00
Virgin 96765		Everything I Own (3 versions)/Use Me				
			1987		3.00	6.00

Brains, The

Label, Number		Title	Year	VG	VG+	NM
Vinyl Albums						
Landslide 1201	EP	Under Streetlights + 3	1982	3.75	7.50	15.00
Mercury SRM-1-3835		The Brains	1980	2.50	5.00	10.00

Label, Number		Title	Year	VG	VG+	NM
45s						
Grey Matter GM 1		Money Changes Everything/Quick with Your Lip				
			1978		2.00	4.00
Grey Matter GM 1	PS	Money Changes Everything/Quick with Your Lip				
			1978		3.00	6.00
First sleeve: Individual photos on back						
Grey Matter GM 1	PS	Money Changes Everything/Quick with Your Lip				
			1978		2.00	4.00
Second sleeve: Group photo on back						
Mercury 76065		Money Changes Everything/Girl in a Magazine				
			1980		1.50	3.00
12-Inch Singles						
Mercury MK 140	DJ	Money Changes Everything/Gold Dust Kids				
			1980	3.75	7.50	15.00
Mercury MK 166	DJ	Dream Life/Eyes of Ice/Asphalt Wonderland/No Tears Tonight				
			1980	3.75	7.50	15.00

Breakdown

7-Inch Extended Play Singles

Label, Number		Title	Year	VG	VG+	NM
Blackout/Noiseville (# unknown)		The '87 Demo E.P.	1990	8.00	16.00	32.00
Yellow vinyl						
Blackout/Noiseville (# unknown)		The '87 Demo E.P.	1990	2.00	4.00	8.00
Blackout/Noiseville (# unknown)						
	PS	The '87 Demo E.P.	1990	2.00	4.00	8.00

Breakfast Club

*New York synth-pop/dance group. Before either recorded, **Madonna** was briefly with the group.*

Vinyl Albums

Label, Number		Title	Year	VG	VG+	NM
MCA 5821		Breakfast Club	1987	2.50	5.00	10.00
45s						
MCA 52954		Right On Track/Right On Track (Local Mix)				
			1986			3.00
MCA 52954	PS	Right On Track/Right On Track (Local Mix)				
			1986			3.00
MCA 53128		Kiss and Tell/Right On Track	1987			3.00
MCA 53128	PS	Kiss and Tell/Right On Track	1987			3.00
MCA 53194		Never Be the Same (Shep Pettibone Mix)/(Dub Version)				
			1987			3.00
MCA 53273		Expressway to Your Heart/Tongue Tied				
			1988			3.00
MCA 53348		Drive My Car (from "License to Drive")/(Instrumental)				
			1988			3.00
12-Inch Singles						
MCA 23687		Right On Track (7 versions)	1986	2.00	4.00	8.00
MCA 23833		Expressway to Your Heart (4 versions)				
			1988	2.00	4.00	8.00

Breeders, The

Dayton, Ohio-based alterna-rock band, led by Kim and Kelley Deal.

45s

Label, Number	Title	Year	VG	VG+	NM
Elektra 64545	Divine Hammer/Cannonball	1994			3.00

Label, Number		Title	Year	VG	VG+	NM

Brickell, Edie, & New Bohemians
Texas alterna-folkie band. Edie eventually went solo.

Vinyl Albums

Geffen 24192		Shooting Rubberbands at the Stars				
			1988	2.50	5.00	10.00
Geffen GHS 24304		Ghost of a Dog	1990	2.50	5.00	10.00
Geffen R 100789		Shooting Rubberbands at the Stars				
			1988	3.00	6.00	12.00
BMG Direct Marketing edition						

45s

Geffen 27580		Circle/Now	1989			3.00
Geffen 27580	PS	Circle/Now	1989			3.00
Geffen 27696		What I Am/I Do	1988			3.00
Geffen 27696	PS	What I Am/I Do	1988			3.00

Brinsley Schwarz
*Early British pub-rock band; **Nick Lowe was a member.***

Vinyl Albums

Capitol ST-589		Brinsley Schwarz	1970	5.00	10.00	20.00
Featuring Nick Lowe and Ian Gomm						
Capitol ST-744		Despite It All	1971	5.00	10.00	20.00
Capitol SWBC-11869	(2)	Brinsley Schwarz	1978	3.75	7.50	15.00
Liberty LN 10145		Silver Pistol	1980	2.50	5.00	10.00
10-track reissue						
Liberty LN 10146		Nervous on the Road	1981	2.50	5.00	10.00
10-track reissue						
United Artists UAS-5566		Silver Pistol	1972	3.75	7.50	15.00
United Artists UAS-5647		Nervous on the Road	1972	3.75	7.50	15.00

45s

United Artists 50915		Nightingale/Silver Pistol	1972		3.00	6.00
United Artists 50976		Nervous on the Road/Happy Doing What We're Doing				
			1972		3.00	6.00

Bronski Beat
*British techno-pop band. Band member Jimmy Somerville went on to form **Communards**.*

Vinyl Albums

MCA 5338		The Age of Consent	1984	3.00	6.00	12.00
MCA 5751		Truthdare, Doubledare	1986	2.50	5.00	10.00
MCA 39038	EP	Hundreds & Thousands	1985	2.50	5.00	10.00

45s

MCA 52494		Smalltown Boy/Memories	1984			3.00
MCA 52494	PS	Smalltown Boy/Memories	1984			3.00
MCA 52565		Why?/Cadillac Car	1985			3.00
MCA 52565	PS	Why?/Cadillac Car	1985			3.00
MCA 52750		Hit That Perfect Beat/I Gave You Everything				
			1985			3.00
MCA 52831		C'mon! C'mon!/Something Special				
			1986			3.00
MCA 52831	PS	C'mon! C'mon!/Something Special				
			1986			3.00

12-Inch Singles

MCA 17063	DJ	Run from Love/Hard Rain	1985	3.00	6.00	12.00
MCA 23521		Smalltown Boy/Infatuation/Memories				
			1984	2.50	5.00	10.00
MCA 23538		Why?/Cadillac Car	1985	3.00	6.00	12.00

Label, Number		Title	Year	VG	VG+	NM
MCA 23550		I Feel Love (source mix)/I Feel Love (cake mix)				
			1985	3.75	7.50	15.00
With Marc Almond (ex-Soft Cell)						
MCA 23605		Hit That Perfect Beat (3 versions)				
			1985	2.50	5.00	10.00
MCA 23630		C'mon C'mon (2 mixes)/Something Special				
			1986		3.00	6.00

Brown, Julie
Los Angeles actress and Valley Girl parodist.

Vinyl Albums

Rhino RNEP 610	EP	Goddess in Progress	1984	3.75	7.50	15.00
Sire 25634		Trapped in the Body of a White Girl				
			1987	2.50	5.00	10.00

45s

Sire 27983		Girl Fight Tonight/Every Boy's Got One				
			1988			3.00
Sire 28251		Trapped in the Body of a White Girl/Will I Make It				
		Through the 80's	1987			3.00

12-Inch Singles

Bulletz (# unknown)		I Like 'Em Big and Stupid/The Homecoming Queen's Got a Gun				
			1982	2.00	4.00	8.00
Sire 20753		Trapped in the Body of a White Girl (3 mixes)/Will I Make It				
		Through the 80's	1987		3.00	6.00
Sire 20865		Girl Fight Tonight/Every Boy's Got One				
			1988		3.00	6.00

Buggles, The
British synth-pop duo: Trevor Horn and Geoffrey Downes. Both later joined Yes. Horn then became an influential producer.

Vinyl Albums

Island ILPS 9585		The Age of Plastic	1980	3.00	6.00	12.00
Island 90090		The Age of Plastic	1983	2.50	5.00	10.00
Reissue						

45s

Carrere 02759	I Am a Camera/Inner City	1982			3.00
Collectables 2600	Video Killed the Radio Star/Pilot of the Airwaves				
		199?			3.00
Reissue; B-side by Charlie Dore					
Island 49114	Video Killed the Radio Star/Kid Dynamo				
		1979		2.00	4.00
Island 49209	Astro Boy (And the Proles on Parade)/Clean Clean				
		1980			3.00
Island 99871	Video Killed the Radio Star/Kid Dynamo				
		1983		3.00	6.00
Stock copies are scarce (deduct 50% for double A-sided promo)					

12-Inch Singles

Island PRO-A-859	DJ	Clean Clean/Living in the Plastic Age				
			1980	2.00	4.00	8.00

Bus Boys
Los Angeles group.

Vinyl Albums

Arista AL 4280	Minimum Wage Rock 'n' Roll	1980	3.00	6.00	12.00

Label, Number		Title	Year	VG	VG+	NM
Arista AL8-8030		American Worker	198?	2.00	4.00	8.00
Reissue						
Arista ALB6-8324		Minimum Wage Rock 'n' Roll	198?	2.00	4.00	8.00
Reissue						
Arista AL 9589		American Worker	1982	3.00	6.00	12.00
Voss/Chrysalis 42915		Money Don't Make No Man	1988	3.00	6.00	12.00
45s						
Arista 0570		Johnny Soul'd Out/Tell the Coach				
			1980		2.00	4.00
Arista 0589		Angie/Did You See Me	1981		2.00	4.00
Arista 1007		Last Forever/(B-side unknown)	1982			3.00
Arista 1034		The Boys Are Back in Town/I Get Lost				
			1983			3.00
Arista 9229		Cleanin' Up the Town/New Shoes				
			1984			3.00
Arista 9409		The Boys Are Back in Town/Cleanin' Up the Town				
			1985			3.00
"Flashback" oldies series						
12-Inch Singles						
Voss 75329		Hard Work (5 versions)	1988	2.00	4.00	8.00

Bush, Kate

British pop/new wave artist.

Label, Number		Title	Year	VG	VG+	NM
Vinyl Albums						
Columbia C 44164		The Sensual World	1989	3.00	6.00	12.00
EMI America SW-17003		The Kick Inside	1978	2.50	5.00	10.00
Reissue of Harvest release						
EMI America SMAS-17008		Lionheart	1978	3.75	7.50	15.00
EMI America ST-17084		The Dreaming	1982	2.50	5.00	10.00
EMI America ST-17115		Never for Ever	1983	2.50	5.00	10.00
EMI America ST-17171		Hounds of Love	1985	7.50	15.00	30.00
Marbled vinyl						
EMI America ST-17171		Hounds of Love	1985	2.50	5.00	10.00
Standard issue						
EMI America PWAS-17242		The Whole Story	1986	3.75	7.50	15.00
EMI America MLP-19004	EP	Kate Bush	1983	3.75	7.50	15.00
Harvest ST-11762		The Kick Inside	1978	6.25	12.50	25.00
45s						
Columbia 73092		Love and Anger/Walk Straight Down the Middle				
			1990		*May be cassette only*	
Columbia 77280		Rubberband Girl/This Woman's Work				
			1993		*Cassette only*	
EMI America 8003		Wuthering Heights/Kite	1978		2.00	4.00
EMI America 8003	PS	Wuthering Heights/Kite	1978	2.00	4.00	8.00
EMI America 8006		The Man with the Child in His Eyes/Moving				
			1978		2.00	4.00
EMI America 8285		Running Up That Hill/Under the Ivy				
			1985			2.00
EMI America 8285	PS	Running Up That Hill/Under the Ivy				
			1985		2.00	4.00
EMI America 8327		The Big Sky/(B-side unknown)	1986			2.00
EMI America 8327	PS	The Big Sky/(B-side unknown)	1986		2.00	4.00
EMI America 8363		Experiment IV/Wuthering Heights (New Vocal)				
			1986			2.00
EMI America 8363	PS	Experiment IV/Wuthering Heights (New Vocal)				
			1986		2.00	4.00

Label, Number		Title	Year	VG	VG+	NM
12-Inch Singles						
EMI America 7865		Running Up That Hill (Extended)/(Instrumental)/Under the Ivy				
			1985	2.50	5.00	10.00
EMI America SPRO-9574/5	DJ	Hounds of Love (3:01)/Hounds of Love (3:44)				
			1985	6.25	12.50	25.00
EMI America SPRO-9892	DJ	Experiment IV (same on both sides)				
			1986	6.25	12.50	25.00
EMI America SPRO-9995	DJ	Cloudbursting (same on both sides)				
			1985	3.00	6.00	12.00
EMI America 19228		Experiment IV/Wuthering Heights/December				
			1986	2.50	5.00	10.00

Butthole Surfers

Punk band formed in San Antonio, Texas in 1981. Also see **P.**

Label, Number		Title	Year	VG	VG+	NM
Vinyl Albums						
Alternative Tentacles VIRUS 32	EP	A Brown Reason to Live	1983	2.00	4.00	8.00
Alternative Tentacles VIRUS 39	EP	PCPPEP	1984	2.00	4.00	8.00
Capitol C1-98798		Independent Worm Saloon	1993	2.50	5.00	10.00
Touch N Go 5		Psychic...Powerless...Another Man's Sac				
			1985	5.00	10.00	20.00
Original on clear vinyl						
Touch N Go 5		Psychic...Powerless...Another Man's Sac				
			1985	2.50	5.00	10.00
Touch N Go 8		Rembrandt Pussyhorse	1986	2.50	5.00	10.00
Touch N Go 14		Cream Corn from the Socket of Devils				
			1985	2.50	5.00	10.00
Touch N Go 19		Locust Abortion Technician	1987	2.50	5.00	10.00
Touch N Go 29		Hairway to Steven	1988	2.50	5.00	10.00
Touch N Go 50		Widowermaker!	1989	2.50	5.00	10.00
45s						
Capitol S7-17514		Who Was In My Room Last Night?/Dancing Fool				
			1993		2.00	4.00
Rough Trade RUS 97-3		Hurdy Gurdy Man/Barking Dogs				
			1990		3.00	6.00
Gold vinyl						
Rough Trade RUS 97-3	PS	Hurdy Gurdy Man/Barking Dogs				
			1990		3.00	6.00
10-Inch Singles						
Capitol SPRO 79612/3	DJ	Chewin' George Lucas' Chocolate/Goofy's Concern/Beat the Press/				
		Ghandi/Neee Neee	1993	3.75	7.50	15.00
12-Inch Singles						
Touch and Go 14		Moving to Florida/Comb/To Parter/Tornadoes				
			1985	2.50	5.00	10.00
Red vinyl						

Buzzcocks, The

Punk band from Manchester, England. Its first gig was as opening act for **The Sex Pistols.**

Label, Number		Title	Year	VG	VG+	NM
Vinyl Albums						
I.R.S. SP-001		Singles Going Steady	1979	3.00	6.00	12.00
I.R.S. SP-009		A Different Kind of Tension	1980	3.00	6.00	12.00
I.R.S. SP-70507	EP	Parts 1-3	1984	2.50	5.00	10.00
I.R.S. SP-70955	DJ	Are Everything/Strange Thing + 4				
			1980	3.75	7.50	15.00

Red vinyl; no cover; some come with numbered sticker

Label, Number		Title	Year	VG	VG+	NM
I.R.S. SP-75001		Singles Going Steady	198?	2.50	5.00	10.00
Reissue of SP-001						
I.R.S. SP-75009		A Different Kind of Tension	198?	2.50	5.00	10.00
Reissue of SP-009						
45s						
I.R.S. 9001		Everybody's Happy Nowadays/Why Can't I Touch It				
			1979		2.50	5.00
I.R.S. 9001	PS	Everybody's Happy Nowadays/Why Can't I Touch It				
			1979		2.50	5.00
I.R.S. 9010		I Believe/Something's Gone Wrong Again				
			1980			3.00
I.R.S. 9010	PS	I Believe/Something's Gone Wrong Again				
			1980			3.00
I.R.S. 9017		Why, She's a Girl from the Chain Store/You Are Everything				
			1980			3.00
I.R.S. 9017	PS	Why, She's a Girl from the Chain Store/You Are Everything				
			1980			3.00
I.R.S. 9019		Strange Thing/Air Waves Dream				
			1980			3.00
I.R.S. 9019	PS	Strange Thing/Air Waves Dream				
			1980			3.00
I.R.S. 9020		Running Free/What Do You Know				
			1981			3.00
I.R.S. 9020	PS	Running Free/What Do You Know				
			1981			3.00

Byrne, David
Of Talking Heads.

Vinyl Albums						
Sire 25022		Music for the Knee Plays	1985	3.00	6.00	12.00
Warner Bros. 25990		Rei Momo	1989	3.00	6.00	12.00
Warner Bros. 26799		Uh-Oh	1992	3.00	6.00	12.00
45s						
Warner Bros. 19919		Dirty Old Town/Good and Evil	1990		*May be cassette only*	
12-Inch Singles						
Luaka Bop PRO-A-4989	DJ	Ava (3 versions)/Nineveh/Machu Picchu				
			1991		3.50	7.00
Luaka Bop 41766		Back in the Box (2 versions)/Gypsy Woman (Live)/				
		A Woman's Secret	1994		3.00	6.00
Sire PRO-A-953		DJThe Jezebel Spirit/America Is Waiting/Help Me Somebody				
			1981	3.00	6.00	12.00
Sire PRO-A-3800	DJ	Make Believe Mambo (4 versions)				
			1989		2.50	5.00
Sire 50034		Big Blue Plymouth (Eyes Wide Open)//Big Business/				
		My Big Hands (Fall Through the Cracks)				
			1982	2.50	5.00	10.00

Byrne, David, and Brian Eno

Vinyl Albums						
Sire SRK 6093		My Life in the Bush of Ghosts	1981	3.50	7.00	14.00

Byrne, David, and Ryuichi Sakamoto
Sakamoto was a member of Yellow Magic Orchestra.

Vinyl Albums						
Virgin 2204	DJ	The Making of The Last Emperor: An Interview with...				
			1988	6.25	12.50	25.00

Label, Number	Title	Year	VG	VG+	NM

C

C.A.R.E. Session, The
*"Cleveland Artists Recording for Ethiopia"; contains **Benjamin Orr** of the **Cars**, etc.*

12-Inch Singles

Blizzard 101	The Eyes of the Children (edited)/The Eyes of the Children (Long)				
		1985	2.00	4.00	8.00

Cabaret Voltaire
British electro-techno-dance trio. An influence on the ambient scene of the 1980s and 1990s.

Vinyl Albums

Caroline CAROL 1331		The Covenant, the Sword, and the Arm of the Lord				
			1985	2.50	5.00	10.00
Caroline CAROL 2451	(2) EP	Drinking Gasoline	1985	2.50	5.00	10.00
Giant GR-16009		Eight Crepuscule Tracks	1988	4.00	8.00	16.00
Manhattan MLT-46999		Code	1987	3.00	6.00	12.00
Restless 71475		Listen Up with Cabaret Voltaire	1990	2.50	5.00	10.00
Restless 71476		The Living Legends	1990	2.50	5.00	10.00
Rough Trade ROUGH US 9		The Voice of America	1980	5.00	10.00	20.00
Rough Trade TRADE US 12	EP	Three Crepuscule Tracks	1981	3.00	6.00	12.00
Rough Trade ROUGH US 15		Red Mecca	1981	5.00	10.00	20.00
Rough Trade ROUGH US 24		Hai! Live in Japan	1982	5.00	10.00	20.00

45s

Rough Trade RT-US-003		Seconds Too Late/Control Addict				
			1981		2.50	5.00
Rough Trade RT-US-003	PS	Seconds Too Late/Control Addict				
			1981		2.50	5.00

12-Inch Singles

Caroline CAROL 2452	(2)	The Drain Train (5 versions)	1986	5.00	10.00	20.00
Mute ED 5562	DJ	Colours (4 mixes)	1991		3.50	7.00

Cale, John
*Ex-member of **The Velvet Underground**.*

Vinyl Albums

A&M SP-4849		Honi Soit	1981	2.50	5.00	10.00
Antilles AN-7063		Guts	198?	2.50	5.00	10.00
Reissue of Island 9459						
Antilles IT-8401		Caribbean Sunset	1984	2.50	5.00	10.00
Antilles IT-8402		John Cale Comes Alive	1984	2.50	5.00	10.00
Columbia C 30131		Church of Anthrax	1971	3.75	7.50	15.00
Columbia CS 1037		Vintage Violence	1970	3.75	7.50	15.00
I.R.S. SP-004		Sabotage/Live	1980	3.75	7.50	15.00
Island IXP-2	DJ	Hear Fear	1975	12.50	25.00	50.00
Promo-only interview album						
Island ILPS 9301		Fear	1975	5.00	10.00	20.00
Island ILPS 9317		Slow Dazzle	1975	3.75	7.50	15.00
Island ILPS 9459		Guts	1977	5.00	10.00	20.00
Reprise MS 2079		The Academy in Peril	1972	3.75	7.50	15.00
Reprise MS 2131		Paris, 1919	1973	6.25	12.50	25.00
ROIR 196		Even Cowgirls Get the Blues	1991			
Listed in Schwann catalog, we're not really sure this exists on vinyl.						
Warner Archives 2079		The Academy in Peril	1993			
Listed in Schwann catalog, we're not really sure this exists on vinyl.						
Warner Bros./Opal 26024		Words for the Dying	1989	2.50	5.00	10.00
Ze/Passport 60019		Music for a New Society	1982	3.00	6.00	12.00

Label, Number		Title	Year	VG	VG+	NM
45s						
A&M 2329		Dead or Alive/Honi Soit	1981			3.00
Columbia 45266		Big White Cloud/Gideon's Bible	1970		3.00	6.00
Reprise 1108		Legs Larry at Television Center/Days of Steam				
			1972		3.00	6.00
Spy/I.R.S. 9008		Mercenaries/Rosegarden Funeral of Sores				
			1979		3.00	6.00
Spy/I.R.S. 9008	PS	Mercenaries/Rosegarden Funeral of Sores				
			1979		3.00	6.00
12-Inch Singles						
A&M 17154	DJ	Dead or Alive/Honi Soit	1981		3.00	6.00

Call, The
California new-wave group.

Label, Number		Title	Year	VG	VG+	NM
Vinyl Albums						
Elektra 60440		Reconciled	1986	2.50	5.00	10.00
Elektra 60739		Into the Woods	1987	2.50	5.00	10.00
Elektra R 141152		Reconciled	1986	3.00	6.00	12.00
RCA Music Service edition						
MCA 6303		Let the Day Begin	1989	2.50	5.00	10.00
Mercury 810 307-1		Modern Romans	1983	2.50	5.00	10.00
Mercury 818 793-1		Some Beyond Dreams	1984	3.00	6.00	12.00
Mercury SRM-1-4037		The Call	1982	3.00	6.00	12.00
45s						
Elektra 69461		I Don't Wanna/Day or Night	1987			3.00
Elektra 69461	PS	I Don't Wanna/Day or Night	1987			3.00
Elektra 69521		Even Now/I Still Believe (Great Design)				
			1986			3.00
Elektra 69546		Everywhere I Go/Tore the Old Place Down				
			1986			3.00
Elektra 69546	PS	Everywhere I Go/Tore the Old Place Down				
			1986			3.00
MCA 53658		Let the Day Begin/Uncovered	1989			3.00
Mercury 811 487-7		Walls Come Down/Upperbirth	1983		2.00	4.00
12-Inch Singles						
Elektra 5168	DJ	Oklahoma/Oklahoma (Live)/I Still Believe (Live)				
			1986		3.50	7.00
Elektra 5234	DJ	I Don't Wanna/I Don't Wanna (Edit)				
			1987		3.50	7.00
Elektra 5250	DJ	In the River (same on both sides)				
			1987		3.00	6.00
Elektra ED 5271	DJ	Walk Walk (CD Version)/Walk Walk (LP Version)				
			1987		3.00	6.00
Mercury MK 198	DJ	War Weary World (same on both sides)				
			1982		3.00	6.00
Mercury MK 229	DJ	Walls Came Down/Destination	1982		3.00	6.00
Mercury MK 242	DJ	Time of Your Life/All About You				
			1983	2.00	4.00	8.00
Mercury PRO 303	DJ	Heavy Hand (same on both sides)				
			1984	2.00	4.00	8.00

Campbell, Ali
Of UB40.

Label, Number		Title	Year	VG	VG+	NM
45s						
Virgin S7-18734		That Look in Your Eyes/Talking Bluebird				
			1995		2.00	4.00

A-side: Introducing Pamela Starks

Label, Number		Title	Year	VG	VG+	NM

Camper Van Beethoven
*Indie-rock heroes of the late 1980s, led by David Lowery, who went on to form **Cracker**.*

Vinyl Albums

Label, Number		Title	Year	VG	VG+	NM
Independent Project 016		Telephone Free Landslide Victory				
			1985	10.00	20.00	40.00
Version 1: Handmade covers, letterpress design, with inserts						
Independent Project 016		Telephone Free Landslide Victory				
			1985	5.00	10.00	20.00
Version 2: With normal covers; 1,175 pressed						
Pitch a Tent 01		II & III	1985	3.75	7.50	15.00
Pitch a Tent 02		Camper Van Beethoven	1986	3.75	7.50	15.00
Pitch a Tent 05		Vampire Can Mating Oven	1987	3.75	7.50	15.00
Virgin 90918		Our Beloved Revolutionary Sweetheart				
			1988	2.50	5.00	10.00
Virgin 91289		Key Lime Pie	1989	2.50	5.00	10.00

45s

Label, Number		Title	Year	VG	VG+	NM
Virgin 99131		Pictures of Matchstick Men/Come On Darkness				
			1990		*Cassette only*	

12-Inch Singles

Label, Number		Title	Year	VG	VG+	NM
Virgin PR 2865	DJ	Pictures of Matchstick Men (same on both sides)				
			1989		3.50	7.00

Candlebox
Seattle pseudo-alternative band.

Vinyl Albums

Label, Number		Title	Year	VG	VG+	NM
Maverick 46076	(2)	Lucy/Candlebox	1995	3.75	7.50	15.00
First two albums packaged together in gatefold sleeve (neither available separately in U.S.)						

45s

Label, Number		Title	Year	VG	VG+	NM
Maverick 18304		You/Pull Away	1994			3.00

Captain Hollywood Project
Techno-dance troupe.

45s

Label, Number		Title	Year	VG	VG+	NM
Imago 25029		More and More (Single Edit)/Underground Mix (Single Edit)				
			1993			3.00

12-Inch Singles

Label, Number		Title	Year	VG	VG+	NM
Imago 25033		All I Want (4 mixes)	1993	2.50	5.00	10.00

Carlisle, Belinda
*Former member of the **Go-Go's**.*

Vinyl Albums

Label, Number		Title	Year	VG	VG+	NM
I.R.S. 5741		Belinda	1986	2.50	5.00	10.00
I.R.S. R 114824		Belinda	1986	3.00	6.00	12.00
RCA Music Service edition						
MCA 6339		Runaway Horses	1989	2.50	5.00	10.00
MCA 42080		Heaven on Earth	1987	2.50	5.00	10.00
MCA R 143541		Heaven on Earth	1987	3.00	6.00	12.00
BMG Direct Marketing edition						
MCA R 173667		Runaway Horses	1989	3.00	6.00	12.00
BMG Direct Marketing edition						

45s

Label, Number		Title	Year	VG	VG+	NM
I.R.S. S45-17262	DJ	Since You've Gone (same on both sides)				
			1987		2.50	5.00
I.R.S. S45-17262	PS	Since You've Gone	1987		2.50	5.00

Label, Number		Title	Year	VG	VG+	NM
I.R.S. 52815		Mad About You/I Never Wanted a Rich Man				
			1986			3.00
I.R.S. 52815	PS	Mad About You/I Never Wanted a Rich Man				
			1986			3.00
I.R.S. 52889		I Feel the Magic/From the Heart				
			1986			3.00
I.R.S. 52889	PS	I Feel the Magic/From the Heart				
			1986			3.00
MCA 53181		Heaven Is a Place on Earth/We Can Change				
			1987			3.00
MCA 53181	PS	Heaven Is a Place on Earth/We Can Change				
			1987			3.00
MCA 53242		I Get Weak/Should I Let You In?				
			1987			3.00
MCA 53242	PS	I Get Weak/Should I Let You In?				
			1987			3.00
MCA 53308		Circle in the Sand/We Can Change				
			1988			3.00
MCA 53308	PS	Circle in the Sand/We Can Change				
			1988			3.00
MCA 53377		I Feel Free/Should I Let You In?1988				3.00
MCA 53377	PS	I Feel Free/Should I Let You In?1988				3.00
MCA 53706		Leave a Light On/Shades of Michelangelo				
			1989	1.50	3.00	6.00

A-side features a guitar solo by George Harrison.

MCA 53783		Summer Rain/Shades of Michelangelo				
			1989			3.00
Virgin S7-17598		It's Too Real (Big Hairy Animal)/Window of the World				
			1993		2.00	4.00

12-Inch Singles

I.R.S. 23629	Mad About You (3 versions)	1986	2.50	5.00	10.00
I.R.S. 23706	Band of Gold (3 versions)	1986	3.00	6.00	12.00

With Freda Payne; gold vinyl

Carpenter, Mary Chapin

Folkish country singer from McLean, Virginia.

Vinyl Albums

Columbia FC 40758	Hometown Girl	1987	2.50	5.00	10.00
Columbia FC 44228	State of the Heart	1989	2.50	5.00	10.00

45s

Columbia 07598	A Lot Like Me/Family Hands	1987			3.00
Columbia 07681	Downtown Train/Just Because	1988			3.00
Columbia 68677	How Do/It Don't Bring You	1989			3.00
Columbia 69051	Never Had It So Good/Other Streets in Other Towns				
		1989			3.00
Columbia 73202	Quittin' Time/Heroes and Heroines				
		1990			3.00
Columbia 73361	Something of a Dreamer/Slow Country Dance				
		1990			3.00
Columbia 73567	You Win Again/The Moon and St. Christopher				
		1990			3.00
Columbia 73699	Right Now/What You Didn't Say1991				3.00
Columbia 73838	Down at the Twist and Shout/Halley Came to Jackson				
		1991			3.00
Columbia 74038	Going Out Tonight/When She's Gone				
		1991			3.00
Columbia 74345	I Feel Lucky/Middle Ground	1992			3.00

Label, Number		Title	Year	VG	VG+	NM
Columbia 74485		Not Too Much to Ask/I Am a Town				
			1992			3.00
A-side: With Joe Difffie						
Columbia 74795		Passionate Kisses/Middle Ground				
			1993			3.00
Columbia 74930		The Hard Way/Goodbye Again	1993			3.00
Columbia 77134		The Bug/Rhythm of the Blues	1993			3.00
Columbia 77316		He Thinks He'll Keep Her/Only a Dream				
			1993			3.00
Columbia 77476		I Take My Chances/Come On Come On				
			1994			3.00
Columbia 77696		Shut Up and Kiss Me/The End of My Pirate Days				
			1994			3.00
Columbia 77780		Tender When I Want to Be/John Doe No. 24				
			1994			3.00
Columbia 77826		House of Cards/Jubilee	1995			3.00
Columbia 77955		Why Walk When You Can Fly/Stones in the Road				
			1995			3.00

Carrasco, Joe "King", and the Crowns

Texas-based roots-rock/new wave/dance band.

Vinyl Albums

Label, Number		Title	Year	VG	VG+	NM
Hannibal HNBL-1308		Joe "King" Carrasco and the Crowns				
			1980	3.00	6.00	12.00
Hannibal HNEP-3301	EP	Party Safari	1981	3.00	6.00	12.00
MCA 5308		Synapse Gap	1982	3.00	6.00	12.00
MCA 5404		Party Weekend	1983	2.50	5.00	10.00
Rounder 9012		Bandido Rock	1987	2.50	5.00	10.00

45s

Label, Number		Title	Year	VG	VG+	NM
Gee Bee GB 101		Party Weekend/Houston El Mover				
			1980		2.00	4.00
Gee Bee GB 101	PS	Party Weekend/Houston El Mover				
			1980		2.00	4.00
MCA 52039		Front Me Some Love/Wanna Get That Feel (Again)				
			1982			3.00
MCA 52081		Don't Let a Woman/That's the Love				
			1982			3.00

Carroll, Jim

*Not the same Jim Carroll as in the **Jim Carroll Band**; listed not because this one is alternative, but as a way to curtail any confusion.*

Vinyl Albums

Label, Number	Title	Year	VG	VG+	NM
A&M SP-4323	Jim Carroll	1971	3.00	6.00	12.00

Carroll, Jim, Band

New York poet-rocker.

Vinyl Albums

Label, Number		Title	Year	VG	VG+	NM
Atco 38-132		Catholic Boy	1980	3.75	7.50	15.00
Atco 38-145		Dry Dreams	1982	2.50	5.00	10.00
Atlantic 80123		I Write Your Name	1984	5.00	10.00	20.00

45s

Label, Number		Title	Year	VG	VG+	NM
Atco 7314		People Who Died/I Want the Angel				
			1980		3.00	6.00
Atco 7323	DJ	Day and Night (same on both sides)				
			1981		2.00	4.00

Stock copy may not exist

Label, Number		Title	Year	VG	VG+	NM
Atlantic 89687	DJ	Sweet Jane (same on both sides)	1984		2.00	4.00
Stock copy may not exist						
12-Inch Singles						
Atlantic 573	DJ	(No More) Luxuries/Voices	1983	3.00	6.00	12.00
Atlantic 593	DJ	Sweet Jane (same on both sides)	1983	3.00	6.00	12.00

Cars, The

*Boston-based new wave/pop group. Extremely popular in the early 1980s. Also see solo releases by **Ric Ocasek, Elliot Easton, and Benjamin Orr.***

Label, Number		Title	Year	VG	VG+	NM
Vinyl Albums						
Elektra 6E-135		The Cars	1978	2.50	5.00	10.00
Elektra 5E-507		Candy-O	1979	2.50	5.00	10.00
No title and artist listed on front cover (information was on a sticker on the shrink wrap)						
Elektra 5E-514		Panorama	1980	2.50	5.00	10.00
Elektra 5E-567		Shake It Up	1981	2.50	5.00	10.00
Elektra 5E-567	PD	Shake It Up	1981	12.50	25.00	50.00
Promo-only picture disc with "KMET-FM" imprinted on back						
Elektra 5E-567	PD	Shake It Up	1981	10.00	20.00	40.00
Promo-only picture disc with blank back						
Elektra 60296		Heartbeat City	1984	2.00	4.00	8.00
Elektra 60296	DJ	Heartbeat City	1984	3.00	6.00	12.00
Promo-only audiophile pressing on Quiex II vinyl						
Elektra 60464		Greatest Hits	1985	2.50	5.00	10.00
Elektra 60747		Door to Door	1987	2.00	4.00	8.00
Elektra R 123334		Candy-O	1979	3.00	6.00	12.00
RCA Music Service edition has "The Cars Candy-O" printed on upper left front cover						
Elektra R 143650		Heartbeat City	1984	2.50	5.00	10.00
RCA Music Service edition						
Elektra R 144033		The Cars	1978	3.00	6.00	12.00
RCA Music Service edition						
Elektra R 153702		Greatest Hits	1985	3.00	6.00	12.00
RCA Music Service edition						
Elektra R 161593		Door to Door	1987	2.50	5.00	10.00
BMG Direct Marketing edition						
Nautilus NR-14		The Cars	1981	7.50	15.00	30.00
Audiophile "Super Disc"						
Nautilus NR-49		Candy-O	1982	7.50	15.00	30.00
Audiophile "Super Disc"						
45s						
Elektra 45118		Let's Go/My Best Friend's Girl	198?			3.00
"Spun Gold" series						
Elektra 45119		Just What I Needed/Good Times Roll 198?				3.00
"Spun Gold" series						
Elektra 45491		Just What I Needed/I'm in Touch with Your World 1978		2.50	5.00	10.00
Red vinyl						
Elektra 45491		Just What I Needed/I'm in Touch with Your World 1978				3.00
Elektra 45491	PS	Just What I Needed/I'm in Touch with Your World 1978			2.50	5.00
Elektra 45537		My Best Friend's Girl/Don't Cha Stop 1978				3.00
Elektra 46014		Good Times Roll/All Mixed Up	1979			3.00
Elektra 46063		Let's Go/That's It	1979			3.00
Elektra 46546		It's All I Can Do/Got a Lot on My Head 1979				3.00
Elektra 46546	PS	It's All I Can Do/Got a Lot on My Head 1979			2.50	5.00
Elektra 46580		Candy-O/Double Life	1980			3.00

Label, Number		Title	Year	VG	VG+	NM
Elektra 47039		Touch and Go/Down Boys	1980			3.00
Elektra 47080		Don't Tell Me No/Don't Go to Pieces				
			1980			3.00
Elektra 47101		Gimme Some Slack/Don't Go to Pieces				
			1981			3.00
Elektra 47250		Shake It Up/Cruiser	1981			3.00
Elektra 47250	PS	Shake It Up/Cruiser	1981			3.00
Elektra 47433		Since You're Gone/Think It Over				
			1982			3.00
Elektra 47433	PS	Since You're Gone/Think It Over				
			1982			3.00
Elektra 47479		Victim of Love/This Could Be Love				
			1982			3.00
Elektra 65983		You Might Think/Magic	198?			3.00
"Spun Gold" series						
Elektra 65984		Drive/Hello Again	198?			3.00
"Spun Gold" series						
Elektra 65996		Shake It Up/Since You're Gone	198?			3.00
"Spun Gold" series						
Elektra 69427		Strap Me In/Door to Door	1988			3.00
Elektra 69432		Coming Up You/Double Trouble				
			1987			2.00
Elektra 69432	PS	Coming Up You/Double Trouble				
			1987			2.00
Elektra 69446		You Are the Girl/Ta Ta Wayo Wayo				
			1987			2.00
Elektra 69446	PS	You Are the Girl/Ta Ta Wayo Wayo				
			1987			2.00
Elektra 69569		I'm Not the One/Heartbeat City	1986			3.00
Elektra 69589		Tonight She Comes/Just What I Needed				
			1985			3.00
Elektra 69657		Why Can't I Have You/Breakaway				
			1985			3.00
Elektra 69681		Hello Again/Hello Again (Dub)	1984			3.00
Elektra 69706		Drive/Stranger Eyes	1984			3.00
Elektra 69724		Magic/I Refuse	1984			3.00
Elektra 69744		You Might Think/Heartbeat City	1984			2.00
Elektra 69744	PS	You Might Think/Heartbeat City	1984			2.00

12-Inch Singles

Label, Number		Title	Year	VG	VG+	NM
Elektra 5014	DJ	Hello Again (Remix)/Hello Again (LP)/Hello Again (Dub)				
			1984		2.50	5.00
Elektra 5264	DJ	Coming Up You (same on both sides)				
			1987		3.00	6.00
Elektra ED 5249	DJ	You Are the Girl (same on both sides)				
			1987		2.50	5.00

Carter, Carlene, and Dave Edmunds
Also see Edmunds, Dave.

45s

Label, Number		Title	Year	VG	VG+	NM
Warner Bros. 49572		Too Bad About Sandy/Baby Ride Easy				
			1980		2.00	4.00

Cash, Roseanne
Daughter of Johnny Cash. A country singer at first, but more recently a neo-folkie.

Vinyl Albums

Label, Number		Title	Year	VG	VG+	NM
Columbia AS 1527	DJ	Interview with Martha Hume	1982	7.50	15.00	30.00
Generic cover with sticker						
Columbia JC 36155		Right or Wrong	1980	2.50	5.00	10.00

Label, Number	Title	Year	VG	VG+	NM
Columbia PC 36155	Right or Wrong	1984	2.00	4.00	8.00
Budget-line reissue with new prefix and "02" added to bar code					
Columbia JC 36965	Seven Year Ache	1981	2.50	5.00	10.00
Columbia PC 36965	Seven Year Ache	1984	2.00	4.00	8.00
Budget-line reissue with new prefix and "02" added to bar code					
Columbia FC 37570	Somewhere in the Stars	1982	2.50	5.00	10.00
Columbia PC 37570	Somewhere in the Stars	1984	2.00	4.00	8.00
Budget-line reissue with new prefix and "02" added to bar code					
Columbia FC 39463	Rhythm and Romance	1985	2.50	5.00	10.00
Columbia FC 40777	King's Record Shop	1987	2.50	5.00	10.00
Columbia OC 45054	Hits 1979-1989	1989	3.00	6.00	12.00
Columbia HC 46965	Seven Year Ache	1981	6.25	12.50	25.00
"Half-Speed Master"					

45s

Label, Number	Title	Year	VG	VG+	NM
Columbia 02463	My Baby Thinks He's a Train/I Can't Resist				
		1981		2.00	4.00
Columbia 02659	Blue Moon with Heartache/Only Human				
		1981		2.00	4.00
Columbia 02937	Ain't No Money/The Feelin'	1982			3.00
Columbia 03131	Seven Year Ache/My Baby Thinks He's a Train				
		1982			3.00
"Golden Oldies" reissue					
Columbia 03283	I Wonder/Oh Yes I Can	1982			3.00
Columbia 03705	It Hasn't Happened Yet/Somewhere in the Stars				
		1983			3.00
Columbia 03868	Blue Moon with Heartache/Ain't No Money				
		1983			3.00
"Golden Oldies" reissue					
Columbia 04809	I Don't Know Why You Don't Want Me/				
	What You Gonna Do About It	1985			3.00
Columbia 04809 PS	I Don't Know Why You Don't Want Me/				
	What You Gonna Do About It	1985			3.00
Columbia 05621	Never Be You/Closing Time	1985			3.00
Columbia 05794	Hold On/Never Gonna Hurt	1986			3.00
Columbia 06159	Second to No One/Never Alone	1986			3.00
Columbia 07200	The Way We Make a Broken Heart/707				
		1987			3.00
Columbia 07624	Tennessee Flat Top Box/Why Don't You Quit Leaving Me Alone				
		1987			3.00
Columbia 07693	It's Such a Small World/Crazy Baby				
		1988			3.00
Rodney Crowell and Roseanne Cash; B-side by Crowell					
Columbia 07746	If You Change Your Mind/Somewhere Sometime				
		1988			3.00
Columbia 07988	Runaway Train/Seven Year Ache	1988			3.00
Columbia 08399	Hold On/Second to No One	1988			3.00
Reissue					
Columbia 08401	I Don't Know Why You Don't Want Me/Never Be You				
		1988			3.00
Reissue					
Columbia 11045	No Memories Hangin' Round/This Has Happened Before				
		1979		2.00	4.00
Duet with Bobby Bare					
Columbia 11188	Couldn't Do Nothin' Right/Seeing Is Believing				
		1980		2.00	4.00
Columbia 11268	Right or Wrong/Take Me, Take Me				
		1980		2.00	4.00
Columbia 11426	Seven Year Ache/Blue Moon with Heartache				
		1981		2.00	4.00
Columbia 68599	I Don't Want to Spoil the Party/Look What Our Love Is Coming To				
		1989			3.00

Label, Number		Title	Year	VG	VG+	NM
Columbia 68599	PS	I Don't Want to Spoil the Party/Look What Our Love Is				
			1989			3.00
Columbia 73054		Black and White/Never Be You	1989			3.00
Columbia 73517		What We Really Want/Portrait	1990			3.00
Columbia 74973		The Wheel/Private Moments	1993			3.00

Catherine Wheel
English rock band.

Vinyl Albums

Label, Number	Title	Year	VG	VG+	NM
Mercury 526 850-1	Happy Days	1995	3.00	6.00	12.00
Clear vinyl					

Cats
Philadelphia power-pop group utterly unknown outside its hometown.

Vinyl Albums

Label, Number	Title	Year	VG	VG+	NM
Elektra 6E-275	Cats	1980	2.50	5.00	10.00

45s

Label, Number	Title	Year	VG	VG+	NM
Elektra 47010	It Doesn't Matter Anymore/The Woman in White				
		1980		2.00	4.00

Chapman, Tracy
Cleveland-born singer-songwriter.

Vinyl Albums

Label, Number	Title	Year	VG	VG+	NM
Elektra 60774	Tracy Chapman	1988	3.00	6.00	12.00
Elektra 60888	Crossroads	1989	2.50	5.00	10.00
Elektra R 142496	Crossroads	1989	3.00	6.00	12.00
BMG Direct Marketing edition					
Elektra R 153582	Tracy Chapman	1988	3.50	7.00	14.00
BMG Direct Marketing edition					

45s

Label, Number		Title	Year	VG	VG+	NM
Elektra 64346		Give Me One Reason/Rape of the World				
			1996			3.00
Most copies have A-side label on both sides (no difference in value)						
Elektra 65938		Fast Car/Talkin' 'Bout a Revolution				
			1989			3.00
"Spun Gold" series						
Elektra 69242		All That You Have Is Your Soul/Material World				
			1990		2.00	4.00
Elektra 69273		Crossroads/Born to Fight	1989			2.00
Elektra 69273	PS	Crossroads/Born to Fight	1989			2.00
Elektra 69356		Baby Can I Hold You/If Not Now				
			1988			2.00
Elektra 69356	PS	Baby Can I Hold You/If Not Now				
			1988			2.00
Elektra 69383		Talkin' 'Bout a Revolution/Behind the Wall				
			1988			2.00
Elektra 69383	PS	Talkin' 'Bout a Revolution/Behind the Wall				
			1988			2.00
Elektra 69412		Fast Car/For You	1988		2.00	4.00
Not issued with picture sleeve in U.S.						

12-Inch Singles

Label, Number		Title	Year	VG	VG+	NM
Elektra 5315	DJ	Talkin' About a Revolution (same on both sides)				
			1988		3.00	6.00
Elektra 5340	DJ	Baby Can I Hold You (same on both sides)				
			1988		3.00	6.00
Elektra ED 5403	DJ	Crossroads (same on both sides)	1989		3.00	6.00

Label, Number		Title	Year	VG	VG+	NM
Elektra 5424	DJ	All That You Have Is Your Soul/				
		All That You Have Is Your Soul (Edit)	1989		2.50	5.00
Elektra 5441	DJ	Born to Fight (same on both sides)				
			1989		3.00	6.00
Elektra 5455	DJ	This Time/This Time (Edit)	1990		3.00	6.00

Cherry, Neneh

New York hip-hop artist.

Vinyl Albums

Virgin 91252		Raw Like Sushi	1989	2.50	5.00	10.00
Virgin R 174031		Raw Like Sushi	1989	3.00	6.00	12.00
BMG Direct Marketing edition						

45s

Virgin S7-56975		Buddy X/Trout	1993		2.50	5.00
*B-side: With Michael Stipe of **R.E.M.***						
Virgin 99153		Heart/Phoney Ladies	1989 *Cassette only*			
Virgin 99154		Manchild/Phoney Ladies	1989			3.00
Virgin 99154	PS	Manchild/Phoney Ladies	1989			3.00
Virgin 99183		Kisses on the Wind/Kisses on the Wind				
			1989			3.00
Virgin 99183	PS	Kisses on the Wind/Kisses on the Wind				
			1989			3.00
Virgin 99231		Buffalo Stance/Buffalo Stance (Electro Shi Mix)				
			1989			3.00
Virgin 99231	PS	Buffalo Stance/Buffalo Stance (Electro Shi Mix)				
			1989			3.00

12-Inch Singles

Virgin 1296	DJ	Buffalo Stance (4 versions)	1989	3.00	6.00	12.00
Virgin 1378	DJ	Kisses on the Wind (6 versions)/Buffalo Blues				
			1989	2.00	4.00	8.00
Virgin 1403	DJ	Manchild (4 versions)/Buffalo Stance (Sukka Mix II)				
			1989	2.00	4.00	8.00
Virgin 12709	DJ	Money Love (2 mixes)/Twisted	1992	2.00	4.00	8.00
Virgin 12776	DJ	Buddy X (6 versions)	1992	2.00	4.00	8.00
Virgin 96532		Kisses on the Wind (6 versions)	1989		3.00	6.00
Virgin 96573		Buffalo Stance (5 versions)	1988		3.00	6.00

China Crisis

45s

A&M 2902		Arizona Sky/Trading in Gold	1987			3.00
A&M 2936		Best Kept Secret	1986			3.00
A&M 2936		Best Kept Secret/The Instigator	1987			3.00
Warner Bros. 28936		Wake Up (King in a Catholic Style)				
			1985			3.00

12-Inch Singles

A&M 17445	DJ	Arizona Sky/Arizona Sky (edit)	1986		2.50	5.00
Epic 03336		African and White/Scream Down at Me				
			1982	2.50	5.00	10.00
Warner Bros. 20172		Working with Fire and Steel (2 versions)/Dockland/Forever				
			1983		3.00	6.00
Warner Bros. PRO-A-2302	DJ	The Highest High/Gift of Freedom				
			1985	3.00	6.00	12.00
Warner Bros. PRO-A-2343	DJ	Wake Up (edit)/Wake Up (LP version)				
			1985	2.00	4.00	8.00

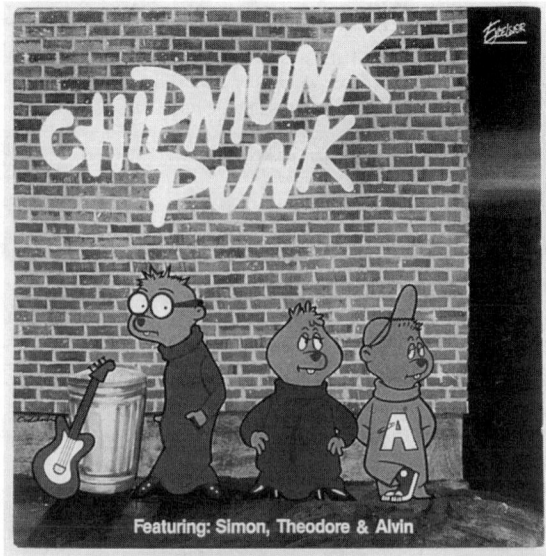

Featuring: Simon, Theodore & Alvin

Many people thought the radio ads were a joke when they first aired in 1980. But yes, the Chipmunks came out of retirement that year with their at-times-hilarious *Chipmunk Punk*. Released on the Excelsior label, just try to find this today. Or harder yet, find either the 45 or 12-inch single that came out of it.

The first American album by The Church, on Capitol, is so obscure that a lengthy discography of the band on the Internet doesn't even list it! The same list does say this came out in Canada, but it most assuredly did have an American release.

Label, Number		Title	Year	VG	VG+	NM

Chipmunks, The

Yes, the Chipmunks! While hardly an alternative group, we had to list the below items because of their collectibility among fans of the genre.

Vinyl Albums

Label, Number		Title	Year	VG	VG+	NM
Excelsior X-6008		Chipmunk Punk	1980	3.75	7.50	15.00

45s

| Excelsior SIS 1002 | | Call Me/Refugee | 1980 | | 2.50 | 5.00 |
| Excelsior SIS 1002 | PS | Call Me/Refugee | 1980 | | 2.50 | 5.00 |

12-Inch Singles

| Excelsior XEP-2000 | DJ | Call Me (Disco Version) (same on both sides) | | | | |
| | | | 1980 | 2.50 | 5.00 | 10.00 |

Church, The

Australian new-wave/pop group.

Vinyl Albums

Label, Number		Title	Year	VG	VG+	NM
Arista 18727-1	(2)	Sometime Anywhere	1994	3.75	7.50	15.00
Arista AL 8521		Starfish	1988	2.50	5.00	10.00
Arista AL 8563		Of Skins and Heart	1988	2.50	5.00	10.00
First U.S. issue of first Australian album						
Arista AL 8564		The Blurred Crusade	1988	2.50	5.00	10.00
First U.S. issue of second Australian album						
Arista AL 8565		Seance	1988	2.50	5.00	10.00
First U.S. issue of third Australian album						
Arista AL 8566		Remote Luxury	1988	2.50	5.00	10.00
Reissue of Warner Bros. 25152						
Arista AL 8567		Heyday	1988	2.50	5.00	10.00
Reissue of Warner Bros. 25370						
Arista AL 8579		Gold Afternoon Fix	1990	2.50	5.00	10.00
Arista ADP 9713	DJ	Sum of the Parts	1988	10.00	20.00	40.00
Interviews and live acoustic tracks						
Arista R 171667		Gold Afternoon Fix	1990	3.00	6.00	12.00
BMG Direct Marketing edition						
Arista R 173703		Starfish	1988	3.00	6.00	12.00
BMG Direct Marketing edition						
Capitol ST-12193		The Church	1982	3.75	7.50	15.00
Warner Bros. 25152		Remote Luxury	1984	3.75	7.50	15.00
Warner Bros. 25370		Heyday	1985	3.75	7.50	15.00

45s

Arista 2027		Metropolis/Much Too Much	1990	*May be cassette-only*		
Arista 9673		Under the Milky Way/Musk	1988			3.00
Arista 9673	PS	Under the Milky Way/Musk	1988			3.00
Arista 9733		Reptile/Under the Milky Way (Acoustic)-Tantalized				
			1988			3.00
Capitol 5087		Bus Driver/Unguarded Moment	1982	2.00	4.00	8.00
Warner Bros. 28700		Columbus/As You Will	1986			3.00
Warner Bros. 28700	PS	Columbus/As You Will	1986		3.00	6.00

12-Inch Singles

Arista ADP 2036	DJ	Terra Nova Cain/Take It Back//Grind (Acoustic Version)				
			1990	3.75	7.50	15.00
Arista 9669		Under the Milky Way/Musk	1988	2.50	5.00	10.00
Arista 9718	DJ	Reptile (Remix) (same on both sides)				
			1988	2.50	5.00	10.00
Arista 9750	DJ	Destination/Destination (Edit)	1988	2.50	5.00	10.00
Warner Bros. PRO-A-2197	DJ	Constant in Opal/Shadow Cabinet				
			1984	3.75	7.50	15.00
Warner Bros. PRO-A-2428	DJ	Tantalized (4:57)/Tantalized (3:58)				
			1985	3.75	7.50	15.00

Label, Number		Title	Year	VG	VG+	NM
Warner Bros. PRO-A-2484	DJ	Columbus (2 versions)/Happy Hunting Ground				
			1986	3.00	6.00	12.00

Ciccone Youth
*Sonic Youth in disguise, this is that band's tribute to **Madonna**.*

45s
New Alliance 030		Burnin' Up/Tuff Titty Rap/Into the Groovey				
			1986	2.50	5.00	10.00
New Alliance 030	PS	Burnin' Up/Tuff Titty Rap/Into the Groovey				
			1986	2.50	5.00	10.00

Clash, The
*British punk band. Also see **Big Audio Dynamite** and **Joe Strummer**.*

Vinyl Albums
Epic AS 913	DJ	Sandinista Now!	1981	5.00	10.00	20.00
Promo-only sampler						
Epic AS 952	DJ	If Music Could Talk (Interchords)				
			1981	7.50	15.00	30.00
Promo-only interview record						
Epic AS 99-1592	PD	Combat Rock	1982	10.00	20.00	40.00
Promo-only picture disc						
Epic AS 1594	DJ	The World According to the Clash				
			1982	10.00	20.00	40.00
Promo-only sampler						
Epic AS 99-1595	DJ	Combat Rock	1982	7.50	15.00	30.00
Camouflage green vinyl promo						
Epic JE 35543		Give 'Em Enough Rope	1978	3.75	7.50	15.00
Script cover; orange label						
Epic JE 35543		Give 'Em Enough Rope	1978	3.75	7.50	15.00
Block letters on cover; orange label						
Epic JE 35543	DJ	Give 'Em Enough Rope	1978	7.50	15.00	30.00
White label promo; timing strip; back cover has one incorrect song title						
Epic JE 36060		The Clash	1979	3.75	7.50	15.00
With bonus single.						
Epic PE 36060		The Clash	1979	2.00	4.00	8.00
Budget-line reissue; no bonus single						
Epic E2 36238	DJ	London Calling	1980	6.25	12.50	25.00
White label promo						
Epic E2 36329	(2)	London Calling	1979	3.75	7.50	15.00
Epic Nu-Disk 4E 36846	10	Black Market Clash	1980	3.75	7.50	15.00
Epic E3X 37037	(3)	Sandinista!	1981	5.00	10.00	20.00
Epic FE 37689		Combat Rock	1982	3.75	7.50	15.00
First pressings contain a commercial in the middle of the song "Inoculated City"						
Epic FE 37689		Combat Rock	1982	2.50	5.00	10.00
Second and later pressings delete commercial during "Inoculated City"						
Epic PE 38540		Black Market Clash	1982	2.50	5.00	10.00
12-inch version of 10-inch record						
Epic FE 40017		Cut the Crap	1985	2.50	5.00	10.00
Epic E2 44025	(2)	The Story of the Clash, Vol. 1	1988	3.75	7.50	15.00
Epic Legacy E3 53191	(3) 10	Super Black Market Clash	1993	5.00	10.00	20.00

45s
Epic AE7 1178	DJ	Gates of the West/Groovy Times				
			1979	2.00	4.00	8.00
Single included with original pressings of the LP "The Clash"						
Epic 02055		The Magnificent Seven/The Magnificent Dance				
			1981		2.50	5.00
(A note on "Should I Stay or Should I Go": All five catalog numbers below have been confirmed!)						
Epic 03006		Should I Stay or Should I Go/Inoculated City				
			1982	2.00	4.00	8.00
Epic 03034		Should I Stay or Should I Go/First Night Back in London				
			1982		3.00	6.00

The Clash's "Should I Stay or Should I Go?" was released on five different Epic numbers with at least two, and perhaps even three or four, different picture sleeves -- and it still didn't make the top 40. This is the sleeve accompanying Epic 03547. Also pictured is the rare three-record 10-inch collection *Super Black Market Clash,* a vinyl-enhanced version (extra tracks on LP) of the CD that was released in 1992.

Label, Number		Title	Year	VG	VG+	NM
Epic 03061		Should I Stay or Should I Go/First Night Back in London				
			1982		2.00	4.00
Epic 03061	PS	Should I Stay or Should I Go/First Night Back in London				
			1982		2.00	4.00
Epic 03088		Train in Vain (Stand By Me)/London Calling				
			1982		2.00	4.00
		Reissue; originals have "Memory Lane" flower petals label (gray label $3 NM)				
Epic 03245		Rock the Casbah/Long Time Jerk				
			1982			3.00
Epic 03547		Should I Stay Or Should I Go?/Cool Confusion				
			1983			3.00
Epic 03547	PS	Should I Stay Or Should I Go?/Cool Confusion				
			1983			3.00
Epic 03571		Should I Stay Or Should I Go?	1983		2.00	4.00
		One-sided budget release				
Epic 05540		Rock the Casbah/Long Time Jerk				
			1984			3.00
		Gray label reissue				
Epic 08470		Rock the Casbah/Should I Stay Or Should I Go				
			1988			3.00
		Reissue				
Epic 50738		White Man in Hammersmith Palais/I Fought the Law				
			1979		2.50	5.00
Epic 50851		Train in Vain (Stand By Me)/London Calling				
			1980		2.00	4.00
Epic 51013		Hitsville U.K./Police on My Back	1981		2.00	4.00

12-Inch Singles

Label, Number		Title	Year	VG	VG+	NM
Epic AS 617	DJ	Gates of the West/Groovy Times/I Fought the Law				
			1979	5.00	10.00	20.00
Epic AS 723	DJ	Clampdown/Lost in the Supermarket/The Card Cheat/				
		London Calling	1979	5.00	10.00	20.00
Epic AS 905	DJ	The Magnificent Seven/Lightning Strikes/One More Time/				
		One More Dub	1980	3.75	7.50	15.00
Epic AS 1464	DJ	Rock the Casbah/Overpowered by Funk/Should I Stay or				
		Should I Go/Death Is a Star	1982	3.75	7.50	15.00
Epic 02036		The Magnificent Dance/The Magnificent Seven/The Call Up/				
		The Cool Out	1981	2.00	4.00	8.00
Epic EAS 2230	DJ	This Is England (same on both sides)				
			1985		3.00	6.00
Epic 02262		This Is Radio Clash/Radio Clash//Outside Broadcast/Radio 5				
			1981	2.00	4.00	8.00
Epic EAS 2277	DJ	Fingerpoppin' (AOR Remix) (same on both sides)				
			1985		3.00	6.00
Epic 03144		Rock the Casbah/Mustapha Dance				
			1982	3.00	6.00	12.00
Epic 06889		This Is Radio Clash/The Magnificent Seven				
			1985		3.00	6.00
		"Mixed Masters" reissue				
Epic 07829		Rock the Casbah/Mustapha Dance				
			1988		3.00	6.00
		"Mixed Masters" reissue				

10-Inch Singles

Label, Number		Title	Year	VG	VG+	NM
Epic AS 749	DJ	Train in Vain (Stand By Me) (same on both sides)				
			1980	6.25	12.50	25.00
Epic AS 788	DJ	Clampdown/Brand New Cadillac/Spanish Bombs				
			1980	6.25	12.50	25.00

Label, Number		Title	Year	VG	VG+	NM

Cock Robin

Los Angeles pop group.

Vinyl Albums

Label, Number		Title	Year	VG	VG+	NM
Columbia BFC 39582		Cock Robin	1985	2.50	5.00	10.00
Columbia PC 39582		Cock Robin	198?	2.00	4.00	8.00
Budget-line reissue						
Columbia FC 40375		After Here Through Midland	1987	2.50	5.00	10.00

45s

Label, Number		Title	Year	VG	VG+	NM
Columbia 04875		When Your Heart Is Weak/Because It Keeps On Working				
			1985			3.00
Columbia 04875	PS	When Your Heart Is Weak/Because It Keeps On Working				
			1985			3.00
Columbia 04875	PS	When Your Heart Is Weak	1985		2.50	5.00
"Demonstration -- Not for Sale" on back						
Columbia 05635		Thought You Were On My Side/A Little Innocence				
			1985			3.00
Columbia 05635	PS	Thought You Were On My Side/A Little Innocence				
			1985			3.00
Columbia 05635	PS	Thought You Were On My Side	1985		2.50	5.00
"Demonstration -- Not for Sale" on back						
Columbia 05720		The Promise You Made/Have You Any Sympathy?				
			1985			3.00
Columbia 05720	PS	The Promise You Made/Have You Any Sympathy?				
			1985			3.00
Columbia 05720	PS	The Promise You Made	1985		2.50	5.00
"Demonstration -- Not for Sale" on back						
Columbia 06143		Once We Might Have Known/More Than Willing				
			1986			3.00
Columbia 07123		Just Around the Corner/Open Book				
			1987			3.00
Columbia 07639		The Biggest Fool of All/Blood of a Saint				
			1987			3.00
Columbia 07639	PS	The Biggest Fool of All/Blood of a Saint				
			1987			3.00
Columbia 73439		It's Only Make Believe/We've Changed				
			1990			*Cassette only*

12-Inch Singles

Label, Number		Title	Year	VG	VG+	NM
Columbia 05363		The Promise You Made	1985		3.00	6.00

Cocteau Twins

Scottish pop/new wave band.

Vinyl Albums

Label, Number		Title	Year	VG	VG+	NM
Capitol SPRO 79066/7	DJ	Sampler	1991	12.50	25.00	50.00
Promo-only 10-song collection						
Capitol C1-90892		Blue Bell Knoll	1988	3.00	6.00	12.00
Capitol C1-93669		Heaven Or Las Vegas	1990	3.00	6.00	12.00
Relativity/4AD 8040		The Pink Opaque	1986	3.00	6.00	12.00
Relativity/4AD 8141	EP	Love's Easy Tears	1986	3.00	6.00	12.00

45s

Label, Number		Title	Year	VG	VG+	NM
Capitol S7-18208		Frosty the Snowman/Winter Wonderland				
			1994		2.50	5.00
Red vinyl						
Capitol 44286		Carolyn's Fingers/Blue Bell Knoll				
			1989		2.50	5.00

12-Inch Singles

Label, Number		Title	Year	VG	VG+	NM
Capitol 15626		Iceblink Luck/Mizake the Mizan/Watchlar				
			1990	3.75	7.50	15.00

Label, Number		Title	Year	VG	VG+	NM
Capitol SPRO-79415/27	DJ	Heaven or Las Vegas/Heaven or Las Vegas (Edit)/Dials				
			1990	3.00	6.00	12.00
Capitol SPRO-79512	DJ	A Kissed Out Red Flatboat (same on both sides)				
			1988	3.75	7.50	15.00
Capitol SPRO-79564	DJ	I Wear Your Ring (same on both sides)				
			1991	3.75	7.50	15.00

Codeine

45s

Sub Pop 155		Realize/Broken-Hearted Wine	1992		2.50	5.00
Clear vinyl						
Sub Pop 155		Realize/Broken-Hearted Wine	1992		2.50	5.00
White vinyl						
Sub Pop 155	PS	Realize/Broken-Hearted Wine	1992		2.50	5.00
#45 in Sub Pop Singles Club series						

Coldcut

*Featuring **Lisa Stansfield** on vocals.*

Vinyl Albums

Tommy Boy 25974		What's That Noise?	1989	3.00	6.00	12.00

45s

Tommy Boy 22848		People Hold On (Radio Mix)/People Hold On (Acapella)				
			1989			3.00
Tommy Boy 22848	PS	People Hold On (Radio Mix)/People Hold On (Acapella)				
			1989			3.00

12-Inch Singles

Tommy Boy 931		People Hold On (5 versions)	1989		3.50	7.00
Tommy Boy 939		People Hold On (6 versions)	1989		3.50	7.00

Collective Soul

Alterna-pop group from Stockbridge, Georgia.

45s

Atlantic 87088		The World I Know/Smashing Young Man				
			1995			3.00
Atlantic 87157		December/Gel	1995			3.00
Atlantic 87237		Shine/Breathe	1994			3.00

Combustible Edison

Modern purveyors of so-called "space age bachelor pad music."

Vinyl Albums

Sub Pop 244		I, Swinger	1994	2.50	5.00	10.00
Sub Pop 313		Schizophonic	1996	2.50	5.00	10.00

45s

Sub Pop 236		Cry Me a River/Satan Says	1993	2.50	5.00	10.00
Sub Pop 236	PS	Cry Me a River/Satan Says	1993	2.50	5.00	10.00
#59 in Sub Pop Singles Club series						

Come

45s

Sub Pop 115		Car/Last Mistake	1991		2.50	5.00
All copies on white vinyl						
Sub Pop 115	PS	Car/Last Mistake	1991		2.50	5.00
#34 in Sub Pop Singles Club series						

Concrete Blonde's 1990 album *Bloodletting* is obscure on vinyl. A promo exists with MCA distribution; the above is a stock copy with Capitol distribution... issued on red vinyl, no less.

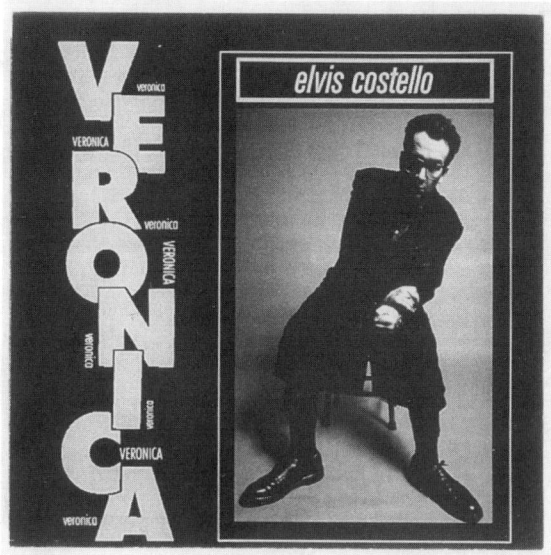

To date, Elvis Costello's last American stock-copy 45 was "Veronica" in 1989. Curiously, with all the excellent recordings he made early in his career, this was his only top 20 hit in America.

Label, Number		Title	Year	VG	VG+	NM

Communards

*Jimmy Somerville's dance-pop project after he left **Bronski Beat**.*

Vinyl Albums

Label, Number		Title	Year	VG	VG+	NM
MCA 5794		Communards	1986	2.50	5.00	10.00
MCA 42106		Red	1987	2.50	5.00	10.00

45s

Label, Number		Title	Year	VG	VG+	NM
MCA 52928		Don't Leave Me This Way/Sanctified	1986			3.00
MCA 52928	PS	Don't Leave Me This Way/Sanctified	1986			3.00
MCA 53224		Never Can Say Goodbye/'77, The Great Escape	1987			3.00
MCA 53224	PS	Never Can Say Goodbye/'77, The Great Escape	1987			3.00

12-Inch Singles

Label, Number		Title	Year	VG	VG+	NM
MCA 23665		Don't Leave Me This Way (3 versions)	1986	2.00	4.00	8.00
MCA 23715		So Cold the Night/When the Walls Come Tumbling Down	1987	2.00	4.00	8.00

Concrete Blonde

*Los Angeles pop/new wave group, led by Johnette Napolitano. Originally known as **Dream 6**.*

Vinyl Albums

Label, Number		Title	Year	VG	VG+	NM
I.R.S. 5835		Concrete Blonde	1987	3.00	6.00	12.00
I.R.S. X1-13037		Bloodletting	1990	5.00	10.00	20.00
Red vinyl						
I.R.S. 82001		Free	1989	3.00	6.00	12.00
I.R.S. 82037	DJ	Bloodletting	1990	6.25	12.50	25.00
Promo-only, sticker on generic cover, black vinyl						

45s

Label, Number		Title	Year	VG	VG+	NM
I.R.S. 52982		Still in Hollywood/Cold Part of Town	1986			3.00
I.R.S. 53053		True/True II (Instrumental)	1987		2.50	5.00
I.R.S. 53053	PS	True/True II (Instrumental)	1987			3.00
I.R.S. 53113		Dance Along the Edge/Make Me Cry	1987		2.50	5.00
I.R.S. 53113	PS	Dance Along the Edge/Make Me Cry	1987			3.00

10-Inch Singles

Label, Number		Title	Year	VG	VG+	NM
Capitol SPRO-79245/6	DJ	Jonestown/Jonestown (Jim Jones Edit)/Simple Twist of Fate	1993	5.00	10.00	20.00

12-Inch Singles

Label, Number		Title	Year	VG	VG+	NM
I.R.S. 17231	DJ	Still in Hollywood/I'll Chew You Up	1986	2.50	5.00	10.00
I.R.S. 17268	DJ	True/Still in Hollywood	1986	2.00	4.00	8.00
I.R.S. 17310	DJ	Dance Along the Edge (Edit)/Dance Along the Edge (LP)	1988	3.75	7.50	15.00
I.R.S. 74001		God Is a Bullet/Free/Little Wing	1989	4.50	9.00	18.00

Cope, Julian

*Ex-leader of **The Teardrop Explodes**.*

Vinyl Albums

Label, Number		Title	Year	VG	VG+	NM
Island 90560		Julian Cope	1987	2.50	5.00	10.00
Island 91025		My Nation Underground	1988	2.50	5.00	10.00

Label, Number		Title	Year	VG	VG+	NM
45s						
Island 99241		Five O'Clock World/S.P.Q.R.	1989			3.00
Island 99241	PS	Five O'Clock World/S.P.Q.R.	1989			3.00
Island 99448		Eve's Volcano/Almost Beautiful Child				
			1987			3.00
Island 99479		World Shut Your Mouth/Umpteenth Unnatural Blues				
			1987			3.00
Island 99479	PS	World Shut Your Mouth/Umpteenth Unnatural Blues				
			1987			3.00
12-Inch Singles						
Island 988	DJ	World Shut Your Mouth (same on both sides)				
			1987		2.50	5.00
Island 1288	DJ	5 O'Clock World/S.P.Q.R.	1988		2.50	5.00
Island 2000	DJ	Trampolene (same on both sides)				
			1987		2.50	5.00
Island 2523	DJ	Charlotte Anne/Charlotte Anne (Edit)				
			1988		3.50	7.00
Island PR12 6667	DJ	Peggy Suicide sampler	1991	3.00	6.00	12.00
Island 868 909-1		Head (2 versions)/Love/Early Risin'				
			1991		3.00	6.00

Copeland, Stewart
*One of **The Police**.*

Label, Number		Title	Year	VG	VG+	NM
Vinyl Albums						
A&M SP 5084		The Rhythmatist	1985	2.50	5.00	10.00
12-Inch Singles						
A&M 12159		Gong Rock (remix)/Gong Rock (dub)				
			1985		3.00	6.00

Copeland, Stewart/Adam Ant

Label, Number		Title	Year	VG	VG+	NM
45s						
I.R.S. 52885		Out of Bounds/Out of Bounds	1986		2.00	4.00
12-Inch Singles						
I.R.S. 17166	DJ	Out of Bounds (extended)/Out of Bounds (LP version)				
			1986	2.00	4.00	8.00

Copeland, Stewart/Stanard Ridgway

Label, Number		Title	Year	VG	VG+	NM
45s						
A&M 2604		Don't Box Me In/Drama at Home				
			1983		2.00	4.00
12-Inch Singles						
A&M 17260	DJ	Don't Box Me In (same on both sides)				
			1983	2.50	5.00	10.00

Costello, Elvis
British pioneer new waver, born Declan McManus. Once one of the most collectible new music artists, his popularity has cooled off.

Label, Number		Title	Year	VG	VG+	NM
Vinyl Albums						
Columbia (no #)	PD	My Aim Is True/This Year's Model				
			1978	12.50	25.00	50.00
Promo-only picture disc; one side is dedicated to each album						
Columbia AS 529	EP	Live at Hollywood High	1978	5.00	10.00	20.00
Promo-only 12-inch version of 7-inch single						
Columbia AS 958	DJ	Tom Snyder Interview	1981	5.00	10.00	20.00

Label, Number		Title	Year	VG	VG+	NM
Columbia AS 1318	DJ	Almost Blue	1981	10.00	20.00	40.00
Radio sampler with introductions by Elvis before each track						
Columbia JC 35037		My Aim Is True	1977	3.75	7.50	15.00
First pressings have yellow back covers						
Columbia JC 35037		My Aim Is True	1978	2.50	5.00	10.00
Second pressings have a white back cover and no bar code						
Columbia PC 35037		My Aim Is True	1984	2.00	4.00	8.00
Reissue						
Columbia JC 35331		This Year's Model	1978	3.00	6.00	12.00
With "Costello" replacing "Columbia" on labels						
Columbia JC 35331		This Year's Model	1978	2.50	5.00	10.00
With standard Columbia label						
Columbia PC 35331		This Year's Model	1984	2.00	4.00	8.00
Reissue						
Columbia JC 35709	DJ	Armed Forces	1979	3.75	7.50	15.00
White label promo, includes bonus 7" single						
Columbia JC 35709		Armed Forces	1979	3.00	6.00	12.00
Stock copy, includes bonus 7" single						
Columbia JC 35709		Armed Forces	1979	2.00	4.00	8.00
Without bonus single						
Columbia PC 35709		Armed Forces	1984	2.00	4.00	8.00
Reissue						
Columbia JC 36347		Get Happy!!	1980	2.50	5.00	10.00
Columbia PC 36347		Get Happy!!	1984	2.00	4.00	8.00
Reissue						
Columbia JC 36839		Taking Liberties	1980	2.50	5.00	10.00
With custom old-style Columbia label						
Columbia JC 36839		Taking Liberties	1980	2.00	4.00	8.00
Columbia PC 36839		Taking Liberties	1984	2.00	4.00	8.00
Reissue						
Columbia JC 37051		Trust	1981	2.50	5.00	10.00
Columbia PC 37051		Trust	1984	2.00	4.00	8.00
Reissue						
Columbia FC 37562		Almost Blue	1981	2.50	5.00	10.00
Columbia PC 37562		Almost Blue	1984	2.00	4.00	8.00
Reissue						
Columbia FC 38157		Imperial Bedroom	1982	2.50	5.00	10.00
Columbia PC 38157		Imperial Bedroom	1984	2.00	4.00	8.00
Reissue						
Columbia FC 38897		Punch the Clock	1983	2.50	5.00	10.00
Columbia FC 39429		Goodbye Cruel World	1984	2.50	5.00	10.00
Columbia FC 40101		The Best of Elvis Costello	1985	3.00	6.00	12.00
Columbia HC 48157		Imperial Bedroom	1982	10.00	20.00	40.00
Half-Speed Mastered edition						
Costello AS 847	EP	Taking Liberties	1980	3.75	7.50	15.00
Promo-only sampler						
Warner Bros. PRO-A-3488	(2) DJ	Spike -- The Elvis Costello Hour	1989	7.50	15.00	30.00
Music and conversation; generic gatefold sleeve with sticker on cover						
Warner Bros. 25848		Spike	1989	2.50	5.00	10.00
Warner Bros. 46198		All This Useless Beauty	1996	2.50	5.00	10.00
Warner Bros. R 100841		Spike	1989	3.00	6.00	12.00
BMG Direct Marketing edition						

45s

Label, Number		Title	Year	VG	VG+	NM
Columbia AE7 1171	DJ	Accidents Will Happen/Alison/Watching the Detectives	1979			3.00
Extra record included in first editions of LP "Armed Forces"						
Columbia AE7 1171	PS	Live at Hollywood High	1979		2.50	5.00
Columbia AE7 1172	DJ	My Funny Valentine/(What's So Funny 'Bout) Peace, Love and Understanding	1980	3.00	6.00	12.00
Red vinyl						
Columbia 02629		A Good Year for the Roses/The Angel Steps Out of Heaven	1981		2.00	4.00

Label, Number		Title	Year	VG	VG+	NM
Columbia 03202		Man Out of Time/(B-side unknown)				
			1982			3.00
Columbia 03269		Man Out of Time	1982		2.50	5.00
One-sided budget release						
Columbia 04045		Everyday I Write the Book/Heathen Town				
			1983			3.00
Columbia 04045	PS	Everyday I Write the Book/Heathen Town				
			1983			3.00
Columbia 04266		Let Them All Talk/Shipbuilding	1983			3.00
Columbia 04502		The Only Flame in Town/Turning the Town Red				
			1984			3.00
Columbia 04502	PS	The Only Flame in Town/Turning the Town Red				
			1984			3.00
Columbia 04625		I Wanna Be Loved/Love Field	1984			3.00
Columbia 05809		Don't Let Me Be Misunderstood/Brand New Hairdo				
			1986			3.00
By "The Costello Show Featuring Elvis Costello"						
Columbia 06059		Lovable/Get Yourself Another Fool				
			1986			3.00
By "The Costello Show Featuring Elvis Costello"						
Columbia 06326		Tokyo Storm Warning/Tokyo Storm Warning				
			1986			3.00
Columbia 10641		Alison/Miracle Man	1977	2.50	5.00	10.00
Contains a remix of "Alison" otherwise unavailable on U.S. vinyl						
Columbia 10696		Watching the Detectives/Blame It on Cain-Mystery Dance				
			1978	2.50	5.00	10.00
Columbia 10705		Alison/Watching the Detectives	1978	2.50	5.00	10.00
Contains the same remix of "Alison" as on Columbia 10641.						
Columbia 10762		This Year's Girl/Big Tears	1978		3.00	6.00
Columbia 10919		Accidents Will Happen/Sunday's Best				
			1979		3.00	6.00
Columbia 11194		I Can't Stand Up for Falling Down/Girls Talk				
			1980		3.00	6.00
Columbia 11251		I Can't Stand Up for Falling Down/Girls Talk//Secondary Modern/				
		King Horse	1980		3.00	6.00
Columbia 11251	PS	I Can't Stand Up for Falling Down/Girls Talk//Secondary Modern/				
		King Horse	1980		3.00	6.00
Columbia 11284		New Amsterdam/Wednesday Week				
			1980		2.00	4.00
Columbia 11389		Gettin' Mighty Crowded/Radio Sweetheart				
			1980		2.00	4.00
Columbia 33401		Accidents Will Happen/Alison	198?		2.00	4.00
"Hall of Fame" reissue						
Columbia 60519		Watch Your Step/Luxembourg	1981		2.00	4.00
Columbia 60519	PS	Watch Your Step/Luxembourg	1981		2.00	4.00
Warner Bros. 22981		Veronica/You're No Good	1989			3.00
Warner Bros. 22981	PS	Veronica/You're No Good	1989			3.00

12-Inch Singles

Label, Number		Title	Year	VG	VG+	NM
Columbia AS 1510	DJ	Man Out of Time/Beyond Belief	1982	3.00	6.00	12.00
Columbia CAS 2310	DJ	Don't Let Me Be Misunderstood (live) (same on both sides)				
			1986	3.75	7.50	15.00
Columbia CAS 2371	DJ	Loveable (same on both sides)	1986	3.50	7.00	
Columbia CAS 2380	DJ	Seven Day Weekend (same on both sides)				
			1986	2.00	4.00	8.00
Columbia CAS 2500	DJ	Tokyo Storm Warning/Tokyo Storm Warning (Part 1)				
			1986		3.00	6.00
Columbia 04115		Everyday I Write the Book (2 versions)//Heathen Town/				
		Night Time	1983	2.00	4.00	8.00
Columbia 05081		The Only Flame in Town (Special Mix)				
			1984	3.00	6.00	12.00
Warner Bros. PRO-A-3424	DJ	Veronica (same on both sides)	1989	3.75	7.50	15.00

Label, Number		Title	Year	VG	VG+	NM

Cotton, Josie
Dallas-born new waver.

Vinyl Albums

Elektra 60140		Convertible Music	1982	2.50	5.00	10.00
Elektra 60309		From the Hip	1984	2.50	5.00	10.00

45s

Elektra 47255		Johnny Are You Queer?/(Let's Do) The Blackout				
			1982		2.50	5.00
Elektra 47481		He Could Be the One/Systematic Way				
			1982		2.50	5.00
Pink vinyl						
Elektra 47481	PS	He Could Be the One/Systematic Way				
			1982		2.50	5.00
Elektra 69748		Jimmy Loves Mary-Anne/No Pictures of Dad				
			1984			3.00
Elektra 69886	DJ	Bye Bye Baby (same on both sides)				
			1982			3.00
May be promo only						

12-Inch Singles

Bomp! 12133		Johnny Are You Queer?/The Blackout				
			1981	3.00	6.00	12.00
Elektra 4958	DJ	Jimmy Loves Mary-Anne (same on both sides)				
			1984		3.50	7.00
Elektra 11538		Johnny Are You Queer?/The Blackout				
			1981	2.50	5.00	10.00
Elektra 67997		Systematic Way/He Could Be the One				
			1982		3.00	6.00

Cowboy Junkies
Country-punk group from Canada, with lead singer Margo Timmins.

Vinyl Albums

Latent Recordings LATEX 4		Whites Off Earth Now!!	1986	7.50	15.00	30.00
Canada-only release						
RCA 8568		The Trinity Session	1988	3.00	6.00	12.00

45s

RCA 8879-7-R		Sweet Jane/200 More Miles	1989		2.50	5.00
RCA 8879-7-R	PS	Sweet Jane/200 More Miles	1989		2.50	5.00
RCA 8997-7-R		Misguided Angel/Postcard Blues	1989		2.50	5.00

12-Inch Singles

RCA 8759	DJ	Sweet Jane (same on both sides)	1988	3.00	6.00	12.00
RCA 8958-1-R		Misguided Angel/Misguided Angel (Live), Sweet Jane (Live) + 2 more live at the Roxy				
			1989	6.25	12.50	25.00

Cracker
*David Lowery's band after **Camper Van Beethoven**.*

Vinyl Albums

Virgin 39012		Kerosene Hat	1993	3.00	6.00	12.00

45s

Virgin S7-17910		Low/Nostalgia	1994			3.00
Virgin S7-18132		Euro-Trash Girl/I Want Everything (Remix Edit)				
			1994			3.00

Label, Number		Title	Year	VG	VG+	NM

Crackerbash

45s

Label, Number		Title	Year	VG	VG+	NM
Sub Pop 158		Nov. 1/Halloween Candy	1992		2.50	5.00
Lavender marbled vinyl						
Sub Pop 158	PS	Nov. 1/Halloween Candy	1992		2.50	5.00
#46 in Sub Pop Singles Club series						

Cramps, The

Pioneer Cleveland-area punk band, they've been at it for 20 years and counting.

Vinyl Albums

Label, Number		Title	Year	VG	VG+	NM
Enigma 21		Smell of Female	1983	3.00	6.00	12.00
Enigma 268	DJ	Stay Sick!	1990	5.00	10.00	20.00
Promo-only version						
Enigma 73543		Stay Sick!	1990	3.00	6.00	12.00
Enigma D1-73617	EP	Creature from the Black Leather Lagoon				
			1990	2.50	5.00	10.00
I.R.S. SP-007		Songs the Lord Taught Us	1980	3.00	6.00	12.00
I.R.S. SP-501	EP	Gravest Hits	1979	6.25	12.50	25.00
I.R.S. SP-70007		Songs the Lord Taught Us	198?	2.50	5.00	10.00
Reissue						
I.R.S. SP-70016		Psychedelic Jungle	1981	3.00	6.00	12.00
I.R.S. SP-70042		Bad Music for Bad People	1984	3.00	6.00	12.00
I.R.S. SP-70501	EP	Gravest Hits	198?	2.50	5.00	10.00
Reissue						
Medicine Label 24592		Flamejob	1994	2.50	5.00	10.00

45s

Label, Number		Title	Year	VG	VG+	NM
I.R.S. 9014		Garbage Man/Drug Train	1980	2.00	4.00	8.00
I.R.S. 9014	PS	Garbage Man/Drug Train	1980	2.00	4.00	8.00
I.R.S. 9021		She Said/Goo Goo Muck	1981	2.00	4.00	8.00
I.R.S. 9021	PS	She Said/Goo Goo Muck	1981	2.00	4.00	8.00
Medicine Label 17932		Naked Girl Falling Down the Stairs/Confessions of a Psycho Cat				
			1995			3.00
Medicine Label 17976		Ultra Twist/No Club Low Wolf	1995			3.00
Medicine Label 18045		Let's Get F*cked Up/How Come You Do Me				
			1994			3.00
Vengeance 666		Surfin' Bird/The Way I Walk	1978	7.50	15.00	30.00
Vengeance 666	PS	Surfin' Bird/The Way I Walk	1978	8.75	17.50	35.00
Vengeance 668		Human Fly/Domino	1978	7.50	15.00	30.00
Vengeance 668	PS	Human Fly/Domino	1978	8.75	17.50	35.00

12-Inch Singles

Label, Number		Title	Year	VG	VG+	NM
Enigma EPRO 253	DJ	Bikini Girls with Machine Guns (same on both sides)				
			1989	2.50	5.00	10.00

Cranberries, The

Irish alterna-rock band with lead singer Dolores O'Riordan.

Vinyl Albums

Label, Number		Title	Year	VG	VG+	NM
Island 524 234-1		To the Faithful Departed	1996	3.00	6.00	12.00
Yellow vinyl, fold-open poster-bag cover; British import for distribution in U.S. (no "Made in England" stickers)						

45s

Label, Number		Title	Year	VG	VG+	NM
Island 854 206-7		Zombie/Ode to My Family	1995			3.00
Island 858 172-7		Linger/Dreams	1994			3.00

Label, Number		Title	Year	VG	VG+	NM

Crash Test Dummies
Canadian rock group.

45s

Arista 12339		Superman's Song/The Voyage	1991		*Cassette only*	
Arista 12654		Mmm Mmm Mmm Mmm/Superman's Song				
			1994		*Cassette only*	

Crenshaw, Marshall
Detroit roots-rocker; has also played John Lennon in Beatlemania and Eddie Cochran in La Bamba.

Vinyl Albums

Warner Bros. BSK 3673		Marshall Crenshaw	1982	3.00	6.00	12.00
Warner Bros. 23873		Field Day	1983	2.50	5.00	10.00
Warner Bros. 25319		Downtown	1985	2.50	5.00	10.00
Warner Bros. 25583		Mary Jean and 9 Others	1987	2.50	5.00	10.00
Warner Bros. 25908		Good Evening	1989	2.50	5.00	10.00

45s

Warner Bros. 22878		Whatever Way the Wind Blows/(B-side unknown)				
			1989			3.00
Warner Bros. 28865		Little Wild One (No. 5)/Like a Vague Memory				
			1985			3.00
Warner Bros. 28865	PS	Little Wild One (No. 5)/Like a Vague Memory				
			1985			3.00
Warner Bros. 29630		Whenever You're On My Mind/Jungle Rock				
			1983			3.00
Warner Bros. 29630	PS	Whenever You're On My Mind/Jungle Rock				
			1983		2.50	5.00
Warner Bros. 29771		Cynical Girl/Rave On-Somebody Like You				
			1983		2.00	4.00
Warner Bros. 29894		There She Goes Again/Usual Thing				
			1982		2.00	4.00
Warner Bros. 29974		Someday, Someway/You're My Favorite Waste of Time				
			1982		2.50	5.00

12-Inch Singles

Shake 104		Something's Gonna Happen/She Can't Dance				
			1981	7.50	15.00	30.00
Warner Bros. PRO-A-2003	DJ	Cynical Girl/Rave On/Somebody Like You				
			1982	3.75	7.50	15.00
Warner Bros. PRO-A-2036	DJ	Whenever You're On My Mind (same on both sides)				
			1983	2.00	4.00	8.00
Warner Bros. PRO-A-2366	DJ	Little Wild One (No. 5) (same on both sides)				
			1985	2.00	4.00	8.00
Warner Bros. PRO-A-2410	DJ	Blues Is King (same on both sides)				
			1985	2.00	4.00	8.00
Warner Bros. PRO-A-2752	DJ	This Is Easy (same on both sides)				
			1987		2.50	5.00
Warner Bros. PRO-A-2793	DJ	Mary Jean (same on both sides)	1987		2.50	5.00

Cretones, The
Backing band for Linda Ronstadt on her bad imitation new-wave LP Mad Love.

Vinyl Albums

Planet P-5		Thin Red Line	1980	2.50	5.00	10.00
Planet P-15		Snap, Snap	1981	2.50	5.00	10.00

45s

Planet 45911		Real Love/Ways of the Heart	1980			3.00
Planet 45911	PS	Real Love/Ways of the Heart	1980			3.00

Label, Number		Title	Year	VG	VG+	NM
Planet 45917		Justine/Mad Love	1980			3.00
Planet 45926		Love Is Turning/Snap! Snap!	1981			3.00

Crime
Los Angeles early punk band.

Vinyl Albums
Planet Pimp OTD 005		Love Us or Hate Us, We Don't Give a Fuck				
			1992	3.00	6.00	12.00

45s
B-Square BSQ 001		Maserati/Gangster Funk	1980	5.00	10.00	20.00
B-Square BSQ 001	PS	Maserati/Gangster Funk	1980	5.00	10.00	20.00
Crime (no #)		Hotwire My Heart/Baby, You're So Repulsive				
			1976	10.00	20.00	40.00
Crime (no #)	PS	Hotwire My Heart/Baby, You're So Repulsive				
			1976	10.00	20.00	40.00
Crime (no #)		Frustration/Murder by Guitar	1977	12.50	25.00	50.00
Crime (no #)	PS	Frustration/Murder by Guitar	1977	12.50	25.00	50.00
Spirit FTD 002		Hotwire My Heart/Baby, You're So Repulsive				
			1990		2.00	4.00
Authorized reissue; 1,000 pressed on blue vinyl						
Spirit FTD 002	PS	Hotwire My Heart/Baby, You're So Repulsive				
			1990		2.00	4.00

Crow, Sheryl
Originally from Missouri, a former backing singer and composer who made good as an alterna-popper.

45s
A&M 31458 0638 7		Can't Cry Anymore/We Do What We Can				
			1995			2.00
A&M 31458 0638 7	PS	Can't Cry Anymore/We Do What We Can				
			1995			2.00
A&M 31458 0836 7		All I Wanna Do/Leaving Las Vegas				
			1994			3.00
A&M 31458 0932 7		Strong Enough/Run, Baby, Run	1995			3.00

Crowded House
*Australian pop group, formed by Neil Finn after the demise of **Split Enz**. Briefly, Neil's brother **Tim Finn** was a member.*

Vinyl Albums
Capitol ST-12485		Crowded House	1987	2.50	5.00	10.00
Capitol C1-48763		Temple of Low Men	1988	3.00	6.00	12.00
Capitol C1-93559		Woodface	1991	3.75	7.50	15.00
Capitol R 114827		Temple of Low Men	1988	3.50	7.00	14.00
BMG Direct Marketing edition						
Capitol R 133277		Crowded House	1987	3.00	6.00	12.00
BMG Direct Marketing edition						

45s
American Pie 9047		Don't Dream It's Over/Something So Strong				
			1990			3.00
Reissue						
Capitol 5614		Don't Dream It's Over/That's What I Call Love				
			1986			3.00
Capitol 5614	PS	Don't Dream It's Over/That's What I Call Love				
			1986		2.50	5.00
Capitol 5634		Mean to Me/Love You 'Til I Die	1986			*Unreleased?*
Capitol 5634	PS	Mean to Me/Love You 'Til I Die	1986			*Unreleased?*

Label, Number		Title	Year	VG	VG+	NM
Capitol 5695		Something So Strong/I Walk Away				
			1987			3.00
Capitol 5695	PS	Something So Strong/I Walk Away				
			1987			3.00
Capitol S7-17706		Nails in My Feet/You Can Touch				
			1994			3.00
Capitol S7-17905		Locked Out/My Sharona	1994		2.00	4.00
B-side by The Knack						
Capitol S7-17966		Distant Sun/Walking on the Spot	1994			3.00
Capitol S7-18041		Private Universe/Black and White Boy				
			1994			3.00
Capitol 44033		World Where You Live/Hole in the River				
			1987			3.00
Capitol 44033	PS	World Where You Live/Hole in the River				
			1987			3.00
Capitol 44083		Now We're Getting Somewhere/Tombstone				
			1987			3.00
Capitol 44083	PS	Now We're Getting Somewhere/Tombstone				
			1987			3.00
Capitol 44164		Better Be Home Soon/Kill Eye	1988			3.00
Capitol 44164	PS	Better Be Home Soon/Kill Eye	1988			3.00
Capitol 44226		Into Temptation/Better Be Home Soon				
			1988			3.00
Capitol 44226	PS	Into Temptation/Better Be Home Soon				
			1988			3.00
Capitol 44406		I Feel Possessed	1989		*May be cassette-only*	
Capitol S7-57699		It's Only Natural/Fame Is	1992			3.00
Capitol 7PRO-79653	DJ	I Feel Possessed (same on both sides)				
			1989		3.00	6.00

Vinyl version appears to be promo-only

12-Inch Singles

Label, Number		Title	Year	VG	VG+	NM
Capitol SPRO-9693/4	DJ	World Where You Live/Mean to Me/Something So Strong				
			1986	3.75	7.50	15.00
Capitol 15240		World Where You Live/Mean to Me/Something So Strong				
			1986	3.00	6.00	12.00
Capitol 15292		Something So Strong/Can't Carry On/I Walk Away				
			1987	2.50	5.00	10.00
Capitol SPRO-79169	DJ	Now We're Getting Somewhere (same on both sides)				
			1987	2.50	5.00	10.00
Capitol SPRO-79774	DJ	Chocolate Cake (same on both sides)				
			1991	2.50	5.00	10.00

Crucifix

Vinyl Albums

Label, Number			Title	Year	VG	VG+	NM
Universal RON 2	EP		Crucifix	1982	10.00	20.00	40.00

Cult, The

British rockers.

Vinyl Albums

Label, Number		Title	Year	VG	VG+	NM
Sire 25259		Love	1985	2.50	5.00	10.00
Sire 25555		Electric	1987	2.50	5.00	10.00
Sire 25871		Sonic Temple	1989	2.50	5.00	10.00
Sire R 101015		Sonic Temple	1989	3.00	6.00	12.00
BMG Direct Marketing edition						
Sire R 134608		Love	1985	3.00	6.00	12.00
RCA Music Service edition						
Sire R 184083		Electric	1987	3.00	6.00	12.00
RCA Music Service edition						
Warner Bros. WBMS-147	DJ	Electric Interview	1987	10.00	20.00	40.00

Label, Number		Title	Year	VG	VG+	NM
45s						
Sire 19926		Sweet Soul Sisters/Soldier Blue	1990		*Cassette only*	
Sire 21945		She Sells Sanctuary/Love Removal Machine				
			198?			3.00
Reissue						
Sire 22873		Edie (Ciao Baby)/Love Removal Machine				
			1989			3.00
Sire 27543		Fire Woman/Automatic Blues	1989			3.00
Sire 27543	PS	Fire Woman/Automatic Blues	1989			3.00
Sire 28290		Lil' Devil/Memphis Hip Shake	1987			3.00
Sire 28290	PS	Lil' Devil/Memphis Hip Shake	1987			3.00
Sire 28820		She Sells Sanctuary/Little Face	1986			3.00
12-Inch Singles						
Reprise PRO-A-5599	DJ	The Witch/The Witch (Edit)	1992	5.00	10.00	20.00
Purple vinyl promo						
Reprise PRO-A-5599	DJ	The Witch/The Witch (Edit)	1992	2.00	4.00	8.00
Regular black vinyl promo						
Sire PRO-A-2394	DJ	She Sells Sanctuary (same on both sides)				
			1985	3.00	6.00	12.00
Sire PRO-A-2427	DJ	Rain (same on both sides)	1985	3.75	7.50	15.00
Sire PRO-A-2691	DJ	Love Removal Machine (7" Edit) (same on both sides)				
			1987		3.50	7.00
Sire PRO-A-2726	DJ	Li'l Devil (same on both sides)	1987		3.00	6.00
Sire PRO-A-2775	DJ	Wildflower/Wildflower (Remix)	1987	3.00	6.00	12.00
Sire PRO-A-3435	DJ	Fire Woman (same on both sides)				
			1989	2.00	4.00	8.00
Sire 20407		She Sells Sanctuary (2 mixes)/Little Face				
			1985	3.75	7.50	15.00
Sire 20641		Love Removal Machine (2 versions)/Wolf Child's Blues				
			1987	2.00	4.00	8.00
Sire 20743		Wildflower (3 versions)	1987	2.50	5.00	10.00
Sire 21195		Fire Woman/Automatic Blues/Messin' Up the Blues				
			1989		3.50	7.00

Culture Club

*Early '80s MTV darlings from England, thanks to a blue-eyed soul sound and the outrageousness of **Boy George**.*

Label, Number		Title	Year	VG	VG+	NM
Vinyl Albums						
Virgin/Epic ARE 38398		Kissing to Be Clever	1982	3.00	6.00	12.00
First pressings do not contain "Time'						
Virgin/Epic FE 38398		Kissing to Be Clever	1983	2.50	5.00	10.00
Early reissue (bar code on back cover has no "02" suffix); also, "Time" has been added						
Virgin/Epic QE 39107		Colour by Numbers	1983	2.50	5.00	10.00
Virgin/Epic 9E9-39237	PD	Colour By Numbers	1983	6.25	12.50	25.00
Virgin/Epic OE 39881		Waking Up with the House on Fire				
			1984	2.50	5.00	10.00
Virgin/Epic 9E9-40005	PD	Waking Up with the House on Fire				
			1984	6.25	12.50	25.00
Virgin/Epic OE 40345		From Luxury to Heartache	1986	2.50	5.00	10.00
Virgin/Epic FE 40913		This Time: The First Four Years	1987	3.00	6.00	12.00
45s						
Epic AE7 1591	DJ	Do You Really Want to Hurt Me (edited intro)/ Do You Really Want to Hurt Me (no intro)				
			1982	2.00	4.00	8.00
Epic 03368		Do You Really Want to Hurt Me/You Know I'm Not Crazy				
			1982			3.00
Not issued with picture sleeve in U.S.						
Epic 03531		Do You Really Want to Hurt Me	1983		2.50	5.00
One-sided budget release						

An American picture sleeve for "Mistake #3" is said to exist, but has not been confirmed. Otherwise, the Culture Club sleeve for "Time (Clock of the Heart)" is the most difficult to find.

Cherie Currie was one of the Runaways. She teamed up with her sister Marie for one album after the all-girl group split up.

Label, Number		Title	Year	VG	VG+	NM
Epic 03796		Time (Clock of the Heart)/Romance Beyond the Alphabet				
			1983			3.00
Epic 03796	PS	Time (Clock of the Heart)/Romance Beyond the Alphabet				
			1983	2.50	5.00	10.00
A reasonably scarce sleeve.						
Epic 03912		I'll Tumble 4 Ya/Mystery Boy	1983			3.00
Epic 03912	PS	I'll Tumble 4 Ya/Mystery Boy	1983			3.00
Epic 04144		Church of the Poison Mind/Mystery Boy				
			1983			3.00
Epic 04144	PS	Church of the Poison Mind/Mystery Boy				
			1983			3.00
Virgin/Epic 04221		Karma Chameleon/That's the Way (I'm Only Trying to Help You)				
			1983			3.00
Virgin/Epic 04221	PS	Karma Chameleon/That's the Way (I'm Only Trying to Help You)				
			1983			3.00
Virgin/Epic 04388		Miss Me Blind/Colour By Numbers				
			1984			3.00
Virgin/Epic 04388	PS	Miss Me Blind/Colour By Numbers				
			1984			3.00
Virgin/Epic 04457		It's a Miracle/Love Twist	1984			3.00
Virgin/Epic 04457	PS	It's a Miracle/Love Twist	1984			3.00
Virgin/Epic 04638		The War Song/La Cancion De Guerra				
			1984			3.00
Virgin/Epic 04638	PS	The War Song/La Cancion De Guerra				
			1984			3.00
Virgin/Epic 04727		Mistake No. 3/Don't Go Down That Street				
			1984			3.00
A U.S. picture sleeve is rumored to exist, but we've been unable to confirm it.						
Virgin/Epic 05847		Move Away/Sexuality	1986			3.00
Virgin/Epic 05847	PS	Move Away/Sexuality	1986			3.00
Virgin/Epic 06133		Gusto Blusto/From Luxury to Heartache				
			1986			3.00
Virgin/Epic 06133	PS	Gusto Blusto/From Luxury to Heartache				
			1986			3.00
Virgin/Epic 08436		Church of the Poison Mind/Do You Really Want to Hurt Me				
			1988			3.00
Reissue						

12-Inch Singles

Label, Number		Title	Year	VG	VG+	NM
Epic AS 1642	DJ	Time/Romance Beyond the Alphabet				
			1983	2.50	5.00	10.00
Epic AS 1752	DJ	Church of the Poison Mind (same on both sides)				
			1983	2.50	5.00	10.00
Epic 03307		Murder Rap Trap/I'm Afraid of Me				
			1982		3.50	7.00
Epic 03393		Do You Really Want to Hurt Me/ Love Is Cold (You Were Never No Good)				
			1982	2.50	5.00	10.00
Epic 03913		I'll Tumble 4 Ya/Man Shake	1983	2.50	5.00	10.00
Epic 04145		Church of the Poison Mind/Mystery Boy				
			1983	2.50	5.00	10.00
Virgin/Epic 04977		Miss Me Blind/It's a Miracle/Colour By Numbers				
			1984		3.50	7.00
Virgin/Epic 05107		The War Song (2 mixes)/La Cancion de Guerra				
			1984		3.50	7.00
Virgin/Epic 05360		Move Away/Sexuality	1986		3.50	7.00
Virgin/Epic 05916		Gusto Blusto (Extended Dance Mix)/Gusto Blusto (Rock Mix)				
			1986		3.00	6.00
Virgin/Epic EAS 2296	DJ	Move Away (same on both sides)	1986		3.50	7.00

Label, Number		Title	Year	VG	VG+	NM

C*nts

*Punk band, sometimes spelled with a "u" replacing the asterisk, and also known as C*nts Live.*

45s

Disturbing (# unknown)		Open Your Mind/Musician in a Bathtub				
			1983	3.75	7.50	15.00
Disturbing (# unknown)	PS	Open Your Mind/Musician in a Bathtub				
			1983	3.75	7.50	15.00
Disturbing (# unknown)		Apocalyptic Breakfast/Turn of the Night				
			1984	3.00	6.00	12.00
Disturbing (# unknown)	PS	Apocalyptic Breakfast/Turn of the Night				
			1984	3.00	6.00	12.00
Disturbing 81480		We're Going to Crash/Penguins Addicted to Molasses				
			1980	5.00	10.00	20.00
Disturbing 81480	PS	We're Going to Crash/Penguins Addicted to Molasses				
			1980	5.00	10.00	20.00
Disturbing 111678		Chemicals in the Mall/Why Do You Live on My Block				
			1978	7.50	15.00	30.00
Disturbing 111678	PS	Chemicals in the Mall/Why Do You Live on My Block				
			1978	7.50	15.00	30.00
Disturbing 112281		There Are Electrical Filaments.../A Date with Disaster				
			1982	2.50	5.00	10.00
Version 1: Green labels						
Disturbing 112281		There Are Electrical Filaments.../A Date with Disaster				
			1982	2.50	5.00	10.00
Version 2: Black labels						
Disturbing 112281		There Are Electrical Filaments.../A Date with Disaster				
			1982	2.25	4.50	9.00
Version 3: Yellow labels						
Disturbing 112281	PS	There Are Electrical Filaments.../A Date with Disaster				
			1982	3.75	7.50	15.00
Version 1: White background, three-piece photocopy art						
Disturbing 112281	PS	There Are Electrical Filaments.../A Date with Disaster				
			1982	5.00	10.00	20.00
Version 1A: Same as above, two extra pieces of "art"						
Disturbing 112281	PS	There Are Electrical Filaments.../A Date with Disaster				
			1982	2.50	5.00	10.00
Version 2: Gray pattern background folder sleeve						
Disturbing 112281	PS	There Are Electrical Filaments.../A Date with Disaster				
			1982	2.25	4.50	9.00
Version 3: White background, photo of band on back						

Cure, The

British gloom-rockers, led by Robert Smith.

Vinyl Albums

A&M SP-4902		Pornography	1982	3.00	6.00	12.00
A&M SP-6020	(2)	Happily Ever After	1981	7.50	15.00	30.00
Elektra 60435		The Head on the Door	1985	3.00	6.00	12.00
Elektra 60477		Standing on a Beach -- The Singles				
			1986	2.50	5.00	10.00
Elektra 60737	(2)	Kiss Me, Kiss Me, Kiss Me	1987	3.75	7.50	15.00
Elektra 60737	(2) DJ	Kiss Me, Kiss Me, Kiss Me	1987	7.50	15.00	30.00
Promo-only audiophile pressing						
Elektra 60783		Faith	1988	2.50	5.00	10.00
Reissue of first U.K. album						
Elektra 60784		Seventeen Seconds	1988	2.50	5.00	10.00
Reissue of second U.K. album						
Elektra 60785		Pornography	1988	2.50	5.00	10.00
Reissue of A&M SP-4902						
Elektra 60786		Boys Don't Cry	1988	2.50	5.00	10.00
Reissue of PVC 7916						

Label, Number		Title	Year	VG	VG+	NM
Elektra 60855		Disintegration	1989	2.50	5.00	10.00
Elektra 60978	(2)	Mixed Up	1990	5.00	10.00	20.00
LP version has one extra track not on CD or cassette						
Elektra 61744	(2)	Wild Mood Swings	1996	3.00	6.00	12.00
Elektra R 101109		Disintegration	1989	3.00	6.00	12.00
BMG Direct Marketing edition						
Elektra R 150024		Standing on a Beach -- The Singles				
			1986	3.00	6.00	12.00
BMG Direct Marketing edition						
Elektra R 242404		Kiss Me, Kiss Me, Kiss Me	1987	4.50	9.00	18.00
BMG Direct Marketing edition						
Elektra R 274190		Mixed Up	1990	6.25	12.50	25.00
BMG Direct Marketing edition						
PVC 7916		Boys Don't Cry	1980	3.75	7.50	15.00
Sire 23928	EP	The Walk	1983	3.00	6.00	12.00
Sire 25076		Japanese Whispers	1983	3.75	7.50	15.00
Sire 25086		The Top	1984	3.75	7.50	15.00

45s

Label, Number		Title	Year	VG	VG+	NM
Elektra 64928		Never Enough/Harold and Joe	1990			3.00
Elektra 65936		Love Song/Fascination Street	1990			3.00
"Spun Gold" reissue						
Elektra 65967		Why Can't I Be You/Hot Hot Hot!!				
			1990			3.00
"Spun Gold" reissue						
Elektra 69249		Lullaby/Homesick	1989			3.00
Elektra 69280		Love Song/2 Late	1989			3.00
First pressing: Red and black label						
Elektra 69280		Love Song/2 Late	1989		2.00	4.00
Second pressing: Gray label. Neither version issued with picture sleeve in U.S.						
Elektra 69300		Fascination Street/Babble	1989			3.00
Elektra 69300	PS	Fascination Street/Babble	1989			3.00
Elektra 69424		Hot Hot Hot!!!/Hey You!!!	1988			3.00
Elektra 69424	PS	Hot Hot Hot!!!/Hey You!!!	1988			3.00
Elektra 69443		Just Like Heaven/Breathe	1987	2.50	5.00	10.00
Sought-after especially by mobile DJs as well as Cure fans, as no reissue exists.						
Elektra 69443	PS	Just Like Heaven/Breathe	1987		2.50	5.00
Elektra 69474		Why Can't I Be You?/Japanese Dream				
			1987		2.00	4.00
Elektra 69474	PS	Why Can't I Be You?/Japanese Dream				
			1987		2.00	4.00
Elektra 69537		Let's Go to Bed/Boys Don't Cry	1986			3.00
Elektra 69537	PS	Let's Go to Bed/Boys Don't Cry	1986			3.00
Elektra 69551		Close to Me/Sinking	1986		2.00	4.00
Elektra 69604		In Between Days (Without You)/Stop Dead				
			1985		2.00	4.00
Elektra 69604	PS	In Between Days (Without You)/Stop Dead				
			1985		2.00	4.00
Sire PRO-A-2022	DJ	Let's Go to Bed (same on both sides)				
			1983	5.00	10.00	20.00
Sire 29376		The Love Cats/Speak My Language				
			1984	2.50	5.00	10.00
Sire 29490		The Walk/The Dream	1983	2.50	5.00	10.00

12-Inch Singles

Label, Number		Title	Year	VG	VG+	NM
Elektra ED 5118	DJ	Close to Me (Extended)/Close to Me (Edit Remix)				
			1985	3.75	7.50	15.00
Elektra ED 5146	DJ	Let's Go to Bed (same on both sides)				
			1986	3.00	6.00	12.00
Elektra ED 5175	DJ	Boys Don't Cry (2:36)/Boys Don't Cry (5:29)				
			1986	3.75	7.50	15.00
Elektra ED 5252	DJ	Just Like Heaven (Remix)/Just Like Heaven (LP Version)				
			1987	4.50	9.00	18.00

Label, Number		Title	Year	VG	VG+	NM
Elektra ED 5273	DJ	Hot Hot Hot (3 versions)	1987	2.00	4.00	8.00
Elektra ED 5374	DJ	Fascination Street (Extended)/Fascination Street (Remix)				
			1989	3.50	7.00	
Elektra ED 5390	DJ	Love Song (same on both sides)	1989	2.00	4.00	8.00
Elektra ED 5398	DJ	Love Song (Remix)/Love Song (Extended Remix)				
			1989	3.00	6.00	12.00
Elektra ED 5418	DJ	Lullaby (3 versions)	1989	3.00	6.00	12.00
Elektra ED 5452	DJ	Pictures of You (4:44)/Pictures of You (8:05)				
			1990	3.00	6.00	12.00
Elektra ED 5489	DJ	Never Enough (2 versions)/Harold and Joe/				
		Let's Go to Bed (Milk Mix)	1990	3.75	7.50	15.00
Elektra ED 5513	DJ	Close to Me (closer mix)/Just Like Heaven (dizzy mix)/				
		Primary (red mix)	1990	3.75	7.50	15.00
Elektra 66595		Close to Me (2 mixes)/Just Like Heaven (Dizzy Mix)				
			1990	2.00	4.00	8.00
Elektra 66604		Never Enough (Big Mix)/Harold and Joe/				
		Let's Go to Bed (Milk Mix)	1990	2.00	4.00	8.00
Elektra 66639		Pictures of You (Extended)/Last Dance (Live)/				
		Fascination Street (Live)	1990	2.00	4.00	8.00
Elektra 666??		Lullaby/Untitled/Homesick (Live)				
			1989	2.00	4.00	8.00
Elektra 66687		Love Song/2 Late/Fear of Ghosts				
			1989	2.50	5.00	10.00
Elektra 66704		Fascination Street/Babble/Out of Mind				
			1989	2.00	4.00	8.00
Elektra 66783		Hot Hot Hot (2 mixes)/Hey You (Extended)				
			1987	2.00	4.00	8.00
Elektra 66793		Just Like Heaven/Breathe/A Chain of Flowers				
			1987	3.00	6.00	12.00
Elektra 66810		Why Can't I Be You (Remix)/A Japanese Dream (vocal extended)				
			1987	2.50	5.00	10.00
Elektra 66856		A Night Like This/New Day/Close to Me/A Man Inside My Mouth				
			1985	4.50	9.00	18.00
Elektra 66882		In Between Days (2 versions)/Stop Dead				
			1985	3.75	7.50	15.00
Sire 20161		The Love Cats (extended)/Speak My Language/Mr. Pink Eyes				
			1983	3.00	6.00	12.00
Sire 29689		Let's Go to Bed (2 versions)/Just One Kiss				
			1983	5.00	10.00	20.00

Curiosity Killed the Cat

London pop/new wavish group.

Vinyl Albums

Mercury 842 010-1		Get Ahead	1989	3.00	6.00	12.00

12-Inch Singles

Mercury 870 101-1		Ordinary Day (2 versions)/Bullet	1987		3.00	6.00
Mercury 888 167-1		Down to Earth/(Instrumental)/Shallow Memory				
			1986	2.00	4.00	8.00
Mercury 888 752-1		Misfit (4 versions)	1986		3.00	6.00

Currie, Cherie and Marie

*Los Angeles sister act. Cherie Currie had been a member of **The Runaways**.*

Vinyl Albums

Capitol ST-12022		Messin' with the Boys	1979	5.00	10.00	20.00

Label, Number		Title	Year	VG	VG+	NM
45s						
Capitol 4754		Since You've Been Gone/Longer Than Forever				
			1979		2.50	5.00
Capitol 4754	PS	Since You've Been Gone/Longer Than Forever				
			1979	2.50	5.00	10.00
Capitol 4841		Secrets/This Time	1980		2.50	5.00
Capitol 4861		All I Want/Messin' with the Boys				
			1980		2.50	5.00

Cutting Crew

British pop group.

Label, Number		Title	Year	VG	VG+	NM
Vinyl Albums						
Virgin 90573		Broadcast	1987	2.50	5.00	10.00
Virgin 91239		The Scattering	1989	2.50	5.00	10.00
Virgin R 101103		The Scattering	1989	3.00	6.00	12.00
BMG Direct Marketing edition						
Virgin R 163456		Broadcast	1987	3.00	6.00	12.00
BMG Direct Marketing edition						
45s						
Virgin 99133		Last Thing	1990		*Cassette only*	
Virgin 99184		Everything But My Pride/Big Noise				
			1989			3.00
Virgin 99215		(Between a) Rock and a Hard Place/Card House				
			1989			3.00
Virgin 99215	PS	(Between a) Rock and a Hard Place/Card House				
			1989			3.00
Virgin 99425		I've Been in Love Before/Life Is a Dangerous Time				
			1987			3.00
Virgin 99425	PS	I've Been in Love Before/Life Is a Dangerous Time				
			1987			3.00
Virgin 99464		One for the Mockingbird/Mirror and a Blade (Live)				
			1987			3.00
Virgin 99464	PS	One for the Mockingbird/Mirror and a Blade (Live)				
			1987			3.00
Virgin 99481		(I Just) Died in Your Arms/For the Longest Time				
			1987			3.00
Virgin 99481	PS	(I Just) Died in Your Arms/For the Longest Time				
			1987			3.00
12-Inch Singles						
Virgin 2686	DJ	(Between a) Rock and a Hard Place/				
		(Between a) Rock and a Hard Place (Edit)				
			1989	2.00	4.00	8.00

D

D'Arby, Terence Trent

British rock and soul singer.

Label, Number	Title	Year	VG	VG+	NM
Vinyl Albums					
Columbia C 40964	Introducing the Hardline According to Terence Trent D'Arby				
		1987	3.00	6.00	12.00
Columbia C 45351	Neither Fish Nor Flesh	1989	2.50	5.00	10.00
45s					
Columbia 07398	If You Let Me Stay/Loving You Is Another Word for Lonely				
		1987			3.00

Label, Number		Title	Year	VG	VG+	NM
Columbia 07398	PS	If You Let Me Stay/Loving You Is Another Word for Lonely				
			1987			3.00
Columbia 07675		Wishing Well/Elevators and Hearts				
			1988			3.00
Columbia 07675	PS	Wishing Well/Elevators and Hearts				
			1988			3.00
Columbia 07911		Sign Your Name/Greasy Chicken				
			1988			3.00
Columbia 07911	PS	Sign Your Name/Greasy Chicken				
			1988			3.00
Columbia 08023		Dance Little Sister (Part One)/Dance Little Sister (Part Two)				
			1988			3.00
Columbia 08023	PS	Dance Little Sister (Part One)/Dance Little Sister (Part Two)				
			1988			3.00
Columbia 73074		This Side of Love/Sad Song for Sister Sarah Serenade				
			1989			3.00
Columbia 73217		To Know Someone Deeply Is to Know Someone Softly/				
		Loose Variations on a Dead Man's Vibe in C Sharp Minor				
			1990	*May be cassette-only*		
Columbia 74963		Do You Love Me Like You Say?/She Kissed Me				
			1993	*Cassette only*		
Columbia 77128		Delicate/She Kissed Me	1993	*Cassette only*		
Columbia 77231		Let Her Down Easy/Come to Me	1993	*Cassette only*		

12-Inch Singles

Label, Number		Title	Year	VG	VG+	NM
Columbia CAS 01070	DJ	Under My Thumb (Live) (same on both sides)				
			198?	3.00	6.00	12.00
May only exist as a test pressing						
Columbia CAS 01141	DJ	Sign Your Name (12" Remix)/Sign Your Name (LP)				
			1988	3.00	6.00	12.00
Columbia CAS 01181	DJ	Sign Your Name (Lee Perry Remix)				
			1987	3.00	6.00	12.00
Advance pressing, no label name on label						
Columbia CAS 2855	DJ	If You Let Me Stay (4 mixes)	1987	2.00	4.00	8.00
Columbia CAS 02888	DJ	Wishing Well (LP Version)/Wishing Well (Cool in the Shade Mix)				
			1987	2.00	4.00	8.00
Columbia 07450		If You Let Me Stay (2 versions)/Loving You Is Another				
		Word for Lonely	1987	2.00	4.00	8.00
Columbia 07543		Wishing Well (Cool in the Shade Mix)/Wonderful World + 1				
			1987	2.00	4.00	8.00
Columbia 07887		Dance Little Sister (3 mixes)	1988	2.00	4.00	8.00
Columbia 74949		Do You Love Me Like You Say? (5 versions)				
			1993	2.00	4.00	8.00

D.N.A. featuring Suzanne Vega

British remixers create a dance-pop hit out of an acapella song.

45s

Label, Number		Title	Year	VG	VG+	NM
A&M/Collectables 8699		Tom's Diner/Tom's Diner (Original Version)				
			1992			3.00
First U.S. 45 of 1990 hit						

12-Inch Singles

Label, Number		Title	Year	VG	VG+	NM
A&M 75021 2342 1		Tom's Diner (12" Version) (7" Version)//(Reprise)				
		(Original Version)	1990	2.00	4.00	8.00
A&M 75021 7305 1	DJ	Rusted Pipe (5 versions)	1991	2.00	4.00	8.00

Label, Number		Title	Year	VG	VG+	NM

Dada
Los Angeles rock band.

45s

I.R.S. S7-19107		I Get High/Dizz Knee Land	1996			3.00

Dale
*Formerly of **Missing Persons**.*

Vinyl Albums

Paisley Park 25577		Riot in English	1988	2.50	5.00	10.00

45s

Paisley Park 27731		Riot in English (Edit)/Riot in English (LP Version)				
			1988			3.00
Paisley Park 28142		Simon Simon/The Perfect Stranger				
			1987			3.00

12-Inch Singles

| Paisley Park 20818 | | Simon Simon (Extended)/Simon Simon (Dub)/The Perfect Stranger | | | | |
| | | | 1988 | 2.00 | 4.00 | 8.00 |

Damned, The
British punkers, they have broken up and re-formed several times.

Vinyl Albums

Frontier 1003		Damned Damned Damned	1987	3.00	6.00	12.00
Reissue of 1976-77 material						
I.R.S. SP-70012		The Black Album	1980	3.00	6.00	12.00
MCA 5966		Anything	1987	3.00	6.00	12.00
MCA 2-8024	(2)	Light at the End of the Tunnel	1988	3.75	7.50	15.00
MCA 39039		Phantasmagoria	1986	3.00	6.00	12.00

45s

I.R.S. 9022		Dr. Jeckyl and Mr. Hyde/Looking at You (Live)				
			1981	2.00	4.00	8.00
I.R.S. 9022		Dr. Jeckyl and Mr. Hyde/Looking at You (Live)				
			1981	2.00	4.00	8.00
MCA 53051		Alone Again Or/In Dulce Decorum				
			1987			3.00
MCA 53051	PS	Alone Again Or/In Dulce Decorum				
			1987			3.00

12-Inch Singles

MCA 17235	DJ	In Dulce Decorum (same on both sides)				
			1986	2.00	4.00	8.00
MCA 23625		Eloise/Beat Girl/Temptation	1986	2.00	4.00	8.00
MCA 23721		Anything/Year of the Jackal/Thanks for the Night				
			1986	2.00	4.00	8.00

Danzig
*Metal band formed by **Glenn Danzig**, ex-**Misfits**.*

Vinyl Albums

American 45647		4	1994	3.00	6.00	12.00
Def American DEF 24208		Danzig	1988	3.00	6.00	12.00
Def American DEF 24281		Lucifuge	1990	3.00	6.00	12.00

12-Inch Singles

| Def American PRO-A-4121 | DJ | Her Black Wings (same on both sides) | | | | |
| | | | 1990 | 2.00 | 4.00 | 8.00 |

Label, Number		Title	Year	VG	VG+	NM

Danzig, Glenn
Member of The Misfits, Samhain and Danzig.

Vinyl Albums
Plan 9 PL9-11		Black Aria	1992	3.00	6.00	12.00

45s
Plan 9 PL 1015		Who Killed Marilyn?/Spook City USA	1981	125.00	250.00	500.00

Black and purple swirl vinyl (25 made); value is conjecture

Plan 9 PL 1015		Who Killed Marilyn?/Spook City USA	1981	33.75	67.50	135.00

Purple vinyl (500 made)

Plan 9 PL 1015		Who Killed Marilyn?/Spook City USA	1981	16.25	32.50	65.00

Black vinyl (5,000 made)

Plan 9 PL 1015	PS	Who Killed Marilyn?/Spook City USA	1981	16.25	32.50	65.00

Das Damen

45s
SST PSST 190	DJ	Reverse Into Tomorrow/Bug	1988	3.75	7.50	15.00

No picture sleeve, but with tour dates insert (deduct 1/3 if insert is missing)

Sub Pop 39		Sad Mile/Making Time	1989	3.00	6.25	12.50

#9 in Sub Pop Singles Club series

Sub Pop 39	PS	Sad Mile/Making Time	1989	3.00	6.25	12.50
Twin/Tone TTR 89139	DJ	Noon Daylight/Damen Dance	1989	2.00	4.00	8.00
Twin/Tone TTR 89139	PS	Noon Daylight/Damen Dance	1989	2.00	4.00	8.00

David and David
Los Angeles duo.

Vinyl Albums
A&M SP 5134		Boomtown	1986	2.50	5.00	10.00
A&M R 183799		Boomtown	1987	3.00	6.00	12.00

RCA Music Service edition

45s
A&M 2857		Welcome to the Boomtown/A Rock for the Forgotten	1986			3.00
A&M 2857	PS	Welcome to the Boomtown/A Rock for the Forgotten	1986			3.00
A&M 2882		Swallowed by the Cracks/All Alone in the Big City	1986			3.00
A&M 2905		Ain't So Easy/Swimming in the Ocean	1987			3.00
A&M 2905	PS	Ain't So Easy/Swimming in the Ocean	1987			3.00

Davis, Martha
Formerly of The Motels.

Vinyl Albums
Capitol CLT-48054		Policy	1988	3.00	6.00	12.00
Capitol CLT-79197/8	DJ	Policy (Radio Cue Card)	1987	6.25	12.50	25.00

45s
Capitol 44058		Don't Tell Me the Time/My Promise	1987			3.00
Capitol 44058	PS	Don't Tell Me the Time/My Promise	1987			3.00

Label, Number		Title	Year	VG	VG+	NM
Capitol 44105		Just Like You/Rebecca				3.00
Capitol 44114		Tell It to the Moon/Bridge of Sighs				
			1987			3.00
Capitol 44114	PS	Tell It to the Moon/Bridge of Sighs				
			1987			3.00
Elektra 69482		We've Never Danced	1987			3.00

12-Inch Singles

Label, Number		Title	Year	VG	VG+	NM
Capitol SPRO 79188	DJ	Just Like You (same on both sides)				
			1987		3.00	6.00

Davis, Martha, and Sly Stone

45s

Label, Number	Title	Year	VG	VG+	NM
A&M 2896	Love and Affection/Black Girls	1986			3.00
B-side by Rae Dawn Chong					

dB's, The

New York City pop-rock group.

Vinyl Albums

Label, Number	Title	Year	VG	VG+	NM
Bearsville 25146	Like This	1984	3.75	7.50	15.00
I.R.S. 42055	The Sound of Music	1987	3.00	6.00	12.00
Rhino R1-70891	Like This	1988	2.50	5.00	10.00
Reissue of Bearsville LP					

45s

Label, Number		Title	Year	VG	VG+	NM
Bearsville 29188		Love Is for Lovers/Darby Hall	1984		2.00	4.00
Car (# unknown)		If and When/I Thought (You Wanted to Know)				
			1978		3.75	7.50
Car (# unknown)	PS	If and When/I Thought (You Wanted to Know)				
			1978		3.75	7.50
I.R.S. 53198		I Lie (Edited)/Sharon	1987			3.00
I.R.S. 53198	PS	I Lie (Edited)/Sharon	1987			3.00
MCA 53468		The Changing Times/21 Jump Street				
			1988			3.00
B-side by Holly Robinson						
Shake 100		Black and White/Soul Kiss Part 1 & 2				
			1980		2.00	4.00
Shake 100	PS	Black and White/Soul Kiss Part 1 & 2				
			1980		2.00	4.00

De La Soul

Psychedelic rappers.

Vinyl Albums

Label, Number		Title	Year	VG	VG+	NM
Tommy Boy 1019		3 Feet High and Rising	1989	2.50	5.00	10.00
Tommy Boy 1029		De La Soul Is Dead	1991	3.75	7.50	15.00
Tommy Boy 1041	(2) DJ	De La Soul Is Dead	1991	6.25	12.50	25.00
Promo-only two-record set						

12-Inch Singles

Label, Number	Title	Year	VG	VG+	NM
Tommy Boy 500	Millie Pulled a Pistol on Santa (2 versions)/Keepin' the Faith				
	(6 versions)	1991	2.00	4.00	8.00
Tommy Boy 586	Breakadawn (3 versions)/Stickabush/Hsubakkits/En Focus				
		1993	2.00	4.00	8.00
Tommy Boy 990	A Roller Skating Jam Named Saturdays (8 mixes)				
		1991	2.00	4.00	8.00

Label, Number		Title	Year	VG	VG+	NM

Dead Boys

Cleveland punk/new wave band. **Stiv Bators later recorded solo.**

Vinyl Albums

Label, Number		Title	Year	VG	VG+	NM
Bomp! 4017		Night of the Living Dead Boys	1981	3.75	7.50	15.00
Sire SR-6038		Young, Loud & Snotty	1977	5.00	10.00	20.00
Sire SRK-6054		We Have Come for Your Children				
			1978	5.00	10.00	20.00

45s

Label, Number		Title	Year	VG	VG+	NM
Sire 1004		Sonic Reducer/Down in Flames	1977	3.00	6.00	12.00
Sire 1004	PS	Sonic Reducer/Down in Flames	1977	3.00	6.00	12.00
Sire 1029		Tell Me/Not Anymore/Ain't Nothin' to Do				
			1978	3.75	7.50	15.00
Sire 1029	PS	Tell Me/Not Anymore/Ain't Nothin' to Do				
			1978	3.75	7.50	15.00

Dead Kennedys

Outrageous San Francisco punk band led by Jello Biafra. Band was a frequent target of would-be censors.

Vinyl Albums

Label, Number	Title	Year	VG	VG+	NM
Alternative Tentacles VIRUS 1	Fresh Fruit for Rotting Vegetables				
		1988	3.00	6.00	12.00
Reissue of I.R.S. album					
Alternative Tentacles VIRUS 5 EP	In God We Trust, Inc.	1981	3.00	6.00	12.00
Alternative Tentacles VIRUS 27	Plastic Surgery Disasters	1982	3.00	6.00	12.00
Alternative Tentacles VIRUS 45	Frankenchrist	1985	2.50	5.00	10.00

Originals have a poster of H.R. Giger's painting Landscape #20, which was involved in an obscenity trial. The poster is still available, but only by mailing in a coupon inside the LP

Label, Number	Title	Year	VG	VG+	NM
Alternative Tentacles VIRUS 50	Bedtime for Democracy	1986	3.00	6.00	12.00

Originals have a newspaper insert

Label, Number	Title	Year	VG	VG+	NM
Alternative Tentacles VIRUS 57	Give Me Convenience or Give Me Death				
		1987	2.50	5.00	10.00
Faulty Products 70014	Fresh Fruit for Rotting Vegetables				
		1982	8.75	17.50	35.00

With nursing home photo on back cover, no reference to I.R.S. on label or cover

Label, Number	Title	Year	VG	VG+	NM
I.R.S./Faulty Products SP-70014	Fresh Fruit for Rotting Vegetables				
		1980	5.00	10.00	20.00

Originals have an orange cover "to distinguish it from imports"

Label, Number	Title	Year	VG	VG+	NM
I.R.S./Faulty Products SP-70014	Fresh Fruit for Rotting Vegetables				
		1980	3.75	7.50	15.00

Reissues have a black front cover, same as imports; it was changed at the insistence of band member Jello Biafra

45s

Label, Number	Title	Year	VG	VG+	NM
Alternative Tentacles VIRUS 2	Too Drunk to Fuck/The Prey	1981	2.00	4.00	8.00
Alternative Tentacles VIRUS 2 PS	Too Drunk to Fuck/The Prey	1981	2.00	4.00	8.00
Picture sleeve and lyric insert					
Alternative Tentacles VIRUS 6	Nazi Punks Fuck Off/Moral Majority				
		1981		3.75	7.50
Alternative Tentacles VIRUS 6 PS	Nazi Punks Fuck Off/Moral Majority				
	1981	3.75			7.50
Lyric sheet and armband in plastic bag, not actually a picture sleeve					
Alternative Tentacles VIRUS 23	Bleed for Me/Life Sentence	1982		2.50	5.00
Alternative Tentacles VIRUS 23 PS	Bleed for Me/Life Sentence	1982		2.50	5.00
Alternative Tentacles VIRUS 28	Halloween/Saturday Night Holocaust				
		1982		2.50	5.00
Alternative Tentacles VIRUS 28 PS	Halloween/Saturday Night Holocaust				
		1982		2.50	5.00
Alternative Tentacles AT-95-41	California Uber Alles/The Man with the Dogs				
		1979	5.00	10.00	20.00
Alternative Tentacles AT-95-41 PS	California Uber Alles/The Man with the Dogs				
		1979	5.00	10.00	20.00

Picture sleeve and lyric insert

Label, Number		Title	Year	VG	VG+	NM
I.R.S./Faulty Products 9016		Holiday in Cambodia/Policetruck				
			1980	2.50	5.00	10.00
I.R.S./Faulty Products 9016	PS	Holiday in Cambodia/Policetruck				
			1980	2.50	5.00	10.00
Optional Music OPT-2		California Uber Alles/The Man with the Dogs				
			1979	3.00	6.00	12.00
Optional Music OPT-2	PS	California Uber Alles/The Man with the Dogs				
			1979	3.00	6.00	12.00
Optional Music OPT-4		Holiday in Cambodia/Policetruck				
			1980	2.50	5.00	10.00
Optional Music OPT-4	PS	Holiday in Cambodia/Policetruck				
			1980	2.50	5.00	10.00
Picture sleeve and lyric insert						
Subterranean SUB 24		Nazi Punks Fuck Off/Moral Majority				
			1981	2.50	5.00	10.00
Subterranean SUB 24	PS	Nazi Punks Fuck Off/Moral Majority				
			1981	2.50	5.00	10.00
Lyric sheet and armband in plastic bag, not actually a picture sleeve						

12-Inch Singles

Label, Number	Title	Year	VG	VG+	NM
Alternative Tentacles VIRUS 23	Bleed for Me/Life Sentence	1982	2.00	4.00	8.00
Alternative Tentacles VIRUS 28	Halloween/Saturday Night Holocaust				
		1982	2.00	4.00	8.00

Dead Milkmen, The

Philadelphia-area punk band. Name was a parody of punk-rock names.

Vinyl Albums

Label, Number		Title	Year	VG	VG+	NM
Enigma D1-73260		Bucky Fellini	1988	3.75	7.50	15.00
Enigma 73351		Beelzebubba	1988	3.75	7.50	15.00
Fever/Enigma 72054		Big Lizard in My Backyard	1985	4.50	9.00	18.00
Restless 72131		Eat Your Paisley	1988	3.75	7.50	15.00

12-Inch Singles

Enigma 039	DJ	Big Time Operator (same on both sides)				
			1987	2.00	4.00	8.00
Enigma EPRO 188	DJ	Smokin' Banana Peels (Edit) (same on both sides)				
			1989	2.00	4.00	8.00
Enigma EPRO 189	DJ	Smokin' Banana Peels (LP version + 3 remixes)				
			1989	2.50	5.00	10.00

Dead Moon

45s

Sub Pop 200		Dirty Noise/Dark Deception	1993		2.50	5.00
Clear vinyl						
Sub Pop 200	PS	Dirty Noise/Dark Deception	1993		2.50	5.00
#53 in Sub Pop Singles Club series						

Dead Or Alive

British synth-pop/dance group. They had the first U.S. hit of a Stock/Aitken/Waterman production.

Vinyl Albums

Epic BFE 40119	Youthquake	1985	3.00	6.00	12.00
Epic FE 40572	Mad, Bad and Dangerous to Know				
		1986	3.00	6.00	12.00
Epic OE 44255	Rip It Up	1988	2.50	5.00	10.00

45s

Epic 04309	What I Want/The Stranger	1984		2.50	5.00
Epic 04573	That's the Way (I Like It)/Do It	1984		2.50	5.00

Label, Number		Title	Year	VG	VG+	NM
Epic 04894		You Spin Me Round (Like a Record)/Misty Circles				
			1985		2.00	4.00
Epic 05607		Lover Come Back to Me/Far Too Hard				
			1985			3.00
Epic 05607	PS	Lover Come Back to Me/Far Too Hard				
			1985			3.00
Epic 05832		My Heart Goes Bang (Get Me to the Doctor)/My Cake And Eat It				
			1986			3.00
Epic 06374		Brand New Lover/In Too Deep	1986			3.00
Epic 06374	PS	Brand New Lover/In Too Deep	1986			3.00
Epic 07022		Something in My House/D.J. Hit That Button				
			1987			3.00
Epic 07022	PS	Something in My House/D.J. Hit That Button				
			1987		3.00	6.00
Epic 08468		You Spin Me Round (Like a Record)/Lover Come Back to Me				
			1988			3.00
Reissue						
Epic 08469		That's the Way (I Like It)/My Heart Goes Bang				
		(Get Me to the Doctor)	1988			3.00
Reissue						
Epic 68885		Come Home With Me Baby/Come Home With Me Baby				
			1989			3.00

12-Inch Singles

Label, Number		Title	Year	VG	VG+	NM
Epic 04202		What I Want (Dance Remix)/The Stranger				
			1983	3.00	6.00	12.00
Epic 04979		I'd Do Anything/I'd Do Anything (Megamix)				
			1983	3.00	6.00	12.00
Epic 05012		That's the Way (I Like It)/Keep That Body Strong				
			1983	2.50	5.00	10.00
Epic 05208		You Spin Me Round (Like a Record)/Misty Circles				
			1985	2.00	4.00	8.00
Epic 05278		Lover Come Back to Me (2 versions)/Far Too Hard				
			1985	2.50	5.00	10.00
Epic 05327		My Heart Goes Bang (2 versions)	1985	2.50	5.00	10.00
Epic 05965		Brand New Lover (3 versions)/In Too Deep (Live)				
			1986	2.00	4.00	8.00
Epic 06750		Something in My House (4 mixes)	1987	2.00	4.00	8.00
Epic 07482		I'll Save You All My Kisses (2 remixes)/				
		I Wanna Be Your Toy (new version)				
			1985	2.00	4.00	8.00
Epic 68777		Come Home with Me Baby (LP)/Come Home with Me Baby				
		(Deadhouse Dub)	1989		3.00	6.00
Epic 73101		Baby Don't Say Goodbye (5 versions)				
			1989	2.00	4.00	8.00

Deadbeats

7-Inch Extended Play Singles

Label, Number		Title	Year	VG	VG+	NM
Dangerhouse IQ 29		Kill the Hippies	1978	6.25	12.50	25.00
Yellow vinyl						
Dangerhouse IQ 29		Kill the Hippies	1978	5.00	10.00	20.00
Dangerhouse IQ 29	PS	Kill the Hippies	1978	5.00	10.00	20.00

Deee-Lite

Neo-psychedelic dance trio.

Vinyl Albums

Label, Number		Title	Year	VG	VG+	NM
Elektra 60957		World Clique	1990	2.50	5.00	10.00
Elektra 61313	(2)	Infinity Within	1992	3.00	6.00	12.00
Elektra 61526	(2)	Dewdrops in the Garden	1994	3.00	6.00	12.00

Label, Number		Title	Year	VG	VG+	NM
45s						
Elektra 64912		Power of Love/Deee-Lite Theme				
			1990		2.00	4.00
Elektra 65930		Groove Is In the Heart/Power of Love				
			1992			3.00
Spun Gold issue; first U.S. 45 of A-side hit						
12-Inch Singles						
Elektra ED 5471	DJ	Groove Is in the Heart (3 mixes)/What Is Love? (3 mixes)				
			1990	2.50	5.00	10.00
Elektra ED 5507	DJ	Power of Love (2 versions)/Build the Bridge/				
		How Do You Say...Love	1990	2.50	5.00	10.00
Elektra ED 5531	DJ	ESP (3 versions)	1990	2.50	5.00	10.00
Elektra ED 5600	(2) DJ	Runaway (7 versions)	1990	3.00	6.00	12.00
Elektra ED 5713	(2) DJ	Call Me (8 versions)	1994	5.00	10.00	20.00
Elektra 66201		Picnic in the Summertime (6 versions)/				
		Music Selector Is the Soul Reflector				
			1994		3.00	6.00
Elektra 66223		Bring Me Your Love (5 versions) + 1				
			1994		3.00	6.00
Elektra 66368		Thank You Everyday (4 versions)	1992	2.00	4.00	8.00
Elektra 66424		Runaway (4 versions)/Rubber Love (2 versions)				
			1992	2.00	4.00	8.00
Elektra 66550		ESP (2 versions)/Good Beat (3 versions)/Riding On Through/				
		Beatapella	1990	2.00	4.00	8.00

Del Amitri

Scottish pop-rock group.

Label, Number		Title	Year	VG	VG+	NM
Vinyl Albums						
A&M SP-5287		Waking Hours	1990	3.00	6.00	12.00
Chrysalis BFV 41499		Del Amitri	1985	3.00	6.00	12.00
45s						
A&M 1485		Kiss This Thing Goodbye/The Return of Maggie Brown				
			1990			*Cassette only*
A&M 31458 1322 7		Tell Her This/Roll to Me	1996			3.00
12-Inch Singles						
A&M SP-17995	DJ	Kiss This Thing Goodbye/The Return of Maggie Brown/				
		Slowly, It's Coming Back	1989	3.00	6.00	12.00
A&M 75021 8076 1	DJ	Stone Cold Sober/Another Letter Home/April the First/				
		More Than You'd Ever Know	1990	3.00	6.00	12.00

Del Fuegos, The

Boston band.

Label, Number		Title	Year	VG	VG+	NM
Vinyl Albums						
RCA 9860		Smoking in the Fields	1989	2.50	5.00	10.00
Slash 25174		The Longest Day	1984	2.50	5.00	10.00
Slash 25339		Boston, Mass.	1985	2.50	5.00	10.00
Slash 25540		Stand Up	1987	2.50	5.00	10.00
45s						
Czech 71		I Can't Sleep/I Always Call Her Back				
			1983	2.00	4.00	8.00
Czech 71	PS	I Can't Sleep/I Always Call Her Back				
			1983	2.00	4.00	8.00
Slash 28262		I'll Sleep with You (Cha Cha D'Amour)/I Can't Take This				
			1987			3.00
Slash 28822		I Still Want You/Hand in Hand	1986			3.00

Label, Number		Title	Year	VG	VG+	NM
Slash 28822	DJ	I Still Want You (LP Version)/I Still Want You (Horny Mix)				
			1986		2.00	4.00
Slash 28822	PS	I Still Want You/Hand in Hand	1986			3.00
12-Inch Singles						
Slash PRO-A-2372	DJ	Don't Run Wild (same on both sides)				
			1985		3.00	6.00
Slash PRO-A-2414	DJ	I Still Want You/I Still Want You (Horny Mix)				
			1985		3.00	6.00
Slash PRO-A-2486	DJ	It's Alright (same on both sides)	1985		3.00	6.00
Slash PRO-A-2681	DJ	Long Slide (same on both sides)	1987		3.00	6.00
Slash PRO-A-2720	DJ	Name Names (same on both sides)				
			1987		3.00	6.00
Slash PRO-A-2769	DJ	Wear It Like a Cape (same on both sides)				
			1987		3.00	6.00

Del Lords, The

Vinyl Albums						
EMI America ST-17183		Johnny Comes Marching Home	1986	3.00	6.00	12.00
Enigma D1-73326		Based on a True Story	1988	2.50	5.00	10.00
45s						
Enigma EPRO 090	DJ	Judas Kiss (Radio Edit)/Judas Kiss (Vocal Edit)				
			1988		3.00	6.00
12-Inch Singles						
Enigma 097	DJ	A Lover's Prayer (same on both sides)				
			1988		3.00	6.00

Depeche Mode

*British synth-pop/new wave band. Original group had Vince Clarke before he left to form **Yaz** and later **Erasure**.*

Vinyl Albums						
Sire SRK 3642		Speak & Spell	1981	3.75	7.50	15.00
Sire PRO-A-5192	(2) DJ	Selections from the Commercially Available Box Sets One and Two				
			1991	6.25	12.50	25.00
Promo-only sampler						
Sire PRO-A-5242	(2) DJ	Selections from the Commercially Available Box Set Three				
			1991	10.00	20.00	40.00
Promo-only sampler						
Sire 23751		A Broken Frame	1982	3.00	6.00	12.00
Sire 23900		Construction Time Again	1983	3.00	6.00	12.00
Sire 25124		People Are People	1984	3.00	6.00	12.00
Sire 25194		Some Great Reward	1984	3.00	6.00	12.00
Sire 25346		Catching Up With Depeche Mode				
			1985	2.50	5.00	10.00
Sire 25429		Black Celebration	1986	2.50	5.00	10.00
Sire 25614		Music for the Masses	1987	2.50	5.00	10.00
Sire 25853	(2)	101	1989	3.75	7.50	15.00
Sire 26081		Violator	1990	3.75	7.50	15.00
Sire R 100560		Catching Up with Depeche Mode				
			1990	3.00	6.00	12.00
BMG Direct Marketing edition; reissue						
Sire R 100598		Music for the Masses	1988	3.00	6.00	12.00
BMG Direct Marketing edition						
Sire R 143674		Catching Up with Depeche Mode				
			1985	3.00	6.00	12.00
RCA Music Service edition						
Sire R 173408		Violator	1990	3.75	7.50	15.00
BMG Direct Marketing edition						

Label, Number		Title	Year	VG	VG+	NM
45s						
Sire 18506		Walking in My Shoes/My Joy	1993			3.00
Sire 18600		I Feel You/One Caress	1993			3.00
Sire 18889		Personal Jesus/Policy of Truth	1992			3.00
First U.S. 45 release of A-side						
Sire 18890		World in My Eyes/Enjoy the Silence				
			1992			3.00
First U.S. 45 release of A-side						
Sire 19580		World in My Eyes	1990		*Cassette only*	
Sire 19842		Policy of Truth/Kaleid	1990			3.00
Sire 19885		Enjoy the Silence/Memphisto	1990			3.00
Sire 19941		Personal Jesus	1990		*Cassette only*	
Sire 21886		Strangelove/Behind the Wheel	198?			3.00
"Back to Back Hits" reissue						
Sire 21994		People Are People/A Question of Lust				
			198?			3.00
"Back to Back Hits" reissue						
Sire 22993		Nothing/Nothing (instrumental)	1989			3.00
Sire 27777		Strangelove/Nothing	1988			3.00
Sire 27777	PS	Strangelove/Nothing	1988			3.00
Sire 27991		Route 66/Behind the Wheel//Behind the Wheel				
			1988			3.00
Sire 27991	PS	Route 66/Behind the Wheel//Behind the Wheel				
			1988			3.00
Sire 28189		Never Let Me Down Again/Pleasure-Little Treasure				
			1987			3.00
Sire 28189	PS	Never Let Me Down Again/Pleasure-Little Treasure				
			1987			3.00
Sire 28366		Strangelove/FPMIP	1987			3.00
Sire 28366	PS	Strangelove/FPMIP	1987			3.00
Sire 28564		But Not Tonight/Stripped	1986			3.00
Sire 28697		A Question of Lust/Christmas Island				
			1986			3.00
Sire 28697	PS	A Question of Lust/Christmas Island				
			1986			3.00
Sire 28835		Share the Disease/Flexible	1985		2.50	5.00
Sire 28918		Master and Servant/(Set Me Free) Remotivate Me				
			1985			3.00
Sire 28918	PS	Master and Servant/(Set Me Free) Remotivate Me				
			1985			3.00
Sire 29221		People Are People/In Your Memory				
			1984			3.00
Sire 29221	PS	People Are People/In Your Memory				
			1984			3.00
Sire 29482		Everything Counts/Work Hard	1983			3.00
Sire 29482	PS	Everything Counts/Work Hard	1983			3.00
Sire 50029		Just Can't Get Enough/Tora, Tora, Tora				
			1982		2.50	5.00
12-Inch Singles						
Sire PRO-A-1084	DJ	Leave in Silence/Photograph/My Secret Garden (2 versions)				
			1982	7.50	15.00	30.00
Sire PRO-A-2221	DJ	Master and Servant (LP version)/Master and Servant				
		(Black and Blue version)	1984	7.50	15.00	30.00
Sire PRO-A-2271	DJ	Blasphemous Rumours/Something to Do/Remotivate Me (Edit)				
			1985	12.50	25.00	50.00
Sire PRO-A-2504	DJ	A Question of Lust (Remix Edit)/A Question of Lust (LP Version)				
			1986	7.50	15.00	30.00
Sire PRO-A-2952	DJ	Behind the Wheel (4 versions)	1987	5.00	10.00	20.00
Sire PRO-A-4507	DJ	World in My Eyes (Single Edit)/World in My Eyes (Oil Tank Mix)				
			1990	3.75	7.50	15.00

Label, Number		Title	Year	VG	VG+	NM
Sire PRO-A-6022	DJ	I Feel You (5 versions)	1993	3.75	7.50	15.00
Sire 20165		Everything Counts (7:23)/Work Hard (6:58)				
			1983	3.00	6.00	12.00
Sire 20214		People Are People (2 mixes)/In Your Memory				
			1984	2.50	5.00	10.00
Sire 20283		Master and Servant/Remotivate Me/Are People People?				
			1984	2.50	5.00	10.00
Sire 20402		It's Called a Heart (3 mixes)/Flexible (Deportation Mix)				
			1985	3.75	7.50	15.00
Sire 20530		A Question of Time/Something to Do (Live)				
			1986	2.50	5.00	10.00
Sire 20578		But Not Tonight (extended)/Breathing In Fumes/ Stripped (Highland Mix)/Black Day				
			1986	2.50	5.00	10.00
Sire 20769		Strangelove (Pain Mix)/Strangelove (7" Mix)/Agent Orange				
			1987	2.50	5.00	10.00
Sire 20858		Behind the Wheel/Route 66 (4 versions)				
			1987	2.50	5.00	10.00
Sire 21022		Strangelove (Remix)/Strangelove (Remix Edit)/Nothing (2 versions)				
			1987	2.50	5.00	10.00
Sire 21183		Everything Counts (2 mixes)/Everything Counts (Live)/ Sacred (Live)/Nothing (Live)	1989	2.50	5.00	10.00
Sire 21534		Policy of Truth (3 versions)/Kaleid				
			1990	2.00	4.00	8.00
Sire 21735		World in My Eyes (3 versions)/Seas of Sin/Happiest Girl				
			1990	2.50	5.00	10.00
Sire 29704		Get the Balance Right//The Great Outdoors/Tora, Tora, Tora				
			1983	2.50	5.00	10.00
Sire 29957		See You (2 versions)/The Meaning of Love/Now This Is Fun				
			1982	5.00	10.00	20.00
Sire 40852		Walking in My Shoes (5 mixes)/My Joy				
			1993	2.00	4.00	8.00
Sire 41058		Condemnation (Live)/Condemnation (Paris Mix)/ Enjoy the Silence (Live)/Halo (Live)/Death's Door/Rush				
			1993	2.00	4.00	8.00
Sire 41362		In Your Room (3 versions)/Higher Love (Adrenaline Mix)				
			1994	2.00	4.00	8.00

Desendants

Seattle punk band. Not to be confused with the mid-80s band spelled "Descendents."

45s

A.O.M. 445		Unnational Anthem/Face Lift	1980	25.00	50.00	100.00

DeVille, Willy

Formerly of Mink DeVille.

45s

A&M 2987		Assassin of Love/I Call Your Name				
			1987			3.00

12-Inch Singles

A&M 17538	DJ	Angel Eyes (same on both sides)				
			1987		3.00	6.00

Label, Number		Title	Year	VG	VG+	NM

Devo
Akron, Ohio-based synth-pop band led by Mark Mothersbaugh.

Vinyl Albums

Label, Number		Title	Year	VG	VG+	NM
Dutch East India DE-112008-1		Smooth Noodle Maps	1991	3.75	7.50	15.00
Red vinyl, 1,000 copies pressed						
Enigma EPRO 326	DJ	Smooth Noodle Maps	1990	5.00	10.00	20.00
Promo only, no picture cover						
Enigma 73303		Total Devo	1988	2.50	5.00	10.00
Enigma 73514		Now It Can Be Told!	1989	2.50	5.00	10.00
Warner Bros. PRO-A-928	EP	Freedom of Choice/Whip It/Be Still/Gates of Steel				
			1980	2.50	5.00	10.00
Promo version of "Dev-O Live"						
Warner Bros. BSK 3239		Q: Are We Not Men? A: We Are Devo!				
			1978	2.50	5.00	10.00
Warner Bros. BSK 3337		Duty Now for the Future	1979	2.50	5.00	10.00
Warner Bros. BSK 3435		Freedom of Choice	1980	2.50	5.00	10.00
Warner Bros. MINI 3548	EP	Dev-O Live	1981	2.50	5.00	10.00
All copies came in plastic sleeve						
Warner Bros. BSK 3595		New Traditionalists	1981	3.75	7.50	15.00
First pressings include bonus 45 (EP 3595) and poster; deduct 1/3 if missing						
Warner Bros. 23741		Oh No! It's Devo	1982	2.50	5.00	10.00
Warner Bros. W1-23741		Oh No! It's Devo	1982	3.00	6.00	12.00
Columbia House version, no easel cutout on back cover						
Warner Bros. 25097		Shout	1984	2.50	5.00	10.00

45s

Label, Number		Title	Year	VG	VG+	NM
Backstreet 52215		Theme from Doctor Detroit/King of Soul				
			1983			3.00
B-side by James Brown						
Booji Boy 7033-14		Jocko Homo/Mongoloid	1977	2.00	4.00	8.00
Booji Boy 7033-14	PS	Jocko Homo/Mongoloid	1977	2.00	4.00	8.00
Booji Boy 72843/75677		Satisfaction/Sloppy	1978			3.00
Still available from Bomp! Records as of 1995 without picture sleeve						
Booji Boy 72843/75677	PS	Satisfaction/Sloppy	1978	2.00	4.00	8.00
Enigma 75023		Disco Dancer/Disco Dancer	1989			3.00
Enigma 75029		Baby Doll (Ivan Ivan Mix)/Baby Doll (Devo Mix)				
			1988			3.00
Enigma 75029	PS	Baby Doll (Ivan Ivan Mix)/Baby Doll (Devo Mix)				
			1988			3.00
Full Moon/Asylum 47204		Working in the Coal Mine/Planet Earth				
			1981			3.00
Full Moon/Asylum 47204	PS	Working in the Coal Mine/Planet Earth				
			1981			3.00
Reflex 5		Bush Whacked	1988			3.00
One-sided flexi-disc given away with Reflex magazine						
Warner Bros. GWB 0400		Whip It/Girl U Want	198?			3.00
Back to Back Hits series						
Warner Bros. EP 3595		Working in the Coal Mine (same on both sides)				
			1981			3.00
Issued with the New Traditionalists LP						
Warner Bros. 8675		(I Can't Get No) Satisfaction/Uncontrollable Urge				
			1978			3.00
Warner Bros. 8745		Come Back Jonee/Praying Hands				
			1979			3.00
Warner Bros. 29133		Are You Experienced/Growing Pains				
			1984			3.00
Warner Bros. 29133	PS	Are You Experienced/Growing Pains				
			1984			3.00
Warner Bros. 29811		That's Good/What I Must Do	1983			3.00
Warner Bros. 29931		Peek-A-Boo/Find Out	1982			3.00
Warner Bros. 29931	PS	Peek-A-Boo/Find Out	1982			3.00
Warner Bros. 49028		Secret Agent Man/Red Eye	1979			3.00

Label, Number		Title	Year	VG	VG+	NM
Warner Bros. 49524		Girl U Want/Mr. B's Ballroom	1980			3.00
Warner Bros. 49550		Whip It/Turn Around	1980			3.00
Warner Bros. 49621		Freedom of Choice/Snowball (Remix)	1980			3.00
Warner Bros. 49621	PS	Freedom of Choice/Snowball (Remix)	1980			3.00
Warner Bros. 49715		Gates of Steel (Live)/Be Still (Live)	1981			3.00
Warner Bros. 49834		Beautiful World/Enough Said	1981			3.00
Warner Bros. 50010		Jerkin' Back 'N' Forth/Mecha Mania Boy	1982			3.00
Warner Bros. 50048		Through Being Cool/Going Under	1982			3.00

12-Inch Singles

Label, Number		Title	Year	VG	VG+	NM
Backstreet L33-1106	DJ	Theme from Doctor Detroit (same on both sides)	1983	2.00	4.00	8.00
Backstreet L33-1113	DJ	Theme from Doctor Detroit (2 versions)/Luv Luv	1983	2.00	4.00	8.00
Backstreet 13968		Theme from Doctor Detroit (2 versions)/Luv Luv	1983	2.00	4.00	8.00
Enigma EPRO 148	DJ	Baby Doll (5 versions)	1988	2.00	4.00	8.00
Enigma EPRO 298	DJ	Post Post-Modern Man (7 versions)	1990	3.00	6.00	12.00
Enigma 75511		Disco Dancer (3 versions)	1988	2.00	4.00	8.00
Enigma 75515		Baby Doll (5 mixes)/Agitated	1988	2.00	4.00	8.00
Enigma 75551		Post Post-Modern Man (7 versions)	1990	2.00	4.00	8.00
Full Moon/Asylum 11523	DJ	Working in a Coal Mine (same on both sides)	1981	2.00	4.00	8.00
Warner Bros. PRO-A-881	DJ	Gates of Steel/Mr's B's Ballroom/Whip It	1980	2.00	4.00	8.00
Warner Bros. PRO-A-993	DJ	Jerkin' Back 'n' Forth//Going Under/Through Being Cool	1981	2.00	4.00	8.00
Warner Bros. PRO-A-1199	DJ	Selections from "Oh No! It's Devo"	1983	3.75	7.50	15.00
Warner Bros. PRO-1-2006	DJ	That's Good/Speed Racer	1983	6.25	12.50	25.00
Promo-only picture disc						
Warner Bros. PRO-A-2217	DJ	Are You Experienced?/Please Please	1984	2.50	5.00	10.00
Warner Bros. 20316		Here to Go (2 versions)/Shout (2 versions)	1985	2.50	5.00	10.00
Warner Bros. 29906		Peek-A-Boo//Peek-A-Boo/Find Out	1982	2.00	4.00	8.00

10-Inch Singles

Label, Number		Title	Year	VG	VG+	NM
Warner Bros. 49826	PD	Beautiful World/Nu'tra Speaks	1981	2.50	5.00	10.00
Shaped picture disc						

Dexy's Midnight Runners

English pop-rock band known for not having any electric guitars or synthesizers.

Vinyl Albums

Label, Number	Title	Year	VG	VG+	NM
Capitol SN-16288	Searching for the Young Soul Rebels	1983	2.00	4.00	8.00
Budget-line reissue					
EMI America SW-17042	Searching for the Young Soul Rebels	1980	3.75	7.50	15.00
Mercury SRM-1-4069	Too-Rye-Ay	1982	2.50	5.00	10.00
Mercury 822 989-1	Don't Stand Me Down	1985	2.50	5.00	10.00

Label, Number		Title	Year	VG	VG+	NM
45s						
Collectables 4826		Come On Eileen/Jackie Wilson Said				
			199?			3.00
Reissue						
Mercury 76189		Come On Eileen/Let's Make This Precious				
			1982			3.00
Mercury 76189	PS	Come On Eileen/Let's Make This Precious				
			1982	2.00	4.00	8.00
A somewhat scarce sleeve.						
Mercury 811 142-7		The Celtic Soul Brothers/Reminisce Pt. 1				
			1983			3.00
Mercury 811 142-7	PS	The Celtic Soul Brothers/Reminisce Pt. 1				
			1983			3.00
Mercury 814 002-7		Jackie Wilson Said (I'm in Heaven When You Smile)/Liars A to Z				
			1983			3.00
12-Inch Singles						
Mercury MK 237	DJ	The Celtic Soul Brothers (same on both sides)				
			1982		3.00	6.00
Mercury MK 247	DJ	The Celtic Soul Brothers/Let's Make This Precious/All in All				
			1982	2.00	4.00	8.00
Mercury PRO 387	DJ	This Is What She's Like/One of Those Things				
			1985	2.00	4.00	8.00
Mercury MDS 4021		Come On Eileen/The Sound of Phil/Let's Make This Precious				
			1982	2.50	5.00	10.00

Dickies, The

Los Angeles-area punk band.

Label, Number		Title	Year	VG	VG+	NM
Vinyl Albums						
A&M SP-4742		The Incredible Shrinking Dickies	1979	3.75	7.50	15.00
A&M SP-4742		The Incredible Shrinking Dickies	1979	5.00	10.00	20.00
First pressing on yellow vinyl						
A&M SP-4796		Dawn of the Dickies	1979	3.75	7.50	15.00
Enigma D1-73289		Second Coming	1989	2.00	4.00	8.00
Enigma D1-73322	EP	Killer Klowns (From Outer Space)				
			1988	2.00	4.00	8.00
PVC 6903		Stukas Over Disneyland	1983	3.00	6.00	12.00
Taang! 56		Locked and Loaded	1991	3.00	6.00	12.00
Triple X 51168		Idjit Savant	1994	2.50	5.00	10.00
45s						
A&M 2092		Silent Night/Sounds of Silence	1978	2.50	5.00	10.00
All copies on white vinyl						
A&M 2092	PS	Silent Night/Sounds of Silence	1978	2.50	5.00	10.00
A&M 2225		Nights in White Satin/Manny, Moe and Jack				
			1980	2.50	5.00	10.00
A&M 2225	PS	Nights in White Satin/Manny, Moe and Jack				
			1980	12.50	25.00	50.00
Withdrawn; shows Dickies in KKK robes						
A&M 2241		Banana Splits (The Tra La La Song)/Sounds of Silence				
			1980	2.50	5.00	10.00
A&M 2241	PS	Banana Splits (The Tra La La Song)/Sounds of Silence				
			1980	2.50	5.00	10.00

Dicks, The

Punk band from Austin, Texas.

Label, Number	Title	Year	VG	VG+	NM
Vinyl Albums					
Alternative Tentacles VIRUS 43	These People	1985	3.75	7.50	15.00
Radical RRR 80351	Recorded Live at Raul's	1980	15.00	30.00	60.00
One side features the Big Boys; the other side, the Dicks					
SST 017	Kill from the Heart	1983	6.25	12.50	25.00

Label, Number		Title	Year	VG	VG+	NM
7-Inch Extended Play Singles						
Radical RRR D1		The Dicks Hate the Police	1979	12.50	25.00	50.00
Radical RRR D1	PS	The Dicks Hate the Police	1979	12.50	25.00	50.00
Radical RRR D2		Peace?	1984		3.75	7.50
Radical RRR D2	PS	Peace?	1984		3.75	7.50

Dictators, The

New York City prototypical punk/metal band.

Vinyl Albums						
Asylum 6E-147		Bloodbrothers	1978	3.00	6.00	12.00
Asylum 7E-1109		Manifest Destiny	1977	3.00	6.00	12.00
Epic KE 33348		The Dictators Go Girl Crazy	1975	3.00	6.00	12.00
45s						
Asylum 45420		Disease/Hey Boys	1977	2.50	5.00	10.00
Asylum 45470		Science Has Gone Too Far/Sleepin' with the T.V. On				
			1978	2.50	5.00	10.00
Asylum 45523		I Stand Tall/Two Much Fun	1978	2.50	5.00	10.00

Didjits

45s						
Sub Pop 241		Dear Junkie/Skull Baby	1993		2.50	5.00
Sub Pop 241	PS	Dear Junkie/Skull Baby	1993		2.50	5.00
#61 in Sub Pop Singles Club series						

Diesel

Pop band from the Netherlands.

Vinyl Albums						
Regency 9603		Watts in a Tank	1981	3.00	6.00	12.00
Original release, distributed by JEM						
Regency SD 19315		Watts in a Tank	1981	2.50	5.00	10.00
Reissue, distributed by Atlantic						
45s						
Regency 7339		Sausalito Summernight/Bite Back				
			1981		2.00	4.00
Regency 7343		Goin' Back to China/The Harness				
			1981			3.00
Regency 7403		Down to the Sunshine	1982			3.00

Difford and Tilbrook

*Chris Difford and Glenn Tilbrook, recording as a duet during a hiatus of their band, **Squeeze**.*

Vinyl Albums						
A&M SP-4985		Difford and Tilbrook	1984	2.50	5.00	10.00
45s						
A&M 2648		Picking Up the Pieces/Within These Walls				
			1984			3.00
A&M 2675		Love's Crashing Waves/Action Speaks Faster				
			1984			3.00
12-Inch Singles						
A&M 17283	DJ	Picking Up the Pieces (same on both sides)				
			1984		3.00	6.00

Label, Number		Title	Year	VG	VG+	NM
Digable Planets						

Rap trio with jazz influences.

Vinyl Albums

Label, Number		Title	Year	VG	VG+	NM
Pendulum E1-30654		Blowout Comb	1994	3.00	6.00	12.00
Pendulum 61414		Reachin' (A New Refutation of Time and Space)				
			1993	3.00	6.00	12.00

45s

Label, Number		Title	Year	VG	VG+	NM
Pendulum S7-18482		Dial 7/Graffiti	1995			3.00
Elektra 64674		Rebirth of Slick (Cool Like Dat)/Where I'm From				
			1993			3.00

12-Inch Singles

Label, Number		Title	Year	VG	VG+	NM
Pendulum 5657	DJ	Nickel Bags (4 versions)/Appointment at the Fat Clinic (2 versions)				
			1993	2.00	4.00	8.00
Pendulum 19945	DJ	9th Wonder (Slicker This Year) (4 versions)				
			1994	2.00	4.00	8.00
Pendulum 66285		Nickel Bags (4 versions)/Appointment at the Fat Clinic (2 versions)				
			1993		3.00	6.00
Pendulum 66318		Where I'm From (6 versions)	1993	2.00	4.00	8.00

Digital Underground

Rap/funk group with fluid membership. 2Pac was briefly a member before he went solo.

Vinyl Albums

Label, Number		Title	Year	VG	VG+	NM
Tommy Boy 964	EP	This Is an E.P. Release	1991	2.00	4.00	8.00
Tommy Boy 1026		Sex Packets	1990	3.00	6.00	12.00
Tommy Boy 1045		Sons of the P.	1991	2.50	5.00	10.00

45s

Label, Number	Title	Year	VG	VG+	NM
Tommy Boy/Collectables 944	The Humpty Dance (same on both sides)				
		1992			3.00

A hit in 1990, this was its first U.S. 45 appearance

12-Inch Singles

Label, Number	Title	Year	VG	VG+	NM
Tommy Boy 513	No Nose Job (3 mixes)	1991	2.00	4.00	8.00
Tommy Boy 587	The Return of the Crazy One (5 versions)/Carry the Way				
		1993	2.00	4.00	8.00
Tommy Boy 590	The Return of the Crazy One (Party Flava Mix)/				
	The Return of the Crazy One (Radio Flava Mix)				
		1993	2.50	5.00	10.00
Tommy Boy 612	Wussup Wit the Luv (3 versions)/Doo Woo You (3 versions)				
		1994		3.00	6.00
Tommy Boy 615	Wussup Wit the Luv (3 versions)/Doo Woo You (3 versions)				
		1994	2.00	4.00	8.00
Tommy Boy 932	Doowutchyalike (4 versions)/Hip Hop Dot (2 versions)				
		1989	2.50	5.00	10.00
Tommy Boy 944	The Humpty Dance (3 mixes)	1989	2.50	5.00	10.00

Dils, The

San Diego punk group.

Vinyl Albums

Label, Number	Title	Year	VG	VG+	NM
Lost 001	The Dils	1990	3.00	6.00	12.00
Triple X 51003	The Dils Live	1987	3.75	7.50	15.00
White vinyl					

45s

Label, Number		Title	Year	VG	VG+	NM
Dangerhouse SLA 268		198 Seconds of The Dils	1977	5.00	10.00	20.00
Dangerhouse SLA 268	PS	198 Seconds of The Dils	1977	5.00	10.00	20.00
What 02		I Hate the Rich/You're Not Blank	1977	4.25	8.75	17.50

Label, Number		Title	Year	VG	VG+	NM
What 02	PS	I Hate the Rich/You're Not Blank	1977	5.50	11.25	22.50
"Dils" in block letters on cover						
What 02	PS	I Hate the Rich/You're Not Blank	1977	4.25	8.75	17.50
"Dils" in angular letters on cover						

Dinosaur Jr

Alternative band featuring J Mascis.

Vinyl Albums

Homestead 015-2		Dinosaur	1985	3.75	7.50	15.00
Released under the name "Dinosaur"						
Sire 45108		Where You Been	1993	3.75	7.50	15.00
Sire 45719		Without a Sound	1994	2.50	5.00	10.00
SST 130		You're Living All Over Me	1987	5.00	10.00	20.00
First released under the name "Dinosaur"						
SST 130		You're Living All Over Me	1987	3.75	7.50	15.00
As "Dinosaur Jr"; purple swirl vinyl						
SST 130		You're Living All Over Me	1987	2.50	5.00	10.00
As "Dinosaur Jr"; black vinyl						
SST 152	EP	Dinosaur Jr	1987	3.00	6.00	12.00
Originals on purple swirl vinyl						
SST 216		Bug	1988	2.50	5.00	10.00
SST 244	EP	Just Like Heaven	1989	2.00	4.00	8.00
SST 275	EP	Fossils	1991	2.00	4.00	8.00
SST 910	10	Dinosaur Jr	1987		3.00	6.00
SST 914	10	Just Like Heaven	1989		3.00	6.00
SST 925	10	Fossils	1991		3.00	6.00

45s

Homestead 032		Repulsion/Bulbs of Passion	1985	2.50	5.00	10.00
Homestead 032	PS	Repulsion/Bulbs of Passion	1985	2.50	5.00	10.00
By "Dinosaur"						
SST 220		Freak Scene/Keep the Glove	1988	2.50	5.00	10.00
Large hole, clear vinyl						
SST 220		Freak Scene/Keep the Glove	1988		2.50	5.00
Small hole, black vinyl						
SST 220	PS	Freak Scene/Keep the Glove	1988		2.50	5.00
SST 244		Just Like Heaven/Throw Down-Chunks	1989	3.00	6.00	12.00
Green vinyl						
SST 244		Just Like Heaven/Throw Down-Chunks	1989			3.00
SST 244	PS	Just Like Heaven/Throw Down-Chunks	1989			3.00
Sub Pop 68		The Wagon/Better Than Gone	1990	15.50	31.25	62.50
200 on purple vinyl						
Sub Pop 68		The Wagon/Better Than Gone	1990	3.00	6.25	12.50
9,800 on white vinyl						
Sub Pop 68	PS	The Wagon/Better Than Gone	1990	3.00	6.25	12.50

Divinyls

Australia pop/new wave group.

Vinyl Albums

	Title	Year	VG	VG+	NM
Chrysalis F1-21627	Temperamental	1989	3.00	6.00	12.00
Chrysalis BVW 41404	Desperate	1983	3.00	6.00	12.00
Chrysalis BFV 41511	What a Life!	1985	3.00	6.00	12.00
Chrysalis BFV 41627	Temperamental	1989	5.00	10.00	20.00

45s

	Title	Year	VG	VG+	NM
Chrysalis 42673	Ring Me Up/Only Lonely	1983			3.00
Chrysalis 43241	Hey Little Boy/Fighting	1988			3.00
Virgin 98873	I Touch Myself/Follow Through	1991		2.50	5.00

Label, Number		Title	Year	VG	VG+	NM
12-Inch Singles						
Chrysalis VAS 1016	DJ	Back to the Wall (same on both sides)				
			1988		2.50	5.00
Chrysalis VAS 1131	DJ	Hey Little Boy/Hey Little Boy (Extended Remix)				
			1988		3.00	6.00
Chrysalis 1689		Only Lonely/Science Fiction	1982	2.00	4.00	8.00
Chrysalis 2156	DJ	Pleasure and Pain (same on both sides)				
			1985	2.00	4.00	8.00
Chrysalis 2247	DJ	In My Life (same on both sides)	1985		3.00	6.00
Chrysalis 2258	DJ	Sleeping Beauty (same on both sides)				
			1985		3.00	6.00
Chrysalis 2283	DJ	Pleasure and Pain (Live)/In My Life (Live)/Sleeping Beauty (Live)				
			1986	5.00	10.00	20.00

Doctor and the Medics

Label, Number	Title	Year	VG	VG+	NM
Vinyl Albums					
I.R.S. 5797	Laughing at the Pieces	1986	3.00	6.00	12.00
45s					
I.R.S. 52880	Spirit in the Sky/Laughing at the Pieces				
		1986		2.00	4.00
I.R.S. 52970	Burn/Barbara Can't Dance	1986			3.00
I.R.S. 53129	Burning Love/Waterloo	1987			3.00
12-Inch Singles					
I.R.S. 23653	Spirit in the Sky/Miracle of Age/Laughing at the Pieces				
		1986		3.00	6.00

Dr. Buzzard's Original Savannah Band

*Multicultural, multiracial group fronted by August Darnell. He later formed **Kid Creole and the Coconuts**.*

Label, Number	Title	Year	VG	VG+	NM
Vinyl Albums					
Elektra 6E-218	James Monroe H.S. Presents Dr. Buzzard's Original Savannah				
	Band Goes to Washington	1979	2.50	5.00	10.00
Passport 6013	Calling All Beatniks	1986	2.50	5.00	10.00
RCA Victor APL1-1504	Dr. Buzzard's Original Savannah Band				
		1976	2.50	5.00	10.00
Reissue on black label with "Nipper" logo					
RCA Victor APL1-1504	Dr. Buzzard's Original Savannah Band				
		1976	3.75	7.50	15.00
Original copies have tan labels					
RCA Victor (# unknown)	Dr. Buzzard's Original Savannah Band Meets King Pennet				
		1978	3.00	6.00	12.00
RCA Victor AYL1-3767	Dr. Buzzard's Original Savannah Band				
		1980	2.00	4.00	8.00
Reissue					
45s					
Collectables 4560	Cherchez La Femme/I'll Play the Fool				
		198?			3.00
Reissue					
Elektra 46607	Didn't I Love You Girl/The Seven Year Itch				
		1980		2.00	4.00
RCA PB-10762	I'll Play the Fool/Sunshower	1976		2.00	4.00
RCA PB-10827	Whispering/Cherchez La Femme/Se Si Bon//Sunshower				
		1976		2.00	4.00
RCA PB-10923	You've Got Something/Lemon in the Honey				
		1977		2.00	4.00
RCA PB-11239	Mister Love//Transistor Madness/Future D.J.				
		1978		2.00	4.00

Label, Number		Title	Year	VG	VG+	NM
RCA GB-11325		Whispering/Cherchez La Femme/Se Si Bon//I'll Play the Fool				
			1978			3.00

Gold Standard Series reissue

Dogs
Detroit punk band.

45s

Detroit 001		Slash Your Face/Fed Up/Are You a Boy or Are You a Girl				
			1978	15.00	30.00	60.00
Detroit 001	PS	Slash Your Face/Fed Up/Are You a Boy or Are You a Girl				
			1978	15.00	30.00	60.00
Dynamic (# unknown)		Younger Point of View/John Rock ('n' Roll Sinclair)				
			1976	25.00	50.00	100.00

Not issued with picture sleeve; some copies have Dogs sticker, insert and press release (add 50% for all)

Dolby, Thomas
*British synthesizer wizard. Originally with **Bruce Woolley and the Camera Club**.*

Vinyl Albums

Capitol ST 12271		The Golden Age of Wireless	1983	2.50	5.00	10.00
Capitol ST-12309		The Flat Earth	1984	2.50	5.00	10.00
EMI Manhattan E1-48075		Aliens Ate My Buick	1988	2.50	5.00	10.00
Harvest ST 12271		The Golden Age of Wireless	1982	3.00	6.00	12.00
Harvest MLP 15007	EP	Blinded by Science	1983	3.00	6.00	12.00

45s

Capitol 5204		She Blinded Me with Science/Flying North				
			1983		2.00	4.00

Not issued with picture sleeve in U.S.

Capitol 5238		Europa and the Pirate Twins/Radio Silence				
			1983			3.00
Capitol 5238	PS	Europa and the Pirate Twins/Radio Silence				
			1983			3.00
Capitol 5321		Hyperactive/Get Out of My Mix	1984			3.00
Capitol 5321	PS	Hyperactive/Get Out of My Mix	1984			3.00
Capitol 5355		Dissidents/I Scare Myself	1984			3.00
Capitol 5374		Dissidents/Dissidents (Dub)	1984			3.00
Capitol 5374	PS	Dissidents/Dissidents (Dub)	1984			3.00
Capitol S7-18904		She Blinded Me with Science/The Politics of Dancing				
			1996			3.00

A-side is different mix than original 45; B-side by Re-Flex

EMI Manhattan 50125		Airhead/Budapest by Blimp	1988			3.00
EMI Manhattan 50125	PS	Airhead/Budapest by Blimp	1988			3.00
EMI Manhattan 50148		Hot Sauce/Salsa Picante	1988			3.00
EMI Manhattan 50148	PS	Hot Sauce/Salsa Picante	1988			3.00
Harvest 5155		Europa and the Pirate Twins/Radio Silence				
			1982	2.50	5.00	10.00
Harvest 5204		She Blinded Me with Science/Flying North				
			1983	2.50	5.00	10.00
MCA 52868		Howard the Duck/Don't Turn Away				
			1986			3.00

Credited to "Dolby's Cube"

MCA 52868	PS	Howard the Duck/Don't Turn Away				
			1986			3.00

Credited to "Dolby's Cube"

12-Inch Singles

Capitol 8561	Get Out of My Mix (2 mixes)	1983		3.00	6.00
Capitol 8576	Hyperactive/Get Out of My Mix	1984	2.00	4.00	8.00
Capitol 8594	Dissidents: The Search for the Truth Pts. 1 and 2				
		1984	2.00	4.00	8.00

Label, Number		Title	Year	VG	VG+	NM
Capitol SPRO 9067/8	DJ	Hyperactive! (5:00)/Hyperactive (4:12)				
			1984	2.50	5.00	10.00
Capitol SPRO 9975	DJ	Get Out of My Mix (2 mixes)	1983	2.00	4.00	8.00
Capitol SPRO 9980	DJ	Airwaves (same on both sides)	1983		3.00	6.00
EMI Manhattan 56086		Airhead (3 mixes)/Budapest by Blimp				
			1988		3.00	6.00
EMI Manhattan 56104		Airheads' Revenge/Revenge Rap/Airhead (2 new mixes)				
			1988		3.00	6.00
EMI Manhattan 56114		Hot Sauce (3 mixes)/Salsa Picante/Get Out of My Mix				
			1988		3.00	6.00
MCA 17165	DJ	Hunger City (same on both sides)	1986		2.50	5.00
As "Dolby's Cube"						
MCA 23645		Howard the Duck (2 versions)/Don't Turn Away				
			1986	2.00	4.00	8.00
As "Dolby's Cube"						

Don Armando's Second Avenue Rhumba Band

*Early version of **Kid Creole and the Coconuts**.*

Vinyl Albums					
Ze 33-005	Don Armando's Second Avenue Rhumba Band				
		1979	4.50	9.00	18.00
45s					
Ze ZEA 45-001	Deputy of Love	1979		2.50	5.00
Ze ZEA 45-305	Winter Love	1980		2.50	5.00

Doug and the Slugs

Vinyl Albums					
Avion AVF 4603	Doug and the Slugs	1987	3.00	6.00	12.00
RCA Victor AFL1-3887	Cognac and Bologna	1981	3.50	7.00	14.00
RCA Victor AFL1-4261	Wrap It	1982	3.50	7.00	14.00
RCA Victor AFL1-4432	Music for the Hard of Thinking	1983	3.50	7.00	14.00
45s					
RCA PB-12167	Too Bad/Chinatown Calculation				
		1981		2.00	4.00
RCA PB-13044	Real Enough/Wrong Kind of Right				
		1982		2.00	4.00
RCA PB-13513	Makin' It Work/St. Laurent Summer				
		1983		2.00	4.00
12-Inch Singles					
RCA JD-12183 DJ	Too Bad (same on both sides)	1981	2.50	5.00	10.00

Dread Zeppelin

Vinyl Albums					
I.R.S. X1-13048	Un-Led-Ed	1990	5.00	10.00	20.00
All copies on gold vinyl					
45s					
Birdcage 45-2690	Whole Lotta Love/Tour-Telvis: A Bad Trip				
		1989	2.50	5.00	10.00
Pink vinyl					
Birdcage 45-2690 PS	Whole Lotta Love/Tour-Telvis: A Bad Trip				
		1989	2.50	5.00	10.00

Label, Number		Title	Year	VG	VG+	NM

Dream 6

*Early incarnation of **Concrete Blonde.***

Vinyl Albums

Label, Number		Title	Year	VG	VG+	NM
Happy Hermit 1983	EP	Dream 6	1983	10.00	20.00	40.00

Dream Academy, The

British dreamy pop band.

Vinyl Albums

Label, Number		Title	Year	VG	VG+	NM
Warner Bros. 25265		The Dream Academy	1985	2.00	4.00	8.00
Warner Bros. 25625		Remembrance Days	1987	2.00	4.00	8.00
Warner Bros. R 154271		The Dream Academy	1986	2.50	5.00	10.00
RCA Music Service edition						

45s

Label, Number		Title	Year	VG	VG+	NM
Reprise 27889		Everybody's Got to Learn Sometime/In Exile (For Rodrigo Rojas) 1988				3.00
Reprise 28118		The Lesson of Love/Here	1988			3.00
Reprise 28118	PS	The Lesson of Love/Here	1988			3.00
Reprise 28750		The Love Parade/A Girl in a Million (For E. Sedgwick) 1986				3.00
Reprise 28750	PS	The Love Parade/A Girl in a Million (For E. Sedgwick) 1986				3.00
Warner Bros. 28199		Indian Summer/Heaven Part 1	1987			3.00
Warner Bros. 28841		Life in a Northern Town/Test Tape No. 3 1985				3.00
Warner Bros. 28841	PS	Life in a Northern Town/Test Tape No. 3 1985				3.00

12-Inch Singles

Label, Number		Title	Year	VG	VG+	NM
Warner Bros. PRO-A-2361	DJ	This World (same on both sides)	1985	2.00	4.00	8.00
Warner Bros. PRO-A-2393	DJ	Life in a Northern Town (same on both sides) 1985		2.50	5.00	10.00
Warner Bros. PRO-A-2439	DJ	The Edge of Forever (same on both sides) 1986		2.00	4.00	8.00

Dream Syndicate, The

Los Angeles-based band of many influences, from the Velvets to psychedelia

Vinyl Albums

Label, Number		Title	Year	VG	VG+	NM
A&M SP-12511		This Is Not the New Dream Syndicate Album...Live 1984		3.00	6.00	12.00
Big Time 10022		Out of the Grey	1985	2.50	5.00	10.00
Down There 2	EP	Sure Thing + 3	1982	5.00	10.00	20.00
Enigma 73341		Ghost Stories	1988	2.00	4.00	8.00
Ruby 807		The Days of Wine and Roses	1982	5.00	10.00	20.00
Slash 23844		The Days of Wine and Roses	1982	3.75	7.50	15.00

45s

Label, Number		Title	Year	VG	VG+	NM
Forced Exposure 004		Ballad of Dwight Frye/Low Rider 1986		7.50	15.00	30.00
Forced Exposure 004	PS	Ballad of Dwight Frye/Low Rider 1986		7.50	15.00	30.00

12-Inch Singles

Label, Number		Title	Year	VG	VG+	NM
Big Time 6014		Out of the Grey/Out of the Grey (Edit) 1986		2.50	5.00	
Big Time 6029		50 in a 25 Zone (2 versions)/Drinking Problem/Blood Money + 1 1987		2.00	4.00	8.00

Label, Number		Title	Year	VG	VG+	NM

Dreams So Real
Rock trio from Athens, Georgia.

Vinyl Albums

Arista 8555		Rough Night in Jericho	1988	2.50	5.00	10.00
Arista AL 8618		Gloryline	1990	2.50	5.00	10.00

45s

Arista 9784		Red Lights (Merry Christmas)/Bearing Witness (Lay Me Down)				
			1988		2.00	4.00
Green vinyl						
Arista 9784	PS	Red Lights (Merry Christmas)/Bearing Witness (Lay Me Down)				
			1988		2.00	4.00
Arista 9794		Bearing Witness (Lay Me Down)/Cinnamon Girl				
			1988			3.00
Coyote (# unknown)		Everywhere Girl/Whirl	1986		2.50	5.00
Coyote (# unknown)	PS	Everywhere Girl/Whirl	1986		2.50	5.00

Drunks with Guns

7-Inch Extended Play Singles

Arch Villain DWG 002		Revolver	1987	12.50	25.00	50.00
Arch Villain DWG 002	PS	Revolver	1987	12.50	25.00	50.00
160 to 200 copies made; beware of bootlegs						
Cheap Beer (# unknown)		Thirst for Knowledge	1986	12.50	25.00	50.00
Cheap Beer (# unknown)	PS	Thirst for Knowledge	1986	12.50	25.00	50.00
300 copies were pressed; beware of bootlegs						
Noiseville 12		Drug Problem	1990	23.75	47.50	95.00
20 pressed on white vinyl; values are conjecture						
Noiseville 12		Drug Problem	1990	23.75	47.50	95.00
20 pressed on clear vinyl; values are conjecture						
Noiseville 12		Drug Problem	1990	5.00	10.00	20.00
480 pressed on black vinyl						
Noiseville 12		Drug Problem	1990		2.50	5.00
Later pressings on orange vinyl						
Noiseville 12	PS	Drug Problem	1990		2.50	5.00

45s

Cheap Beer (# unknown)		Blood Bath/Punched in the Head-I Got the Gun				
			1985	12.50	25.00	50.00
Cheap Beer (# unknown)	PS	Blood Bath/Punched in the Head-I Got the Gun				
			1985	12.50	25.00	50.00
300 copies were pressed; beware of bootlegs						
Dental Records 02		Zombie/Leprosy-Enemy	1987	6.25	12.50	25.00
Dental Records 02	PS	Zombie/Leprosy-Enemy	1987	6.25	12.50	25.00
500 were pressed						
Orphanage 15		Headgiver/Tomorrow We Kill-Cock Breeder				
			198?		2.00	4.00
Blue vinyl (all copies)						
Orphanage 15	PS	Headgiver/Tomorrow We Kill-Cock Breeder				
			198?		2.00	4.00

Dukes of Stratosphear, The
Actually XTC.

Vinyl Albums

Geffen GHS 24169		Psonic Psunspot	1987	3.00	6.00	12.00

12-Inch Singles

Geffen PRO-A-2840	DJ	Vanishing Girl (same on both sides)				
			1987		3.00	6.00

Label, Number		Title	Year	VG	VG+	NM

Duran Duran

*British new wave/pop stars and early MTV pinups. Also see **Arcadia; The Power Station; Taylor, Andy; Taylor, Roger.***

Vinyl Albums

Label, Number		Title	Year	VG	VG+	NM
Capitol ST-12158		Duran Duran	1983	2.50	5.00	10.00
Reissue, with new cover and "Is There Something I Should Know"						
Capitol ST-12211		Rio	1983	2.50	5.00	10.00
Version 3: Capitol logo replaces Harvest logo on back cover						
Capitol ST-12310		Seven and the Ragged Tiger	1983	2.50	5.00	10.00
Capitol SWAV-12374		Arena	1984	2.50	5.00	10.00
With booklet (deduct 25% if cut out)						
Capitol PJ-12540		Notorious	1986	2.50	5.00	10.00
Capitol SPRO-79097/8	EP	Duran Goes Dutch	1987	12.50	25.00	50.00
Promo-only five-song EP recorded live in Rotterdam						
Capitol C1-90958		Big Thing	1988	2.50	5.00	10.00
Capitol C1-93178		Decade	1989	2.50	5.00	10.00
Capitol C1-94292		Liberty	1990	3.00	6.00	12.00
Capitol R 100682		Big Thing	1988	3.00	6.00	12.00
BMG Direct Marketing edition						
Capitol R 114794		Notorious	1987	3.00	6.00	12.00
RCA Music Service edition						
Capitol R 134452		Duran Duran	1983	3.00	6.00	12.00
RCA Music Service edition; with "Is There Something I Should Know?"						
Capitol R 140395		Arena	1984	3.00	6.00	12.00
RCA Music Service edition						
Capitol R 163452		Rio	1983	3.00	6.00	12.00
RCA Music Service edition						
Capitol R 163458		Liberty	1990	3.00	6.00	12.00
BMG Direct Marketing edition						
Capitol R 173573		Decade	1989	3.00	6.00	12.00
BMG Direct Marketing edition						
Harvest ST-12158		Duran Duran	1981	3.75	7.50	15.00
Harvest ST-12211		Rio	1982	3.75	7.50	15.00
Version 1: Harvest logo on lower back cover, no mention of remixes by David Kershenbaum						
Harvest ST-12211		Rio	1982	3.00	6.00	12.00
Version 2: Harvest logo on lower back cover, with remixes by David Kershenbaum						
Harvest MLP-15006	EP	Carnival	1982	6.25	12.50	25.00
Imports of this are relatively common and worth much less.						
Mobile Fidelity 1-182		Seven and the Ragged Tiger	1985	7.50	15.00	30.00
Original Master Recording						

45s

Label, Number		Title	Year	VG	VG+	NM
Capitol 5215		Rio/Hold Back the Rain	1983			3.00
Capitol 5215	PS	Rio/Hold Back the Rain	1983		3.00	6.00
Capitol 5233		Is There Something I Should Know/Careless Memories				
			1983			3.00
Capitol 5233	PS	Is There Something I Should Know/Careless Memories				
			1983		2.00	4.00
Capitol 5290		Union of the Snake/Secret Oktober				
			1983			3.00
Custom label						
Capitol 5290	PS	Union of the Snake/Secret Oktober				
			1983			3.00
Capitol 5309		New Moon on Monday/Tiger Tiger				
			1984			3.00
Capitol 5309	PS	New Moon on Monday/Tiger Tiger				
			1984			3.00
Capitol 5345		The Reflex/New Religion	1984		2.00	4.00
Capitol 5345	PS	The Reflex/New Religion	1984	2.00	4.00	8.00
Foldout poster sleeve						
Capitol 5345	PS	The Reflex/New Religion	1984		2.00	4.00
Standard picture sleeve; though less sought-after, this is actually much scarcer than the poster						

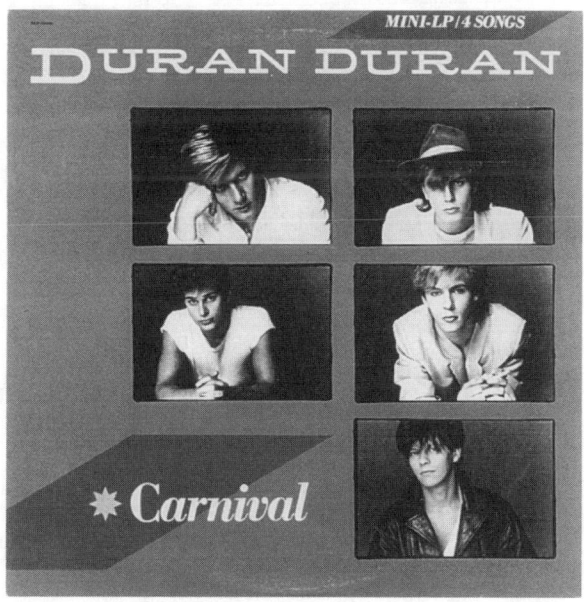

Duran Duran's early American releases are highly sought-after and often fetch handsome prices. The first issue of the "Rio" 45 (Harvest B-5175) has a completely different mix than either the LP or the later hit 45 on Capitol, not to mention the custom label. Also hard to find is the four-song remix album *Carnival*. Easily obtained on European or Japanese imports, the American version is the most pricey of the band's regular 12-inch releases ($25).

Label, Number		Title	Year	VG	VG+	NM
Capitol 5417		The Wild Boys/(I'm Looking for) Cracks in the Pavement				
			1984			3.00
Capitol 5417	PS	The Wild Boys/(I'm Looking for) Cracks in the Pavement				
			1984			3.00
Capitol 5438		Save a Prayer/Save a Prayer (From the Arena)				
			1985			3.00
Capitol 5438	PS	Save a Prayer/Save a Prayer (From the Arena)				
			1985			3.00
Capitol 5475		A View to a Kill/A View to a Kill (That Fatal Kiss)				
			1985			3.00
Capitol 5475	PS	A View to a Kill/A View to a Kill (That Fatal Kiss)				
			1985		2.00	4.00
Capitol 5648		Notorious/Winter Marches On	1986			3.00
Capitol 5648	DJ	Notorious (same on both sides)	1986	2.50	5.00	10.00
Clear vinyl in heavy clear plastic sleeve						
Capitol 5648	PS	Notorious/Winter Marches On	1986			3.00
Capitol 5670		Skin Trade/We Need You	1987			3.00
Capitol 5670	DJ	Skin Trade (same on both sides)	1987	2.50	5.00	10.00
Red vinyl in heavy clear plastic sleeve						
Capitol 5670	PS	Skin Trade/We Need You	1987			3.00
American all-red sleeve						
Capitol 5670	PS	Skin Trade/We Need You	1987	6.25	12.50	25.00
Canada-only nude sleeve						
Capitol S7-17316		Come Undone/Skin Trade	1993			3.00
Capitol S7-17438		Too Much Information/Drowning Man				
			1993			3.00
Capitol S7-18488		White Lines/Watching the Detectives				
			1995			3.00
Capitol S7-18577		Perfect Day/Success	1995			3.00
Capitol 44001		Meet El Presidente/Vertigo (Do the Demolition)				
			1987			3.00
Capitol 44001	DJ	Meet El Presidente (same on both sides)				
			1987	2.50	5.00	10.00
White vinyl in heavy clear plastic sleeve						
Capitol 44001	PS	Meet El Presidente/Vertigo (Do the Demolition)				
			1987		2.00	4.00
Foldout poster sleeve						
Capitol 44237		I Don't Want Your Love/(instrumental)				
			1988			3.00
Capitol 44237	PS	I Don't Want Your Love/(instrumental)				
			1988			3.00
Capitol 44287		All She Wants Is/Medley: I Believe-All I Need to Know				
			1988			3.00
Capitol 44287	PS	All She Wants Is/Medley: I Believe-All I Need to Know				
			1988			3.00
Capitol 44337		Do You Believe in Shame?/Edge of America-Lakeshore Driving				
			1989			3.00
Capitol 44337	PS	Do You Believe in Shame?/Edge of America-Lakeshore Driving				
			1989			3.00
Capitol S7-56945		Ordinary World/Save a Prayer	1993			3.00
Harvest 5017		Planet Earth/To the Shore	1981	6.25	12.50	25.00
Harvest 5070		Girls on Film/Faster Than Light	1981	6.25	12.50	25.00
Harvest 5134		Hungry Like the Wolf (3:23)/Careless Memories				
			1982	3.00	6.00	12.00
Harvest 5175		Rio/Hold Back the Rain	1982	3.00	6.00	12.00
Custom label						
Harvest 5195		Hungry Like the Wolf (4:11)/Hungry Like the Wolf (5:14)				
			1982			3.00
Harvest 5195	PS	Hungry Like the Wolf (4:11)/Hungry Like the Wolf (5:14)				
			1982	2.50	5.00	10.00
A fairly scarce sleeve						

Label, Number		Title	Year	VG	VG+	NM
12-Inch Singles						
Capitol 8567		Union of the Snake//Union of the Snake (Single Version)/				
		Secret Oktober	1983	2.00	4.00	8.00
Capitol SPRO-9060	DJ	New Moon on Monday (same on both sides)				
			1983	3.00	6.00	12.00
Capitol SPRO-9093/4	DJ	The Reflex (LP)/The Reflex (Single)/The Reflex (Live)/				
		Religion (Live)New	1984	3.75	7.50	15.00
Capitol SPRO-9315	DJ	Save a Prayer (4 versions)	1984	3.75	7.50	15.00
Capitol SEAX-12352	PD	The Reflex (Dance Mix)	1984	5.00	10.00	20.00
Picture disc with embossed outer sleeve; deduct 25% if cover is missing						
Capitol 15264		Notorious (Extended)/Notorious (45 RPM Mix)/				
		Winter Marches On	1986	3.00	6.00	12.00
Capitol 15266		Notorious (Latin Rascals Mix)/Notorious (Single Version)/				
		Winter Marches On	1986	3.75	7.50	15.00
Capitol 15274		Skin Trade (2 versions)/We Need You				
			1986	2.50	5.00	10.00
Capitol 15320	(2)	Master Mixes: American Science/Vertigo/Skin Trade				
			1986	10.00	20.00	40.00
Capitol 15417		I Don't Want Your Love (3 mixes)	1988	2.00	4.00	8.00
Capitol 15434		All She Wants Is (3 mixes)/I Believe/All I Need				
			1988	2.00	4.00	8.00
Capitol 15456		Do You Believe in Shame/Krush Brothers LSD Edit/Notorious				
			1989	2.50	5.00	10.00
		(Live)/Drug (Alternate Version)				
Capitol 15546		Decadance (2 mixes)/Burning the Ground				
			1989	2.50	5.00	10.00
Capitol 15612		Violence of Summer (4 mixes)/Throb (instrumental)				
			1990	2.00	4.00	8.00
Capitol 15995		Drowning Man (5 versions)	1993	2.50	5.00	10.00
Capitol SPRO-79008/9	DJ	Presidential Suite (3 remixes of Meet El Presidente)/Skin Trade				
		(2 remixes)	1987	3.75	7.50	15.00
Capitol SPRO-79269/70	DJ	Too Much Information (4 mixes)				
			1993	3.75	7.50	15.00
Capitol SPRO-79529	DJ	Do You Believe in Shame (same on both sides)				
			1989	2.00	4.00	8.00
Capitol SPRO-79544	(2) DJ	White Lines (8 mixes)	1994	3.00	6.00	12.00
Harvest SPRO-9636	DJ	Planet Earth (Club Version)/Planet Earth (Radio Version)				
			1981	7.50	15.00	30.00
Harvest SPRO-9662	DJ	Careless Memories//Is There Anyone Out There/Girls on Film				
			1981	7.50	15.00	30.00
Harvest SPRO-9680	DJ	Girls On Film (Club Version)/Girls On Film (Radio Version)				
			1981	5.00	10.00	20.00
Harvest SPRO-9786/7	DJ	Hungry Like the Wolf/Lonely in Your Nightmare/Rio				
			1982	5.00	10.00	20.00

Dury, Ian, and the Blockheads

British new wave/dance group.

	Title	Year	VG	VG+	NM
Vinyl Albums					
Polydor PD1-6337	Lord Upminster	1981	3.50	7.00	14.00
Stiff STF 0002	New Boots and Panties	1978	2.50	5.00	10.00
Stiff USE 02	New Boots and Panties	1980	2.50	5.00	10.00
Reissue of Stiff 0002					
Stiff USE 17	Juke Box Dury	1981	3.00	6.00	12.00
Stiff/Epic JE 36104	Do It Yourself	1979	3.00	6.00	12.00
Stiff/Epic JE 36998	Laughter	1980	3.00	6.00	12.00
45s					
Stiff SS 1000	Wake Up and Make Love to Me/Billericay Dickie				
		1978		2.00	4.00

Label, Number		Title	Year	VG	VG+	NM
Stiff/Epic 50726		Hit Me With Your Rhythm Stick/ There Ain't Half Been Some Clever Bastards				
			1979		2.00	4.00
Stiff/Epic 50726	PS	Hit Me With Your Rhythm Stick/ There Ain't Half Been Some Clever Bastards				
			1979		2.00	4.00
Stiff/Epic 50800		Reasons to Be Cheerful Pt. 3/ Hit Me With Your Rhythm Stick (Dance Version)				
			1979		2.00	4.00
Stiff/Epic AE7 1190	DJ	Reasons for Promotion Pt. 3	1979	2.50	5.00	10.00
With Tom Couch and Eddie Gorodetsky						

12-Inch Singles

Label, Number		Title	Year	VG	VG+	NM
Stiff SP 19	DJ	Wake Up and Make Love to Me/Billericay Dickie				
			1978	3.00	6.00	12.00
Stiff/Epic AE 819	DJ	Hit Me With Your Rhythm Stick/Clever Bastards				
			1978	3.00	6.00	12.00
Stiff/Epic 50779		Hit Me With Your Rhythm Stick/Reasons to Be Cheerful Pt. 3				
			1979	3.75	7.50	15.00

Dwarves

Vinyl Albums

Label, Number		Title	Year	VG	VG+	NM
Sub Pop 67		Blood, Guts and Pussy	1990	5.00	10.00	20.00
First 1,000 on red vinyl						
Sub Pop 67		Blood, Guts and Pussy	1990	2.50	5.00	10.00
Sub Pop 126		Thank Heaven for Little Girls	1991	2.50	5.00	10.00
Sub Pop 197		Sugar Fix	1993	2.50	5.00	10.00

7-Inch Extended Play Singles

Label, Number		Title	Year	VG	VG+	NM
Sub Pop 81		Drugstore	1990	2.50	5.00	10.00
Purple vinyl						
Sub Pop 81		Drugstore	1990		2.50	5.00
Sub Pop 81	PS	Drugstore	1990	2.50	5.00	10.00
With "Fuck you up and get high" pin						
Sub Pop 81	PS	Drugstore	1990		2.50	5.00
Without pin						

45s

Label, Number		Title	Year	VG	VG+	NM
Sub Pop 50		She's Dead/Fuckhead	1990	5.50	11.25	22.50
White vinyl pressing of 1,500						
Sub Pop 50		She's Dead/Fuckhead	1990		3.75	7.50
Black vinyl pressing of 1,500						
Sub Pop 50	PS	She's Dead/Fuckhead	1990		3.75	7.50
#16 in Sub Pop Singles Club series						
Sub Pop 113		Lucky Tonight	1991		2.50	5.00
All copies on orange vinyl						
Sub Pop 113	PS	Lucky Tonight	1991		2.50	5.00
Sub Pop 183		Underworld/Lies	1993		2.50	5.00
Sub Pop 183	PS	Underworld/Lies	1993		2.50	5.00
Sub Pop 183-5		Underworld/Lies	1993	3.00	6.25	12.50
Special 5-inch single pressing on orange vinyl						
Sub Pop 183-5	PS	Underworld/Lies	1993	3.00	6.25	12.50
Picture sleeve for the above						
Sub Pop 195		Anybody Out There	1993		2.50	5.00
Sub Pop 195	PS	Anybody Out There	1993		2.50	5.00

Label, Number		Title	Year	VG	VG+	NM

E

Earle, Steve

Alternative country/rock/folk artist.

Vinyl Albums

Label, Number		Title	Year	VG	VG+	NM
Epic FE 39226		Early Tracks	1987	3.50	7.00	14.00
MCA 5713		Guitar Town	1986	2.50	5.00	10.00
MCA 5998		Exit 0	1987	2.50	5.00	10.00
MCA R 143506		Exit 0	1987	3.00	6.00	12.00
BMG Direct Marketing edition						
MCA R 154072		Guitar Town	1986	3.00	6.00	12.00
RCA Music Service edition						
Uni 7		Copperhead Road	1988	2.50	5.00	10.00
Uni R 100679		Copperhead Road	1988	3.00	6.00	12.00
BMG Direct Marketing edition						

7-Inch Extended Play Singles

Label, Number		Title	Year	VG	VG+	NM
LSI 8209		Nothin' But You/Continental Trailways Blues/Squeeze Me In/ My Baby Worships Me	1982	5.00	10.00	20.00
LSI 8209	PS	Pink and Black	1982	5.00	10.00	20.00

45s

Label, Number		Title	Year	VG	VG+	NM
Epic 04070		Nothin' But You/Continental Trailways Blues	1983		2.50	5.00
Epic 04307		Squeeze Me In/The Devil's Right Hand	1984		2.50	5.00
Epic 04666		What'll You Do About Me/Cry Myself to Sleep	1984		2.50	5.00
Epic 04784		A Little Bit in Love/The Crush	1985			3.00
Epic 04784	PS	A Little Bit in Love/The Crush	1985			3.00
Epic 04784	PS	A Little Bit in Love	1985		3.00	6.00
"Demonstration -- Not for Sale" on back						
MCA 52785		Hillbilly Highway/Down the Road	1986			3.00
MCA 52856		Guitar Town/Little Rock 'N' Roller	1986			3.00
MCA 52920		Someday/Hillbilly Highway	1986			3.00
MCA 53011		Goodbye's All We Got Left/Good Ol' Boy (Gettin' Tough)	1987			3.00
MCA 53103		Nowhere Road/I Ain't Ever Satisfied	1987			3.00
MCA 53182		Sweet Little '66/Angry Young Man	1987			3.00
MCA 53249		Six Days on the Road/The Week of Living Dangerously	1988			3.00
MCA 53532		Guitar Town/Hillbilly Highway	1988			3.00
"Double Hit" reissue						
MCA 53608		Someday/Goodbye's All We Got Left to Say	1988			3.00
"Double Hit" reissue						

12-Inch Singles

Label, Number		Title	Year	VG	VG+	NM
MCA 17129	DJ	Someday/Fearless Heart/Good Ol' Boy	1986		3.00	6.00
MCA 17327	DJ	I Ain't Ever Satisfied (same on both sides)	1987		3.00	6.00
MCA 23693		Someday/State Trooper (Live)/Good Ol' Boy (Live)	1986	2.00	4.00	8.00

Label, Number		Title	Year	VG	VG+	NM

Easton, Elliot
Member of The Cars.

Vinyl Albums
| Elektra 60393 | | Change No Change | 1985 | 2.50 | 5.00 | 10.00 |

45s
Elektra 69645		Shayla/(Wearing Down) Like a Wheel				
			1985			3.00
Elektra 69652		(Wearing Down) Like a Wheel/The Hard Way				
			1985			3.00

12-Inch Singles
Elektra ED 5033	DJ	(Wearing Down) Like a Wheel (same on both sides)				
			1985		2.50	5.00
Elektra 5050	DJ	Shayla (same on both sides)	1985		2.50	5.00

Eat, The
Miami-based punk rockers.

7-Inch Extended Play Singles
| Giggling Hitler (#unknown) | | God Punishes The Eat | 1980 | 12.50 | 25.00 | 50.00 |
| Giggling Hitler (#unknown) | PS | God Punishes The Eat | 1980 | 12.50 | 25.00 | 50.00 |

Sleeve with baseball card and lyrics insert; other inserts include a 45 adaptor, photos, a sticker and (in some) a $1 rebate offer (each adds another 10% to value)

45s
Giggling Hitler (#unknown)		Communist Radio/Catholic Love (Live)				
			1979	18.75	37.50	75.00
Giggling Hitler (#unknown)	PS	Communist Radio/Catholic Love (Live)				
			1979	18.75	37.50	75.00

Echo and the Bunnymen
English new wave trio.

Vinyl Albums
Sire SRK-3569		Heaven Up Here	1981	2.50	5.00	10.00
Sire SRK-6096		Crocodiles	1980	2.50	5.00	10.00
Sire 23770		Porcupine	1983	2.50	5.00	10.00
Sire 23987	EP	The Echo	1983	2.50	5.00	10.00
Sire 25084		Ocean Rain	1984	3.00	6.00	12.00
Sire 25360		Songs to Learn and Sing	1986	3.00	6.00	12.00
Sire 25597		Echo and the Bunnymen	1987	2.50	5.00	10.00

45s
Sire 28113		Bed Bugs and Ballyhoo/Run, Run, Run (Live)				
			1988			2.50
Sire 28113	PS	Bed Bugs and Ballyhoo/Run, Run, Run (Live)				
			1988			2.50
Sire 28260		Lips Like Sugar/Rollercoaster	1987			3.00
Sire 28260	PS	Lips Like Sugar/Rollercoaster	1987			3.00
Sire 28791		Bring On the Dancing Horses/Read It in Books				
			1986			2.50
Sire 28791	PS	Bring On the Dancing Horses/Read It in Books				
			1986			2.50
Sire 29288		Seven Seas/Angels and Devils	1984			3.00
Sire 29664		The Cutter/Gods Will Be Gods	1983			3.00

12-Inch Singles
Sire PRO-A-2164	DJ	Seven Seas/Silver	1984	3.00	6.00	12.00
Sire PRO-A-2398	DJ	Bring On the Dancing Horses/Bring On the Dancing Horses (7")				
			1985	2.50	5.00	10.00

Label, Number		Title	Year	VG	VG+	NM
Sire PRO-A-2774	DJ	New Direction (same on both sides)				
			1987		3.00	6.00
Sire PRO-A-2977	DJ	Bedbugs and Ballyhoo (2 versions)				
			1987		3.00	6.00
Sire 20203		Killing Moon (all night version)/Killing Moon (Live)/				
		Do It Clean (Live)	1983	3.00	6.00	12.00
Sire 20784		Lips Like Sugar (3 versions)/Rollercoaster				
			1987		3.00	6.00
Sire 20838		Bedbugs and Ballyhoo (2 versions)/Run Run Run/Paint It Black/				
		Friction	1988		3.00	6.00

Eddie and the Subtitles

Los Angeles punk band.

Vinyl Albums

13th Story (no #)		Dead Drunks Don't Dance	1983	6.25	12.50	25.00
No Label (no #)		Skeletons in the Closet	1981	10.00	20.00	40.00

45s

(No label or number)		Louie, Louie/American Society	1980	7.50	15.00	30.00
(No label or number)	PS	Louie, Louie/American Society	1980	7.50	15.00	30.00
Folder sleeve in plastic bag						

Edmunds, Dave

*British roots-rocker with a 25-year career. Also a member of **Rockpile**.*

Vinyl Albums

Atlantic PR 320	DJ	College Network	1978	12.50	25.00	50.00
Promo-only interview album						
Capitol C1-90372		Closer to the Flame	1990	3.75	7.50	15.00
Columbia AS99 1725	PD	Information	1983	6.25	12.50	25.00
Promo-only picture disc						
Columbia FC 37930		D.E. 7th	1982	3.00	6.00	12.00
Columbia PC 37930		D.E. 7th	198?	2.00	4.00	8.00
Budget-line reissue ("02" added to bar code on back cover)						
Columbia FC 38651		Information	1983	3.00	6.00	12.00
Columbia PC 38651		Information	198?	2.00	4.00	8.00
Budget-line reissue ("02" added to bar code on back cover)						
Columbia FC 39273		Riff Raff	1984	2.50	5.00	10.00
Columbia FC 40603		I Hear You Rockin'	1987	2.50	5.00	10.00
Columbia PC 40603		I Hear You Rockin'	198?	2.00	4.00	8.00
Budget-line reissue ("02" added to bar code on back cover)						
MAM 3		Rockpile	1972	10.00	20.00	40.00
RCA Victor LPL1-5003		Subtle as a Flying Mallet	1975	3.00	6.00	12.00
RCA AYL1-4238		Subtle as a Flying Mallet	1982	2.50	5.00	10.00
Reissue (black label, dog near top)						
Swan Song SS 8418		Get It	1977	3.75	7.50	15.00
Swan Song SS 8505		Trax on Wax 4	1978	3.75	7.50	15.00
Swan Song SS 8507		Repeat When Necessary	1979	3.75	7.50	15.00
Swan Song SS 8510		The Best of Dave Edmunds	1981	3.00	6.00	12.00
Swan Song SD 16034		Twangin'	1981	3.00	6.00	12.00

45s

Capitol 44525		Closer to the Flame/Stay with Me Tonight				
			1990		*May be cassette-only*	
Capitol 7PRO-79973	DJ	Closer to the Flame (same on both sides)				
			1990	2.50	5.00	10.00
Columbia 02960		From Small Things (Big Things One Day Come)/				
		Warmed Over Kisses (Left Over Love)				
			1982		2.00	4.00
Columbia 03428		Run Rudolph Run/Deep in the Heart of Texas				
			1982		2.00	4.00

Label, Number		Title	Year	VG	VG+	NM
Columbia 03428	PS	Run Rudolph Run/Deep in the Heart of Texas				
			1982	2.00	4.00	8.00
A reasonably scarce sleeve						
Columbia 03877		Slipping Away/Don't Call Me Tonight				
			1983			3.00
Columbia 04080		Information/What Have I Got to Do to Win				
			1983			3.00
Columbia 04585		Something About You/You Can't Get Enough				
			1984			3.00
Columbia 04700		Breaking Out/How Could I Be So Wrong				
			1984			3.00
Columbia 04762		High School Nights/Porky's Revenge				
			1985			2.50
Columbia 04762	PS	High School Nights/Porky's Revenge				
			1985			2.50
Columbia 04887		Queen of the Hop/I Don't Want to Do It				
			1985	5.00	10.00	20.00
B-side by George Harrison, thus accounting for this 45's value						
Columbia 04923		Do You Want to Dance/Don't Call Me Tonight				
			1985			3.00
Columbia 05487		Run Rudolph Run/From Small Things (Big Things One Day Come)				
			198?			3.00
"Golden Oldies" reissue						
Columbia 06599		The Wanderer/Information	1987			3.00
Columbia 07040		Paralyzed/Here Comes the Weekend				
			1987			3.00
MAM 3601		I Hear You Knocking/Black Bill	1970	2.00	4.00	8.00
MAM 3608		I'm Coming Home/Country Roll	1971		3.00	6.00
MAM 3611		Blue Monday/I'll Get Along	1971		3.00	6.00
MCA 53256		Gonna Move/Red River Rock	1988			2.50
B-side by Silicon Teens						
MCA 53256	PS	Gonna Move/Red River Rock	1988			2.50
B-side by Silicon Teens						
RCA Victor 74-0882		Baby I Love You/Maybe	1973		3.00	6.00
RCA Victor LPBO-5000		Born to Be with You/Pick Axe Rag				
			1973		3.00	6.00
RCA Victor PB-10118		Let It Be Me/Need a Shot of Rhythm and Blues				
			1974		2.50	5.00
Swan Song 70113		I Knew the Bride/Little Darlin'	1978		2.00	4.00
Swan Song 70116		Get Out of Denver/Work Out Suits				
			1978		2.00	4.00
Swan Song 70118		Trouble Boys/What Looks Best on You				
			1978		2.00	4.00
Swan Song 71001		Girls Talk/Creature from the Black Lagoon				
			1979		2.50	5.00
Swan Song 71002		Crawling from the Wreckage/Queen of Hearts				
			1979		2.50	5.00
Swan Song 72000		Almost Saturday Night/You'll Never Get Me Up				
			1981			3.00
Swan Song 72000	PS	Almost Saturday Night/You'll Never Get Me Up				
			1981			3.00
Swan Song 72003		The Race Is On/Singin' the Blues	1981		2.50	5.00
Backing group: Stray Cats						

12-Inch Singles

Label, Number		Title	Year	VG	VG+	NM
Columbia AS 1660	DJ	Slipping Away (same on both sides)	1982	2.00	4.00	8.00
Columbia AS 1911	DJ	Something About You (same on both sides)				
			1984		3.00	6.00
Columbia CAS 2077	DJ	Do You Want to Dance (same on both sides)				
			1985		3.00	6.00
Columbia CAS 02598	DJ	The Wanderer/Dave Edmunds Mega-Mix				
			1986		3.00	6.00

Label, Number		Title	Year	VG	VG+	NM

Edmunds, Dave, and Nick Lowe

45s

Columbia AE7-1219	DJ	Nick Lowe and Dave Edmunds Sing The Everly Brothers				
			1980	2.50	5.00	10.00

Bonus EP included in the Rockpile LP Seconds of Pleasure

Elastica
British alterna-rockers.

Vinyl Albums

DGC 24728		Elastica	1995	2.50	5.00	10.00

45s

Sub Pop 275		Stutter/Pussycat	1994	2.50	5.00	10.00
Sub Pop 275	PS	Stutter/Pussycat	1994	2.50	5.00	10.00

Produced by Sub Pop for export to the U.K.

Electronic
*Side project of **Johnny Marr (ex-The Smiths**) and Bernard Summer (of **New Order**). Also has **Pet Shop Boys** involvement.*

45s

Warner Bros. 19161		Feel Every Beat	1992		*Cassette only*	
Warner Bros. 19880		Getting Away With It/Lucky Bag	1990		2.00	4.00

12-Inch Singles

Warner Bros. 21832		Get the Message (3 versions)/Free Will (extended)				
			1991	2.00	4.00	8.00
Warner Bros. 40159		Feel Every Beat (5 versions)/Lean to the Inside				
			1991	2.00	4.00	8.00
Warner Bros. 40562		Disappointed (3 versions)/Gangster (Ibi Mix)				
			1992	2.00	4.00	8.00

Elfman, Danny
Of Oingo Boingo.

Vinyl Albums

MCA 5535		So-Lo	1984	2.50	5.00	10.00

45s

MCA 52560		Gratitude/Tough as Nails	1985			3.00
MCA 52560	PS	Gratitude/Tough as Nails	1985			3.00
Warner Bros. 22756		The Batman Theme (Edit)/The Batman Theme (Action Mix)				
			1989			3.00
Warner Bros. 22756	PS	The Batman Theme (Edit)/The Batman Theme (Action Mix)				
			1989			3.00

12-Inch Singles

MCA L33-1249	DJ	Gratitude (3 versions)	1984	3.00	6.00	12.00
MCA L33-1260	DJ	Gratitude (Remix) (same on both sides)				
			1985	2.50	5.00	10.00
MCA 23532		Gratitude (3 versions)	1984	2.50	5.00	10.00

Elvis Brothers, The

Vinyl Albums

Portrait BFR 38865		Movin' Up	1983	3.00	6.00	12.00

45s

Portrait 04106		Hidden in a Heartbeat/Full Speed Straight Ahead				
			1983			3.00

Label, Number		Title	Year	VG	VG+	NM
Portrait 04106	PS	Hidden in a Heartbeat/Full Speed Straight Ahead				
			1983			3.00
Portrait 04106	PS	Hidden in a Heartbeat	1983		2.50	5.00
"Demonstration -- Not for Sale" on back						
Portrait 04879		Somebody Call the Police/Crosswinds				
			1985			3.00
Recession 88144		Motormouth/Rock for It	1993			2.50
Green vinyl, small center hole						
Recession 88144	PS	Motormouth/Rock for It	1993			2.50

Ely, Joe

*One-time member of **Jimmie Dale and the Flatlanders**. Too country to make it as a rocker, too rock to make it on the country charts.*

Vinyl Albums

Hightone 8008		Lord of the Highway	1987	2.50	5.00	10.00
Hightone 8015		Dig All Night	1988	2.50	5.00	10.00
MCA 2242		Joe Ely	1977	4.00	8.00	16.00
MCA 2333		Honky Tonk Masquerade	1978	4.00	8.00	16.00
MCA 3080		Down on the Drag	1979	4.00	8.00	16.00
Originals have a gatefold sleeve						
MCA 5262		Live Shots	1981	3.00	6.00	12.00
MCA 5480		Hi-Res	1984	3.00	6.00	12.00
MCA R 124826		Live at Liberty Lunch	1990	3.75	7.50	15.00
BMG Music Service edition						
Southcoast 5183		Musta Notta Gotta Lotta	1981	3.00	6.00	12.00

45s

MCA 40666		All My Love/Mardi Gras Waltz	1976		2.00	4.00
MCA 40709		Gambler's Bride/Tennessee's Not the State I'm In				
			1977		2.00	4.00
MCA 40870		Fingernails/Because of the Wind	1978		2.00	4.00
MCA 40906		Honky Tonk Masquerade/Johnny Blues				
			1978		2.00	4.00
MCA 40956		Cornbread Moon/She Never Spoke Spanish to Me				
			1978		2.00	4.00
South Coast 51102		Musta Notta Gotta Lotta/Rock Me My Baby				
			1981		2.00	4.00

12-Inch Singles

Hightone 1001	DJ	Lord of the Highway (same on both sides)				
			1987		3.00	6.00
Hightone 1002	DJ	My Baby Thinks She's French (same on both sides)				
			1987		2.50	5.00
Southcoast L33 1168	DJ	What's Shakin' Tonight (same on both sides)				
			1984		3.00	6.00

EMF

Alternative techno-funk/rock group from England.

Vinyl Albums

EMI E1-96238		Schubert Dip	1991	3.00	6.00	12.00

45s

(EMI) 7PRO 4786	DJ	Lies/Strange Brew (Live)	1991	3.00	6.00	12.00
Maroon label, small hole, no label name on label						
EMI S7-56801		There Here/It's You That Leaves Me Dry				
			1992			3.00
EMI S7-57799		Unbelievable/Search and Destroy				
			1992		3.00	6.00

Label, Number		Title	Year	VG	VG+	NM
12-Inch Singles						
EMI SPRO 04669	DJ	It's You (5 versions)	1992	2.50	5.00	10.00
EMI SPRO 04774/81	DJ	Lies (3 mixes)	1990	2.50	5.00	10.00
EMI SPRO 04810	DJ	Lies (Head the Ball Mix)	1991	7.50	15.00	30.00
Promo-only pressing on clear vinyl; 250 made						
EMI 56209		Unbelievable (6 versions)	1991	2.00	4.00	8.00
EMI 56223		Lies (3 mixes)/Strange Brew (Live)/Head the Ball				
			1991	2.00	4.00	8.00

English Beat, The

British ska band (known there as The Beat, but had to alter their name in the U.S.), evolved into a pop-rock group.

Label, Number		Title	Year	VG	VG+	NM
Vinyl Albums						
I.R.S. SP-70032		Special Beat Service	1982	2.50	5.00	10.00
I.R.S. SP-70040		What Is Beat?	1983	2.50	5.00	10.00
I.R.S. SP-70606		I Just Can't Stop It	1983	2.50	5.00	10.00
Reissue of Sire album of the same name						
I.R.S. SP-70607		Wha'ppen?	1983	2.50	5.00	10.00
Reissue of Sire album of the same name						
Sire SRK-3567		Wha'ppen	1981	3.75	7.50	15.00
Sire SRK-6091		I Just Can't Stop It	1980	3.75	7.50	15.00
45s						
I.R.S. 9909		Save It for Later/Jeanette	1982		2.00	4.00
I.R.S. 9909	PS	Save It for Later/Jeanette	1982		2.00	4.00
I.R.S. 9913		I Confess/March of the Swivel Heads				
			1983		2.00	4.00
Sire 49265		Tears of a Clown/Twist and Crawl				
			1980	2.00	4.00	8.00
12-Inch Singles						
I.R.S. 70408		I Confess (remix)/Jeanette	1982		3.00	6.00
I.R.S. 70964		Save It for Later/Sole Salvation	1982	3.00	6.00	12.00
I.R.S. 70970		Too Nice to Talk To (2 versions)/Best Friend				
			1982		3.00	6.00
Sire PRO-A-874	DJ	Tears of a Clown/Hands Off...She's Mine/Twist and Crawl				
			1980	3.75	7.50	15.00
Sire PRO-A-988	DJ	Too Nice to Talk To/Mirror in the Bathroom/Walk Away				
			1981	3.00	6.00	12.00

Enigma

Romanian by way of Germany, Enigma is Michael Cretu. Uses unusual samples to a dance beat.

Label, Number		Title	Year	VG	VG+	NM
45s						
Charisma 98806		Mea Culpa Part 2 (Catholic Version)/Mea Culpa Part 2				
		(Orthodox Version)	1991		2.00	4.00
Charisma 98864		Sadeness Part 1/Sadeness Part 1(Meditation Mix)				
			1991		2.00	4.00
Virgin S7-17911		Return to Innocence/Return to Innocence (380 Midnight Mix)				
			1994		2.00	4.00
12-Inch Singles						
Charisma 1591	DJ	Sadeness (4 versions)	1990	2.00	4.00	8.00
Charisma 1647	DJ	Mea Culpa Pt. 2 (4 versions)	1990	2.00	4.00	8.00
Charisma 14174	DJ	Age of Loneliness (3 mixes)	1994	2.00	4.00	8.00

Label, Number	Title	Year	VG	VG+	NM

Eno, Brian

Originally with Roxy Music, as a solo artist influenced the whole ambient scene. He also produced many of the more mainstream acts in this book.

Vinyl Albums

Label, Number	Title	Year	VG	VG+	NM
Antilles AN-7001	No Pussyfooting	1973	3.75	7.50	15.00
By Robert Fripp and Eno					
Antilles AN-7018	Evening Star	1975	3.00	6.00	12.00
By Robert Fripp and Eno					
Antilles AN-7030	Discreet Music	1975	3.00	6.00	12.00
Antilles AN-7070	Music for Films	1978	3.75	7.50	15.00
Editions EG ENO-1	Here Come the Warm Jets	1982	2.50	5.00	10.00
Reissue					
Editions EG ENO-2	Taking Tiger Mountain (By Strategy)				
		1982	2.50	5.00	10.00
Reissue					
Editions EG EGBS-2 (11)	Working Backwards: 1983-1973	1984	15.00	30.00	60.00
Boxed set of nine albums plus Music For Films II and Rarities 12"					
Editions EG ENO-3	Another Green World	1982	2.50	5.00	10.00
Reissue					
Editions EG ENO-4	Before and After Science	1982	2.50	5.00	10.00
Reissue					
Editions EG ENO-5	Apollo: Atmospheres and Soundtracks				
		1983	2.50	5.00	10.00
Editions EG EGED-20	Ambient 4 -- On Land	1982	2.50	5.00	10.00
Editions EG EGED-37	The Pearl	1984	3.00	6.00	12.00
By Harold Budd and Brian Eno					
Editions EG EGS-102	No Pussyfooting	1982	2.50	5.00	10.00
By Robert Fripp and Eno; reissue					
Editions EG EGS-103	Evening Star	1982	2.50	5.00	10.00
By Robert Fripp and Eno; reissue					
Editions EG EGS-105	Music for Films	1982	2.50	5.00	10.00
Reissue					
Editions EG EGS-107	Fourth World Volume 1: Possible Musics				
		1980	3.00	6.00	12.00
With Jon Hassell					
Editions EG EGS-201	Ambient #1 -- Music for Airports	1982	3.00	6.00	12.00
Reissue					
Editions EG EGS-202	Ambient 2 -- The Plateaux of Mirrors				
		1982	3.00	6.00	12.00
By Harold Budd and Brian Eno					
Editions EG EGS-301	Pavilion of Dreams	1982	3.00	6.00	12.00
By Harold Budd and Brian Eno					
Editions EG EGS-303	Discreet Music	1983	3.00	6.00	12.00
Reissue					
Island ILPS 9268	Here Come the Warm Jets	1973	3.00	6.00	12.00
Island ILPS 9309	Taking Tiger Mountain (By Strategy)				
		1974	3.00	6.00	12.00
Island ILPS 9351	Another Green World	1975	3.00	6.00	12.00
Double the value if four lithographs are included with the package.					
Island ILPS 9478	Before and After Science	1977	3.00	6.00	12.00
Jem ENO DJ DJ	Music for Airplay	1981	12.50	25.00	50.00
Promo-only 10-track sampler					
Opal/Warner Bros. 25769	Music for Films, Vol. III	1988	2.50	5.00	10.00
Opal/Warner Bros. 26421	Wrong Way Up	1990	2.50	5.00	10.00
With John Cale					
PVC 7908	Ambient #1 -- Music for Airports				
		1979	3.00	6.00	12.00

12-Inch Singles

Label, Number	Title	Year	VG	VG+	NM
Opal 40539	Fractal Zoom (6 versions)/The Roll, The Choke				
		1992	2.00	4.00	8.00

Label, Number		Title	Year	VG	VG+	NM

Eno, Brian, and David Byrne

12-Inch Singles

Sire PRO-A-953	DJ	The Jezebel Spirit/America Is Waiting/Help Me Somebody				
			1981		3.00	6.00

Erasure

*English synth-pop duo formed by Vincent Clarke (ex-**Depeche Mode, Yaz**).*

Vinyl Albums

Mute/Elektra 5621	DJ	Abba-esque (Remixes)	1992	6.25	12.50	25.00
Promo-only vinyl; remixes of 4-song EP; no special jacket						
Sire 25354		Wonderland	1987	3.00	6.00	12.00
Sire 25554		The Circus	1987	3.00	6.00	12.00
Sire 25667	(2)	The Two Ring Circus	1988	3.75	7.50	15.00
Sire 25730		The Innocents	1988	2.50	5.00	10.00
Sire 25904	EP	Crackers International	1989	2.00	4.00	8.00
Sire 26026		Wild!	1989	2.50	5.00	10.00
Sire R 101009		The Innocents	1988	3.00	6.00	12.00
BMG Music Service edition						

45s

Sire 19837		Star	1990		*Cassette only*	
Sire 21863		Chains of Love/A Little Respect				
			199?			3.00
Reissue						
Sire 22721		Blue Savannah/91 Steps	1989		*Cassette only*	
Sire 22879		Stop!/Ship of Fools	1989			3.00
Sire 27738		A Little Respect/Like Zsa Zsa Gabor				
			1988			3.00
Sire 27738	PS	A Little Respect/Like Zsa Zsa Gabor				
			1988			3.00
Sire 27844		Chains of Love/Don't Suppose	1988			3.00
Sire 27844	PS	Chains of Love/Don't Suppose	1988			3.00
Sire 28238		Victim of Love/Soldier's Return	1987			3.00
Sire 28238	PS	Victim of Love/Soldier's Return	1987			3.00
Sire 28362		Sometimes/It Doesn't Have to Be	1987		2.50	5.00
Sire 28614		Oh L'Amour/Gimme! Gimme! Gimme!				
			1986		2.50	5.00
Sire 28728		Push Me Shove Me/Who Needs Love Like That				
			1986		2.50	5.00
Sire PRO-S-3409	DJ	She Won't Be Home (Lonely Christmas)/				
		God Rest Ye Merry Gentlemen	1988	3.00	6.00	12.00
Released with promo insert (add 50%), no picture sleeve						

12-Inch Singles

Mute/Elektra 5716	DJ	I Love Saturday (4 remixes)	1994	3.75	7.50	15.00
Sire PRO-A-3151	DJ	Chains of Love (7" Remix)/Chains of Love (Long Remix)				
			1988	3.75	7.50	15.00
Sire PRO-A-3186	DJ	Chains of Love (6 mixes)	1988	3.75	7.50	15.00
Sire PRO-A-3365	DJ	A Little Respect (6 versions)	1988	3.75	7.50	15.00
Sire PRO-A-3471	DJ	Stop (12" Version)/Stop (7" Version)				
			1988	3.75	7.50	15.00
Sire PRO-A-3601	DJ	Blue Savannah (3 versions)	1989	4.50	9.00	18.00
Sire 20210		Never Never/Stop-Start	1983	3.75	7.50	15.00
Sire 20404		Who Needs Love (Like That) (2 remixes)/Push Me Shove Me/				
		Heavenly Action	1985	2.50	5.00	10.00
Sire 20488		Oh L'Amour (Funky Sisters Remix)/Gimme Gimme Gimme/				
		March Down the Line	1986	2.50	5.00	10.00
Sire 20614		Sometimes (2 remixes)	1987	2.00	4.00	8.00
Sire 20740		Victim of Love (3 versions)/Soldiers Return				
			1987	2.00	4.00	8.00
Sire 20822		The Circus (4 remixes)	1987	2.00	4.00	8.00

Label, Number	Title	Year	VG	VG+	NM
Sire 20953	Chains of Love (3 versions)/The Good, The Bad/Don't Suppose				
		1988		3.00	6.00
Sire 21059	A Little Respect (4 remixes)/Like Zsa Zsa Gabor				
		1988	2.50	5.00	10.00
Sire 21356	Drama (2 versions)/Sweet Sweet Baby (2 versions)/				
	Paradise (2 versions)	1989		3.00	6.00
Sire 21428	Blue Savannah (3 versions)/Runaround on the Underground/				
	Supernature/No GDM	1989		3.00	6.00
Sire 21558	Star (3 versions)/Dreamlike State (24 Hour Technicolor Mix)				
		1990		3.00	6.00
Sire 40123	Chorus (3 mixes)/Snappy (2 mixes)				
		1991	2.00	4.00	8.00
Sire 40344	Breath of Life (6 versions)/Waiting for Sex				
		1991		3.00	6.00
Sire 40721	Who Needs Love (Like That) (3 versions)/				
	The Circus (Gladiator Mix)/Sometimes				
		1992	2.00	4.00	8.00

Eurogliders

Australian pop-rock group.

Vinyl Albums

Columbia BFC 39588	This Island	1984	2.50	5.00	10.00
Columbia BFC 40269	Absolutely	1986	2.50	5.00	10.00

45s

Columbia 04626	Heaven (Must Be There)/Waiting for You				
		1984			3.00
Columbia 04747	Another Day in the Big World/Cold Comfort				
		1985			3.00
Columbia 05797	Can't Wait to See You/I Like to Hear It				
		1986			3.00
Columbia 06105	Absolutely/So Tough	1986			3.00

Eurythmics

*British synth-pop duo of **Annie Lennox** and **Dave Stewart**, formerly of **The Tourists**.*

Vinyl Albums

Arista AL 8606	We Too Are One	1989	3.00	6.00	12.00
RCA Victor ABL1-5371	1984 (For the Love of Big Brother)				
		1984	3.00	6.00	12.00
RCA Victor AFL1-4681	Sweet Dreams (Are Made of This)				
		1983	3.00	6.00	12.00
RCA Victor AFL1-4917	Touch	1984	3.00	6.00	12.00
RCA Victor CPL1-5086 EP	Touch Dance	1983	3.00	6.00	12.00
RCA Victor AJL1-5429	Be Yourself Tonight	1985	3.00	6.00	12.00
RCA Victor DJL1-5707 DJ	Rough and Tough -- Live at the Roxy				
		1986	7.50	15.00	30.00
Promo-only 4-song live album					
RCA Victor AJL1-5827	Revenge	1986	3.00	6.00	12.00
RCA 6794-1-R	Savage	1987	3.00	6.00	12.00

45s

Arista 2243	Sweet Dreams (Are Made of This) '91/				
	The King and Queen of America	1991			3.00
Arista 9880	Don't Ask Me Why/Rich Girl	1989			2.00
Arista 9880 PS	Don't Ask Me Why/Rich Girl	1989			2.00
Arista 9917	Angel/Precious	1989			3.00
Arista 9939	Baby's Gonna Cry/Baby's Gonna Cry (Acoustic)				
		1990			3.00
RCA 5058-7-R	Thorn in My Side/In This Town	1986			3.00
RCA 5058-7-R PS	Thorn in My Side/In This Town	1986			3.00

Label, Number		Title	Year	VG	VG+	NM
RCA 5177		Missionary Man/Thorn in My Side				
			1987			3.00
Reissue						
RCA 5361-7-R		I Need a Man/Heaven	1987			3.00
RCA 5361-7-R	PS	I Need a Man/Heaven	1987			3.00
RCA 7615-7-R		You Have Placed a Chill in My Heart/Wide Eyed Girl				
			1988			3.00
RCA 7615-7-RAA	DJ	You Have Placed a Chill in My Heart (Chill Mix)/				
		You Have Placed a Chill in My Heart				
			1988		2.00	4.00
RCA 7615-7-RAA	PS	You Have Placed a Chill in My Heart (Chill Mix)/				
		You Have Placed a Chill in My Heart				
			1988	5.00	10.00	20.00
A very scarce sleeve						
RCA 7615-7-RX		You Have Placed a Chill in My Heart (Chill Mix)/				
		You Have Placed a Chill in My Heart				
			1988	2.50	5.00	10.00
RCA PB-13533		Sweet Dreams (Are Made of This)/I Could Give You (A Mirror)				
			1983			3.00
RCA PB-13533	PS	Sweet Dreams (Are Made of This)/I Could Give You (A Mirror)				
			1983		2.50	5.00
RCA PB-13618		Love Is a Stranger/Monkey, Monkey				
			1983			3.00
RCA PB-13618	PS	Love Is a Stranger/Monkey, Monkey				
			1983	2.00	4.00	8.00
A reasonably scarce sleeve						
RCA PB-13695		Right By Your Side/Right By Your Side (Party Mix)				
			1984			3.00
RCA PB-13695	PS	Right By Your Side/Right By Your Side (Party Mix)				
			1984			3.00
RCA PB-13725		Here Comes the Rain Again/Paint a Rumour				
			1984			3.00
RCA PB-13725	PS	Here Comes the Rain Again/Paint a Rumour				
			1984			3.00
RCA GB-13790		Sweet Dreams (Are Made of This)/Love Is a Stranger				
			1984			3.00
Gold Standard Series reissue						
RCA PB-13800		Who's That Girl?/Aqua	1984			3.00
RCA PB-13800	PS	Who's That Girl?/Aqua	1984			3.00
RCA PB-13956		Sexcrime (Nineteen Eighty-Four)/I Did It Just the Same				
			1984			3.00
RCA PB-13956	PS	Sexcrime (Nineteen Eighty-Four)/I Did It Just the Same				
			1984			3.00
RCA PB-14015		Julia (Extended)/Theme from 1984 (Sexcrime) (Special Radio Edit)				
			1985			3.00
RCA PB-14015	PS	Julia (Extended)/Theme from 1984 (Sexcrime) (Special Radio Edit)				
			1985			3.00
RCA GB-14063		Here Comes the Rain Again/Right By Your Side				
			1985			3.00
Gold Standard Series reissue						
RCA PB-14078		Would I Lie to You?/Here Comes That Sinking Feeling				
			1985			3.00
RCA PB-14078	PS	Would I Lie to You?/Here Comes That Sinking Feeling				
			1985			3.00
RCA PB-14160		There Must Be An Angel (Playing with My Heart)/Grown Up Girls				
			1985			3.00
RCA PB-14160	PS	There Must Be An Angel (Playing with My Heart)/Grown Up Girls				
			1985			3.00
RCA PB-14284		It's Alright (Baby's Coming Back)/Conditioned Soul				
			1986			3.00
RCA PB-14284	PS	It's Alright (Baby's Coming Back)/Conditioned Soul				
			1986			3.00

Label, Number		Title	Year	VG	VG+	NM
RCA GB-14338		Would I Lie to You?/There Must Be An Angel (Playing with My Heart)	1986			3.00
Gold Standard Series reissue						
RCA PB-14414		Missionary Man/Take Your Pain Away	1986			3.00
RCA PB-14414	PS	Missionary Man/Take Your Pain Away	1986			3.00
12-Inch Singles						
RCA 5726-1-RDAA	DJ	When Tomorrow Comes (same on both sides)	1986	2.00	4.00	8.00
RCA 5771	DJ	Thorn in My Side (same on both sides)	1986	2.00	4.00	8.00
RCA 6820-1-RD		I Need a Man (2 mixes)/(I Love to Dance to) Beethoven (2 mixes)	1987	2.00	4.00	8.00
RCA 6986	DJ	You Have Placed a Chill in My Heart (same on both sides)	1987		3.00	6.00
RCA 7644-1-RDAB		You Have Placed a Chill in My Heart (Dance)/ Here Comes the Rain Again (Live)/Wide Eyed Girl	1988	3.00	6.00	12.00
RCA PD-13502		Sweet Dreams (Are Made of This)/I Could Give You (A Mirror)	1983	2.50	5.00	10.00
RCA PD-13622		Love Is a Stranger (LP)//Love Is a Stranger (Live)/The Walk (Live)	1983	3.75	7.50	15.00
RCA PD-13629		Love Is a Stranger (Club Mix)//Let's Just Close Our Eyes/ Monkey, Monkey	1983	3.00	6.00	12.00
RCA PD-13696		Right By Your Side/Right By Your Side (Special Mix)	1984	2.50	5.00	10.00
RCA JD-13711	DJ	Here Comes the Rain Again (same on both sides)	1984	3.00	6.00	12.00
RCA PW-13726		Here Comes the Rain Again//This City Never Sleeps (live)/ Paint a Rumour	1984	2.00	4.00	8.00
RCA PW-13801		Who's That Girl?//Aqua/Jennifer	1984	2.50	5.00	10.00
RCA JD-13803	DJ	Who's That Girl? (Long)/Who's That Girl? (Short)	1984	2.50	5.00	10.00
RCA JR-13837	DJ	Who's That Girl? (Live) (same on both sides)	1984	3.00	6.00	12.00
RCA PD-13848		The First Cut/Cool Blues/Paint a Rumour/Regret	1983	2.00	4.00	8.00
RCA PD-13957		Sexcrime (Nineteen Eighty-Four) (Extended)//Sexcrime (Single Version)/I Did It Just the Same	1984	2.50	5.00	10.00
RCA JR-13961	DJ	Sexcrime (Nineteen Eighty-Four) (same on both sides)	1984	3.00	6.00	12.00
RCA PD-14016		Julia (Extended)/Ministry of Love (Extended)	1985	2.50	5.00	10.00
RCA PD-14079		Would I Lie to You? (extended)/Here Comes That Sinking Feeling	1985	2.50	5.00	10.00
RCA JD-14080	DJ	Would I Lie to You? (same on both sides)	1985	2.00	4.00	8.00
RCA JD-14143	DJ	Love You Like a Ball and Chain (same on both sides)	1985	2.00	4.00	8.00
RCA PD-14161		There Must Be An Angel (Playing with My Heart)/Grown Up Girls	1985	2.50	5.00	10.00
RCA PW-14287		It's Alright (Baby's Coming Back)//Conditioned Soul/ Tout Les Garcons Et Les Filles	1986	2.50	5.00	10.00
RCA JD-14389	DJ	Missionary Man (same on both sides)	1986		3.00	6.00
RCA PD-14409		Missionary Man (Extended)/Take Your Pain Away	1986	2.00	4.00	8.00

Label, Number		Title	Year	VG	VG+	NM

Eurythmics and Aretha Franklin

45s

RCA PB-14214		Sisters Are Doin' It for Themselves/I Love You Like a Ball and Chain	1985			3.00
B-side by Eurythmics						
RCA PB-14214	PS	Sisters Are Doin' It for Themselves/I Love You Like a Ball and Chain	1985			3.00

12-Inch Singles

RCA JR-14206	DJ	Sisters Are Doin' It for Themselves (same on both sides)	1985	2.00	4.00	8.00
RCA PW-14243		Sisters Are Doin' It for Themselves/I Love You Like a Ball and Chain	1985	2.00	4.00	8.00
B-side by Eurythmics						

Eurythmics and Etta James

12-Inch Singles

Capitol 15453		Avenue D (3 versions)	1989	2.00	4.00	8.00

Everclear

Alterna-rock trio.

Vinyl Albums

Capitol/TimKerr C1 30929		Sparkle and Fade	1995	2.50	5.00	10.00
Green vinyl; originals include bonus 7-inch single, priced separately						

7-Inch Extended Play Singles

Capitol/TimKerr 7PRO-79594		Live on the Radio	1995			2.00
Red vinyl; bonus with first pressings of the LP "Sparkle and Fade"						
Capitol/TimKerr 7PRO-79594 PS		Live on the Radio	1995			2.00

45s

Capitol S7-19018		Santa Monica/Heroin Girl (Acoustic)	1996			3.00

Everything But The Girl

British duo.

Vinyl Albums

Atlantic 82057		The Language of Life	1990	3.00	6.00	12.00
Sire 25214		Everything But The Girl	1984	2.50	5.00	10.00
Sire 25274		Love Not Money	1985	3.00	6.00	12.00
Sire 25494		Baby, the Stars Shine Bright	1986	3.00	6.00	12.00
Sire 25721		Idlewild	1988	2.50	5.00	10.00

45s

Sire 27892		I Always Was Your Girl/Hang Out the Flags	1988		2.00	4.00
Sire 28526		Don't Leave Me Behind/Draining the Bar	1986		2.00	4.00

12-Inch Singles

Sire PRO-A-2605	DJ	Don't Leave Me Behind (same on both sides)	1986		3.50	7.00

Label, Number		Title	Year	VG	VG+	NM

F

Fabulous Poodles

English rock foursome.

Vinyl Albums

Epic JE 35666		Mirror Stars	1978	2.50	5.00	10.00
Epic JE 36256		Think Pink	1979	2.50	5.00	10.00

45s

Epic 50666		Mirror Star/Tit Photographer Blues				
			1979		2.00	4.00
Epic 50720		Work Shy/Toytown People	1979		2.00	4.00
Epic 50823		Man with Money/B Movies	1980		2.00	4.00
Epic 50835		Bionic Man/Suicide Bridge	1980		2.00	4.00

12-Inch Singles

Epic AS 718	DJ	Pink City Twist/Bionic Man	1979	2.50	5.00	10.00

Faith No Man

*Band later evolved into **Faith No More**.*

45s

Ministry of Propaganda FNM 1	Quiet in Heaven/Song of Liberty	1983	5.00	10.00	20.00
Ministry of Propaganda FNM 1PS	Quiet in Heaven/Song of Liberty	1983	5.00	10.00	20.00

Faith No More

San Francisco heavy/rock/rap/you name it band.

Vinyl Albums

Mordam FNM 1		We Care a Lot	1985	5.00	10.00	20.00
Slash 25559		Introduce Yourself	1987	2.50	5.00	10.00
Slash 25878		The Real Thing	1989	2.50	5.00	10.00
Slash 45723	(2)	King for a Day/Fool for a Lifetime				
			1995	3.00	6.00	12.00

45s

Epic 77193	Another Body Murdered (Remix)/Another Body Murdered				
	(Album Version)	1993			*Cassette only*
Reprise 18569	Easy/Das Schutzenfest	1993			3.00
Reprise 18733	A Small Victory	1993			*Cassette only*
Reprise 18832	Midlife Crisis	1993			*Cassette only*
Slash 17868	Evidence/Get Out	1995			3.00
Slash 18891	Epic/Falling to Pieces	1993			3.00
Reissue; first appearance of B-side on U.S. 45					
Slash 19813	Epic/Edge of the World	1990		2.00	4.00
Warner Bros. 28287	We Care a Lot/Spirit	1987		2.00	4.00

12-Inch Singles

Slash PRO-A-2702	DJ	We Care a Lot (2 mixes)/Annie's Song				
			1987	3.00	6.00	12.00
Slash PRO-A-2823	DJ	Chinese Arithmetic (radio)/Chinese Arithmetic (Kick Scream Mix)				
			1987	2.00	4.00	8.00
Slash PRO-A-3559	DJ	From Out of Nowhere (same on both sides)				
			1989		3.00	6.00
Slash PRO-A-5757	DJ	A Small Victory (3 versions)/Malpractice				
			1992	3.00	6.00	12.00

A rare 1991 promo 7-inch single of "Lies," EMF's American follow-up to "Unbe-lievable." This appears to be its only appearance on an American 7-inch. It actually plays at 33 1/3 rpm!

An obviously home-made sleeve, pretty typical of one-shot D.I.Y. records, housed the first single by Faith No Man. Over a period of time, the band evolved into Faith No More. The record and sleeve combined can fetch $40.

Label, Number		Title	Year	VG	VG+	NM

Faithfull, Marianne

Original British Invasion performer, she returned, after years of exile, as a punk/new wave artist.

Vinyl Albums

Label, Number		Title	Year	VG	VG+	NM
ABKCO 75471		Greatest Hits	1988	2.50	5.00	10.00
Reissue of London PS 547						
Island PRO 794	EP	Blazing Away Sampler	1990	5.00	10.00	20.00
Promo-only sampler for radio						
Island ILPS 9570		Broken English	1979	2.50	5.00	10.00
Island ILPS 9648		Dangerous Acquaintances	1981	2.50	5.00	10.00
Island 90039		Broken English	1983	2.00	4.00	8.00
Reissue						
Island 90066		A Child's Adventure	1983	2.50	5.00	10.00
Island 90066	DJ	A Child's Adventure	1983	3.75	7.50	15.00
Promo-only Quiex II audiophile pressing						
Island 90613		Strange Weather	1987	2.50	5.00	10.00
London PS 423	S	Marianne Faithfull	1965	3.75	7.50	15.00
London PS 452	S	Go Away from My World	1965	5.00	10.00	20.00
London PS 482	S	Faithfull Forever	1966	5.00	10.00	20.00
London PS 547		Greatest Hits	1969	3.75	7.50	15.00
London LL 3423	M	Marianne Faithfull	1965	5.00	10.00	20.00
London LL 3452	M	Go Away from My World	1965	3.75	7.50	15.00
London LL 3482	M	Faithfull Forever	1966	3.75	7.50	15.00
Mobile Fidelity 1-235		Broken English	1995	5.00	10.00	20.00
Original Master Recording						

45s

Label, Number		Title	Year	VG	VG+	NM
Collectables 2605		Broken English/Why D'Ya Do It	199?			3.00
Reissue						
Collectables 4238		As Tears Go By/Gloria	199?			3.00
Reissue; B-side by Them						
Island 49121		Broken English/Brain Drain	1979		2.50	5.00
Island 49873		Sweetheart/For Beauty's Sake	1981		2.00	4.00
Island 94997		Broken English/Why D'Ya Do It?	198?		2.00	4.00
Gold label "Revival of the Fittest" series						
London 1022		Sister Morphine/Something Better	1969	25.00	50.00	100.00
Promo worth about 50% of these values.						
London 9697		As Tears Go By/Greensleeves	1964	3.00	6.00	12.00
London 9731		Come and Stay with Me/What Have I Done Wrong	1965	2.50	5.00	10.00
London 9759		This Little Bird/Morning Sun	1965	2.50	5.00	10.00
London 9780		Summer Nights/The Sha-La-La Song	1965	2.50	5.00	10.00
London 9802		Go Away from My World/Oh Look Around You	1965	2.50	5.00	10.00
London 9802	PS	Go Away from My World/Oh Look Around You	1965	5.00	10.00	20.00
London 20012		Counting/Tomorrow's Calling	1966	2.50	5.00	10.00
London 20012	PS	Counting/Tomorrow's Calling	1966	5.00	10.00	20.00
London 20020		Is This What I Get for Loving You/Tomorrow's Calling	1966	2.50	5.00	10.00

12-Inch Singles

Label, Number		Title	Year	VG	VG+	NM
Antilles AN 801		Broken English (5:59)/Why D'Ya Do It	1979	2.50	5.00	10.00
Island DMD 627	DJ	Blue Millionaire (Long)/Blue Millionaire (Short)	1983	2.00	4.00	8.00

Label, Number		Title	Year	VG	VG+	NM

Fall, The

British new-wave band formed in 1977 and with almost constant personnel changes.

Vinyl Albums

Label, Number		Title	Year	VG	VG+	NM
Beggars Banquet 2430-1-H		458489	1990	2.50	5.00	10.00
Beggars Banquet 6897-1-H		The Frenz Experiment	1988	2.50	5.00	10.00
Beggars Banquet 9582-1-H		I Am Kurious Oranj	1988	2.50	5.00	10.00
Beggars Banquet 9807-1-H		Seminal Live	1989	2.50	5.00	10.00
I.R.S. SP-003		Live at the Witch Trials	1979	5.00	10.00	20.00
I.R.S./Faulty COPE-2		Early Years 77-79	1981	3.75	7.50	15.00
Matador OLE 55-1		The Infotainment Scan	1993	2.50	5.00	10.00
Matador OLE 95-1		Middle Class Revolt	1994	2.50	5.00	10.00
PVC 8932		The Wonderful and Frightening World of The Fall				
			1984	4.00	8.00	16.00
PVC 8940		This Nation's Saving Grace	1985	3.75	7.50	15.00
Rough Trade TRADE 3/10	10	Slates	1981	3.00	6.00	12.00
10-inch EP						
Rough Trade ROUGH US 8		Grotesque (After the Gramme)	1981	3.75	7.50	15.00

12-Inch Singles

Label, Number		Title	Year	VG	VG+	NM
PVC 5909		Rollin' Danny/Couldn't Get Ahead/Vixen/Barmy				
			1986	2.00	4.00	8.00
RCA 7617-1	DJ	Victoria (same on both sides)	1988		3.00	6.00
RCA 8826-1-HDAA	DJ	New Big Prinz (same on both sides)				
			1988		3.00	6.00

Farm, The

Liverpool five-person rock group.

45s

Label, Number		Title	Year	VG	VG+	NM
Sire 18809		Rising Sun	1993		*Cassette only*	
Sire 19209		Groovy Train/Stepping Stone	1991			3.00

12-Inch Singles

Label, Number		Title	Year	VG	VG+	NM
Sire PRO-A-4798	DJ	All Together Now (6 versions)	1991	2.50	5.00	10.00
Sire PRO-A-4935	DJ	Groovy Train (5 versions)	1991	2.50	5.00	10.00
Sire PRO-A-5898	DJ	Love See No Colour (4 versions)				
			1992	2.00	4.00	8.00

Fastbacks, The

*With drummer Duff McKagan, pre-**Guns N' Roses**, on the No Threes records.*

7-Inch Extended Play Singles

Label, Number		Title	Year	VG	VG+	NM
No Threes 009		In the Summer/You Can't Be Happy/Everything That I Don't Need/				
		Queen of Eyes	1989		3.75	7.50
No Threes 009	PS	In the Summer/You Can't Be Happy/Everything That I Don't Need/				
		Queen of Eyes	1989		3.75	7.50
Smilin' Ears 009	(2)	Live in America	199?		3.75	7.50
Smilin' Ears 009	PS	Live in America	199?		3.75	7.50

45s

Label, Number		Title	Year	VG	VG+	NM
No Threes 005		It's Your Birthday/You Can't Be Happy				
			1981	7.50	15.00	30.00
No Threes 005	PS	It's Your Birthday/You Can't Be Happy				
			1981	7.50	15.00	30.00
Sub Pop 104	(2)	Impatience/Whatever Happened To/Above the Sunrise/My Letters				
			1991	5.50	11.25	22.50
One red, one green vinyl record						
Sub Pop 104	(2)	Impatience/Whatever Happened To/Above the Sunrise/My Letters				
			1991		3.75	7.50
Two black vinyl records						

Label, Number		Title	Year	VG	VG+	NM
Sub Pop 104	PS	Impatience/Whatever Happened To/Above the Sunrise/My Letters				
			1991		3.75	7.50
Fold-out poster sleeve						

Fear
San Francisco punk band.

Vinyl Albums

Restless 72039		More Beer	1985	3.75	7.50	15.00
Slash 23933		The Record	1982	2.50	5.00	10.00
Slash SR 111		The Record	1982	5.00	10.00	20.00

45s

Criminal Records (no #)		I Love Livin' in the City/Now Your Dead				
			1978	61.50	125.00	250.00
Criminal Records (no #)	PS	I Love Livin' in the City/Now Your Dead				
			1978	61.50	125.00	250.00
Slash 900		Fuck Christmas/*uck Christmas	1979	7.50	15.00	30.00
Not issued with picture sleeve; add 20% for plain white sleeve rubber-stamped with Christmas tree						

Feelies, The
New York/New Jersey-based punk/new wave outfit.

Vinyl Albums

A&M SP-5214		Only Life	1988	3.00	6.00	12.00
A&M 75021 5344 1		Time for a Witness	1991	3.00	6.00	12.00
A&M 75021 7413 1	DJ	Paint It Black + 5	1990	3.75	7.50	15.00
Promo-only 6-song sampler						
Coyote/TwinTone TTC 8673		The Good Earth	1986	3.00	6.00	12.00
Stiff USE-4		Crazy Rhythms	1980	7.50	15.00	30.00
Price is for an actual U.S. pressing. Most copies sold in U.S. were U.K. copies with stickers.						

12-Inch Singles

A&M 17627	DJ	Away (Edit)/Dancing Barefoot	1988	2.00	4.00	8.00

Ferry Aid
Another charity group, this one was put together by Paul McCartney to aid families of the victims of the Zeebrugge (England) ferry sinking.

45s

Profile 5147		Let It Be/Let It Be (Gospel Jam Mix)				
			1987	2.50	5.00	10.00
Profile 5147	PS	Let It Be/Let It Be (Gospel Jam Mix)				
			1987	2.50	5.00	10.00

12-Inch Singles

Profile 7147		Let It Be/Let It Be (Mega Message Mix)				
			1987	3.75	7.50	15.00

Ferry, Bryan
Of Roxy Music.

Vinyl Albums

Atlantic SD 7304	These Foolish Things	1973	3.75	7.50	15.00
Atlantic SD 18113	Another Time, Another Place	1974	3.75	7.50	15.00
Atlantic SD 18187	Let's Stick Together	1976	3.00	6.00	12.00
Atlantic SD 18216	In Your Mind	1977	3.00	6.00	12.00
Atlantic SD 19205	The Bride Stripped Bare	1978	3.00	6.00	12.00
Reprise 25598	Bete Noire	1988	3.00	6.00	12.00
Warner Bros. 25082	Boys and Girls	1985	3.00	6.00	12.00

Label, Number		Title	Year	VG	VG+	NM
45s						
Atlantic 3017		A Hard Rain's Gonna Fall/2 HB	1974		2.50	5.00
Atlantic 3351		Let's Stick Together (Let's Work Together)/Sea Breezes				
			1976		2.00	4.00
Atlantic 3364		Heart on My Sleeve/Re-Make, Re-Model				
			1976		2.00	4.00
Atlantic 3399		Tokyo Joe/As the World Turns	1977		2.00	4.00
Atlantic 3539		Sign of the Times/Can't Let Go	1978		2.00	4.00
MCA 52788		Is Your Love Strong Enough/Windswept				
			1986			3.00
MCA 52788	PS	Is Your Love Strong Enough/Windswept				
			1986			3.00
Reprise 28116		Limbo (Brooklyn Version)/Limbo (Latin Version)				
			1988			3.00
Reprise 28116	PS	Limbo (Brooklyn Version)/Limbo (Latin Version)				
			1988			3.00
Reprise 28117		Kiss and Tell/Zamba	1988			3.00
Reprise 28117	PS	Kiss and Tell/Zamba	1988			3.00
Reprise 28172		The Right Stuff/The Right Stuff (Brooklyn Mix)				
			1987			3.00
Virgin S7-18133		Mamouna/Don't Stop the Dance (Live)				
			1994		2.00	4.00
Warner Bros. 28582		Help Me/Broken Wings	1986			3.00
Warner Bros. 28582	PS	Help Me/Broken Wings	1986			3.00
Warner Bros. 28887		Don't Stop the Dance/Nocturne	1985			3.00
Warner Bros. 28887	PS	Don't Stop the Dance/Nocturne	1985			3.00
Warner Bros. 28990		Slave to Love/Valentine	1985			3.00
Warner Bros. 28990	PS	Slave to Love/Valentine	1985			3.00
12-Inch Singles						
MCA 23620		Is Your Love Strong Enough (2 versions)/Windswept				
			1986	2.00	4.00	8.00
Reprise PRO-A-2852	DJ	The Right Stuff (same on both sides)				
			1987		3.00	6.00
Reprise 20799		The Right Stuff (3 mixes)	1987		3.00	6.00
Reprise 20841		Kiss and Tell (3 versions)/Zamba				
			1988	2.50	5.00	10.00
With picture cover; deduct 40% if cover is missing						
Reprise 20846		Limbo (2 versions)/Bete Noire	1989	2.50	5.00	10.00
Warner Bros. PRO-A-2304	DJ	Slave to Love (Long)/Slave to Love (Short)				
			1985	2.00	4.00	8.00
Warner Bros. PRO-A-2352	DJ	Don't Stop the Dance/Don't Stop the Dance (Edit)				
			1985	2.00	4.00	8.00
Warner Bros. PRO-A-2577	DJ	Help Me (same on both sides)	1986	3.00	6.00	12.00
Warner Bros. 20385		Don't Stop the Dance/Slave to Love				
			1985		3.00	6.00

Figures on a Beach

Boston techno-pop band.

Vinyl Albums						
Metro America 1002	EP	Swimming	1983	2.50	5.00	10.00
Sire 25596		Standing on Ceremony	1987	2.50	5.00	10.00
Sire 25804		Figures on a Beach	1989	2.00	4.00	8.00
45s						
Sire 22870		Accidentally Fourth Street (Gloria)/Get Serious				
			1989			3.00
Sire 27628		You Ain't Seen Nothing Yet/Independence Day				
			1989			3.00
Sire 27628	PS	You Ain't Seen Nothing Yet/Independence Day				
			1989			3.00

Label, Number		Title	Year	VG	VG+	NM
Sire 28270		No Stars/Eternal Repetition	1987			3.00
12-Inch Singles						
Metro America 1004		Breathless (3 mixes)	1984		3.00	6.00
Sire PRO-A-2745	DJ	No Stars (same on both sides)	1987		3.00	6.00
Sire 20793		No Stars (3 versions)/Eternal Repetition				
			1987		3.00	6.00
Sire 21131		You Ain't Seen Nothing Yet (5 versions)				
			1989		3.00	6.00
Sire 21260		Accidentally 4th Street (2 versions)/Get Serious				
			1989		3.00	6.00

Filter

*Cleveland industrial-rock duo, with former members of **Nine Inch Nails**.*

Vinyl Albums						
Reprise 45864		Short Bus	1995	2.50	5.00	10.00

Fine Young Cannibals

*British pop band, one of the two splinter groups from **The English Beat**.*

Vinyl Albums						
I.R.S. 5683		Fine Young Cannibals	1986	2.50	5.00	10.00
I.R.S. 6273		The Raw and the Cooked	1989	2.50	5.00	10.00
I.R.S. 10125		The Raw and the Remix	1990	3.00	6.00	12.00
I.R.S. R 101068		The Raw and the Cooked	1989	3.00	6.00	12.00
BMG Direct Marketing edition						
I.R.S. R 143927		Fine Young Cannibals	1986	3.00	6.00	12.00
BMG Direct Marketing edition						
45s						
I.R.S. 53483		She Drives Me Crazy/Pull the Sucker Off				
			1988			3.00
I.R.S. 53483	PS	She Drives Me Crazy/Pull the Sucker Off				
			1988		2.00	4.00
I.R.S. 53639		Good Thing/Social Security	1989		2.50	5.00
Slight premium because B-side is a doo-wop-style non-LP track						
I.R.S. 53686		I'm Not the Man I Used to Be/Don't Let It Get You Down				
			1989			3.00
I.R.S. 53695		Don't Look Back/As Hard As It Is				
			1989			3.00
I.R.S. 53789		I'm Not Satisfied/Wade in the Water				
			1990			3.00
MCA 52760		Johnny Come Home/Love for Sale				
			1986			3.00
MCA 52760	PS	Johnny Come Home/Love for Sale				
			1986			3.00
MCA 52836		Suspicious Minds/Pick Up Your Ears				
			1986			3.00
MCA 52836	PS	Suspicious Minds/Pick Up Your Ears				
			1986			3.00
MCA 52981		Ever Fallen in Love/Move to Work				
			1986			3.00
MCA 52981	PS	Ever Fallen in Love/Move to Work				
			1986			3.00
12-Inch Singles						
I.R.S. 17763	DJ	She Drives Me Crazy/She Drives Me Crazy (7:05 remix)				
			1989	2.00	4.00	8.00
I.R.S. 23926		She Drives Me Crazy (4 remixes)				
			1989		3.00	6.00
I.R.S. 23959		Good Thing (4 versions)	1989		3.00	6.00
I.R.S. 23979		Don't Look Back (2 versions)/You Never Know				

Label, Number		Title	Year	VG	VG+	NM
			1989	2.00	4.00	8.00
I.R.S. 24009		I'm Not Satisfied (5 versions)	1990	2.00	4.00	8.00
I.R.S. 53950		Johnny Come Home (2 versions)/Johnny Takes a Trip				
			1990	2.00	4.00	8.00
MCA 17075	DJ	Johnny Come Home (same on both sides)				
			1986	2.00	4.00	8.00
MCA 17124	DJ	Suspicious Minds (same on both sides)				
			1986	2.50	5.00	10.00
MCA 17259	DJ	Ever Fallen in Love (same on both sides)				
			1986	2.00	4.00	8.00
MCA 23578		Johnny Come Home (Extended)/Blue (Dance)/Wade in the Water				
			1986	2.00	4.00	8.00
MCA 23626		Suspicious Minds (2 mixes)/Prick Up Your Ears/				
		Johnny Come Home (That Other Mix)				
			1986	2.00	4.00	8.00
MCA 23707		Ever Fallen in Love (3 versions)	1986		3.50	7.00

Finn, Tim

*Australian -- member of both **Split Enz** and **Crowded House** at different times.*

Vinyl Albums

A&M SP-4972		Escapade	1983	2.50	5.00	10.00
Capitol C1-48735		Tim Finn	1989	2.50	5.00	10.00
Virgin 90879		Big Canoe	1988	2.50	5.00	10.00

45s

A&M 2572		Through the Years/Grand Adventure				
			1983			3.00
A&M 2597		Made My Day/Grand Adventure	1983			3.00
Capitol S7-17515		Persuasion/Hit the Ground Running				
			1993			3.00
Capitol 44339		How'm I Gonna Sleep/Cruel Black Crow				
			1989			3.00
Capitol 44339	PS	How'm I Gonna Sleep/Cruel Black Crow				
			1989			3.00

12-Inch Singles

Capitol SPRO-79558	DJ	Crescendo (same on both sides)	1989		2.50	5.00

fIREHOSE

*California band with former members of **The Minutemen**. Also see **Mike Watt**.*

Vinyl Albums

Columbia C 47839		Flyin' the Flannel	1991	3.00	6.00	12.00
SST 079		Ragin' Full-On	1986	3.00	6.00	12.00
SST 115		If'n	1987	3.00	6.00	12.00
SST 131	EP	Sometimes	1988		3.00	6.00
SST 235		fROMOHIO	1989	3.00	6.00	12.00

7-Inch Extended Play Singles

(no label) fHYPE-1	DJ	Flyin' the Flannel/Epoxy, For Example/O'er the Town of Pedro/				
		Too Long	1991	2.00	4.00	8.00
Not issued with picture sleeve						

45s

SST PSST-079	DJ	Brave Captain/Perfect Pairs	1986	2.50	5.00	10.00
Not issued with picture sleeve						

12-Inch Singles

SST PRO 235	DJ	Time with You (same on both sides)				
			1989	2.50	5.00	10.00

Label, Number		Title	Year	VG	VG+	NM

Fishbone

Black funk/thrash band from Los Angeles.

Vinyl Albums

Label, Number		Title	Year	VG	VG+	NM
Columbia CAS 2235	EP	New and Improved Bonin' + 4	1990	3.00	6.00	12.00
Promo-only five-song sampler						
Columbia B6C 40032	EP	Fishbone	1985	3.00	6.00	12.00
Columbia BFC 40333		In Your Face	1986	3.00	6.00	12.00
Columbia FC 40891		Truth and Soul	1988	3.00	6.00	12.00
Columbia 4C 44097	EP	It's a Wonderful Life (Gonna Have a Good Time)				
			1987	2.50	5.00	10.00
Columbia C 46142	(2)	The Reality of My Surroundings	1991	3.75	7.50	15.00

45s

Label, Number		Title	Year	VG	VG+	NM
Columbia 04922		? (Modern Industry)/V.T.T.L.O.T.S.D.G.F.				
			1985		2.00	4.00
Columbia 08500		Freddie's Dead/Question of Life	1988		2.00	4.00
Columbia 73549		New and Improved Bonin'/In the Name of Swing/Love and Bullshit/				
		Hide Behind My Glasses/Bonin' in the Jungle				
			1990			*Cassette only*

12-Inch Singles

Label, Number		Title	Year	VG	VG+	NM
Columbia CAS 2076	DJ	? (Modern Industry) (LP version)/? (Modern Industry) (Dance Mix)				
			1985	2.50	5.00	10.00
Columbia CAS 3082	DJ	Sunless Saturday/Fishy Swa Ska/Understand Me				
			1991		3.00	6.00
Columbia 05223		? (Modern Industry) (3 versions)	1984	3.00	6.00	12.00
Columbia CAS 5252	DJ	Swim (3 versions)	1993	3.00	6.00	12.00
Columbia 05326		Party at Ground Zero (2 versions)/Skanking to the Beat				
			1985	2.50	5.00	10.00
Columbia 05984		When Problems Arise (3 versions)				
			1986	2.00	4.00	8.00
Columbia 08172		Freddie's Dead (5 mixes)	1988	2.00	4.00	8.00

Fishbone and Curtis Mayfield

45s

Label, Number		Title	Year	VG	VG+	NM
Arista 9806		He's a Flyguy/(Instrumental)	1989			2.00
Arista 9806	PS	He's a Flyguy/(Instrumental)	1989			3.00

12-Inch Singles

Label, Number		Title	Year	VG	VG+	NM
Arista 9812		He's a Flyguy (3 versions)	1988		3.00	6.00

Fixx, The

London techno-pop/new wave band.

Vinyl Albums

Label, Number		Title	Year	VG	VG+	NM
MCA 5345		Shuttered Room	1982	3.00	6.00	12.00
MCA 5417		Reach the Beach	1983	2.50	5.00	10.00
Reissue						
MCA L33-1212	DJ	Phantoms	1984	3.75	7.50	15.00
Promo-only with band-member intros						
MCA L33-1213	DJ	Phantoms	1984	3.75	7.50	15.00
MCA 5507		Phantoms	1984	2.50	5.00	10.00
MCA 5705		Walkabout	1986	2.50	5.00	10.00
MCA 10205		Ink	1991	3.00	6.00	12.00
MCA 39001		Reach the Beach	1983	3.50	7.00	14.00
MCA 42008		React	1987	2.50	5.00	10.00
MCA R 153353		Phantoms	1984	3.00	6.00	12.00
RCA Music Service edition						
MCA R 164166		React	1987	3.00	6.00	12.00
BMG Direct Marketing edition						

Label, Number		Title	Year	VG	VG+	NM
MCA R 164380		Walkabout	1986	3.00	6.00	12.00
RCA Music Service edition						
RCA 8566-1-R		Calm Animals	1989	2.50	5.00	10.00
45s						
American Pie 9116		One Thing Leads to Another/Saved by Zero				
			199?			3.00
Reissue						
Impact 54028		How Much Is Enough/(Excerpts)				
			1991			*Cassette only*
Impact 54106		No One Has to Cry/(Excerpts)	1991			*Cassette only*
MCA 52106		Stand or Fall/Sinking Island	1982		2.00	4.00
MCA 52167		Red Skies/Is It By Instinct	1982		2.00	4.00
MCA 52213		Saved by Zero/Going Overboard				
			1983			3.00
MCA 52213	PS	Saved by Zero/Going Overboard	1983			3.00
MCA 52264		One Thing Leads to Another/Opinions				
			1983			3.00
MCA 52264	PS	One Thing Leads to Another/Opinions				
			1983			3.00
MCA 52316		The Sign of Fire/Saved by Zero	1983			3.00
MCA 52316	PS	The Sign of Fire/Saved by Zero	1983			3.00
MCA 52444		Are We Ourselves?/Deeper and Deeper				
			1984			3.00
MCA 52444	PS	Are We Ourselves?/Deeper and Deeper				
			1984			3.00
MCA 52498		Sunshine in the Shade/Question	1984			3.00
MCA 52498	DJ	Sunshine in the Shade (same on both sides)				
			1984	2.50	5.00	10.00
Yellow vinyl						
MCA 52498	PS	Sunshine in the Shade/Question	1984			3.00
MCA 52529		Less Cities, More Moving People/Woman on a Train				
			1984			3.00
MCA 52832		Secret Separation/Sense of Adventure				
			1986			3.00
Not issued with picture sleeve in U.S.						
MCA 52902		Built for the Future/Camphor	1986			3.00
MCA 53066		Red Skies/Built for the Future	1987			3.00
RCA 8837-7-R		Driven Out/Shred of Evidence	1988			3.00
RCA 8837-7-R	PS	Driven Out/Shred of Evidence	1988			3.00
12-Inch Singles						
MCA L33 1102	DJ	Red Skies (same on both sides)	1983	3.75	7.50	15.00
Red vinyl						
MCA L33 1109	DJ	Saved by Zero (Remix)/Outside	1983	3.00	6.00	12.00
MCA L33 1128	DJ	One Thing Leads to Another (8:00 and 3:23)/The Sign of Fire				
			1983	6.25	12.50	25.00
Blue vinyl						
MCA L33 1128	DJ	One Thing Leads to Another (8:00 and 3:23)/The Sign of Fire				
			1983	3.00	6.00	12.00
Black vinyl						
MCA L33 1146	DJ	The Sign of Fire/One Thing Leads to Another (Live)/				
		Saved by Zero (Live)	1983	2.50	5.00	10.00
MCA L33 1184	DJ	Deeper and Deeper (2 versions) + 2				
			1984		3.00	6.00
The "+2" are by Marilyn Martin and Fire Inc., respectively						
MCA L33 1186	DJ	Deeper and Deeper (same on both sides)				
			1984		3.00	6.00
MCA L33 1230	DJ	Less Cities, More Moving People (7:09) (same on both sides)				
			1984		3.00	6.00
MCA L33 1252	DJ	Sunshine in the Shade (Live) (same on both sides)				
			1984		3.00	6.00

Label, Number		Title	Year	VG	VG+	NM
MCA 17027	DJ	A Letter to Both Sides (same on both sides)				
			1985		2.50	5.00
MCA 17175	DJ	Built for the Future (same on both sides)				
			1986		2.50	5.00
MCA 17181	DJ	Built for the Future (3 versions)	1986		3.00	6.00
MCA 17304	DJ	Red Skies (Long)/Red Skies (Short)				
			1987		3.50	7.00

Flaming Lips, The

Oklahoma City punk/alternative band.

Vinyl Albums

Label, Number		Title	Year	VG	VG+	NM
Lovely Sorts of Death (#unknown)		Bag Full of Thoughts	1984	17.50	35.00	70.00
Green vinyl; dark brown background on jacket						
Lovely Sorts of Death (#unknown)		Bag Full of Thoughts	1984	12.50	25.00	50.00
Green vinyl; black background on jacket						
Pink Dust 72173		Here It Is	1986	8.75	17.50	35.00
Originals on white vinyl						
Pink Dust 72188	EP	The Flaming Lips	1985	6.25	12.50	25.00
Originals on lavender vinyl						
Restless 72207		Oh My Gawd, The Flaming Lips	1987	5.00	10.00	20.00
Clear vinyl, gatefold sleeve						
Restless 72350		Telepathic Surgery	1989	2.50	5.00	10.00
Restless 72359		In a Priest Driven Ambulance	1990	2.50	5.00	10.00
Warner Bros. 45334		Transmissions from the Satellite Heart				
			1993	2.50	5.00	10.00
Warner Bros. 45911		Clouds Taste Metallic	1995	2.50	5.00	10.00

45s

Label, Number		Title	Year	VG	VG+	NM
Sub Pop 28		Strychnine/Drug Machine/				
		What's So Funny 'Bout Peace, Love and Understanding				
			1989	5.00	10.00	20.00
Sub Pop 28	PS	Strychnine/Drug Machine/				
		What's So Funny 'Bout Peace, Love and Understanding				
			1989	5.00	10.00	20.00
Warner Bros. PRO-S-5452	DJ	Ballrooms of Mars/Sudden Death				
			1991	6.25	12.50	25.00
"Soil Samples #6" on gray vinyl; B-side by Mr. Bungle						
Warner Bros. 18131		She Don't Use Jelly/Turn It On	1994		2.00	4.00

Flash And The Pan

From Australia, a duo of former members of The Easybeats, who had done "Friday on My Mind" in the 1960s.

Vinyl Albums

Label, Number	Title	Year	VG	VG+	NM
Epic ARE 37725	Headlines	1982	3.00	6.00	12.00
Epic BFE 39618	Early Morning Wake-Up Call	1984	2.00	4.00	8.00
Epic JE 36018	Flash And The Pan	1979	3.50	7.00	14.00
Epic JE 36432	Lights in the Night	1980	2.50	5.00	10.00

45s

Label, Number	Title	Year	VG	VG+	NM
Epic 03316	Where Were You/Hey Jimmy	1982		2.00	4.00
Epic 50715	Hey, St. Peter/Walking in the Rain				
		1979		2.00	4.00
Epic 50761	Down Among the Dead Men/The Man Who Knew the Answer				
		1979		2.00	4.00
Epic 50882	Media Man/Captain Beware	1980		2.00	4.00
Epic 50920	Welcome to the Universe/Lights in the Night				
		1980		2.00	4.00

Label, Number		Title	Year	VG	VG+	NM
Midland Int'l. JB-10934	DJ	Hey, St. Peter (Short)/Hey, St. Peter (Long)				
			1977	2.00	4.00	8.00
Midland Int'l. MB-10934		Hey, St. Peter/Walking in the Rain				
			1977	3.00	6.00	12.00

12-Inch Singles

Label, Number		Title	Year	VG	VG+	NM
Epic AE 761	DJ	Media Man (2 versions)/Welcome to the Universe/Restless				
			1980	2.00	4.00	8.00
Epic 03546		Waiting for a Train (Short)/Waiting for a Train (Long)				
			1983	2.00	4.00	8.00
Epic 05118		Midnight Man/(Instrumental)	1984		3.50	7.00

Flesh For Lulu

British punk band.

Vinyl Albums

Label, Number		Title	Year	VG	VG+	NM
Capitol C1-48217		Long Live the New Flesh	1987	3.00	6.00	12.00
Capitol SPRO 79992	DJ	Final Vinyl (Every Little Word + 7 Live)				
			1989	5.00	10.00	20.00
Red vinyl; sticker on generic cover						
Capitol C1-90232		Plastic Fantastic	1989	3.00	6.00	12.00

45s

Label, Number		Title	Year	VG	VG+	NM
Capitol 44074		Postcards from Paradise/Dumbest Things (Live In Your Living Room)	1987			3.00
Capitol 44165		I Go Crazy/Siamese Twist	1988			3.00
Capitol 44165	PS	I Go Crazy/Siamese Twist	1988			3.00
MCA 53036		I Go Crazy/The Shiest Time	1987			3.00
B-side by The Apartments						
MCA 53036	PS	I Go Crazy/The Shiest Time	1987			3.00
B-side by The Apartments						

12-Inch Singles

Label, Number		Title	Year	VG	VG+	NM
Capitol 15337		Postcards from Paradise (3 versions)/I'm Not Like Everybody Else				
			1987	2.00	4.00	8.00
Capitol 15556		Every Little Word (4 versions)	1989		3.00	6.00
Capitol SPRO 79347	DJ	I Go Crazy (same on both sides)	1987	2.50	5.00	10.00
MCA 17280	DJ	I Go Crazy (same on both sides)	1987		3.00	6.00
MCA 23736		I Go Crazy (3 versions)	1987		3.00	6.00

Flesheaters

*Los Angeles punk band; members later played in X and **The Blasters**.*

Vinyl Albums

Label, Number		Title	Year	VG	VG+	NM
Homestead (# unknown)		Prehistoric Hits Vol. 1	198?	3.00	6.00	12.00
Homestead 124-1		Live	1988	2.50	5.00	10.00
Ruby JRR 805		Forever Came Today	1982	5.00	10.00	20.00
Ruby JRR-101		A Minute to Pray, a Second to Die				
			1981	5.00	10.00	20.00
SST 094		Greatest Hits	1986	3.00	6.00	12.00
SST 094		Destroyed by Fire/Greatest Hits	1991	2.50	5.00	10.00
Reissue with new name						
SST 264		Prehistoric Fits (Volume 2)	1990	3.00	6.00	12.00
SST 273	(2)	Dragstrip Riot	1991	3.00	6.00	12.00
Upsetter UP 56		A Hard Road to Follow	1983	7.50	15.00	30.00
Upsetter UPCJ-34		No Questions Asked	1980	10.00	20.00	40.00

7-Inch Extended Play Singles

Label, Number		Title	Year	VG	VG+	NM
Upsetter (no #)		Flesheaters	1978	7.50	15.00	30.00
Upsetter (no #)	PS	Flesheaters	1978	7.50	15.00	30.00

Label, Number		Title	Year	VG	VG+	NM

Flipper

San Francisco punk group.

Vinyl Albums

Label, Number		Title	Year	VG	VG+	NM
Subterranean SUB 25		Generic Flipper	1981	3.00	6.00	12.00
Subterranean SUB 42		Gone Fishin'	1982	3.00	6.00	12.00
Subterranean SUB 53		Public Flipper Ltd.	1985	3.00	6.00	12.00

45s

Label, Number		Title	Year	VG	VG+	NM
Subterranean SUB 23		Sexbomb/Brainwash	1981		3.00	6.00
Subterranean SUB 23	PS	Sexbomb/Brainwash	1981		3.00	6.00
Subterranean SUB 35		Get Away/The Old Lady That Swallowed the Fly				
			1982		3.00	6.00
Subterranean SUB 35	PS	Get Away/The Old Lady That Swallowed the Fly				
			1982		3.00	6.00
Thermidor/		Love Canal/Ha Ha Ha	1980		3.00	6.00
Subterranean T 1/SUB 7						
Thermidor/	PS	Love Canal/Ha Ha Ha	1980		3.00	6.00
Subterranean T 1/SUB 7						

Flirts, The

Vinyl Albums

Label, Number		Title	Year	VG	VG+	NM
CBS Associated BFZ 40197		Blondes, Brunettes and Redheads	1985	2.50	5.00	10.00
CBS Associated BFZ 40419		Questions of the Heart	1986	2.50	5.00	10.00
O 1		10 Cents a Dance	1982	3.75	7.50	15.00
Preppy 1217	EP	Heartbreak USA	1984	3.00	6.00	12.00
Telefon 8001		Made in America	1984	3.00	6.00	12.00

45s

Label, Number		Title	Year	VG	VG+	NM
CBS Associated 05629		You and Me/Prop	1985			3.00
CBS Associated 05849		New Toy/I Wanna Wear Your Ring				
			1986			3.00
CBS Associated 06345		All You Ever Think About Is (Sex)/				
		All You Ever Think About Is (Sex)				
			1986			3.00
O ORS 1001		Jukebox	1980	2.00	4.00	8.00

12-Inch Singles

Label, Number		Title	Year	VG	VG+	NM
CBS Associated 05284		You and Me (3 versions)	1985		3.00	6.00
CBS Associated 05334		New Toy (2 mixes)	1985		3.00	6.00
CBS Associated 05914		Miss You (3 versions)	1986	2.00	4.00	8.00
CBS Associated 05952		All You Ever Think About Is (Sex) (2 versions)				
			1986	2.00	4.00	8.00
O 720		Passion (9:03)/Passion (5:03)	1982	2.50	5.00	10.00
O 723		We Just Want to Dance (2 versions)				
			1983		3.00	6.00
O 1203		After School (4 versions)	1989		3.00	6.00
Popular POP 16		A Thing Called Love (4 versions)				
			1988	2.00	4.00	8.00
Telefon TE 3		Helpless (7:43)/Helpless (3:55)	1984	2.00	4.00	8.00
Telephone 5		Dancing Madly Backwards/Temptation				
			1986	2.00	4.00	8.00

Flock of Seagulls, A

British synth-pop band.

Vinyl Albums

Label, Number		Title	Year	VG	VG+	NM
Jive 1007-1-J		A Flock of Seagulls	1986	2.00	4.00	8.00
Reissue						
Jive 1008-1-J		Listen	1986	2.00	4.00	8.00
Reissue						

Label, Number		Title	Year	VG	VG+	NM
Jive 1009-1-J		A Dream Come True	1986	2.50	5.00	10.00
Jive 1034-1-J		The Best of A Flock of Seagulls	1987	3.00	6.00	12.00
Jive JL8-8013		Listen	1983	3.00	6.00	12.00
Jive JL8-8250		The Story of a Young Heart	1984	2.50	5.00	10.00
Jive 66000		A Flock of Seagulls	1982	3.50	7.00	14.00

45s

Label, Number		Title	Year	VG	VG+	NM
Jive 102		I Ran (So Far Away)/Pick Me Up	1982		2.50	5.00
Not issued with picture sleeve in U.S.						
Jive 2003		Space Age Love Song/Windows	1982		2.00	4.00
Jive 2003	PS	Space Age Love Song/Windows	1982		2.00	4.00
Jive 2006		Wishing (If I Had a Photograph of You)/Committed	1983		2.00	4.00
Jive 2006	PS	Wishing (If I Had a Photograph of You)/Committed	1983		2.00	4.00
Jive 9018		Wishing (If I Had a Photograph of You)/Committed	1983			3.00
Jive 9018	PS	Wishing (If I Had a Photograph of You)/Committed	1983			3.00
Jive 9069		(It's Not Me) Talking/I Ran	1983			3.00
Jive 9220		The More You Live, The More You Love/Lost Control	1984			3.00
Jive 9220	PS	The More You Live, The More You Love/Lost Control	1984			3.00

12-Inch Singles

Label, Number		Title	Year	VG	VG+	NM
GNP Crescendo GNPS 1208		Magic (4 versions)	1989	2.00	4.00	8.00
Jive 9061		(It's Not Me) Talking/Nightmares	1983	2.50	5.00	10.00
Jive 9079	DJ	(It's Not Me) Talking (same on both sides)	1983	2.00	4.00	8.00
Jive 9221		The More You Live/The More You Live (Full Moon Mix)	1984	2.00	4.00	8.00
Jive 9463		Heartbeat Like a Drum (3 versions)/Effect of the Sun	1986		3.00	6.00
Jive 12002		Space Age Love Song/I Ran	1982	3.50	7.00	14.00
Jive 12014		Wishing (If I Had a Photograph of You)/The Flight of Yuri Gagarin/ Rosenmontag/Committed	1983	2.50	5.00	10.00
Jive VK 22001		Telecommunication/Tanglimara/You Can Run/ Modern Love Is Automatic/DNA	1981	3.00	6.00	12.00

Flying Lizards, The

British techno-pop/new wave group. Their version of "Money" must be heard to be believed.

Vinyl Albums

Label, Number		Title	Year	VG	VG+	NM
Virgin VA 13137		The Flying Lizards	1980	3.00	6.00	12.00

45s

Label, Number		Title	Year	VG	VG+	NM
Virgin 67003		Money/Money B	1979		2.00	4.00
Virgin 67003	PS	Money/Money B	1979		2.00	4.00
Virgin 67006		TV/Tube	1980		2.00	4.00
Virgin 67006	PS	TV/Tube	1980		2.00	4.00

12-Inch Singles

Label, Number		Title	Year	VG	VG+	NM
Virgin DK-4809		Money/Summertime Blues	1980	3.00	6.00	12.00

Foo Fighters

*With Dave Grohl, formerly of **Nirvana**.*

Vinyl Albums

Label, Number		Title	Year	VG	VG+	NM
Roswell/Capitol C1-34027		Foo Fighters	1995	2.50	5.00	10.00

Label, Number		Title	Year	VG	VG+	NM
12-Inch Singles						
Capitol/Roswell SPRO 79641/2	DJ	Exhausted/Winnebago	1995	2.50	5.00	10.00

Fordham, Julia

45s						
Virgin 99224		Comfort of Strangers/I Know	1989			3.00

4 Out of 5 Doctors

Vinyl Albums						
Nemperor JZ 36575		4 Out of 5 Doctors	1981	3.00	6.00	12.00
Nemperor ARZ 37700		Second Opinion	1982	2.50	5.00	10.00
45s						
Nemperor 01048		Modern Man/New Wave Girls	1981		2.00	4.00
Nemperor 02716		Call Me at Home/Never Say Die	1982		2.00	4.00
Nemperor 7538		I Want Her/Opus 10	1980		2.00	4.00

Frankie Goes To Hollywood

*British band assembled by Trevor Horn (ex-**Buggles**) and featuring **Holly Johnson**.*

Vinyl Albums						
Atlantic (# unknown)		Bang...The Greatest Hits of Frankie Goes to Hollywood				
			1994	3.00	6.00	12.00
Island 90232	(2)	Welcome to the Pleasuredome	1985	3.75	7.50	15.00
Island 90546		Liverpool	1986	2.00	4.00	8.00
Island R 120202		Liverpool	1986	2.50	5.00	10.00
RCA Music Service edition						
45s						
Island PR 695	DJ	Relax (same on both sides)	1983	3.00	6.00	12.00
Island PR 976	DJ	Rage Hard (Remix) (same on both sides)				
			1986	2.50	5.00	10.00
Island 99486		Warriors of the Wasteland (Edited Mix)/ Warriors of the Wasteland (Extended Mix)				
			1986			3.00
Island 99486	PS	Warriors of the Wasteland (Edited Mix)/ Warriors of the Wasteland (Extended Mix)				
			1986			3.00
Island 99502		Rage Hard/(Don't Lose What's Left) Of Your Little Mind				
			1986			3.00
Island 99653		Welcome to the Pleasuredome/Relax International (Live)				
			1985			3.00
Island 99653	PS	Welcome to the Pleasuredome/Relax International (Live)				
			1985			3.00
Island 99695		Two Tribes/One February Friday	1984			3.00
Island 99695	PS	Two Tribes/One February Friday	1984			3.00
Island 99805		Relax/One September Monday	1983		3.00	6.00
Original single mix (time 3:02), dark purple label, no picture sleeve						
Island 99805		Relax/One September Monday	1983		2.00	4.00
New single mix (time 3:55), dark purple label, no picture sleeve						
Island 99805		Relax/One September Monday	1983			3.00
New single mix (time 3:55), light blue label, only some have picture sleeves						
Island 99805	PS	Relax/One September Monday	1983		2.50	5.00
Only released with later editions of the single						
12-Inch Singles						
Island PR 657	DJ	Two Tribes (same on both sides)	1984	2.00	4.00	8.00
Island DMD 691	DJ	Relax (7:20, 3:56 and 4:24 versions)				
			1983	7.50	15.00	30.00

Label, Number		Title	Year	VG	VG+	NM
Island PR 696	DJ	Relax (same on both sides)	1984	3.00	6.00	12.00
Island PR 706	DJ	Welcome to the Pleasuredome (Edit)/Relax (Live)				
			1985	12.50	25.00	50.00
Clear vinyl, with letter from Island Records						
Island DMD 830	DJ	Welcome to the Pleasuredome (2 versions)/				
		Relax International (Live)	1985	4.50	9.00	18.00
Island PR 945	DJ	Rage Hard (Remix) (same on both sides)				
			1986		3.00	6.00
Island PR 999	DJ	Warriors of the Wasteland (2 mixes)				
			1986	2.00	4.00	8.00
Island 96799		Warriors of the Wasteland (9:42)/Warriors of the Wasteland (8:11)				
			1986		3.00	6.00
Island 96806		Rage Hard/Suffragette City/Your Little Mind				
			1986		3.00	6.00
Island 96931		Two Tribes (2 versions)/One February Friday/War				
			1984		3.00	6.00
Island 96975		Relax (3 versions)	1983	2.50	5.00	10.00

Frogs, The

*Openly gay band; also appears on the B-side of a **Pearl Jam** single.*

45s

Matador ELO 069-7		Here Comes Santa's Pussy//Have a Merry X-Mas/Snow Kisses				
			1995			2.50
Green vinyl, small hole						
Matador ELO 069-7	PS	Here Comes Santa's Pussy//Have a Merry X-Mas/Snow Kisses				
			1995			2.50

Fugazi

Washington, D.C.-area indie rock hardcore group. Despite many offers, they remain with their own truly independent label.

Vinyl Albums

Dischord 30	EP	Fugazi	1988	1.25	2.50	5.00
Dischord 35	EP	Margin Walker	1989	1.25	2.50	5.00
Dischord 44		Repeater	1990	2.00	4.00	8.00
Dischord 60		Steady Diet of Nothing	1991	2.00	4.00	8.00
Dischord 70		In On the Kill Taker	1993	2.00	4.00	8.00
Dischord 90-V		Red Medicine	1995	2.00	4.00	8.00

45s

Dischord 43		Joe #1/Break In/Song #1	1990			2.50
Dischord 43	PS	Joe #1/Break In/Song #1	1990			2.50
Sub Pop 52		Joe #1/Break In/Song #1	1989	18.75	37.50	75.00
Green vinyl pressing of 1,200						
Sub Pop 52		Joe #1/Break In/Song #1	1989	6.25	12.50	25.00
Black vinyl pressing of 800						
Sub Pop 52	PS	Joe #1/Break In/Song #1	1989	6.25	12.50	25.00
#14 in Sub Pop Singles Club series						

Fun Boy Three

*Splinter group from **The Specials**.*

Vinyl Albums

Chrysalis CHS 1383		Fun Boy Three	1982	3.00	6.00	12.00
Chrysalis PV 41383		Fun Boy Three	1984	2.00	4.00	8.00
Reissue						
Chrysalis B6V 41417		Waiting	1983	2.50	5.00	10.00
Chrysalis PV 41417		Waiting	1986	2.00	4.00	8.00
Reissue						

Label, Number		Title	Year	VG	VG+	NM
45s						
Chrysalis 42710		Our Lips Are Sealed/We're All Having Fun				
			1983		2.00	4.00
12-Inch Singles						
Chrysalis 2570		It Ain't What You Do/Funrama	1982	3.00	6.00	12.00
Includes **Bananarama**						
Chrysalis 42689		Our Lips Are Sealed (3 versions)	1983	3.00	6.00	12.00

G

Gabriel, Peter

Former lead singer of Genesis, his music remains highly interesting, much more so than his former band-mates'.

Vinyl Albums						
Atco SD 36-147		Peter Gabriel	1977	3.75	7.50	15.00
(The "Solsbury Hill" album) -- Original pressing has yellow labels (deduct 1/3 for later pressings)						
Atlantic SD-19181		Peter Gabriel	1978	3.75	7.50	15.00
(The "D.I.Y." album)						
Geffen GHS 2011		Peter Gabriel (Security)	1982	2.50	5.00	10.00
Geffen GHS 2011	DJ	Peter Gabriel (Security)	1982	3.75	7.50	15.00
Promo-only Quiex II audiophile pressing						
Geffen GHSP 2035		Peter Gabriel	1983	2.50	5.00	10.00
Reissue of Mercury album						
Geffen 2GHS 4012	(2)	Plays Live	1983	3.75	7.50	15.00
Geffen GHS 24070		Birdy (Soundtrack)	1985	2.50	5.00	10.00
Geffen GHS 24088		So	1986	2.50	5.00	10.00
Geffen 24206		Passion: Music for "The Last Temptation of Christ"				
			1989	3.75	7.50	15.00
Geffen R 114764		So	1986	3.00	6.00	12.00
BMG Direct Marketing edition						
Geffen R 153801		Peter Gabriel (Security)	1982	3.00	6.00	12.00
RCA Music Service edition						
Geffen R 243372	(2)	Plays Live	1983	4.50	9.00	18.00
RCA Music Service edition						
Mercury SRM-1-3848		Peter Gabriel	1980	3.00	6.00	12.00
(The "Games Without Frontiers" album)						
Nautilus Super Disc 16615		Peter Gabriel	1980	25.00	50.00	100.00
Which "Peter Gabriel" album is this?						
45s						
Atco 7079		Solsbury Hill/Moribund the Burgermeister				
			1977	2.50	5.00	10.00
Atlantic 3479		D.I.Y. (Do It Yourself)/Mother of Violence				
			1978	2.50	5.00	10.00
Atlantic 89668		Walk Through the Fire/Making a Big Mistake				
			1984		2.00	4.00
Atlantic 89668	PS	Walk Through the Fire/Making a Big Mistake				
			1984		2.00	4.00
Geffen GGEF 0481		Shock the Monkey/Solsbury Hill (Live)				
			198?			3.00
Reissue						
Geffen 19136		Digging in the Dirt/Quiet Steam	1992		2.00	4.00
Geffen 19145		Steam/Games Without Frontiers (DB Mix)				
			1992		2.00	4.00
Geffen 28247		Red Rain/I Go Swimming	1987			3.00
Geffen 28247	PS	Red Rain/I Go Swimming	1987			3.00
Geffen 28463		Don't Give Up/Curtains	1987			3.00
*A-side: Peter Gabriel/ **Kate Bush***						
Geffen 28463	PS	Don't Give Up/Curtains	1987			3.00

Label, Number		Title	Year	VG	VG+	NM
Geffen 28503		Big Time/We Do What We're Told (milgram's 37)				
			1986			3.00
Geffen 28503	PS	Big Time/We Do What We're Told (milgram's 37)				
			1986			3.00
Geffen 28622		In Your Eyes/In Your Eyes (Special Mix)				
			1986			3.00
Geffen 28622	PS	In Your Eyes/In Your Eyes (Special Mix)				
			1986			3.00
Geffen 28718		Sledgehammer/Don't Break This Rhythm				
			1986			3.00
Geffen 28718	PS	Sledgehammer/Don't Break This Rhythm				
			1986			3.00
Geffen 29542		Solsbury Hill (Live)/I Go Swimming				
			1983		2.50	5.00
Geffen 29883		Shock the Monkey/Soft Dog	1982		2.50	5.00
Mercury 76063		Games Without Frontiers/Lead a Normal Life				
			1980		2.00	4.00
Mercury 76063	PS	Games Without Frontiers/Lead a Normal Life				
			1980	3.00	6.00	12.00
Mercury 76086	DJ	I Don't Remember (same on both sides)				
			1980	2.00	4.00	8.00
Stock copy may not exist						
WTG 68936		In Your Eyes/Skankin' to the Beat	1989		2.00	4.00
B-side by **Fishbone**						
WTG 68977		In Your Eyes/In Your Eyes (Live Version)				
			1989			3.00

12-Inch Singles

Label, Number		Title	Year	VG	VG+	NM
Atlantic PR 310	DJ	Do It Yourself (D.I.Y.) (same on both sides)				
			1978	5.50	11.00	22.00
Atlantic 609	DJ	Walk Through the Fire (Remix) (same on both sides)				
			1984	3.00	6.00	12.00
Geffen PRO-A-1062	DJ	Shock the Monkey/I Have the Touch/Kiss of Life				
			1982	2.50	5.00	10.00
Geffen PRO-A-2044	DJ	I Go Swimming (Live)/No Self Control (Live)/D.I.Y. (Live)/				
		I Don't Remember (Live)	1984	3.00	6.00	12.00
Geffen PRO-A-2462	DJ	Sledgehammer (Edit)/Sledgehammer (LP Version)				
			1986	3.00	6.00	12.00
Geffen PRO-A-2625	DJ	Big Time (same on both sides)	1986	2.50	5.00	10.00
Geffen PRO-A-2689	DJ	Don't Give Up (Edit)/Don't Give Up (LP Version)				
			1986	2.50	5.00	10.00
Geffen 4488	DJ	Steam (4 versions)	1992	3.75	7.50	15.00
Geffen 20456		Sledgehammer (2 remixes)/Don't Break this Rhythm/				
		I Have the Touch (Remix)	1986	2.50	5.00	10.00
Geffen 20535		In Your Eyes (2 versions)/Biko	1986	2.00	4.00	8.00
Geffen 20600		Big Time (Dance Mix)/In Your Eyes (Special Mix)/				
		We Do What We're Told	1986	2.00	4.00	8.00
Geffen 20749		Red Rain/Ga Ga/Walk Through the Fire				
			1987	2.00	4.00	8.00
Geffen 20804		Biko (Video Mix)/Biko (Edit)/No More Apartheid				
			1987	3.00	6.00	12.00
Geffen 29863		Shock the Monkey (Long)/Shock the Monkey (Short)				
			1982	3.00	6.00	12.00
Mercury MK 157	DJ	I Don't Remember/And Through the Wire				
			1980	7.50	15.00	30.00

Gang of Four

Leeds (England)-based new wave band. Broke up in 1984, partially reunited in 1988.

Vinyl Albums

Label, Number		Title	Year	VG	VG+	NM
Warner Bros. BSK 3446		Entertainment!	1980	3.00	6.00	12.00
Warner Bros. BSK 3494		Gang of Four	1980	2.50	5.00	10.00

Label, Number		Title	Year	VG	VG+	NM
Warner Bros. BSK 3565		Solid Gold	1981	2.50	5.00	10.00
Warner Bros. MINI 3646	EP	Another Day, Another Dollar	1982	2.00	4.00	8.00
Warner Bros. 23683		Songs of the Free	1982	2.50	5.00	10.00
Warner Bros. 23936		Hard	1983	2.50	5.00	10.00
45s						
Warner Bros. 29449		Is It Love/Arabic	1983		2.00	4.00
Warner Bros. 29921		I Love a Man in a Uniform/I Will Be a Good Boy				
			1982		2.00	4.00
12-Inch Singles						
Polydor 922	DJ	Cadillac (2 versions)/Favourites	1991	2.00	4.00	8.00
Polydor 925	DJ	Don't Fix What Ain't Broke (same on both sides)				
			1991	2.00	4.00	8.00
Warner Bros. PRO-A-1050	DJ	I Love a Man in a Uniform (2 versions)/Call Me Up				
			1982		3.50	7.00
Warner Bros. PRO-A-2081	DJ	Is It Love (Long Mix)/Is It Love (Short)/Man with a Good Car				
			1983		3.50	7.00
Warner Bros. 20174		Is It Love (Remix)/(Instrumental)	1983		3.00	6.00
Warner Bros. 29907		I Love a Man in a Uniform (Remix)/				
		I Love a Man in a Uniform (Dub)	1982	2.00	4.00	8.00

Garbage

Madison, Wisconsin-based alternative band featuring Butch Vig, ace alterna-producer, as one of its members.

Vinyl Albums						
Almo Sounds 80004	(2)	Garbage	1995	3.00	6.00	12.00

Gears, The

Los Angeles power-pop/punk group.

Vinyl Albums						
Playgems GS 6471		Rockin' at Ground Zero	1980	7.50	15.00	30.00
45s						
Four Speed (# unknown)		Let's Go to the Beach/Hard Rock/Don't Be Afraid to Pogo				
			1979	25.00	50.00	100.00
Four Speed (# unknown)	PS	Let's Go to the Beach/Hard Rock/Don't Be Afraid to Pogo				
			1979	25.00	50.00	100.00

Geldof, Bob

*Former leader of **The Boomtown Rats** and mastermind of **Band Aid**.*

Vinyl Albums						
Atlantic 1010	DJ	Questions and Answers (Interview)				
			1987	2.50	5.00	10.00
Atlantic 81687		Deep in the Heart of Nowhere	1986	2.50	5.00	10.00
45s						
Atlantic 89261		Heartless Heart/Pulled Apart by Horses				
			1987			3.00
Atlantic 89309		Love Is Like a Rocket/Pulled Apart by Horses				
			1986			3.00
Atlantic 89309	PS	Love Is Like a Rocket/Pulled Apart by Horses				
			1986			3.00
Atlantic 89341		This Is the World Calling/Talk Me Up				
			1986			3.00
Atlantic 89341	PS	This Is the World Calling/Talk Me Up				
			1986			3.00

Label, Number		Title	Year	VG	VG+	NM
12-Inch Singles						
Atlantic 2026	DJ	Heartless Heart/Pulled Apart by Horses				
			1986	2.00	4.00	8.00

Gene Loves Jezebel
British techno-pop duo.

Label, Number		Title	Year	VG	VG+	NM
Vinyl Albums						
Geffen 141	DJ	Discover Interview	1986	6.25	12.50	25.00
Geffen 4192	EP	Remix Sampler	1990	5.00	10.00	20.00
Promo-only collection						
Geffen GHS 24118		Discover	1986	2.50	5.00	10.00
Geffen GHS 24165		Promise	1988	2.50	5.00	10.00
Geffen GHS 24171		The House of Dolls	1988	2.50	5.00	10.00
Geffen GHS 24260		Kiss of Life	1990	3.00	6.00	12.00
Relativity 8075	EP	Desire	1985	2.00	4.00	8.00
Relativity EMC 8036		Immigrant	1985	2.50	5.00	10.00
45s						
Geffen 28104		Suspicion/Showing Crazy	1988			3.00
Geffen 28183		Motion of Love/Bugg's Bruises	1987			3.00
Geffen 28183	PS	Motion of Love/Bugg's Bruises	1987			3.00
12-Inch Singles						
Geffen PRO-A-2800	DJ	Suspicion (same on both sides)	1987	2.50	5.00	10.00
Geffen PRO-A-2998	DJ	Twenty Killer Hurts (3 versions)	1987	2.00	4.00	8.00
Geffen 4157	DJ	Tangled Up in You (2 mixes)/Jealous (2 mixes)				
			1990	2.50	5.00	10.00
Geffen 20519		Heartache/Heartache (extended)/Before Doubt/Deli Babies				
			1986	2.00	4.00	8.00
Geffen 20744		The Motion of Love (Jezebel Mix)/Buggs Bruises/Vagabond				
			1987	2.50	5.00	10.00
Geffen 20929		Suspcion (Jezebel Mix)/Twenty Killer Hurts (Killer 12")				
			1987	2.50	5.00	10.00

General Public
*Splinter group from **The English Beat**.*

Label, Number		Title	Year	VG	VG+	NM
Vinyl Albums						
I.R.S. 5782		Hand to Mouth	1986	2.50	5.00	10.00
I.R.S. SP 70046		...All the Rage	1984	2.50	5.00	10.00
I.R.S. R 142295		Hand to Mouth	1986	3.00	6.00	12.00
RCA Music Service edition						
45s						
Epic 77866		Rainy Days/Blow Hard	1995			3.00
I.R.S. 9934		Tenderness/Limited Balance	1984			3.00
I.R.S. 9934	PS	Tenderness/Limited Balance	1984			3.00
I.R.S. 9935		Never You Done That/All the Rage				
			1985			3.00
I.R.S. 9935	PS	Never You Done That/All the Rage				
			1985			3.00
I.R.S. 9937		Hot Your Cool/Day-to-Day (Live)				
			1985			3.00
I.R.S. 52941		Too Much or Nothing/Taking the Day Off				
			1986			3.00
I.R.S. 52941	PS	Too Much or Nothing/Taking the Day Off				
			1986			3.00
I.R.S. 53016		Come Again/Cheque in the Post	1987			3.00
12-Inch Singles						
Epic Soundtrax 77460	(2)	I'll Take You There (8 versions)	1994	6.25	12.50	25.00

Label, Number		Title	Year	VG	VG+	NM
I.R.S. 17192	DJ	Too Much or Nothing (Long)/Too Much or Nothing (Short)				
			1986		2.50	5.00
I.R.S. 17271	DJ	Come Again (same on both sides)1986			3.00	6.00
I.R.S. 23683		Too Much or Nothing (5 versions)1986			2.50	5.00
I.R.S. 23734		In Conversation (4 versions)	1987		2.50	5.00
I.R.S. 70413		Tenderness/Never You Done That (2 versions)				
			1983	2.50	5.00	10.00
I.R.S. 70415		So Hot You're Cool (2 versions)/Day to Day				
			1984	2.50	5.00	10.00
I.R.S. 70980		Tenderness (Dance Mix)/Tenderness (Radio Version)				
			1984	2.50	5.00	10.00
I.R.S. 70984		Never You Done That/Burning Bright (Edit)				
			1985		3.00	6.00
I.R.S. 70986		So Hot You're Cool (Hot)/So Hot You're Cool (Cool)				
			1984		3.00	6.00

Generation X

*Early British punk group, featuring **Billy Idol**.*

Vinyl Albums

Label, Number	Title	Year	VG	VG+	NM
Chrysalis CHR 1169	Generation X	1978	4.00	8.00	16.00
Chrysalis CHR 1193	Valley of the Dolls	1979	4.00	8.00	16.00
Chrysalis CHR 1327	Kiss Me Deadly	1981	4.00	8.00	16.00
Chrysalis FV 41169	Generation X	1984	3.00	6.00	12.00
Reissue					
Chrysalis FV 41193	Valley of the Dolls	1984	3.00	6.00	12.00
Reissue					
Chrysalis FV 41327	Kiss Me Deadly	1985	3.00	6.00	12.00
Reissue					

Germs, The

Los Angeles punk band. Appeared in the movie The Decline of Western Civilization.

Vinyl Albums

Label, Number		Title	Year	VG	VG+	NM
Mohawk SCALP-001		Recorded Live at the Whiskey, June, 1977				
			1981	12.50	25.00	50.00
First edition: Numbered edition, with sticker						
Mohawk SCALP-001		Recorded Live at the Whiskey, June, 1977				
			1981	5.00	10.00	20.00
Second edition: Un-numbered edition, with sticker						
Slash SR-103		(GI)	1981	3.75	7.50	15.00
Slash SREP 108		What We Do Is Secret	1981	3.75	7.50	15.00
Slash 23932		(GI)	1983	3.00	6.00	12.00
Reissue						

45s

Label, Number		Title	Year	VG	VG+	NM
Iloki ILSO 101		Forming/Sexboy	1990		3.75	7.50
1,000 copies, all on clear vinyl						
Iloki ILSO 101	PS	Forming/Sexboy	1990		3.75	7.50
Slash 101		Lexicon Devil/Circle One/No God				
			1978	5.00	10.00	20.00
Slash 101	PS	Lexicon Devil/Circle One/No God				
			1978	5.00	10.00	20.00
What 01		Forming/Sex Boy	1977	5.00	10.00	20.00
What 01	PS	Forming/Sex Boy	1977	5.00	10.00	20.00
With lyric insert						

Gilmore, Jimmie Dale

*Former leader of **Jimmie Dale and the Flatlanders**. **Country rocker**.*

Vinyl Albums

Label, Number	Title	Year	VG	VG+	NM
Hightone HT-8011	Fair and Square	1988	2.50	5.00	10.00

Label, Number		Title	Year	VG	VG+	NM
Hightone HT-8018		Jimmie Dale Gilmore	1989	2.50	5.00	10.00

Gin Blossoms

Alterna-rock/pop group from Tempe, Arizona.

Vinyl Albums

A&M 75021 5369 1	EP	Up and Crumbling	1991	3.75	7.50	15.00
San Jacinto DRAM 019		Dusted	1989	5.00	10.00	20.00
With picture insert and biographical material						

45s

A&M 31458 0418 7		Found Out About You/Hey Jealousy				
			1993		2.50	5.00
A&M 31458 0862 7		Allison Road/Until I Fall Away	1994			3.00
A&M 31458 1380 7		Follow You Down/Til I Hear It from You				
			1996			3.00
A&M 8735		Hey Jealousy/Found Out About You				
			1996			3.00
Oldies reissue						

Gina Go-Go

*Despite the name, has nothing to do with Gina Schock of the **Go-Go's**.*

45s

Capitol 44233		I Can't Face the Fact/I Can't Face the Fact				
			1988			3.00
Capitol 44434		(Gotta Be) The Only One (Radio Edit)/				
		(Gotta Be) The Only One (Radio Remix)				
			1989			3.00

Gits, The

Seattle-based grunge/hardcore band with several female lead singers over the years.

Vinyl Albums

C/Z 051		Frenching the Bully	199?	6.25	12.50	25.00
Red vinyl						

45s

Big Flaming Ego 06		Precious Blood/Seaweed/Kings and Queens				
			1990	2.50	5.00	10.00
Big Flaming Ego 06	PS	Precious Blood/Seaweed/Kings and Queens				
			1990	2.50	5.00	10.00
Broken Rekids SKIP 4		Second Skin/Social Love	1991	2.00	4.00	8.00
Purple vinyl						
Broken Rekids SKIP 4	PS	Second Skin/Social Love	1991	2.00	4.00	8.00

Go West

British pop-rock duo.

Vinyl Albums

Chrysalis FV 41495		Go West	1985	2.50	5.00	10.00
Chrysalis FV 41550		Dancing on the Couch	1987	2.50	5.00	10.00

45s

Chrysalis 42850		We Close Our Eyes/Missing Persons				
			1985			3.00
Chrysalis 42850	PS	We Close Our Eyes/Missing Persons				
			1985			3.00
Chrysalis 42865		Call Me/Haunted	1985			3.00
Chrysalis 42865	PS	Call Me/Haunted	1985			3.00
Chrysalis 42903		Eye to Eye/Man in My Mirror	1985			3.00

Label, Number		Title	Year	VG	VG+	NM
Chrysalis 42903	PS	Eye to Eye/Man in My Mirror	1985			3.00
Chrysalis 43141		Don't Look Down -- The Sequel/Let's Build a Boat				
			1987			3.00
Chrysalis 43141	PS	Don't Look Down -- The Sequel/Let's Build a Boat				
			1987			3.00
EMI S7-17636		Tracks of My Tears/One Way Street				
			1993			3.00
EMI S7-56948		Faithful/King of Wishful Thinking				
			1993		2.00	4.00

First release of B-side on U.S. 45 (hit charts in 1990)

12-Inch Singles

Label, Number		Title	Year	VG	VG+	NM
Chrysalis VAS 2760	DJ	Don't Look Down (3 versions)	1987		3.50	7.00
Chrysalis 42853		We Close Our Eyes (5:55)/We Close Our Eyes (3:48)				
			1985	2.50	5.00	10.00
Chrysalis 42871		Call Me (Remix)/We Close Our Eyes (Remix)				
			1985	3.00	6.00	12.00
Chrysalis 42900		Eye to Eye (3 versions)	1985	2.00	4.00	8.00

Go-Go's

*California-based all-female pop-rock group. Broke up in 1985 and reunited in 1994. Also see **Carlisle, Belinda; House of Schock; The Graces; Wiedlin, Jane**.*

Vinyl Albums

Label, Number		Title	Year	VG	VG+	NM
I.R.S. SP 70021		Beauty and the Beat	1981	3.00	6.00	12.00
First pressings with peach-colored cover and light label						
I.R.S. SP 70021		Beauty and the Beat	1981	2.00	4.00	8.00
Second pressings with dark blue cover and darker label						
I.R.S. SP 70031		Vacation	1982	2.00	4.00	8.00
I.R.S. SP 70041		Talk Show	1984	2.00	4.00	8.00
I.R.S. R 151667		Talk Show	1984	2.50	5.00	10.00
RCA Music Service edition						

45s

Label, Number		Title	Year	VG	VG+	NM
I.R.S. 8001	PD	We Got the Beat/Our Lips Are Sealed				
			1982	2.50	5.00	10.00
7-inch picture disc						
I.R.S. 8690		Our Lips Are Sealed/We Got the Beat				
			198?			3.00
Amnesia Series reissue						
I.R.S. 8691		Vacation/Cool Jerk	198?			3.00
Amnesia Series reissue						
I.R.S. 9901		Our Lips Are Sealed/Surfing and Spying				
			1981			3.00
I.R.S. 9901	PS	Our Lips Are Sealed/Surfing and Spying				
			1981		3.00	6.00
I.R.S. 9903		We Got the Beat/Can't Stop the World				
			1982			3.00
I.R.S. 9903	PS	We Got the Beat/Can't Stop the World				
			1982			3.00
I.R.S. 9907		Vacation/Beatnik Beach	1982			3.00
I.R.S. 9907	PS	Vacation/Beatnik Beach	1982			3.00
I.R.S. 9910		Get Up and Go/Speeding	1982			3.00
I.R.S. 9910	PS	Get Up and Go/Speeding	1982			3.00
I.R.S. 9911		This Old Feeling/It's Everything But Partytime				
			1982			3.00
I.R.S. 9911	PS	This Old Feeling/It's Everything But Partytime				
			1982			3.00
Die-cut "Go-Go's" sleeve (yellow)						
I.R.S. 9926		Head Over Heels/Good for Gone				
			1984			3.00

Label, Number		Title	Year	VG	VG+	NM
I.R.S. 9926	PS	Head Over Heels/Good for Gone				
			1984			3.00
I.R.S. 9928		Turn to You/I'm With You	1984			3.00
I.R.S. 9928	PS	Turn to You/I'm With You	1984			3.00
I.R.S. 9933		Yes or No/Mercenary	1984			3.00
I.R.S. S7-18490		Good Girl/The Whole World Lost Its Head				
			1995			3.00

12-Inch Singles

Label, Number		Title	Year	VG	VG+	NM
I.R.S. 70956	DJ	Our Lips Are Sealed/Tonight/We Got the Beat				
			1981	2.00	4.00	8.00
I.R.S. 70959	DJ	We Got the Beat/How Much More				
			1982	2.00	4.00	8.00
I.R.S. 70961	DJ	Vacation/Beatnik Beach	1982	2.00	4.00	8.00
I.R.S. 70973	DJ	Head Over Heels (same on both sides)				
			1984	2.00	4.00	8.00
I.R.S. 70977		Turn to You/I'm the Only One	1984	2.00	4.00	8.00
I.R.S. 75021 7480 1	DJ	Cool Jerk (6 versions)	1990	2.00	4.00	8.00

Gomm, Ian

*Ex-member of **Brinsley Schwarz**.*

Vinyl Albums

Label, Number	Title	Year	VG	VG+	NM
Stiff/Epic JE 36103	Gomm with the Wind	1979	3.00	6.00	12.00
Stiff/Epic JE 36433	What a Blow	1980	3.00	6.00	12.00

45s

Label, Number	Title	Year	VG	VG+	NM
Stiff/Epic 50747	Hold On/Another Year	1979		2.00	4.00
Stiff/Epic 50802	Hooked on Love/Chicken Run	1979		2.00	4.00

Goo Goo Dolls

Buffalo, New York-based punk/alternative band.

Vinyl Albums

Label, Number	Title	Year	VG	VG+	NM
Enigma D1-73406	JED	1989	4.00	8.00	16.00

45s

Label, Number	Title	Year	VG	VG+	NM
Warner Bros. 18512	We Are the Normal/Another Second Time Around				
		1993			3.00

Gordon, Robert

*Neo-rockabilly artist formerly with **Tuff Darts**.*

Vinyl Albums

Label, Number		Title	Year	VG	VG+	NM
Private Stock PS-2030		Robert Gordon with Link Wray	1977	4.00	8.00	16.00
Private Stock PS-7008		Fresh Fish Special	1978	4.00	8.00	16.00
RCA Victor AFL1-3294		Rock Billy Boogie	1979	5.00	10.00	20.00
Original pressing on white vinyl						
RCA Victor AFL1-3294		Rock Billy Boogie	1979	3.00	6.00	12.00
RCA Victor AFL1-3296		Robert Gordon with Link Wray	1979	3.00	6.00	12.00
Reissue						
RCA Victor AFL1-3299		Fresh Fish Special	1979	3.00	6.00	12.00
Reissue						
RCA Victor DJL1-3411	DJ	Essential Robert Gordon	1979	7.50	15.00	30.00
Promo-only live album with tracks from Tuff Darts						
RCA Victor AFL1-3523		Bad Boy	1980	3.00	6.00	12.00
RCA Victor AFL1-3773		Are You Gonna Be the One	1981	3.00	6.00	12.00
RCA Victor AFL1-4380		Too Fast to Live, Too Young to Die				
			1982	3.00	6.00	12.00

45s

Label, Number	Title	Year	VG	VG+	NM
Private Stock 45,156	Red Hot/Sweet Surrender	1977		3.00	6.00

Label, Number		Title	Year	VG	VG+	NM
Private Stock 45,191		Sea Cruise/If This Is Wrong	1978		3.00	6.00
With Link Wray						
Private Stock 45,203		Fire/If This Is Wrong	1979		2.50	5.00
Private Stock 45,203	PS	Fire/If This Is Wrong	1979		2.50	5.00
RCA PB-11452		Blue Christmas/Fire	1978		2.50	5.00
With Link Wray						
RCA PB-11471		It's Only Make Believe/Rock Billy Boogie				
			1979		2.50	5.00
RCA PB-11608		Black Slacks/Walk On By	1979		2.50	5.00
RCA PB-11919		Born to Lose/Need You	1980		2.50	5.00
RCA PB-12239		Someday, Someway/Drivin' Wheel				
			1981		2.50	5.00
RCA PB-13399		Something's Gonna Happen/Flying Saucers Rock and Roll				
			1982		2.50	5.00

Gore, Martin
Member of Depeche Mode.

Vinyl Albums

Sire 25980	EP	Counterfeit	1989	2.00	4.00	8.00

Gories

45s

Sub Pop 134		Give Me Some Money/You Don't Love Me				
			1991		3.00	6.00
All copies on red vinyl						
Sub Pop 134	PS	Give Me Some Money/You Don't Love Me				
			1991		3.00	6.00
#36 in Sub Pop Singles Club series						

Gorilla

Vinyl Albums

Thrill Jockey 003		Deal With It	1993	2.50	5.00	10.00

45s

Sub Pop 119		Detox Man/Sober	1991		2.50	5.00
All copies on gray vinyl						
Sub Pop 119	PS	Detox Man/Sober	1991		2.50	5.00
#35 in Sub Pop Singles Club series						

Government Issue
Washington, D.C. hardcore band.

7-Inch Extended Play Singles

Dischord 4		Legless Bull	1981	8.75	17.50	35.00
Dischord 4	PS	Legless Bull	1981	8.75	17.50	35.00
1,000 copies were pressed						

Graces, The
Featuring Charlotte Caffey, ex-Go-Go's.

Vinyl Albums

A&M SP-5265		Perfect View	1989	2.50	5.00	10.00

45s

A&M 1440		Lay Down Your Arms/Out in the Field				
			1989			*Cassette only*
A&M 1453		Perfect View/Out in the Field	1989			*Cassette only*

Label, Number		Title	Year	VG	VG+	NM

Grandmaster Flash/Grandmaster Melle Mel and the Furious Five

Pioneer hip-hop group from New York City. Group has splintered and re-formed many times. Most of the splintering has revolved around turntable spinner Grandmaster Flash and lead rapper Grandmaster Melle Mel. All of their known records are listed below without discriminating.

45s

Label, Number		Title	Year	VG	VG+	NM
Atlantic 89659		Beat Street Breakdown/Beat Street Breakdown				
			1984			3.00
Atlantic 89659	PS	Beat Street Breakdown/Beat Street Breakdown				
			1984			3.00
Elektra 69380		Magic Carpet Ride/On the Strength				
			1988			3.00
Elektra 69400		Fly Girl/Gold In Effect	1988			3.00
Elektra 69416		Gold/Back in the Old Days of Hip-Hop				
			1988			3.00
Elektra 69459		All Wrapped Up/Kid Named Flash				
			1987			3.00
Elektra 69490		U Know What Time It Is/Bus Dis (Woo)				
			1987			3.00
Elektra 69530		Behind Closed Doors/Lies	1986			3.00
Elektra 69552		Style (Peter Gunn Theme)/(Instrumental)				
			1986			3.00
Elektra 69617		Who's That Lady?/Alternate Groove				
			1985			3.00
Elektra 69643		Girls Love the Way He Spins/Larry's Dance Theme				
			1985			3.00
Elektra 69677		Sign of the Times/Larry's Dance Theme				
			1984			3.00
MCA 52740		Vice/Chase	1985			3.00
MCA 52740	PS	Vice/Chase	1985			3.00
Sugar Hill 756		Freedom/(instrumental)	1980	2.50	5.00	10.00
Sugar Hill 759		The Birthday Party/(instrumental)				
			1979	2.50	5.00	10.00
Sugar Hill 92011		We Don't Work for Free/(Instrumental)				
			1984			3.00

12-Inch Singles

Label, Number		Title	Year	VG	VG+	NM
Elektra 5079	DJ	Alternative Groove (3 versions)	1985		3.50	7.00
Elektra 5134	DJ	Style (Peter Gunn Theme) (3 versions)				
			1986		3.50	7.00
Elektra 5154	DJ	Behind Closed Doors (2 versions)				
			1986		2.50	5.00
Elektra 5233	DJ	All Wrapped Up (3 versions)	1987		2.50	5.00
Elektra 5279	DJ	Gold (6 versions)	1988		3.00	6.00
Elektra ED 5301	DJ	Fly Girl (6 versions)	1988		3.00	6.00
Elektra 5319	DJ	Magic Carpet Ride (3 versions)	1988		3.00	6.00
Elektra 66825		U Know What Time It Is (2 versions)/Bus Dis				
			1987		3.00	6.00
Elektra 66857		Style (Peter Gunn Theme) (3 versions)				
			1986		3.00	6.00
New Day 529		White Lines '89 Part 2 (3 versions)				
			1989	2.50	5.00	10.00
Posse 1234		What's the Matter with Your World (3 versions)				
			1989		3.00	6.00
Sugar Hill 457		New York, New York/(Instrumental)				
			1983	2.00	4.00	8.00
Sugar Hill 465		White Lines (Don't Don't Do It) (4 versions)				
			1983	2.50	5.00	10.00
Sugar Hill 549		Freedom/(Instrumental)	1980	2.50	5.00	10.00
Sugar Hill 555		The Birthday Party (same on both sides)				
			1981	2.50	5.00	10.00
Sugar Hill 569		It's Nasty (Genius of Love) (7:49)/It's Nasty (Genius of Love) (8:15)				
			1981	2.50	5.00	10.00
Sugar Hill 574		Flash to the Beat (Part 1 and 2)	1982	2.50	5.00	10.00
Sugar Hill 584		The Message/(Instrumental)	1982	2.50	5.00	10.00

Label, Number	Title	Year	VG	VG+	NM
Sugar Hill 594	The Message II/(Instrumental)	1982		3.50	7.00
Sugar Hill 32009	White Lines (Don't Don't Do It)/Melle Mel's Groove				
		1983	3.00	6.00	12.00
Sugar Hill 32016	Jesse/(Instrumental)	1984	2.00	4.00	8.00
Sugar Hill 32019	Beat Street/Internationally Known Parts 1 & 2				
		1982	2.00	4.00	8.00
Sugar Hill 32025	We Don't Work for Free (same on both sides)				
		1984	2.50	5.00	10.00
Sugar Hill 32033	Step Off (6:52)/Step Off (4:32)	1984	2.00	4.00	8.00
Sugar Hill 32039	The Mega-Melle Mix/World War III				
		1985	2.50	5.00	10.00
Sugar Hill 32044	King of the Streets (3 versions)	1985	2.50	5.00	10.00
Sugar Hill 32058	Vice/World War III	1985	2.00	4.00	8.00
Sugar Hill 32504	Freedom/New York, New York	1985	3.00	6.00	12.00
"Old Gold" reissue					
Sugar Hill 32505	The Message/The Birthday Party	1985	2.50	5.00	10.00
"Old Gold" reissue					
Sugar Hill 32508	White Lines (Don't Don't Do It)/Scorpio				
		1985	2.50	5.00	10.00
"Old Gold" reissue					
Vinyl Albums					
Elektra 60389	They Said It Couldn't Be Done	1985	2.50	5.00	10.00
Elektra 60723	Ba-Dop-Boom-Bang	1987	2.50	5.00	10.00
Elektra 60769	On the Strength	1988	2.50	5.00	10.00
New Day ND 222	Piano	1989	2.50	5.00	10.00
Sugar Hill 268	The Message	1982	3.75	7.50	15.00

Great Buildings

*Los Angeles pop-rock group. Two members of Great Buildings formed **The Rembrandts**.*

Vinyl Albums					
Columbia NJC 36920	Great Buildings	1980	3.75	7.50	15.00
45s					
Columbia 02008	Combat Zone/Hold On Something				
		1981		3.00	6.00
12-Inch Singles					
Columbia AS 927 DJ	Combat Zone + 2	1981		3.00	6.00

Green Day

Neo-punk band from Berkeley, California.

Vinyl Albums					
Lookout 22	39/Smooth	1990	2.50	5.00	10.00
Lookout 46	Kerplunk	1992	2.50	5.00	10.00
Reprise 45529 DJ	Dookie	1994	8.75	17.50	35.00
Promo version on clear green vinyl in plain white cover					
Reprise 45529 DJ	Dookie	1994	7.50	15.00	30.00
Promo version on milky pale-green vinyl					
Reprise 45529	Dookie	1994	3.75	7.50	15.00
Original stock issue on black vinyl					
Reprise 45529	Dookie	1995	2.50	5.00	10.00
Reissue on pink vinyl					
Reprise 46046	Insomniac	1995	2.50	5.00	10.00
7-Inch Extended Play Singles					
Lookout 17	1,000 Hours/Dry Ice//Only of You/The One I Want				
		1989			3.00
Lookout 17 PS	1,000 Hours	1989			3.00
Lookout 35	Paper Lanterns/Why Do You Want Him?//409 In Your Coffeemaker/				
	Knowledge	1990	5.00	10.00	20.00
First pressing of 1,000 on blue vinyl					
Lookout 35	Paper Lanterns/Why Do You Want Him?//409 In Your Coffeemaker/				
	Knowledge	1990			2.00

Label, Number		Title	Year	VG	VG+	NM
Lookout 35	PS	Slappy	1990		2.50	5.00

45s

Reprise 17941		When I Come Around/Basket Case				
			1995			3.00

10-Inch Singles

Reprise 41656		Longview/Going to Pasalaqua (Live)//F.O.D. (Live)/				
		Christy Road (Live)	1994	2.50	5.00	10.00

Green vinyl 10-inch single in clear plastic sleeve with sticker

Green Jelly

Heavy/silly band originally known as Green Jello until the lawyers got involved.

45s

Zoo 14093		Three Little Pigs/Electric Harley House (Of Love)				
			1993		2.00	4.00
Zoo 141??		Anarchy in the U.K./Green Jelly Theme				
			1993			3.00

Green Magnet School

45s

Sub Pop 136		Singed/Slipper	1991		2.50	5.00
All copies on clear gold vinyl; A-side plays at 33 1/3, B-side at 45						
Sub Pop 136	PS	Singed/Slipper	1991		2.50	5.00
#38 in Sub Pop Singles Club series						

Green River

*Seminal Seattle grunge band. Its members went on to form **Mother Love Bone, Mudhoney** and **Pearl Jam.***

Vinyl Albums

Homestead 031		Come On Down	198?	3.00	6.00	12.00
Originals do not have a UPC code (deduct 25% if UPC is there)						
Sub Pop 11	EP	Dry as a Bone	1987	12.50	25.00	50.00
First 2,000 copies have yellow inserts						
Sub Pop 11	EP	Dry as a Bone	1987	8.75	17.50	35.00
Later copies have pink inserts						
Sub Pop 15	EP	Rehab Doll	1988	8.75	17.50	35.00
First 1,000 copies on green vinyl						
Sub Pop 15	EP	Rehab Doll	1988	6.25	12.50	25.00

45s

Tasque Force ICP 01		Together We'll Never/Ain't Nothing to Do				
			1984	31.25	62.50	125.00
500 pressed on green vinyl; no picture sleeve						

Guadalcanal Diary

Marietta, Georgia-based pop-rock group.

Vinyl Albums

DB 73		Walking in the Shadow of the Big Man				
			1984	5.00	10.00	20.00
Elektra 60429		Walking in the Shadow of the Big Man				
			1985	2.50	5.00	10.00
Elektra 60478		Jamboree	1986	2.50	5.00	10.00
Elektra 60752		2X4	1987	2.50	5.00	10.00
Elektra 60848		Flip-Flop	1989	2.00	4.00	8.00
Elektra 60848	DJ	Flip-Flop	1989	2.50	5.00	10.00
Promo-only white label audiophile vinyl						
Entertainment on Disc EOD 102EP		Watusi Rodeo	1983	4.00	8.00	16.00

Label, Number		Title	Year	VG	VG+	NM
45s						
Elektra 69316		Always Saturday/Kiss of Fire	1989			3.00
12-Inch Singles						
Elektra ED 5071	DJ	Trail of Tears (same on both sides)				
			1985		3.00	6.00
Elektra ED 5155	DJ	Lonely Street (same on both sides)				
			1986		2.50	5.00
Elektra ED 5172	DJ	Spirit Train (same on both sides)				
			1986		2.50	5.00
Elektra ED 5256	DJ	Litany (same on both sides)	1987		2.50	5.00
Elektra ED 5272	DJ	Lips of Steel (same on both sides)				
			1987		2.50	5.00
Elektra ED 5291	DJ	Get Over It (same on both sides)				
			1987		2.50	5.00
Elektra ED 5359	DJ	Always Saturday (Edit)/Always Saturday (LP Version)				
			1989		2.50	5.00
Elektra ED 5379	DJ	Pretty Is As Pretty Does (same on both sides)				
			1989		2.50	5.00

Guided By Voices

Dayton, Ohio noise band, almost progressive but definitely low-fi.

Vinyl Albums					
GBV 0001	Devil Between My Toes	1987	31.25	62.50	125.00
Halo (# unknown)	Self Inflicted Aerial Nostalgia	1989	10.00	20.00	40.00
Halo 1	Sandbox	1987	18.75	37.50	75.00
I Wanna Records (#unknown) EP	Forever Since Breakfast	1986	18.75	37.50	75.00
Rockathon (# unknown)	Propeller	199?	18.75	37.50	75.00

Hand-colored cover with nature-book paste-on

Guns N' Roses

Heavy-metal antiheroes; Duff McKagan was a graduate of the early Seattle punk scene.

Vinyl Albums						
Geffen XXXG 24148		Appetite for Destruction	1988	10.00	20.00	40.00

Original banned "rape cover"; the XXXG prefix is on the cover only; all copies of the record use the GHS prefix

Geffen GHS 24148		Appetite for Destruction	1988	2.50	5.00	10.00
Geffen GHS 24198		G N' R Lies	1988	2.50	5.00	10.00
Geffen GEF 24415	(2)	Use Your Illusion I	1991	5.00	10.00	20.00
Geffen GEF 24420	(2)	Use Your Illusion II	1991	5.00	10.00	20.00
Geffen GEF 24617		The Spaghetti Incident?	1993	3.75	7.50	15.00

Orange vinyl

Geffen R 100805	G N' R Lies	1988	3.00	6.00	12.00

BMG Direct Marketing edition

Geffen R 170348	Appetite for Destruction	1987	3.00	6.00	12.00

BMG Direct Marketing edition

Uzi Suicide USR 001	EP	Live ?!*@ Like a Suicide	1986	25.00	50.00	100.00

45s				
Geffen 19027	Don't Cry/Don't Cry (Alt. Lyrics)			
		1991	2.00	4.00
Geffen 19039	You Could Be Mine/Civil War	1991	2.00	4.00
Geffen 19067	November Rain/Sweet Child O' Mine			
		1992	2.00	4.00

The longest 45 version of a Top 10 hit in chart history (8:40)

Geffen 19114	Live and Let Die/Live and Let Die (Live)			
		1991	2.00	4.00
Geffen 19142	Yesterdays/Yesterdays (Live in Las Vegas)			
		1992	2.00	4.00

Label, Number		Title	Year	VG	VG+	NM
Geffen 19266		Since I Don't Have You/				
		You Can't Put Your Arms Around a Memory				
			1993		2.00	4.00
Geffen 21901		Sweet Child O' Mine/Welcome to the Jungle				
			1989			3.00
Reissue						
Geffen 22869		Nightrain/Reckless Life	1989		2.00	4.00
Geffen 22996		Patience/Rocket Queen	1989		2.00	4.00
Geffen 22996	PS	Patience/Rocket Queen	1989		2.00	4.00
Geffen 27570		Paradise City/Move to the City	1989		2.00	4.00
Geffen 27570	PS	Paradise City/Move to the City	1989		2.00	4.00
Geffen 27759		Welcome to the Jungle/Mr. Brownstone				
			1988		2.00	4.00
Geffen 27759	PS	Welcome to the Jungle/Mr. Brownstone				
			1988		2.00	4.00
Geffen 27963		Sweet Child O' Mine/It's So Easy				
			1988		2.00	4.00
Geffen 27963	PS	Sweet Child O' Mine/It's So Easy				
			1988		2.00	4.00

Picture discs were fairly common in the late 1970s. This one by the Go-Go's, a stock release, came out in 1982 on a 7-inch single and is worth about $10.

Discovered just in time to add to this book is this interesting item from Green Day: a 10-inch, swirly-green vinyl copy of its first mainstream airplay hit, "Longview." It came with three otherwise unavailable live tracks and a special plastic sleeve with a sticker.

Label, Number		Title	Year	VG	VG+	NM

H

Hagen, Nina

Originally from East Berlin, East Germany, this new-wave artist eventually ended up in Los Angeles.

Vinyl Albums

Label, Number		Title	Year	VG	VG+	NM
Columbia 3C 36817	10	TV Glotzer	1980	3.00	6.00	12.00
Columbia ARC 38008		Nunsexmonkrock	1982	3.00	6.00	12.00
Columbia PC 38008		Nunsexmonkrock	198?	2.50	5.00	10.00
Reissue with new prefix						

12-Inch Singles

Label, Number		Title	Year	VG	VG+	NM
Columbia 04265		New York New York (English)//Zarah/ New York New York (German)	1983	2.50	5.00	10.00
Columbia 05010		Zarah (Remix)/Zarah (Dub)	1983	3.00	6.00	12.00
Columbia 05211		Universal Radio (3 mixes)	1985	2.50	5.00	10.00
Columbia AS 1506	DJ	Smack Jack/Cosma Shiva/Born in Xlxax	1982	2.50	5.00	10.00

Haircut One Hundred

*British new wave/pop band with lead vocals by **Nick Heyward**.*

Vinyl Albums

Label, Number		Title	Year	VG	VG+	NM
Arista AL 6600		Pelican West	1982	3.75	7.50	15.00
Arista ALB6-8330		Pelican West	198?	3.00	6.00	12.00
Reissue						

45s

Label, Number		Title	Year	VG	VG+	NM
Arista 0672		Love Plus One/Favourite Shirts (Boy Meets Girl)	1982		2.00	4.00
Arista 0708	DJ	Favourite Shirts (Boy Meets Girl) (same on both sides)	1982		2.00	4.00
Stock copy may not exist						

12-Inch Singles

Label, Number		Title	Year	VG	VG+	NM
Arista SP-139	DJ	Fantastic Day (Extended)/Ski Club/Love's Got Me (Extended)/ Calling Captain Autumn (Extended)	1982	2.00	4.00	8.00

Halo of Flies

Minneapolis garage-punk band.

45s

Label, Number		Title	Year	VG	VG+	NM
Amphetamine Reptile (1)		Rubber Room/Thoughts in a Booth/3 More Quarters	1985	37.50	75.00	150.00
Numbered edition of 300						
Amphetamine Reptile (1)	PS	Rubber Room/Thoughts in a Booth/3 More Quarters	1985	37.50	75.00	150.00
With insert						
Amphetamine Reptile SCALE 2		Snapping Back Roscoe Bottles: DDT Fin 13-PCP/Can't Touch Her	1985	25.00	50.00	100.00
Numbered edition of 400						
Amphetamine Reptile SCALE 2PS		Snapping Back Roscoe Bottles: DDT Fin 13-PCP/Can't Touch Her	1985	25.00	50.00	100.00
With lyrics						
Amphetamine Reptile SCALE 3		M.D. 20-20/Pipebomb/Sinner Sings	1986	18.75	37.50	75.00
Yellow vinyl (300 made)						
Amphetamine Reptile SCALE 3		M.D. 20-20/Pipebomb/Sinner Sings	1986	6.25	12.50	25.00
Black vinyl (1,700 made)						

Label, Number		Title	Year	VG	VG+	NM
Amphetamine Reptile SCALE 3PS		M.D. 20-20/Pipebomb/Sinner Sings				
			1986	6.25	12.50	25.00
Amphetamine Reptile SCALE 5		Richie's Dog/How Does It Feel to Feel				
			1986	6.25	12.50	25.00
Amphetamine Reptile SCALE 5PS		Richie's Dog/How Does It Feel to Feel				
			1986	6.25	12.50	25.00
Amphetamine Reptile SCALE 13		No Time/You Get Nothing	1987	5.00	10.00	20.00
Amphetamine Reptile SCALE 13	PS	No Time/You Get Nothing	1987	5.00	10.00	20.00
Amphetamine Reptile SCALE 19		Death of a Fly/Sit It Out/There Ain't No Hell				
			1988	3.75	7.50	15.00
Amphetamine Reptile SCALE 19	PS	Death of a Fly/Sit It Out/There Ain't No Hell				
			1988	3.75	7.50	15.00
Amphetamine Reptile SCALE 35		Tired and Cold/Wasted Time	1990	2.50	5.00	10.00
Amphetamine Reptile SCALE 35		Tired and Cold/Wasted Time	1990	6.25	12.50	25.00
Amphetamine Reptile SCALE 35	PS	Tired and Cold/Wasted Time	1990	2.50	5.00	10.00
Amphetamine Reptile SCALE 36		Jagged Time Lapse/She's Just Fifteen				
			1991		3.75	7.50
Amphetamine Reptile SCALE 36		Jagged Time Lapse/She's Just Fifteen				
			1991	6.75	13.75	27.50
Amphetamine Reptile SCALE 36	PS	Jagged Time Lapse/She's Just Fiftee				
			1991		3.75	7.50
Forced Exposure FE-019		Human Fly/I'ma Big	1989	5.00	10.00	20.00
Forced Exposure FE-019	PS	Human Fly/I'ma Big	1989	5.00	10.00	20.00
Siltbreeze 1		Richie's Dog/Garbage Rock/Ballad of Extreme Hate				
			1989	3.00	6.25	12.50
Siltbreeze 1	PS	Richie's Dog/Garbage Rock/Ballad of Extreme Hate				
			1989	3.00	6.25	12.50

First pressings have a numbered insert; add 80% if insert is enclosed

Happy Mondays
English dance-pop group.

Vinyl Albums

Elektra 60854		Bummed	1989	2.50	5.00	10.00

12-Inch Singles

Elektra ED 5469	DJ	Step On (4 versions)	1990	2.00	4.00	8.00
Elektra ED 5522	DJ	Loose Fit (4:21)/Loose Fit (6:15)				
			1991	2.00	4.00	8.00
Elektra ED 5537	DJ	Bob's Yer Uncle (2 mixes)	1990		3.00	6.00
Elektra ED 5637	DJ	Sunshine and Love (3 mixes)	1992	2.00	4.00	8.00
Elektra 66363		Stinkin' Thinkin' (2 remixes)	1992		3.50	7.00
Elektra 66624		Step On (4 versions)	1990	2.00	4.00	8.00
Elektra 66691		Wrote for Luck + 3	1989		3.00	6.00

Harrison, Jerry
*Member of **Talking Heads**.*

Vinyl Albums

Sire SRK 3631	The Red and the Black	1981	2.50	5.00	10.00
Sire 25663	Casual Gods	1988	2.50	5.00	10.00
Sire 25943	Walk on Water	1990	2.50	5.00	10.00

45s

Sire 27977	Rev It Up/Bobby (Aboriginal Mix)				
		1988			3.00

Label, Number		Title	Year	VG	VG+	NM
12-Inch Singles						
Sire PRO-A-3165	DJ	Man with a Gun (2 versions)	1988		3.00	6.00
Sire 20897		Rev It Up (2 versions)/Bobby	1988		2.50	5.00

Harry, Debbie

*Former lead singer of **Blondie**. Some of her later records were released under the name Deborah Harry.*

Vinyl Albums						
Chrysalis CHR 1347		Koo Koo	1981	2.50	5.00	10.00
Chrysalis FV 41347		Koo Koo	1983	2.00	4.00	8.00
Reissue						
Geffen GHS 24123		Rockbird	1986	2.50	5.00	10.00
Geffen R 124347		Rockbird	1986	3.00	6.00	12.00
RCA Music Service edition						
Sire 25938		Def, Dumb & Blonde	1989	2.50	5.00	10.00
45s						
Chrysalis 2526		Backfired/Military Rap	1981			3.00
Chrysalis 2526	PS	Backfired/Military Rap	1981			3.00
Chrysalis 2554		The Jam Was Moving/Inner City Spillover				
			1981			3.00
Chrysalis 42745		Rush, Rush, Rush/Dance, Dance, Dance				
			1983			3.00
Chrysalis 42745	PS	Rush, Rush, Rush/Dance, Dance, Dance				
			1983			3.00
Chrysalis 43328		Denis (The '88 Remix)/Rapture (Teddy Riley Remix)				
			1988			3.00
Chrysalis 43328	PS	Denis (The '88 Remix)/Rapture (Teddy Riley Remix)				
			1988			3.00
Geffen 28476		In Love with Love/Secret Life	1987			3.00
Geffen 28476	PS	In Love with Love/Secret Life	1987			3.00
Geffen 28546		French Kissin'/Rockbird	1986			3.00
Geffen 28546	PS	French Kissin'/Rockbird	1986			3.00
Reprise 27792		Liar, Liar/Queen of Voodoo	1988			3.00
B-side by Voodooist Corporation						
Reprise 27792	PS	Liar, Liar/Queen of Voodoo	1988			3.00
Sire 19998		Sweet and Low	1990			*Cassette only*
Sire 22816		I Want That Man/Bike Boy	1989			3.00
12-Inch Singles						
Chrysalis 32		Chrome/Under Arrest	1981	3.75	7.50	15.00
Chrysalis 33		Backfired (Long)/Backfired (Short)				
			1981		3.50	7.00
Chrysalis 2547		Backfired (Long Version)/Military Rap				
			1981		3.00	6.00
Chrysalis 42741		Rush Rush (Extended)/Rush Rush (Dub Mix)				
			1983		3.50	7.00
Geffen PRO-A-2594	DJ	French Kissin' (Remix)/French Kissin' (LP Version)				
			1986		3.50	7.00
Geffen 20391		Feel the Spin (extended)/Feel the Spin (Dub)				
			1985		3.00	6.00
Geffen 20575		French Kissin' (3 versions)/Rockbird				
			1986		3.00	6.00
Geffen 20654		In Love with Love (3 versions)	1987		3.00	6.00
Sire 21322		I Want That Man (3 versions)/Bika Boy (CD Version)				
			1989		3.00	6.00
Sire 21492		Sweet and Low (5 mixes)/Lovelight				
			1989	2.00	4.00	8.00
Sire 41000		I Can See Clearly (5 versions)	1993		3.00	6.00

Label, Number		Title	Year	VG	VG+	NM

Harvey, PJ

Polly Jean Harvey. Alternative rocker.

Vinyl Albums

Label, Number		Title	Year	VG	VG+	NM
Island 524 085-1		To Bring You My Love	1995	3.75	7.50	15.00

Hatfield, Juliana, Three

*Alterna-rocker formerly with **Blake Babies**.*

45s

Mammoth MR 0053		My Sister//A Dame with a Rod/Put It Away				
			1993		2.50	5.00
Gray vinyl; limited edition of 1,500						
Mammoth MR 0053	PS	My Sister//A Dame with a Rod/Put It Away				
			1993		2.50	5.00

Hawkins, Sophie B.

*New York-based singer-songwriter, formerly with the touring band of **Bryan Ferry**.*

45s

Columbia 74164		Damn I Wish I Was Your Lover/Don't Stop Swaying				
			1992		2.00	4.00
Columbia 74349		California Here I Come/Saviour Child				
			1992			3.00
Columbia 74747		I Want You/Live and Let Love	1992			3.00

12-Inch Singles

| Columbia CAS 6237 | DJ | Right Beside You (4 versions) | 1994 | 2.50 | 5.00 | 10.00 |

Hay, Colin James

*Former lead singer with **Men At Work**.*

Vinyl Albums

Columbia FC 40611		Looking for Jack	1987	2.50	5.00	10.00
MCA 6346		Wayfaring Sons	1990	2.50	5.00	10.00
As "Colin Hay Band"						

45s

Columbia 06580		Hold Me/Home Sweet Home	1987			3.00
Columbia 06580	PS	Hold Me/Home Sweet Home	1987			3.00
Columbia 07042		Can I Hold You?/Nature of the Heart				
			1987			3.00
Columbia 07265		Looking for Jack/These Are Our Finest Days				
			1987			3.00

Hayzi Fantayzee

English new-wave pop-rock duo.

Vinyl Albums

| RCA AFL1-4823 | | Battle Hymns for Children Singing | | | | |
| | | | 1983 | 3.00 | 6.00 | 12.00 |

45s

RCA PB-13534		Shiny Shiny/Shiny Shiny Bon Temps				
			1983		2.50	5.00
RCA PB-13534	PS	Shiny Shiny/Shiny Shiny Bon Temps				
			1983		2.50	5.00
RCA PB-13633		Sister Friction/Here Comes the Beast				
			1983		2.50	5.00

Label, Number		Title	Year	VG	VG+	NM
12-Inch Singles						
RCA PD-13432		John Wayne Is Big Leggy (Groovy Long Version)/				
		Sabres of Paradise	1983	6.25	12.50	25.00
RCA PD-13523		Shiny Shiny Dance/Shiny Shiny Bon Temps				
			1983	5.00	10.00	20.00
RCA PD-13634		Sister Friction (Remix)/Jimmy Jive/Here Comes the Beast				
			1983	5.00	10.00	20.00

Heartbreakers, The

Johnny Thunders' group post-New York Dolls. No relation to Tom Petty's band.

45s						
Max's Kansas City 213		All By Myself/Milk Me	1979	6.25	12.50	25.00

Heaven 17

British techno-pop band. A splinter group from the pre-fame Human League.

Vinyl Albums						
Arista AL 6606		Heaven 17	1982	3.00	6.00	12.00
Arista AL8-8007		Heaven 17	1983	2.50	5.00	10.00
Reissue						
Arista AL8-8020		Luxury Gap	1983	2.50	5.00	10.00
Arista AL8-8259		How Men Are	198?	2.50	5.00	10.00
Caroline 1393		Teddy Bear Duke & Psycho	1988	2.50	5.00	10.00
Virgin 90569		Pleasure One	1986	2.50	5.00	10.00
45s						
Arista 1050		Let Me Go/I'm Your Money	1983			3.00
Arista 9027		We Live So Fast/Best Kept Secret				
			1983			3.00
Arista 9027	PS	We Live So Fast/Best Kept Secret				
			1983			3.00
Arista 9096		Crushed by the Wheels of Industry/Lady Ice and Mr. Hex				
			1983			3.00
Arista 9271		Sunset Now/Counterforce	1984			3.00
Virgin 99468		Contendors/Excerpts from "Diary of a Contender"				
			1987			3.00
12-Inch Singles						
Arista 0723		Who Will Stop the Rain (Extended)/Who Will Stop the Rain (Dub)/				
		Height of Fighting (Remix)	1982	2.50	5.00	10.00
Arista 9030		We Live So Fast (2 versions)/Temptation				
			1983	2.50	5.00	10.00
Arista 9074		Crushed by the Wheels of Industry/Lady Ice and Mr. Hex				
			1983		3.00	6.00
Arista 9269		Sunset Now/Counterforce I (Extended)				
			1984		3.00	6.00
Arista 9306		This Is Mine (3 versions)	1984		3.00	6.00
Virgin 1049	DJ	(Big) Trouble (2 versions)	1986		3.00	6.00
Virgin 12667	DJ	Penthouse and Pavement (4 versions)				
			1993	2.00	4.00	8.00
Virgin 96766		Trouble (At Mill Mix)/(Big) Trouble				
			1986	2.00	4.00	8.00
Virgin 96790		Contenders (4 versions)	1987		3.00	6.00

Helios Creed

45s						
Amphetamine Reptile SCALE 33		The Warming/Your Spaceman	1990		3.75	7.50

Label, Number		Title	Year	VG	VG+	NM
Amphetamine Reptile SCALE 33		The Warming/Your Spaceman	1990	6.75	13.75	27.50
Amphetamine Reptile SCALE 33	PS	The Warming/Your Spaceman	1990		3.75	7.50
Sub Pop 30		Nothing Wrong/The Sky	1989	3.75	7.50	15.00
Sub Pop 30	PS	Nothing Wrong/The Sky	1989	3.75	7.50	15.00
#5 in Sub Pop Singles Club series						

Hell, Richard, and the Voidoids

Early New York new wave act.

Vinyl Albums

Red Star RED 801		Destiny Street	1982	3.75	7.50	15.00
Richard Hell solo						
Sire SRK 6037		Blank Generation	1977	5.00	10.00	20.00

7-Inch Extended Play Singles

Shake SHK 101		Don't Die/Time//That's All I Know (Right Now)/ Love Comes in Spurts	1980	3.00	6.25	12.50
B-side tracks by Neon Boys						
Shake SHK 101	PS	Don't Die/Time//That's All I Know (Right Now)/ Love Comes in Spurts	1980	3.00	6.25	12.50

45s

Ork 81976		I Could Live With You in Another World/Blank Generation/ You Gotta Lose	1977	3.75	7.50	15.00
Ork 81976	PS	I Could Live With You in Another World/Blank Generation/ You Gotta Lose	1977	3.75	7.50	15.00
Sire 1003		Blank Generation/Love Comes in Spurts	1977	2.50	5.00	10.00
Sire 1003	PS	Blank Generation/Love Comes in Spurts	1977	2.50	5.00	10.00

Helmet

Minneapolis-area noise-rock.

45s

Amphetamine Reptile SCALE 22		Born Annoying/Rumble	1989	6.25	12.50	25.00
Amphetamine Reptile SCALE 22	PS	Born Annoying/Rumble	1989	6.25	12.50	25.00
Amphetamine Reptile SCALE 41		Unsung/Your Head	1990	2.50	5.00	10.00
Amphetamine Reptile SCALE 41		Unsung/Your Head	1990	2.50	5.00	10.00
Amphetamine Reptile SCALE 41	PS	Unsung/Your Head	1990	2.50	5.00	10.00
Amphetamine Reptile SCALE 55		Primitive/Born Annoying	1992			3.00
Amphetamine Reptile SCALE 55	PS	Primitive/Born Annoying	1992			3.00

Herman, Pee Wee

Real name: Paul Reubens. Comic, Saturday morning TV host and darling of the MTV set.

45s

Columbia 07301		Surfin' Bird/My Beach	1987			3.00
B-side by Surf Punks						
Columbia 07301	PS	Surfin' Bird/My Beach	1987			3.00

Label, Number		Title	Year	VG	VG+	NM

Hersh, Kristin
Member of Throwing Muses.

45s

Warner Bros. PRO-S-4663	DJ	Counting Backwards (Live)/Counting Sheep (Live)				
			1991	2.50	5.00	10.00

"Soil Samples" series; B-side by the Judybats; green vinyl

Heyward, Nick
Formerly of Haircut One Hundred.

Vinyl Albums

Arista AL8-8106		Nick Heyward	1983	2.50	5.00	10.00
Reprise 25758		I Love You Avenue	1988	2.50	5.00	10.00

45s

Arista 9072		Whistle Down the Wind/Two Make It True				
			1983			3.00
Reprise 27835		You're My World/Pizza Tears	1988			3.00

12-Inch Singles

Reprise 20988		You're My World (3 versions)/Pizza Tears				
			1988	2.00	4.00	8.00

Hindu Love Gods
Features Bill Berry, Peter Beck and Mike Mills of R.E.M. with Warren "Werewolves of London" Zevon as lead singer.

Vinyl Albums

Giant 24406		Hindu Love Gods	1990	3.75	7.50	15.00

45s

I.R.S. 52867		Gonna Have a Good Time Tonight/Narrator				
			1986	2.00	4.00	8.00
I.R.S. 52867	PS	Gonna Have a Good Time Tonight/Narrator				
			1986	2.00	4.00	8.00

Hipsway
Scottish dance-pop group with a former member of Altered Images.

45s

Columbia 06579		The Honeythief/Forbidden	1986			3.00
Columbia 06579	PS	The Honeythief/Forbidden	1986			3.00
Columbia 07118		Ask the Lord/Set This Day Apart				
			1987			3.00
Columbia 07118	PS	Ask the Lord/Set This Day Apart				
			1987			3.00
Columbia 07330		Long White Car/Upon a Thread	1987			3.00

12-Inch Singles

Columbia 05988		The Honeythief (3 versions)	1986		3.00	6.00
Columbia 06801		Ask the Lord (3 versions)	1987		3.00	6.00

Hitchcock, Robyn, and the Egyptians
Robyn Hitchcock, formerly of the Soft Boys, was a cult hero among certain rock fans. The below also includes solo work.

Vinyl Albums

A&M SP-5182		Globe of Frogs	1988	2.50	5.00	10.00
A&M SP-5241		Queen Elvis	1989	2.50	5.00	10.00

Label, Number		Title	Year	VG	VG+	NM
Glass Fish/Relativity 8082		I Often Dream of Trains	1986	2.50	5.00	10.00
First U.S. issue of U.K. album						
Glass Fish/Relativity 8083		Groovy Decoy	1986	2.50	5.00	10.00
First U.S. issue of U.K. album						
Glass Fish/Relativity 8088		Black Snake Diamond Role	1986	2.50	5.00	10.00
First U.S. issue of U.K. album						
Glass Fish/Relativity 8089		Invisible Hitchcock	1986	2.50	5.00	10.00
Glass Fish/Relativity 8130		Element of Light	1986	2.50	5.00	10.00
Relativity 8056		Gotta Let This Hen Out	1985	3.00	6.00	12.00
Relativity 8074	PD	Exploding in Silence	1986	4.50	9.00	18.00
Picture-disc EP						
Slash 25316		Fegmania!	1985	3.75	7.50	15.00
Twin/Tone TTR 89175		Eye	1989	2.50	5.00	10.00

45s

Label, Number		Title	Year	VG	VG+	NM
A&M 1409		Madonna of the Wasps/Ruling Class				
			1989	2.50	5.00	10.00
A&M 3023		Balloon Man/A Globe of Frogs (Electric)				
			1988		2.00	4.00
Relativity 8076	DJ	Heaven/Listening to the Higsons				
			1985	2.50	5.00	10.00

12-Inch Singles

Label, Number		Title	Year	VG	VG+	NM
A&M SP-17530	DJ	Balloon Man/A Globe of Frogs (Electric)/The Ghost Ship				
Green vinyl			1988	3.75	7.50	15.00
A&M SP-17537DJ		Balloon Man (same on both sides)				
			1988	2.50	5.00	10.00
A&M SP-17549DJ		Flesh Number One/Legalized Murder				
Blue vinyl			1988	3.75	7.50	15.00
A&M SP-17697	DJ	Madonna of the Wasps/One Long Pair of Eyes (Acoustic)/				
		More Than This	1989	3.00	6.00	12.00
A&M SP-17729	DJ	One Long Pair of Eyes (Edit)/The Ghost in You (Live)/				
		Freeze (Sunset Mix)	1989	4.50	9.00	18.00
A&M SP-17765	DJ	Interview with Deidre O'Donoghue				
			1989	3.00	6.00	12.00
A&M 75021 7271 1	DJ	So You Think You're in Love/Watch Your Intelligence				
			1991	2.50	5.00	10.00
A&M 75021 7277 1	DJ	Dark Green Energy + 2	1991	2.50	5.00	10.00
A&M 75021 7300 1	DJ	Oceanside + 2	1991	2.50	5.00	10.00
Relativity 8130		Somewhere Apart/If You Were a Priest				
			1987	2.50	5.00	10.00

Hole

*Seattle female grunge-rock band led by Courtney Love, ex-wife of Kurt Cobain of **Nirvana**.*

45s

Label, Number		Title	Year	VG	VG+	NM
DGC 19379		Doll Parts/Plump (Live)	1994		2.00	4.00
Sub Pop 93		Dicknail/Burn Black	1991	11.25	22.50	45.00
First 3,500 on gray marble vinyl						
Sub Pop 93		Dicknail/Burn Black	1991		2.50	5.00
Sub Pop 93	PS	Dicknail/Burn Black	1991		2.50	5.00
Sympathy for the Record		Retard Girl//Phonebillsong/Johnnie's in the Bathroom				
Industry 53			1990	9.25	18.75	37.50
First pressing on pink vinyl						
Sympathy for the Record		Retard Girl//Phonebillsong/Johnnie's in the Bathroom				
Industry 53			1990			2.50
Sympathy for the Record	PS	Retard Girl//Phonebillsong/Johnnie's in the Bathroom				
Industry 53			1990			2.50
Tim/Kerr 947081		Miss World/Over the Edge	1994		2.00	4.00
Pink vinyl						
Tim/Kerr 947081	PS	Miss World/Over the Edge	1994		2.00	4.00

Label, Number		Title	Year	VG	VG+	NM

Holly and the Italians
Holly Beth Vincent, originally from Chicago, and her backing band.

Vinyl Albums

Virgin ARE 38287		Holly and the Italians	1982	2.50	5.00	10.00
Virgin NFE 37359		The Right to Be Italian	1981	2.50	5.00	10.00

45s

Virgin 02482		Miles Away/Means to an End	1981		2.00	4.00

12-Inch Singles

Epic 03173		For What It's Worth/Dangerously	1982	2.50	5.00	10.00

Holly Beth Vincent solo

Hollywood Squares, The
Los Angeles punk band.

45s

Square (no #)		Hillside Strangler/Hollywood Square	1978	16.25	32.50	65.00
Square (no #)	PS	Hillside Strangler/Hollywood Square	1978	16.25	32.50	65.00

Plain sleeve with rubber-stamp on it

Honeymoon Killers

45s

Sub Pop 51		Get It Hot/Gettin' Hot	1989	10.00	20.00	40.00
Red vinyl pressing of 1,200						
Sub Pop 51		Get It Hot/Gettin' Hot	1989	5.00	10.00	20.00
Black vinyl pressing of 800						
Sub Pop 51	PS	Get It Hot/Gettin' Hot	1989	5.00	10.00	20.00
#13 in Sub Pop Singles Club series						

Honeymoon Suite
Canadian pop-rock band.

Vinyl Albums

Warner Bros. 25098		Honeymoon Suite	1984	2.50	5.00	10.00
Warner Bros. 25293		The Big Prize	1986	2.50	5.00	10.00
Warner Bros. 25652		Racing After Midnight	1988	2.50	5.00	10.00
Warner Bros. R 144489		The Big Prize	1986	3.00	6.00	12.00
RCA Music Service edition						
Warner Bros. R 162140		Racing After Midnight	1988	3.00	6.00	12.00
BMG Direct Marketing edition						

45s

Warner Bros. 27791		Cold Look/Love Fever	1988			3.00
Warner Bros. 27935		Love Changes Everything/Fast Company	1988			3.00
Warner Bros. 28379		Lethal Weapon/Take My Hand	1987			3.00
Warner Bros. 28670		What Does It Take/Words in the Wind	1986			3.00
Warner Bros. 28670	PS	What Does It Take/Words in the Wind	1986			3.00
Warner Bros. 28779		Feel It Again/Wounded	1986			3.00
Warner Bros. 28992		Face to Face/Stay In the Night	1985			3.00
Warner Bros. 29109		Burning in Love/Turn My Head	1985			3.00
Warner Bros. 29208		New Girl Now/It's Your Heart	1984			3.00
Warner Bros. 29208	PS	New Girl Now/It's Your Heart	1984			3.00

Label, Number		Title	Year	VG	VG+	NM
12-Inch Singles						
Warner Bros. PRO-A-2165	DJ	New Girl Now/Wave Babies	1984	2.00	4.00	8.00
Warner Bros. PRO-A-2202	DJ	Burning in Love (same on both sides)				
			1984	2.00	4.00	8.00
Warner Bros. PRO-A-2437	DJ	Feel It Again (same on both sides)	1985		3.00	6.00
Warner Bros. PRO-A-2515	DJ	What Does It Take (same on both sides)				
			1985		3.00	6.00
Warner Bros. PRO-A-2539	DJ	All Along You Knew (LP version)/				
		All Along You Knew (Single Version)				
			1985		3.00	6.00

Hoodoo Gurus

*Australian new wave band. Includes a former member of **Divinyls**.*

Label, Number		Title	Year	VG	VG+	NM
Vinyl Albums						
A&M SP 5012		Stone Age Romeos	1983	3.00	6.00	12.00
Big Time 009		Mars Needs Guitars	1985	3.00	6.00	12.00
Elektra 60485		Mars Needs Guitars	1986	2.50	5.00	10.00
Reissue of Big Time LP						
Elektra 60728		Blow Your Cool	1987	2.50	5.00	10.00
RCA 9781-1-R		Magnum Cum Louder	1989	2.50	5.00	10.00
45s						
A&M 2670		I Want You Back/Death Ship	1984		3.00	6.00
Big Time BTS 1503		Bittersweet/Mars Needs Guitars	1985		2.50	5.00
Big Time BTS 1503	PS	Bittersweet/Mars Needs Guitars	1985		2.50	5.00
Big Time BTS 1588		Like Wow -- Wipeout/Bring the Hoodoo Down				
			1985		2.50	5.00
Big Time BTS 1588	PS	Like Wow -- Wipeout/Bring the Hoodoo Down				
			1985		2.50	5.00
Elektra 69440		What's My Scene/Heart of Darkness				
			1987			3.00
Elektra 69481		Good Times/Heart of Darkness	1987			3.00
Elektra 69481	PS	Good Times/Heart of Darkness	1987			3.00
Elektra 69536		Death Defying (Ooh-Wee)/Turkey Dinner				
			1986			3.00
Elektra 69544		Bittersweet/Bring the Hoodoo Down				
			1986			3.00
12-Inch Singles						
A&M 17286	DJ	I Want You Back (Edit) (same on both sides)				
			1984		3.00	6.00
Big Time 1001	DJ	Bittersweet (same on both sides)	1985		3.00	6.00
Big Time 1002	DJ	Poison Pen (same on both sides)	1985		2.50	5.00
Elektra 5151	DJ	Death Defying (Remix) (same on both sides)				
			1985		3.00	6.00
Elektra 5215	DJ	Good Times (same on both sides)				
			1987		3.00	6.00
Elektra 5235	DJ	Out That Door (same on both sides)				
			1987		2.50	5.00
Elektra 5255	DJ	What's My Scene (same on both sides)				
			1987		2.50	5.00
RCA 8998-1		Come Anytime/Hallucination/Where's the Hit?				
			1989		2.50	5.00

Label, Number		Title	Year	VG	VG+	NM

Hooters

Philadelphia-area pop-rock band. Pre-Columbia material was more ska-oriented than later pop stuff. Members Rob Hyman and Eric Bazilian were formerly in **Baby Grand**. *They also assisted the solo debut of* **Cyndi Lauper**. *Bazilian wrote "One of Us" for Joan Osborne.*

Vinyl Albums

Label, Number		Title	Year	VG	VG+	NM
Antenna HOO 83		Amore	1983	5.00	10.00	20.00
Columbia BFC 39912		Nervous Night	1985	3.00	6.00	12.00
Columbia FC 39912		Nervous Night	1985	2.50	5.00	10.00
Reissue with new prefix						
Columbia OC 40659		One Way Home	1987	2.50	5.00	10.00
Columbia C 45058		Zig Zag	1989	2.50	5.00	10.00

45s

Label, Number		Title	Year	VG	VG+	NM
Antenna HOO 84		Hangin' on a Heartbeat/Concubine	1984	2.50	5.00	10.00
Antenna HOO 84	PS	Hangin' on a Heartbeat/Concubine	1984	2.50	5.00	10.00
Columbia 04854		All You Zombies/Nervous Night	1985		2.00	4.00
Not issued with picture sleeve in U.S.						
Columbia 05568		And We Danced/Blood from a Stone	1985			3.00
Columbia 05568	PS	And We Danced/Blood from a Stone	1985			3.00
Columbia 05730		Day By Day/South Ferry Road	1985			3.00
Columbia 05730	PS	Day By Day/South Ferry Road	1985			3.00
Columbia 05854		Where Do the Children Go/Nervous Night	1986			3.00
Columbia 05854	PS	Where Do the Children Go/Nervous Night	1986			3.00
Columbia 07241		Johnny B/Lucy in the Sky with Diamonds	1987			3.00
Non-LP B-side						
Columbia 07241	PS	Johnny B/Lucy in the Sky with Diamonds	1987			3.00
Columbia 07607		Satellite/One Way Home	1987			3.00
Columbia 07607	PS	Satellite/One Way Home	1987			3.00
Columbia 07666		Karla with a K/Washington's Day	1988			3.00
Columbia 08384		And We Danced/All You Zombies	1988			3.00
Reissue						
Columbia 73013		500 Miles/The House of Wolfgang	1989			3.00
Backing vocals on A-side: Peter, Paul and Mary						
Columbia 73235		Brother, Don't You Walk Away/A Man Understands	1990		*Cassette only*	
Columbia 73320		Heaven Laughs/Mr. Big Baboon	1990		*Cassette only*	
Eighty Percent HOO 80		Fightin' on the Same Side/Wireless	1980	2.50	5.00	10.00
Eighty Percent HOO 80	PS	Fightin' on the Same Side/Wireless	1980	2.50	5.00	10.00
Eighty Percent HOO 82		All You Zombies (Live)/Rescue Me	1982	2.50	5.00	10.00
Eighty Percent HOO 82	PS	All You Zombies (Live)/Rescue Me	1982	2.50	5.00	10.00

12-Inch Singles

Label, Number		Title	Year	VG	VG+	NM
Columbia AS 2043	DJ	All You Zombies (long & short)	1985	3.75	7.50	15.00
Columbia CAS 2232	DJ	Day by Day (same on both sides)	1985		3.00	6.00
Columbia CAS 2734	DJ	Johnny B (same on both sides)	1987		3.00	6.00

Label, Number		Title	Year	VG	VG+	NM

Hootie & The Blowfish

South Carolina-based pop-rock band.

Vinyl Albums

Atlantic 82613		Cracked Rear View	1995	3.00	6.00	12.00
Red vinyl						
Atlantic 82886		Fairweather Johnson	1996	2.50	5.00	10.00

45s

Atlantic 87074		Old Man & Me (When I Get to Heaven)/ Before the Heartache Rolls In	1996			2.00
Small center hole, photo label						
Atlantic 87074	PS	Old Man & Me (When I Get to Heaven)/ Before the Heartache Rolls In	1996			2.00
Cardboard sleeve						
Atlantic 87095		Time/Only Wanna Be With You	1995			3.00
Atlantic 87231		Let Her Cry/Hold My Hand	1995			3.00

Hothouse Flowers

Soul-oriented band from Dublin, Ireland.

Vinyl Albums

London 085	DJ	Conversation and Music with Hothouse Flowers				
			1988	3.75	7.50	15.00
London 828 101-1		People	1988	3.00	6.00	12.00
London 884-1	DJ	Live	1990	6.25	12.50	25.00
Six-song promo-only live EP						

45s

London 886 279-7		Don't Go/Saved	1988			2.50
London 886 279-7	PS	Don't Go/Saved	1988			2.50
London 886 317-7		I'm Sorry/Mountains	1988			2.50
London 886 317-7	PS	I'm Sorry/Mountains	1988			2.50

12-Inch Singles

London 604	DJ	Don't Go (same on both sides)	1988		3.00	6.00
London PRO 715	DJ	Feet on the Ground (LP and Live)/Carrickfergus/Better and Better				
			1988	2.50	5.00	10.00

House of Pain

White-boy rappers from Los Angeles -- no, they're not from Ireland despite their shamrock motif.

Vinyl Albums

Tommy Boy 1056		House of Pain	1992	3.00	6.00	12.00

45s

Sub Pop 188		Shamrocks and Shenanigans (In the Dirt Mix)/ Shamrocks and Shenanigans (Buds & Brew Mix)				
All copies on "lucky green vinyl"			1992	2.50	5.00	10.00
Sub Pop 188	PS	Shamrocks and Shenanigans (In the Dirt Mix)/ Shamrocks and Shenanigans (Buds & Brew Mix)				
			1992	2.50	5.00	10.00
Tommy Boy 526		Jump Around (same on both sides)	1992		2.00	4.00
With no "Collectables" logo on label						
Tommy Boy 526		Jump Around (same on both sides)	1993			3.00
With "Collectables" logo on label						
Tommy Boy 543		Shamrocks and Shenanigans (Boom Shalock Lock Boom) (LP Version)/same (Butch Vig Mix)				
			1992			3.00
Tommy Boy 556		Who's the Man?/Kick Some	1993			3.00

Label, Number		Title	Year	VG	VG+	NM
12-Inch Singles						
Tommy Boy 548		Shamrocks and Shenanigans (5 versions)/ Put Your Head Out (Clean LP Version) 1992	1992	2.00	4.00	8.00
Tommy Boy 556		Put On Your Sh*t Kickers (4 versions) 1993	1993	2.00	4.00	8.00
Tommy Boy 556		Who's the Man? (2 versions)/Put On Your Sh*t Kickers (2 versions) 1993	1993	2.00	4.00	8.00
Tommy Boy 623		On Point (5 versions)	1994		3.00	6.00
Uptown 2606	DJ	Who's the Man? (same on both sides) 1993	1993		3.50	7.00

House of Schock

*Featuring Gina Schock, formerly of the **Go-Go's**.*

Label, Number		Title	Year	VG	VG+	NM
Vinyl Albums						
Capitol C1-46925		House of Schock	1988	2.50	5.00	10.00
45s						
Capitol 44135		Middle of Nowhere/World Goes 'Round 1988	1988			3.00
Capitol 44135	PS	Middle of Nowhere/World Goes 'Round 1988	1988			3.00
Capitol 44202		Love in Return/Middle of Nowhere 1988	1988			3.00
12-Inch Singles						
Capitol SPRO-79277	DJ	Middle of Nowhere (same on both sides) 1988	1988		2.50	5.00

Housemartins, The

Label, Number		Title	Year	VG	VG+	NM
Vinyl Albums						
Elektra 60501		London 0 Hull 4	1986	2.50	5.00	10.00
Elektra 60761		The People Who Grinned Themselves to Death 1987	1987	2.50	5.00	10.00
Elektra 60761	DJ	The People Who Grinned Themselves to Death 1987	1987	3.00	6.00	12.00
Promo-only audiophile pressing						
45s						
Elektra 69436		Caravan of Love/When I First Met Jesus 1987	1987			3.00
Elektra 69436	PS	Caravan of Love/When I First Met Jesus 1987	1987			3.00
Elektra 69491		Flag Day/The Mighty Ship	1987			3.00
Elektra 69515		Happy Hour/The Mighty Ship	1986			3.00
12-Inch Singles						
Elektra 5174	DJ	Happy Hour (same on both sides)1986	1986		3.50	7.00

Human League

*British synth-pop group. First of the new-wave groups to hit Number One on the Billboard Hot 100. Two early members left and created **Heaven 17**.*

Label, Number		Title	Year	VG	VG+	NM
Vinyl Albums						
A&M SP6-4892		Dare	1981	2.50	5.00	10.00
A&M SP-4923		Hysteria	1984	2.50	5.00	10.00
A&M SP-5129		Crash	1986	2.50	5.00	10.00
A&M SP-5227		Greatest Hits	1989	2.50	5.00	10.00
A&M SP-12501	EP	Fascination!	1983		3.00	6.00
A&M R 100837		Greatest Hits	1989	3.00	6.00	12.00
BMG Direct Marketing edition						

Travelogue, from 1980, appears to be the first Human League album to have seen release in America. Not commonly known to exist, this came out on the Virgin International label here.

This single by Minneapolis indie-rock heroes Husker Du is still available from SST Records.

Label, Number		Title	Year	VG	VG+	NM
A&M R 162455		Crash	1986	3.00	6.00	12.00
RCA Music Service edition						
A&M 75021 5316 1		Romantic?	1990	3.00	6.00	12.00
Virgin 90880		Travelogue	1988	2.50	5.00	10.00
Virgin 90881		Reproduction	1988	2.50	5.00	10.00
First issue of early U.K. album						
Virgin International VI 2160		Travelogue	1980	3.75	7.50	15.00

45s

Label, Number		Title	Year	VG	VG+	NM
A&M 2397		Don't You Want Me/Seconds	1982			3.00
A&M 2397	PS	Don't You Want Me/Seconds	1982		3.00	6.00
A somewhat scarce sleeve						
A&M 2425		Love Action (I Believe in Love)/Hard Times	1982			3.00
A&M 2425	PS	Love Action (I Believe in Love)/Hard Times	1982			3.00
A&M 2449		Things That Dreams Are Made Of/ Things That Dreams Are Made Of (instrumental)	1982			3.00
B-side by "League Unlimited Orchestra"						
A&M 2508		Don't You Want Me/Don't You Want Me (instrumental)	1982			3.00
B-side by "League Unlimited Orchestra"						
A&M 2547		(Keep Feeling) Fascination/Total Panic	1983			3.00
A&M 2547	PS	(Keep Feeling) Fascination/Total Panic	1983			3.00
A&M 2587		Mirror Man/Non-Stop	1983			3.00
A&M 2587	PS	Mirror Man/Non-Stop	1983			3.00
A&M 2641		The Lebanon/Thirteen	1984			3.00
A&M 2641	PS	The Lebanon/Thirteen	1984			3.00
A&M 2650		Don't You Know I Want You/Thirteen	1984			3.00
A&M 2657		Louise/The World Tonight	1984			3.00
A&M 2661	DJ	Life on Your Own (same on both sides)	1984		2.50	5.00
No stock copies issued						
A&M 2861		Human/Human (instrumental)	1986			3.00
A&M 2861	PS	Human/Human (instrumental)	1986			3.00
A&M 2893		I Need Your Loving/Are You Ever Coming Back?	1986			3.00
A&M 2893	PS	I Need Your Loving/Are You Ever Coming Back?	1986			3.00
A&M 2918		Love Is All That Matters/Love Is All That Matters (instrumental)	1987			3.00
A&M 2934		Jam/Are You Ever Coming Back?	1987			3.00
A&M 8635		(Keep Feeling) Fascination/Mirror Man	198?			3.00
Reissue						
A&M 8647		Don't You Want Me/Love Action (I Believe in Love)	198?			3.00
Reissue						
A&M 8670		Human/Love Is All That Matters	198?			3.00
Reissue						
EastWest 64443		Tell Me When/Kimi Nu Mune Kyum	1995		2.00	4.00

12-Inch Singles

Label, Number		Title	Year	VG	VG+	NM
A&M 12045		Don't You Want Me (Extended)/Love Action	1982	3.00	6.00	12.00
A&M 12049		Hard Times (Vocal & Instrumental)/ Love Action (Vocal & Instrumental)	1981		3.00	6.00
A&M 12197		Human (3 versions)	1986	2.00	4.00	8.00

Label, Number		Title	Year	VG	VG+	NM
A&M 12213		I Need Your Loving (4 versions)	1986	2.00	4.00	8.00
A&M 12227		Love Is All That Matters (4 versions)				
			1984		3.00	6.00
A&M 17227	DJ	(Keep Feeling) Fascination (4:56)/(Keep Feeling) Fascination (6:12)				
			1983	2.00	4.00	8.00
A&M 17276	DJ	The Lebanon/The Lebanon (Single Version)				
			1984	2.00	4.00	8.00
EastWest 5731	DJ	Tell Me When (4 versions)	1995	2.00	4.00	8.00

Humans, The

Northern California new-wave band.

Vinyl Albums

Label, Number		Title	Year	VG	VG+	NM
I.R.S. SP-17900	EP	The Humans	1980	2.50	5.00	10.00
Promo-only 12-inch with die-cut sleeve						
I.R.S. SP-70025		The Humans (Happy Hour)	1981	2.50	5.00	10.00

45s

Label, Number		Title	Year	VG	VG+	NM
Beat HIT 1234		I Live in the City/Earthling//Electric Bodies/Play				
			1979	2.00	4.00	8.00
Beat HIT 1234	PS	I Live in the City/Earthling//Electric Bodies/Play				
			1979	2.00	4.00	8.00
I.R.S. 7700		I Live in the City/Play//Tracy/Pipeline				
			1980	2.00	4.00	8.00
I.R.S. 7700	PS	I Live in the City/Play//Tracy/Pipeline				
			1980	2.00	4.00	8.00
Gatefold sleeve with 12-page booklet						
I.R.S. 9009		Wild Thing/I Live in the City	1980		2.00	4.00

12-Inch Singles

Label, Number		Title	Year	VG	VG+	NM
I.R.S. 70957	DJ	Don't Be Afraid of the Dark/Get You Tonight/Lightning				
			1981		2.50	5.00

Huns, The

Austin, Texas punk band. Made one record, then split up.

45s

Label, Number		Title	Year	VG	VG+	NM
God 001		Busy Kids/Glad He's Dead	1979	18.75	37.50	75.00
God 001	PS	Busy Kids/Glad He's Dead	1979	18.75	37.50	75.00
Oversized sleeve with insert						

Hunters & Collectors

Melbourne, Australia band.

12-Inch Singles

Label, Number		Title	Year	VG	VG+	NM
A&M 12076		Talking to a Stranger (2 versions)/Run Run Run				
			1982		3.00	6.00
I.R.S. 17224	DJ	Throw Your Arms/Say Goodbye/Anybody				
			1986		3.00	6.00
I.R.S. 17634	DJ	Back on the Breadline (same on both sides)				
			1988		2.50	5.00
I.R.S. 17705	DJ	Faraway Man (Live)/Say Goodbye (Live)/				
		Back on the Breadline (Live)/Parting Glass (Live)				
			1988	2.50	5.00	10.00

Husker Du

Highly influential Minneapolis indie-rock legends of the 1980s. Also see **Mould, Bob.**

Vinyl Albums

Label, Number		Title	Year	VG	VG+	NM
New Alliance 007		Land Speed Record	1982	6.25	12.50	25.00

Label, Number		Title	Year	VG	VG+	NM
New Alliance 007		Land Speed Record	1982	3.00	6.00	12.00
Second pressing, "Marketed by SST" on cover						
Reflex #D		Everything Falls Apart	1982	10.00	20.00	40.00
SST 020	EP	Metal Circus	1983	2.00	4.00	8.00
SST 027	(2)	Zen Arcade	1984	3.75	7.50	15.00
SST PSST E27	DJ	Eight Miles High/6 from Zen Arcade	1984	7.50	15.00	30.00
Promo sampler, etched design on side 1, sticker cover						
SST 031		New Day Rising	1985	2.50	5.00	10.00
SST 055		Flip Your Wig	1985	2.50	5.00	10.00
SST 195		Land Speed Record	198?	2.50	5.00	10.00
Reissue of New Alliance 007						
SST 908	10	Metal Circus	199?	2.00	4.00	8.00
SST 915	10	Eight Miles High/Makes No Sense at All	199?	2.00	4.00	8.00
Warner Bros. WBMS-145	DJ	The Warehouse Interview	1987	6.25	12.50	25.00
Promo only, part of the Warner Bros. Music Show series						
Warner Bros. PRO-A-2719	DJ	Warehouse: Songs and Stories	1987	2.00	4.00	8.00
Promo-only four-song sampler						
Warner Bros. 25385		Candy Apple Grey	1986	3.00	6.00	12.00
Warner Bros. 25544	(2)	Warehouse: Songs and Stories	1987	3.00	6.00	12.00

45s

Label, Number		Title	Year	VG	VG+	NM
New Alliance 010		In a Free Land/What Do I Want/M.I.C.	1982	7.50	15.00	30.00
New Alliance 010	PS	In a Free Land/What Do I Want/M.I.C.	1982	7.50	15.00	30.00
Reflex 38285		Statues/Amusement (Live)	1980	9.25	18.75	37.50
Reflex 38285	PS	Statues/Amusement (Live)	1980	9.25	18.75	37.50
SST 025		Eight Miles High/Masochism World (Live)	1984			2.00
SST 025	PS	Eight Miles High/Masochism World (Live)	1984			2.00
Still in print as of 1995						
SST PSST 031	DJ	Celebrated Summer/New Day Rising	1984	3.75	7.50	15.00
SST PSST 031	PS	Celebrated Summer/New Day Rising	1984	3.75	7.50	15.00
Rubber-stamped sleeve with sticker and enclosed press release						
SST 051		Makes No Sense at All/Love Is All Around	1985			2.00
SST 051	PS	Makes No Sense at All/Love Is All Around	1985			2.00
Still in print as of 1995						

12-Inch Singles

Label, Number		Title	Year	VG	VG+	NM
Warner Bros. PRO-A-2524	DJ	Sorry Somehow (same on both sides)	1986	2.00	4.00	8.00
Warner Bros. PRO-A-2654	DJ	Could You Be the One (same on both sides)	1987		3.50	7.00

I

Ice Cube

A founding member of gangsta rap group N.W.A.

Vinyl Albums

Label, Number		Title	Year	VG	VG+	NM
Priority 57120		AmeriKKKa's Most Wanted	1990	3.00	6.00	12.00
Priority 57155		Death Certificate	1991	3.00	6.00	12.00
Priority 57185		The Predator	1992	3.00	6.00	12.00
Priority 7230	EP	Kill at Will	1990	2.00	4.00	8.00

Label, Number		Title	Year	VG	VG+	NM
Priority P1-53876		Lethal Injection	1993	2.50	5.00	10.00
Priority P1-53921		Bootlegs & B-Sides	1994	2.50	5.00	10.00
12-Inch Singles						
Priority 50795		Bop Gun (One Nation)/Bop Gun (One Nation) (Edit)/				
		Down for Whatever	1994	2.50	5.00	10.00
Priority 50828		What Can I Do? (3 versions)	1994	2.50	5.00	10.00
Priority 7046		You Know How We Do It/(Instrumental)				
			1994	2.00	4.00	8.00

Ice-T

*One of the original "gangsta rappers." Also created a controversial heavy-metal band called **Body Count.***

Vinyl Albums						
Rhyme Syndicate 53858		Home Invasion	1993	2.50	5.00	10.00
Sire PRO-A-4959	(2) DJ	O.G. Original Gangster	1991	10.00	20.00	40.00
Promo-only radio-ready version of album otherwise unavailable on U.S. vinyl						
Sire 25602		Rhyme Pays	1987	2.50	5.00	10.00
Sire 25765		Power	1988	3.00	6.00	12.00
Sire 26028		The Iceberg/Freedom of Speech...Just Watch What You Say				
			1989	3.00	6.00	12.00

45s						
Sire 18629		Gotta Lotta Love	1993			*Cassette only*
Sire 19991		What You Wanna Do?/The Girl Tried to Kill Me				
			1990			*Cassette only*
Sire 19994		Freedom of Speech/You Played Yourself				
			1990			3.00
Sire 22810		Lethal Weapon/Heartbeat	1989		2.00	4.00
Sire 27574		High Rollers/Hunted Child	1989		2.00	4.00
Sire 27768		I'm Your Pusher/Girls L.G.B.N.A.F.				
			1988		2.00	4.00
Sire 27768	PS	I'm Your Pusher/Girls L.G.B.N.A.F.				
			1988		2.00	4.00
Sire 27902		Colors/Squeeze the Trigger	1988		2.50	5.00
Sire 27902	PS	Colors/Squeeze the Trigger	1988		2.50	5.00
Sire 28126		Somebody Gotta Do It/Our Most Requested Record				
			1988		2.50	5.00

12-Inch Singles						
Electrobeat EB 002		Killers/Killers (Instrumental)/Body Rock (2 versions)				
			198?	3.75	7.50	15.00
Giant PRO-A-4643	DJ	New Jack Hustler (3 versions)	1991	2.00	4.00	8.00
Priority 7023		That's How I'm Livin' (4 versions)/99 Problems (2 versions)				
			1993		3.00	6.00
Rhino 393		Ice-A Mix (7:00)/Ice-A-Tek (5:00)				
			198?	2.00	4.00	8.00
Sire 20711		Make It Funky (3 versions)/Sex (2 versions)				
			1987	2.50	5.00	10.00
Sire 20805		Somebody Gotta Do It (2 versions)/				
		Our Most Requested Record (2 versions)				
			1987		3.00	6.00
Sire 21149		High Rollers/The Hunted Child (3 versions)/Power (Remix)/				
		Power (Instrumental)	1989		2.00	4.00	8.00
Sire 21325		Lethal Weapon (2 versions)/This One's for Me/Heartbeat				
			1989		2.00	4.00	8.00
Sire 21704		Dick Tracy (4 versions)	1990		3.00	6.00
Sire 40104		Original Gangster (3 versions)/Bitches 2 (2 versions)				
			1991		2.00	4.00	8.00
Sire 40131		Lifestyles of the Rich and Infamous (3 versions)/				
		The Tower (2 versions)	1991		3.00	6.00

Label, Number		Title	Year	VG	VG+	NM
Sire 40210		Ricochet (2 versions)/Mind Over Matter (Remix)				
			1991		3.00	6.00
Sire 40737		Gotta Lotta Love (3 versions)	1992		3.00	6.00
Sire PRO-A-5143	DJ	Ricochet (3 versions)/Mind Over Matter (4 versions)				
			1991	2.00	4.00	8.00
Sire PRO-A-5367	DJ	Mind Over Matter (4 versions)	1991	2.00	4.00	8.00
TechnoHop 10		Ya Don't Quit (3 versions)	1986	3.00	6.00	12.00
TechnoHop 13		Dog'n the Wax (3 versions)/6 in the Morning				
			1986	3.75	7.50	15.00

Icehouse

Australian pop-rock band. Took its name from one of its early songs after discovering its original name, Flowers, was already claimed.

Vinyl Albums

Label, Number	Title	Year	VG	VG+	NM
Chrysalis CHR 1350	Icehouse	1981	3.00	6.00	12.00
Chrysalis CHR 1390	Primitive Man	1982	3.00	6.00	12.00
Chrysalis F1-21680	Great Southern Land	1989	3.00	6.00	12.00
Chrysalis FV 41350	Icehouse	198?	2.00	4.00	8.00
Reissue of CHS 1350					
Chrysalis 5V 41436	Fresco	1983	2.50	5.00	10.00
Five-track LP, with same songs on both sides					
Chrysalis FV 41458	Sidewalk	1983	2.50	5.00	10.00
Chrysalis BFV 41527	Measure for Measure	1986	2.50	5.00	10.00
Chrysalis FV 41592	Man of Colours	1987	2.50	5.00	10.00
Chrysalis R 100935	Great Southern Land	1989	3.00	6.00	12.00
BMG Direct Marketing edition					
Chrysalis R 143633	Man of Colours	1987	3.00	6.00	12.00
BMG Direct Marketing edition					
Chrysalis R 144571	Measure for Measure	1986	3.00	6.00	12.00
RCA Music Service edition					

45s

Label, Number		Title	Year	VG	VG+	NM
Chrysalis 2530		We Can Get Together/Not My Mind				
			1981		2.50	5.00
Chrysalis 2530	PS	We Can Get Together/Not My Mind				
			1981		2.50	5.00
Chrysalis 2556		Walls/(B-side unknown)	1981		2.00	4.00
Chrysalis 2568		Can't Help Myself/(B-side unknown)				
			1981		2.00	4.00
Chrysalis 23414		Touch the Fire/Great Southern Land				
			1989			3.00
Chrysalis 42670		Hey Little Girl/(B-side unknown)	1983		2.00	4.00
Chrysalis 42978		No Promises/(B-side unknown)	1986		2.00	4.00
Chrysalis 43057		Cross the Border/(B-side unknown)				
			1986		2.00	4.00
Chrysalis 43156		Crazy/No Promises	1987			3.00
Chrysalis 43156	PS	Crazy/No Promises	1987			3.00
Chrysalis 43201		Electric Blue/Over My Head	1988			3.00
Chrysalis 43201	PS	Electric Blue/Over My Head	1988			3.00
Chrysalis 43240		My Obsession/Your Confession	1988			3.00
Chrysalis 43240	PS	My Obsession/Your Confession	1988			3.00

12-Inch Singles

Label, Number		Title	Year	VG	VG+	NM
Chrysalis 37		Can't Help Myself (2 versions)	1981	2.50	5.00	10.00
Chrysalis 42		Uniform (extended)/Hey Little Girl/Mysterious Thing				
			1982	2.50	5.00	10.00
Chrysalis AS 1859	DJ	Taking the Town (same on both sides)				
			1984	2.00	4.00	8.00
Chrysalis VAS 2305	DJ	No Promises (same on both sides)				
			1986		3.50	7.00
Chrysalis VAS 2362	DJ	No Promises (3 versions)	1986	2.50	5.00	10.00

Label, Number		Title	Year	VG	VG+	NM
Chrysalis VAS 2389	DJ	Cross the Border/Iva Davies Interview				
			1986	2.50	5.00	10.00
Released with cue sheets						
Chrysalis VAS 2519	DJ	Paradise (2 versions)/No Promises (Live)/Cross the Border (Live)				
			1986		3.00	6.00
Chrysalis VAS 2899	DJ	Electric Blue (3 versions)	1988	3.75	7.50	15.00
Blue vinyl promo						
Chrysalis 42731		Hey Little Girl (2 versions)	1983	2.00	4.00	8.00
Chrysalis 43009		No Promises (3 versions)	1986	2.00	4.00	8.00
Chrysalis 43062		Cross the Border (3 versions)	1986		3.00	6.00

Icicle Works

British rock trio from Liverpool.

Vinyl Albums

Label, Number	Title	Year	VG	VG+	NM
Arista AL6-8202	Icicle Works	1984	2.50	5.00	10.00
Beggars Banquet 6447-1-H	If You Want to Defeat Your Enemy, Sing His Song				
		1987	3.00	6.00	12.00

45s

Label, Number	Title	Year	VG	VG+	NM
Arista 9155	Whisper to a Scream (Birds Fly)/In the Dance the Shaman Led				
		1984			3.00

12-Inch Singles

Label, Number		Title	Year	VG	VG+	NM
Arista ADP 9187		Whisper to a Scream (Birds Fly) (3 mixes)				
			1983	3.00	6.00	12.00
Arista 9217	DJ	In the Cauldron of Love (same on both sides)				
			1984	2.00	4.00	8.00
RCA 6444	DJ	Understanding Jane (same on both sides)				
			1987	2.00	4.00	8.00
RCA 8772		The Kiss Off (3 versions)	1988		2.50	5.00

Idol, Billy

Leather-lunged and leather-clad pop-new wave star, originally with **Generation X.**

Vinyl Albums

Label, Number		Title	Year	VG	VG+	NM
Chrysalis CHR 1377		Billy Idol	1982	3.00	6.00	12.00
Chrysalis VAS 2610	DJ	Interview	1983	3.75	7.50	15.00
Chrysalis CEP 4000	EP	Don't Stop	1981	3.00	6.00	12.00
Chrysalis F1-21735		Charmed Life	1990	3.00	6.00	12.00
Chrysalis FV 41377		Billy Idol	1983	2.50	5.00	10.00
Reissue						
Chrysalis FV 41450		Rebel Yell	1983	2.50	5.00	10.00
Chrysalis FV 41514		Whiplash Smile	1986	2.50	5.00	10.00
Chrysalis OV 41620		Vital Idol	1987	2.50	5.00	10.00
Chrysalis R 104806		Billy Idol	1982	3.00	6.00	12.00
RCA Music Service edition						
Chrysalis R 124674		Rebel Yell	1984	3.00	6.00	12.00
RCA Music Service edition						
Chrysalis R 153899	EP	Don't Stop	1981	3.00	6.00	12.00
RCA Music Service edition						
Chrysalis R 154038		Vital Idol	1987	3.00	6.00	12.00
BMG Direct Marketing edition						
Chrysalis R 154108		Whiplash Smile	1986	3.00	6.00	12.00
RCA Music Service edition						
Chrysalis R 162264		Charmed Life	1990	3.50	7.00	14.00
BMG Direct Marketing edition						

45s

Label, Number	Title	Year	VG	VG+	NM
Chrysalis 2488	Dancing with Myself/Turn and Walk Away				
		1981	2.50	5.00	10.00
Label credit: "Billy Idol and Gen X"					
Chrysalis 2543	Mony Mony/Baby Talk	1981	2.50	5.00	10.00

Label, Number		Title	Year	VG	VG+	NM
Chrysalis 2605		Hot in the City/Hole in the Wall	1982		2.50	5.00
Chrysalis 2605	PS	Hot in the City/Hole in the Wall	1982		2.50	5.00
Chrysalis S7-17403		Shock to the System/Heroin	1993			3.00
Chrysalis S7-17516		Wasteland/Neuromancer	1993			3.00
Chrysalis S7-19027		Dancing with Myself/Catch My Fall	1996			3.00
Reissue						
Chrysalis 23509		Cradle of Love/311 Man	1990		2.00	4.00
Chrysalis 23509	PS	Cradle of Love/311 Man	1990		2.00	4.00
Chrysalis 23571		L.A. Woman/(B-side unknown)	1990		2.00	4.00
Chrysalis 42648		White Wedding/Dead on Arrival	1982		2.00	4.00
Chrysalis 42697		White Wedding/Dead on Arrival	1983		2.00	4.00
Chrysalis 42723		Dancing with Myself/Love Calling	1983		2.00	4.00
Label credit: "Billy Idol and Gen X"						
Chrysalis 42762		Rebel Yell/Crank Call	1983			3.00
Chrysalis 42762	PS	Rebel Yell/Crank Call	1983			3.00
Chrysalis 42786		Eyes Without a Face/Blue Highway	1984			3.00
Chrysalis 42786	PS	Eyes Without a Face/Blue Highway	1984			3.00
Chrysalis 42809		Flesh For Fantasy/The Dead Next Door	1984			3.00
Chrysalis 42809	PS	Flesh For Fantasy/The Dead Next Door	1984			3.00
Chrysalis 42840		Catch My Fall/(B-side unknown)	1984			3.00
Chrysalis 42955		Rebel Yell/Blue Highway	1985			3.00
Silver label reissue						
Chrysalis 42956		Eyes Without a Face/Flesh For Fantasy	1985			3.00
Silver label reissue						
Chrysalis 43024		To Be a Lover/All Summer Single	1986			3.00
Chrysalis 43024	PS	To Be a Lover/All Summer Single	1986			3.00
Chrysalis 43087		Don't Need a Gun/Fatal Charm	1986			3.00
Chrysalis 43087	PS	Don't Need a Gun/Fatal Charm	1986			3.00
Chrysalis 43114		Sweet Sixteen/Beyond Belief	1987			3.00
Chrysalis 43114	PS	Sweet Sixteen/Beyond Belief	1987			3.00
Chrysalis 43161		Mony Mony "Live"/Shakin' All Over "Live"	1987		2.00	4.00
Chrysalis 43161	PS	Mony Mony "Live"/Shakin' All Over "Live"	1987		2.00	4.00
Non-LP tracks (both sides!)						
Chrysalis 43203		Hot in the City/Catch My Fall	1988			3.00
Chrysalis 43203	PS	Hot in the City/Catch My Fall	1988			3.00
12-Inch Singles						
Chrysalis AS 1761	DJ	Rebel Yell (same on both sides)	1983		3.50	7.00
Chrysalis AS 1831	DJ	Blue Highway (same on both sides)	1983		3.00	6.00
Chrysalis AS 1856	DJ	Eyes Without a Face (LP version)/Eyes Without a Face (single)	1984	2.00	4.00	8.00
Chrysalis AS 1894	DJ	Flesh For Fantasy (2 versions)	1984	2.50	5.00	10.00
Chrysalis AS 1901	DJ	Flesh For Fantasy (2 versions)	1984		3.00	6.00
Chrysalis VAS 2449	DJ	To Be a Lover (same on both sides)	1986	2.00	4.00	8.00
Chrysalis VAS 2672	DJ	Sweet Sixteen (same on both sides)	1987	2.00	4.00	8.00
Chrysalis EPC 5002		White Wedding Part 2/White Wedding Part 1 & 2	1982	3.75	7.50	15.00
White vinyl						

Label, Number		Title	Year	VG	VG+	NM
Chrysalis 24826	(2) DJ	Heroin (9 versions)	1994	3.75	7.50	15.00
White vinyl promo-only release						
Chrysalis 42685		White Wedding Part 2/White Wedding Part 1 & 2				
			1982	2.50	5.00	10.00
Reissue of white vinyl version (EPC 5002)						
Chrysalis 42810		Flesh for Fantasy (2 mixes)	1984	3.75	7.50	15.00
Chrysalis 43025		To Be a Lover (2 versions)/All Summer Single				
			1986	2.50	5.00	10.00
Chrysalis 43090		Don't Need a Gun (2 remixes)/Fatal Charm				
			1986	3.00	6.00	12.00

Iggy and the Stooges

Iggy Pop and his early Detroit-based proto-punk band, the Stooges.

Vinyl Albums

Label, Number		Title	Year	VG	VG+	NM
Bomp! 1018		Kill City	1978	2.00	4.00	8.00
By "Iggy Pop and James Williamson"						
Columbia KC 32111		Raw Power	1973	12.50	25.00	50.00
Elektra EKS 74051		The Stooges	1969	12.50	25.00	50.00
By "The Stooges"; value is for original red-label pressings (butterfly label, deduct 60%)						
Elektra EKS 74101		Fun House	1970	12.50	25.00	50.00
By "The Stooges"; value is for original red-label pressings (butterfly label, deduct 60%)						
Import/Bomp! 1015		Metallic K.O.	1977	4.50	9.00	18.00
Import/Bomp! 1018		Kill City	1978	3.00	6.00	12.00
By "Iggy Pop and James Williamson"; original issue on green vinyl						

7-Inch Extended Play Singles

Label, Number		Title	Year	VG	VG+	NM
Bomp! 114		Jesus Loves the Stooges	1977		3.75	7.50
Bomp! 114	PS	Jesus Loves the Stooges	1977		3.75	7.50

45s

Label, Number		Title	Year	VG	VG+	NM
Bomp! 139		I Got a Right/Gimme Some Skin	1991			2.00
Bomp! 139	PS	I Got a Right/Gimme Some Skin	1991			2.00
Siamese 001		I Got a Right/Gimme Some Skin	1977	6.25	12.50	25.00
Siamese 001		I Got a Right/Gimme Some Skin	1977	2.50	5.00	10.00
Second pressing: "Siamese" in fake Asian lettering with iguana logo						
Siamese 001	PS	I Got a Right/Gimme Some Skin	1977		3.00	6.00
Only issued with Bomp!-distributed copies; has "Iggy & & The Stooges" on cover						

12-Inch Singles

Label, Number		Title	Year	VG	VG+	NM
Bomp! 12139		I Got a Right/Gimme Some Skin	1991		2.50	5.00

Iggy Pop

Punk-rock founding father. Also see Iggy and the Stooges.

Vinyl Albums

Label, Number		Title	Year	VG	VG+	NM
A&M SP-5145		Blah Blah Blah	1986	2.50	5.00	10.00
A&M SP-5198		Instinct	1988	2.50	5.00	10.00
A&M SP-17641	DJ	Live at the Channel 7/19/88	1988	10.00	20.00	40.00
Numbered, rubber-stamped promo-only edition						
A&M R 134099		Blah Blah Blah	1986	3.00	6.00	12.00
RCA Music Service edition						
Animal 6000		Zombie Birdhouse	1982	3.00	6.00	12.00
Animal FV 41399		Zombie Birdhouse	1983	2.00	4.00	8.00
Reissue						
Arista SP-115	EP	Special Rock Club Versions	1981	4.50	9.00	18.00
Promo-only remixes of 4 songs from the "Party" LP						
Arista AL 4237		New Values	1979	3.75	7.50	15.00
Arista AB 4259		Soldier	1980	3.00	6.00	12.00
Arista AL5-8172		Soldier	198?	2.00	4.00	8.00
Reissue						
Arista AL5-8189		Party	198?	2.00	4.00	8.00
Reissue						

Label, Number		Title	Year	VG	VG+	NM
Arista AL 9572		Party	1981	3.00	6.00	12.00
Pair PDL2-1051	(2)	Iggy Pop	1986	3.00	6.00	12.00
Compilation of RCA Victor material						
RCA Victor APL1-2275		The Idiot	1977	4.50	9.00	18.00
RCA Victor AFL1-2488		Lust for Life	1977	4.50	9.00	18.00
RCA Victor AFL1-2796		TV Eye -- 1977 Live	1978	3.00	6.00	12.00
RCA Victor AFL1-4957		Choice Cuts	1984	3.75	7.50	15.00
Virgin 91381		Brick by Brick	1990	2.50	5.00	10.00

45s

Label, Number		Title	Year	VG	VG+	NM
A&M 2874		Cry for Love/Winners and Losers				
			1986		2.00	4.00
A&M 2909		Real Wild Child (Wild One)/Little Miss Emperor				
			1987		2.00	4.00
RCA PB-10989		Baby/Sister Midnight	1977		3.00	6.00

12-Inch Singles

Label, Number		Title	Year	VG	VG+	NM
A&M 12203		Cry for Love (Extended)/Cry for Love (7" edit)/Little Miss Emperor				
			1986	2.00	4.00	8.00
A&M 17426	DJ	Cry for Love (same on both sides)				
			1986		3.00	6.00
A&M 17444	DJ	Isolation (same on both sides)	1986	2.00	4.00	8.00
A&M 17446	DJ	Real Wild Child (2 mixes)	1986	2.00	4.00	8.00
A&M 17608	DJ	Cold Metal (2 mixes)/Tough Baby (2 mixes)				
			1988	2.00	4.00	8.00
Arista SP-81	DJ	Knocking 'Em Down/Ambition/Loco Mosquito				
			1980	5.00	10.00	20.00

Indigo Girls

Female alterna-folk duo.

Vinyl Albums

Label, Number		Title	Year	VG	VG+	NM
Epic AE 1481	EP	Kid Fears/Closer to Fine/Center Stage/Prince of Darkness				
			1989	7.50	15.00	30.00
Promo-only with tour-dates sticker on white cardboard cover						
Epic EAS 2201	DJ	Shades of Indigo: An Interview by Shawn Colvin				
			1990	10.00	20.00	40.00
Epic FE 45044		Indigo Girls	1989	5.00	10.00	20.00
Epic E 46820		Nomads*Indians*Saints	1990	5.00	10.00	20.00
Epic E 57621		Swamp Ophelia	1994	7.50	15.00	30.00
All copies autographed on the label by the Indigo Girls						

45s

Label, Number	Title	Year	VG	VG+	NM
Epic 68912	Closer to Fine/Cold As Ice	1989	2.50	5.00	10.00
Epic 73003	Land of Canaan/Never Stop	1989	2.50	5.00	10.00
Epic 73255	Get Together/Finlandia	1990			*Cassette only*
Epic 73607	Hammer and a Nail/Welcome Me (Live)				
		1990			*Cassette only*
Epic 74326	Galileo/Ghost/Joking/Love Will Come to You/Jonas & Ezekiel				
		1992			*Cassette only*
Epic 74434	Joking/Airplane	1992			*Cassette only*

Injections, The

Semi-legendary central California punk band.

45s

Label, Number	Title	Year	VG	VG+	NM
Radio Active 04	Prison Walls/Lies	1980	50.00	100.00	200.00
Not issued with picture sleeve					

Label, Number		Title	Year	VG	VG+	NM

Inmates, The
British punkish rock band.

Vinyl Albums

| Polydor PD1-6241 | | First Offence | 1979 | 3.00 | 6.00 | 12.00 |
| Polydor PD1-6302 | | Shot in the Dark | 1980 | 3.00 | 6.00 | 12.00 |

45s

Polydor 2032		Dirty Water/I Can't Sleep	1979		2.00	4.00
Polydor 2058		Back in History/The Walk	1980		2.00	4.00
Polydor 2152		(I Thought I Heard a) Heartbeat/Show You My Way				
			1980		2.00	4.00

12-Inch Singles

| Polydor 123 | DJ | The Walk/Dirty Water | 1979 | 2.50 | 5.00 | 10.00 |

Innocent, The
*With Trent Reznor, pre-**Nine Inch Nails**.*

Vinyl Albums

| Red Label 7300 | | Livin' in the Street | 1985 | 6.25 | 12.50 | 25.00 |

Inside Out (California band)
*Later became **Rage Against The Machine**.*

7-Inch Extended Play Singles

Revelation 19		Burning Fight	1988	5.50	11.25	22.50
Blue vinyl						
Revelation 19		Burning Fight	1988		3.75	7.50
Black vinyl						
Revelation 19	PS	Burning Fight	1988		3.75	7.50

Inside Out (New York band)
Punkish metal band. Altered its name to prevent confusion with the California group of the same name, then the California group changed its name entirely!

45s

Noiseville 3		Above All/Beat Life/Cracking Up				
			1989	9.25	18.75	37.50
Blue vinyl						
Noiseville 3		Above All/Beat Life/Cracking Up				
			1989	5.50	11.25	22.50
Red vinyl						
Noiseville 3		Above All/Beat Life/Cracking Up				
			1989	3.00	6.25	12.50
Black vinyl						
Noiseville 3		Above All/Beat Life/Cracking Up				
			1989		2.50	5.00
Reissue as "Inside Out NY"						
Noiseville 3	PS	Above All/Beat Life/Cracking Up				
			1989	3.00	6.25	12.50
Noiseville 3	PS	Above All/Beat Life/Cracking Up				
			1989		2.50	5.00
Reissue as "Inside Out NY"						

Insults, The
Punk band from the music hotbed of Watsonville, California.

7-Inch Extended Play Singles

| Insults 0001 | | Thrasher Go Home | 1982 | 5.00 | 10.00 | 20.00 |
| Insults 0001 | PS | Thrasher Go Home | 1982 | 5.00 | 10.00 | 20.00 |

Label, Number		Title	Year	VG	VG+	NM
45s						
Ric-Mer (# unknown)		Population Zero/Zombie Lover	1979	11.25	22.50	45.00
Ric-Mer (# unknown)	PS	Population Zero/Zombie Lover	1979	11.25	22.50	45.00
Sick Sound (# unknown)		Stiff Love/Tax War/I'm a Doper	1979	15.00	30.00	60.00
Sick Sound (# unknown)	PS	Stiff Love/Tax War/I'm a Doper	1979	15.00	30.00	60.00

INXS

Australian pop-rock band.

Label, Number		Title	Year	VG	VG+	NM
Vinyl Albums						
Atco 90072		Shabooh Shoobah	1983	3.00	6.00	12.00
Atco 90115	EP	Dekadance	1983	3.75	7.50	15.00
Atco 90160		The Swing	1984	3.00	6.00	12.00
Atco 90184		INXS	1984	3.00	6.00	12.00
U.S. issue of 1980 Australian album						
Atco 90185		Underneath the Colours	1984	3.00	6.00	12.00
U.S. issue of 1981 Australian album						
Atlantic 81277		Listen Like Thieves	1985	2.50	5.00	10.00
Atlantic 81796		Kick	1987	2.50	5.00	10.00
Atlantic 82140		X	1990	2.50	5.00	10.00
Atlantic 82294	(2)	Live Baby Live	1991	5.00	10.00	20.00
Columbia House version (only U.S. vinyl pressing)						
Atlantic R 114468		Listen Like Thieves	1985	3.00	6.00	12.00
RCA Music Service edition						
Atlantic R 153606		Kick	1987	3.00	6.00	12.00
BMG Direct Marketing edition						
Atlantic R 164378		X	1990	3.00	6.00	12.00
BMG Direct Marketing edition						
45s						
Atco 99703		Burn for You/Johnson's Aeroplane	1984		2.00	4.00
Atco 99703	PS	Burn for You/Johnson's Aeroplane	1984		2.00	4.00
Atco 99731		I Send a Message/Mechanical	1984		2.00	4.00
Atco 99731	PS	I Send a Message/Mechanical	1984		2.00	4.00
Atco 99766		Original Sin/Stay Young	1984		2.00	4.00
Atco 99766	PS	Original Sin/Stay Young	1984		2.00	4.00
Atco 99833		To Look at You/Sax Thing	1983		2.00	4.00
Atco 99833	PS	To Look at You/Sax Thing	1983		2.00	4.00
Atco 99874		Don't Change/Long in Tooth	1983		2.00	4.00
Atco 99874	PS	Don't Change/Long in Tooth	1983		2.00	4.00
Atco 99905		The One Thing/Phantom of the Opera	1983		2.00	4.00
Atco 99905	PS	The One Thing/Phantom of the Opera	1983		2.00	4.00
Atlantic 84926		New Sensation/Never Tear Us Apart	199?			3.00
"Oldies Series" reissue						
Atlantic 84927		Need You Tonight/Devil Inside	199?			3.00
"Oldies Series" reissue						
Atlantic 84967		What You Need/This Time	198?			3.00
"Oldies Series" reissue						
Atlantic 87784		Disappear/Middle Beast	1990			3.00
Atlantic 87784	PS	Disappear/Middle Beast	1990			3.00
Atlantic 87860		Suicide Blonde/Everybody Wants U Tonight	1990			3.00
Not issued with picture sleeve in U.S.						
Atlantic 89038		Never Tear Us Apart/Different World	1988			3.00
Atlantic 89038	PS	Never Tear Us Apart/Different World	1988			3.00
Atlantic 89080		New Sensation/Guns in the Sky	1988			3.00

Label, Number		Title	Year	VG	VG+	NM
Atlantic 89080	PS	New Sensation/Guns in the Sky	1988			3.00
Atlantic 89144		Devil Inside/On the Rocks	1988			3.00
Atlantic 89144	PS	Devil Inside/On the Rocks	1988			3.00
Atlantic 89188		Need You Tonight/I'm Comin' Home	1987			3.00
Atlantic 89188	PS	Need You Tonight/I'm Comin' Home	1987			3.00
Atlantic 89418		Kiss the Dirt (Falling Off the Mountain)/Six Knots	1986			3.00
Atlantic 89429		Listen Like Thieves/Begotten	1986			3.00
Atlantic 89429	PS	Listen Like Thieves/Begotten	1986			3.00
Atlantic 89460		What You Need/Sweet as Sin	1986			3.00
Atlantic 89460	PS	What You Need/Sweet as Sin	1986			3.00
Atlantic 89497		This Time/I'm Over You	1985			3.00
Atlantic 89497	PS	This Time/I'm Over You	1985			3.00

12-Inch Singles

Label, Number		Title	Year	VG	VG+	NM
Atco PR 481	DJ	The One Thing (Extended)/The One Thing (Edit)	1983	2.00	4.00	8.00
Atco PR 499	DJ	Don't Change (same on both sides)	1982	3.00	6.00	12.00
Atco PR 527	DJ	To Look at You (long & short)	1983	3.75	7.50	15.00
Atco PR 586	DJ	Original Sin (3 versions)	1984	5.00	10.00	20.00
Atco PR 618	DJ	I Send a Message (Remix)/I Send a Message (LP Version)	1984	3.00	6.00	12.00
Atco PR 639	DJ	Burn for You (3 versions)	1984	3.00	6.00	12.00
Atco 96957		Original Sin (2 versions)/Stay Young/Just Keep Walking	1984	3.00	6.00	12.00
Atlantic 788	DJ	This Time (same on both sides)	1985		3.50	7.00
Atlantic PR 824	DJ	What You Need (same on both sides)	1985	2.00	4.00	8.00
Atlantic PR 865	DJ	Listen Like Thieves (same on both sides)	1985	2.00	4.00	8.00
Atlantic 885	DJ	Kiss the Dirt (same on both sides)	1985	3.00	6.00	12.00
Atlantic 910	DJ	What You Need/What You Need (Extended)	1985	3.00	6.00	12.00
Atlantic 936	DJ	Listen Like Thieves (3 versions)	1985	2.00	4.00	8.00
Atlantic 1137	DJ	Devil Inside (Remix)/Devil Inside (Edit)/On the Rocks	1987		3.00	6.00
Atlantic 1172	DJ	New Sensation (3 versions)	1988	2.00	4.00	8.00
Atlantic 1550	DJ	Suicide Blonde (4 mixes)	1990	2.00	4.00	8.00
Atlantic 1616	DJ	Bitter Tears (Lorimer Remix)/(Instrumental)	1990	2.00	4.00	8.00
Atlantic 1933	DJ	Taste It (3 versions)	1992	3.75	7.50	15.00
Atlantic 2078	DJ	Please (You Got That...) (3 dub versions)/Freedom Deep (12" Version)	1993	3.75	7.50	15.00
Atlantic PR 2116	DJ	Need You Tonight (same on both sides)	1987	2.00	4.00	8.00
Atlantic PR 2191	DJ	Devil Inside (LP version)/Devil Inside (edit)	1987	2.00	4.00	8.00
Atlantic 86080		Bitter Tears (Lorimer Remix)/(Instrumental)/The Other Side	1990		3.00	6.00
Atlantic 86563PD *Picture disc*		New Sensation (Nick's 12" Mix)/Guns in the Sky (Kick Ass Mix)	1988	5.00	10.00	20.00
Atlantic 86622		Devil Inside (Remix)/Devil Inside (Edit)/On the Rocks	1987	2.50	5.00	10.00
Atlantic 86645		Need You Tonight-Mediate/I'm Coming (Home)	1987	2.00	4.00	8.00
Atlantic 86818		Listen Like Thieves (Extended)/(Instrumental)/Different World/Begotten	1985	3.00	6.00	12.00
Atlantic 86832		What You Need (2 mixes)/Melting in the Sun/Burn for You	1985	2.50	5.00	10.00

Label, Number		Title	Year	VG	VG+	NM

INXS & Jimmy Barnes

45s

Label, Number		Title	Year	VG	VG+	NM
Atlantic 89237		Good Times/Laying Down the Law				
			1987			3.00
Atlantic 89237	PS	Good Times/Laying Down the Law				
			1987			3.00

12-Inch Singles

Atlantic PR 2050	DJ	Good Times (same on both sides)				
			1986	2.00	4.00	8.00

Iowa Beef Experience
Corn-fed (and beef- fed) Iowa punks. (You thought they were from Hawaii?)

7-Inch Extended Play Singles

Smudged BDA 005		Vulcans Ode to Metal Cough	1987	3.00	6.25	12.50
Smudged BDA 005	PS	Vulcans Ode to Metal Cough	1987	3.00	6.25	12.50

45s

Noiseville 24		Trailer Court/Dope Smoking Red Necks from Cedar Rapids				
			198?	2.00	4.00	8.00
400 on red vinyl with piece of beef jerky						
Noiseville 24		Trailer Court/Dope Smoking Red Necks from Cedar Rapids				
			198?			3.00
Black vinyl, no jerky						
Noiseville 24	PS	Trailer Court/Dope Smoking Red Necks from Cedar Rapids				
			198?		3.50	7.00
Red and white sleeves (first 800)						
Noiseville 24	PS	Trailer Court/Dope Smoking Red Necks from Cedar Rapids				
			198?			3.00
Black and white sleeves						
Rave 029		New South Old Lies/Octopus	1992	6.25	12.50	25.00
Rave 029	PS	New South Old Lies/Octopus	1992	6.25	12.50	25.00
Sympathy For The Record Industry 139		Jubilix/Nitro Burning Funny Cow	199?		2.00	4.00
Sympathy For The Record Industry 139	PS	Jubilix/Nitro Burning Funny Cow	199?		2.00	4.00

Iron Cross
Washington, D.C. hardcore band.

7-Inch Extended Play Singles

Skinflint 2		Hated and Proud	1983	5.00	10.00	20.00
Skinflint 2	PS	Hated and Proud	1983	5.00	10.00	20.00
Skinflint/Dischord 1 (8 1/2)		Skinhead Glory	1982	15.00	30.00	60.00
Green vinyl						
Skinflint/Dischord 1 (8 1/2)		Skinhead Glory	1982	5.00	10.00	20.00
Black vinyl						
Skinflint/Dischord 1 (8 1/2)	PS	Skinhead Glory	1982	5.00	10.00	20.00

Isaak, Chris
California-based neo-rockabilly artist with a touch of Roy Orbison thrown in.

Vinyl Albums

Reprise 25837		Heart Shaped World	1989	3.00	6.00	12.00
Warner Bros. 25256		Silvertone	1985	3.00	6.00	12.00
Warner Bros. 25336		Chris Isaak	1987	3.00	6.00	12.00

45s

Reprise 17781		Go Walking Down There/Things Go Wrong				
			1995			3.00

Label, Number		Title	Year	VG	VG+	NM
Reprise 17872		Somebody's Crying/Changed Your Mind				
			1995			3.00
Reprise 18263		Dark Moon/Except the New Girl	1993			3.00
Reprise 18462		Solitary Man/5:15	1993			3.00
Reprise 18604		Can't Do a Thing (To Stop Me)/Lonely with a Broken Heart				
			1993			3.00
Reprise 19704		Wicked Game/(instrumental)	1990		2.50	5.00
Warner Bros. 28907		Gone Ridin' (Theme from American Flyers)/Tears				
			1985		2.00	4.00
Warner Bros. 28971		Livin' for Your Lovin'/Talk to Me				
			1985		2.00	4.00
Warner Bros. 29073		Dancin'/Unhappiness	1985		2.00	4.00
12-Inch Singles						
Warner Bros. PRO-A-2265	DJ	Dancin'/Gone Ridin'	1985	2.00	4.00	8.00
Warner Bros. PRO-A-2332	DJ	Livin' for Your Lover (same on both sides)				
			1985	2.00	4.00	8.00
Warner Bros. PRO-A-2359	DJ	Gone Ridin' (same on both sides)	1985	2.00	4.00	8.00
Warner Bros. PRO-A-2682	DJ	You Owe Me Some Kind of Love (same on both sides)				
			1987	2.00	4.00	8.00
Warner Bros. PRO-A-2736	DJ	Heart Full of Soul (same on both sides)				
			1987	2.00	4.00	8.00

Ism

Punk band from Long Island.

45s						
S.I.N. 003		I Think I Love You/A7	1983	5.00	10.00	20.00
S.I.N. 003	PS	I Think I Love You/A7	1983	5.00	10.00	20.00
With mail-order insert						
S.I.N. 716		Attack/Queen Jap	1980	3.00	6.25	12.50
B-side is "King Tut" with new lyrics						
S.I.N. 716	PS	Attack/Queen Jap	1980	3.00	6.25	12.50

J

Jackson, Joe

Eclectic British singer. Began as a new-waver, but has dabbled in most other kinds of music as well.

Vinyl Albums						
A&M SP-3187		Look Sharp!	198?	2.00	4.00	8.00
Reissue of SP-4743						
A&M SP-3221		I'm the Man	198?	2.00	4.00	8.00
Reissue of SP-4794						
A&M SP-3241		Beat Crazy	198?	2.00	4.00	8.00
Reissue of SP-4837						
A&M SP-3271		Joe Jackson's Jumpin' Jive	198?	2.00	4.00	8.00
Reissue of SP-4871						
A&M SP-3286		Body and Soul	1986	2.00	4.00	8.00
Reissue of SP-5000						
A&M SP-3666	(2)	Look Sharp!	1979	4.50	9.00	18.00
Two 10-inch records in gatefold sleeve with button						
A&M SP-3908		Will Power	1987	3.00	6.00	12.00
A&M SP-4743		Look Sharp!	1979	3.00	6.00	12.00
A&M SP-4794		I'm the Man	1979	2.50	5.00	10.00
A&M SP-4837		Beat Crazy	1980	2.50	5.00	10.00
A&M SP-4871		Joe Jackson's Jumpin' Jive	1981	2.50	5.00	10.00
A&M SP-4906		Night and Day	1982	2.50	5.00	10.00
A&M SP-4931		Mike's Murder [Soundtrack]	1983	3.00	6.00	12.00
A&M SP-5000		Body and Soul	1984	2.50	5.00	10.00
A&M SP-5249		Blaze of Glory	1989	2.50	5.00	10.00

Label, Number		Title	Year	VG	VG+	NM
A&M SP-6021	(2)	Big World	1986	3.75	7.50	15.00
A&M SP-6706	(2)	Live: 1980-1986	1988	3.75	7.50	15.00
A&M R 101141		Blaze of Glory	1989	3.00	6.00	12.00
BMG Direct Marketing edition						
A&M R 209597	(2)	Live 1980-1986	1987	4.50	9.00	18.00
BMG Direct Marketing edition						
A&M R 244331	(2)	Big World	1986	4.50	9.00	18.00
RCA Music Service edition						
Mobile Fidelity 1-080		Night and Day	1982	7.50	15.00	30.00
Original Master Recording						

45s

Label, Number		Title	Year	VG	VG+	NM
A&M 1207		Memphis (Live)/Look Sharp (Live)				
			1988			3.00
A&M 1228		(He's a) Shape in a Drape/Speedway				
			1988			3.00
A&M 1404		19 Forever/Acropolis Now	1989		2.00	4.00
A&M 2132		Is She Really Going Out with Him?/(Do the) Instant Mash				
			1979		2.00	4.00
A&M 2132	PS	Is She Really Going Out with Him?/(Do the) Instant Mash				
			1979		2.50	5.00
A&M 2186		It's Different for Girls/Come On	1979		2.00	4.00
A&M 2186	PS	It's Different for Girls/Come On	1979		2.00	4.00
A&M 2209		I'm the Man/Come On	1979		2.00	4.00
A&M 2276		One to One/Enough Is Not Enough				
			1980		2.00	4.00
A&M 2365		Jumpin' Jive/Knock Me a Kiss	1981		2.00	4.00
A&M 2428		Steppin' Out/Chinatown	1982			3.00
A&M 2428	PS	Steppin' Out/Chinatown	1982			3.00
A&M 2510		Breaking Us in Two/Target	1982			3.00
A&M 2510	PS	Breaking Us in Two/Target	1982			3.00
A&M 2548		Another World/Otro Mundo	1983			3.00
A&M 2601		Memphis/Breakdown	1983			3.00
A&M 2601	PS	Memphis/Breakdown	1983			3.00
A&M 2628		You Can't Get What You Want (Till You Know What You Want)/				
		Cha Cha Loco	1984			3.00
A&M 2628	PS	You Can't Get What You Want (Till You Know What You Want)/				
		Cha Cha Loco	1984			3.00
A&M 2635		Happy Landing/Loisaida	1984			3.00
A&M 2635	PS	Happy Landing/Loisaida	1984			3.00
A&M 2673		Be My No. 2/Heart of Ice	1984			3.00
A&M 2829		Right and Wrong/Breaking Us in Two				
			1986			3.00
A&M 2829	PS	Right and Wrong/Breaking Us in Two				
			1986			3.00
A&M 2847		Home Town/I'm the Man (Live)	1986			3.00
A&M 2944		Nocturne/Will Power	1987			3.00
A&M SP-18000	(5)	I'm the Man	1979	5.00	10.00	20.00

Boxed set of five 7" singles with small holes and picture sleeves, comprising the album of the same name

12-Inch Singles

Label, Number		Title	Year	VG	VG+	NM
A&M 17201	DJ	Steppin' Out (LP version)/Steppin' Out (edit)				
			1982	2.00	4.00	8.00
A&M 17374	DJ	Right and Wrong (4:35)/Right and Wrong (4:11)				
			1986		3.00	6.00
A&M 17375	DJ	Wild West/Right and Wrong/Home Town/Tonight				
			1986		3.00	6.00
A&M 17395	DJ	Home Town (same on both sides)	1986		3.00	6.00

Label, Number		Title	Year	VG	VG+	NM

Jam, The

*British punk/new wave band. Leader Paul Weller later formed **The Style Council**.*

Vinyl Albums

Label, Number		Title	Year	VG	VG+	NM
Polydor PX1-503	EP	The Jam	1982	3.00	6.00	12.00
Polydor PX1-506	EP	The Bitterest Pill	1982	3.00	6.00	12.00
Polydor PD1-6110		In the City	1977	6.25	12.50	25.00
Polydor PD1-6129		This Is the Modern World	1978	5.00	10.00	20.00
Polydor PD1-6188		All Mod Cons	1979	3.75	7.50	15.00
Polydor PD1-6249		Setting Sons	1980	3.75	7.50	15.00
Polydor PD1-6315		Sound Affects	1981	3.75	7.50	15.00
Polydor PD1-6349		The Gift	1982	3.00	6.00	12.00
Polydor PD1-6365		Dig the New Breed	1982	2.50	5.00	10.00
Polydor 810 751-1	EP	Beat Surrender	1982	2.50	5.00	10.00
Polydor 815 537-1	(2)	Snap!	1983	3.75	7.50	15.00
Polydor 817 124-1		In the City	198?	2.50	5.00	10.00
Reissue						
Polydor 823 281-1		This Is the Modern World	198?	2.50	5.00	10.00
Reissue						

45s

Label, Number		Title	Year	VG	VG+	NM
Polydor 14442		In the City/Takin' My Love	1977	2.50	5.00	10.00
Polydor 14462		I Need You (For Someone)/In the City	1978	2.00	4.00	8.00
Polydor 14553		The Butterfly Collector/Strange Town	1979	2.50	5.00	10.00
Yellow vinyl stock copy						
Polydor 14553	DJ	The Butterfly Collector (same on both sides)	1979	2.00	4.00	8.00
Yellow vinyl promo						
Polydor 14566		Down in the Tube Station at Midnight/Mr. Clean	1979		3.00	6.00
Polydor 2051		Eton Rifles/Smithers-Jones	1980		3.00	6.00
Polydor 2074		(Love Is Like a) Heat Wave/Saturday's Kids	1980		3.00	6.00
Polydor 2155		Start/When You're Young	1980		3.00	6.00
Polydor 2155	PS	Start/When You're Young	1980	2.00	4.00	8.00
Polydor 2206		Town Called Malice/Precious	1982		3.00	6.00
Polydor PRO 145	DJ	Going Underground/Dreams of Children	1980	2.00	4.00	8.00

12-Inch Singles

Label, Number		Title	Year	VG	VG+	NM
Polydor 180	DJ	Town Called Malice (same on both sides)	1982	2.50	5.00	10.00

James

British alterna-pop group, best known in the States for their song "Laid" (not on vinyl here).

Vinyl Albums

Label, Number		Title	Year	VG	VG+	NM
Sire 25437		Stutter	1986	2.50	5.00	10.00

12-Inch Singles

Label, Number		Title	Year	VG	VG+	NM
Sire PRO-A-3127	DJ	What For?/James Who? (interview)	1988	2.50	5.00	10.00

Jane's Addiction

*Los Angeles punk band. After it broke up, two members created **Porno for Pyros** and another joined **Red Hot Chili Peppers**.*

Vinyl Albums

Label, Number		Title	Year	VG	VG+	NM
Triple X 51004		Jane's Addiction	1987	3.75	7.50	15.00

Label, Number		Title	Year	VG	VG+	NM
Warner Bros. PRO-A-3369	DJ	Words and Music	1988	10.00	20.00	40.00
Promo-only interview album						
Warner Bros. 25727		Nothing's Shocking	1988	3.00	6.00	12.00
Warner Bros. 25993		Ritual de lo Habitual	1990	3.00	6.00	12.00
First cover, with drawing						
Warner Bros. 26223		Ritual de lo Habitual	1990	2.50	5.00	10.00
Second cover, all white with text of First Amendment						

45s

Label, Number		Title	Year	VG	VG+	NM
Warner Bros. 19574		Been Caught Stealing/Had a Dad	1991		*Cassette only*	
Warner Bros. 27520		Mountain Song/Standing in the Shower...Thinking				
			1989	2.50	5.00	10.00
Warner Bros. 27520	PS	Mountain Song/Standing in the Shower...Thinking				
			1989	2.50	5.00	10.00

12-Inch Singles

Label, Number		Title	Year	VG	VG+	NM
Warner Bros. 21559		Stop/I Would For You (Demo)/Three Days				
			1990	2.50	5.00	10.00
Warner Bros. 21736		Been Caught Stealing (2 versions)/Had a Dad (Demo)				
			1990		3.00	6.00

Japan

*London new-wave band led by **David Sylvian**.*

Vinyl Albums

Label, Number		Title	Year	VG	VG+	NM
Ariola America SW-50037		Adolescent Sex	1978	5.00	10.00	20.00
Ariola America SW-50047	EP	Obscure Alternatives	1979	3.75	7.50	15.00
Virgin/Epic ARE 37914		Japan	1982	2.50	5.00	10.00

45s

Label, Number		Title	Year	VG	VG+	NM
Ariola America 7727		Sometimes I Feel So Low/Love Is Infectious				
			1979	2.00	4.00	8.00
Ariola America 7756		Life in Tokyo/Love Is Infectious	1979	2.00	4.00	8.00

12-Inch Singles

Label, Number		Title	Year	VG	VG+	NM
Ariola America PRO 7727	DJ	Sometimes I Feel So Low (same on both sides)				
			1978	5.00	10.00	20.00
Ariola America PRO 7756	DJ	Life in Japan (Long)/Life in Japan (Short)				
			1979	2.50	5.00	10.00
Virgin/Epic 02756		Canton/Visions of China	1981	2.00	4.00	8.00

Jayhawks, The

*Roots-rock band from Minneapolis. Broke up about the time they were finally starting to get national atten-
tion.*

Vinyl Albums

Label, Number	Title	Year	VG	VG+	NM
American 43006	Tomorrow the Green Grass	1995	2.50	5.00	10.00

Jazzy Jeff and Fresh Prince

*Rap duo. Records appeared under the above name, "DJ Jazzy Jeff and the Fresh Prince," and "DJ Jazzy
Jeff."*

Vinyl Albums

Label, Number		Title	Year	VG	VG+	NM
Jive 1026-1-J		Rock the House	1986	2.50	5.00	10.00
Reissued in 1989 with same catalog number and one new track						
Jive 1091-1-J	(2)	He's the D.J., I'm the Rapper	1988	3.00	6.00	12.00
Without "Nightmare on My Street" disclaimer on cover						
Jive 1091-1-J RE	(2)	He's the D.J., I'm the Rapper	1988	4.00	8.00	16.00
With "Nightmare on My Street" disclaimer on cover (much scarcer than original)						
Jive 1188-1-J		And in This Corner...	1989	2.50	5.00	10.00
Jive 1392-1-J		Homebase	1991	3.00	6.00	12.00
Jive JL6-8399		On Fire	1985	3.00	6.00	12.00

Label, Number		Title	Year	VG	VG+	NM
Jive 41489-1		Code Red	1993	3.00	6.00	12.00
LP in generic black cover with center hole and sticker						
Word Up WDLP-0001		Rock the House	1985	6.25	12.50	25.00
45s						
Jive 1029-7		The Magnificent Jazzy Jeff/(Instrumental)				
			1987		2.00	4.00
Jive 1042-7		A Touch of Jazz/(Instrumental)	1987		2.00	4.00
Jive 1099-7		Parents Just Don't Understand/(Instrumental)				
			1988			3.00
Jive 1099-7	PS	Parents Just Don't Understand/(Instrumental)				
			1988			3.00
Jive 1124-7		A Nightmare on My Street/(Instrumental)				
			1988			3.00
Jive 1124-7	PS	A Nightmare on My Street/(Instrumental)				
			1988			3.00
Jive 1147-7		Girls Ain't Nothin' But Trouble/Brand New Funk				
			1988			3.00
Jive 1147-7	PS	Girls Ain't Nothin' But Trouble/Brand New Funk				
			1988			3.00
Jive 1282-7		I Think I Can Beat Mike Tyson/(Instrumental)				
			1989			3.00
Jive 1282-7	PS	I Think I Can Beat Mike Tyson/(Instrumental)				
			1989			3.00
Jive 1465-4		Summertime (LP Version)/Summertime (D.J. Jazzy Jeff's Mix)				
			1991			*Cassette only*
Jive 9329		King Heroin (Don't Mess with Heroin)/(instrumental)				
			1985		2.00	4.00
Label credit: "DJ Jazzy Jeff"						
Jive 9377		Mix So I Can Go Crazy	1985		2.00	4.00
Label credit: "DJ Jazzy Jeff"						
Jive 9428		Fire/We Just Want to Have Fun	1985		2.00	4.00
Label credit: "DJ Jazzy Jeff"						
12-Inch Singles						
Jive 1030		The Magnificent Jazzy Jeff/(Instrumental)/Megadope Mix				
			1987	2.50	5.00	10.00
Jive 1040		A Touch of Jazz (3 mixes)	1987	2.50	5.00	10.00
Jive 1092-1		Parents Just Don't Understand (4 mixes)				
			1988	2.00	4.00	8.00
Jive 1125-1		A Nightmare on My Street (4 mixes)				
			1988	2.00	4.00	8.00
Jive 1146-1		Girls Ain't Nothin' But Trouble (3 mixes)/				
		Brand New Funk (4 mixes)	1988		3.00	6.00
Jive 1313-1		The Groove (6 mixes)	1989		3.00	6.00
Jive 1442-1		Summertime (6 mixes)	1991		3.00	6.00
Jive 9330		King Heroin (Don't Mess with Heroin) (3 mixes)				
			1985		3.00	6.00
Label credit: "DJ Jazzy Jeff"						
Jive 9378		Mix So I Can Go Crazy (2 versions)/Rock It (2 versions)				
			1985	2.00	4.00	8.00
Label credit: "DJ Jazzy Jeff"						
Jive 9427		Fire (2 mixes)/We Just Want to Have Fun				
		(Gangster Boogie Dub Mix)	1985	2.00	4.00	8.00
Label credit: "DJ Jazzy Jeff"						
Jive 42050		You Saw My Blinker/You Saw My Blinker (Edit)				
			1992		3.50	7.00
Jive 42182		I'm Looking for the One (5 versions)				
			1993	2.00	4.00	8.00
Jive 42202		I Wanna Rock (7 versions)	1994		3.50	7.00
Pow Wow 430		Real Hip Hop My Man (4 versions)				
			1988	2.00	4.00	8.00
Label credit: "Jazzy Jeff"						

Label, Number		Title	Year	VG	VG+	NM
Word Up WD-001		Girls Ain't Nothing But Trouble (4 versions)				
			1985	3.00	6.00	12.00
Word Up WD-002		Guys Ain't Nothing But Trouble (same on both sides)				
			1985	3.75	7.50	15.00
Word Up WD-003		Just One of Those Days (same on both sides)				
			1985	3.75	7.50	15.00

Jeffreys, Garland

New York singer-songwriter who's done rock, R&B and reggae. You try to classify him.

Vinyl Albums

Label, Number		Title	Year	VG	VG+	NM
A&M SP-4629		Ghost Writer	1977	3.00	6.00	12.00
A&M SP-4778		American Boy and Girl	1979	2.50	5.00	10.00
Epic PE 36983		Escape Artist	1981	2.50	5.00	10.00
Epic FE 37436		Rock 'N' Roll Adult	1981	2.50	5.00	10.00
Epic ARE 38190		Guts for Love	1983	2.50	5.00	10.00

7-Inch Extended Play Singles

Label, Number		Title	Year	VG	VG+	NM
Epic AE7 1223	DJ	Escapades	1981	2.00	4.00	8.00
Epic AE7 1223	PS	Escapades	1981	2.00	4.00	8.00

45s

Label, Number		Title	Year	VG	VG+	NM
A&M 1934		Wild in the Streets/Ghost Writer				
			1977		2.00	4.00
A&M 1952		New York Skyline/Cool Down Boy				
			1977		2.00	4.00
A&M 2030		One-Eyed Jack/Reelin'	1978		2.00	4.00
A&M 2074		She Didn't Lie/Scream in the Night				
			1979		2.00	4.00
A&M 2178		American Boy and Girl/Livin' for Me				
			1979		2.00	4.00
A&M 2244		American Boy and Girl/Matador	1980		2.00	4.00
Arista 0119		The Disco Kid Part 1/The Disco Kid Part 2				
			1975		2.50	5.00
Atlantic 2948		She Didn't Lie/Lon Chaney	1973		2.50	5.00
Atlantic 2981		Wild in the Streets/Lon Chaney	1973		2.50	5.00
Epic AE7 1225	DJ	Interview with Garland Jeffreys	1981	2.00	4.00	8.00
Epic AE7 1225	PS	Interview with Garland Jeffreys	1981	2.00	4.00	8.00
Epic 02073		Modern Lovers/Spanish Manners	1981			3.00
Epic 02173		R.O.C.K./Miami Beach	1981			3.00
Epic 03189		Surrender/Rebel Love	1982			3.00
Epic 03687		Rebel Love/What Does It Take (To Win Your Love)				
			1983			3.00
Epic 51008		96 Tears/Escape Goat Dab	1981			3.00

12-Inch Singles

Label, Number		Title	Year	VG	VG+	NM
Epic AS 962	DJ	Modern Lovers/R.O.C.K./Ghost of a Chance				
			1981	2.50	5.00	10.00
RCA 62175		Hail Hail Rock 'N' Roll (5 versions)				
			1992	2.00	4.00	8.00
RCA 62295		The Answer (6 versions)	1992	2.50	5.00	10.00

Jesus and Mary Chain, The

Glasgow, Scotland-based new wave/pop band.

Vinyl Albums

Label, Number	Title	Year	VG	VG+	NM
Reprise 25383	Psychocandy	1985	2.50	5.00	10.00
Warner Bros. 25656	Darklands	1987	2.50	5.00	10.00
Warner Bros. 25729	Barbed Wire Kisses	1988	2.50	5.00	10.00
Warner Bros. 26015	Automatic	1989	2.50	5.00	10.00

Several A&M Records albums were released in formats other than the standard 12-inch LP. Joe Jackson's second album, *I'm the Man*, saw release here in a boxed set of five 7-inch records with individual picture sleeves and an enclosed poster ($20).

After every major label, and a lot of minor ones, turned her down, Joan Jett created her own label, Blackheart, to release her debut. This original LP can be found for as little as $20 or as much as $100 depending on the source.

Label, Number		Title	Year	VG	VG+	NM
45s						
Rough Trade RTUS 006		Upside Down/Vegetable Man	1984	2.00	4.00	8.00
Rough Trade RTUS 006	PS	Upside Down/Vegetable Man	1984	2.00	4.00	8.00
Warner Bros. 19891		Head On/Penetration	1990		2.00	4.00
Warner Bros. 27754		Surfin' USA (Summer Mix)/Kill Surf City				
			1988		2.00	4.00
Warner Bros. 27754	PS	Surfin' USA (Summer Mix)/Kill Surf City				
			1988		2.00	4.00
12-Inch Singles						
Def American PRO-A-5340	DJ	Reverence (4 versions)	1992	3.75	7.50	15.00
Reprise 20714		April Skies (Long Version)/Kill Surf City				
			1987	2.00	4.00	8.00
Warner Bros. 20931		Sidewalking (2 versions)/Taste of Candy (Live)/April Skies (Live)				
			1988	3.75	7.50	15.00
Warner Bros. PRO-A-2857	DJ	Happy When It Rains (same on both sides)				
			1987	2.00	4.00	8.00
Warner Bros. PRO-A-2857	DJ	Happy When It Rains (same on both sides)				
			1987	2.00	4.00	8.00
Warner Bros. PRO-A-3750	DJ	Blues from a Gun (same on both sides)				
			1989	3.00	6.00	12.00

Jesus Jones

British pop-rock group. Its two biggest hit singles, "Right Here, Right Now" and "Real Real Real," remain unavailable on U.S. 45s.

Vinyl Albums						
SBK 05348	DJ	A Conversation with Jesus	1990	5.00	10.00	20.00
Generic cover with sticker						
45s						
EMI S7-56970		The Devil You Know/Zeroes and Ones				
			1993		2.00	4.00
12-Inch Singles						
SBK 19742		Real Real Real (3 mixes)	1991	2.00	4.00	8.00

Jett, Joan, and the Blackhearts

*Born in Philadelphia, raised in Baltimore, settled on Long Island. Originally with **The Runaways**; also produced **The Germs** before becoming a leather-clad rocker and godmother of the "riot grrrl" movement. Some of the below records only list Joan Jett's name on the label.*

Vinyl Albums					
Blackheart JJ 707	Joan Jett	1980	10.00	20.00	40.00
Value is an average; an unusually wide range of values was reported					
Blackheart BFZ 40544	Good Music	1986	3.00	6.00	12.00
Blackheart FZ 44146	Up Your Alley	1988	2.50	5.00	10.00
Blackheart Z 45473	The Hit List	1990	3.00	6.00	12.00
Blackheart Z 47488	Notorious	1991	3.00	6.00	12.00
Boardwalk NB1-33251	Bad Reputation	1982	2.50	5.00	10.00
Reissue of FW 37065					
Boardwalk NB1-33243	I Love Rock-n-Roll	1982	2.50	5.00	10.00
First pressing, with "Little Drummer Boy"					
Boardwalk NB1-33243	I Love Rock-n-Roll	1982	3.00	6.00	12.00
Second pressing, with "Oh Woe Is Me"					
Boardwalk FW 37065	Bad Reputation	1981	3.00	6.00	12.00
Essentially a reissue of Blackheart JJ 707					
MCA 5437	Album	1983	3.00	6.00	12.00
MCA 5476	Glorious Results of a Misspent Youth				
		1984	3.00	6.00	12.00

Label, Number		Title	Year	VG	VG+	NM
MCA R 163731		Glorious Results of a Misspent Youth				
			1984	4.00	8.00	16.00
RCA Music Service edition						
Reprise 45567		Pure and Simple	1994	3.00	6.00	12.00
45s						
Blackheart 06336		Good Music/Fantasy	1986			3.00
Blackheart 06336	PS	Good Music/Fantasy	1986			3.00
Blackheart 06692		Light of Day/Roadrunner (Radio On)				
			1987			3.00
As "The Barbusters"						
Blackheart 06692	PS	Light of Day/Roadrunner (Radio On)				
			1987			3.00
As "The Barbusters"						
Blackheart 07919		I Hate Myself for Loving You/Love Is Pain (Live)				
			1988			3.00
Blackheart 07919	PS	I Hate Myself for Loving You/Love Is Pain (Live)				
			1988			3.00
Blackheart 08095		Little Liar/What Can I Do for You				
			1988			3.00
Blackheart 08095	PS	Little Liar/What Can I Do for You				
			1988			3.00
Blackheart 73215		Dirty Deeds/Let It Bleed	1990	2.00	4.00	8.00
Blackheart 73314		Love Hurts/Handiman	1990		*Cassette only*	
Blackheart F-15		Spinster//Go Home/Hostility	1994		2.50	5.00
Blue vinyl, small center hole						
Blackheart F-15	PS	Spinster//Go Home/Hostility	1994			3.00
Both this and FR-15 (below) have the same picture sleeve						
Blackheart FR-15		Spinster//Go Home/Hostility	1994			3.00
Blue vinyl, large center hole						
Boardwalk 5706		You Don't Own Me/Jezebel	1981	2.00	4.00	8.00
Boardwalk NBS-7-086	DJ	Little Drummer Boy (same on both sides)				
			1981	3.75	7.50	15.00
Boardwalk NB7-11-135		I Love Rock 'N Roll/You Don't Know What You've Got				
			1982			3.00
Boardwalk NB7-11-135	PS	I Love Rock 'N Roll/You Don't Know What You've Got				
			1982	2.50	5.00	10.00
A fairly scarce picture sleeve						
Boardwalk NB7-11-144		Crimson and Clover/Oh Woe Is Me				
			1982			3.00
Boardwalk NB7-11-144	PS	Crimson and Clover/Oh Woe Is Me				
			1982			3.00
Boardwalk NB 11-150-7		Do You Wanna Touch Me (Oh Yeah)/Victim of Circumstance				
			1982			3.00
Boardwalk NB 11-150-7	PS	Do You Wanna Touch Me (Oh Yeah)/Victim of Circumstance				
			1982			3.00
Def Jam 07630		She's Lost You/Hazy Shade of Winter				
			1987			3.00
*B-side by **Bangles***						
Def Jam 07630	PS	She's Lost You/Hazy Shade of Winter				
			1987			3.00
*B-side by **Bangles***						
Epic Associated 74067		Don't Surrender/Don't Surrender (The Most Excellent Mix)				
			1991		*Cassette only*	
MCA 52240		Fake Friends/Nite Time	1983			3.00
"Nite Time" has a locked groove. In other words, if left on an automatic turntable, it'll just keep playing...						
MCA 52240	PS	Fake Friends/Nite Time	1983			3.00
MCA 52254		Fake Friends/Handy Man	1983		2.00	4.00
Evidently a jukebox single with a different flip side so the needle wouldn't get stuck!						
MCA 52272		Everyday People/Why Can't We Be Happy				
			1983			3.00
MCA 52272	PS	Everyday People/Why Can't We Be Happy				
			1983			3.00

Label, Number		Title	Year	VG	VG+	NM
MCA 52472		I Love You Love/Talkin' 'Bout My Bab				
			1984			3.00
MCA 52472	PS	I Love You Love/Talkin' 'Bout My Baby				
			1984			3.00
Reprise 18245		I Love Rock 'N Roll/Activity Grrrl				
			1994			3.00
Warner Bros. 17637		Love Is All Around/Rubber & Glue				
			1996			3.00

12-Inch Singles

Label, Number		Title	Year	VG	VG+	NM
Blackheart BH 007	DJ	Light of Day/Roadrunner	1987	5.00	10.00	20.00
Blackheart ZAS 1094	DJ	I Hate Myself for Loving You (same on both sides)				
			1988	3.00	6.00	12.00
Blackheart ZAS 2517	DJ	Good Music (3:29)/Good Music (5:45)				
			1985	3.00	6.00	12.00
Blackheart ZAS 2559	DJ	Roadrunner/You Got Me Floatin'/This Means War				
			1986	5.00	10.00	20.00
Blackheart ZAS 4256	DJ	Don't Surrender (6:42)/Don't Surrender (4:04)				
			1991	3.00	6.00	12.00
Boardwalk 005	DJ	Little Drummer Boy/Victim of Circumstance				
			1981	5.00	10.00	20.00
Boardwalk 012	DJ	Crimson and Clover (AOR Remix) (same on both sides)				
			1982	3.75	7.50	15.00
Boardwalk 019	DJ	Do You Wanna Touch Me (Oh Yeah)/Summertime Blues				
			1982	3.75	7.50	15.00
MCA L33-1117	DJ	Fake Friends (same on both sides)				
			1983	2.50	5.00	10.00
MCA L33-1121	DJ	Everyday People (Short)/Everyday People (Long)				
			1983	2.00	4.00	8.00
MCA L33-1247	DJ	I Love You Love/New Orleans/Little Drummer Boy				
			1984	3.75	7.50	15.00
MCA 13973		Everyday People/Star Star	1983	5.00	10.00	20.00

Jimmie Dale and the Flatlanders

Jimmie Dale Gilmore and Joe Ely were members of this seminal country-rock/roots band.

Vinyl Albums

Label, Number	Title	Year	VG	VG+	NM
Plantation 22	One Road More	1972			
May exist only as an 8-track tape. Should an LP exist, its value would be in the hundreds.					
Rounder SS-34	More a Legend Than a Band	1990	3.00	6.00	12.00
As "The Flatlanders"; reissue of Plantation material					

45s

Label, Number	Title	Year	VG	VG+	NM
Plantation 92	Dallas/Tonight I'm Gonna Go Downtown				
		1972	12.50	25.00	50.00
Plantation 106	Jole Blon/You've Never Seen Me Cry				
		1972		*Not known to exist*	

Jo Jo Zep and the Falcons

Vinyl Albums

Label, Number	Title	Year	VG	VG+	NM
A&M SP-4968	Cha	1983	2.00	4.00	8.00
Columbia JC 36642	Screaming Targets	1980	3.00	6.00	12.00
Columbia NFC 37047	Step Lively	1981	2.50	5.00	10.00

45s

Label, Number	Title	Year	VG	VG+	NM
A&M 2578	The Losing Game/Competition	1983	2.00	4.00	8.00
Columbia 02341	But It's Alright/I Will Return	1981		2.00	4.00
Columbia 02645	Gimme Little Sign/I Will Return	1981		2.00	4.00
Columbia 11319	Hit and Run/Nosey Parker/Thin Line				
		1980		2.00	4.00

Label, Number		Title	Year	VG	VG+	NM
12-Inch Singles						
A&M 17249	DJ	The Losing Game (3 versions)	1983	2.00	4.00	8.00
Columbia AS 820	DJ	Hit and Run/The Shape I'm In	1979	3.00	6.00	12.00

Johansen, David

*Former member of **The New York Dolls**. Later became pseudo-lounge lizard **Buster Poindexter**.*

Label, Number		Title	Year	VG	VG+	NM
Vinyl Albums						
Blue Sky AS 519	DJ	The David Johansen Group Live				
			1978	7.50	15.00	30.00
Blue Sky AS 1281	DJ	Live and Sampler	1981	3.00	6.00	12.00
Promo-only four-song sampler						
Blue Sky JZ 34926		David Johansen	1978	2.50	5.00	10.00
Blue Sky JZ 36082		In Style	1979	2.50	5.00	10.00
Blue Sky FZ 36589		Here Comes the Night	1981	2.50	5.00	10.00
Blue Sky ARZ 38004		Live It Up	1982	2.50	5.00	10.00
Passport PB-6043		Sweet Revenge	1984	2.50	5.00	10.00
45s						
Blue Sky 02584		She Loves Strangers/Here Comes the Night				
			1981			3.00
Blue Sky 2771		Funky But Chic/The Rope	1978		2.00	4.00
Blue Sky 2781		Melody/Reckless Crazy	1979		2.00	4.00
Blue Sky 2789		Swaheto Woman/She Knew She Was Falling in Love				
			1980		2.00	4.00
Blue Sky 03003		Medley: We Gotta Get Out of This Place-Don't Bring Me Down/				
		Bohemian Love Dad	1982			3.00
Blue Sky 03382		Melody/Here Comes the Night	1982			3.00
Reissue						
12-Inch Singles						
Blue Sky AS 740	DJ	Swaheto Woman (Long)/Swaheto Woman (Short)				
			1979	3.75	7.50	15.00
Blue Sky AS 972	DJ	Here Comes the Night/You Fool You/ + 2				
			1981		3.00	6.00
Passport 4112		King of Babylon (Extended)/Stinkin' Rich + 1				
			1985	2.00	4.00	8.00

Johnson, Holly

*Formerly of **Frankie Goes to Hollywood**.*

Label, Number		Title	Year	VG	VG+	NM
Vinyl Albums						
Uni 603		Blast	1988	2.50	5.00	10.00
12-Inch Singles						
Uni 8017		Love Train (2 versions)/Murder in Paradise				
			1988		2.50	5.00

Jones, Howard

British synth-pop star.

Label, Number		Title	Year	VG	VG+	NM
Vinyl Albums						
Elektra 60346		Human's Lib	1984	3.00	6.00	12.00
Elektra 60390		Dream Into Action	1985	3.00	6.00	12.00
Elektra 60466	EP	Action Replay	1986	2.50	5.00	10.00
Elektra 60499		One to One	1986	3.00	6.00	12.00
Elektra 60794		Cross That Line	1989	2.50	5.00	10.00
Elektra 60794	DJ	Cross That Line	1989	2.50	5.00	10.00
Promo-only white label audiophile vinyl						
Elektra R 133246	EP	Action Replay	1986	3.00	6.00	12.00
RCA Music Service edition						

Label, Number		Title	Year	VG	VG+	NM
Elektra R 134013		One to One	1986	3.00	6.00	12.00
RCA Music Service edition						
Elektra R 143992		Dream into Action	1985	3.00	6.00	12.00
RCA Music Service edition						
45s						
Elektra 65948		Everlasting Love/The Prisoner	1992			3.00
"Spun Gold" reissue						
Elektra 65968		You Know I Love You...Don't You?/All I Want				
			198?			3.00
"Spun Gold" reissue						
Elektra 65976		Things Can Only Get Better/Like to Get to Know You Well				
			198?			3.00
"Spun Gold" reissue						
Elektra 65977		New Song/What Is Love	198?			3.00
"Spun Gold" reissue						
Elektra 65977		No One Is to Blame/Life in One Day				
			198?			3.00
"Spun Gold" reissue						
Elektra 69288		The Prisoner/Rubber Morals	1989			3.00
Elektra 69308		Everlasting Love/The Brutality of Fact				
			1989			3.00
Elektra 69308	PS	Everlasting Love/The Brutality of Fact				
			1989			3.00
Elektra 69479		Will You Still Be There/Will You Still Be There (Acoustic)				
			1987			3.00
Elektra 69494		All I Want/Dig This Well Deep	1987			3.00
Elektra 69494	PS	All I Want/Dig This Well Deep	1987			3.00
Elektra 69512		You Know I Love You...Don't You?/Roll Right Up				
			1986			3.00
Elektra 69512	PS	You Know I Love You...Don't You?/Roll Right Up				
			1986			3.00
Elektra 69549		No One Is to Blame/The Chase	1986			3.00
Elektra 69549	PS	No One Is to Blame/The Chase	1986			3.00
Elektra 69598		Like to Get to Know You Well/Equality				
			1985			3.00
Elektra 69631		Life in One Day/Learning How to Love				
			1985			3.00
Elektra 69631	PS	Life in One Day/Learning How to Love				
			1985			3.00
Elektra 69651		Things Can Only Get Better/Why Look for the Key				
			1985			3.00
Elektra 69651	PS	Things Can Only Get Better/Why Look for the Key				
			1985			3.00
Elektra 69705		Pearl in the Shell/Don't Always Look at the Rain				
			1984			3.00
Elektra 69737		What Is Love/It Just Doesn't Matter				
			1984			3.00
Elektra 69737	PS	What Is Love/It Just Doesn't Matter				
			1984			3.00
Elektra 69766		New Song/Conditioning	1984			3.00
Elektra 69766	PS	New Song/Conditioning	1984			3.00
12-Inch Singles						
Elektra 4944	DJ	New Song (2 versions)/Conditioning/Change the Man				
			1983	2.50	5.00	10.00
Elektra 4965	DJ	What Is Love (Long)/What Is Love (Short)				
			1983		2.50	5.00
Elektra 4992	DJ	Pearl in the Shell (Long)/Pearl in the Shell (Short)				
			1984	2.00	4.00	8.00
Elektra 5043	DJ	Things Can Only Get Better/Things Can Only Get Better (Remix)				
			1985	2.00	4.00	8.00

Label, Number		Title	Year	VG	VG+	NM
Elektra 5065	DJ	Life in One Day/Life in One Day (Remix Part 1 & 2)				
			1985		3.00	6.00
Elektra 5091	DJ	Like to Get to Know You Well (Short)/				
		Like to Get to Know You Well (Long)				
			1985	2.50	5.00	10.00
Elektra 5178	DJ	You Know I Love You...Don't You?/				
		You Know I Love You...Don't You? (Edit)				
			1986		3.00	6.00
Elektra 5207	DJ	All I Want (2 versions)/				
		You Know I Love You... Don't You? (Live)				
			1986		2.50	5.00
Elektra 5385	DJ	The Prisoner (3 versions)	1989	2.00	4.00	8.00
Elektra 66695		The Prisoner/Rubber Morals/Have You Heard the News				
			1989	2.00	4.00	8.00
Elektra 66831		You Know I Love You...Don't You (3 versions)/Roll Right Up				
			1986		3.00	6.00
Elektra 66895		Life in One Day/Life in One Day (Remix Part 1 & 2)				
			1985		3.00	6.00
Elektra 66915		Things Can Only Get Better (2 versions)/What Is Love/New Song				
			1985	2.00	4.00	8.00
Elektra 66977		New Song (Extended)/Conditioning/Change the Ma				
			1983	2.00	4.00	8.00

Jones, Oran "Juice"

His soul/rap hit "The Rain" was the first mega-hit for rap/funk label Def Jam Records.

Vinyl Albums						
Def Jam BFC 40367		Juice	1986	3.00	6.00	12.00
45s						
Def Jam 06209		The Rain/Your Song	1986		2.00	4.00
Def Jam 06389		Curiosity/Here I Go Again	1986			3.00
Def Jam 06687		Here I Go Again/1.2.1	1987			3.00
Def Jam 07391		Cold Spendin' My Money/(Instrumental)				
			1987			3.00
Def Jam 07656		I Just Can't Say Goodbye/Not on the Outside				
			1987			3.00
Def Jam 68736		The Rain/Your Song	1989			3.00
Reissue						
OBR 73023		To Be Immortal/Pipedreams	1989			3.00
OBR 73274		Shanique/Dollar and a Dream	1990		*Cassette only*	
12-Inch Singles						
Def Jam 05968		Curiosity (2 versions)/Here I Go Again				
			1986		3.50	7.00
Def Jam 06730		Here I Go Again/1.2.1	1986		3.00	6.00
Def Jam 06960		Cold Spendin' My Money/(Instrumental)				
			1987		3.00	6.00
OBR 73172		Dollar and a Dream (3 versions)/Shanique (3 versions)/				
		To Be Immortal	1990		3.00	6.00

Jonestown

Minneapolis grunge band.

45s						
C/Z 031		Recall/Screw Crude	1991		2.50	5.00
C/Z 031	PS	Recall/Screw Crude	1991		2.50	5.00
Project A-Bomb (# unknown)		Sugar Ship/Eczema	1990		3.00	6.00
Project A-Bomb (# unknown)	PS	Sugar Ship/Eczema	1990		3.00	6.00
Skidmark 1		Crusty Rug/Tri-State Breeders Co-Op				
			1990	3.00	6.25	12.50

Label, Number		Title	Year	VG	VG+	NM
Skidmark 1	PS	Crusty Rug/Tri-State Breeders Co-Op				
			1990	5.50	11.25	22.50
First 100 have colored-in sleeves						
Skidmark 1	PS	Crusty Rug/Tri-State Breeders Co-Op				
			1990	3.00	6.25	12.50
Without colored-in sleeve						

Joy Division
*British gloom-synth rockers. After lead singer Ian Curtis' suicide, the remaining members became **New Order**.*

Vinyl Albums						
Factory FACT US 1		Unknown Pleasures	1979	3.75	7.50	15.00
Factory FACT US 6		Closer	1980	12.50	25.00	50.00
Purple tint vinyl						
Factory FACT US 6		Closer	1980	6.25	12.50	25.00
Red tint vinyl						
Warner Bros. 25747		Substance	1988	2.50	5.00	10.00
Warner Bros. 25840		Unknown Pleasures	1989	2.50	5.00	10.00
Reissue of FACT US 1						
Warner Bros. 25841		Closer	1989	2.50	5.00	10.00
Reissue of FACT US 6						
45s						
Factory FACUS 23		Love Will Tear Us Apart/These Days				
			1980	3.00	6.25	12.50
Factory FACUS 23	DJ	Love Will Tear Us Apart/These Days				
			1980	25.00	50.00	100.00
Factory FACUS 23	PS	Love Will Tear Us Apart/These Days				
			1980	3.00	6.25	12.50
Factory 28		Komakino/Incubation/Dub	1980	3.75	7.50	15.00
Flexi-disc with no picture sleeve, "Evatone" on label						
Factory 28		Komakino/Incubation/Dub	1980	2.50	5.00	10.00
Flexi-disc, with below picture sleeve						
Factory 28	PS	Komakino/Incubation/Dub	1980	6.25	12.50	25.00
Numbered sleeve from fanzine "The Other Sound"						
12-Inch Singles						
Factory FACUS 2		She's Lost Control/Atmosphere	1979	2.50	5.00	10.00

Label, Number		Title	Year	VG	VG+	NM

K

Kajagoogoo

*British synth-pop band produced by Nick Rhodes of **Duran Duran**. Lead singer was **Limahl**.*

Vinyl Albums

EMI America ST-17094		White Feathers	1983	3.00	6.00	12.00

45s

EMI America 8161		Too Shy/Take Another View	1983			3.00
EMI America 8161	PS	Too Shy/Take Another View	1983		2.50	5.00
EMI America 8171		Hang On Now/Kajagoogoo	1983			3.00
EMI America 8171	PS	Hang On Now/Kajagoogoo	1983			3.00

12-Inch Singles

EMI America 7806		Too Shy (midnight mix)/Another View				
			1982	3.00	6.00	12.00

Katrina and the Waves

Formed in Britain, this pop-rock band had two Americans and two Brits. One of the Brits was Kimberley Rew, ex-Soft Boys.

Vinyl Albums

Capitol ST-12400		Katrina and the Waves	1985	2.50	5.00	10.00
Capitol ST-12478		Waves	1986	2.50	5.00	10.00
SBK K1-92649		Break of Hearts	1989	2.50	5.00	10.00

45s

American Pie 9044		Walking on Sunshine/Do You Want Crying				
			198?			3.00
Reissue						
Capitol 5450		Do You Want Crying/Maniac House				
			1985			3.00
Capitol 5450	PS	Do You Want Crying/Maniac House				
			1985			3.00
Capitol 5466		Walking on Sunshine/Going Down to Liverpool				
			1985			3.00
Capitol 5466	PS	Walking on Sunshine/Going Down to Liverpool				
			1985			3.00
Capitol 5528		Que Te Quiero/He's a Charmer	1985			3.00
Capitol 5528	PS	Que Te Quiero/He's a Charmer	1985			3.00
Capitol 5566		Is That It?/I Really Taught Me to Watusi				
			1986			3.00
Capitol 5566	PS	Is That It?/I Really Taught Me to Watusi				
			1986			3.00
Capitol 5593		Sun Street/(A Man Only Needs) One Woman				
			1986			3.00
SBK 07303		That's the Way/Love Calculator	1989			3.00
SBK 07303	PS	That's the Way/Love Calculator	1989			3.00
SBK 07310		Rock N Roll Girl/Rene (Live)	1989			3.00
SBK 07310	PS	Rock N Roll Girl/Rene (Live)	1989			3.00

12-Inch Singles

Capitol SPRO 9359	DJ	Do You Want Crying (Extended Mix)/				
		Do You Want Crying (Single Version)				
			1985		3.00	6.00
Capitol SPRO 9372/3	DJ	Walking on Sunshine (5:37)/Walking on Sunshine (4:00)				
			1985	2.50	5.00	10.00
Capitol SPRO 9413	DJ	Red Wine and Whiskey (same on both sides)				
			1985	2.50	5.00	10.00
Red vinyl						

Label, Number		Title	Year	VG	VG+	NM
Capitol SPRO 9514	DJ	Que Te Quiero (same on both sides)				
			1985	2.00	4.00	8.00
Capitol SPRO 9645	DJ	Is That It/Is That It (extended)	1986		3.00	6.00
Capitol SPRO 9716	DJ	Lovely Lindsay (same on both sides)				
			1986		3.00	6.00
SBK 05311	DJ	That's the Way (same on both sides)				
			1989		3.50	7.00

Kid Creole and the Coconuts

Soul/funk/new wave group with August Darnell as ringleader. Also see **Dr. Buzzard's Original Savannah Band** *and* **Don Armando's Second Avenue Rhumba Band.**

Vinyl Albums

Antilles AN 7078		Off the Coast of Me	1980	3.00	6.00	12.00
Sire SRK 3534		Fresh Fruit in Foreign Places	1981	3.00	6.00	12.00
Sire SRK 3681		Wise Guy	1982	2.50	5.00	10.00
Sire 23977		Doppelganger	1983	2.50	5.00	10.00
Sire 25298		In Praise of Older Women and Other Crimes				
			1985	2.50	5.00	10.00
Sire 25579		I, Too, Have Seen the Woods	1987	2.50	5.00	10.00

45s

Atlantic 89664	DJ	My Male Curiosity (edit)/My Male Curiosity (LP)				
			1984		2.00	4.00
Apparently, no stock copy exists						
Columbia 73256		The Sex of It/He's Takin' the Rap				
			1990			*Cassette only*
Columbia 73452		I Love Girls/Ode to a Coloured Man				
			1990			*Cassette only*
Columbia 73975		(She's a) Party Girl/Baby Doc	1991			*Cassette only*
Musician 69306		People Will Talk/(B-side unknown)				
			1989			3.00
Sire 28959		Endicott/Dowopsalsaboprock	1985			3.00
Sire 29468		If You Wanna Be Happy/The Seven Year Itch				
			1983			3.00
Sire 29738		Annie, I'm Not Your Daddy/Imitation				
			1983			3.00
Sire 29738	PS	Annie, I'm Not Your Daddy/Imitation				
			1983			3.00
Sire 29909		Love We Have/Stool Pigeon	1982			3.00
Sire 49811		Going Places/In the Jungle	1981			3.00
Sire 50069		I'm a Wonderful Thing, Baby/No Fish Today				
			1982			3.00

12-Inch Singles

Antilles 806		Yolanda/Mr. Softee	1980	3.00	6.00	12.00
Atlantic PR 610	DJ	My Male Curiosity (same on both sides)				
			1984	2.00	4.00	8.00
Columbia 69204		The Sex of It (4 versions)	1990	2.00	4.00	8.00
Columbia 73514		I Love Girls (4 mixes)/Girls I Love Dub				
			1990		3.00	6.00
Musician 5369	DJ	People Will Talk	1989		3.00	6.00
Sire PRO-A-969	DJ	Going Places/In the Jungle/Table Manners				
			1981	2.50	5.00	10.00
Sire PRO-A-1026	DJ	I'm a Wonderful Thing, Baby/I'm a Wonderful Thing, Baby (Edit)				
			1982		3.50	7.00
Sire PRO-A-1064	DJ	Stool Pigeon (Extended)/Annie, I'm Not Your Daddy/I'm Corrupt				
			1982		3.50	7.00
Sire PRO-A-2005	DJ	Annie, I'm Not Your Daddy (Long)/ Annie, I'm Not Your Daddy (Short)				
			1983		3.00	6.00
Sire 20351		Endicott/Dowopsalsaboprock	1985		3.00	6.00

Label, Number		Title	Year	VG	VG+	NM
Sire 20403		Caroline Was a Drop Out/You Can't Keep a Good Man Down				
			1986		3.00	6.00
Sire 20789		Dancin' at the Bains Douches (3 versions)				
			1987		3.00	6.00

Killdozer

45s

Label, Number		Title	Year	VG	VG+	NM
Amphetamine Reptile		Her Mother's Sorrow/Short Eyes	199?	8.25	16.75	33.50
SCALE 24						
Yellow vinyl						
Amphetamine Reptile		Her Mother's Sorrow/Short Eyes	199?		3.75	7.50
SCALE 24						
Amphetamine Reptile	PS	Her Mother's Sorrow/Short Eyes	199?		3.75	7.50
SCALE 24						
Touch N Go 39	(5)	For Ladies Only	199?	12.50	25.00	50.00
Five singles in gatefold package with fold-open book						
Touch N Go 44		Lupus/Nasty	199?			3.00
Touch N Go 44	PS	Lupus/Nasty	199?			3.00
Touch N Go 122		The Pig Was Cool/Unbelievable	199?			3.00
Touch N Go 122	PS	The Pig Was Cool/Unbelievable	199?			3.00

Kingbees, The

West Coast power-pop/rock group.

Vinyl Albums

Label, Number	Title	Year	VG	VG+	NM
RSO RS1-3075	The Kingbees	1980	3.75	7.50	15.00
RSO RS1-3097	The Big Rock	1981	3.75	7.50	15.00

45s

Label, Number	Title	Year	VG	VG+	NM
RSO 1032	My Mistake/Once Is Not Enough				
		1980		2.00	4.00
RSO 1050	Shake-Bop	1980		2.00	4.00
RSO 1062	She Can't "Make Up" Her Mind/Stick It Out				
		1981		2.00	4.00

10-Inch Singles

Label, Number	Title	Year	VG	VG+	NM
Last Minute LMP1 007	Just Like That/If I Want To	1982	5.00	10.00	20.00
As "Jamie James and the Kingbees"					

Kings, The

Toronto-based pop-rock group.

Vinyl Albums

Label, Number	Title	Year	VG	VG+	NM
Elektra 6E-277	The Kings Are Here	1980	3.75	7.50	15.00
Elektra 5E-543	Amazon Beach	1981	2.50	5.00	10.00

45s

Label, Number	Title	Year	VG	VG+	NM
Elektra 47006	Switchin' to Glide/My Habit	1980		2.50	5.00
Elektra 47052	Switchin' to Glide/This Beat Goes On				
		1980			3.00
Elektra 47110	Don't Let Me Know/Partyitis	1981			3.00
Elektra 47213	All the Way/Loading Zone	1981			3.00

12-Inch Singles

Label, Number	Title	Year	VG	VG+	NM
Elektra AS 11528	All the Way/Equal Noise	1981	2.50	5.00	10.00

"Klark Kent" was the alter ego of Stewart Copeland of the Police. This is the American picture sleeve for the obscure "Away from Home" on the Kryptone/I.R.S. label ($10 for record and sleeve together).

A rare picture sleeve for a rare reissue, "My Sharona" by The Knack is on Side A and "Tempted" by Squeeze is on Side 1 (sic). It was issued by RCA to promote the movie *Reality Bites* in 1994, and the record and sleeve already fetch $5 each.

Label, Number		Title	Year	VG	VG+	NM

Klark Kent

*"Klark Kent" is **Stewart Copeland** of **The Police** in disguise.*

Vinyl Albums

Kryptone/I.R.S. SP 70600	EP	Music Madness from the Kinetic Kid				
			1980	4.50	9.00	18.00

Green vinyl 10" in die-cut 12" sleeve

45s

Kryptone/I.R.S. 9012		Away from Home/Office Talk	1980		2.50	5.00
Green vinyl, custom label, small hole						
Kryptone/I.R.S. 9012	PS	Away from Home/Office Talk	1980		2.50	5.00

KLF, The

*Bizarre British samplers. Originally known as the JAM's. Also recorded as **The Timelords**.*

Vinyl Albums

Wax Trax! 7155		Chill Out	1991	3.75	7.50	15.00

45s

Arista 2230		3 A.M. Eternal (Live at the S.S.L.)/				
		3 A.M. Eternal (Guns of Mu Mu)	1991		2.00	4.00
Arista 12365		What Time Is Love/Build a Fire	1991			3.00
Arista 12382		Last Train to Transcentral (Live from the Lost Continent)/				
		Make It Rain	1991		*Cassette only*	
Arista 12401		Justified and Ancient (Stand By the JAMs)/Justified and Ancient				
			1991		2.00	4.00

A-side guest vocalist: Tammy Wynette

12-Inch Singles

Arista 2231		3 A.M. Eternal (4 mixes)	1991	2.00	4.00	8.00
Arista 12366		America: What Time Is Love/What Time Is Love (2 mixes)				
			1991		3.00	6.00
Arista 12383		Last Train to Transcentral (3 mixes)				
			1991	2.00	4.00	8.00
Arista 12403		Justified and Ancient (4 mixes)	1991	2.00	4.00	8.00

Knack, The

*Probably not the same as **The** "My Sharona" **Knack**; also probably not The Knack that were on Capitol in the 1960s.*

45s

Atco 7051		Pick It Up/Always	1976		2.50	5.00

Knack, The

Widely scorned when they were ultra-popular, The Knack actually was a pretty decent power-pop/new wave band.

Vinyl Albums

Capitol SO-11948		Get the Knack	1979	3.00	6.00	12.00
Capitol SOO-12045		...But the Little Girls Understand	1980	2.50	5.00	10.00
Capitol ST-12168		Round Trip	1981	2.50	5.00	10.00

45s

Capitol 4731		My Sharona/Let Me Out	1979		2.00	4.00
Capitol 4731	PS	My Sharona/Let Me Out	1979		3.00	6.00
Capitol 4771		Good Girls Don't/Frustrated	1979		2.00	4.00
A-side contains different lyrics from LP version in three places						
Capitol 4771	PS	Good Girls Don't/Frustrated	1979		3.00	6.00
Capitol 4822		Baby Talks Dirty/End of the Game				
			1980		2.00	4.00

Label, Number		Title	Year	VG	VG+	NM
Capitol 4822	PS	Baby Talks Dirty/End of the Game				
			1980	2.50	5.00	10.00
Capitol 4853		Can't Put a Price on Love/Rave Up				
			1980		2.00	4.00
Not issued with picture sleeve in U.S.						
Capitol 5054		Pay the Devil (Ooo, Baby, Ooo)/Lil' Cal's Big Mistake				
			1981		2.00	4.00
Capitol 5054	PS	Pay the Devil (Ooo, Baby, Ooo)/Lil' Cal's Big Mistake				
			1981		2.00	4.00
Capitol 5078		Boys Go Crazy/We Are Waiting	1981		2.00	4.00
Capitol S7-17905		My Sharona/Locked Out	1994		2.00	4.00
B-side by Crowded House						
RCA 62800		My Sharona/Tempted	1994		2.50	5.00
B-side by Squeeze						
RCA 62800	PS	My Sharona/Tempted	1994		2.50	5.00
B-side by Squeeze						
12-Inch Singles						
Capitol SPRO 9713	DJ	Art War/Africa/Pay the Devil	1981		3.00	6.00
Capitol SPRO-9712	DJ	Art War (same on both sides)	1981		3.00	6.00

Kraftwerk

German synthesizer group, an influence to most who came after them.

Label, Number		Title	Year	VG	VG+	NM
Vinyl Albums						
Capitol ST-11457		Radio-Activity	1975	4.00	8.00	16.00
Capitol SW 11603		Trans-Europe Express	1977	4.00	8.00	16.00
Capitol SW-11728		The Man-Machine	1978	4.00	8.00	16.00
Capitol SN-16301		Trans-Europe Express	198?	2.50	5.00	10.00
Reissue						
Capitol SN-16302		The Man-Machine	198?	2.50	5.00	10.00
Reissue						
Capitol SN-16380		Radio-Activity	1986	2.50	5.00	10.00
Reissue						
Elektra 60789		Computer World	1988	2.00	4.00	8.00
Reissue						
Elektra 60797		Autobahn	1988	2.00	4.00	8.00
Still another reissue of this album						
Elektra 60798		Electric Cafe	1988	2.00	4.00	8.00
Reissue						
Elektra 60869	(2)	The Mix	1991	3.00	6.00	12.00
Mercury SRM-1-3704		Autobahn	1977	3.75	7.50	15.00
Reissue of Vertigo VEL-2003						
Vertigo VEL-2003		Autobahn	1974	5.00	10.00	20.00
Vertigo VEL-2006		Ralf & Florian	1976	4.00	8.00	16.00
Recorded in 1973						
Warner Bros. HS 3549		Computer World	1981	2.50	5.00	10.00
Warner Bros. 25326		Autobahn	1985	3.00	6.00	12.00
Another reissue of Vertigo VEL-2003						
Warner Bros. 25525		Electric Cafe	1986	3.00	6.00	12.00
45s						
Capitol 4211		Radioactivity/Antenna	1976		2.50	5.00
Capitol 4211	PS	Radioactivity/Antenna	1976	2.00	4.00	8.00
Capitol 4460		Trans-Europe Express/Franz Schubert				
			1977		2.50	5.00
Capitol 4620		Neon Lights/The Robots	1978		2.50	5.00
Vertigo 203		Autobahn/Morgan Spaziergance	1975	2.00	4.00	8.00
Vertigo 204		Mitternacht (Midnight)/Kometen Melodie (Comet Melody 2)				
			1975	2.00	4.00	8.00
Warner Bros. 28441		The Telephone Call/Der Telefon Anruf				
			1987			3.00

Label, Number		Title	Year	VG	VG+	NM
Warner Bros. 28441	PS	The Telephone Call/Der Telefon Anruf				
			1987			3.00
Warner Bros. 28532		Musique Non-Stop (Long)/Musique Non-Stop (Short)				
			1986			2.00
Warner Bros. 28532	PS	Musique Non-Stop (Long)/Musique Non-Stop (Short)				
			1986			2.00
Warner Bros. 29342		Tour de France (Remix)/Tour de France (French)				
			1984			3.00
Warner Bros. 49723		Pocket Calculator/Dentaku	1981		2.50	5.00
Yellow vinyl						
Warner Bros. 49723	PS	Pocket Calculator/Dentaku	1981		2.50	5.00
Plastic sleeve that goes with yellow vinyl pressing						
Warner Bros. 49723		Pocket Calculator/Dentaku	1981			3.00
Warner Bros. 49795		Numbers/Computer Love	1981			3.00

12-Inch Singles

Label, Number		Title	Year	VG	VG+	NM
Capitol 8502		Showroom Dummies (6:00)/Les Mannequins (6:02)				
			1977	5.00	10.00	20.00
Capitol 8526		Neon Lights (9:03)/The Model	1978	6.25	12.50	25.00
Elektra ED 5551	DJ	Robotnik/The Robots/Robotronik	1991	3.00	6.00	12.00
Warner Bros. PRO-A-951	DJ	Pocket Calculator/Dentaku	1981	3.00	6.00	12.00
Warner Bros. 20549		Musique Nonstop (LP Version)/Musique Nonstop (7" Version)				
			1986	2.00	4.00	8.00

Kravitz, Lenny
Singer-songwriter.

Vinyl Albums

Label, Number	Title	Year	VG	VG+	NM
Virgin 39169	Are You Gonna Go My Way	1993	6.25	12.50	25.00
Clear-vinyl LP plus bonus CD with 8 unreleased tracks					
Virgin 91290	Let Love Rule	1989	3.00	6.00	12.00

45s

Label, Number	Title	Year	VG	VG+	NM
Virgin S7-17445	Believe/For the First Time	1993			3.00
Virgin S7-17711	Heaven Help/Spinning Around Over You				
		1994			3.00

Kreviss

45s

Label, Number		Title	Year	VG	VG+	NM
Sub Pop 149		Going to Hell//You Heard It All/Broken Flowers				
			1992		2.50	5.00
B-side by Mecca Normal; green marbled vinyl						
Sub Pop 149	PS	Going to Hell//You Heard It All/Broken Flowers				
			1992		2.50	5.00
#42 in Sub Pop Singles Club series						

Krush Groove All-Stars
*Fat Boys, **Run-D.M.C.**, Sheila E and Kurtis Blow.*

45s

Label, Number	Title	Year	VG	VG+	NM
Warner Bros. 28843	Krush Groove/Kold Krush	1985		2.00	4.00

L

L.L. Cool J
Rapper; one of the first to have major hits among white mainstream audiences.

Vinyl Albums

Label, Number	Title	Year	VG	VG+	NM
Def Jam FC 40239	Radio	1985	3.00	6.00	12.00

Label, Number		Title	Year	VG	VG+	NM
Def Jam FC 40793		Bigger and Deffer	1987	2.50	5.00	10.00
Def Jam OC 45173		Walking with a Panther	1989	2.50	5.00	10.00
Def Jam C 46888		Mama Said Knock You Out	1990	2.50	5.00	10.00
Def Jam C 53325	(2)	14 Shots to the Dome	1993	3.75	7.50	15.00
Def Jam 523 845-1		Mr. Smith	1995	2.50	5.00	10.00

45s

Label, Number		Title	Year	VG	VG+	NM
Def Jam 05665		I Can't Live Without My Radio/I Can Give You More				
			1985			3.00
Def Jam 05840		Rock the Bells/El Shabazz	1986			3.00
Def Jam 06061		You'll Rock/I Need a Beat	1986			3.00
Def Jam 07120		I'm Bad/Get Down	1987			3.00
Def Jam 07350		I Need Love/My Rhyme Ain't Done				
			1987			3.00
Def Jam 07620		Go Cut Creator Go/Kanday	1987			3.00
Def Jam 07679		Going Back to Cali/Jack the Ripper				
			1988			3.00
Def Jam 07679	PS	Going Back to Cali/Jack the Ripper				
			1988			3.00
Def Jam 08380		I Can't Live Without My Radio/Rock the Bells				
			1988			3.00
Reissue						
Def Jam 08381		I Need Love/I'm Bad	1988			3.00
Reissue						
Def Jam 68902		I'm That Type of Guy/It Gets No Rougher				
			1989			3.00
Def Jam 69056		One Shot of Love/Big Ole Butt	1989			3.00
Def Jam 73207		Jingling Baby/Illegal Search	1990			*Cassette only*
Def Jam 73457		The Boomin' System (Radio 1)/				
		The Boomin' System (Underground Mix)				
			1990			*Cassette only*
Def Jam 73609		Around the Way Girl/Mama Said Knock You Out				
			1991			3.00
Def Jam 73820		6 Minutes of Pleasure/Eat 'Em Up L Chill				
			1991			*Cassette only*
Def Jam 74811		Now I'm Comin'/Buckin' Em Down/Now I'm Comin'				
			1993			*Cassette only*
Def Jam 74984		Back Seat (Of My Jeep)/Pink Cookies in a Plastic Bag Getting				
		Crushed by Buildings	1993			*Cassette only*
Def Jam 77098		Stand By Your Man/Soul Survivor				
			1993			*Cassette only*
Def Jam 576 120-7		Doin It (On the Air)/Hey Lover (Radio Edit)				
			1996			3.00
Def Jam 577 494-7		Hey Lover (Radio Edit) (same on both sides)				
			1995			3.00
Featuring Boyz II Men						

12-Inch Singles

Label, Number		Title	Year	VG	VG+	NM
Def Jam CAS 05010	DJ	Now I'm Comin'/(Instrumental)	1993	2.00	4.00	8.00
Def Jam CAS 05193	DJ	Pink Cookies in a Plastic Bag Getting Crushed by Buildings/				
		Funkadelic Relic	1992	2.00	4.00	8.00
Def Jam 05291		I Can Give You More (vocal)/(Instrumental)/				
		I Can't Live Without My Radio	1985		3.00	6.00
Def Jam 05349		Rock the Bells (Special Version)/Rock the Bells				
			1985	2.00	4.00	8.00
Def Jam 07476		Co Cut Creator Go/Kanday	1987	2.00	4.00	8.00
Def Jam 68792		I'm That Type of Guy/It Gets No Rougher				
			1989	2.00	4.00	8.00
Def Jam 73281		6 Minutes of Pleasure (3 versions)/Eat 'Em Up L-Chill (3 versions)				
			1991	2.00	4.00	8.00
Def Jam 73458		The Boomin' System (3 mixes)	1990	2.00	4.00	8.00
Def Jam 73610		Around the Way Girl (5 mixes)	1990	2.00	4.00	8.00

Label, Number		Title	Year	VG	VG+	NM
Def Jam 73703		Mama Said Knock You Out (7 mixes)				
			1991	2.00	4.00	8.00
Def Jam 74810		Now I'm Comin' (2 mixes)/Buckin' Em Down (2 mixes)				
			1993	2.00	4.00	8.00
Def Jam 74983		Pink Cookies in a Plastic Bag Getting Crushed by Buildings				
		(4 mixes)/Back Seat	1993	2.00	4.00	8.00
Def Jam 77097		Stand By Your Man (6 mixes)/Soul Survivor				
			1993	2.50	5.00	10.00
MCA 54246		Strictly Business (4 versions)	1991		3.00	6.00
Motown 18371	DJ	To Da Break of Dawn (4 mixes)	1990		3.00	6.00
Uptown 1696	DJ	Strictly Business (4 mixes)	1991	2.00	4.00	8.00

L7

Female punk band from Los Angeles.

Vinyl Albums

Epitaph 86401		L7	1988	12.50	25.00	50.00
Slash 45624		Hungry for Stink	1994	3.00	6.00	12.00
Sub Pop 79	EP	Smell the Magic	1990	10.00	20.00	40.00
First 1,000 on purple vinyl						
Sub Pop 79	EP	Smell the Magic	1990	3.00	6.00	12.00

45s

Slash PRO-S-7783	DJ	Can I Run/Baggage (Live)	1995		2.50	5.00
Sub Pop 58		Shove/Packin' a Rod	1990	5.00	10.00	20.00
Green vinyl pressing of 1,200						
Sub Pop 58		Shove/Packin' a Rod	1990	2.50	5.00	10.00
Black vinyl pressing of 1,800						
Sub Pop 58	PS	Shove/Packin' a Rod	1990	2.50	5.00	10.00
#15 in Sub Pop Singles Club series						

Laddin, Hilary

Los Angeles-based guitar-rock punk artist.

45s

What 101		The Sell/City of Fame	1980	6.25	12.50	25.00
What 101	PS	The Sell/City of Fame	1980	6.25	12.50	25.00

Lane, Robin, and the Chartbusters

Boston-based new wave band.

Vinyl Albums

Reron 77	EP	Heart Connection	1984	3.00	6.00	12.00
Robin Lane solo						
Warner Bros. BSK 3424		Robin Lane and the Chartbusters	1980	3.75	7.50	15.00
Warner Bros. BSK 3537		Imitation Life	1981	3.75	7.50	15.00
Warner Bros. MINI 3495		Five Live	1980	3.75	7.50	15.00

45s

Deli Platters RLC 1		When Things Go Wrong/Why Do You Tell Lies/The Letter				
			1979	2.50	5.00	10.00
Deli Platters RLC 1	PS	When Things Go Wrong/Why Do You Tell Lies/The Letter				
			1979	2.50	5.00	10.00
Warner Bros. 49246		When Things Go Wrong/Many Years Ago				
			1980		2.00	4.00
Warner Bros. 49246	PS	When Things Go Wrong/Many Years Ago				
			1980		2.00	4.00
Warner Bros. 49546		Don't Cry/Waitin' in Line	1980		2.00	4.00
Warner Bros. 49742		Solid Rock/Say Goodbye	1981		2.00	4.00

Label, Number		Title	Year	VG	VG+	NM

lang, k.d.

Just your average Canadian lesbian vegetarian country singer who has become more of a singer-songwriter over the years.

Vinyl Albums

Label, Number		Title	Year	VG	VG+	NM
Bumstead BUM-842		A Truly Western Experience	1984	15.00	30.00	60.00
Canadian import						
Bumstead BUM-862		A Truly Western Experience	1984	5.00	10.00	20.00
Canadian import; reissue of Bumstead 842						
Sire PRO-A-3120	DJ	The Making of Shadowland	1988	6.25	12.50	25.00
Sire 25441		Angel with a Lariat	1987	2.50	5.00	10.00
Sire 25724		Shadowland	1988	2.50	5.00	10.00
Sire 25877		Absolute Torch and Twang	1989	2.50	5.00	10.00
Sire R 134567		Shadowland	1988	3.00	6.00	12.00
BMG Direct Marketing edition						
Sire R 160100		Angel with a Lariat	1987	3.00	6.00	12.00
BMG Direct Marketing edition						
Warner Bros. 46034		All You Can Eat	1995	2.50	5.00	10.00

45s

Label, Number		Title	Year	VG	VG+	NM
Sire 18289		Just Keep Me Moving/In Perfect Dreams				
			1994			3.00
Sire 18608		Miss Chatelaine/Outside Myself	1993			3.00
Sire 18942		Constant Craving/Season of Hollow Soul				
			1992			3.00
Sire 19683		Mind of Love	1993			Cassette only
Sire 19793		Seven Lonely Days/Ridin' the Rails				
			1990			3.00
Sire 22932		Full Moon of Love/Wallpaper Waltz				
			1989			3.00
Sire 27813		Lock, Stock and Teardrop/Don't Let the Stars Get In Your Eyes				
			1988			3.00
Sire 27919		I'm Down to My Last Cigarette/Western Stars				
			1988			3.00
Sire 27919	PS	I'm Down to My Last Cigarette/Western Stars				
			1988			3.00
Sire 28338		Turn Me Around/Diet of Strange Places				
			1987			3.00
Sire 28465		Rose Garden/High Time for a Detour				
			1987			3.00
Warner Bros. 17747		If I Were You/Get Some	1995			3.00

12-Inch Singles

Label, Number		Title	Year	VG	VG+	NM
Sire PRO-A-2697	DJ	Turn Me Round (same on both sides)				
			1987	2.50	5.00	10.00
Sire PRO-A-6052	DJ	Miss Chatelaine (4 remixes)	1992	3.75	7.50	15.00
Sire 41197		Just Keep Me Moving (5 versions)/In Perfect Dreams				
			1993	2.50	5.00	10.00
Sire 41379		Lifted by Love (4 versions)/No More Tears (3 versions)				
			1994	2.00	4.00	8.00

Last, The

Los Angeles guitar-rock band.

45s

Label, Number		Title	Year	VG	VG+	NM
Backlash 001		She Don't Know Why I'm Here/Bombing of London				
			1978	7.50	15.00	30.00
Backlash 001	PS	She Don't Know Why I'm Here/Bombing of London				
			1978	7.50	15.00	30.00
Backlash 003		L.A. Explosion/Hitler's Brother	1978	2.00	4.00	8.00
Backlash 003	PS	L.A. Explosion/Hitler's Brother	1978	2.00	4.00	8.00

Never released in America was k.d. lang's debut album, *A Truly Western Experience*. Its original issue on Bumstead 842 goes for $60, a reissue on Bumstead 862 for $20.

Released in 1994, Live's LP *Throwing Copper* is one of those that unexpectedly came out on vinyl here. The band's earlier releases evidently did not.

Label, Number		Title	Year	VG	VG+	NM
Bomp! 119		She Don't Know Why I'm Here/Bombing of London				
			1978			3.00
Bomp! 119	PS	She Don't Know Why I'm Here/Bombing of London				
			1978			3.00
Bomp! 126		Every Summer's Day/Slavedriver				
			1979		3.00	6.00
Bomp! 126	PS	Every Summer's Day/Slavedriver				
			1979		3.00	6.00
Warfrat (# unknown)		Up in the Air/Wrong Turn/Leper Colony				
			1982		2.50	5.00
Red label						
Warfrat (# unknown)		Up in the Air/Wrong Turn/Leper Colony				
			1982		2.00	4.00
Yellow label						
Warfrat (# unknown)	PS	Up in the Air/Wrong Turn/Leper Colony				
			1982		2.50	5.00
Black and yellow sleeve (with red label release)						
Warfrat (# unknown)	PS	Up in the Air/Wrong Turn/Leper Colony				
			1982		2.00	4.00
Black and orange sleeve (with yellow label release)						

Last Rights

Boston punk band.

45s

Taang! 2		Chunks/So Ends Our Night	1984	4.50	9.00	18.00
Taang! 2	PS	Chunks/So Ends Our Night	1984	16.25	32.50	65.00
"Hitler" version on green paper						
Taang! 2	PS	Chunks/So Ends Our Night	1984	16.25	32.50	65.00
"Hitler" version: two-piece white outersleeve over regular white sleeve						
Taang! 2	PS	Chunks/So Ends Our Night	1984	4.50	9.00	18.00
White cardboard with band member "Choke" swinging the mike stand						
Taang! 2	PS	Chunks/So Ends Our Night	1984	4.50	9.00	18.00
Shirtless "Choke" edition, another live shot						
Taang! 2	PS	Chunks/So Ends Our Night	1984	6.75	13.50	27.00
Mike stand edition with four inserts with a different photo						

Laughner, Peter

*Member of **Pere Ubu**.*

45s

Forced Exposure FE-018		Cinderella Backstreet/White Light White Heat				
			1987	2.50	5.00	10.00
Pre-Pere Ubu recordings from 1973-75						
Forced Exposure FE-018	PS	Cinderella Backstreet/White Light White Heat				
			1987	2.50	5.00	10.00

Lauper, Cyndi

*New wave/pop phenomenon of the mid-1980s, thanks to her odd look and wonderful hit songs. Formerly with **Blue Angel**.*

Vinyl Albums

Portrait BFR 38930		She's So Unusual	1983	2.50	5.00	10.00
Portrait 9R9 39610	PD	She's So Unusual	1984	7.50	15.00	30.00
Portrait OR 40313		True Colors	1986	2.50	5.00	10.00
Epic OE 44318		A Night to Remember	1989	3.00	6.00	12.00

45s

Epic 07940		Hole in My Heart (All the Way to China)/Boy Blue				
			1988			3.00
Epic 07940	PS	Hole in My Heart (All the Way to China)/Boy Blue				
			1988			3.00

Label, Number		Title	Year	VG	VG+	NM
Epic 08443		True Colors/What's Going On	1988			3.00
Reissue						
Epic 68759		I Drove All Night/Maybe He'll Know				
			1989			3.00
Epic 68945		My First Night Without You/Unabbreviated Love				
			1989			3.00
Epic 73031		A Night to Remember/Insecurious	1989			3.00
Epic 74942		Who Let In the Rain/Cold	1993			3.00
Epic 77233		That's What I Think/That's What I Think (Live)				
			1993			3.00
Portrait 04120		Girls Just Want to Have Fun/Right Track Wrong Train				
			1983			3.00
Portrait 04120	PS	Girls Just Want to Have Fun/Right Track Wrong Train				
			1983	2.00	4.00	8.00
Portrait 04120	PS	Girls Just Want to Have Fun	1983	2.00	4.00	8.00
"Demonstration -- Not for Sale" on back						
Portrait 04432		Time After Time/I'll Kiss You	1984			3.00
Portrait 04516		She Bop/Witness	1984			3.00
Portrait 04516	PS	She Bop/Witness	1984			3.00
Portrait 04639		All Through the Night/Witness	1984			3.00
Portrait 04639	PS	All Through the Night/Witness	1984			3.00
Portrait 04737		Money Changes Everything (Studio)/				
		Money Changes Everything (Live)	1984			3.00
Portrait 04737	PS	Money Changes Everything (Studio)/				
		Money Changes Everything (Live)	1984			3.00
Portrait 04918		The Goonies 'R' Good Enough/What a Thrill				
			1985			3.00
Portrait 04918	PS	The Goonies 'R' Good Enough/What a Thrill				
			1985			3.00
Portrait 05480		Girls Just Want to Have Fun/Time After Time				
			198?			3.00
Reissue						
Portrait 05537		She Bop/All Through the Night	198?			3.00
Reissue						
Portrait 06247		True Colors/Heading for the Moon				
			1986			3.00
Portrait 06247	PS	True Colors/Heading for the Moon				
			1986			3.00
Portrait 06431		Change of Heart/Witness	1986			3.00
Portrait 06431	PS	Change of Heart/Witness	1986			3.00
Portrait 06970		What's Going On/One Track Mind				
			1987			3.00
Portrait 06970	PS	What's Going On/One Track Mind				
			1987			3.00
Portrait 07181		Boy Blue/The Faraway Nearby	1987			3.00
Portrait 07181	PS	Boy Blue/The Faraway Nearby	1987	2.00	4.00	8.00
12-Inch Singles						
Epic 77234		That's What I Think (6 versions)	1993		3.50	7.00
Portrait AS 2084	DJ	The Goonies 'R' Good Enough (same on both sides)				
			1985		3.00	6.00
Portrait AS 2450	DJ	True Colors (same on both sides)	1986		3.00	6.00
Portrait AS 2560	DJ	Change of Heart (AOR Mix) (same on both sides)				
			1986		3.00	6.00
Portrait 04121		Girls Just Want to Have Fun/Money Changes Everything				
			1983	3.00	6.00	12.00
Portrait 04971		Girls Just Want to Have Fun/Fun With V. Knutson/Extra Fun				
			1984		3.00	6.00
Portrait 05011		She Bop (Remix)/(Instrumental)	1984		3.00	6.00
Portrait 05246		The Goonies 'R' Good Enough (Dance Version)/				
		The Goonies 'R' Good Enough (Dub)				
			1985		3.00	6.00

Label, Number		Title	Year	VG	VG+	NM
Portrait 05974		Change of Heart/(Instrumental)/Heartbeats/Witness				
			1986		3.00	6.00
Portrait 06740		What's Going On (3 versions)/One Track Mind				
			1986	2.00	4.00	8.00

Lazy Cowgirls

Guitar-rock/pop band.

45s

Label, Number		Title	Year	VG	VG+	NM
Bomp! 137		Sock It To Me Santa/Goddamn Bottle				
			1986		3.50	7.00
Bomp! 137	PS	Sock It To Me Santa/Goddamn Bottle				
			1986		3.50	7.00
Sub Pop 43		Loretta/Hybrid Moments	1989	6.25	12.50	25.00
1,000 copies on clear vinyl						
Sub Pop 43		Loretta/Hybrid Moments	1989		2.50	5.00
Black vinyl						
Sub Pop 43	PS	Loretta/Hybrid Moments	1989		2.50	5.00
#11 in Sub Pop Singles Club series						
Sympathy For The Record		Haven't Had a Drink/Platypus Man				
Industry 006			198?	3.00	6.25	12.50
Sympathy For The Record	PS	Haven't Had a Drink/Platypus Man				
Industry 006			198?	3.00	6.25	12.50
Sympathy For The Record		The Long Goodbye/Who Are the Mystery Girls/Crazy Arms				
Industry 25			198?			3.00
Sympathy For The Record		The Long Goodbye/Who Are the Mystery Girls/Crazy Arms				
Industry 25			198?		2.50	5.00
Sympathy For The Record	PS	The Long Goodbye/Who Are the Mystery Girls/Crazy Arms				
Industry 25			198?			3.00
Sympathy For The Record	PS	The Long Goodbye/Who Are the Mystery Girls/Crazy Arms				
Industry 25			198?		2.50	5.00

Lemonheads, The

Boston-based pop-rock group led by Evan Dando.

Vinyl Albums

Label, Number		Title	Year	VG	VG+	NM
Atlantic SAM 1267	DJ	Come On Feel the Lemonheads	1993	5.00	10.00	20.00
Promo-only four-song sampler						
Atlantic 82137		Lovey	1990	3.00	6.00	12.00
Atlantic 82537		Come On Feel the Lemonheads	1993	3.00	6.00	12.00
Taang! 15		Hate Your Friends	1987	5.00	10.00	20.00
First pressing: Black vinyl, yellow lettering on sleeve, yellow label						
Taang! 15		Hate Your Friends	1987	4.50	9.00	18.00
Second pressing: Black vinyl, red lettering on sleeve, yellow label						
Taang! 15		Hate Your Friends	1987	4.00	8.00	16.00
Third pressing: Black vinyl, red lettering on sleeve, red label						
Taang! 15		Hate Your Friends	1987	3.50	7.00	14.00
Fourth pressing: Black vinyl, red lettering on sleeve, blue and green label						
Taang! 15		Hate Your Friends	1987	3.00	6.00	12.00
Fifth pressing: Yellow vinyl, yellow lettering on sleeve, yellow label						
Taang! 15		Hate Your Friends	1987	2.50	5.00	10.00
None of the above (current pressings)						
Taang! 23		Creator	1988	2.50	5.00	10.00
Taang! 32		Lick	1989	2.50	5.00	10.00

7-Inch Extended Play Singles

Label, Number		Title	Year	VG	VG+	NM
Armory Arms/Huh-Bag 1/2		Laughing All the Way to the Bank				
			1986	12.50	25.00	50.00
Armory Arms/Huh-Bag 1/2	PS	Laughing All the Way to the Bank				
			1986	12.50	25.00	50.00
Also has lyric insert; both record and sleeve have been counterfeited						

Label, Number		Title	Year	VG	VG+	NM
45s						
Atlantic PR 5336	DJ	Style/Acoustic Rick James Style	1993		3.00	6.00
White label promo with small hole						
Atlantic PR 5336	PS	Style/Acoustic Rick James Style	1993		3.00	6.00
Taang! 31		Luka//Strange/Mad	1989	3.00	6.00	12.00
Red vinyl						
Taang! 31		Luka//Strange/Mad	1989	2.00	4.00	8.00
Blue/yellow vinyl						
Taang! 31		Luka//Strange/Mad	1989		3.00	6.00
Blue vinyl						
Taang! 31		Luka//Strange/Mad	1989		2.00	4.00
White vinyl						
Taang! 31		Luka//Strange/Mad	1989			3.00
Black vinyl						
Taang! 31	PS	Luka//Strange/Mad	1989			3.00
With "Colored Vinyl Limited Edition" sticker						
The Bob 44		Confetti (acoustic demo)	1993	2.00	4.00	8.00
Yellow flexi-disc included with The Bob magazine						
12-Inch Singles						
Atlantic SAM 1126	DJ	Confetti (Remix)/My Drug Buddy	1992	2.00	4.00	8.00
Atlantic SAM 1164	DJ	Mrs. Robinson/Being Around	1992	2.00	4.00	8.00
Atlantic SAM 1253	DJ	Into Your Arms/Miss Otis Regrets	1993	2.00	4.00	8.00
Atlantic 3499	DJ	Half the Time/Left for Dead/Li'l Seed	1990	2.00	4.00	8.00

Lennox, Annie

*Formerly of **Eurythmics**.*

		Title	Year	VG	VG+	NM
45s						
Arista 12419		Why/Primitive	1992		*Cassette only*	
Arista 12452		Walking on Broken Glass	1992		*Cassette only*	
Arista 12508		Little Bird/Love Song for a Vampire	1992		*Cassette only*	
Arista 12804		No More "I Love You's"/Ladies of the Canyon	1995			3.00
Non- LP B-side						
Arista 12850		A Whiter Shade of Pale/No More "I Love You's" (Remix)	1995			3.00

Lennox, Annie, and Al Green

		Title	Year	VG	VG+	NM
45s						
A&M 1255		Put a Little Love in Your Heart/A Great Big Piece of Love	1988			3.00
B-side by Spheres of Celestial Influence						
A&M 1255	PS	Put a Little Love in Your Heart/A Great Big Piece of Love	1988			3.00
12-Inch Singles						
A&M 12288		Put a Little Love in Your Heart (3 versions)	1988	2.00	4.00	8.00

Les Thugs

		Title	Year	VG	VG+	NM
45s						
Sub Pop 29		Chess and Crimes/Sunday Time	1989	5.00	10.00	20.00
#4 in Sub Pop Singles Club series						
Sub Pop 29	PS	Chess and Crimes/Sunday Time	1989	5.00	10.00	20.00

Label, Number		Title	Year	VG	VG+	NM

Let's Active
*Guitar-pop band led by Mitch Easter, original producer for **R.E.M.***

Vinyl Albums

I.R.S. 5703		Big Plans for Everybody	1986	2.00	4.00	8.00
I.R.S. SP-70505	EP	Afoot	1983	3.00	6.00	12.00
I.R.S. SP-70648		Cypress	1984	2.50	5.00	10.00

12-Inch Singles

I.R.S. 17133	DJ	In Little Ways/Talking to Myself/Last Chance Town				
			1986		2.50	5.00
I.R.S. 17627	DJ	Every Dog Has Its Day (same on both sides)				
			1988		2.50	5.00
I.R.S. 70981	DJ	Blue Line (same on both sides)	1984		3.00	6.00
I.R.S. 70983	DJ	Water's Part/Blue Line	1984	2.00	4.00	8.00

Lethal Yellow
Florida-based hardcore punk.

7-Inch Extended Play Singles

TPOS/Stench 009		Declaration of Retardation	1983	7.50	15.00	30.00
TPOS/Stench 009	PS	Declaration of Retardation	1983	7.50	15.00	30.00
Yellow sleeve						
TPOS/Stench 009	PS	Declaration of Retardation	1983	7.50	15.00	30.00
Pink sleeve						

Letters to Cleo
Boston-based alterna-pop group.

45s

Giant 17823	Awake/Acid Jed	1995		2.00	4.00
Yellow vinyl					
Giant 17913	Here & Now/Big Star	1995			3.00

Level 42
British synth-pop dance group.

Vinyl Albums

A&M SP-4995	Standing in the Light	1984	3.00	6.00	12.00
Polydor PD1-6359	The Pursuit of Accidents	1982	4.00	8.00	16.00
Polydor R 160226	Running in the Family	1987	3.50	7.00	14.00
BMG Direct Marketing edition					
Polydor 810 015-1	The Pursuit of Accidents	1986	2.00	4.00	8.00
Reissue					
Polydor 813 865-1	Standing in the Light	1986	2.00	4.00	8.00
Reissue					
Polydor 821 935-1	Level 42	1986	3.00	6.00	12.00
First U.S. issue of early U.K. LP					
Polydor 823 542-1	True Colours	1986	3.00	6.00	12.00
Polydor 827 487-1	World Machine	1986	3.00	6.00	12.00
Polydor 831 593-1	Running in the Family	1987	3.00	6.00	12.00
Polydor 837 247-1	Staring at the Sun	1988	2.50	5.00	10.00
Polydor 841 399-1	Level Best	1989	2.50	5.00	10.00

45s

A&M 2631	Micro-Kid/Standing in the Light				
		1984		2.50	5.00
A&M 2667	The Sun Goes Down (Living It Up)/Dance On Heavy Weather				
		1984		2.50	5.00
Collectables 4831	Something About You/Lessons in Love				
		199?			3.00
Reissue					

Label, Number		Title	Year	VG	VG+	NM
Polydor 2207		Turn It On/Star Child	1982		2.50	5.00
Polydor 2221		Love Games/Weave Your Spell	1982		2.50	5.00
Polydor 811 538-7		Last Chance/Chinese Way	1983		2.50	5.00
Polydor 871 438-7		Tracie/Man	1989			3.00
Polydor 883 362-7		Something About You/	1985			3.00
Polydor 883 956-7		Lessons in Love/Hot Water (Live)				
			1986			3.00
Polydor 883 956-7	PS	Lessons in Love/Hot Water (Live)				
			1986			3.00
Polydor 885 155-7		Hot Water	1986			3.00
Polydor 885 284-7		Leaving Me Now/Sleep on My Heart				
			1986			3.00
Polydor 885 957-7		Running in the Family/Fashion Fever				
			1987			3.00
Polydor 885 957-7	PS	Running in the Family/Fashion Fever				
			1987			3.00
Polydor 887 136-7		To Be with You Again/Physical Presence (Live)				
			1987			3.00
Polydor 887 277-7		It's Over/MICR Kid	1987			3.00

12-Inch Singles

Label, Number		Title	Year	VG	VG+	NM
A&M 12091		Micro-Kid (Extended)/Micro-Kid (Dub)				
			1983	3.00	6.00	12.00
Polydor 492	DJ	Lessons in Love (same on both sides)				
			1987	3.00	6.00	12.00
Polydor PDD 520		Starchild/Turn It On	1981	4.50	9.00	18.00
Polydor PRO 522-1	DJ	Running in the Family (same on both sides)				
			1987	3.00	6.00	12.00
Polydor PD 525		Weave Your Spell (long and short versions)				
			1981	3.00	6.00	12.00
Polydor 811 537-1		The Chinese Way (3 mixes)	1983	3.75	7.50	15.00
Polydor 883 362-1		Something About You (Long)/Coup D'Etat				
			1985	3.00	6.00	12.00
Polydor 885 155-1		Hot Water (Mastermix 10:21)/Hot Water (LP)/Hot Water (Live)				
			1985	2.50	5.00	10.00
Polydor 885 471-1		World Machine (Remix)/World Machine (Dub)				
			1985	2.00	4.00	8.00
Polydor 885 706-1		Lessons in Love (3 versions)/Freedom Someday				
			1987	3.00	6.00	12.00

Levy, Marcy

Detroit-based singer. Co-wrote several late-1970s Eric Clapton hits. Under the name Marcella Detroit, became one-half of Shakespear's Sister.

45s

Label, Number		Title	Year	VG	VG+	NM
Epic 03035		Close to Her/Waiting on You	1982			3.00
RSO 1047		Help Me/(Instrumental)	1980		2.00	4.00
With Robin Gibb						
RSO 1047	PS	Help Me/(Instrumental)	1980		2.00	4.00

Lewd, The

West Coast punk band.

Vinyl Albums

Label, Number		Title	Year	VG	VG+	NM
ICI CF 200		American Wino	1982	10.00	20.00	40.00

45s

Label, Number		Title	Year	VG	VG+	NM
Scratched 101		Kill Yourself/Trash Can Baby/Pay or Die				
			1978	9.25	18.75	37.50
Scratched 101	PS	Kill Yourself/Trash Can Baby/Pay or Die				
			1978	9.25	18.75	37.50

Label, Number		Title	Year	VG	VG+	NM

Lightning Seeds, The
British studio group.

Vinyl Albums

MCA 6404		Cloudcuckooland	1990	3.00	6.00	12.00

45s

MCA 79059		All I Want/Persuasion	1990		2.00	4.00

12-Inch Singles

MCA 24016		Pure/All I Want/Joy/Love Explosion				
			1990	2.00	4.00	8.00

Limahl
*Formerly of **Kajagoogoo**.*

Vinyl Albums

EMI America ST-17142		Don't Suppose	1985	2.50	5.00	10.00
EMI America ST-17194		Colour All My Days	1986	2.50	5.00	10.00

45s

EMI America 8230		Never Ending Story/Ivory Tower				
			1984			3.00
EMI America 8230	PS	Never Ending Story/Ivory Tower				
			1984			3.00
EMI America 8277		Only for Love	1983			3.00
EMI America 8318		Love in Your Eyes	1986			3.00
EMI America 8318	PS	Love in Your Eyes	1986			3.00

12-Inch Singles

EMI America 7854		Never Ending Story (Club Mix)/(Instrumental)				
			1984	2.00	4.00	8.00
EMI America 7861		Only for Love (3 Versions)	1983		3.00	6.00

Lime Spiders

7-Inch Extended Play Singles

Virgin 99393	DJ	Space Cadet/Just One Solution/Action Women/Stone Free				
			1987	3.00	6.25	12.50
Promo-only live versions; green vinyl						
Virgin 99393	PS	Space Cadet/Just One Solution/Action Women/Stone Free				
			1987	3.00	6.25	12.50

Live
York, Pennsylvania rock group.

Vinyl Albums

Radioactive 10997		Throwing Copper	1994	2.50	5.00	10.00

Living Colour
Metal/pop band led by guitar wizard Vernon Reid.

Vinyl Albums

Epic FE 44099		Vivid	1988	3.00	6.00	12.00
Epic E 46202		Time's Up	1990	5.00	10.00	20.00
Yellow vinyl						

45s

Epic 68548		Glamour Boys/Cult of Personality (Live)				
			1989			3.00
Epic 68611		Cult of Personality/Funny Vibe	1989			3.00

Label, Number		Title	Year	VG	VG+	NM
Epic 68934		Open Letter (To a Landlord)/Talkin' About a Revolution				
			1989			3.00
Epic 73575		Type/Should I Stay Or Should I Go				
			1990		2.00	4.00
Non-LP B-side						
Epic 73660		Love Rears Its Ugly Head/Love Rears Its Ugly Head				
		(Soulpower Edit)	1991			*Cassette only*
Epic 73800		Solace of You/Someone Like You				
			1991			3.00
Epic 77046		Nothingness/Nothingness (Colour Mix)				
			1993			*Cassette only*
12-Inch Singles						
Epic EAS 01074	DJ	Middleman (same on both sides)	1988		3.50	7.00
Epic EAS 01265	DJ	Cult of Personality + 4 live songs				
			1988	2.50	5.00	10.00
Epic EAS 2147	DJ	Type/Final Solution/Sailin' On (Live)				
			1990	4.50	9.00	18.00
Promo-only on yellow vinyl with picture cover						
Epic EAS 04952	DJ	Leave It Alone/Hemp	1992	2.50	5.00	10.00
Red vinyl						
Epic EAS 5140	DJ	Auslander (4 versions)	1993	2.50	5.00	10.00
Epic EAS 6296	DJ	Sunshine of Your Love/Sunshine of Your Love				
		(Adrian Sherwood Remix)	1994		3.50	7.00
Epic 73677		Love Rears Its Ugly Head (2 mixes)/Elvis Is Dead (2 mixes)				
			1991		3.50	7.00

Loeb, Lisa, and Nine Stories

Pop-rock group first featured on the (non-vinyl) soundtrack to the movie Reality Bites.

Label, Number	Title	Year	VG	VG+	NM
Vinyl Albums					
Geffen GEF 24734	Tails	1996	3.00	6.00	12.00
45s					
Geffen 19388	Do You Sleep?/When All the Stars Were Falling				
		1995			3.00
Geffen 19393	Taffy/Sandalwood	1996			3.00

Londonbeat

British dance-pop group.

Label, Number	Title	Year	VG	VG+	NM
Vinyl Albums					
Radioactive 10192	In the Blood	1991	3.00	6.00	12.00
12-Inch Singles					
Radioactive/MCA 53992	I've Been Thinking About You (6 mixes)				
		1991	2.00	4.00	8.00

Lone Justice

*Country-rock group featuring **Maria McKee**.*

Label, Number		Title	Year	VG	VG+	NM
Vinyl Albums						
Geffen GHS 24060		Lone Justice	1985	2.50	5.00	10.00
Geffen GHS 24122		Shelter	1986	2.50	5.00	10.00
45s						
Geffen 28470		I Found Love/If You Don't Like Pain				
			1987			3.00
Geffen 28520		Shelter/Belfry	1986			3.00
Geffen 28520	PS	Shelter/Belfry	1986			3.00
Geffen 28965		Sweet Sweet Baby (I'm Falling)/Don't Toss Us Away				
			1985			3.00

Label, Number		Title	Year	VG	VG+	NM
Geffen 28965	PS	Sweet Sweet Baby (I'm Falling)/Don't Toss Us Away				
			1985			3.00
Geffen 29023		Ways to Be Wicked/Cactus Rose	1985			3.00
Geffen 29023	PS	Ways to Be Wicked/Cactus Rose	1985			3.00

12-Inch Singles

Label, Number		Title	Year	VG	VG+	NM
Geffen PRO-A-2275	DJ	Ways to Be Wicked (same on both sides)				
			1985		2.50	5.00
Geffen PRO-A-2329	DJ	Sweet Sweet Baby/Sweet Sweet Baby (Remix)				
			1985		3.00	6.00
Geffen PRO-A-2596	DJ	Shelter (same on both sides)	1986		3.00	6.00
Geffen PRO-A-2645	DJ	I Found Love (same on both sides)				
			1986		3.00	6.00
Geffen 20570		Shelter/Belfry/I Can't Look Back	1988	2.00	4.00	8.00

Lonely Moans
Early grunge band.

45s

Label, Number		Title	Year	VG	VG+	NM
Amphetamine Reptile SCALE 14		Rockinerd/Welcome Home	1988	5.00	10.00	20.00
Amphetamine Reptile SCALE 14	PS	Rockinerd/Welcome Home	1988	5.00	10.00	20.00
Sub Pop 46		Shoot the Cool/Texas Love Goat	1989	3.00	6.00	12.00
Red vinyl first pressing of 1,200						
Sub Pop 46		Shoot the Cool/Texas Love Goat	1989			3.00
Black vinyl second pressing of 800						
Sub Pop 46	PS	Shoot the Cool/Texas Love Goat	1989	3.00	6.00	12.00
#12 in Sub Pop Singles Club series						

Lords of the New Church
*British group led by Cleveland native **Stiv Bators**.*

Vinyl Albums

Label, Number		Title	Year	VG	VG+	NM
I.R.S. 5726		Killer Lords	1986	3.00	6.00	12.00
I.R.S. SP-70029		The Lords of the New Church	1982	3.75	7.50	15.00
I.R.S. SP-70039		Is Nothing Sacred?	1983	3.00	6.00	12.00
I.R.S. SP-70049		The Method to Our Madness	1984	3.00	6.00	12.00
As "The Lords"						

45s

Label, Number		Title	Year	VG	VG+	NM
I.R.S. 9908		Open Your Eyes/A Question of Temperature				
			1982		2.00	4.00
I.R.S. 9921		Live for Today/Girls Girls Girls	1983		2.00	4.00
I.R.S. 9921	PS	Live for Today/Girls Girls Girls	1983		2.00	4.00

12-Inch Singles

Label, Number		Title	Year	VG	VG+	NM
I.R.S. 70409		Live for Today/Opening Nightmares/Dreams and Desires				
			1983	2.50	5.00	10.00
I.R.S. 70962	DJ	Holy War/Open Your Eyes	1982	2.00	4.00	8.00
I.R.S. 70985	DJ	The Method to My Madness (same on both sides)				
			1985	4.50	9.00	18.00

Los Lobos
Los Angeles Hispanic-American band. Utterly unclassifiable.

Vinyl Albums

Label, Number		Title	Year	VG	VG+	NM
New Vistas 1001		Just Another Band from East L.A.				
			1978	25.00	50.00	100.00
Slash 23963	EP	And a Time to Dance	1983	3.00	6.00	12.00
Slash 25177		How Will the Wolf Survive?	1984	3.00	6.00	12.00
Slash 25523		By the Light of the Moon	1987	3.00	6.00	12.00

Label, Number		Title	Year	VG	VG+	NM
Slash 25790		La Pistola y El Corazon	1988	3.00	6.00	12.00
Slash 26131		The Neighborhood	1990	3.00	6.00	12.00
Slash R 144507		By the Light of the Moon	1987	3.50	7.00	14.00
RCA Music Service edition						
45s						
Slash 21942		La Bamba/Come On, Let's Go	198?			3.00
"Back to Back Hits" reissue						
Slash 28186		Come On, Let's Go/Ooh My Head				
			1987			3.00
Slash 28336		La Bamba/Charlena	1987			3.00
Slash 28336	PS	La Bamba/Charlena	1987			3.00
Slash 28390		Set Me Free (Rosalie)/Tears of God				
			1987			3.00
Slash 28464		One Time One Night/All I Wanted to Do Was Dance				
			1987			3.00
Slash 29093		Will the Wolf Survive?/The Breakdown				
			1985			3.00
Slash 29093	PS	Will the Wolf Survive?/The Breakdown				
			1985			3.00
Warner Bros. 18659		Kiko and Lavender Moon	1993		*Cassette only*	
12-Inch Singles						
Slash PRO-A-2226	DJ	Don't Worry Baby/Will the Wolf Survive?				
			1984		3.50	7.00
Slash PRO-A-2252	DJ	Will the Wolf Survive? (Remix Edit)/				
		Will the Wolf Survive? (LP Version)				
			1984		3.50	7.00
Slash PRO-A-2640	DJ	Shakin' Shakin' Shakes (same on both sides)				
			1986	2.00	4.00	8.00
Slash PRO-A-2685	DJ	Is That All There Is (same on both sides)				
			1987		3.50	7.00
Slash PRO-A-2690	DJ	Set Me Free (Rosa Lee) (same on both sides)				
			1987		2.50	5.00
Slash PRO-A-2737	DJ	La Bamba/La Bamba (Fade)	1987	2.00	4.00	8.00

Love and Rockets

*British synth-rock band with three former members of **Bauhaus**.*

Vinyl Albums						
Beggars Banquet 9715-1-R		Love and Rockets	1989	2.50	5.00	10.00
Big Time/RCA 6011-1-B		Express	1986	3.00	6.00	12.00
Big Time/RCA 6058-1-B8		Earth.Sun.Moon	1987	2.50	5.00	10.00
RCA 8507-1-R		Seventh Dream of Teenage Heaven				
			1988	2.50	5.00	10.00
45s						
Big Time 6069-7-B		No New Tale to Tell/Earth, Sun, Moon				
			1987		2.50	5.00
Big Time 8956-7-R		So Alive/Dreamtime	1989			3.00
Big Time 8956-7-R	PS	So Alive/Dreamtime	1989			3.00
Big Time 9045-7-R		No Big Deal/No Words No More				
			1989			3.00
12-Inch Singles						
Big Time 6018		Kundalini Express/Lucifer Sam/Holiday on the Moon				
			1986	2.50	5.00	10.00
Big Time 6018	DJ	Kundalini Express (same on both sides)				
			1986	2.00	4.00	8.00
Big Time 6023		All in My Mind (electric)/All in My Mind (acoustic)				
			1986	2.50	5.00	10.00
Big Time 6035	DJ	Ball of Confusion (same on both sides)				
			1986	2.00	4.00	8.00

Label, Number		Title	Year	VG	VG+	NM
Big Time 6038		Ball of Confusion (3 mixes)/All in My Mind				
			1986	2.50	5.00	10.00
Big Time 6063	DJ	No New Tale to Tell (same on both sides)				
			1987	2.50	5.00	10.00
Big Time 6067	DJ	Mirror People (same on both sides)				
			1987	2.50	5.00	10.00
Big Time 6070		Mirror People (5 versions)	1987	3.00	6.00	12.00
Big Time 6071	DJ	Waiting for the Flood (same on both sides)				
			1987	2.50	5.00	10.00
RCA 8758	DJ	Dog End of the Day Gone By (2 versions)/Interview				
			1988	3.75	7.50	15.00
RCA 9041		Rock and Roll Babylon/No New Tale to Tell (Live)/				
		Ball of Confusion (Live)	1989	5.00	10.00	20.00
RCA 9097		No Big Deal (2 versions)/1000 Watts of Your Love/				
		No Words No More	1989	2.50	5.00	10.00

Love Battery

45s

Sub Pop 135		Foot (Alt.)/Mr. Soul	1991		2.00	4.00
Sub Pop 135	PS	Foot (Alt.)/Mr. Soul	1991		2.00	4.00
#37 in Sub Pop Singles Club series						

10-Inch Singles

Atlas 69712 0050		Nehru Jacket/Illuminated Man/Red Onion				
			1994	3.00	6.00	12.00
Blue vinyl promo						

Lovett, Lyle

Country-rock singer.

Vinyl Albums

MCA/Curb 5748		Lyle Lovett	1986	2.50	5.00	10.00
MCA/Curb 17355	EP	Not Exactly Mr. Showbiz	1987	3.00	6.00	12.00
Promo-only five-song EP with special sleeve						
MCA/Curb 42028		Pontiac	1988	2.50	5.00	10.00
MCA/Curb 42263		Lyle Lovett and His Large Band	1989	2.50	5.00	10.00
MCA/Curb R 100932		Lyle Lovett And His Large Band	1989	3.00	6.00	12.00
BMG Direct Marketing edition						
MCA/Curb R 133603		Lyle Lovett	1986	3.00	6.00	12.00
RCA Music Service edition						
MCA/Curb R 153258		Pontiac	1988	3.00	6.00	12.00
BMG Direct Marketing edition						

45s

MCA 52818		Farther Down the Line/Why I Don't Know				
			1986			3.00
MCA 52818	DJ	Farther Down the Line (same on both sides)				
			1986	2.00	4.00	8.00
Green vinyl						
MCA 79025		Here I Am/Nobody Knows Me	1990			3.00
MCA/Curb 52951		Cowboy Man/The Waltzing Fool	1986			3.00
MCA/Curb 52951	DJ	Cowboy Man (same on both sides)				
			1986	2.00	4.00	8.00
Clear vinyl						
MCA/Curb 53030		God Will/An Acceptable Level of Ecstasy (The Wedding Song)				
			1987			3.00
MCA/Curb 53102		Why I Don't Know/If I Were the Man You Wanted				
			1987			3.00
MCA/Curb 53157		Give Back My Heart/Simple Song				
			1987			3.00
MCA/Curb 53246		She's No Lady/Pontiac	1988			3.00

Label, Number		Title	Year	VG	VG+	NM
MCA/Curb 53316		I Loved You Yesterday/L.A. County				
			1988			3.00
MCA/Curb 53401		If I Had a Boat/Black and Blue	1988			3.00
MCA/Curb 53471		I Married Her Just Because She Looks Like You/If I Had a Boat				
			1988			3.00
MCA/Curb 53611		Stand By Your Man/Wallisville Road				
			1989			3.00
MCA/Curb 53650		Nobody Knows Me/Here I Am	1989			3.00
MCA/Curb 53703		If I Were the Man You Wanted/Cryin' Shame				
			1989			3.00
SBK S7-56996		Stand By Your Man/The Crying Game				
			1993		2.00	4.00
B-side by Boy George; red vinyl						
SBK S7-56996		Stand By Your Man/The Crying Game				
			1993			3.00
B-side by Boy George; black vinyl						

Lovich, Lene

New wave singer, born in America, moved to England as a teenager.

Vinyl Albums

Label, Number		Title	Year	VG	VG+	NM
Stiff/Epic JE 36102		Stateless	1979	5.00	10.00	20.00
Red vinyl						
Stiff/Epic JE 36102		Stateless	1979	3.00	6.00	12.00
Stiff/Epic JE 36308		Flex	1980	3.00	6.00	12.00
Stiff/Epic 5E 37452	EP	New Toy	1981	3.75	7.50	15.00
Stiff/Epic ARE 38399		No Man's Land	1983	2.50	5.00	10.00

45s

Label, Number	Title	Year	VG	VG+	NM
Stiff/Epic 03499	It's You, Only You (Mein Schmerz)/Blue				
		1983		2.50	5.00
Stiff/Epic 03863	Blue Hotel/Savages	1983		2.50	5.00
Stiff/Epic 50725	Lucky Number/Lucky Number (Slavic Dance Version)				
		1979		3.00	6.00
Stiff/Epic 50767	Home/The Writing on the Wall	1979		3.00	6.00
Stiff/Epic 50866	The Night/Monkey Talk (Live)	1980		3.00	6.00

12-Inch Singles

Label, Number	Title	Year	VG	VG+	NM
CBS Special Products P 20135	Lucky Number/New Toy	1987	3.00	6.00	12.00
Pathfinder PTF 8009	Wonderland (4 versions)	1989		3.00	6.00
Stiff/Epic 03342	It's You, Only You (Remix)/It's You, Only You (Dub)				
		1982	2.00	4.00	8.00
Stiff/Epic 03799	Blue Hotel (Dance Mix)/Blue Hotel				
		1983	2.50	5.00	10.00

Lowe, Nick

*Pop/rock/new wave performer from England. Also was with **Brinsley Schwarz and Rockpile**.*

Vinyl Albums

Label, Number		Title	Year	VG	VG+	NM
Columbia AS 1400	DJ	An Interrogation of Nick Lowe	1990	6.25	12.50	25.00
Promo-only interview album						
Columbia JC 35529		Pure Pop for Now People	1978	5.00	10.00	20.00
Columbia PC 35529		Pure Pop for Now People	198?	2.00	4.00	8.00
Budget-line reissue						
Columbia JC 36087		Labour of Lust	1979	2.50	5.00	10.00
Columbia PC 36087		Labour of Lust	198?	2.00	4.00	8.00
Budget-line reissue						
Columbia FC 37932		Nick the Knife	1982	3.00	6.00	12.00
Columbia PC 37932		Nick the Knife	198?	2.00	4.00	8.00
Budget-line reissue						
Columbia FC 38589		The Abominable Showman	1983	3.00	6.00	12.00

Label, Number		Title	Year	VG	VG+	NM
Columbia PC 38589		The Abominable Showman	1986	2.00	4.00	8.00
Budget-line reissue						
Columbia FC 39371		Nick Lowe and His Cowboy Outfit				
			1984	3.00	6.00	12.00
Columbia PC 39371		Nick Lowe and His Cowboy Outfit				
			1986	2.00	4.00	8.00
Budget-line reissue						
Columbia FC 39958		The Rose of England	1985	3.00	6.00	12.00
Columbia FC 40381		Pinker and Prouder Than Previous				
			1988	3.50	7.00	14.00
Reprise 26132		Party of One	1990	3.00	6.00	12.00

45s

Label, Number		Title	Year	VG	VG+	NM
Columbia 02813		Stick It Where the Sun Don't Shine/My Heart Hurts				
			1982			3.00
Columbia 03837		Wish You Were Here/How Do You Talk to An Angel				
			1983			3.00
Columbia 03837	DJ	Cool Reaction (same on both sides)				
			1983			3.00
Columbia 04486		Half a Boy and Half a Man/Awesome				
			1984			3.00
Columbia 05570		I Knew the Bride (When She Used to Rock and Roll)/				
		Long Walk Back	1985			3.00
Columbia 07734		Lovers Jamboree/Crying in My Sleep				
			1988			3.00
Columbia 10734		So It Goes/Heart of the City (Live)	1978		2.50	5.00
Columbia 10844		(I Love the Sound of) Breaking Glass/Endless Sleep				
			1978		2.50	5.00
Columbia 11018		Cruel to Be Kind/Endless Grey Ribbon				
			1979		2.50	5.00
Columbia 11131		Switch Board Susan/Basin Street	1979		2.50	5.00
Columbia 33398		Cruel to Be Kind/So It Goes	198?			3.00
"Hall of Fame" reissue						

12-Inch Singles

Label, Number		Title	Year	VG	VG+	NM
Columbia AS 921	DJ	Without Love (same on both sides)	198?	2.00	4.00	8.00
Nick Lowe with Johnny Cash and Dave Edmunds						
Columbia AS 1626	DJ	Raging Eyes (same on both sides)	1983		2.50	5.00
Columbia AS 1876	DJ	Half a Boy and Half a Man (same on both sides)				
			1984		2.50	5.00
Columbia CAS 2171	DJ	I Knew the Bride (When She Used to Rock and Roll)				
		(same on both sides)	1985	2.00	4.00	8.00
Columbia CAS 2923	DJ	Lover's Jamboree (same on both sides)				
			1988		2.50	5.00

Lubricated Goat

45s

Label, Number		Title	Year	VG	VG+	NM
Sub Pop 65		Meeting My Head/20th Century Rake				
			1990		2.50	5.00
Black vinyl pressing of 1,500						
Sub Pop 65		Meeting My Head/20th Century Rake				
			1990	3.75	7.50	15.00
Gold vinyl pressing of 2,000						
Sub Pop 65	PS	Meeting My Head/20th Century Rake				
			1990		2.50	5.00
#18 in Sub Pop Singles Club series						

Label, Number		Title	Year	VG	VG+	NM

Luchs Brothers

*Chicago punk band, imitators of the **Sex Pistols**.*

45s

Label, Number		Title	Year	VG	VG+	NM
Retread 0001		Kill Me I'm Rotten/Losing My Lunch Over You				
			1978	5.00	10.00	20.00
Retread 0001	PS	Kill Me I'm Rotten/Losing My Lunch Over You				
			1978	5.00	10.00	20.00

Lunch, Lydia

*From Rochester, New York. Originally with **Teenage Jesus and the Jerks**.*

Vinyl Albums

Label, Number	Title	Year	VG	VG+	NM
Ruby JRR 806	13.13	1982	7.50	15.00	30.00
Ze/Buddah 33006	Queen of Siam	1980	7.50	15.00	30.00

Luscious Jackson

*Female rockers. Drummer Kate Schellenbach had played behind the **Beastie Boys** in the early years.*

Vinyl Albums

Label, Number		Title	Year	VG	VG+	NM
Grand Royal GR 001	EP	In Search of Manny	1993	2.00	4.00	8.00
Grand Royal GR 009		Natural Ingredients	1994	2.50	5.00	10.00

45s

Label, Number	Title	Year	VG	VG+	NM
Capitol S7-18581	Here/Citysong	1995			3.00

12-Inch Singles

Label, Number		Title	Year	VG	VG+	NM
Capitol SPRO 79482/99	DJ	Deep Shag (3 versions)/Daddy	1994	2.00	4.00	8.00
Cream vinyl promo copy						

Luxurious Bags

45s

Label, Number		Title	Year	VG	VG+	NM
Twisted Village 1008		Powerline/Airpocket/Sad Banjo Eyed				
			1991	3.75	7.50	15.00
Twisted Village 1008	PS	Powerline/Airpocket/Sad Banjo Eyed				
			1991	3.75	7.50	15.00
Numbered edition of 500						

Label, Number		Title	Year	VG	VG+	NM

M

M

*One-man synth-pop band. Real name: **Robin Scott**.*

Vinyl Albums

Label, Number		Title	Year	VG	VG+	NM
Sire SRK 3672		Famous Last Words	1982	2.50	5.00	10.00
Sire SRK 6084		New York-London-Paris-Munich				
			1979	3.00	6.00	12.00
Sire SRK 6099		The Official Secrets Act	1981	2.50	5.00	10.00

45s

Label, Number		Title	Year	VG	VG+	NM
Sire 49033		Pop Muzik/M Factor	1979		2.00	4.00
Sire 49033	DJ	Pop Muzik (Long)/Pop Muzik (Short)				
			1979		2.50	5.00
Sire 49033	PS	Pop Muzik/M Factor	1979		3.00	6.00
Sire 49136		Moonlight and Muzak/Woman Make Man				
			1979		2.00	4.00
Sire 49206		That's the Way the Money Goes/Satisfy Your Lust				
			1980		2.00	4.00
Sire 49687		Join the Party/Working for the Corporation				
			1981		2.00	4.00

12-Inch Singles

Label, Number		Title	Year	VG	VG+	NM
Sire PRO-A-842	DJ	Moonlight and Muzak/Woman Make Man				
			1979	2.00	4.00	8.00
Sire PRO-A-851	DJ	That's the Way the Money Goes 1 & 2/Cowboys and Indians				
			1980		3.00	6.00
Sire DSRE 8887		Pop Muzik/M Factor	1979	3.00	6.00	12.00

M/A/R/R/S

British techno-funk group and sampling wizards.

45s

Label, Number		Title	Year	VG	VG+	NM
4th & B'Way 7452		Pump Up the Volume (Radio Edit)/Anitina				
			1987		2.00	4.00
No mention of "Bright Lights Big City" on label						
4th & B'Way 7452		Pump Up the Volume (From Bright Lights Big City)/Anitina				
			1987			3.00
4th & B'Way 7452	PS	Pump Up the Volume (From Bright Lights Big City)/Anitina				
			1987			3.00
Both versions have same picture sleeve						
Collectables 2610		Pump Up the Volume/(instrumental)				
			199?			3.00
Reissue						

12-Inch Singles

Label, Number		Title	Year	VG	VG+	NM
4th & B'Way 452		Pump Up the Volume (4 versions)/Anitina				
			1987	2.00	4.00	8.00

MacGowan, Shane, and the Popes

*New band from ex-member of **The Pogues**.*

45s

Label, Number		Title	Year	VG	VG+	NM
ZTT/Warner Bros. 17782		Nancy Whiskey/That Woman's Got Me Drinking				
			1995			3.00

Label, Number		Title	Year	VG	VG+	NM

Mad Daddies

45s

Label, Number		Title	Year	VG	VG+	NM
Sub Pop 35		Alligator Wine/Take Me Back to Woodstock				
			1989		2.50	5.00
Sub Pop 35	PS	Alligator Wine/Take Me Back to Woodstock				
#7 in Sub Pop Singles Club series			1989		2.50	5.00

Mad, The

New York City punk group.

45s

Label, Number		Title	Year	VG	VG+	NM
Disgusting 123		Fried Egg//The Hell/Disgusting	1979	12.50	25.00	50.00
Disgusting 123	PS	Fried Egg//The Hell/Disgusting	1979	12.50	25.00	50.00
Disgusting 781		Eyeball/I Hate Music	1979	12.50	25.00	50.00
Disgusting 781	PS	Eyeball/I Hate Music	1979	12.50	25.00	50.00

Madness

British ska band.

Vinyl Albums

Label, Number		Title	Year	VG	VG+	NM
Geffen GHS 4003		Madness	1983	2.50	5.00	10.00
Geffen GHS 4022		Keep Moving	1984	2.50	5.00	10.00
Geffen GHS 24079		Mad Not Mad	1985	2.50	5.00	10.00
Sire SRK 6085		One Step Beyond	1979	3.00	6.00	12.00
Sire SRK 6094		Absolutely	1980	2.50	5.00	10.00

45s

Label, Number		Title	Year	VG	VG+	NM
Geffen GGEF 0466		Our House/It Must Be Love	198?			3.00
Reissue						
Geffen 29350		The Sun and the Rain/Time for Tea				
			1984			3.00
Geffen 29350	PS	The Sun and the Rain/Time for Tea				
			1984			3.00
Geffen 29562		It Must Be Love/Calling Cards	1983			3.00
Geffen 29562	PS	It Must Be Love/Calling Cards	1983			3.00
Geffen 29668		Our House/Cardiac Arrest	1983			3.00
Geffen 29668	PS	Our House/Cardiac Arrest	1983			3.00
Sire 0204		One Step Beyond/Mistakes	1979	2.50	5.00	10.00
Canada-only single						
Sire 49205		Madness/Mistakes	1980		2.50	5.00

12-Inch Singles

Label, Number		Title	Year	VG	VG+	NM
Geffen PRO-A-2122	DJ	The Sun and the Rain/Wings of a Dove/Keep Moving				
			1984		3.00	6.00
Geffen 29667		Our House (Extended Dance Version)/Our House (Dub Version)				
			1983	2.50	5.00	10.00
Sire PRO-A-852	DJ	One Step Beyond/My Girl/Madness				
			1980	3.75	7.50	15.00

Madonna

Dance-pop queen. One of the first female artists to control her own image, thus setting the stage for all who followed. And the singles are good to classic.

Vinyl Albums

Label, Number		Title	Year	VG	VG+	NM
Maverick PRO-A-5904	DJ	Erotica	1992	12.50	25.00	50.00
Promo-only 2-record set						
Maverick PRO-A-7311	DJ	Bedtime Stories	1994	12.50	25.00	50.00
Promo-only 2-record set on pink vinyl						
Sire PRO-A-2892		You Can Dance	1987	7.50	15.00	30.00
Promo-only; contains single edits of the seven songs on the stock editions						

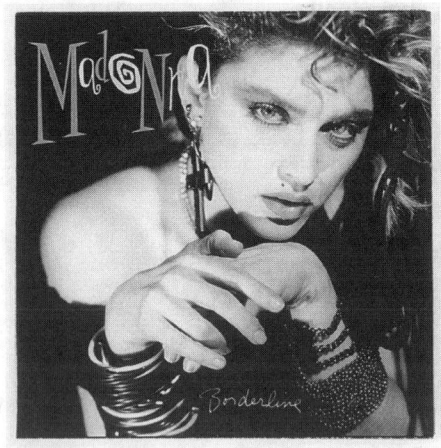

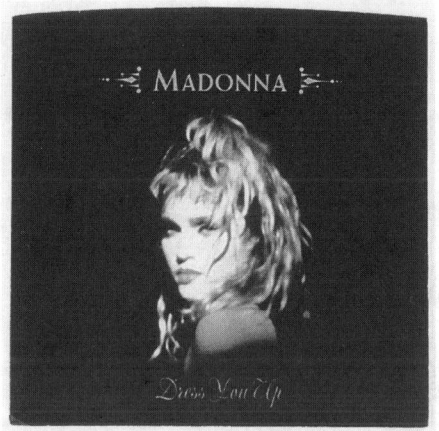

Most Madonna picture sleeves are common, but these three aren't. "Borderline," her first in America, folds open into a poster. "Dress You Up," strangely, was only spottily available. Each fetches up to $50. "Keep It Together," from 1990, is rarely seen and was her last U.S. picture sleeve. Fewer of them exist than either of the other two, but it's not as valuable because it's not as well known as a rarity.

Label, Number		Title	Year	VG	VG+	NM
Sire 23867		Madonna	1983	5.00	10.00	20.00
First pressing with 4:48 version of "Burning Up"						
Sire 23867		Madonna	1983	2.50	5.00	10.00
Second pressing with 3:49 version of "Burning Up"						
Sire W1-23867		Madonna	1984	3.75	7.50	15.00
Columbia House edition						
Sire 25157		Like a Virgin	1984	15.00	30.00	60.00
White vinyl with silver colored spine						
Sire 25157		Like a Virgin	1984	12.50	25.00	50.00
White vinyl with cream colored spine						
Sire 25157		Like a Virgin	1984	2.50	5.00	10.00
Sire W1-25157		Like a Virgin	1985	3.75	7.50	15.00
Columbia House edition						
Sire 25442		True Blue	1986	3.00	6.00	12.00
With poster						
Sire 25442		True Blue	1986	2.00	4.00	8.00
Without poster						
Sire W1-25442		True Blue	1986	3.75	7.50	15.00
Columbia House edition; issued with poster						
Sire 25535		You Can Dance	1987	3.00	6.00	12.00
With gold obi "Madonna and Dancing"						
Sire 25535		You Can Dance	1987	2.00	4.00	8.00
Without gold obi						
Sire W1-25535		You Can Dance	1987	3.75	7.50	15.00
Columbia House edition; not issued with obi						
Sire 25844		Like a Prayer	1989	2.50	5.00	10.00
Sire W1-25844		Like a Prayer	1989	3.75	7.50	15.00
Columbia House edition						
Sire 26209		I'm Breathless	1990	2.50	5.00	10.00
Sire W1-26209		I'm Breathless	1990	3.75	7.50	15.00
Columbia House edition						
Sire 26440	(2)	The Immaculate Collection	1990	3.75	7.50	15.00
Sire W1-26440	(2)	The Immaculate Collection	1990	5.00	10.00	20.00
Columbia House edition						
Sire R 100572		I'm Breathless	1990	3.75	7.50	15.00
BMG Direct Marketing edition						
Sire R 101029		Like a Prayer	1989	3.75	7.50	15.00
BMG Direct Marketing edition						
Sire R 134536		You Can Dance	1987	3.75	7.50	15.00
RCA Music Service edition; <u>not</u> issued with obi						
Sire R 143811		True Blue	1986	3.75	7.50	15.00
RCA Music Service edition; issued with poster						
Sire R 161153		Like a Virgin	1985	3.75	7.50	15.00
RCA Music Service edition						
Sire R 164288		Madonna	1984	3.75	7.50	15.00
RCA Music Service edition						
Sire R 254164	(2)	The Immaculate Collection	1990	5.00	10.00	20.00
BMG Direct Marketing edition						

45s

Label, Number		Title	Year			NM
Geffen GGEF 0540		Gambler/Crazy for You	198?			3.00
"Back to Back Hits" series; first issue of A-side on U.S. 45						
Geffen 29051		Crazy for You/No More Words	1985			3.00
B-side by Berlin						
Geffen 29051	PS	Crazy for You/No More Words	1985			3.00
Maverick 17714		Love Don't Live Here Anymore (Soulpower Radio Remix)/ Love Don't Live Here Anymore (Album Remix)	1996			3.00
Maverick 17719		You'll See/Live to Tell (Live Edit)	1995			3.00
Maverick 17882		Human Nature/Sanctuary	1995			3.00
Maverick 17926		Bedtime Story/Survival	1995			3.00
Maverick 18000		Take a Bow/Take a Bow (In Da Soul Mix)	1994			3.00
Maverick 18035		Secret/Secret (instrumental)	1994			3.00

Label, Number		Title	Year	VG	VG+	NM
Maverick 18247		I'll Remember/Secret Garden	1994			3.00
Maverick 18505		Rain/Waiting	1993			3.00
Maverick 18639		Deeper and Deeper/Deeper and Deeper (instrumental)				
			1992			3.00
Maverick 18650		Bad Girl/Fever	1993			3.00
Maverick 18782		Erotica/Erotica (instrumental)	1992			3.00
Sire GSRE 0494		Borderline/Holiday	198?			3.00
"Back to Back Hits" reissue						
Sire GSRE 0506		Live a Virgin/Lucky Star	198?			3.00
"Back to Back Hits" reissue						
Sire GSRE 0507		Material Girl/Angel	198?			3.00
"Back to Back Hits" reissue						
Sire GSRE 0539		Into the Groove/Dress You Up	198?			3.00
"Back to Back Hits" series; first issue of A-side on U.S. 45						
Sire PRO-S-2023	DJ	Physical Attraction/Physical Attraction				
			1983	2.50	5.00	10.00
Sire 18822		This Used to Be My Playground/ This Used to Be My Playground (Long Version)				
			1992			3.00
Sire 19485		Justify My Love/Express Yourself 1990				
			1990			3.00
Sire 19490		Rescue Me/Rescue Me (Alternate Single Mix)				
			1990			3.00
Sire 19789		Hanky Panky/More	1990			3.00
Sire 19863		Vogue (Single Version)/Vogue (Bette Davis Dub)				
			1990			3.00
Sire 19986		Keep It Together/Keep It Together (instrumental)				
			1990			3.00
Sire 19986	PS	Keep It Together/Keep It Together (instrumental)				
			1990	3.75	7.50	15.00
Much scarcer than this value indicates, this so far is the last Madonna picture sleeve in the U.S.						
Sire 21860		Express Yourself/Cherish	199?			3.00
"Back to Back Hits" reissue						
Sire 21861		Like a Prayer/Oh Father	199?			3.00
"Back to Back Hits" reissue						
Sire 21940		Who's That Girl/Causing a Commotion				
			198?			3.00
"Back to Back Hits" reissue						
Sire 21941		La Isla Bonita/Open Your Heart	198?			3.00
"Back to Back Hits" reissue						
Sire 21985		Live to Tell/True Blue	198?			3.00
"Back to Back Hits" reissue						
Sire 21986		Papa Don't Preach/Everybody	198?			3.00
"Back to Back Hits" reissue						
Sire 22723		Oh Father/Pray for Spanish Eyes	1989			3.00
Not issued with picture sleeve in U.S.						
Sire 22883		Cherish/Supernatural	1989			3.00
Sire 22883	PS	Cherish/Supernatural	1989			3.00
Sire 22948		Express Yourself/The Look of Love				
			1989			3.00
Sire 22948	PS	Express Yourself/The Look of Love				
			1989			3.00
Sire 27539		Like a Prayer/Act of Contrition	1989			3.00
Sire 27539	DJ	Like a Prayer (7" Remix Edit)/Like a Prayer (7" Version with Fade)				
			1989	2.50	5.00	10.00
Sire 27539	PS	Like a Prayer/Act of Contrition	1989			3.00
Sire 28224		Causing a Commotion/Jimmy, Jimmy				
			1987			3.00
Sire 28224	PS	Causing a Commotion/Jimmy, Jimmy				
			1987			3.00
Sire 28341		Who's That Girl?/White Heat	1987			3.00
Sire 28341	PS	Who's That Girl?/White Heat	1987			3.00

Label, Number		Title	Year	VG	VG+	NM
Sire 28425		La Isla Bonita/La Isla Bonita (instrumental)				
			1987			3.00
Sire 28425	PS	La Isla Bonita/La Isla Bonita (instrumental)				
			1987			3.00
Sire 28508		Open Your Heart/White Heat	1986			3.00
Sire 28508	PS	Open Your Heart/White Heat	1986			3.00
Sire 28591		True Blue/Ain't No Big Deal	1986		2.50	5.00
Blue vinyl						
Sire 28591	PS	True Blue/Ain't No Big Deal	1986		2.50	5.00
"Limited edition blue vinyl pressing" on sleeve						
Sire 28591		True Blue/Ain't No Big Deal	1986			3.00
Sire 28591	PS	True Blue/Ain't No Big Deal	1986			3.00
No mention of limited edition on sleeve						
Sire 28660		Papa Don't Preach/Pretender	1986			3.00
Sire 28660	PS	Papa Don't Preach/Pretender	1986			3.00
Sire 28717		Live to Tell/Live to Tell (instrumental)				
			1986			3.00
Sire 28717	PS	Live to Tell/Live to Tell (instrumental)				
			1986			3.00
Sire 28919		Dress You Up/Shoo-Be-Doo	1985			3.00
Sire 28919	PS	Dress You Up/Shoo-Be-Doo	1985	12.50	25.00	50.00
Sire 29008		Angel/Angel (12" Remix Edit)	1985			3.00
Sire 29008	PS	Angel/Angel (12" Remix Edit)	1985			3.00
Sire 29083		Material Girl/Pretender	1985			3.00
Sire 29083	PS	Material Girl/Pretender	1985			3.00
Sire 29177		Lucky Star/I Know It	1984		2.00	4.00
Sire 29210		Like a Virgin/Stay	1984			3.00
Sire 29210	PS	Like a Virgin/Stay	1984			3.00
Sire 29354		Borderline/Think of Me	1984		2.00	4.00
Sire 29354	PS	Borderline/Think of Me	1984	12.50	25.00	50.00
Fold-out poster sleeve						
Sire 29478		Holiday/Holiday (instrumental)	1983		2.00	4.00
Sire 29841		Everybody/Everybody (instrumental)				
Deduct 50% for promo copy			1982	2.50	5.00	10.00

12-Inch Singles

Label, Number		Title	Year	VG	VG+	NM
Maverick PRO-A-5665	DJ	Erotica (LP version)/Erotica (Radio Edit)				
			1992	3.75	7.50	15.00
Maverick PRO-A-5860	(2) DJ	Erotica (11 versions)	1992	7.50	15.00	30.00
Promo-only two-record set						
Maverick PRO-A-5928	(2) DJ	Deeper and Deeper (12 versions)				
			1992	10.00	20.00	40.00
Promo-only two-record set						
Maverick PRO-A-7600	DJ	Bedtime Story (4 versions)	1995	3.75	7.50	15.00
Maverick 40585		Erotica (6 mixes)	1992	2.00	4.00	8.00
Maverick 40722		Deeper and Deeper (6 mixes)	1992	2.00	4.00	8.00
Maverick 40793		Bad Girl/Fever (5 mixes)	1993	2.00	4.00	8.00
Maverick 40988		Rain (2 mixes)/Up Down Suite/Waiting				
			1993	2.00	4.00	8.00
Maverick 41355		I'll Remember (4 mixes)	1994	2.00	4.00	8.00
Maverick 41772		Secret (5 mixes)	1994	2.00	4.00	8.00
Maverick 41887		Take a Bow (5 mixes)	1994		3.00	6.00
Maverick 41895		Bedtime Story (5 mixes)	1995		3.00	6.00
Sire PRO-A-2069	DJ	Lucky Star/Holiday	1983	7.50	15.00	30.00
Sire PRO-A-2120	DJ	Borderline (New Mix 6:54)/(Instrumental)				
			1984	10.00	20.00	40.00
Sire PRO-A-2223	DJ	Like a Virgin (Extended Remix) (same on both sides)				
			1984	7.50	15.00	30.00
Sire PRO-A-2257	DJ	Material Girl (same on both sides)				
			1985	6.25	12.50	25.00
Sire PRO-A-2292	DJ	Angel (3:40 and 6:15)	1985	3.00	6.00	12.00
Sire PRO-A-2353	DJ	Dress You Up (12" Formal Mix) (same on both sides)				
			1985	3.00	6.00	12.00

Label, Number		Title	Year	VG	VG+	NM
Sire PRO-A-2517	DJ	Papa Don't Preach/Papa Don't Preach (edit)				
			1986	3.75	7.50	15.00
Sire PRO-A-3791	DJ	Keep It Together (4 versions)	1990	3.00	6.00	12.00
Sire PRO-A-4582	DJ	Justify My Love (same on both sides)				
			1990	3.00	6.00	12.00
Sire PRO-A-4613	DJ	Justify My Love (4 versions)	1990	5.00	10.00	20.00
Sire PRO-A-4710	(2) DJ	Rescue Me (7 versions)	1990	7.50	15.00	30.00
Promo-only two-record set						
Sire 20212		Borderline/Lucky Star	1984	2.50	5.00	10.00
Sire 20239		Like a Virgin/Stay	1984		3.00	6.00
Sire 20304		Material Girl/Pretender	1985	2.00	4.00	8.00
Sire 20335		Angel/Into the Groove	1985	2.00	4.00	8.00
Sire 20369		Dress You Up (2 mixes)/Shoo-Be-Doo				
			1985	2.00	4.00	8.00
Sire 20461		Live to Tell (Long)/Live to Tell (Edit)/Live to Tell (Instrumental)				
			1986	2.00	4.00	8.00
Sire 20492		Papa Don't Preach/Pretender	1986		3.00	6.00
Sire 20533		True Blue (2 mixes)/Ain't No Big Deal (2 mixes)				
			1986	2.00	4.00	8.00
Sire 20597		Open Your Heart (2 mixes)/White Heat				
			1986	2.00	4.00	8.00
Sire 20633		La Isla Bonita (2 mixes)	1987		3.00	6.00
Sire 20692		Who's That Girl (2 mixes)/White Heat				
			1987	2.00	4.00	8.00
Sire 20762		Causing a Commotion (3 mixes)/Jimmy Jimmy				
			1987	2.50	5.00	10.00
Sire 21170		Like a Prayer (5 mixes)/Act of Contrition				
			1989	2.50	5.00	10.00
Sire 21225		Express Yourself (4 mixes)	1989		3.00	6.00
Sire 21427		Keep It Together (6 mixes)	1990		3.00	6.00
Sire 21513		Vogue (3 mixes)	1990		3.00	6.00
Sire 21577		Hanky Panky (2 mixes)/More	1990		3.00	6.00
Sire 21813		Rescue Me (4 mixes)	1991	2.00	4.00	8.00
Sire 21820		Justify My Love (3 mixes)/Express Yourself				
			1990	2.00	4.00	8.00
Sire 29715		Burning Up/Physical Attraction	1983	2.50	5.00	10.00
Sire 29899		Everybody/Everybody (Dub)	1982	2.50	5.00	10.00

Magazine

British new-wave band.

Vinyl Albums

I.R.S. SP-70015		Play	1981	3.00	6.00	12.00
I.R.S. SP-70020		Magic, Murder and the Weather	1981	3.00	6.00	12.00
I.R.S. SP-70030		After the Fact	1982	2.50	5.00	10.00
Virgin VA 13144		The Correct Use of Soap	1980	2.50	5.00	10.00
Virgin 90891		Rays & Hail 1978-1981	1987	3.00	6.00	12.00
Virgin International VI-2100		Real Life	1978	3.75	7.50	15.00
Virgin International VI-2121		Secondhand Daylight	1979	2.50	5.00	10.00

45s

I.R.S. 9023		About the Weather/In the Dark	1981		2.50	5.00

12-Inch Singles

I.R.S. SP-70404		About the Weather/In the Dark/The Operative				
			1981		3.00	6.00
Virgin International VIDJ 1	DJ	The Light Pours Out of Me/Cut-Out Shapes				
			1979	3.75	7.50	15.00

Label, Number		Title	Year	VG	VG+	NM

Maggots, The
U.S. punk band.

7-Inch Extended Play Singles
Wiggleteens 37689		Tammy Wynette/2-2-79/Rough Dub				
			1980	7.50	15.00	30.00
Wiggleteens 37689	PS	Tammy Wynette/2-2-79/Rough Dub				
			1980	7.50	15.00	30.00

Maids, The
U.S. punk band.

45s
| Anemic 1 | | Back to Bataan/I Do I Do | 1979 | 15.00 | 30.00 | 60.00 |
| Anemic 1 | PS | Back to Bataan/I Do I Do | 1979 | 15.00 | 30.00 | 60.00 |

Mars, Chris
*Ex-member of **The Replacements**.*

Vinyl Albums
| Smash 513 198-1 | DJ | Horseshoes and Hand Grenades | 1992 | 5.00 | 10.00 | 20.00 |
| *Vinyl is promo-only* | | | | | | |

Martha and the Muffins
Canadian pop/new wave group. Most of the RCA recordings were under the name "M+M".

Vinyl Albums
| RCA Victor AFL1-4664 | | Danseparc | 1983 | 2.50 | 5.00 | 10.00 |
| Virgin VA 13145 | | Metro Music | 1980 | 2.50 | 5.00 | 10.00 |

45s
RCA 5041-7-R		Song in My Head/The Work Is a Ball				
			1986			3.00
RCA PB-13473		Danseparc/Whatever Happened to Radio Valve Road?				
			1983		2.00	4.00
RCA PB-13824		Black Stations-White Stations/XOA OHO				
			1984			3.00
RCA PB-14028		Cooling the Medium (Remixed Edited Version)/Big Trees				
			1985			3.00
Virgin 68000		Echo Beach/(B-side unknown)	1981		2.50	5.00
Virgin 68000	PS	Echo Beach/(B-side unknown)	1981		2.50	5.00

12-Inch Singles
RCA PD-13476		Danseparc (Every Day It's Tomorrow)/These Dangerous Machines				
			1983	2.00	4.00	8.00
RCA PD-13802		Black Stations-White Stations (4 mixes)				
			1984		3.00	6.00
RCA PD-13920		Cooling the Medium (Remix)/Cooling the Medium (Dub)/				
		Come Out and Dance	1984		3.00	6.00

Matchheads, The
San Francisco band.

45s
| Artiste (# unknown) | | Cadillac/Pearl Harbor/Fat Bitch | 1981 | 12.50 | 25.00 | 50.00 |
| Artiste (# unknown) | PS | Cadillac/Pearl Harbor/Fat Bitch | 1981 | 12.50 | 25.00 | 50.00 |

Label, Number		Title	Year	VG	VG+	NM

Mavericks, The

Country-rock band with a touch of Tex-Mex, flamenco and Roy Orbison... No wonder they don't get much country radio airplay.

Vinyl Albums

MCA 11257		Music for All Occasions	1995	2.50	5.00	10.00

45s

MCA 54464		This Broken Heart/Excuse Me (I Think I've Got a Heartache)				
			1992			3.00
MCA 54520		I Got You/A Better Way	1992			3.00
MCA 54748		What a Crying Shame/The Things You Said to Me				
			1993			3.00
MCA 54780		O What a Thrill/Ain't Found Nobody				
			1994			3.00
MCA 54909		There Goes My Heart/Just a Memory				
			1994			3.00
MCA 54975		I Should Have Been True/The Losing Side of Me				
			1995			3.00
MCA 55026		All That Heaven Will Allow/Pretend				
			1995			3.00
MCA 55080		Here Comes the Rain/I'm Not Gonna Cry for You				
			1995			3.00
MCA 55154		All You Ever Do Is Bring Me Down/Volver, Volver				
			1996			3.00

Mazzy Star

California male-female alterna-rock duo.

45s

Capitol S7-18300		She's My Baby/Fade Into You	1995			3.00

12-Inch Singles

Rough Trade US 77		Blue Flower (same on both sides)				
			1990	3.00	6.00	12.00

MC5

Punk-rock pioneers from Detroit.

Vinyl Albums

Alive 0005	10	Power Trip	1994		3.00	6.00
Alive 0008	10	Ice Pick Slim/Mad Like Eldridge Cleaver				
			1994		3.00	6.00
Atlantic SD 8247		Back in the U.S.A.	1970	12.50	25.00	50.00
Atlantic SD 8285		High Time	1971	12.50	25.00	50.00
Elektra EKS-74042		Kick Out the Jams	1969	12.50	25.00	50.00
Gatefold cover with John Sinclair liner notes in center spread; brownish label						
Elektra EKS-74042		Kick Out the Jams	1969	5.00	10.00	20.00
All other editions						
Total Energy 2001	10	The American Ruse	1994		3.00	6.00

45s

A-Square 333		Looking at You/Borderline	1967	20.00	40.00	80.00
500 copies of this record were pressed						
A-Square 333	PS	Looking at You/Borderline	1967	10.00	20.00	40.00
AMG 1000	DJ	I Can Only Give You Everything (same on both sides)				
			1966	12.50	25.00	50.00
AMG 1001		I Can Only Give You Everything/I Just Don't Know				
			1969	12.50	25.00	50.00
Black label						

Label, Number		Title	Year	VG	VG+	NM
AMG 1001		I Can Only Give You Everything/One of the Guys				
			1969	12.50	25.00	50.00
Yellow label						
Atlantic 2678		Tonight/Looking at You	1969	3.75	7.50	15.00
Atlantic 2724		The American Ruse/Shakin' Street				
			1970	3.75	7.50	15.00
Elektra MC5-1	DJ	Kick Out the Jams/Motor City Is Burning				
			1968	10.00	20.00	40.00
Distributed free at Fillmore East concert 12/12/68; A-side is an alternate take						
Elektra 45648		Kick Out the Jams/Motor City Is Burning				
			1969	5.00	10.00	20.00

McCann, Edwin

45s

Label, Number	Title	Year	VG	VG+	NM
Lava 98141	Solitude/Alive	1995			3.00
A-side: With Darius Rucker of Hootie and the Blowfish					

McKee, Maria

*Formerly with **Lone Justice**.*

Vinyl Albums

Label, Number	Title	Year	VG	VG+	NM
Geffen GHS 24229	Maria McKee	1989	2.50	5.00	10.00

45s

Label, Number	Title	Year	VG	VG+	NM
Geffen 22800	To Miss Someone/(B-side unknown)				
		1989			3.00

McLachlan, Sarah

Canadian singer-songwriter.

Vinyl Albums

Label, Number	Title	Year	VG	VG+	NM
Arista AL 8594	Touch	1989	2.50	5.00	10.00

45s

Label, Number	Title	Year	VG	VG+	NM
Arista 9804	Vox/Touch	1989			3.00
Arista 12390	Into the Fire	1991			*Cassette only*
Arista 12662	Possession/Black/Fear/Mary	1994			*Cassette only*

12-Inch Singles

Label, Number	Title	Year	VG	VG+	NM
Arista 9805	Vox (4 versions)	1989		3.00	6.00

Meat Puppets

Phoenix indie-rock heroes of the 1980s, now with a major.

Vinyl Albums

Label, Number		Title	Year	VG	VG+	NM
London 1109	10	Raw Meat	199?	5.00	10.00	20.00
Promo-only five-song 10-inch EP						
London 828 484-1		Too High to Die	1994	3.00	6.00	12.00
Includes bonus 10-inch EP (double value for DJ stamp on cover)						
Mercury 828 665-1		No Joke!	1995	2.50	5.00	10.00
SST 009		Meat Puppets	1982	3.75	7.50	15.00
SST 019		Meat Puppets II	1984	3.00	6.00	12.00
SST 039		Up on the Sun	1985	3.00	6.00	12.00
SST 049	10	Out My Way	1986	2.00	4.00	8.00
SST 100		Mirage	1986	3.00	6.00	12.00
SST 150		Huevos	1987	2.50	5.00	10.00
SST 253		Monsters	1989	2.50	5.00	10.00
SST 265	(2)	No Strings Attached	1990	4.00	8.00	16.00

Label, Number		Title	Year	VG	VG+	NM
7-Inch Extended Play Singles						
SST 044		In a Car/Big House/Dolfin Field/Out in the Gardiner/Foreign Lawns				
			1985			2.50
Reissue of World Imitation EP						
SST 044	PS	In a Car	1985			2.50
World Imitation PRC-1		In a Car/Big House/Dolfin Field/Out in the Gardiner/Foreign Lawns				
			1981	5.00	10.00	20.00
World Imitation PRC-1	PS	In a Car	1981	5.00	10.00	20.00
45s						
London PRO 943	DJ	Sam/Bali Ha'i	1991		2.50	5.00
London PRO 943	PS	Sam/Bali Ha'i	1991		2.50	5.00
SST E 39	DJ	Swimming Ground/Up on the Sun				
			1985		3.00	6.00
SST E 39	PS	Swimming Ground/Up on the Sun				
			1985		3.00	6.00
Stamped sleeve promoting upcoming LP						
12-Inch Singles						
SST 100		I Am a Machine/Get On Down	1987	2.00	4.00	8.00
SST 150		Paradise/I Can't Be Counted On	1987	2.00	4.00	8.00

Meatmen, The

Punk band.

Label, Number		Title	Year	VG	VG+	NM
Vinyl Albums						
Homestead 009		War of the Superbikes	198?	3.75	7.50	15.00
Touch N Go TGLP 001		We're the Meatmen...And You Suck				
			198?	6.25	12.50	25.00
7-Inch Extended Play Singles						
Touch N Go (no #)		Blood Sausage	1982	9.25	18.75	37.50
Contains a, shall we say, tasteful Beatles novelty song, "1 Down 3 to Go"						
Touch N Go (no #)	PS	Blood Sausage	1982	9.25	18.75	37.50
Touch N Go 8		Crippled Children Suck	1982	9.25	18.75	37.50
Touch N Go 8	PS	Crippled Children Suck	1982	9.25	18.75	37.50
With insert						
45s						
Vintage Meat (no #)		Wine Wenches & Wheels/Lesbian Death Dirge				
			198?	5.00	10.00	20.00
1983 recordings released later						
Vintage Meat (no #)	PS	Wine Wenches & Wheels/Lesbian Death Dirge				
			198?	5.00	10.00	20.00
Limited edition of 1,000, autographed						

Meaty Buys

Chicago punk band.

Label, Number		Title	Year	VG	VG+	NM
45s						
Disturbing 020279		New Freedumb/Criminal Mind	1979	15.00	30.00	60.00
Disturbing 020279	PS	New Freedumb/Criminal Mind	1979	15.00	30.00	60.00

Mecca Normal

Label, Number		Title	Year	VG	VG+	NM
45s						
Sub Pop 149		You Heard It All/Broken Flowers//Going to Hell				
			1992		2.50	5.00
B-side by Kreviss; marbled green vinyl						
Sub Pop 149	PS	You Heard It All/Broken Flowers//Going to Hell				
			1992		2.50	5.00
#42 in Sub Pop Singles Club series						

Label, Number		Title	Year	VG	VG+	NM

Melvins, The

Early Seattle grunge-rockers.

7-Inch Extended Play Singles

Label, Number		Title	Year	VG	VG+	NM
C/Z 1705		Easy As It Was	1986	6.25	12.50	25.00
C/Z 1705	PS	Easy As It Was	1986	6.25	12.50	25.00

45s

Label, Number		Title	Year	VG	VG+	NM
Boner BR 21		Sweet Young Thing Ain't Sweet No More/I Dreamed I Dream				
			1989	6.25	12.50	25.00
B-side by Steel Pole Bathtub; orange vinyl						
Boner BR 21	PS	Sweet Young Thing Ain't Sweet No More/I Dreamed I Dream				
			1989	6.25	12.50	25.00
Leopard Gecko LG 004		Oven/Revulsion/We Reach	1989	5.00	10.00	20.00
Originals on pink vinyl						
Leopard Gecko LG 004	PS	Oven/Revulsion/We Reach	1989	5.00	10.00	20.00
With insert of cut-out clothes						
Make 'em Bleed and Suffer		Symptom of the Universe/Hate the Police (Live)				
(no #)			1988	6.25	12.50	25.00
Make 'em Bleed and Suffer	PS	Symptom of the Universe/Hate the Police (Live)				
(no #)			1988	6.25	12.50	25.00
Rise RR 76	PD	Hooch/Sky Pup	1993	3.75	7.50	15.00
Most of these picture discs were used as promos						
Rise RR 76	PS	Hooch/Sky Pup	1993	3.75	7.50	15.00
Fold-around silk-screened sleeve by Frank Kozik						
Slap a Ham 13		Love Canal/Someday	199?	2.50	5.00	10.00
5" single with clear vinyl						
Slap a Ham 13	PS	Love Canal/Someday	199?	2.50	5.00	10.00
Plastic bag with stickers on both sides						
Sympathy For The Record		With Yo Heart, Not Yo Hands/4-Letter Woman/Anal Satan				
Industry 81			199?		2.00	4.00
Sympathy For The Record	PS	With Yo Heart, Not Yo Hands/4-Letter Woman/Anal Satan				
Industry 81			199?		2.00	4.00

Men At Work

*Australian pop-rock/new wave band. Lead singer **Colin James Hay** later recorded as a solo artist.*

Vinyl Albums

Label, Number		Title	Year	VG	VG+	NM
Columbia A2S 1650		(2) DJ Cargo (World Premiere Weekend)				
			1983	3.75	7.50	15.00
Promo-only two-record package of interviews and music						
Columbia ARC 37978		Business as Usual	1982	2.50	5.00	10.00
Columbia FC 37978		Business as Usual	1982	2.00	4.00	8.00
New prefix to reflect list-price increase						
Columbia QC 38660		Cargo	1983	2.50	5.00	10.00
Columbia PC 38660		Cargo	198?	2.00	4.00	8.00
Reissue with new prefix						
Columbia FC 40078		Two Hearts	1985	2.00	4.00	8.00
Columbia HC 47978		Business as Usual	1983	3.75	7.50	15.00
"Half-Speed Master"						
Columbia HC 48660		Cargo	1983	3.75	7.50	15.00
"Half-Speed Master"						

45s

Label, Number		Title	Year	VG	VG+	NM
Columbia AE7 1633	DJ	Overkill (same on both sides)	1983		2.50	5.00
Columbia AE7 1633	PS	Overkill (same on both sides)	1983		2.50	5.00
Special color sleeve, different from stock version						
Columbia 02888		Who Can It Be Now?/Anyone for Tennis				
			1982		2.00	4.00
Columbia 03303		Down Under/Crazy	1982		2.00	4.00
Columbia 03373		Down Under	1982		2.50	5.00
One-sided budget release						

Label, Number		Title	Year	VG	VG+	NM
Columbia 03552		Be Good Johnny/Fig	1983			
Cancelled? (This was released as a single in Canada, but whether with this catalog number is unknown.)						
Columbia 03795		Overkill/Till the Money Runs Out				
			1983			3.00
Columbia 03795	PS	Overkill/Till the Money Runs Out				
			1983			3.00
Columbia 03959		It's a Mistake/Shintano	1983			3.00
Columbia 03959	PS	It's a Mistake/Shintano	1983			3.00
Columbia 04111		Dr. Heckyll & Mr. Jive/I Like To (Live)				
			1983			3.00
Columbia 04111	PS	Dr. Heckyll & Mr. Jive/I Like To (Live)				
			1983			3.00
Columbia 04111	PS	Dr. Heckyll & Mr. Jive	1983		2.50	5.00
"Demonstration -- Not for Sale" on rear						
Columbia 04929		Everything I Need/Sail to You	1985			3.00
Columbia 04929	PS	Everything I Need/Sail to You	1985			3.00
Columbia 04929	PS	Everything I Need	1985		2.50	5.00
"Demonstration -- Not for Sale" on rear						
Columbia 05454		Maria/Snakes and Ladders	1985			3.00
Columbia 05454	PS	Maria/Snakes and Ladders	1985			3.00
Columbia 05649		Hard Luck Story/Snakes and Ladders				
			1985			3.00

12-Inch Singles

Label, Number		Title	Year	VG	VG+	NM
Columbia (no #)	DJ	Who Can It Be Now? (same on both sides)				
			1982	3.00	6.00	12.00
Columbia AS 1608	DJ	Be Good Johnny (same on both sides)				
			1983	2.00	4.00	8.00
Columbia AS 1634	DJ	Overkill (same on both sides)	1983	2.00	4.00	8.00
Columbia AS 1749	DJ	Dr. Heckyll & Mr. Jive/Upstairs at My House (Live)/				
		I Like To(Live)	1983	2.00	4.00	8.00
Columbia CAS 2073	DJ	Everything I Need (same on both sides)				
			1985	2.00	4.00	8.00
Columbia CAS 2152	DJ	Maria (same on both sides)	1985		3.00	6.00
Columbia CAS 2189	DJ	Hard Luck Story/Hard Luck Story (Single Version)				
			1985	2.50	5.00	10.00
Columbia 03977		It's a Mistake//Who Can It Be Now/F19				
			1983	3.00	6.00	12.00
Columbia 05216		Everything I Need (extended)/Everything I Need (7")				
			1985	2.00	4.00	8.00

Men Without Hats

Canadian synth-pop group.

Vinyl Albums

Label, Number		Title	Year	VG	VG+	NM
Backstreet 5436		Rhythm of Youth	1983	2.50	5.00	10.00
Reissue						
Backstreet 39002		Rhythm of Youth	1983	3.00	6.00	12.00
MCA 5487		Folk of the 80's, Part 3	1984	2.50	5.00	10.00
Mercury 842 000-1		In the 21st Century	1989	2.50	5.00	10.00
Stiff TEES-12-01	EP	Folk of the 80's	1981	7.50	15.00	30.00
Reissue of Trend 10-inch EP						
Trend HATS-001	10	Folk of the 80's	1981	10.00	20.00	40.00
10-inch four-song EP; possibly released only in Canada						

45s

Label, Number		Title	Year	VG	VG+	NM
Backstreet 52232		The Safety Dance/Living in China				
			1983			3.00
Backstreet 52232	PS	The Safety Dance/Living in China				
			1983		2.50	5.00
A moderately tough sleeve to find.						

Label, Number		Title	Year	VG	VG+	NM
MCA 52293		I Like/Things in My Life	1983			3.00
MCA 52293	PS	I Like/Things in My Life	1983			3.00
MCA 52332		I've Got the Message/Great Ones Remember				
			1983			3.00
MCA 52460		Where Do the Boys Go?/Unsatisfaction				
			1984			3.00
Mercury 870 153-7		Moonbeam/Jenny Wore Black	1988			3.00
Mercury 870 153-7	PS	Moonbeam/Jenny Wore Black	1988			3.00
Mercury 870 432-7		Walk on Water/Lose My Way	1988			3.00
Mercury 888 859-7		Pop Goes the World/End of the World				
			1987			3.00
Mercury 888 859-7	PS	Pop Goes the World/End of the World				
			1987			3.00

12-Inch Singles

Backstreet 13969		The Safety Dance (extended)/Antarctica				
			1983	2.50	5.00	10.00
MCA L33-1164	DJ	I Got the Message (long)/I Got the Message (short)				
			1983		3.00	6.00
MCA L33-1217	DJ	Where Do the Boys Go/Where Do the Boys Go (Extended)				
			1984		3.00	6.00
MCA 23513		Where Do the Boys Go (2 versions)				
			1984	2.00	4.00	8.00
Mercury 870 153-1		Moonbeam (5 versions)	1988	2.50	5.00	10.00
Mercury 888 859-1		Pop Goes the World (4 versions)	1987	2.50	5.00	10.00
Stiff TEES-12-08		Nationale 7/Freeways	1981	3.00	6.00	12.00

Men, The

*Originally known as **The Mentally Ill**.*

Vinyl Albums

	Title	Year	VG	VG+	NM
Snat-5 2001	Hermeneutics	1981	6.25	12.50	25.00

Mental As Anything

Vinyl Albums

		Title	Year	VG	VG+	NM
A&M SP-4921		If You Leave Me, Can I Come Too?				
			1982	3.00	6.00	12.00
A&M SP-4946		Creatures of Leisure	1983	3.00	6.00	12.00
Columbia BFC 40299		Fundamental	1985	2.50	5.00	10.00
Columbia C 45367		Cyclone Raymond	1989	2.50	5.00	10.00
Columbia FC 44144		Mouth to Mouth	1988	2.50	5.00	10.00

45s

A&M 2503		Too Many Times/Let's Cook	1982			3.00
A&M 2514		If You Leave Me, Can I Come Too?/Let's Cook				
			1982			3.00
A&M 2592		Brain Brain/Not Enough	1983			3.00
Columbia 05798		Live It Up/Good Friday	1986			3.00
Columbia 05798	PS	Live It Up/Good Friday	1986			3.00
Columbia 06168		You're So Strong/Splashing	1986			3.00
Columbia 07763		Don't Tell Me Now/The Mad King				
			1988			3.00

12-Inch Singles

A&M 17234	DJ	If You Leave Me, Can I Come Too? (same on both sides)				
			1982		3.00	6.00
A&M 17247	DJ	Brain Brain (Remix)/Brain Brain (Edit)				
			1983		3.00	6.00
Columbia 05923		You're So Strong (3 versions)	1984		2.50	5.00

Label, Number		Title	Year	VG	VG+	NM

Mentally Ill, The
*Chicago punk band, later changed its name to **The Men**.*

45s

Autistic MI 1		Gacy's Place/Padded Cell/Tumor Boy				
			1979	7.50	15.00	30.00
Autistic MI 1	PS	Gacy's Place/Padded Cell/Tumor Boy				
			1979	7.50	15.00	30.00

Mercury Rev

Vinyl Albums

| Columbia C 53030 | | Yerself Is Steam | 1992 | 3.00 | 6.00 | 12.00 |

10-Inch Singles

| Columbia 74907 | | The Hum Is Coming from Her/So There | | | | |
| | | | 1993 | | 3.00 | 6.00 |

Michael, George
*Former lead singer of **Wham!** Blue-eyed soulster and international pinup boy.*

Vinyl Albums

Columbia OC 40867		Faith	1987	2.50	5.00	10.00
Columbia C 46898		Listen Without Prejudice (Volume 1)				
			1990	3.00	6.00	12.00

45s

Columbia 05888		A Different Corner/A Different Corner (instrumental)				
			1986			3.00
Columbia 05888	PS	A Different Corner/A Different Corner (instrumental)				
			1986			3.00
Columbia 07164		I Want Your Sex (Rhythm 1 Lust)/				
		I Want Your Sex (Rhythm 2 Brass in Love)				
			1987			3.00
Columbia 07164	PS	I Want Your Sex (Rhythm 1 Lust)/				
		I Want Your Sex (Rhythm 2 Brass in Love)				
			1987			3.00
Columbia 07623		Faith/Hand to Mouth	1987			*May not exist*
Columbia 07623		Faith/Faith (instrumental)	1987			3.00
Columbia 07623	PS	Faith/Faith (instrumental)	1987			3.00
Columbia 07682		Father Figure/Father Figure (instrumental)				
			1988			3.00
Columbia 07682	PS	Father Figure/Father Figure (instrumental)				
			1988			3.00
Columbia 07773		One More Try/Look At Your Hands				
			1988			3.00
Columbia 07773	PS	One More Try/Look At Your Hands				
			1988			3.00
Columbia 07941		Monkey/Monkey (instrumental)	1988			3.00
Columbia 07941	PS	Monkey/Monkey (instrumental)	1988			3.00
Columbia 08050		Kissing a Fool/Kissing a Fool (instrumental)				
			1988			3.00
Columbia 08050	PS	Kissing a Fool/Kissing a Fool (instrumental)				
			1988			3.00
Columbia 68704		A Different Corner/A Different Corner (instrumental)				
			1989			3.00
Reissue						
Columbia 73512		Praying for Time/If You Were My Woman				
			1990			3.00
Columbia 73559		Freedom/Fantasy	1990			3.00
Columbia 73663		Waiting for That Day/Mothers Pride				
			1991			3.00

Label, Number	Title	Year	VG	VG+	NM
Columbia 73799	Soul Free/Cowboys and Angels	1991			*Cassette only*
Columbia 74086	Don't Let the Sun Go Down on Me/ I Believe (When I Fall in Love It Will Be Forever)	1991			3.00
A-side: With Elton John					
Columbia 74114	Faith/Hand to Mouth	1991			3.00
Reissue					
Columbia 74115	One More Try/Look at Your Hands	1991			3.00
Reissue					
Columbia 74353	Too Funky/Crazyman Dance	1992			3.00
DreamWorks SKG 59000	Jesus to a Child/One More Try (Live Gospel Version)	1996			3.00
DreamWorks SKG 59001	Fastlove/I'm Your Man '96	1996			3.00

12-Inch Singles

Label, Number	Title	Year	VG	VG+	NM
Columbia 06814	I Want Your Sex (Monogamy Mix 13:13)/Hard Day	1987		3.00	6.00
Columbia 07466	Hard Day (Special Remix)/Hard Day (Edit)/ I Want Your Sex (Monogamy Mix)	1987	2.00	4.00	8.00
Columbia 07547	Father Figure//Love's In Need of Love Today (Live)/ Father Figure (Instrumental)	1987	2.50	5.00	10.00
Columbia 07849	Monkey (3 versions)	1988		3.00	6.00
Columbia 73584	Freedom (2 mixes)/Fantasy	1990	2.50	5.00	10.00
Columbia 74352	Too Funky (2 mixes)/Too Jazzy/Crazyman Dance	1992	2.50	5.00	10.00

Midnight Oil

Australian pop-rock group.

Vinyl Albums

Label, Number	Title	Year	VG	VG+	NM
Columbia BFC 38996	10,9,8,7,6,5,4,3,2,1	1983	3.00	6.00	12.00
Columbia BFC 39987	Red Sails in the Sunset	1984	3.00	6.00	12.00
Columbia BFC 40967	Diesel and Dust	1987	3.00	6.00	12.00
Columbia FC 40967	Diesel and Dust	1988	2.50	5.00	10.00
Reissue; "02" added to rear-cover bar code					
Columbia C 45398	Blue Sky Mining	1990	3.00	6.00	12.00
All copies on blue vinyl					

45s

Label, Number		Title	Year	VG	VG+	NM
Columbia 04349		The Power and the Passion/Tin Legs and Tin Mines	1984			3.00
Columbia 04349	PS	The Power and the Passion/Tin Legs and Tin Mines	1984			3.00
Columbia 04349	PS	The Power and the Passion	1984		2.50	5.00
"Demonstration -- Not for Sale" on rear						
Columbia 04470		Read About It/Outside World	1984			3.00
Columbia 07433		Beds Are Burning/Bullroarer	1987		2.00	4.00
With copyright notice "1987 Midnight Oil"						
Columbia 07433		Beds Are Burning/Bullroarer	1987			3.00
With copyright notice "1987 CBS Records Pty. Ltd."						
Columbia 07964		The Dead Heart/Kosciusko	1988			3.00
Columbia 07964	PS	The Dead Heart/Kosciusko	1988			3.00
Columbia 08093		Dreamworld/Progress	1988			3.00
Columbia 08093	PS	Dreamworld/Progress	1988			3.00
Columbia 73250		Blue Sky Mine/Wedding Cake Island	1990			*Cassette only*
Columbia 73336		Forgotten Years/You May Not Be Released	1990			*Cassette only*
Columbia 74933		Truganini/Drums of Heaven	1993			3.00
Columbia 77090		Outbreak of Love/Ships of Freedom	1993			3.00

Label, Number		Title	Year	VG	VG+	NM
12-Inch Singles						
Columbia AS 1746	DJ	The Power and the Passion/Read About It/U.S. Forces				
			1982	2.00	4.00	8.00
Columbia CAS 2020	DJ	Blue Sky Mine (Food On Table Mix) (same on both sides)				
			1990	2.00	4.00	8.00
Columbia CAS 2107	DJ	Best of Both Worlds (same on both sides)				
			1984	3.00	6.00	12.00
Columbia CAS 2911	DJ	Beds Are Burning (same on both sides)				
			1987	3.00	6.00	12.00
Columbia 04238		The Power and the Passion/Glitch Baby Glitch				
			1983	2.50	5.00	10.00
Columbia 04976		The Power and the Passion/Glitch Baby/Wedding Cake				
			1983	2.00	4.00	8.00

Mighty Joe Young

Grunge-rockers. This is <u>not</u> early **Stone Temple Pilots.**

45s						
Powerhaus MJ 004		(There'll Be Other Girls) Hoss/Chump				
			1989	3.75	7.50	15.00
1,000 copies were pressed						
Powerhaus MJ 004	PS	(There'll Be Other Girls) Hoss/Chump				
			1989	62.50	125.00	250.00

Only 25 came with picture sleeves; value is conjecture

Mighty Lemon Drops, The

British pop-rock group.

Vinyl Albums		Title	Year	VG	VG+	NM
Reprise 26017		Laughter	1989	2.50	5.00	10.00
Sire 25532		The Mighty Lemon Drops	1986	2.50	5.00	10.00
Sire 25595		Out of Hand	1987	2.50	5.00	10.00
Sire 25788		Happy Head	1988	2.50	5.00	10.00
45s						
Sire 27906		Inside Out/Head on the Block	1988			3.00
12-Inch Singles						
Sire PRO-A-2639	DJ	My Biggest Thrill (same on both sides)				
			1986		2.50	5.00
Sire PRO-A-2791	DJ	Out of Hand (Extended)/Out of Hand (LP Version)				
			1987		2.50	5.00
Sire PRO-A-2963	DJ	Inside Out (12")/Inside Out (7")	1988		2.50	5.00
Sire PRO-A-3103	DJ	Fall Down (Remix)/Inside Out (Live)/Mighty Lemon Talk				
			1988		2.50	5.00
Sire PRO-A-3751	DJ	Into the Heart of Love (LP)/Into the Heart of Love (Edit)				
			1989		2.50	5.00

Mighty Mighty Bosstones

Boston-based ska-rock band.

Vinyl Albums		Title	Year	VG	VG+	NM
Taang! 44		Devils Night Out	1991	3.75	7.50	15.00
Taang! 49		More Noise & Other Disturbances				
			1991	3.75	7.50	15.00
45s						
Mercury 858 894-7		Detroit Rock City/Detroit Rock City				
			1994		2.00	4.00
B-side by Kiss; small center hole; green vinyl						
Mercury 858 894-7	PS	Detroit Rock City/Detroit Rock City				
			1994		2.00	4.00

Label, Number		Title	Year	VG	VG+	NM
12-Inch Singles						
Mercury 1156	DJ	Kinder Words/Chocolate Pudding/Pirate Ship				
			1994	2.50	5.00	10.00

Ministry
Chicago techno-rock group.

Label, Number		Title	Year	VG	VG+	NM
Vinyl Albums						
Arista AL 6608		With Sympathy	1983	3.50	7.00	14.00
Arista AL6 8016		With Sympathy	198?	2.50	5.00	10.00
Reissue						
Sire 25309		Twitch	1986	2.50	5.00	10.00
Sire 25799		The Land of Rape and Honey	1988	2.50	5.00	10.00
Sire 26004		The Mind Is a Terrible Thing to Taste				
			1989	2.50	5.00	10.00
Warner Bros. 45838		Filth Pig	1996	2.50	5.00	10.00
Wax Trax! 035		Twelve Inch Singles 1981-84	1985	3.75	7.50	15.00
45s						
Arista 9021		Revenge/She's Got a Cause	1983		3.00	6.00
Arista 9068		I Wanted to Tell Her/A Walk in the Park				
			1983		3.00	6.00
12-Inch Singles						
Arista CP 726		Work for Love (3 mixes)	1983	3.75	7.50	15.00
Arista 9037		Work for Love/For Love	1983	3.75	7.50	15.00
Arista 9062		Revenge/Effigy/I Wanted to Tell Her				
			1983	3.75	7.50	15.00
Arista 9102		I Wanted to Tell Her (Tongue Tied Mix)/I Wanted to Tell Her				
			1983	3.75	7.50	15.00
Sire PRO-A-3322	DJ	Stigmata/Tonight We Murder	1988	3.00	6.00	12.00
Sire 20401		Over the Shoulder/Isle of Man (Version 2)/Twitch (Version 2)				
			1986	2.00	4.00	8.00
Sire 21113		Stigmata/Tonight We Murder	1988	2.50	5.00	10.00
Sire 21384		Burning Inside/Thieves/Smothered Hope				
			1989	2.50	5.00	10.00
Sire 40211		Jesus Built My Hot Rod (2 mixes)/TV Song				
			1991	2.50	5.00	10.00
Wax Trax! 003		Cold Life/Cold Life (Dub)/I'm Falling/Primental				
			1985	3.00	6.00	12.00
Wax Trax! 007		Every Day (Is Halloween)/All Day				
			198?	3.00	6.00	12.00
Wax Trax! 009		Nature of Love/Nature of Love (Cruelty Mix)				
			1985	2.00	4.00	8.00
Wax Trax! 020		Halloween (Remix)/Nature of Outtakes				
			1985	2.50	5.00	10.00
Wax Trax! 110072X		I'm Falling/Cold Life/Primental	1982	3.75	7.50	15.00

Mink DeVille
*American power-pop band, featuring **Willy DeVille**.*

Label, Number	Title	Year	VG	VG+	NM
Vinyl Albums					
Atlantic SD 19311	Coup De Grace	1981	3.00	6.00	12.00
Atlantic 80115	Where Angels Fear to Tread	1983	2.50	5.00	10.00
Atlantic 81623	Sportin' Life	1985	2.00	4.00	8.00
Capitol ST-11631	Mink DeVille	1977	3.00	6.00	12.00
Capitol SW-11780	Return to Magenta	1978	3.00	6.00	12.00
Capitol ST-11955	Le Chat Bleu	1980	3.00	6.00	12.00
Capitol SN-16281	Savoir Faire	1982	2.00	4.00	8.00
Budget-line reissue of self-titled album					
Capitol SN-16282	Return to Magenta	1982	2.00	4.00	8.00
Budget-line reissue					

Label, Number		Title	Year	VG	VG+	NM
45s						
Atlantic 3864		You Better Move On/She Was Made in Heaven				
			1981			3.00
Atlantic 3880		Maybe Tomorrow	1981		2.00	4.00
Atlantic 89443		Italian Shoes	1986			3.00
Atlantic 89470		I Must Be Dreaming/In the Heart of the City				
			1985			3.00
Atlantic 89682		Pick Up the Pieces/Demasiado Corazon				
			1983			3.00
Atlantic 89750		Each Word's a Beat of My Heart/River of Tears				
			1983			3.00
Capitol 4461		Mixed-Up, Shook-Up Girl/Spanish Stroll				
			1977		2.00	4.00
Capitol 4510		Little Girl/Cadillac Walk	1977		2.00	4.00
Capitol 4607		Guardian Angel/Easy Slider	1978		2.00	4.00
Capitol 4938		Lipstick Traces/Just to Walk That Little Girl Home				
			1980		2.00	4.00
12-Inch Singles						
Atlantic 402	DJ	You Better Move On/Just Give Me One Good Reason				
			1981	2.00	4.00	8.00
Atlantic 412	DJ	Maybe Tomorrow/Maybe Tomorrow (Live)				
			1981	2.00	4.00	8.00
Atlantic 551	DJ	Each Word's a Beat of My Heart/Are You Lonely Tonight				
			1983	2.00	4.00	8.00
Atlantic 598	DJ	Pick Up the Pieces/Demasiado Corazon/Lily's Daddy				
			1983	2.00	4.00	8.00

Minor Threat

Washington, D.C. hardcore band; mutated into **Fugazi.**

Vinyl Albums						
Dischord 10		Out of Step	1983	12.50	25.00	50.00
First stock pressing, black back cover with lyrics						
Dischord 10		Out of Step	1983	5.00	10.00	20.00
Dischord 10	DJ	Out of Step	1983	125.00	250.00	500.00
Test pressing of 50; black silkscreen cover with sheep logo; paste-on back cover; blank labels; plain innersleeve with rubber stamp. Value is negotiable.						
Dischord 12		Minor Threat	1984	3.75	7.50	15.00

7-Inch Extended Play Singles						
Dischord 3		Filler/I Don't Wanna Hear It/Seeing Red/Straight Edge// Small Man, Big Mouth/Screaming at a Wall/Bottled Violence/ Minor Threat	1981	8.75	17.50	35.00
First pressing of 1000: Yellow label						
Dischord 3		Filler/I Don't Wanna Hear It/Seeing Red/Straight Edge// Small Man, Big Mouth/Screaming at a Wall/Bottled Violence/ Minor Threat	1981	8.75	17.50	35.00
Second pressing of 1000: Blue label						
Dischord 3		Filler/I Don't Wanna Hear It/Seeing Red/Straight Edge// Small Man, Big Mouth/Screaming at a Wall/Bottled Violence/ Minor Threat	1981	7.50	15.00	30.00
Third and fourth pressings: Silver label						
Dischord 3	PS	Minor Threat	1981	8.75	17.50	35.00
First pressing of 1000: Red cover						
Dischord 3	PS	Minor Threat	1981	8.75	17.50	35.00
Second pressing of 1000: Yellow cover						
Dischord 3	PS	Minor Threat	1981	8.75	17.50	35.00
Third pressing of 1000: Green cover						
Dischord 3	PS	Minor Threat	1981	7.50	15.00	30.00
Fourth pressing of 2000: Blue cover						

Label, Number		Title	Year	VG	VG+	NM
Dischord 5		In My Eyes/Out of Step//Guilty of Being White/Steppin' Stone				
			1981	8.75	17.50	35.00
First pressing of 1000: Red vinyl						
Dischord 5		In My Eyes/Out of Step//Guilty of Being White/Steppin' Stone				
			1981	8.75	17.50	35.00
Black vinyl, yellow label						
Dischord 5		In My Eyes/Out of Step//Guilty of Being White/Steppin' Stone				
			1981	7.50	15.00	30.00
Black vinyl, blue label						
Dischord 5	PS	In My Eyes/Out of Step//Guilty of Being White/Steppin' Stone				
			1981	11.25	22.50	45.00
First 125 issued with photocopied cover						
Dischord 5	PS	In My Eyes/Out of Step//Guilty of Being White/Steppin' Stone				
			1981	8.75	17.50	35.00
Printed, as opposed to photocopied, sleeve						
Dischord 5	PS	In My Eyes/Out of Step//Guilty of Being White/Steppin' Stone				
			1981	7.50	15.00	30.00
Heavy cover stock, as opposed to thinner paper stock						

45s

Dischord 15		Salad Days/Stumped/Good Guys	1985		2.50	5.00
Dischord 15	PS	Salad Days/Stumped/Good Guys	1985		2.50	5.00

Minutemen

*Punk band from San Pedro, California. Member **Mike Watt** also recorded solo and was in splinter group* **fIREHOSE.**

Vinyl Albums

New Alliance 017		The Politics of Time	1984	3.00	6.00	12.00
SST 004		The Punch Line	1981	5.00	10.00	20.00
Original copies have white labels						
SST 004		The Punch Line	1981	3.00	6.00	12.00
SST 014		What Makes a Man Start Fires?	1983	2.50	5.00	10.00
SST 014		What Makes a Man Start Fires?	1983	3.75	7.50	15.00
Original version has yellow labels and no UPC code						
SST 016	EP	Buzz or Howl Under the Influence of Heat				
			1983	2.50	5.00	10.00
SST PSST E28	DJ	Excerpts from Double Nickels on the Dime				
			1984	6.25	12.50	25.00
One-sided promo LP with etched B-side and sticker on blank cover						
SST 028	(2)	Double Nickels on the Dime	1984	3.00	6.00	12.00
SST 034	EP	Project Mersh	1985	2.50	5.00	10.00
SST 058		3-Way Tie (For Last)	1985	3.00	6.00	12.00
SST 068	(2)	Ballot Result	1987	3.00	6.00	12.00
SST 277		The Politics of Time	198?	2.50	5.00	10.00
Reissue of New Alliance 017						

7-Inch Extended Play Singles

Reflex #L		Tour-Spiel	1984	3.00	6.25	12.50
Reflex #L	PS	Tour-Spiel	1984	3.00	6.25	12.50
SST 002		Paranoid Time	1980		3.00	6.00
SST 002	PS	Paranoid Time	1980		3.00	6.00
Thermidor 8		Bean-Spill	1981	2.00	4.00	8.00
Came in generic Thermidor sleeve (add 25%)						

45s

New Alliance 004		Joy/Black Sheep//More Joy	1981		3.00	6.00
New Alliance 004	PS	Joy/Black Sheep//More Joy	1981		3.00	6.00
SST PSST E58		Courage/What Is It?/Stories	1985	2.00	4.00	8.00
SST PSST E58	PS	Courage/What Is It?/Stories	1985	3.00	6.00	12.00
Rubberstamped sleeve						
SST 214		Joy/Black Sheep//More Joy	199?			2.00
Reissue of New Alliance 004						
SST 214	PS	Joy/Black Sheep//More Joy	199?			2.00

Label, Number		Title	Year	VG	VG+	NM

Misfits, The

*Legendary punk band featuring **Glenn Danzig**. <u>Warning</u>: Almost all the Misfits' singles have been counter-feited because of their collectibility. When in doubt, check with a reputable dealer in alternative/punk music.*

Vinyl Albums

Label, Number		Title	Year	VG	VG+	NM
Caroline 7511		Static Age	1995	3.00	6.00	12.00
Caroline 7515		Collection II	1995	3.00	6.00	12.00
Plan 9 PL9-02		Earth A.D.	1983	12.50	25.00	50.00
100 on green vinyl						
Plan 9 PL9-02		Earth A.D.	1983	6.25	12.50	25.00
200 on clear vinyl						
Plan 9 PL9-02		Earth A.D.	1983	6.25	12.50	25.00
200 on yellow vinyl						
Plan 9 PL9-02		Earth A.D.	1983	6.25	12.50	25.00
200 on purple vinyl						
Plan 9 PL9-02		Earth A.D.	1983	3.00	6.00	12.00
At least 10,000 on black vinyl (distributed by Caroline)						
Plan 9 PL9-03	EP	Die, Die My Darling	1984	6.25	12.50	25.00
500 on purple vinyl						
Plan 9 PL9-03	EP	Die, Die My Darling	1984	6.25	12.50	25.00
500 on white vinyl (distributed by Caroline)						
Plan 9 PL9-03	EP	Die, Die My Darling	1984	3.00	6.00	12.00
Common issue on black vinyl (distributed by Caroline)						
Plan 9 PL9-06		Legacy of Brutality	1986	25.00	50.00	100.00
16 (!!) on pink vinyl						
Plan 9 PL9-06		Legacy of Brutality	1986	6.25	12.50	25.00
500 on white vinyl						
Plan 9 PL9-06		Legacy of Brutality	1986	6.25	12.50	25.00
500 on red vinyl						
Plan 9 PL9-06		Legacy of Brutality	1986	3.00	6.00	12.00
Common issue on black vinyl (distributed by Caroline)						
Plan 9 PL9-08	EP	Evilive	1987	6.25	12.50	25.00
2,000 on green vinyl						
Plan 9 PL9-08	EP	Evilive	1987	3.00	6.00	12.00
Common issue on black vinyl (distributed by Caroline)						
Plan 9 PL9-09		Misfits	1988	3.00	6.00	12.00
Ruby/Slash JRR 804		Walk Among Us	1982	12.50	25.00	50.00
Original red cover; has custom innersleeve and insert						
Ruby/Slash JRR 804		Walk Among Us	1982	12.50	25.00	50.00
Purple cover with innersleeve and insert						
Slash 25756		Walk Among Us	1988	3.00	6.00	12.00
Reissue of JRR 804						

7-Inch Extended Play Singles

Label, Number		Title	Year	VG	VG+	NM
Plan 9 PL 1019		Evilive	1982	12.50	25.00	50.00
Yellow label						
Plan 9 PL 1019		Evilive	1982	10.00	20.00	40.00
Orange label						
Plan 9 PL 1019	PS	Evilive	1982	18.75	37.50	75.00
Numbered sleeves (800 were made)						
Plan 9 PL 1019	PS	Evilive	1982	10.00	20.00	40.00
Unnumbered sleeves (1,400)						
Plan 9 PL 1019	(3)	Evilive	1982	87.50	175.00	350.00
33 sets of 3 each with individual sleeves of the three band members, available through the Fiend Club (fan club)						

45s

Label, Number		Title	Year	VG	VG+	NM
Blank A 101		Cough Cool/She	1977	37.50	75.00	150.00
500 copies were pressed						
Blank A 101	PS	Cough Cool/She	1977	37.50	75.00	150.00
Plan 9 PL 1001		Bullet/We Are 138/Attitude/Hollywood Babylon				
			1978	25.00	50.00	100.00
8,000 on black vinyl						
Plan 9 PL 1001		Bullet/We Are 138/Attitude/Hollywood Babylon				
			1978	31.25	62.50	125.00
2,000 on red vinyl						

Label, Number		Title	Year	VG	VG+	NM
Plan 9 PL 1001	PS	Bullet/We Are 138/Attitude/Hollywood Babylon	1978	10.00	20.00	125.00
First edition with gatefold and lyric sheet						
Plan 9 PL 1001	PS	Bullet/We Are 138/Attitude/Hollywood Babylon	1978	31.25	62.50	125.00
Second edition with new back cover "Better Dead in Red"						
Plan 9 PL 1009		Horror Business/Teenagers from Mars/Children in Heat	1979	15.00	30.00	60.00
5,000 on yellow vinyl						
Plan 9 PL 1009		Horror Business/Teenagers from Mars/Children in Heat	1979	50.00	100.00	200.00
25 (!!) on black vinyl; value is conjecture						
Plan 9 PL 1009	PS	Horror Business/Teenagers from Mars/Children in Heat	1979	25.00	50.00	100.00
With insert						
Plan 9 PL 1009	PS	Horror Business/Teenagers from Mars/Children in Heat	1979	15.00	30.00	60.00
Without insert						
Plan 9 PL 1010		Night of the Living Dead/Where Eagles Dare/Ratt Fink	1979	12.50	25.00	50.00
Plan 9 PL 1010	PS	Night of the Living Dead/Where Eagles Dare/Ratt Fink	1979	12.50	25.00	50.00
Plan 9 PL 1013		London Dungeon/Horror Hotel/Ghouls Night Out	1981	12.50	25.00	50.00
3,000 with gray label						
Plan 9 PL 1013		London Dungeon/Horror Hotel/Ghouls Night Out	1981	12.50	25.00	50.00
7,000 with orange label						
Plan 9 PL 1013		London Dungeon/Horror Hotel/Ghouls Night Out	1981	12.50	25.00	50.00
Second pressing: 400 on white vinyl						
Plan 9 PL 1013		London Dungeon/Horror Hotel/Ghouls Night Out	1981	12.50	25.00	50.00
Second pressing: 400 on black vinyl						
Plan 9 PL 1013	PS	3 Hits from Hell: London Dungeon/Horror Hotel/Ghouls Night Out	1981	12.50	25.00	50.00
Plan 9 PL 1017		Halloween I/Halloween II	1981	10.00	20.00	40.00
Plan 9 PL 1017	PS	Halloween I/Halloween II	1981	8.75	17.50	35.00
Without lyric sheet						
Plan 9 PL 1017	PS	Halloween I/Halloween II	1981	10.00	20.00	40.00
With lyric sheet						

Misfits, The (Different group)

Upstate New York punk band, changed its name to The Tragics to prevent confusion with the better-known outfit above.

45s

Black & White (no #)		Pretty Boy/Laughing Lover/Mommi I'm a Misfit/ When I Was Young	1982	12.50	25.00	50.00
Black & White (no #)	PS	Pretty Boy/Laughing Lover/Mommi I'm a Misfit/ When I Was Young	1982	12.50	25.00	50.00

Most picture sleeves have a sticker with the band's new name, The Tragics

Missing Persons

*Los Angeles pop/new wave band. Dale Bozzio, lead singer, later recorded under the name **Dale**.*

Vinyl Albums

Capitol ST-12228		Spring Session M	1982	3.00	6.00	12.00
Capitol ST-12315		Rhyme & Reason	1984	2.50	5.00	10.00
Capitol ST-12465		Color in Your Life	1986	2.50	5.00	10.00
Capitol MLP-15001	EP	Missing Persons	1982	3.00	6.00	12.00

Label, Number		Title	Year	VG	VG+	NM
Capitol SN-16359		Rhyme & Reason	1985	2.00	4.00	8.00
Budget-line reissue						
Capitol SN-16460		Spring Session M	1987	2.00	4.00	8.00
Budget-line reissue						

7-Inch Extended Play Singles

Label, Number		Title	Year	VG	VG+	NM
Komos (# unknown)		I Like Boys	1980	6.25	12.50	25.00
Komos (# unknown)	PS	I Like Boys	1980	6.25	12.50	25.00

45s

Label, Number		Title	Year	VG	VG+	NM
American Pie 9036		Words/Wildflower	198?			3.00
Reissue; B-side by Skylark						
Capitol 5127		Words/Hello, I Love You	1982			3.00
Capitol 5127	PS	Words/Hello, I Love You	1982			3.00
Capitol 5161		Destination Unknown/No Way Out	1982			3.00
Capitol 5161	PS	Destination Unknown/No Way Out	1982			3.00
Capitol 5200		Windows/Rock And Roll Suspension	1983			3.00
Capitol 5200	PS	Windows/Rock And Roll Suspension	1983			3.00
Capitol 5212		Walking in L.A./Mental Hopscotch	1983			3.00
Capitol 5326		Give/Clandestine People	1984			3.00
Capitol 5326	PS	Give/Clandestine People	1984			3.00
Capitol 5358		Right Now/Racing Against Time	1984			3.00
Capitol 5381		Surrender Your Heart/All Fall Down	1985			3.00
Capitol 5381	PS	Surrender Your Heart/All Fall Down	1985			3.00
Capitol S7-18874		Destination Unknown/Windows	1995			3.00
Reissue						

12-Inch Singles

Label, Number		Title	Year	VG	VG+	NM
Capitol 8582		Give (dance mix)/Clandestine People	1984	2.50	5.00	10.00
Capitol SPRO 9081/2	DJ	Give (Long)/Give (Short)	1984	3.75	7.50	15.00
Capitol SPRO 9123	DJ	Right Now (same on both sides)	1984	2.50	5.00	10.00
Capitol SPRO 9187	DJ	Surrender Your Heart (same on both sides)	1984		3.00	6.00
Capitol SPRO 9721	DJ	I Can't Think About Dancing (Extended)/ I Can't Think About Dancing	1986	2.00	4.00	8.00
Capitol SPRO 9837/8	DJ	Destination Unknown/Walking in L.A.	1982	5.00	10.00	20.00
Capitol SPRO 9853	DJ	Color in Your Life/Go Against the Flow	1986	2.00	4.00	8.00
Capitol SPRO 9885	DJ	Windows (same on both sides)	1982	2.50	5.00	10.00
Capitol 15233		I Can't Think About Dancing (3 versions)/Face to Face	1988		3.00	6.00

Mr. Bungle

*Side project by a former member of **Faith No More**.*

Vinyl Albums

Label, Number		Title	Year	VG	VG+	NM
Warner Bros. 45963		Disco Volante	1995	2.50	5.00	10.00
Originals have bonus 7-inch single (listed separately)						

45s

Label, Number		Title	Year	VG	VG+	NM
Warner Bros. PRO-S-5452	DJ	Sudden Death/Ballrooms of Mars	1991	6.25	12.50	25.00

"Soil Samples #6" on gray vinyl; B-side by the Flaming Lips

Label, Number		Title	Year	VG	VG+	NM
Warner Bros. PRO-S-7829	DJ	Platypus/The Legendary Paper Project by the Secret Chiefs Trio				
			1995			3.00
Bonus 45 with LP "Disco Volante"						

Mr. Epp and the Calculations
*With Mark Arm, pre-**Green River** and **Mudhoney**.*

7-Inch Extended Play Singles
Pravda 711		Of Course I'm Happy	1982	7.50	15.00	30.00
Pravda 711	PS	Of Course I'm Happy	1982	7.50	15.00	30.00

Moby
Techno-rave composer and DJ.

12-Inch Singles
Elektra 5695	DJ	Hymn (4 remixes)	1995	2.00	4.00	8.00
Elektra 5725	(2) DJ	Everytime You Touch Me (8 versions)				
			1995	6.25	12.50	25.00
Promo-only two-record set						
Elektra 66180		Feeling So Real (4 versions)/				
		Everytime You Touch Me (Remix Parts)				
			1995		3.00	6.00
Instinct 240		Drop a Beat (2 mixes)/Electricity	1994	2.00	4.00	8.00

Models, The
Australian pop-rock group.

Vinyl Albums
Geffen GHS 24100		Out of Mind Out of Sight	1986	3.00	6.00	12.00
Windsong BXL1-3642		Yes With My Body	1980	3.00	6.00	12.00

45s
Geffen 28644		Cold Fever/Preacher from the Black Lagoon/				
		Out of Mind, Out of Sight	1986			3.00
Geffen 28762		Out of Mind, Out of Sight/Down in the Garden				
			1986			3.00
Geffen 28762	PS	Out of Mind, Out of Sight/Down in the Garden				
			1986			3.00
Windsong CB-12046		Yes With My Body/What a Lovin' Man				
			1980		2.00	4.00

12-Inch Singles
Geffen PRO-A-2421	DJ	Out of Mind Out of Sight (long)/Out of Mind Out of Sight (short)				
			1985	2.00	4.00	8.00
Geffen PRO-A-2521	DJ	Cold Fever/Cold Fever (Extended)				
			1986	2.00	4.00	8.00
Geffen 20434		Cold Fever (extended)/Out of Mind Out of Sight (Live)/				
		Hear Motion (Extended)/Preacher from the Black Lagoon				
			1986	2.50	5.00	10.00
Geffen 20435		Out of Mind, Out of Sight/Seeing Is Believing/Tropic of Cancer				
			1985		3.00	6.00

Modern English
English new wave/synth-rock group.

Vinyl Albums
Sire 23821		After the Snow	1982	2.50	5.00	10.00
Sire 25066		Ricochet Days	1984	2.50	5.00	10.00
Sire 25343		Stop Start	1986	2.50	5.00	10.00

Label, Number		Title	Year	VG	VG+	NM
45s						
Sire 28741		Ink and Paper/Love Forever	1986			3.00
Sire 29339		Hands Across the Sea/Reflection	1984			3.00
Sire 29598		Carry Me Down/Someone's Calling				
			1983			3.00
Sire 29775		I Melt with You/After the Snow	1983		2.50	5.00
12-Inch Singles						
Sire PRO-A-2035	DJ	Someone's Calling (Edit)/Carry Me Down (Edit)				
			1983	2.00	4.00	8.00
Sire PRO-A-2429	DJ	Ink and Paper (same on both sides)				
			1986	2.50	5.00	10.00
Sire 29836		I Melt with You/Someone's Calling/Life in the Glasshouse				
			1982	3.00	6.00	12.00

Monkeywrench

45s						
Sub Pop 139		Bottle Up and Go/Cold Cold World (No Organ) & Out				
			1992	3.75	7.50	15.00
Clear red vinyl						
Sub Pop 139		Bottle Up and Go/Cold Cold World (No Organ) & Out				
			1992		2.50	5.00
Sub Pop 139	PS	Bottle Up and Go/Cold Cold World (No Organ) & Out				
			1992		2.50	5.00

Mono Men

7-Inch Extended Play Singles						
Estrus ES 718		Booze	1991	10.00	20.00	40.00
Any color vinyl other than green or black						
Estrus ES 718		Booze	1991	7.50	15.00	30.00
Green vinyl						
Estrus ES 718		Booze	1991		2.50	5.00
Estrus ES 718	PS	Booze	1991	2.50	5.00	10.00
Sympathy For The Record		Took That Thing	1992		3.75	7.50
Industry 164						
Sympathy For The Record	PS	Took That Thing	1992		3.75	7.50
Industry 164						
45s						
Estrus ES 71		Burning Bush/Rat Fink	1989	6.75	13.75	27.50
Gold vinyl						
Estrus ES 71		Burning Bush/Rat Fink	1989		3.75	7.50
Estrus ES 71	PS	Burning Bush/Rat Fink	1989		3.75	7.50
Estrus ES 74		I Don't Care/Jezebel	1990	5.00	10.00	20.00
Green vinyl						
Estrus ES 74		I Don't Care/Jezebel	1990	3.75	7.50	15.00
Purple vinyl						
Estrus ES 74		I Don't Care/Jezebel	1990	2.50	5.00	10.00
Estrus ES 74	PS	I Don't Care/Jezebel	1990	3.75	7.50	15.00
Purple and gold sleeve						
Estrus ES 74	PS	I Don't Care/Jezebel	1990	3.75	7.50	15.00
Three-color sleeve						
Estrus ES 74	PS	I Don't Care/Jezebel	1990		2.50	5.00
Black and gold sleeve						
Estrus ES 74	DJ	I Don't Care/Jezebel	1990	7.50	15.00	30.00
Promos on black vinyl, no picture sleeve						
Lucky LK 004		Don't Know Yet//Lie Detector/Jack the Ripper				
			199?		2.00	4.00
Lucky LK 004	PS	Don't Know Yet//Lie Detector/Jack the Ripper				
			199?		2.00	4.00
Rekkids (no #)		He's Waiting/Boss Hoss	1992		3.75	7.50

Label, Number		Title	Year	VG	VG+	NM
Rekkids (no #)	PS	He's Waiting/Boss Hoss	1992		3.75	7.50
Rise RR 72		I'm Hangin'/Teen Dogs in Trouble	199?	3.00	6.25	12.50
Rise RR 72	PS	I'm Hangin'/Teen Dogs in Trouble	199?	3.00	6.25	12.50
Wrap-around silk-screen sleeve						
Sub Pop 159		Skin and Bones/Comanche	1992	3.00	6.25	12.50
Bright blue vinyl						
Sub Pop 159	PS	Skin and Bones/Comanche	1992	3.00	6.25	12.50
#47 in Sub Pop Singles Club series						

Monochrome Set

British punk/new wave band.

45s

I.R.S. 9002		Alphaville/He's Frank	1979	3.00	6.25	12.50
I.R.S. 9002	PS	Alphaville/He's Frank	1979	3.00	6.25	12.50

Monster Magnet

Rockers from Red Bank, New Jersey.

45s

A&M MM 1	DJ	Cage Around the Sun/Superjudge	1993		3.75	7.50
Sky blue vinyl						
A&M MM 1	PS	Cage Around the Sun/Superjudge	1993		3.75	7.50
Circuit CIRCA 7001		Lizard Johnny/Freak Shop USA	1989	13.75	27.50	55.00
Red vinyl						
Circuit CIRCA 7001		Lizard Johnny/Freak Shop USA	1989	5.00	10.00	20.00
Circuit CIRCA 7001	PS	Lizard Johnny/Freak Shop USA	1989	5.00	10.00	20.00
Primo Scree SCREE 2		Murder/Tractor	1990	9.25	18.75	37.50
Green vinyl						
Primo Scree SCREE 2		Murder/Tractor	1990	3.00	6.25	12.50
Primo Scree SCREE 2	DJ	Murder/Tractor	1990	5.50	11.25	22.50
Primo Scree SCREE 2	PS	Murder/Tractor	1990	3.00	6.25	12.50

Moore, Thurston

Of Sonic Youth.

Vinyl Albums

	Title	Year	VG	VG+	NM
DGC 24810	Psychic Hearts	1995	2.50	5.00	10.00

Morissette, Alanis

Canadian alterna-punk singer. Had two pop albums on MCA Canada (neither on vinyl) that gave her the nickname of "The Canadian Debbie Gibson"!

45s

	Title	Year	VG	VG+	NM
Maverick 17698	Ironic/Forgiven (Live)	1996			3.00

Morrissey

*Former brooding lead singer of **The Smiths**.*

Vinyl Albums

	Title	Year	VG	VG+	NM
Sire 25699	Viva Hate	1988	3.00	6.00	12.00
Sire R 153729	Viva Hate	1988	4.00	8.00	16.00
BMG Direct Marketing edition					

Label, Number		Title	Year	VG	VG+	NM
45s						
Sire 18789		Tomorrow	1993		*Cassette only*	
Sire 27837		Everyday Is Like Sunday/Disappointed				
			1988		2.50	5.00
Sire 27907		Suedehead/I Know Very Well How I Got My Name				
			1988		2.50	5.00
12-Inch Singles						
Sire 20877		Suedehead/I Know Very Well.../Hairdresser on Fire				
			1988	3.00	6.00	12.00
Sire 20986		Everyday Is Like Sunday/Sister I'm a Poet/Disappointed/				
		I Never Will Marry	1988	3.75	7.50	15.00
Sire 21163		The Last of the Famous International Playboys/Lucky Lisp/				
		Michael Bones	1989	3.75	7.50	15.00
Sire 21232		Interesting Drug/Such a Little Thing.../Sweet and Tender...				
			1989	3.00	6.00	12.00
Sire 21424		Ouija Board, Ouija Board/Yes, I Am Blind/East West				
			1989	3.00	6.00	12.00
Sire 21529		November Spawned a Monster/He Knows I'd Love to See Him/				
		Girl Least Likely To	1990	2.50	5.00	10.00
Sire 40043		Our Frank/Journalists Who Lie/Tony the Pony				
			1991	2.50	5.00	10.00
Sire 40580		Tomorrow/Let the Right One Slip In/There Speaks a True Friend				
			1992	2.50	5.00	10.00

Motels, The

*California pop-new wave band, with lead singer **Martha Davis**.*

Label, Number		Title	Year	VG	VG+	NM
Vinyl Albums						
Capitol ST-11996		The Motels	1979	2.50	5.00	10.00
Capitol ST-12070		Careful	1980	2.50	5.00	10.00
Capitol ST-12177		All Four One	1982	2.50	5.00	10.00
Capitol ST-12177	DJ	All Four One	1982	3.75	7.50	15.00
Promo-only high-grade vinyl pressing (different front cover)						
Capitol ST-12288		Little Robbers	1983	2.50	5.00	10.00
Capitol SJ-12378		Shock	1985	2.50	5.00	10.00
Capitol SN-16343		The Motels	1985	2.00	4.00	8.00
Budget-line reissue						
Capitol SN-16347		Careful	1985	2.00	4.00	8.00
Budget-line reissue						
Capitol SN-16355		Little Robbers	1985	2.00	4.00	8.00
Budget-line reissue						
Capitol SN-16420		All Four One	198?	2.00	4.00	8.00
Budget-line reissue						
45s						
American Pie 9045		Only the Lonely/Suddenly Last Summer				
			198?			3.00
Reissue						
Capitol 4796		Total Control/Love Don't Help	1979		2.50	5.00
Capitol 4796	PS	Total Control/Love Don't Help	1979		2.50	5.00
Capitol 4896		Danger/Cry Baby	1980		2.50	5.00
Capitol 4937		Envy/Whose Problem	1980		2.50	5.00
Capitol 5114		Only the Lonely/Change My Mind				
			1982			3.00
Capitol 5114	PS	Only the Lonely/Change My Mind				
			1982		2.00	4.00
A moderately tough sleeve to find						
Capitol 5149		Take the L/Mission of Mercy	1982			3.00
Capitol 5149	PS	Take the L/Mission of Mercy	1982			3.00
Capitol 5182		Forever Mine/So L.A.	1982			3.00
Capitol 5182	PS	Forever Mine/So L.A.	1982			3.00

Label, Number		Title	Year	VG	VG+	NM
Capitol 5246		Remember the Nights/Mission of Mercy				
			1983			3.00
Capitol 5246	PS	Remember the Nights/Mission of Mercy				
			1983			3.00
Capitol 5271		Suddenly Last Summer/Some Things Never Change				
			1983			3.00
Capitol 5271	PS	Suddenly Last Summer/Some Things Never Change				
			1983			3.00
Capitol 5497		Shame/Save the Last Dance for Love				
			1985			3.00
Capitol 5497	PS	Shame/Save the Last Dance for Love				
			1985			3.00
Capitol 5529		Shock/In the Jungle (Concrete Jungle)				
			1985			3.00
Capitol 5529	PS	Shock/In the Jungle (Concrete Jungle)				
			1985			3.00

12-Inch Singles

Label, Number		Title	Year	VG	VG+	NM
Capitol SPRO 9048	DJ	Remember the Nights (same on both sides)				
			1983		3.50	7.00
Capitol SPRO 9267	DJ	Total Control/Your Place or Mine	1979	2.50	5.00	10.00
Capitol SPRO 9436	DJ	Shame/Shame (Extended Mix)	1985		3.00	6.00
Capitol SPRO 9515	DJ	Shock (same on both sides)	1985		3.00	6.00

Mother Love Bone

*Seattle grunge band formed from the wreckage of **Green River**. Just before their only full-length LP was released, lead singer Andrew Wood died.The remaining members were founding members of **Pearl Jam**.*

Vinyl Albums

Label, Number		Title	Year	VG	VG+	NM
Polydor 843 191-1		Apple	1990	12.50	25.00	50.00
Stardog 839 011-1	EP	Shine	1989	12.50	25.00	50.00
Four songs on side one, the same four songs on side two						

12-Inch Singles

Label, Number		Title	Year	VG	VG+	NM
Mercury PRO 900	DJ	Shangri La (same on both sides)	1990	5.00	10.00	20.00

Mothers of Invention, The

*See **Zappa, Frank***

Motors, The

British new wave group.

Vinyl Albums

Label, Number	Title	Year	VG	VG+	NM
Virgin VA 13139	Tenement Steps	1980	2.50	5.00	10.00
Virgin JZ 35348	Approved by the Motors	1978	2.50	5.00	10.00
Virgin PZ 34924	The Motors	1977	3.00	6.00	12.00

45s

Label, Number		Title	Year	VG	VG+	NM
Virgin ZS8 9515		Dancing the Night Away/Whiskey and Wine				
			1977		2.00	4.00
Virgin ZS8 9517		Cold Love/Phoney Heaven	1977		2.00	4.00
Virgin ZS8 9519		Airport/Mamma Rock 'N' Roller	1978		2.00	4.00
Virgin ZS8 9520		Forget About You/Breathless	1978		2.00	4.00
Virgin ZS8 9521		Today/The Hustler	1978		2.00	4.00
Virgin 67007		Love and Loneliness/Time for Makeup				
			1980			3.00
Virgin 67007	PS	Love and Loneliness/Time for Makeup				
			1980			3.00

Label, Number		Title	Year	VG	VG+	NM

Mould, Bob

*Formerly with **Husker Du**. Also see **Sugar**.*

Vinyl Albums

Label, Number		Title	Year	VG	VG+	NM
Virgin PR 3512	EP	Rust Bucket Coliseum	1990	4.50	9.00	18.00
Promo-only five-track release						
Virgin 91240		Workbook	1989	2.50	5.00	10.00
Virgin 91395		Black Sheets of Rain	1990	3.00	6.00	12.00

45s

Label, Number	Title	Year	VG	VG+	NM
Virgin 99190	See a Little Light/All Those People Know				
		1989		2.00	4.00

12-Inch Singles

Label, Number		Title	Year	VG	VG+	NM
Virgin 2685	DJ	See a Little Light (same on both sides)				
			1989		3.00	6.00
Virgin 2929	DJ	Wishing Well/If You're True + 4 live tracks				
			1989	6.25	12.50	25.00

Moving Pictures

Australian pop-rock group.

45s

Label, Number		Title	Year	VG	VG+	NM
Geffen 22859		What About Me/Joni and the Romeo				
			1989			3.00
Reissue						
Network 69952		What About Me/Joni and the Romeo				
			1982			3.00
Network 69952	PS	What About Me/Joni and the Romeo				
			1982		3.00	6.00

Not a particularly common sleeve

Moyet, Alison

*Former lead singer of **Yaz**.*

Vinyl Albums

Label, Number	Title	Year	VG	VG+	NM
Columbia BFC 39956	Alf	1985	2.50	5.00	10.00
Columbia BFC 40653	Raindancing	1987	2.50	5.00	10.00
Columbia C 47841	Hoodoo	1991	3.00	6.00	12.00

45s

Label, Number		Title	Year	VG	VG+	NM
Columbia 04781		Invisible/Hitch Hike	1985			3.00
Columbia 04781	PS	Invisible/Hitch Hike	1985			3.00
Columbia 05411		Resurrection/Baby I Do	1985			3.00
Columbia 05614		For You Only/Money Mile	1985			3.00
Columbia 05614	PS	For You Only/Money Mile	1985			3.00
Columbia 07019		Is This Love?/Blow Wind Blow	1987			3.00
Columbia 07365		Weak in the Presence of Beauty/To Work On You				
			1987			3.00

12-Inch Singles

Label, Number		Title	Year	VG	VG+	NM
Columbia AS 2029	DJ	Invisible (3:56)/Invisible (5:55)	1984	2.00	4.00	8.00
Columbia AS 2103	DJ	Love Resurrection/Love Resurrection (7")				
			1984	2.00	4.00	8.00
Columbia CAS 2177	DJ	For You Only (same on both sides)				
			1985	2.00	4.00	8.00
Columbia CAS 2679	DJ	Is This Love/Is This Love (Remix)				
			1986		3.00	6.00
Columbia CAS 4116	DJ	Hoodoo (4 versions)	1991	2.00	4.00	8.00
Columbia 05163		Invisible (Transparent Mix)/Hitch Hike				
			1984	2.00	4.00	8.00

Label, Number		Title	Year	VG	VG+	NM
Columbia 05237		Love Resurrection (Remix)/Baby I Do				
			1985	2.00	4.00	8.00
Columbia 06773		Is This Love (2 versions)/Blow Wind Blow				
			1986	2.00	4.00	8.00

Mudhoney

Seattle grunge-rockers, one of the two bands that emerged from the splintered **Green River**.

Vinyl Albums						
Reprise 45840		My Brother the Cow	1994	2.50	5.00	10.00
Sub Pop 21	EP	Superfuzz Bigmuff	1988	7.50	15.00	30.00
With poster						
Sub Pop 21	EP	Superfuzz Bigmuff	1988	5.00	10.00	20.00
Without poster						
Sub Pop 44		Mudhoney	1989	7.50	15.00	30.00
First 3,000 have gatefold sleeve and poster						
Sub Pop 44		Mudhoney	1989	5.00	10.00	20.00
Without gatefold and poster						
Sub Pop 105		Every Good Boy Deserves Fudge	1991	2.50	5.00	10.00
Sub Pop 105 PD	PD	Every Good Boy Deserves Fudge	1991	7.50	15.00	30.00
Picture disc -- limited edition of 2,500						
45s						
Amphetamine Reptile		She's Just Fifteen/Jagged Time Lapse				
SCALE 36			1991		3.75	7.50
Amphetamine Reptile		She's Just Fifteen/Jagged Time Lapse				
SCALE 36			1991	6.75	13.75	27.50
Amphetamine Reptile	PS	She's Just Fifteen/Jagged Time Lapse				
SCALE 36			1991		3.75	7.50
Fox 10012		Pump It Up/Stomp	1994		2.50	5.00
B-side by George Clinton/Parliament Funkadelic						
Fox 10012	PS	Pump It Up/Stomp	1994		2.50	5.00
B-side by George Clinton/Parliament Funkadelic						
Make 'em Bleed and Suffer		Hate the Police (Live)/Symptom of the Universe				
(no #)			1988	6.25	12.50	25.00
Make 'em Bleed and Suffer	PS	Hate the Police (Live)/Symptom of the Universe				
(no #)			1988	6.25	12.50	25.00
Reprise PRO-S-5740	DJ	Suck You Dry/Deception Pass	1992	3.75	7.50	15.00
Reprise PRO-S-6025	DJ	Blinding Sun/King Sandbox	1993	3.75	7.50	15.00
Promo-only on 1970s-style Reprise brown label						
Sub Pop 18		Touch Me I'm Sick/Sweet Young Thing				
			1988	22.50	45.00	90.00
First 800 were pressed on brown vinyl						
Sub Pop 18		Touch Me I'm Sick/Sweet Young Thing				
			1988	50.00	100.00	200.00
Any of accidental purple, red, yellow or blueish vinyl pressings						
Sub Pop 18		Touch Me I'm Sick/Sweet Young Thing				
			1988	25.00	50.00	100.00
Standard black vinyl pressing, toilet label						
Sub Pop 18		Touch Me I'm Sick/Sweet Young Thing				
			1988		3.75	7.50
Regular Sub Pop label, black vinyl						
Sub Pop 18	PS	Touch Me I'm Sick/Sweet Young Thing				
			1988		3.75	7.50
Only accompanied regular Sub Pop label pressings						
Sub Pop 26		Halloween/Touch Me I'm Sick	1988	3.75	7.50	15.00
B-side by Sonic Youth; last 2,500 on black vinyl						
Sub Pop 26		Halloween/Touch Me I'm Sick	1988	12.50	25.00	50.00
B-side by Sonic Youth; first 500 on clear vinyl						
Sub Pop 26	PS	Halloween/Touch Me I'm Sick	1988	5.00	10.00	20.00
#2 in Sub Pop Singles Club series						
Sub Pop 33		You Got It/Burn It Clean	1989	3.75	7.50	15.00
White vinyl						

Label, Number		Title	Year	VG	VG+	NM
Sub Pop 33		You Got It/Burn It Clean	1989	2.50	5.00	10.00
Sub Pop 33	PS	You Got It/Burn It Clean	1989	6.25	12.50	25.00
Foldout poster sleeve						
Sub Pop 33	PS	You Got It/Burn It Clean	1989		2.50	5.00
Regular picture sleeve						
Sub Pop 44a		This Gift/Baby Help Me Forget				
			1989		2.50	5.00
Sub Pop 44a		This Gift/Baby Help Me Forget	1989	7.50	15.00	30.00
Purple vinyl						
Sub Pop 44a	PS	This Gift/Baby Help Me Forget	1989		2.50	5.00
Sub Pop 63		Thorn/You're Gone/You Make Me Die				
			1990	5.00	10.00	20.00
First 3,000 on pink vinyl						
Sub Pop 63		Thorn/You're Gone/You Make Me Die				
			1990		2.50	5.00
Sub Pop 63	PS	Thorn/You're Gone/You Make Me Die				
			1990		2.50	5.00
Sub Pop 95		Let It Slide//Ounce of Deception/Checkout Time				
			1991	6.25	12.50	25.00
Clear chartreuse vinyl						
Sub Pop 95		Let It Slide//Ounce of Deception/Checkout Time				
			1991			3.00
Sub Pop 95	PS	Let It Slide//Ounce of Deception/Checkout Time				
			1991		2.50	5.00
Sub Pop 248		Tonight I'm Gonna Go Downtown/Blinding Sun				
			1994		3.75	7.50
B-side by Jimmie Dale Gilmore						
Sub Pop 248	PS	Tonight I'm Gonna Go Downtown/Blinding Sun				
			1994		3.75	7.50
B-side by Jimmie Dale Gilmore						

Mummies, The

Punk band.

7-Inch Extended Play Singles

			Year	VG	VG+	NM
Planet Pimp PP-002		Larry Winther and His Mummies Live at Pony Express Pizza				
			1992	2.50	5.00	10.00
Black vinyl, first pressing						
Planet Pimp PP-002		Larry Winther and His Mummies Live at Pony Express Pizza				
			1992		3.75	7.50
Gold vinyl, second pressing						
Planet Pimp PP-002	PS	Larry Winther and His Mummies Live at Pony Express Pizza				
			1992	2.50	5.00	10.00
First sleeve: Band surrounded by topless women						
Planet Pimp PP-002	PS	Larry Winther and His Mummies Live at Pony Express Pizza				
			1992		3.75	7.50
Second sleeve: Numbered edition						
Pre-B.S. 45001		That Girl	1990	9.25	18.75	37.50
Pre-B.S. 45001	PS	That Girl	1990	9.25	18.75	37.50
Rekkids 005		Greg Lowery	1989	6.25	12.50	25.00
Rekkids 005	PS	Greg Lowery	1989	6.25	12.50	25.00

45s

			Year	VG	VG+	NM
Estrus ES 79		Out of Our Tree/Tall Cool One	1991	9.25	18.75	37.50
Red vinyl						
Estrus ES 79		Out of Our Tree/Tall Cool One	1991	3.00	6.25	12.50
Estrus ES 79	PS	Out of Our Tree/Tall Cool One	1991	3.00	6.25	12.50
Rekkids 001		Skinny Minnie/You Can't Sit Down				
			1989	6.25	12.50	25.00
Rekkids 001	PS	Skinny Minnie/You Can't Sit Down				
			1989	6.25	12.50	25.00
Telstar 006		Stronger Than Dirt/Your Love	1992		2.50	5.00
Telstar 006	PS	Stronger Than Dirt/Your Love	1992		2.50	5.00

Label, Number		Title	Year	VG	VG+	NM

Musical Cast of Toys, The
*Featuring Wendy and Lisa, former cohorts of **Prince**, with guest vocal by **Seal**.*

45s

| Geffen 19146 | | The Closing of the Year/(instrumental) | | | | |
| | | | 1992 | | | 3.00 |

Musical Youth
English kiddie-pop reggae-ska group.

Vinyl Albums

| MCA 5389 | | The Youth of Today | 1983 | 2.50 | 5.00 | 10.00 |
| MCA 5454 | | Different Style | 1983 | 2.50 | 5.00 | 10.00 |

45s

MCA 52149		Pass the Dutchie/Give Love a Chance				
			1982			3.00
MCA 52149	PS	Pass the Dutchie/Give Love a Chance				
			1982			3.00
MCA 52203		Never Gonna Give You Up/Rub 'N' Dub				
			1983			3.00
MCA 52216		Heartbreaker/Rockers	1983			3.00
MCA 52312		She's Trouble/Yard Style	1983			3.00
MCA 52312	PS	She's Trouble/Yard Style	1983			3.00
MCA 52364		Tell Me Why/What Cha Talking 'Bout				
			1984			3.00

12-Inch Singles

MCA L33-1108	DJ	Heartbreaker (short)/Heartbreaker (long)				
			1983	2.50	5.00	10.00
MCA L33-1147	DJ	She's Trouble/Incommunicado	1983	2.50	5.00	10.00
MCA 13965		Never Gonna Give You Up/Mirror Mirror/Rub N Dub				
			1983		3.00	6.00
MCA 13986		She's Trouble (2 versions)/Sixteen				
			1983	2.50	5.00	10.00

Mutants
San Francisco-based punk/new wave act.

45s

415 Records 34859		New Dark Ages/Insect Lounge/New Drug				
			1978	5.00	10.00	20.00
415 Records 34859	PS	New Dark Ages/Insect Lounge/New Drug				
			1978	5.00	10.00	20.00

My Bloody Valentine
New wave band from Dublin, Ireland.

Vinyl Albums

| Relativity (# unknown) | | Isn't Anything | 1989 | 5.00 | 10.00 | 20.00 |

12-Inch Singles

Relativity 88561-1016-1		Soft as Snow/Feed Me With Your Kiss/You're Still in a Dream/				
		Slow/Instrumental	1989	5.00	10.00	20.00
Sire PRO-A-4512	DJ	Soon/Glider/Don't Ask Why/Off Your Face				
			1990	2.00	4.00	8.00

Myrick, Gary, and the Figures
American new-wave band.

Vinyl Albums

| Epic AS 912 | DJ | Talks in Stereo | 1981 | 10.00 | 20.00 | 40.00 |

Side one has studio tracks, side two has live versions of songs on side one

Label, Number		Title	Year	VG	VG+	NM
Epic AS 1389	DJ	Live Sampler	1982	4.00	8.00	16.00
Four live tracks, including one unreleased song						
Epic NJE 36524		Gary Myrick and the Figures	1980	3.00	6.00	12.00
Epic JE 36524		Gary Myrick and the Figures	1981	2.50	5.00	10.00
Reissue with amended prefix						
Epic ARE 37429		Living in a Movie	1981	2.50	5.00	10.00
Epic B5E 38637	EP	Language	1983	2.50	5.00	10.00
Geffen GHS 24076		Stand for Love	1985	2.50	5.00	10.00

7-Inch Extended Play Singles

Label, Number		Title	Year	VG	VG+	NM
Epic AE7 1207	DJ	She Talks in Stereo/Ever Since the World Began// Deep in the Heartland/The Party	1980	2.00	4.00	8.00

45s

Label, Number		Title	Year	VG	VG+	NM
Epic AE7 1303	DJ	Living in a Movie/My Girl (It's Simple)	1981		2.50	5.00
Epic AE7 1303	PS	Living in a Movie/My Girl (It's Simple)	1981		2.50	5.00
"Film can" sleeve with bio insert						
Epic 04009		Message Is You/Glamorous	1983			3.00
Epic 50937		She Talks in Stereo/Model	1980			3.00
Geffen 28905		When Angels Kiss/I Was a Painted Picture	1985			3.00

12-Inch Singles

Label, Number		Title	Year	VG	VG+	NM
Epic AS 1694	DJ	Guitar, Talk, Love & Drums (Extended Special Version)/ same (Short Special Version)	1983	2.50	5.00	10.00
Geffen PRO-A-2349	DJ	When Angels Kiss/I Stand for Love	1985	2.00	4.00	8.00
Geffen PRO-A-2403	DJ	Hearts Pound (Like a Rhythm Machine) (same on both sides)	1985	2.00	4.00	8.00

N

Naked Eyes

British synth-pop duo.

Vinyl Albums

Label, Number		Title	Year	VG	VG+	NM
EMI America ST-17089		Naked Eyes	1983	3.00	6.00	12.00
EMI America ST-17116		Fuel for the Fire	1984	2.50	5.00	10.00

45s

Label, Number		Title	Year	VG	VG+	NM
American Pie 9062		Always Something There to Remind Me/Bluer Than Blue	198?			3.00
Reissue; B-side by Michael Johnson						
American Pie 9064		Promises, Promises/Giving It Up for Your Love	198?			3.00
Reissue; B-side by Delbert McClinton						
EMI America 8155		Always Something There to Remind Me/The Time Is Now	1983		2.00	4.00
EMI America 8170		Promises, Promises/A Very Hard Act to Follow	1983		2.00	4.00
EMI America 8170	PS	Promises, Promises/A Very Hard Act to Follow	1983		2.00	4.00
EMI America 8183		When the Lights Go Out/Low Life	1983		2.00	4.00
EMI America 8219		(What) In the Name of Love/Two Heads Together	1984		2.00	4.00
EMI America 8219	PS	(What) In the Name of Love/Two Heads Together	1984		2.00	4.00

Label, Number		Title	Year	VG	VG+	NM
12-Inch Singles						
EMI America 7832		(What) In the Name of Love (3 versions)				
			1984	2.00	4.00	8.00
EMI America SPRO 9923	DJ	Always Something There to Remind Me (Remix)/				
		Voices in My Head	1983	2.00	4.00	8.00

Naked Raygun
Chicago punk band.

Vinyl Albums						
Homestead 008		Throb Throb	1984	4.50	9.00	18.00
First edition has lyric sheet						
Homestead 008		Throb Throb	1984	3.00	6.00	12.00
Second edition has lyric innersleeve						
Ruthless 03	EP	Basement Screams	1983	20.00	40.00	80.00
7-Inch Extended Play Singles						
Ruthless (# unknown)		Flammable Solid	1983	12.50	25.00	50.00
Ruthless (# unknown)	PS	Flammable Solid	1983	12.50	25.00	50.00
With stickered cover and parchment lyric sheet						
45s						
Sandpounder (# unknown)		Vanilla Blue/Slim	198?			3.00
Blue and white vinyl						
Sandpounder (# unknown)	PS	Vanilla Blue/Slim	198?			3.00

Naked Skinnies
*With Mark Eitzel, later of **American Music Club.***

45s						
Naked House (# unknown)		All My Life/This Is the Beautiful Night				
			1981	9.00	18.00	36.00
Naked House (# unknown)	PS	All My Life/This Is the Beautiful Night				
			1981	9.00	18.00	36.00

Naughty By Nature
Rap group.

Vinyl Albums						
Tommy Boy TBLP-1051		Naughty By Nature	1991	3.75	7.50	15.00
Tommy Boy TBLP-1069		19NaughtyIII	1993	3.75	7.50	15.00
Tommy Boy TBLP-1111		Poverty's Paradise	1995	3.00	6.00	12.00
45s						
Tommy Boy 512		O.P.P./Everything's Gonna Be Alright				
			1991		2.50	5.00
Original on green and bluish label						
Tommy Boy 512		O.P.P./Everything's Gonna Be Alright				
			1991			3.00
Reissue on white label						
Tommy Boy 554		Hip Hop Hooray (same on both sides)				
			1993			3.00
Tommy Boy 670		Craziest (same on both sides)	1995			3.00
Tommy Boy 682		Feel Me Flow (same on both sides)				
			1995			3.00
12-Inch Singles						
Soul 2125		Uptown Anthem (3 versions)	1991		3.50	7.00
Tommy Boy 569		It's On (4 versions)/Hip Hop Hooray (Pete Rock Remix)				
			1993		3.50	7.00

Label, Number		Title	Year	VG	VG+	NM

NdegeOcello, Me'Shell
Singer-bassist. Female duet on John Mellencamp's version of "Wild Night."

Vinyl Albums

Maverick PRO-A-6622	(2) DJ	Plantation Lullabies	1993	5.00	10.00	20.00
Promo-only U.S. vinyl release						

45s

Maverick 18326		If That's Your Boyfriend (He Wasn't Last Night)/ Two Lonely Hearts (On the Subway)				
			1993			3.00

12-Inch Singles

Maverick PRO-A-6485	DJ	Dred Loc (same on both sides)	1993	2.00	4.00	8.00
Maverick PRO-A-6852	DJ	Outside Your Door (3 versions)	1993	2.00	4.00	8.00
Maverick 41039		Dred Loc (5 versions)	1993	2.00	4.00	8.00
Maverick 41316		If That's Your Boyfriend (He Wasn't Last Night) (same on both sides)	1993		3.00	6.00

Necros
From Maumee, Ohio, outside Toledo. In 1982, it was written of them: "They are loud, fast, young and ugly." 'Nuff said.

Vinyl Albums

Restless (# unknown)		Tangled Up	1986	3.00	6.00	12.00
Touch N Go 2		Conquest for Death	1983	10.00	20.00	40.00

7-Inch Extended Play Singles

Touch N Go 001		Sex Drive/Police Brutality//Better Never Than Late/Caste System				
			1981	62.50	125.00	250.00
Touch N Go 001	PS	Sex Drive/Police Brutality//Better Never Than Late/Caste System				
			1981	62.50	125.00	250.00
Beware! Both record and sleeve have been heavily bootlegged.						
Touch N Go 14422		Conquest for Death	1983	7.50	15.00	30.00
Touch N Go 14422	PS	Conquest for Death	1983	7.50	15.00	30.00
Touch N Go/Dischord 13118		I.Q. 32	1981	10.00	20.00	40.00
Touch N Go/Dischord 13118	PS	I.Q. 32	1981	10.00	20.00	40.00

45s

Gasatanka JC 9019		Tangled Up/The Nile Song	1985	2.50	5.00	10.00
Gasatanka JC 9019	PS	Tangled Up/The Nile Song	1985	2.50	5.00	10.00

Ned's Atomic Dustbin
British alterna-rock band.

12-Inch Singles

Chaos CAS 5239	DJ	Saturday Night (one-sided)	1993	2.50	5.00	10.00

Negativland
From Berkeley, California, a noise and sample band.

Vinyl Albums

Seeland 001		Negativland	1981	3.75	7.50	15.00
Every copy has a different cover						
Seeland 002		Points	1982	3.00	6.00	12.00
Seeland 002		Points	1982	12.50	25.00	50.00
Blue vinyl						
Seeland 003		A Big 10-8 Place	1985	3.00	6.00	12.00
SST 133		Escape from Noise	1987	4.50	9.00	18.00
With booklet						
SST 252		Helter Stupid	1989	3.00	6.00	12.00

Label, Number		Title	Year	VG	VG+	NM
SST 272	EP	U2	1990	25.00	50.00	100.00
Withdrawn thanks to pressure from the record company of U2 (the band)						
SST 292	EP	Guns	1992	2.00	4.00	8.00

Nena

German singer.

Vinyl Albums

Epic BFE 39294		99 Luftballons	1984	3.00	6.00	12.00
Epic PE 39294		99 Luftballons	198?	2.00	4.00	8.00
Budget-line reissue with new prefix						
Epic FE 40144		It's All in the Game	1985	2.50	5.00	10.00

45s

Epic 04108		99 Luftballons/Just a Dream	1983		*May not exist*	
Epic 04108		99 Luftballons/99 Red Ballons	1983		2.50	5.00
B-side label had "Balloons" misspelled						
Epic 04108		99 Luftballons/99 Red Balloons	1983			3.00
B-side label corrects spelling error						
Epic 04440		Just a Dream/Rette Mich	1984			3.00
Epic 04542		Kino (At the Movies)/Kino (At the Movies) (German Version)				
			1984			3.00
Epic 08472		99 Luftballons/99 Red Balloons	1988			3.00
Reissue						

12-Inch Singles

Epic 04109		99 Luftballons/99 Red Balloons	1983		*May not exist*	
Epic 04109		99 Luftballons/Just a Dream	1983		3.00	6.00

Neon Boys

*Neon Boys later became **Television**.*

7-Inch Extended Play Singles

Shake SHK 101		That's All I Know (Right Now)/Love Comes in Spurts//Don't Die/				
		Time	1980	3.00	6.25	12.50
B-side tracks by Richard Hell and the Voidoids						
Shake SHK 101	PS	That's All I Know (Right Now)/Love Comes in Spurts//Don't Die/				
		Time	1980	3.00	6.25	12.50

Nerves, The

*California power-pop group. Members later joined **The Beat** and **The Plimsouls**. And yes, that's the song **Blondie** later recorded...*

7-Inch Extended Play Singles

Nerves 4501		Hanging on the Telephone	1976	5.00	10.00	20.00
Nerves 4501	PS	Hanging on the Telephone	1976	5.00	10.00	20.00

Nervous Eaters

Boston new-wave band.

Vinyl Albums

Ace of Hearts 1007		Hot Steel and Acid	1986	2.50	5.00	10.00
Elektra 6E-282		Nervous Eaters	1980	3.75	7.50	15.00

45s

Elektra 47025		No Sleep Tonite/Last Chance	1980	5.00	10.00	20.00
Elektra 47025	DJ	No Sleep Tonite (mono/stereo)	1980	3.75	7.50	15.00
Elektra 47072		Loretta/Get Stuffed	1980	5.00	10.00	20.00
Elektra 47072	DJ	Loretta (mono/stereo)	1980	3.75	7.50	15.00
Rat 528-G		Just Head/Get Stuffed	1979	10.00	20.00	40.00
Rat 5282		Loretta/Rock with Me	1979	2.50	5.00	10.00

Nervous Eaters were a Boston new-wave band that never gained the acclaim of their Elektra counterparts, The Cars. But the former band's records have become quite collectible. Even though not issued with a picture sleeve, a stock copy of "Loretta" on Elektra goes for $20.

No record in the history of Sub Pop Records has been in print longer than Nirvana's 1990 45 "Sliver"/ "Dive" (the rear of the picture sleeve is pictured above). It's been issued at least five different times with two variations of the picture sleeve, and it's *still* available.

Label, Number		Title	Year	VG	VG+	NM
Rat 5282	PS	Loretta/Rock with Me	1979	10.00	20.00	40.00
First pressing has cardboard sleeve						
Rat 5282	PS	Loretta/Rock with Me	1979	2.50	5.00	10.00

New Order

*English synth-pop-dance group formed by the surviving members of **Joy Division**. Also see **Electronic**.*

Vinyl Albums

Label, Number		Title	Year	VG	VG+	NM
Factory FACT US 8	EP	1981-1982	1983	5.00	10.00	20.00
Factory FAC US 12		Power, Corruption and Lies	1983	3.00	6.00	12.00
Factory FAC US 50		Movement	1981	5.00	10.00	20.00
Qwest 25289		Low Life	1985	2.50	5.00	10.00
Qwest 25308		Power, Corruption and Lies	1985	2.50	5.00	10.00
Reissue						
Qwest 25511		Brotherhood	1986	2.50	5.00	10.00
Qwest 25621	(2)	Substance	1987	3.75	7.50	15.00
Qwest 25845		Technique	1989	3.00	6.00	12.00
Qwest R 100938		Technique	1989	3.50	7.00	14.00
BMG Music Service edition						

45s

Label, Number		Title	Year	VG	VG+	NM
Factory (# unknown)		Procession/Everything's Gone Green	1982		2.50	5.00
Factory (# unknown)	PS	Procession/Everything's Gone Green	1982		2.50	5.00
American edition has a different color sleeve than British edition (UK press worth 25% less)						
Qwest PRO-S-3464	DJ	Fine Time (7" Edit)/Round and Round (Edit)	1989	2.00	4.00	8.00
Qwest 18586		Regret/Regret (New Order Mix)	1993			3.00
Qwest 21887		True Faith/Blue Monday 1988	198?			3.00
Reissue						
Qwest 27524		Round & Round/Best and Marsh	1989			3.00
Qwest 27524	PS	Round & Round/Best and Marsh	1989			3.00
Qwest 27979		Blue Monday 1988/Touched by the Hand of God	1988			3.00
Qwest 27979	PS	Blue Monday 1988/Touched by the Hand of God	1988			3.00
Qwest 28271		True Faith/1963	1987			3.00
Qwest 28271	PS	True Faith/1963	1987			3.00
Qwest 28421		Bizarre Love Triangle/Every Little Bit Counts	1987	2.50	5.00	10.00
Scarce on stock copy						
Qwest 28421	DJ	Bizarre Love Triangle (same on both sides)	1987	2.50		5.00
Qwest 28968		The Perfect Kiss/The Perfect Kiss (instrumental)	1985		3.00	6.00

12-Inch Singles

Label, Number		Title	Year	VG	VG+	NM
A&M 12174		Shellshock/Thieves Like Us	1986	2.00	4.00	8.00
Factory FACTUS 10		Blue Monday/The Beach	1983	2.00	4.00	8.00
Qwest PRO-A-2342	DJ	The Perfect Kiss (edit)/The Perfect Kiss (live)	1985	2.50	5.00	10.00
Qwest PRO-A-2784	DJ	True Faith (LP Version)/True Faith (Edit)	1987	2.50	5.00	10.00
Qwest PRO-A-3037	DJ	Blue Monday '88 (Club Mix)/Touched by the Hand of God (Remix) (Dub)	1988	2.50	5.00	10.00
Qwest PRO-A-6276	(2) DJ	World (The Price of Love) (8 versions)	1993	6.25	12.50	25.00
Promo-only two-record set						
Qwest PRO-A-6318	DJ	Ruined in a Day (6 versions)	1993	5.00	10.00	20.00
Qwest PRO-A-6729	DJ	Spooky (6 versions)	1993	3.75	7.50	15.00

Label, Number		Title	Year	VG	VG+	NM
Qwest 20330		Perfect Kiss/The Kiss of Death/Perfect Pit				
			1985	2.00	4.00	8.00
Qwest 20390		Sub Culture (3 versions)	1985	3.00	6.00	12.00
Qwest 20546		Bizarre Love Triangle (2 mixes)/I Don't Care/State of the Nation				
			1986	3.00	6.00	12.00
Qwest 20733		True Faith (Morning Sun Extended)/True Faith (Dub)/1963				
			1987	3.00	6.00	12.00
Qwest 20869		Blue Monday '88 (12") (Dub)/Touched by the Hand of God				
		(Remix) (Dub)	1988	2.50	5.00	10.00
Qwest 21062		Round & Round (3 mixes)/Best and Marsh				
			1989	2.00	4.00	8.00
Qwest 21107		Fine Time (5 versions)/Don't Do It				
			1988		3.00	6.00
Qwest 21582		World in Motion (4 versions)	1990		3.00	6.00
Qwest 40760		Regret (4 versions)	1993	2.00	4.00	8.00
Qwest 41313		Spooky (6 versions)	1993	2.00	4.00	8.00
Streetwise 2213		Confusion (4 versions)	1984	2.00	4.00	8.00

New York Dolls

*Seminal Big Apple punk-glam band. See **David Johanson**, **Sylvain Sylvain** and **The Heartbreakers**.*

Vinyl Albums

Mercury SRM-1-675		New York Dolls	1973	5.00	10.00	20.00
Mercury SRM-1-1001		In Too Much Too Soon	1974	5.00	10.00	20.00
Mercury 826 094-1		Night of the Living Dolls	1985	3.00	6.00	12.00

45s

Mercury DJ-378	DJ	Trash (mono/stereo)	1973	3.75	7.50	15.00
Mercury DJ-378	PS	Trash (mono/stereo)	1973	18.75	37.50	75.00
Promo-only numbered sleeve						
Mercury DJ-387	DJ	Personality Crisis (mono/stereo)	1973	3.75	7.50	15.00
Mercury 73414		Trash/Personality Crisis	1973	15.00	30.00	60.00
Mercury 73414	PS	Trash/Personality Crisis	1973	3.75	7.50	15.00
Mercury 73478		Stranded in the Jungle/Who Are the Mystery Girls				
			1974	3.75	7.50	15.00
Mercury 73615		Puss 'N' Boots/Showmen	1974	5.00	10.00	20.00

Next, The

Texas punk band.

7-Inch Extended Play Singles

Sharp (# unknown)		Make It Quick	1979	18.75	37.50	75.00
Sharp (# unknown)	PS	Make It Quick	1979	18.75	37.50	75.00
Actually a 15x22 poster with the white side facing out, wrapped around the record						
Sharp (# unknown)	PS	Make It Quick	1979	22.50	45.00	90.00
A few copies of the poster had "The Next -- Make It Quick" stamped on the white side						
Sharp (# unknown)		Kick Ass	1980	15.00	30.00	60.00
Sharp (# unknown)	PS	Kick Ass	1980	15.00	30.00	60.00
With sleeve and poster						

Nine Inch Nails

*Industrial/gloom band led by Trent Reznor. Reznor was in a band called **The Innocent**. Two early NIN members joined **Filter**.*

Vinyl Albums

Nothing/TVT 2610		Pretty Hate Machine	1990	5.00	10.00	20.00
Nothing/TVT/Interscope PR 5509	(2) DJ	The Downward Spiral	1994	6.25	12.50	25.00
Promo-only two-record set						

Label, Number		Title	Year	VG	VG+	NM
12-Inch Singles						
Nothing/TVT/Interscope 2117 (2) DJ		Closer to God (6 versions)/Memorabilia/March of the F*ckheads/				
		Heresy	1994	6.25	12.50	25.00
Promo-only two-record set						
Nothing/TVT/Interscope	DJ	Happiness in Slavery (4 versions)	1994	3.75	7.50	15.00
DMD 1941						

999

British new wave band. Some records came out under the name "Nine Nine Nine."

Label, Number	Title	Year	VG	VG+	NM
Vinyl Albums					
Polydor PD1-6256	Biggest Prize in Sport	1980	3.50	7.00	14.00
Polydor PD1-6307	Biggest Tour in Sport	1980	3.50	7.00	14.00
Polydor PD1-6322	Concrete	1981	3.00	6.00	12.00
PVC 7999	High Energy Plan	1979	3.00	6.00	12.00
45s					
Polydor 2076	Boiler/Hollywood	1980	3.75	7.50	15.00
Polydor 2172	Obsessed/Fortune Teller	1981	3.75	7.50	15.00

Label, Number		Title	Year	VG	VG+	NM
12-Inch Singles						
Polydor PRO 155	DJ	Mercy Mercy/That's the Way It Goes/Obsessed/Taboo				
			1981	2.50	5.00	10.00

94 East

*Minneapolis band; **Prince** and Andre Cymone in the early days.*

Label, Number	Title	Year	VG	VG+	NM
Vinyl Albums					
Hot Pink HLP 3223	Minneapolis Genius -- 94 East	1986	10.00	20.00	40.00
Recordings made in 1977; deduct 25% for cut-outs					
45s					
Hot Pink 3223	Just Another Sucker/(B-side unknown)				
		1986		3.00	6.00
Polydor 14414	Be My Fortune Teller/I Just Wanna Be				
		1977			
Record not known to exist, even as a promo.					

Nirvana

*Seattle grunge-rock band. Lead singer was Kurt Cobain (misspelled numerous ways over the years on the records). After Cobain's suicide, band member Dave Grohl appeared with **Backbeat Band** and **Foo Fighters**.*

Label, Number	Title	Year	VG	VG+	NM
Vinyl Albums					
DGC 24425	Nevermind	1991	5.00	10.00	20.00
DGC 24504	Incesticide	1992	5.00	10.00	20.00
DGC 24607	In Utero	1993	5.00	10.00	20.00
DGC 24727	MTV Unplugged in New York	1994	3.00	6.00	12.00
All copies on white vinyl					
Mobile Fidelity 1-258	Nevermind	1996	5.00	10.00	20.00
Original Master Recording					
Sub Pop 34	Bleach	1989	12.50	25.00	50.00
First 1,000 were pressed on white vinyl					
Sub Pop 34	Bleach	1989	7.50	15.00	30.00
With poster					
Sub Pop 34	Bleach	1989	5.00	10.00	20.00
Red vinyl					
45s					
Communion 23	Here She Comes Now/Venus in Furs				
		1991	3.00	6.25	12.50
B-side by The Melvins; blue vinyl					

Label, Number		Title	Year	VG	VG+	NM
Communion 23		Here She Comes Now/Venus in Furs				
			1991	3.00	6.25	12.50
B-side by The Melvins; green vinyl						
Communion 23	PS	Here She Comes Now/Venus in Furs				
			1991	3.00	6.25	12.50
B-side by The Melvins						
DGC 19050		Smells Like Teen Spirit/Even In His Youth				
			1991	2.00	4.00	8.00
DGC 19120		Come As You Are/Drain You	1992	2.00	4.00	8.00
DGC 19134		Lithium/Been a Son	1992		*Cassette only*	
Sub Pop 23		Love Buzz/Big Cheese	1988	18.75	37.50	75.00
Sub Pop 23	PS	Love Buzz/Big Cheese	1988	18.75	37.50	75.00
Hand-numbered edition of 1,000; #1 in Sub Pop Singles Club series						
Sub Pop 73		Sliver/Dive	1990	10.00	20.00	40.00
First 3,000 on blue vinyl						
Sub Pop 73		Sliver/Dive	1990	12.50	25.00	50.00
Clear pink/lavender vinyl						
Sub Pop 73		Sliver/Dive	1990	2.50	5.00	10.00
Black vinyl, no California address on label						
Sub Pop 73		Sliver/Dive	1990		3.50	7.00
Later issues on pale yellow vinyl with California address on label						
Sub Pop 73		Sliver/Dive	1990			3.00
Still later issues on black vinyl with California address on label						
Sub Pop 73	PS	Sliver/Dive	1990	2.50	5.00	10.00
Original picture sleeves were fold-over, not seam sealed						
Sub Pop 73	PS	Sliver/Dive	1990			3.00
Later picture sleeves were seam sealed						
Sub Pop 97		Molly's Lips (Live)/Candy	1991	2.50	5.00	10.00
B-side by Fluid; black vinyl						
Sub Pop 97		Molly's Lips (Live)/Candy	1991	8.75	17.50	35.00
B-side by Fluid; green vinyl						
Sub Pop 97	PS	Molly's Lips (Live)/Candy	1991	2.50	5.00	10.00
B-side by Fluid; #27 in Sub Pop Singles Club series						

12-Inch Singles

Label, Number		Title	Year	VG	VG+	NM
DGC 4344	DJ	Smells Like Teen Spirit/Even In His Youth/Aneurysm				
			1991	5.00	10.00	20.00
Promo only on yellow vinyl						
DGC 4416	DJ	Come As You Are (same on both sides)				
			1991	3.75	7.50	15.00
DGC 4558	DJ	Heart-Shaped Box/Gallons of Rubbin' Alcohol				
			1993	3.00	6.00	12.00

Nixon, Mojo, and Skid Roper

Bizarre rock duo.

Vinyl Albums

Label, Number		Title	Year	VG	VG+	NM
Enigma ST-73272		Bo-Day-Shus!!!	1987	3.00	6.00	12.00
Restless 72056		Mojo Nixon and Skid Roper	1985	3.00	6.00	12.00
Restless 72127		Frenzy	1986	3.00	6.00	12.00
Restless 72185	EP	Get Out of My Way	1986	2.50	5.00	10.00
Clear vinyl						

12-Inch Singles

Label, Number		Title	Year	VG	VG+	NM
Enigma 054	DJ	I'm Gonna Dig Up Howlin' Wolf (same on both sides)				
			1987		3.00	6.00

Noel

Dance-pop singer from the Bronx.

Vinyl Albums

Label, Number		Title	Year	VG	VG+	NM
4th & B'Way 4009		Noel	1988	2.50	5.00	10.00

Label, Number		Title	Year	VG	VG+	NM
45s						
4th & B'Way 7439		Silent Morning/(Instrumental)	1987			3.00
4th & B'Way 7439	PS	Silent Morning/(Instrumental)	1987			3.00
4th & B'Way 7458		Like a Child	1988			3.00
4th & B'Way 7458	PS	Like a Child	1988			3.00
Collectables 2611		Silent Morning/Like a Child	199?			3.00
Reissue						
12-Inch Singles						
4th & B'Way 439		Silent Morning (4 versions)	1987		3.00	6.00
4th & B'Way 458		Like a Child (6 versions)	1988		3.00	6.00
4th & B'Way 469	DJ	Out of Time (4 versions)	1988		3.00	6.00
4th & B'Way 481	DJ	Change (5 versions)	1989	2.00	4.00	8.00

Normal, The

One-man band: Daniel Miller of Mute Records.

45s						
Sire 1044		T.V.O.D./Warm Leatherette	1978		2.00	4.00
Sire 1044	PS	T.V.O.D./Warm Leatherette	1978		2.00	4.00

Numan, Gary

British synth-pop performer, formerly with Tubeway Army (those records also are listed below).

Label, Number	Title	Year	VG	VG+	NM
Vinyl Albums					
Atco SD 32-103	Telekon	1980	2.50	5.00	10.00
Atco SD 32-106	Tubeway Army: The First Album				
		1980	2.50	5.00	10.00
First American issue of U.K. debut					
Atco SD 38-117	Replicas	1979	2.50	5.00	10.00
With Tubeway Army					
Atco SD 38-120	The Pleasure Principle	1979	3.00	6.00	12.00
Atco SD 38-143	Dance	1981	2.50	5.00	10.00
Atco 90014	I, Assassin	1982	3.00	6.00	12.00
I.R.S. 82003	New Anger	1988	2.50	5.00	10.00
Numa 1005	Strange Charm	1985	2.50	5.00	10.00
45s					
Atco 7206	Are Friends Electric?/You Are In My Vision				
		1979		2.00	4.00
Atco 7211	Cars/Metal	1980		2.00	4.00
Atco 7308	I Die; You Die/Sleep by Windows				
		1980		2.00	4.00
Atco 7316	Remind Me to Smile	1981		2.00	4.00
Atlantic 13224	Cars/I Die; You Die	198?			3.00
"Oldies Series" reissue					
12-Inch Singles					
I.R.S. 13824	My World Storm (2 versions)/Are Friends Electric (2 versions)				
		1991	2.50	5.00	10.00

Nuns, The

San Francisco pop/punk band.

Label, Number	Title	Year	VG	VG+	NM
Vinyl Albums					
Bomp! 4010	The Nuns	1980	3.00	6.00	12.00
Posh Boy 105	The Nuns	1980	2.50	5.00	10.00
Same album as the Bomp! release					
45s					
415 Records S-0001	Savage/Decadent Jew/Suicide Child				
		1978	5.00	10.00	20.00

Label, Number		Title	Year	VG	VG+	NM
415 Records S-0001	PS	Savage/Decadent Jew/Suicide Child				
			1978	5.00	10.00	20.00
Rosco (no #)		The Beat/Media Control	1979	3.75	7.50	15.00
Rosco (no #)	PS	The Beat/Media Control	1979	3.75	7.50	15.00
Rosco 4166		World War III/Cock in My Pocket				
			1980	3.75	7.50	15.00
Rosco 4166	PS	World War III/Cock in My Pocket				
			1980	3.75	7.50	15.00

Insert and rubberstamped sleeve

O

O'Connor, Sinead
British singer-songwriter.

Vinyl Albums

	Title	Year	VG	VG+	NM
Chrysalis F1-21612	The Lion and the Cobra	1989	2.50	5.00	10.00
Reissue					
Chrysalis F1-21759	I Do Not Want What I Haven't Got				
		1990	3.00	6.00	12.00
Chrysalis R 133512	I Do Not Want What I Haven't Got				
		1990	3.50	7.00	14.00
BMG Direct Marketing edition					
Ensign/Chrysalis BFV 41612	The Lion and the Cobra	1987	2.00	4.00	8.00
Ensign/Chrysalis R 163660	The Lion and the Cobra	1988	2.50	5.00	10.00
BMG Direct Marketing edition					

45s

	Title	Year	VG	VG+	NM
Chrysalis S7-18397	Thank You for Hearing Me/Fire on Babylon				
		1995			3.00
Chrysalis 23488	Nothing Compares 2 U/Jump in the River				
		1990		2.50	5.00
Scarce stock copy; sometimes believed not to exist on U.S. 45, but it does					
Chrysalis 23528	The Emperor's New Clothes	1990		2.00	4.00
Chrysalis 43207	Mandinka/Drank Before the War	1988		2.00	4.00
Chrysalis 43330	Jump in the River/Jerusalem	1988		2.00	4.00
Chrysalis S7-57993	Success Has Made a Failure of Our Home/				
	You Do Something to Me	1992			3.00

12-Inch Singles

		Title	Year	VG	VG+	NM
Chrysalis VAS 2967	DJ	Mandinka (same on both sides)	1987	2.50	5.00	10.00
Chrysalis 43309		Jump Into the River (2 versions)/Jerusalem				
			1987		3.50	7.00
Ensign 1062	DJ	Jerusalem (same on both sides)	1988	2.50	5.00	10.00
Ensign/Chrysalis 23568		The Emperor's New Clothes (3 versions)/				
		I Am Stretched Out on Your Grave (3 versions)				
			1990	2.50	5.00	10.00

Oakey, Philip and Giorgio Moroder
*Solo recording by member of **The Human League**.*

45s

		Title	Year	VG	VG+	NM
A&M 2755		Goodbye Bad Times/(Instrumental)				
			1985			3.00
A&M 2755	PS	Goodbye Bad Times/(Instrumental)				
			1985			3.00
Epic 04618		Together in Electric Dreams/Madeline's Theme				
			1984			3.00

12-Inch Singles

	Title	Year	VG	VG+	NM
A&M 12141	Goodbye Bad Times/(Instrumental)				
		1985	2.00	4.00	8.00

Label, Number		Title	Year	VG	VG+	NM

Oasis
British band, part of the "New Britpop" scene.

45s

Epic 78216		Wonderwall/Round Are Way	1996			3.00

Ocasek, Ric
*Formerly with **The Cars**; lead singer on most of their hits.*

Vinyl Albums

Geffen GHS 2022		Beatitude	1983	3.00	6.00	12.00
Geffen 24098		This Side of Paradise	1986	2.50	5.00	10.00
Geffen R 144634		This Side of Paradise	1986	3.00	6.00	12.00
RCA Music Service edition						

45s

Geffen 28504		True to You/Hello Darkness	1986			3.00
Geffen 28504	PS	True to You/Hello Darkness	1986			3.00
Geffen 28617		Emotion in Motion/P.F.J.	1986			3.00
Geffen 28617	PS	Emotion in Motion/P.F.J.	1986			3.00
Geffen 29625		Jimmy Jimmy/Quick One	1983			3.00

12-Inch Singles

Geffen PRO-A-2002	DJ	Prove/Connect Up to Me	1983		2.50	5.00
Geffen PRO-A-2629	DJ	True to You (same on both sides)	1986		2.50	5.00
Geffen PRO-A-2646	DJ	Keep On Laughing (same on both sides)				
			1986		2.50	5.00
Geffen 20114		Connect Up to Me/Jimmy Jimmy	1983		2.50	5.00

Off Broadway USA
Oak Park, Illinois power-pop band.

Vinyl Albums

Atlantic SD 19263		On	1980	3.00	6.00	12.00
Atlantic SD 19287		Quick Turns	1981	2.50	5.00	10.00

45s

Atlantic 3647		Stay in Time/Full Moon Turn My Head Around				
			1980		2.00	4.00
Atlantic 3668		Bad Indication/Oh, Boy!	1980			3.00
Atlantic 3781		Automatic	1980			3.00
Atlantic 3799		Are You Alone	1981			3.00

Offspring
Neo-punk band.

Vinyl Albums

Epitaph 86432		Smash	1994	2.50	5.00	10.00

Oingo Boingo
*British new-wave band featuring the considerable talents of **Danny Elfman**.*

Vinyl Albums

A&M SP-3250		Only a Lad	1984	2.00	4.00	8.00
Reissue						
A&M SP-3251		Nothing to Fear	1984	2.00	4.00	8.00
Reissue						
A&M SP-3252		Good for Your Soul	1984	2.00	4.00	8.00
Reissue						
A&M SP-4863		Only a Lad	1981	2.50	5.00	10.00
A&M SP-4903		Nothing to Fear	1982	2.50	5.00	10.00

Label, Number		Title	Year	VG	VG+	NM
A&M SP-4959		Good for Your Soul	1983	2.50	5.00	10.00
A&M SP-5217		Skeletons in the Closet	1988	2.50	5.00	10.00
I.R.S. 70400	10	Only a Lad	1980	3.00	6.00	12.00
Six-song 10-inch EP						
I.R.S. 70400		Only a Lad	1980	3.00	6.00	12.00
Limited edition 12" version						
MCA 5665		Dead Man's Party	1985	3.00	6.00	12.00
MCA 5811		BOI-NGO	1987	2.50	5.00	10.00
MCA 6365		Dark at the End of the Tunnel	1990	2.50	5.00	10.00
MCA 8030	(2)	Boingo Alive	1988	3.75	7.50	15.00
MCA L33-18137	PD	Dark at the End of the Tunnel	1990	10.00	20.00	40.00
Promo-only picture disc						

45s

Label, Number		Title	Year	VG	VG+	NM
A&M 2439		Islands/Private Life	1982		2.00	4.00
A&M 2504	DJ	Whole Day Off (stereo)/Whole Day Off (mono)				
			1982		2.00	4.00
Apparently, no stock copy exists						
A&M 2610		Wake Up (It's 1984)/No Spill Blood				
			1983		2.00	4.00
MCA 42013	(5)	BOI-NGO	1987	10.00	20.00	40.00
Boxed set of five 45s, comprising the album of the same name						
MCA 52633		Weird Science/Weird Mama	1985			3.00
MCA 52633	PS	Weird Science/Weird Mama	1985			3.00
MCA 52726		Just Another Day/Dead Man's Party				
			1985			3.00
MCA 52726	PS	Just Another Day/Dead Man's Party				
			1985			3.00
MCA 52789		Stay/Heard Somebody Cry	1986			3.00
MCA 52789	PS	Stay/Heard Somebody Cry	1986			3.00
MCA 53050		Not My Slave/Where Do All My Friends Go				
			1987			3.00
MCA 53050	PS	Not My Slave/Where Do All My Friends Go				
			1987			3.00
MCA 53105		We Close Our Eyes/Where Do All My Friends Go				
			1987			3.00
MCA 53105	PS	We Close Our Eyes/Where Do All My Friends Go				
			1987			3.00

12-Inch Singles

Label, Number		Title	Year	VG	VG+	NM
A&M 17203	DJ	Private Life/Whole Day Off/Nothing to Fear				
			1982	2.50	5.00	10.00
A&M 17240	DJ	Wake Up (It's 1984) (long/short)	1983	2.00	4.00	8.00
MCA 17022	DJ	Weird Science (3:45) (same on both sides)				
			1985	2.50	5.00	10.00
MCA 17048	DJ	Weird Science (6:00)/Weird Science (6:38)				
			1985	2.50	5.00	10.00
MCA 17078	DJ	Just Another Day (5:10)/Just Another Day (3:58)				
			1985	2.50	5.00	10.00
MCA 17193	DJ	Pain (same on both sides)	1986		3.00	6.00
MCA 17288	DJ	Not My Slave (same on both sides)				
			1987		3.50	7.00
MCA 17660	DJ	Winning Side/Cinderella Undercover				
			1988		3.00	6.00
MCA 18005	DJ	Flesh and Blood (3 versions)	1989	3.00	6.00	12.00
MCA 23574		Weird Science (3:45)/Weird Science (6:38)				
			1985		3.50	7.00
MCA 23638		Dead Man's Party/Stay	1986	3.00	6.00	12.00
MCA 23696		Pain (4 mixes)	1986		3.00	6.00
MCA 23752		Not My Slave (7:40)/Not My Slave (5:52)				
			1987	2.50	5.00	10.00
MCA 24022		Out of Control (6 versions)	1990		3.00	6.00

Label, Number		Title	Year	VG	VG+	NM

Ono, Yoko

*Avant-garde artist and wife of John Lennon; an unlikely influence on new wave music (listen to "Rock Lob-ster" by **The B-52's** for proof). Most of the below records were recorded with John; the value is because of his involvement, not Yoko's.*

Vinyl Albums

Label, Number		Title	Year	VG	VG+	NM
Apple SW-3362		Live Peace in Toronto 1969	1970	7.50	15.00	30.00
By "The Plastic Ono Band" -- without calendar						
Apple SW-3362		Live Peace in Toronto 1969	1970	10.00	20.00	40.00
By "The Plastic Ono Band" -- with calendar						
Apple SW-3373		Yoko Ono Plastic Ono Band	1970	3.75	7.50	15.00
Apple SVBB-3380	(2)	Fly	1971	6.50	12.50	25.00
Apple SVBB-3392	(2)	Some Time in New York City	1972	7.50	15.00	30.00
By John and Yoko						
Apple SVBB-3399	(2)	Approximately Infinite Universe	1973	6.25	12.50	25.00
Apple SW 3412		Feeling the Space	1973	3.75	7.50	15.00
Apple T-5001		Two Virgins -- Unfinished Music No. 1	1968	37.50	75.00	150.00
Both John Lennon and Yoko -- price with die-cut bag						
Apple T-5001		Two Virgins -- Unfinished Music No. 1	1968	37.50	75.00	150.00
Both John Lennon and Yoko -- price with brown bag						
Apple T-5001		Two Virgins -- Unfinished Music No. 1	1968	12.50	25.00	50.00
Both John Lennon and Yoko -- price without brown bag						
Apple T-5001		Two Virgins -- Unfinished Music No. 1	1985	3.75	7.50	15.00
Both John Lennon and Yoko -- reissue, flat label						
Capitol SVBB-3392	(2)	Some Time in New York City	197?	6.25	12.50	25.00
By John and Yoko -- reissue						
Capitol ST-12239		Live Peace in Toronto 1969	1982	2.50	5.00	10.00
By "The Plastic Ono Band" -- reissue, purple Capitol label						
Capitol ST-12239		Live Peace in Toronto 1969	1983	12.50	25.00	50.00
By "The Plastic Ono Band" -- reissue, black Capitol label						
Capitol C1-91425		Double Fantasy	1989	5.00	10.00	20.00
Very briefly available reissue						
Geffen GHS 2001		Double Fantasy	1980	2.50	5.00	10.00
Seven tracks by Yoko, seven by John Lennon; off-white label; titles on back cover out of order						
Geffen GHS 2001		Double Fantasy	1981	3.00	6.00	12.00
Off-white label, titles in order on the back cover						
Geffen GHS 2001		Double Fantasy	1981	18.75	37.50	75.00
Columbia House edition (all have corrected back cover) with "CH" on label						
Geffen GHS 2001		Double Fantasy	1981	3.00	6.00	12.00
Columbia House edition (all have corrected back cover) without "CH" on label						
Geffen GHS 2001		Double Fantasy	1986	12.50	25.00	50.00
Same as above, but with black Geffen label						
Geffen GHS 2004		Season of Glass	1981	3.00	6.00	12.00
Geffen R 104689		Double Fantasy	1981	10.00	20.00	40.00
RCA Music Service edition						
Nautilus NR-47		Double Fantasy	1982	15.00	30.00	60.00
Half-speed master						
Nautilus NR-47		Double Fantasy	1982	500.00	1,000.00	2,000.00
Half-speed master; alternate experimental cover with yellow and red added to black and white front						
Polydor PD1-6364		It's Alright	1982	2.50	5.00	10.00
Polydor 817 160-1		Milk and Honey	1983	2.50	5.00	10.00
With John Lennon						
Polydor 817 238-1		Heart Play (Unfinished Dialogue)	1983	3.00	6.00	12.00
Interviews with John Lennon and Yoko Ono						
Polydor 823 289-1		It's Alright	1984	2.00	4.00	8.00
Reissue						
Polydor 827 530-1		Starpeace	1985	3.00	6.00	12.00
Zapple ST-3357		Life with the Lions -- Unfinished Music No. 2	1969	6.25	12.50	25.00
Both John Lennon and Yoko						

Label, Number		Title	Year	VG	VG+	NM
45s						
Apple GM/OYB-1	DJ	Greenfield Morning/Open Your Box	1971	200.00	400.00	800.00
Exactly six copies made for the personal use of Yoko Ono						
Apple 1809		Give Peace a Chance/Remember Love	1969		2.50	5.00
As "Plastic Ono Band"; Yoko sings backup on A-side, lead on B-side						
Apple 1809	PS	Give Peace a Chance/Remember Love	1969	3.00	6.00	12.00
As "Plastic Ono Band"						
Apple 1813		Don't Worry Kyoko (Mummy's Only Looking for a Hand in the Snow)/Cold Turkey	1969		2.50	5.00
As "Plastic Ono Band"; Yoko only on A-side						
Apple 1813	PS	Don't Worry Kyoko (Mummy's Only Looking for a Hand in the Snow)/Cold Turkey	1969	18.75	37.50	75.00
As "Plastic Ono Band"						
Apple 1818		Who Has Seen the Wind?/Instant Karma! (We All Shine On)	1970		2.00	4.00
As "Yoko Ono Lennon"; B-side by "John Ono Lennon". Value is for most common version.						
Apple 1818	PS	Who Has Seen the Wind?/Instant Karma! (We All Shine On)	1970	3.00	6.00	12.00
As "Yoko Ono Lennon"; B-side by "John Ono Lennon"						
Apple 1827		Why/Mother	1970	2.00	4.00	8.00
As "Yoko Ono/Plastic Ono Band"; B-side by "John Lennon/Plastic Ono Band"						
Apple 1827	PS	Why/Mother	1970	25.00	50.00	100.00
As "Yoko Ono/Plastic Ono Band"; B-side by "John Lennon/Plastic Ono Band"						
Apple 1830		Touch Me/Power to the People	1971	2.00	4.00	8.00
As "Yoko Ono/Plastic Ono Band"; B-side by "John Lennon/Plastic Ono Band"						
Apple 1830	PS	Touch Me/Power to the People	1971	7.50	15.00	30.00
As "Yoko Ono/Plastic Ono Band"; B-side by "John Lennon/Plastic Ono Band"						
Apple 1839		Mrs. Lennon/Midsummer New York	1971		3.50	7.00
As "Yoko Ono/Plastic Ono Band"						
Apple 1842		Happy Xmas (War Is Over)/Listen, the Snow Is Falling	1971	3.75	7.50	15.00
As "John & Yoko/Plastic Ono Band with the Harlem Community Choir"; green vinyl, faces label						
Apple 1842		Happy Xmas (War Is Over)/Listen, the Snow Is Falling	1971	2.50	5.00	10.00
As "John & Yoko/Plastic Ono Band with the Harlem Community Choir"; green vinyl, Apple label						
Apple 1842	PS	Happy Xmas (War Is Over)/Listen, the Snow Is Falling	1971	5.00	10.00	20.00
As "John & Yoko/Plastic Ono Band with the Harlem Community Choir"						
Apple 1848		Sisters O Sisters/Woman Is the Nigger of the World	1972	2.00	4.00	8.00
As "Yoko Ono/Plastic Ono Band..."; B-side by "John Lennon/Plastic Ono Band..."						
Apple 1848	PS	Sisters O Sisters/Woman Is the Nigger of the World	1972	6.25	12.50	25.00
As "Yoko Ono/Plastic Ono Band..."; B-side by "John Lennon/Plastic Ono Band..."						
Apple 1853		Now or Never/Move On Fast	1972	3.50	7.00	
Apple 1853	PS	Now or Never/Move On Fast	1972	2.00	4.00	8.00
Apple 1859		Death of Samantha/Yang Yang	1973		3.50	7.00
Apple 1867		Woman Power/Men, Men, Men	1973		3.50	7.00
Apple/Americom 1809-P/M-435		Give Peace a Chance/Remember Love	1969	187.50	375.00	750.00
As "Plastic Ono Band"; four-inch flexi-disc sold in vending machines						
Capitol S7-17644		Happy Xmas (War Is Over)/Listen, the Snow Is Falling	1994		2.00	4.00
Green vinyl (all copies)						
Capitol S7-18550		Never Say Goodbye/We're All Water	1995			3.00
Geffen PRO-S-935	DJ	Walking on Thin Ice (3:23)/Walking on Thin Ice (5:58)	1981	2.50	5.00	10.00

Label, Number		Title	Year	VG	VG+	NM
Geffen 29855		Happy Xmas (War Is Over)/Beautiful Boy (Darling Boy)				
			1982		2.50	5.00
B-side by John Lennon						
Geffen 29855	PS	Happy Xmas (War Is Over)/Beautiful Boy (Darling Boy)				
			1982		2.50	5.00
B-side by John Lennon						
Geffen 49604		Kiss Kiss Kiss/(Just Like) Starting Over				
			1980		2.00	4.00
B-side by John Lennon						
Geffen 49604	PS	Kiss Kiss Kiss/(Just Like) Starting Over				
			1980		2.00	4.00
B-side by John Lennon						
Geffen 49644		Beautiful Boys/Woman	1980		2.00	4.00
B-side by John Lennon						
Geffen 49644	PS	Beautiful Boys/Woman	1980		2.00	4.00
B-side by John Lennon						
Geffen 49683		Walking on Thin Ice/It Happened				
			1981		2.00	4.00
Geffen 49683	PS	Walking on Thin Ice/It Happened				
			1981		2.00	4.00
Includes picture sleeve and lyric insert						
Geffen 49695		Yes, I'm Your Angel/Watching the Wheels				
			1981		2.00	4.00
B-side by John Lennon						
Geffen 49695	PS	Yes, I'm Your Angel/Watching the Wheels				
			1981		2.00	4.00
B-side by John Lennon						
Geffen 49802		No, No, No/Will You Touch Me	1981		2.00	4.00
Geffen 49802	PS	No, No, No/Will You Touch Me	1981		2.00	4.00
Geffen 49849		Goodbye Sadness/I Don't Know Why				
			1981		2.00	4.00
Polydor 2224		My Man/Let the Tears Dry	1982			3.00
Polydor 2224	PS	My Man/Let the Tears Dry	1982			3.00
Polydor 817 254-7		O' Sanity/Nobody Told Me	1983		2.00	4.00
B-side by John Lennon						
Polydor 817 254-7	PS	O' Sanity/Nobody Told Me	1983		2.00	4.00
B-side by John Lennon						
Polydor 821 107-7		Sleepless Night/I'm Stepping Out	1984		2.00	4.00
B-side by John Lennon						
Polydor 821 107-7	PS	Sleepless Night/I'm Stepping Out	1984		2.00	4.00
B-side by John Lennon						
Polydor 821 204-7		Your Hands/Borrowed Time	1984		2.50	5.00
B-side by John Lennon						
Polydor 821 204-7	PS	Your Hands/Borrowed Time	1984		2.50	5.00
B-side by John Lennon						
Polydor 883 455-7		Hell in Paradise/(B-side unknown)				
			1985			3.00
Polydor 883 455-7	PS	Hell in Paradise/(B-side unknown)				
			1985			3.00

12-Inch Singles

Label, Number		Title	Year	VG	VG+	NM
Geffen PRO-A-934	DJ	Walking on Thin Ice (3:23)/Walking on Thin Ice (5:58)				
			1981	3.75	7.50	15.00
Polydor 192	DJ	My Man/Let the Tears Dry	1982		3.00	6.00
Polydor 883 455-1	DJ	Hell in Paradise (3 versions)	1985		3.00	6.00
Polydor 883 872-1	DJ	Walking on Thin Ice (Remix)/Cape Clear (2 versions)				
			1986	3.00	6.00	12.00

Orchestral Manoeuvres in the Dark

British synth-pop duo also known as "OMD."

Vinyl Albums

Label, Number	Title	Year	VG	VG+	NM
A&M SP6-5027	Junk Culture	1984	2.50	5.00	10.00

Label, Number		Title	Year	VG	VG+	NM
A&M SP-5077		Crush	1985	2.50	5.00	10.00
A&M SP-5144		The Pacific Age	1986	2.50	5.00	10.00
A&M SP-5186		The Best of O.M.D.	1988	2.50	5.00	10.00
A&M R 114546		The Pacific Age	1986	3.00	6.00	12.00
RCA Music Service edition						
A&M R 184156		The Best of O.M.D.	1988	3.00	6.00	12.00
BMG Direct Marketing edition						
Virgin 90611		Orchestral Manoeuvres in the Dark				
			1987	2.00	4.00	8.00
Reissue						
Virgin 90612		Organisation	1987	2.00	4.00	8.00
Reissue						
Virgin 91006		Dazzle Ships	1988	2.00	4.00	8.00
Reissue						
Virgin/Epic FE 37411		Orchestral Manoeuvres in the Dark				
			1981	3.00	6.00	12.00
Virgin/Epic ARE 37721		Architecture and Morality	1981	3.00	6.00	12.00
Virign/Epic BFE 38543		Dazzle Ships	1983	2.50	5.00	10.00
45s						
A&M 1209		Secret/Telegraph (Live)	1988			3.00
A&M 1209	PS	Secret/Telegraph (Live)	1988			3.00
A&M 2671		Locomotion/Her Body in My Soul				
			1984			3.00
A&M 2746		So in Love/Concrete Hands	1985			3.00
A&M 2746	PS	So in Love/Concrete Hands	1985			3.00
A&M 2794		Secret/Firegun	1985			3.00
A&M 2794	PS	Secret/Firegun	1985			3.00
A&M 2811		If You Leave/La Femme Accident				
			1986			3.00
A&M 2811	PS	If You Leave/La Femme Accident				
			1986		2.00	4.00
A&M 2872		(Forever) Live and Die/This Town				
			1986		2.00	4.00
First pressing: White stock label						
A&M 2872		(Forever) Live and Die/This Town				
			1986			3.00
Second pressing: Black label						
A&M 2872	PS	(Forever) Live and Die/This Town				
			1986			3.00
A&M 2897		We Love You/We Love You	1986		2.00	4.00
A&M 3002		Dreaming/Satellite	1988			3.00
A&M 3002	PS	Dreaming/Satellite	1988			3.00
A&M 8669		If You Leave/Secret	198?			3.00
Reissue						
Virgin S7-17597		Dream of Me (Based on "Love's Theme")/Strange Situations				
			1993		2.00	4.00
Virgin/Epic 02766		Souvenir/New Stone Age	1982		2.50	5.00
Virgin/Epic 03891		Telegraph/This Is Helena	1983		2.50	5.00
12-Inch Singles						
A&M 12108		Locomotion/Her Body in My Soul/The Avenue				
			1984	2.00	4.00	8.00
A&M 12120		Tesla Girls (3 versions)	1984	2.50	5.00	10.00
A&M 12143		So in Love (3:29)/So in Love (5:40)				
			1985	3.00	6.00	12.00
A&M 12161		Secret (remix)/Firegun/The Naive Daughters of Golden West				
			1985	2.50	5.00	10.00
A&M 12176		If You Leave (Remix)/La Femme Accident				
			1986	3.75	7.50	15.00
A&M 12202		(Forever) Live and Die (2 mixes)/This Town				
			1986	2.50	5.00	10.00
A&M 12215		We Love You (3 versions)	1986	2.50	5.00	10.00

Label, Number		Title	Year	VG	VG+	NM
A&M 12258		Dreaming (3 versions)/Satellite	1988	2.50	5.00	10.00
A&M 12272		Secret (3 versions)/Telegraph (Live)				
			1988	2.00	4.00	8.00
A&M 12285		Brides of Frankenstein (remix)/Brides of Frankenstein (dub)				
			1988		3.50	7.00
A&M 17367	DJ	If You Leave/Pretty in Pink	1986	2.50	5.00	10.00
		B-side by Psychedelic Furs; promo from movie "Pretty in Pink"				
A&M 17428	DJ	(Forever) Live and Die (same on both sides)				
			1986	2.50	5.00	10.00
A&M 17441	DJ	We Love You (7")/We Love You (Remix)				
			1986		3.00	6.00
Virgin 1665		Pandora's Box (4 versions)/Sugar Tax				
			1991	2.00	4.00	8.00
Virgin 1802		Sailing on the Seven Seas (5 versions)				
			1991	2.00	4.00	8.00
Virgin 12777	DJ	Stand Above Me (3 versions)	1993	2.50	5.00	10.00
Virgin/Epic AE 1247	DJ	Enola Gay/Messages	1980	3.75	7.50	15.00
Virgin/Epic AE 1403	DJ	Georgia/Souvenir/She's Leaving/Joan of Arc				
			1981	3.75	7.50	15.00
Virgin/Epic AE 1658	DJ	Telegraph (LP version)/Telegraph (Edit)/Radio Waves				
			1983	3.00	6.00	12.00

Orr, Benjamin

Formerly of The Cars.

Vinyl Albums

Elektra 60460		The Lace	1986	2.50	5.00	10.00
Elektra R 152406		The Lace	1986	3.00	6.00	12.00
		RCA Music Service edition				

45s

Elektra 65970		Stay the Night/Too Hot to Stop	198?			3.00
		"Spun Gold" reissue				
Elektra 69493		Too Hot to Stop/The Lace	1987			3.00
Elektra 69506		Stay the Night/That's the Way	1986			3.00
Elektra 69506	PS	Stay the Night/That's the Way	1986			3.00

12-Inch Singles

Elektra 5200	DJ	Too Hot to Stop (same on both sides)				
			1986		2.50	5.00

Otto's Chemical Lounge

Tom Hazelmyer and John Anglim, pre-Halo of Flies.

7-Inch Extended Play Singles

Reflex #H		Fire	1983	9.25	18.75	37.50
Reflex #H	PS	Fire	1983	9.25	18.75	37.50

Outfield, The

British pop-rock group with a sound somewhat like the early Police.

Vinyl Albums

Columbia BFC 40027		Play Deep	1985	2.50	5.00	10.00
Columbia OC 40619		Bangin'	1987	2.50	5.00	10.00
Columbia OC 44449		Voices of Babylon	1989	2.50	5.00	10.00
MCA 10111		Diamond Days	1990	2.50	5.00	10.00

45s

Columbia 05447		Say It Isn't So/Mystery Man	1985		2.00	4.00
Columbia 05796		Your Love/61 Seconds	1986			3.00
Columbia 05796	PS	Your Love/61 Seconds	1986			3.00

Label, Number		Title	Year	VG	VG+	NM
Columbia 05894		All the Love in the World/Taking My Chances				
			1986			3.00
Columbia 05894	PS	All the Love in the World/Taking My Chances				
			1986			3.00
Columbia 06295		Everytime You Cry/Tiny Lights	1986			3.00
Columbia 06295	PS	Everytime You Cry/Tiny Lights	1986			3.00
Columbia 07170		Since You've Been Gone/Better Than Nothing				
			1987			3.00
Columbia 07170	PS	Since You've Been Gone/Better Than Nothing				
			1987			3.00
Columbia 07384		No Surrender/Playground	1987			3.00
Columbia 07384	PS	No Surrender/Playground	1987			3.00
Columbia 08426		Say It Isn't So/Mystery Man	1988			3.00
Reissue						
Columbia 68601		Voices of Babylon/Inside Your Skin				
			1989			3.00
Columbia 68943		My Paradise/Somewhere in America '89				
			1989			3.00
MCA 54432		Winning It All/Your Love (Acoustic)				
			1992			3.00

Oxo

West Coast pop group.

Label, Number		Title	Year	VG	VG+	NM
Vinyl Albums						
Geffen GHS 4001		Oxo	1982	3.00	6.00	12.00
45s						
Geffen 29495		My Pride/Waiting for You	1983			3.00
Geffen 29601		Dance All Night/Wanna Be Your Love				
			1983			3.00
Geffen 29765		Whirly Girl/In the Stars	1983			3.00
Geffen 29765	PS	Whirly Girl/In the Stars	1983			3.00
12-Inch Singles						
Geffen PRO-A-2015	DJ	Whirly Girl/My Ride	1983		2.50	5.00

Label, Number		Title	Year	VG	VG+	NM

P

P

*Includes actor Johnny Depp and Gibby Haynes (**Butthole Surfers**).*

Vinyl Albums

| Capitol C1-32942 | | P | 1995 | 2.50 | 5.00 | 10.00 |

P.M. Dawn

Spacey rap duo.

Vinyl Albums

| Gee Street 6768 | | (2) DJ The Bliss Album | 1993 | 5.00 | 10.00 | 20.00 |
| *Promo-only vinyl edition* | | | | | | |

45s

Gee Street/Island 854 408-7		Downtown Venus/She Dreams Persistent Maybes				
			1995			3.00
Gee Street/Island 854 476-7		Sometimes I Miss You So Much (LP Version)/				
		Sometimes I Miss You So Much (Dallas Austin Remix)				
			1995			3.00
Island 862 024-7		Looking Through Patient Eyes/The Ways of the Wind				
			1993			3.00

12-Inch Singles

Gee Street 862 025-1		Looking Through Patient Eyes (3 mixes)/Paper Doll (2 mixes)				
			1993	2.00	4.00	8.00
Gee Street 862 217-1		Looking Through Patient Eyes (3 mixes)/Plastic (Radio Mix)				
			1993	2.00	4.00	8.00
Gee Street 862 475-1		The Ways of the Wind (4 versions)				
			1993		3.00	6.00
Gee Street 864 967-1		Plastic (4 versions)	1992	2.00	4.00	8.00
Gee Street 866 095-1		Set Adrift on Memory Bliss (2 versions)/				
		Watchers Point of View (2 versions)				
			1991		3.00	6.00
Gee Street 868 319-1		A Watcher's Point of View (3 versions)/Twisted Mellow				
			1991		3.50	7.00

P.O.L. (Parade of Losers)

45s

| Giant 17878 | | Stupid/Attitude Check | 1995 | | | 3.00 |

Pagans, The

Punk band.

45s

Bona Fide 7004		Don't Leave Me Alone/Real Worl				
			1987	5.00	10.00	20.00
Red vinyl (all copies)						
Bona Fide 7004	PS	Don't Leave Me Alone/Real World				
			1987	5.00	10.00	20.00
Poster sleeve, numbered edition of 200						
Drome DR-1		Street Where Nobody Lives/What's This Shit Called Love?				
			1978	3.00	6.25	12.50
Drome DR-1	PS	Street Where Nobody Lives/What's This Shit Called Love?				
			1978	15.50	31.25	62.50
Drome DR-1	PS	Street Where Nobody Lives/What's This Shit Called Love?				
			1987	3.00	6.25	12.50
New picture sleeve with original records (500 made)						

Label, Number		Title	Year	VG	VG+	NM
Drome DR-5		Not Now No Way/I Juvenile	1979	10.00	20.00	40.00
Drome DR-5		Not Now No Way/I Juvenile	1987	2.50	5.00	10.00
New record manufactured by Treehouse, accompanied by original picture sleeve						
Drome DR-5	PS	Not Now No Way/I Juvenile	1979	2.50	5.00	10.00
Drome DR-7		Dead End America/Little Black Egg				
			1979	10.00	20.00	40.00
Drome DR-7		Dead End America/Little Black Egg				
			1987	2.50	5.00	10.00
New record manufactured by Treehouse, accompanied by original picture sleeve						
Drome DR-7	PS	Dead End America/Little Black Egg				
			1979	2.50	5.00	10.00
Neck 002		Six & Change/Six & Change	1977	43.75	87.50	175.00
Neck 002	PS	Six & Change/Six & Change	1977	43.75	87.50	175.00
250 copies were made						
Treehouse PR 01	DJ	(Us and) All Our Friends Are So Messed Up/Heart of Stone				
			1988	6.25	12.50	25.00
Clear vinyl						
Treehouse PR 01	DJ	(Us and) All Our Friends Are So Messed Up/Heart of Stone				
			1988	2.50	5.00	10.00
Black vinyl						
Treehouse PR 01	PS	(Us and) All Our Friends Are So Messed Up/Heart of Stone				
			1988	6.25	12.50	25.00
Green sleeve						
Treehouse PR 01	PS	(Us and) All Our Friends Are So Messed Up/Heart of Stone				
			1988	2.50	5.00	10.00
Blue sleeve						
Treehouse 003		Dead End America 87/Secret Agent Man				
			1987	3.00	6.25	12.50
Treehouse 003	PS	Dead End America 87/Secret Agent Man				
			1987	3.00	6.25	12.50
Treehouse 021		Her Name Was Jane/I Do	1990	6.75	13.75	27.50
Red vinyl						
Treehouse 021		Her Name Was Jane/I Do	1990		3.75	7.50
Black vinyl						
Treehouse 021	PS	Her Name Was Jane/I Do	1990		3.75	7.50

Pain Teens

Noisy, grungy group from San Antonio, Texas.

7-Inch Extended Play Singles

Label, Number		Title	Year	VG	VG+	NM
Smilin' Ear SE 001		Lady of Flame	1990	8.75	17.50	35.00
Pink vinyl						
Smilin' Ear SE 001		Lady of Flame	1990	3.75	7.50	15.00
Smilin' Ear SE 001	PS	Lady of Flame	1990	3.75	7.50	15.00

45s

Label, Number		Title	Year	VG	VG+	NM
C/Z 034		Sacrificial Shack/Sweetheart	1992		3.75	7.50
C/Z 034	PS	Sacrificial Shack/Sweetheart	1992		3.75	7.50
Rave 024		Bondage/1066	1991	3.75	7.50	15.00
Red vinyl; B-side by God And Texas						
Rave 024		Bondage/1066	1991		2.50	5.00
Black vinyl; B-side by God And Texas						
Rave 024	PS	Bondage/1066	1991		2.50	5.00
Spank 01		Hangman's Rope/Kill Switch	1991	5.00	10.00	20.00
B-side by Lost						
Spank 01	PS	Hangman's Rope/Kill Switch	1991	5.00	10.00	20.00
Sub Pop 148		Death Row Eyes/The Smell	1992	6.25	12.50	25.00
210 on aqua vinyl						
Sub Pop 148		Death Row Eyes/The Smell	1992	3.75	7.50	15.00
1,841 on blue vinyl						
Sub Pop 148		Death Row Eyes/The Smell	1992	3.75	7.50	15.00
1,234 on white vinyl						

Label, Number		Title	Year	VG	VG+	NM
Sub Pop 148	PS	Death Row Eyes/The Smell	1992	3.75	7.50	15.00
#43 in Sub Pop Singles Club series						

Parker, Graham
*British pub-rocker, with backing band **The Rumour** on most of his early records.*

Vinyl Albums

Arista SP-63	DJ	Live Sparks	1979	5.00	10.00	20.00
Arista AL 4223		Squeezing Out Sparks	1979	3.00	6.00	12.00
Arista AL8-8023		The Real Macaw	1983	2.50	5.00	10.00
Arista AL6-8352		The Real Macaw	1985	2.00	4.00	8.00
Budget-line reissue						
Arista AL6-8356		The Up Escalator	1985	2.00	4.00	8.00
Budget-line reissue						
Arista AL6-8363		Squeezing Out Sparks	1985	2.00	4.00	8.00
Budget-line reissue						
Arista AL6-8374		Another Grey Area	1985	2.00	4.00	8.00
Budget-line reissue						
Arista AL6-8391		Look Back in Anger	1985	2.50	5.00	10.00
Arista AL 9517		The Up Escalator	1980	2.50	5.00	10.00
Arista AL 9589		Another Grey Area	1982	2.50	5.00	10.00
Elektra 60388		Steady Nerves	1985	2.50	5.00	10.00
Mercury SRM-2-100	(2)	The Parkerilla	1978	4.50	9.00	18.00
Originals have gatefold sleeves						
Mercury SRM-1-1095		Howlin' Wind	1976	3.75	7.50	15.00
Mercury SRM-1-1117		Heat Treatment	1976	3.75	7.50	15.00
Mercury SRM-1-3706		Stick to Me	1977	3.75	7.50	15.00
Mercury 824 808-1		Stick to Me	1985	3.00	6.00	12.00
Reissue with new number						
Mercury 826 097-1		Pourin' It All Out: The Mercury Years	1985	3.00	6.00	12.00
RCA 8316-1-R		The Mona Lisa's Sister	1988	2.50	5.00	10.00
RCA 9876-1-R		Human Soul	1989	2.50	5.00	10.00

45s

Arista 0420		Local Girls/I Want You Back	1979		2.00	4.00
Arista 0420	PS	Local Girls/I Want You Back	1979		2.00	4.00
Arista 0439		Mercury Poisoning/I Want You Back (Alive)	1979		2.00	4.00
Arista 0523		Stupefaction/Women in Charge	1980		2.00	4.00
Arista 0523	PS	Stupefaction/Women in Charge	1980		2.00	4.00
Arista 0549		Endless Nights/No Holding Back	1980		2.00	4.00
A-side: Guest vocals by Bruce Springsteen						
Arista 0652		Temporary Beauty/No More Excuses	1981		2.00	4.00
Arista 0687		You Hit the Spot/Habit Worth Forming	1982			3.00
Arista 9065		Life Gets Better/Beyond a Joke	1983			3.00
Mercury DJ-491	DJ	Hold Back the Night (same on both sides)	1977	3.00	6.00	12.00
Mercury DJ-531	DJ	Stick to Me (same on both sides)	1977	3.00	6.00	12.00
Mercury 73834		Soul Shoes/You've Got to Be Kidding	1976	2.00	4.00	8.00
Mercury 73876		Heat Treatment/Back Door Love	1976	2.00	4.00	8.00
Mercury 73970		Stick to Me/The Heat in Harlem	1977	2.00	4.00	8.00
Mercury 74000		Hold Back the Night/(Let Me Get) Sweet on You//White Honey/ Soul Shoes	1977		2.50	5.00
Pink vinyl						
Mercury 74000		Hold Back the Night/(Let Me Get) Sweet on You//White Honey/ Soul Shoes	1977		3.50	7.00
Black vinyl; scarcer than pink version						
Mercury 74000	PS	"The Pink Parker": Hold Back the Night/(Let Me Get) Sweet on You/ White Honey/Soul Shoes	1977		2.50	5.00

Label, Number		Title	Year	VG	VG+	NM
12-Inch Singles						
Arista SP-41	DJ	Mercury Poisoning (one-sided)	1979	3.00	6.00	12.00
Gray vinyl with custom labels						
Arista SP-54	DJ	Local Girls/I Want You Back (Alive)	1979		3.00	6.00
Arista SP-65	DJ	Mercury Poisoning/I Want You Back (Alive)	1979	3.00	6.00	12.00
Arista SP-118	DJ	Temporary Beauty/No More Excuses (Instrumental)	1982		3.50	7.00
Arista SP-130	DJ	You Hit the Spot/You Hit the Spot (Extended)	1982		3.00	6.00
Arista 9098	DJ	You Can't Take Love for Granted (2 versions)	1983		3.00	6.00
Elektra ED 5040	DJ	Wake Up (Next to You) (Long Version)/Wake Up (Next to You) (Short Version)	1984		2.50	5.00
Elektra ED 5078	DJ	The Weekend's Too Short (same on both sides)	1985		2.50	5.00
Mercury MK-28	DJ	Hold Back the Night/(Let Me Get) Sweet on You//White Honey/Soul Shoes	1977	7.50	15.00	30.00
RCA 8336-1	DJ	Start a Fire (LP version)/Start a Fire (Edit)	1988		3.00	6.00
RCA 8685-1	DJ	Don't Let It Break You Down (same on both sides)	1988		3.00	6.00
RCA 9178-RD		Everything Goes (extended)/That Thing Is Rockin'	1990	2.50	5.00	10.00

Passengers

*Includes **U2, Brian Eno** and guest star Luciano Pavarotti.*

Label, Number		Title	Year	VG	VG+	NM
Vinyl Albums						
Island 524 166-1		Original Soundtracks 1	1995	2.50	5.00	10.00

Pavement

Punk band from Stockton, California.

Label, Number		Title	Year	VG	VG+	NM
7-Inch Extended Play Singles						
Drag City DC 02		Demolition Plot J-7	1990	3.00	6.25	12.50
Drag City DC 02	PS	Demolition Plot J-7	1990	3.00	6.25	12.50
45s						
Drag City DC 9		Summer Babe//Mercy Snack/Baptiss Blacktick	1990	2.50	5.00	10.00
Drag City DC 9	PS	Summer Babe//Mercy Snack/Baptiss Blacktick	1990	2.50	5.00	10.00
Treble Kicker TK 001		Slay Tracks: You're Killing Me/Box Elder	1989	12.50	25.00	50.00
Treble Kicker TK 001	PS	Slay Tracks: You're Killing Me/Box Elder	1989	12.50	25.00	50.00
Numbered edition of 1,000; already has been counterfeited						

Pearl Harbour and the Explosions

American new-wave group.

Label, Number		Title	Year	VG	VG+	NM
Vinyl Albums						
Warner Bros. BSK 3404		Pearl Harbor and the Explosions	1980	3.00	6.00	12.00
Warner Bros. BSK 3515		Don't Follow Me, I'm Lost Too	1981	2.50	5.00	10.00
*Pearl Harbour solo, with members of **The Clash***						
45s						
415 Records S-0003		Drivin'/Release It	1979		2.00	4.00
415 Records S-0003	PS	Drivin'/Release It	1979		2.00	4.00

Label, Number		Title	Year	VG	VG+	NM
Warner Bros. 49143		You Got It (Release It)/Busy Little B Side				
			1979		2.00	4.00
Warner Bros. 49207		Drivin'/The Big One	1980		2.00	4.00
12-Inch Singles						
Island 96883		Flirt/Killer Joe	1985	2.50	5.00	10.00
Warner Bros. PRO-A-843	DJ	You Got It/Drivin'/Busy B Side	1979		3.00	6.00

Pearl Jam

Eddie Vedder and company, from Seattle. Also see **Green River; Mother Love Bone; Three Fish.**

Vinyl Albums						
Epic Associated Z 47857		Ten	1991	2.50	5.00	10.00
Album not released on U.S. vinyl until 1994						
Epic E 53136		Vs.	1993	2.50	5.00	10.00
Epic E 66900		Vitalogy	1994	2.50	5.00	10.00
45s						
Epic ZS7 4906	DJ	Sonic Reducer/Ramblings Continued				
			1992	5.00	10.00	20.00
Epic ZS7 4906	PS	Sonic Reducer/Ramblings Continued				
			1992	5.00	10.00	20.00
Picture sleeve front states "Who Killed Rudolph?"						
Epic ZS7 5610	DJ	Angel/Ramblings	1993	3.75	7.50	15.00
Epic ZS7 5610	PS	Angel/Ramblings	1993	3.75	7.50	15.00
Epic 77771		Spin the Black Circle/Tremor Christ				
			1994			3.00
Epic 77771	PS	Spin the Black Circle/Tremor Christ				
			1994			3.00
Epic 77772		Not for You/Out of My Mind	1995			3.00
Epic 77772	PS	Not for You/Out of My Mind	1995			3.00
Epic 77873		Immortality/Rearviewmirror	1995			3.00
B-side by **The Frogs**						
Epic 77873	PS	Immortality/Rearviewmirror	1995			3.00
Epic 78199		I Got I.D./Long Road	1995			2.00
With Neil Young						
Epic 78199	PS	I Got I.D./Long Road	1995			2.00
"Merkinball" cardboard sleeve						
Epic Associated ZS7 4354	DJ	Let Me Sleep (Christmas Time)/Ramblings				
			1991	5.00	10.00	20.00
Small hole, plays at 33 1-3 RPM						
Epic Associated ZS7 4354	PS	Let Me Sleep (Christmas Time)/Ramblings				
			1991	5.00	10.00	20.00
Epic Associated 74745		Jeremy/Alive	1992	5.00	10.00	20.00

White label; deleted upon release, then briefly available again in 1995 before it was replaced by a gray-label reissue ($3 NM)

Penn, Michael

Older brother of actor Sean Penn. Alterna-rocker.

Vinyl Albums						
RCA 9692-1-R		March	1989	2.50	5.00	10.00
45s						
RCA 2512-7-R		This & That/No Myth (Acoustic Version)				
			1990			3.00
RCA 9111-7-R		No Myth/Big House	1989			2.00
RCA 9111-7-R	PS	No Myth/Big House	1989			2.00

Officially, no Pearl Jam 45s were released in the United States until 1994's "Spin the Black Circle"/ "Tremor Christ." But in the fall of 1992, Epic Associated released "Jeremy"/ "Alive" for about a day until it was recalled. It later re-surfaced after Collectables Records did a gray-label reissue of the two songs from *Ten,* but the white label still goes for at least $20. The other one above was part of a series meant for the band's fan club. The first of these, "Let Me Sleep (Christmas Time)," is the most difficult to locate, as it came out around Christmas of 1991, when the band had just released its debut album.

Label, Number		Title	Year	VG	VG+	NM

Pere Ubu

*Cleveland's pioneer new wave band. Also see **Laughner, Peter.***

Vinyl Albums

Label, Number		Title	Year	VG	VG+	NM
Blank 001		The Modern Dance	1978	8.75	17.50	35.00
Chrysalis CHR 1207		Dub Housing	1979	6.25	12.50	25.00
Enigma D1-73343		The Tenement Years	1988	3.00	6.00	12.00
Fontana 838 237-1		Cloudland	1989	3.00	6.00	12.00
Rough Trade ROUGH US 4		The Art of Walking	1980	8.75	17.50	35.00
First 1,800 were incorrectly mastered						
Rough Trade ROUGH US 4		The Art of Walking	1980	6.25	12.50	25.00
Revised version: Vocal added on "Arabia"; "Miles" is shortened						
Rough Trade ROUGH US 7		The Modern Dance	1981	6.25	12.50	25.00
Reissue of Blank 001						
Rough Trade ROUGH US 10		390 Degrees of Simulated Stereo	1981	5.00	10.00	20.00
Rough Trade ROUGH US 21		The Song of the Bailing Man	1982	5.00	10.00	20.00

45s

Label, Number		Title	Year	VG	VG+	NM
Hearthan HR-101		30 Seconds Over Tokyo/Heart of Darkness				
			1975	12.50	25.00	50.00
First issue: Black label						
Hearthan HR-101		30 Seconds Over Tokyo/Heart of Darkness				
			1975	8.75	17.50	35.00
Second issue: Brown on white label						
Hearthan HR-101	PS	30 Seconds Over Tokyo/Heart of Darkness				
			1975	25.00	50.00	100.00
First 1,000 issued with picture sleeve						
Hearthan HR-102		Final Solution/Cloud 149	1976	6.25	12.50	25.00
Hearthan HR-102	PS	Final Solution/Cloud 149	1976	30.00	75.00	150.00
First 600 issued with picture sleeve						
Hearthan HR-103		Street Waves/My Dark Ages	1976	6.25	12.50	25.00
Hearthan HR-103	PS	Street Waves/My Dark Ages	1976	12.50	25.00	50.00
Most issued with picture sleeve						
Hearthan HR-104		The Modern Dance/Heaven	1977	6.25	12.50	25.00
Hearthan HR-104	PS	The Modern Dance/Heaven	1977	12.50	25.00	50.00
First 1,000 issued with picture sleeve						
Rough Trade RT US 004		Not Happy/Lonesome Cowboy Dave				
			1981	2.50	5.00	10.00
Rough Trade RT US 004	PS	Not Happy/Lonesome Cowboy Dave				
			1981	3.75	7.50	15.00

12-Inch Singles

Label, Number		Title	Year	VG	VG+	NM
Fontana PRO 747	DJ	Breathe/Bang the Drum/Over My Head/Universal Vibration				
			1989	2.50	5.00	10.00
Restless 72340		We Have the Technology/Postman Drove a Caddy/The B Side				
			1988		3.00	6.00

Pet Shop Boys

*British synth-pop duo. Also see **Electronic.***

Vinyl Albums

Label, Number		Title	Year	VG	VG+	NM
EMI America PW-17193		Please	1986	3.00	6.00	12.00
EMI America SQ-17246		Disco	1986	3.00	6.00	12.00
EMI America R 164390		Please	1986	3.50	7.00	14.00
BMG Direct Marketing edition						
EMI E1-28105		Disco 2	1994	3.00	6.00	12.00
EMI Manhattan 04233	(3) DJ	Special Limited Edition: Introspective Club Mixes				
			1988	10.00	20.00	40.00
Promo-only set of three 12" records of remixes						
EMI Manhattan ELJ-46972		Actually	1987	3.00	6.00	12.00
EMI Manhattan E1-90263	(2)	Actually	1988	5.00	10.00	20.00
Limited double-LP set with extra record of remixes						
EMI Manhattan E1-90868		Introspective	1989	3.00	6.00	12.00

Label, Number		Title	Year	VG	VG+	NM
EMI Manhattan R 100681		Introspective	1988	3.50	7.00	14.00
BMG Direct Marketing edition						
EMI Manhattan R 153678		Actually	1987	3.50	7.00	14.00
BMG Direct Marketing edition						

45s

Label, Number		Title	Year	VG	VG+	NM
EMI S7-17492		Can You Forgive Her/I Want to Wake Up				
			1993		2.00	4.00
EMI S7-17708		Go West/Yesterday, When I Was Mad				
			1994		2.00	4.00
EMI S7-18736		Paninaro '95/Girls & Boys (Live in Rio)				
			1995		2.00	4.00
EMI S7-57696		Was It Worth It/Miserablism	1992		2.00	4.00
A-side is dub version, perhaps released in error						
EMI America 8307		West End Girls/A Man Could Get Arrested				
			1986		2.00	4.00
EMI America 8307	PS	West End Girls/A Man Could Get Arrested				
			1986		2.00	4.00
EMI America 8321		Opportunities (Let's Make Lots of Money)/In the Night				
			1986	2.50	5.00	10.00
EMI America 8321	PS	Opportunities (Let's Make Lots of Money)/In the Night				
			1986	2.50	5.00	10.00
Withdrawn shortly after release						
EMI America 8330		Opportunities (Let's Make Lots of Money)/Was That What It Was				
			1986		2.00	4.00
EMI America 8330	PS	Opportunities (Let's Make Lots of Money)/Was That What It Was				
			1986		2.00	4.00
EMI America 8338		Love Comes Quickly/That's My Impression				
			1986		2.00	4.00
EMI America 8338	PS	Love Comes Quickly/That's My Impression				
			1986		2.00	4.00
EMI America 8355		Suburbia/Jack the Lad	1986		2.00	4.00
EMI America 8355	PS	Suburbia/Jack the Lad	1986		2.00	4.00
EMI America 43027		It's a Sin/You Know Where You Went Wrong				
			1987		2.00	4.00
EMI America 43027	PS	It's a Sin/You Know Where You Went Wrong				
			1987		2.00	4.00
EMI Manhattan 50107		What Have I Done to Deserve This?/A New Life				
			1987		2.00	4.00
Vocal guest: Dusty Springfield						
EMI Manhattan 50107	PS	What Have I Done to Deserve This?/A New Life				
			1987		2.00	4.00
EMI Manhattan 50123		Always on My Mind/Do I Have To?				
			1988		2.00	4.00
Not issued with picture sleeve in U.S.						
EMI Manhattan 50161		Domino Dancing/Don Juan	1988		2.00	4.00
EMI Manhattan 50161	PS	Domino Dancing/Don Juan	1988		2.00	4.00
EMI Manhattan 50171		Left to My Own Devices/The Sound of the Atom Splitting				
			1988		2.00	4.00
EMI Manhattan 50171	PS	Left to My Own Devices/The Sound of the Atom Splitting				
			1988	2.00	4.00	8.00

12-Inch Singles

Label, Number		Title	Year	VG	VG+	NM
Bobcat 05019		West End Girls/One More Chance				
			1984	7.50	15.00	30.00
Early versions of these songs, produced by Bobby O(rlando)						
EMI SPRO 04690	DJ	So Hard (4 mixes)	1990	2.50	5.00	10.00
EMI SPRO 04727	DJ	How Can You Expect to Be Taken Seriously (5 versions)				
			1991	2.50	5.00	10.00
EMI 56194		So Hard (3 mixes)/It Must Be Obvious				
			1990	3.00	6.00	12.00

Label, Number		Title	Year	VG	VG+	NM
EMI 56204		How Can You Expect to Be Taken Seriously? (3 mixes)/ Being Boring/We All Feel Better in the Dark				
			1990	3.00	6.00	12.00
EMI 56234		DJ Culture (2 versions)/Music for Boys 1 & 2				
			1991	2.50	5.00	10.00
EMI 56243		Was It Worth It (12")/Was It Worth It (Dub)/Miserabilism (2 versions)	1992	2.00	4.00	8.00
EMI 56279		Can You Forgive Her (5 mixes)	1992	2.00	4.00	8.00
EMI America SPRO 9669	DJ	Opportunities (Let's Make Lots of Money) (same on both sides)				
			1985	5.00	10.00	20.00
EMI America SPRO 9925	DJ	Suburbia (2 versions)	1986	2.50	5.00	10.00
EMI America 19208		West End Girls (Dance Mix)/A Man Could Get Arrested/ West End Girls	1985	3.75	7.50	15.00
EMI America 19215		Opportunities (Let's Make Lots of Money) (3 remixes)/ Was That What It Was	1986	2.00	4.00	8.00
EMI America 19218		Love Comes Quickly (3 mixes)/That's My Impression (Disco Mix)				
			1986	3.00	6.00	12.00
EMI America 19226		Suburbia (The Full Horror)/Suburbia (Edit)/Jack the Lad				
			1986	2.00	4.00	8.00
EMI America 19256		It's a Sin (4 mixes)/You Know Where You Went Wrong				
			1987	3.00	6.00	12.00
EMI America 56080		What Have I Done to Deserve This?/Rent				
			1987		3.00	6.00
EMI Manhattan SPRO 04013/4	DJ	What Have I Done to Deserve This (2 mixes)/Rent/I Want a Dog				
			1988	6.25	12.50	25.00
EMI Manhattan SPRO 04051	DJ	Always On My Mind (5 versions)/Do I Have To				
			1988	4.00	8.00	16.00
EMI Manhattan SPRO 04231/2	DJ	I'm Not Scared/I Want a Dog	1988	3.75	7.50	15.00
EMI Manhattan 56089		Always on My Mind (2 remixes)/Do I Have To?				
			1988	2.50	5.00	10.00
EMI Manhattan 56116		Domino Dancing (3 mixes)/Don Juan (Disco Mix)				
			1988	2.50	5.00	10.00
EMI Manhattan 56121		Left to My Own Devices (2 mixes)/The Sound of the Atom Splitting				
			1988	3.00	6.00	12.00

Phair, Liz

Female rocker from New Haven, Connecticut.

Vinyl Albums

Matador OLE 51-1	(2)	Exile in Guyville	1992	3.00	6.00	12.00
Matador OLE 107-1		Whip-Smart	1994	2.50	5.00	10.00

45s

Matador OLE 103-7		Supernova/Combo Platter	1994		2.00	4.00
Blue vinyl, small center hole						
Matador OLE 103-7	PS	Supernova/Combo Platter	1994		2.00	4.00
Minty Fresh MF-4		Carnivore/Carnivore (Raw Version)				
			1993	3.75	7.50	15.00
First pressing: 1,000 on clear red vinyl						
Minty Fresh MF-4		Carnivore/Carnivore (Raw Version)				
			1993	3.75	7.50	15.00
Second pressing: 1,000 on red/blue vinyl						
Minty Fresh MF-4	PS	Carnivore/Carnivore (Raw Version)				
			1993	3.75	7.50	15.00

Pickett, Charlie, and the Eggs

Fort Lauderdale, Florida trash-rockers.

45s

Open 1		Feelin'/White Light White Heat	1981	3.75	7.50	15.00

Label, Number		Title	Year	VG	VG+	NM
Open 1	PS	Feelin'/White Light White Heat	1981	3.75	7.50	15.00
Open 2		If This Is Love Can I Get My Money Back/Slow Death				
			1981	4.50	9.00	18.00
Open 2		If This Is Love Can I Get My Money Back (Remixed Version)/				
		Slow Death	1982	5.00	10.00	20.00
Open 2	PS	If This Is Love Can I Get My Money Back (Remixed Version)/				
		Slow Death	1981	4.50	9.00	18.00

Pigbag
British new-wave group.

12-Inch Singles

Stiff TEES 12??		Papa's Got a Brand New Pigbag/Whoops/Sunny Day				
			1981	2.00	4.00	8.00
Stiff TEES 1213		Getting Up (2 mixes)/Giggling Mud/Go Cat				
			1982	2.00	4.00	8.00
Y USA 5		The Big Bean/Scumda	1982	2.50	5.00	10.00

Pigface

45s

Sub Pop 240		Empathy/Steamroller	1993		2.50	5.00
Sub Pop 240	PS	Empathy/Steamroller	1993		2.50	5.00
#60 in Sub Pop Singles Club series						

Piscopo, Joe
Comedian, former member of the "Saturday Night Live" troupe.

45s

Columbia 03253		I Love Rock and Roll (Medley)/The First Rehearsal				
			1982			3.00
Columbia 03253	PS	I Love Rock and Roll (Medley)/The First Rehearsal				
			1982			3.00
Columbia 04939		Honeymooners Rap/Fat Boy	1985			3.00
Columbia 04939	PS	Honeymooners Rap/Fat Boy	1985			3.00

12-Inch Singles

Columbia 03254		I Love Rock and Roll (Medley)/The First Rehearsal				
			1982	2.00	4.00	8.00
Columbia 05224		Honeymooners Rap (3 versions)	1985		3.50	7.00
Columbia CAS 2092	DJ	Honeymooners Rap/Honeymooners Rap (Captain Video Version)				
			1985	2.00	4.00	8.00

Pixies
*Boston alterna-rock group. Member Kim Deal, with sister Kelley, formed **The Breeders**.*

Vinyl Albums

4AD/Rough Trade RTUS 38		Surfer Rosa	198?	5.00	10.00	20.00
Elektra 60856		Doolittle	1989	2.50	5.00	10.00
Elektra 60856	DJ	Doolittle	1989	3.00	6.00	12.00
Promo-only on audiophile vinyl						
Elektra 60963		Bossanova	1990	2.50	5.00	10.00
Elektra/4AD PR-8127	DJ	Live	1989	12.50	25.00	50.00
Promo-only seven-song live collection of mostly songs from their pre-Elektra days						

45s

Elektra 69287		Here Comes Your Man/Into the White				
			1989	2.00	4.00	8.00

Label, Number		Title	Year	VG	VG+	NM
12-Inch Singles						
Elektra ED 5386	DJ	Here Comes Your Man (same on both sides)				
			1989		3.00	6.00
Elektra ED 5476	DJ	Velouria/Make Believe/I've Been Waiting for You/The Thing				
			1990	2.50	5.00	10.00

Planet P

Group of session musicians with Tony Carey as lead singer. Also known as Planet P Project.

Vinyl Albums						
Geffen GHS 4000		Planet P	1983	3.00	6.00	12.00
MCA L33-1227	EP	Pink World	1984	3.00	6.00	12.00
Promo-only pink vinyl EP						
MCA 8019	(2)	Pink World	1984	5.00	10.00	20.00
45s						
Geffen 29705		Why Me?/Only You and Me	1983			3.00
Geffen 29705	PS	Why Me?/Only You and Me	1983			3.00
MCA 52515		What I See/Beyond the Barrier	1984			3.00
MCA 52515	DJ	What I See (same on both sides)	1984	2.00	4.00	8.00
Pink vinyl						

Planet Patrol

*Funk group. Not the same as **Planet P**.*

Vinyl Albums						
Tommy Boy TBLP-1002		Planet Patrol	1986	3.00	6.00	12.00
Originals on colored vinyl						
12-Inch Singles						
Tommy Boy 837		I Didn't Know I Loved You (vocal and instrumental)/				
		Play at Your Own Risk	1983	2.00	4.00	8.00
Tommy Boy 846		Danger Zone (3 versions)	1984	2.00	4.00	8.00

Plasmatics

*Outrageous New York band, fronted by chainsaw-wielding **Wendy O. Williams**.*

Vinyl Albums						
Capitol ST-12237		Coup d'Etat	1982	3.75	7.50	15.00
PVC 6908		Metal Priestess	1983	3.75	7.50	15.00
Reissue of Stiff WOW-666						
PVC 8929		Beyond the Valley of 1984	1983	3.75	7.50	15.00
Reissue of Stiff USE-11						
Stiff USE-9		New Hope for the Wretched	1980	6.25	12.50	25.00
Stiff USE-11		Beyond the Valley of 1984	1981	6.25	12.50	25.00
Stiff WOW-666	EP	Metal Priestess	1981	6.25	12.50	25.00
Vice Squad VS 105/106	EP	Meet the Plasmatics	1979	6.25	12.50	25.00
45s						
Vice Squad VS 101/102		Butcher Baby/Fast Food Service/Concrete Shoes				
			1978	5.00	10.00	20.00
All copies on red vinyl						
Vice Squad VS 101/102	PS	Butcher Baby/Fast Food Service/Concrete Shoes				
			1978	5.00	10.00	20.00
Vice Squad VS 103/104		Dream Lover/Corruption/Want You Baby				
			1978	5.00	10.00	20.00
All copies on purple vinyl						
Vice Squad VS 103/104	PS	Dream Lover/Corruption/Want You Baby				
			1978	5.00	10.00	20.00

Label, Number		Title	Year	VG	VG+	NM

Plastic Idols
American punk band.

45s
Vision 23		I.U.D./Sophistication	1979	3.00	6.00	12.00
Vision 23	PS	I.U.D./Sophistication	1979	3.00	6.00	12.00
Vision 25		Einstein Experience/Uncircumcised Twin/Siamese Lust				
			1980	5.00	10.00	20.00
Vision 25	PS	Einstein Experience/Uncircumcised Twin/Siamese Lust				
			1980	5.00	10.00	20.00

Platinum Blonde
Canadian rock band.

Vinyl Albums
Epic BFE 40147		Alien Shores	1985	2.50	5.00	10.00
Epic BFE 40949		Contact	1987	2.50	5.00	10.00

45s
Epic 05593		Crying Over You/It Ain't Love Anyway				
			1985			3.00
Epic 05593		Crying Over You/It Ain't Love Anyway				
			1985			3.00
Epic 05593	PS	Crying Over You/It Ain't Love Anyway				
			1985			3.00
Epic 05804		Somebody Somewhere/Red Light				
			1985			3.00
Epic 07606		Contact/Tough Enough	1987			3.00

Plimsouls, The
Los Angeles new wave/pop act.

Vinyl Albums
Beat BE-1001	EP	Zero Hour	1980	3.75	7.50	15.00
Geffen GHS 4002		Everywhere at Once	1983	3.00	6.00	12.00
Planet 13		The Plimsouls	1981	3.75	7.50	15.00

45s
Geffen 29496		Oldest Story in the World/Hobo	1983	2.50	5.00	10.00
Geffen 29600		A Million Miles Away/Play the Breaks				
			1983		2.00	4.00
Geffen 29600	PS	A Million Miles Away/Play the Breaks				
			1983	3.00	6.00	12.00
Planet 47923		Now/When You Find Out	1981	7.50	15.00	30.00
Planet 47930		Zero Hour//Hush Hush/Dizzy Miss Lizzie				
			1981	15.00	30.00	60.00
Shaky City 134		A Million Miles Away/I'll Get Lucky				
			1982		2.00	4.00
Shaky City 134	PS	A Million Miles Away/I'll Get Lucky				
			1982		2.00	4.00

12-Inch Singles
Geffen PRO-A-2068	DJ	A Million Miles Away/The Oldest Story/Magic Touch				
			1983	3.00	6.00	12.00
Shaky City 12134		A Million Miles Away/I'll Get Lucky				
			1982	5.00	10.00	20.00

Plugz
Los Angeles punk band.

Vinyl Albums
Fatima 80		Better Luck	1981	3.00	6.00	12.00

Label, Number		Title	Year	VG	VG+	NM
Plug/Real Life 001		Electrify Me	1979	5.00	10.00	20.00
45s						
Fatima 79		La Bamba/Achin'	1981	3.75	7.50	15.00
Fatima 79	PS	La Bamba/Achin'	1981	3.75	7.50	15.00
Slash 102		Move/Let Go/Mindless Contentment				
			1978	5.00	10.00	20.00
Slash 102	PS	Move/Let Go/Mindless Contentment				
			1978	25.00	50.00	100.00
Black on yellow sleeve with band photo and lyrics						
Slash 102	PS	Move/Let Go/Mindless Contentment				
			1978	5.00	10.00	20.00
Gray folder with necktie and "Singi" button artwork						

Pogo the Clown
With former members of **Halo of Flies**.

45s						
Amphetamine Reptile SCALE 15		Lederhosen/Sesame Street	1988	5.00	10.00	20.00
Amphetamine Reptile SCALE 15	PS	Lederhosen/Sesame Street	1988	5.00	10.00	20.00

Pogues, The
Punk-folk group from England, originally fronted by **Shane MacGowan**.

Vinyl Albums						
Enigma ST-73225		Red Roses for Me	1986	3.00	6.00	12.00
Stiff/MCA 36015	EP	Poguetry in Motion	1986	3.00	6.00	12.00
Stiff/MCA 5744		Rum, Sodomy and the Lash	1985	3.00	6.00	12.00
12-Inch Singles						
Island 2607	DJ	Yeah ,Yeah, Yeah, Yeah, Yeah (2 versions)/The Limerick Rake				
			1988		3.50	7.00
Island 96578		Yeah, Yeah, Yeah, Yeah, Yeah (2 versions)/The Limerick Rake				
			1988		3.50	7.00

Poi Dog Pondering
Not from Hawaii, but from Austin, Texas. Eclectic band.

Vinyl Albums						
Columbia CAS 1856	DJ	Interchords	1989	5.00	10.00	20.00
Promo-only interview and music						
Columbia CAS 2219	EP	Untitled (Fruitless)	1990	3.75	7.50	15.00
Promo-only six-song sampler						
Texas Hotel 16	EP	Circle Around the Sun + 3	198?	2.00	4.00	8.00
45s						
Columbia CS7 2000	DJ	Big Beautiful Spoon/Sugarbush Cushman				
			1990	2.00	4.00	8.00
12-Inch Singles						
Columbia CAS 1777	DJ	Living with the Dreaming Body/Fact of Life				
			1989		3.00	6.00
Columbia CAS 1995	DJ	U Li La Lu/Bury Me Deep	1990	2.00	4.00	8.00
One-sided 12-inch with etched B-side						

Poindexter, Buster
**David Johansen** in disguise.

Vinyl Albums						
RCA 6633-1-R		Buster Poindexter	1987	3.00	6.00	12.00

Label, Number		Title	Year	VG	VG+	NM
RCA 9665-1-R		Buster Goes Berserk	1989	3.00	6.00	12.00

45s

Label, Number		Title	Year	VG	VG+	NM
RCA 2572-7-R		Under the Sea/Debourge Yourself				
			1990			3.00
RCA 5357-7-R		Hot Hot Hot/Cannibal	1987			3.00
RCA 5357-7-R	PS	Hot Hot Hot/Cannibal	1987			3.00
RCA 6893-7	DJ	Zat You Santa Claus/Hot Hot Hot				
			1987			3.00
RCA 7638-7-R		Oh Me Oh My (I'm a Fool for You Baby)/Cannibal				
			1988			3.00
RCA 8914-7-R		Hit the Road Jack/Heart of Gold	1989			3.00
RCA 9007-7-R		All Night Party (Hot Mix)/All Night Party (Power Mix)				
			1989			3.00
RCA 9195-7-R		Under the Sea/Debourge Yourself				
			1990			3.00

12-Inch Singles

Label, Number	Title	Year	VG	VG+	NM
RCA 2531	International Playboy (5 versions)	1990		3.00	6.00
RCA 6726	Are You Lonely for Me/House of the Rising Sun				
		1987	2.00	4.00	8.00
RCA 8708-1	Cannibal (4 versions)/Hot Hot Hot ('88 version)				
		1988		2.50	5.00
RCA 9002-1	All Night Party (5 versions)	1989		3.00	6.00

Poison Idea

Portland, Oregon hardcore group.

7-Inch Extended Play Singles

Label, Number		Title	Year	VG	VG+	NM
American Leather 001		Darby Crash Rides Again	1988	3.75	7.50	15.00
Blue vinyl						
American Leather 001	PS	Darby Crash Rides Again	1988	3.75	7.50	15.00
Black and white sleeve						
Fatal Erection TR-001		Pick Your King	1983	9.25	18.75	37.50
First pressing on clear vinyl						
Fatal Erection TR-001		Pick Your King	1983	5.00	10.00	20.00
Second pressing on black vinyl						
Fatal Erection TR-001		Pick Your King	1983	3.00	6.25	12.50
Third pressing on blue vinyl						
Fatal Erection TR-001	PS	Pick Your King	1983	9.25	18.75	37.50
First sleeve: white with two inserts						
Fatal Erection TR-001	PS	Pick Your King	1983	5.00	10.00	20.00
Second sleeve: Blue, no inserts						
Fatal Erection TR-001	PS	Pick Your King	1983	3.00	6.25	12.50
Third sleeve: Cream or white, no inserts						
Shitfool (# unknown)		Filth Kick	1988	3.00	6.00	12.00
Shitfool (# unknown)	PS	Filth Kick	1988	3.00	6.00	12.00
2,000 pressed						

45s

Label, Number		Title	Year	VG	VG+	NM
American Leather 002	PD	Just to Get Away/Kick Out the Jams				
			198?	3.75	7.50	15.00
American Leather 003		Discontent/Jailhouse Stomp	1990		2.50	5.00
American Leather 003	PS	Discontent/Jailhouse Stomp	1990		2.50	5.00
Sub Pop 86		We Got the Beat/Taken by Surprise				
			1990	5.50	11.25	22.50
First 3,000 on mint green vinyl						
Sub Pop 86		We Got the Beat/Taken by Surprise				
			1990		3.75	7.50
Last 1,500 on black vinyl						
Sub Pop 86	PS	We Got the Beat/Taken by Surprise				
			1990		3.75	7.50
#25 in Sub Pop Singles Club series						

Label, Number		Title	Year	VG	VG+	NM

Police, The

*British new wavers, at first reggae-influenced, later a pop phenomenon. Also see **Sting; Stewart Copeland; Andy Summers; Klark Kent.***

Vinyl Albums

Label, Number		Title	Year	VG	VG+	NM
A&M SP-3311		Outlandos d'Amour	198?	2.00	4.00	8.00
Reissue						
A&M SP-3312		Reggatta da Blanc	198?	2.00	4.00	8.00
Reissue						
A&M SP-3713	10 (2)	Reggatta da Blanc	1979	7.50	15.00	30.00
Two 10" records with poster						
A&M SP-3720		Zenyatta Mondatta	1980	2.50	5.00	10.00
A&M SP-3730	DJ	Ghost in the Machine	1981	250.00	500.00	1,000.00
Special prototype picture disc that lights up when placed on a turntable. Truly bizarre.						
A&M SP-3730		Ghost in the Machine	1982	2.50	5.00	10.00
A&M SP-3735		Synchronicity	1983	7.50	15.00	30.00
Black & white cover						
A&M SP-3735		Synchronicity	1983	5.00	10.00	20.00
With gold, silver and bronze color bands on cover; used on audiophile pressings						
A&M SP-3735		Synchronicity	1983	2.50	5.00	10.00
With blue, yellow and red color bands; 93 versions of this cover exist, none more valuable than any other						
A&M SP-3902		Every Breath You Take -- The Singles	1986	2.50	5.00	10.00
A&M SP-4753		Outlandos d'Amour	1979	3.00	6.00	12.00
A&M SP-4792		Reggatta da Blanc	1979	3.00	6.00	12.00
A&M R 123571		Ghost in the Machine	1981	3.00	6.00	12.00
RCA Music Service edition						
A&M R 124159		Outlandos d'Amour	1979	3.00	6.00	12.00
RCA Music Service edition						
A&M R 130108		Zenyatta Mondatta	1980	3.00	6.00	12.00
RCA Music Service edition						
A&M R 134070		Synchronicity	1983	3.00	6.00	12.00
RCA Music Service edition						
A&M R 153349		Reggatta da Blanc	1979	3.00	6.00	12.00
RCA Music Service edition						
A&M R 173924		Every Breath You Take -- The Singles	1986	3.00	6.00	12.00
BMG Direct Marketing edition						
Nautilus NR-19		Zenyatta Mondatta	1981	8.75	17.50	35.00
Audiophile "Super Disc"						
Nautilus NR-40		Ghost in the Machine	1982	8.75	17.50	35.00
Audiophile "Super Disc"						

45s

Label, Number		Title	Year	VG	VG+	NM
A&M (# unknown)	PD	Roxanne/Can't Stand Losing You	1979	2.50	5.00	10.00
Badge-shaped picture disc						
A&M (no #)	(5) DJ	The Police File	1985	12.50	25.00	50.00
Boxed set of five "A&M Memories" singles released to radio. Price is mostly for the box.						
A&M 2096		Roxanne/Dead End Job	1978		3.00	6.00
Not issued with picture sleeve in U.S.						
A&M 2147		Can't Stand Losing You/No Time This Time	1979		2.50	5.00
A&M 2147	PS	Can't Stand Losing You/No Time This Time	1979	2.50	5.00	10.00
A&M 2190		Message in a Bottle/Landlord	1979		2.50	5.00
A&M 2190	PS	Message in a Bottle/Landlord	1979	2.50	5.00	10.00
Fold-out poster sleeve						
A&M 2218		Bring On the Night/Visions of the Night	1980		2.50	5.00
A&M 2275		De Do Do Do, De Da Da Da/Friends	1980		2.00	4.00
Standard A&M brown and silver late-1970s label						

Label, Number		Title	Year	VG	VG+	NM
A&M 2275		De Do Do Do, De Da Da Da/Friends	1980			3.00
Yellowish custom label with blueish triangle (most common version)						
A&M 2275		De Do Do Do, De Da Da Da/Friends	1980		2.00	4.00
Red custom label with silver triangle						
A&M 2275	PS	De Do Do Do, De Da Da Da/Friends	1980		3.00	6.00
Actually a title sleeve with large center hole						
A&M 2301		Don't Stand So Close to Me/A Sermon	1981			3.00
A&M 2301	PS	Don't Stand So Close to Me/A Sermon	1981			3.00
A&M 2371		Every Little Thing She Does Is Magic/Shambelle	1981			3.00
A&M 2371	PS	Every Little Thing She Does Is Magic/Shambelle	1981			3.00
A&M 2390		Spirits in the Material World/Flexible Strategies	1982			3.00
A&M 2390	PS	Spirits in the Material World/Flexible Strategies	1982			3.00
A&M 2408		Secret Journey/Darkness	1982			3.00
A&M 2408	PS	Secret Journey/Darkness	1982			3.00
A&M 2542		Every Breath You Take/Murder by Numbers	1983			3.00
A&M 2542	PS	Every Breath You Take/Murder by Numbers	1983			3.00
A&M 2569		King of Pain/Someone to Talk To	1983			3.00
A&M 2569	PS	King of Pain/Someone to Talk To	1983			3.00
A&M 2571		Synchronicity II/Once Upon a Daydream	1983			3.00
A&M 2571	PS	Synchronicity II/Once Upon a Daydream	1983			3.00
A&M 2614		Wrapped Around Your Finger/Tea in the Sahara (Live)	1984			3.00
A&M 2614	PS	Wrapped Around Your Finger/Tea in the Sahara (Live)	1984			3.00
A&M 2879		Don't Stand So Close to Me '86/Don't Stand So Close to Me (Live)	1986			3.00
A&M 2879	PS	Don't Stand So Close to Me '86/Don't Stand So Close to Me (Live)	1986			3.00
A&M 2908		Walking on the Moon/Message in a Bottle	1986		2.50	5.00
A&M 2908	PS	Walking on the Moon/Message in a Bottle	1986		2.50	5.00
A&M PR-4400	PD	Message in a Bottle/Message in a Bottle (Live)	1980	2.50	5.00	10.00
Star-shaped badge picture disc in folder; promo only						
A&M PR-4401	PD	Don't Stand So Close to Me/De Do Do Do, De Da Da Da	1981	2.50	5.00	10.00
Star-shaped badge picture disc in folder; promo only						
A&M 8622		Roxanne/Can't Stand Losing You	198?			3.00
Reissue						
A&M 8631		De Do Do Do, De Da Da Da/Don't Stand So Close to Me	198?			3.00
Reissue						
A&M 8633		Every Little Thing She Does Is Magic/Spirits in the Material World	198?			3.00
Reissue						

Label, Number		Title	Year	VG	VG+	NM
A&M 8640		Every Breath You Take/Wrapped Around Your Finger				
			198?			3.00
Reissue						
A&M 8649		King of Pain/Synchronicity II	198?			3.00
Reissue						
A&M 25000		De Do Do Do, De Da Da Da (Japanese)/				
		De Do Do Do, De Da Da Da (Spanish)				
			1981		2.50	5.00
A&M 25000	PS	De Do Do Do, De Da Da Da (Japanese)/				
		De Do Do Do, De Da Da Da (Spanish)				
			1981		2.50	5.00
A&M 75021 8738 7		Canary in a Coalmine/Message in a Bottle				
			1996			3.00

Oldies reissue; first appearance of A-side on U.S. 45

12-Inch Singles						
A&M SP-12207		Don't Stand So Close to Me '86 (2 versions)/				
		Don't Stand So Close to Me (Original & Live)				
			1986	2.00	4.00	8.00
A&M SP-17122	DJ	Message in a Bottle//Message in a Bottle (Live)/Landlord				
			1979	5.00	10.00	20.00
A&M SP-17137	DJ	Voices Inside My Head/When the World Is Running Down...				
			1980	2.00	4.00	8.00
A&M SP-17173	DJ	One World (Not Three)/Too Much Information				
			1981	2.50	5.00	10.00
A&M SP-17182	DJ	Spirits in the Material World/Secret Journey				
			1981	3.00	6.00	12.00
A&M SP-17230	DJ	Every Breath You Take (same on both sides)				
			1983	2.50	5.00	10.00
A&M SP-17432	DJ	Don't Stand So Close to Me '86 (same on both sides)				
			1986		3.50	7.00
A&M SP-17449	DJ	Walking on the Moon (same on both sides)				
			1986	2.00	4.00	8.00

Pop Will Eat Itself

British psychedelic/rap/rock/who knows what else group.

Vinyl Albums						
Nothing 95887		Amalgamation	1994	2.50	5.00	10.00
Rough Trade ROUGH US 22		Now for a Feast	198?	4.00	8.00	16.00
12-Inch Singles						
Nothing 2141		RSVP (4 versions)	1994	3.00	6.00	12.00
RCA 2732		Dance of the Mad (2 versions)/Preaching to the Perverted/				
		Touched by the Hand of God	1990	2.50	5.00	10.00
RCA 2763		X, Y & Zee (3 versions)	1991	3.00	6.00	12.00
RCA 2845		Another Man's Rhubarb (3 versions)				
			1990	2.50	5.00	10.00
RCA 9001		Can U Dig It? (4 versions)	1989	3.00	6.00	12.00
RCA 9009	DJ	Can U Dig It?/Can You Dig It? (7" English Mix)				
			1989	2.50	5.00	10.00

Porno for Pyros

*Includes two former members of **Jane's Addiction**.*

Vinyl Albums						
Warner Bros. 45228		Porno for Pyros	1993	3.00	6.00	12.00

Label, Number		Title	Year	VG	VG+	NM

Poster Children

45s

Sub Pop 88		Pointed Stick/Thinner-Stronger	1990			3.50
Last 1,500 on black vinyl						
Sub Pop 88		Pointed Stick/Thinner-Stronger	1990		3.75	7.50
First 3,000 on reddish vinyl						
Sub Pop 88	PS	Pointed Stick/Thinner-Stronger	1990			3.50
#24 in Sub Pop Singles Club series						
Warner Bros. PRO-S-????	DJ	He's My Star//Childlike and Evergreen/Someone Else's Song				
			1995		3.50	7.00

"Soil Samples #19" promo on white vinyl; B-side by Wilco

Power Station, The

*Side project of **Duran Duran** members **John Taylor** and **Andy Taylor,** with vocalist Robert "Addicted to Love" Palmer.*

Vinyl Albums

Capitol SJ-12380		The Power Station	1985	2.50	5.00	10.00
Capitol R 123577		The Power Station	1985	3.00	6.00	12.00
RCA Music Service edition						

45s

Capitol 5444		Some Like It Hot/The Heat Is On				
			1985			3.00
Capitol 5444	PS	Some Like It Hot/The Heat Is On				
			1985			3.00
Capitol 5479		Get It On/Go To Zero	1985			3.00
Capitol 5479	PS	Get It On/Go To Zero	1985			3.00
Capitol 5511		Communication/Murderess	1985			3.00
Capitol 5511	PS	Communication/Murderess	1985			3.00

12-Inch Singles

Capitol 8646		Get It On (2 versions)/Go to Zero	1985	2.50	5.00	10.00
Capitol SPRO-9344	DJ	Some Like It Hot/Some Like It Hot (7" Mix)				
			1985	2.50	5.00	10.00
Capitol 15204		Communication (Special Dub Mix)/Murderess				
			1985	2.00	4.00	8.00

Prefab Sprout

British rock band.

Vinyl Albums

Epic BFE 40100		Two Wheels Good	1985	2.50	5.00	10.00
Epic BFE 44208		From Langley Park to Memphis	1988	2.50	5.00	10.00
Epic E 46132		Jordan: The Comeback	1990	3.00	6.00	12.00
Portrait BFR 39872		Swoon	1984	2.50	5.00	10.00

45s

Epic 05464		When Love Breaks Down/The Yearning Loins				
			1985			3.00
Epic 05464	PS	When Love Breaks Down/The Yearning Loins				
			1985			3.00
Epic 05769		Appetite/When the Angels	1986			3.00
Epic 07922		Cars and Girls/Vendetta	1988			3.00
Epic 07922	PS	Cars and Girls/Vendetta	1988			3.00

12-Inch Singles

Epic EAS 01020	DJ	The Golden Calf (Remix)/The Golden Calf (LP version)				
			1988		2.50	5.00
Epic AS 2236	DJ	Faron (2 versions)/Appetite	1985		2.50	5.00
Epic 74743		If You Don't Love Me (5 mixes)	1992		3.00	6.00

Label, Number		Title	Year	VG	VG+	NM

Pretenders

British new-wave band with frequent membership turnover, with American lead singer Chrissie Hynde the constant.

Vinyl Albums

Label, Number		Title	Year	VG	VG+	NM
Nautilus NR-38		Pretenders	1982	7.50	15.00	30.00
Audiophile "Super Disc"						
Sire MINI 3563	EP	Extended Play	1981	2.50	5.00	10.00
Sire SRK 3572		Pretenders II	1981	2.50	5.00	10.00
Sire SRK 6083		Pretenders	1980	2.50	5.00	10.00
Sire 23980		Learning to Crawl	1983	2.50	5.00	10.00
Sire 23980	DJ	Learning to Crawl	1983	3.00	6.00	12.00
Promo-only Quiex II pressing						
Sire 25488		Get Close	1986	2.50	5.00	10.00
Sire 25664		The Singles	1987	2.50	5.00	10.00
Sire 26219		Packed!	1990	3.00	6.00	12.00
Sire R 133248		The Singles	1987	3.00	6.00	12.00
BMG Direct Marketing edition						
Sire R 144453		Get Close	1986	3.00	6.00	12.00
RCA Music Service edition						
Warner Bros. WBMS-142	DJ	Get Close Interview	1987	5.00	10.00	20.00
Part of "The Warner Bros. Music Show" series						

45s

Label, Number		Title	Year	VG	VG+	NM
American Pie 9014		Stop Your Sobbing/Talk of the Town				
			198?			3.00
Reissue label; first appearance of B-side on U.S. stock 45						
MCA 54615		I'm Not in Love/I'm Not in Love (instrumental)				
			1993			3.00
Polydor 887 816-7		Window of the World/1969	1988			3.00
Polydor 887 816-7	PS	Window of the World/1969	1988			3.00
Sire GSRE 0448		Back on the Chain Gang/My City Was Gone				
			198?			3.00
"Back to Back Hits" reissue						
Sire GSRE 0474		Brass in Pocket/Middle of the Road				
			198?			3.00
"Back to Back Hits" reissue						
Sire GSRE 0496		Show Me/Thin Line Between Love and Hate				
			198?			3.00
"Back to Back Hits" reissue						
Sire PRO-S-942	DJ	Message of Love/Talk of the Town				
			1981	2.50	5.00	10.00
Sire 18160		I'll Stand By You/Rebel Rock Me				
			1994			3.00
Sire 18163		Night in My Veins/Angel of the Morning				
			1994			3.00
Sire 19820		Never Do That	1990		*Cassette only*	
Sire 28354		Hymn to Her (She Will Always Carry On)/Tradition of Love				
			1987			3.00
Sire 28354	PS	Hymn to Her (She Will Always Carry On)/Tradition of Love				
			1987			3.00
Sire 28496		My Baby/Room Full of Mirrors	1987			3.00
Sire 28496	PS	My Baby/Room Full of Mirrors	1987			3.00
Sire 28630		Don't Get Me Wrong/Dance!	1986			3.00
Sire 28630	PS	Don't Get Me Wrong/Dance!	1986			3.00
Sire 29249		Thin Line Between Love and Hate/Time the Avenger				
			1984			3.00
Sire 29249	PS	Thin Line Between Love and Hate/Time the Avenger				
			1984			3.00
Sire 29317		Show Me/Fast or Slow (The Law Is The Law)				
			1984			3.00
Sire 29317	PS	Show Me/Fast or Slow (The Law Is The Law)				
			1984			3.00

Label, Number		Title	Year	VG	VG+	NM
Sire 29444		Middle of the Road/2000 Miles	1983			3.00
Sire 29444	PS	Middle of the Road/2000 Miles	1983			3.00
Sire 29840		Back on the Chain Gang/My City Was Gone				
			1982			3.00
Sire 29840	PS	Back on the Chain Gang/My City Was Gone				
			1982			3.00
Sire 49181		Brass in Pocket (I'm Special)/Space Invader				
			1980		2.00	4.00
Not issued with picture sleeve in U.S.						
Sire 49506		Stop Your Sobbing/Phone Call	1980	2.00	4.00	8.00
Sire 49506	PS	Stop Your Sobbing/Phone Call	1980		2.00	4.00
Sire 49533		Kid/Tattooed Love Boys	1980		2.00	4.00
Sire 49819		Louie Louie/In the Sticks	1981		2.00	4.00
Sire 49819	PS	Louie Louie/In the Sticks	1981		2.00	4.00
Sire 49861		I Go to Sleep/Waste Not Want Not				
			1981		2.00	4.00
Warner Bros. 28259		If There Was a Man/Into Vienna	1987			3.00
B-side by John Barry						
Warner Bros. 28259	PS	If There Was a Man/Into Vienna	1987			3.00

12-Inch Singles

Label, Number		Title	Year	VG	VG+	NM
Polydor 632	DJ	Windows of the World/1969	1988	2.00	4.00	8.00
Sire PRO-A-1085	DJ	Back on the Chain Gang/My City Was Gone				
			1982	2.00	4.00	8.00
Sire PRO-A-2106	DJ	Middle of the Road/2000 Miles	1983		3.00	6.00
Sire PRO-A-2128	DJ	Show Me/Time the Avenger	1984		3.50	7.00
Sire PRO-A-2154	DJ	Thin Line Between Love and Hate/Thumbelina				
			1984		3.50	7.00
Sire PRO-A-2627	DJ	Room Full of Mirrors (same on both sides)				
			1986		3.00	6.00
Sire PRO-A-2677	DJ	Tradition of Love (long)/Tradition of Love (edit)				
			1986		3.00	6.00
Sire PRO-A-2732	DJ	Hymn to Her (Edit)/Hymn to Her (LP Version)				
			1986		3.50	7.00

Pretty Poison

New wave, later dance-pop, group from Camden, New Jersey: Jade Starling and Whey Cooler.

Vinyl Albums

Label, Number		Title	Year	VG	VG+	NM
Svengali SRPP-1	EP	Laced	1984	5.00	10.00	20.00
Virgin 90885		Catch Me I'm Falling	1987	2.50	5.00	10.00
Virgin R 144099		Catch Me I'm Falling	1988	3.00	6.00	12.00
BMG Direct Marketing edition						

45s

Label, Number		Title	Year	VG	VG+	NM
Poison Pops (no #)		Gimme Gimme (Your Autograph)/Kill You				
			1981	2.50	5.00	10.00
Small center hole; original paper sleeve has handwritten phone number						
Poison Pops (no #)	PS	Gimme Gimme (Your Autograph)/Kill You				
			1981	2.50	5.00	10.00
Svengali 2913		Expiration/The Realm of Existence				
			1981		3.00	6.00
Plays at 33 1/3 rpm						
Svengali 2913	PS	Expiration/The Realm of Existence				
			1981		3.00	6.00
Fold-over sleeve						
Virgin 99310		When I Look Into Your Eyes/When I Look Into Your Eyes				
		(Hip Hop Mix)	1988			3.00
Virgin 99350		Nightime/Nightime (Spanish Mix)				
			1988			3.00
Virgin 99350	PS	Nightime/Nightime (Spanish Mix)				
			1988	2.50	5.00	10.00

Label, Number		Title	Year	VG	VG+	NM
Virgin 99416		Catch Me (I'm Falling)/Catch Me (I'm Falling) Spanish Mix				
			1987			3.00
Virgin 99416	PS	Catch Me (I'm Falling)/Catch Me (I'm Falling) Spanish Mix				
			1987		3.50	7.00
Lips sleeve						
Virgin 99416	PS	Catch Me (I'm Falling)/Catch Me (I'm Falling) Spanish Mix				
			1987		2.50	5.00
"Hiding Out" sleeve						
12-Inch Singles						
Svengali SR 8403		Nightime (Dance Mix)//Nightime/				
		In the Heat of the Night (Dub Mix)				
			1984	2.50	5.00	10.00
Svengali SR 8704		Catch Me (I'm Falling) (5 versions)				
			1987	6.25	12.50	25.00
Virgin 1080	DJ	Catch Me (I'm Falling) (4 versions)				
			1987	2.00	4.00	8.00
Virgin 1100	DJ	Catch Me (I'm Falling) (Spanish Ultimix) (same on both sides)				
			1987		3.00	6.00
Virgin 1143	DJ	Nightime (4 versions)	1988		2.50	5.00
Virgin 1190	DJ	Nightime (4 versions)	1988		3.00	6.00
Virgin 1204	DJ	When I Look Into Your Eyes (3 versions)/				
		Nightime (Welcome to Our House Mix)				
			1988		2.50	5.00

Primal Scream

Glasgow, Scotland rock/punk band.

Label, Number		Title	Year	VG	VG+	NM
45s						
Sire 18189		Rocks/Everybody Needs Somebody				
			1994			3.00
12-Inch Singles						
Sire PRO-A-4513	DJ	Come Together (3 versions)/Loaded (3 versions) + 2				
			1990	2.00	4.00	8.00

Prince

Needs no introduction. In recent years has changed his name to an unpronounceable symbol. Some of his records feature him with the Revolution, others with the New Power Generation, still others with the N.P.G. He also has done duets (those are noted when the other artist is credited). He has written and produced for many other artists, often under pseudonyms, and he played synthesizer on Stevie Nicks' "Stand Back."

Label, Number		Title	Year	VG	VG+	NM
Vinyl Albums						
NPG/Bellmark 71003	EP	The Beautiful Experience	1994	2.50	5.00	10.00
Paisley Park 25286		Around the World in a Day	1985	2.50	5.00	10.00
Original copies have a fold-over flap (deduct 25% or more if missing)						
Paisley Park 25395		Parade	1986	2.00	4.00	8.00
Paisley Park 25577	(2)	Sign "O" The Times	1987	3.75	7.50	15.00
Paisley Park W1-25577	(2)	Sign "O" The Times	1987	4.50	9.00	18.00
Columbia House edition						
Paisley Park 25677		The Black Album	1987	500.00	1,000.00	2,000.00
Withdrawn prior to release, though a few copies escaped. Numerous counterfeits exist on other labels and colored vinyl.						
Paisley Park 25677DJ	(2) DJ	The Black Album	1987	750.00	1,500.00	3,000.00
Entire album on two 12-inch records that play at 45 RPM						
Paisley Park 25720		Lovesexy	1988	3.00	6.00	12.00
Paisley Park 25720DJ	DJ	Lovesexy	1988	4.00	8.00	16.00
Gold stamped and stickered cover (no UPC) with promo labels						
Paisley Park 27493	(2)	Graffiti Bridge	1990	3.75	7.50	15.00
Also includes The Time, Tevin Campbell						
Paisley Park R 124370		Around the World in a Day	1985	3.00	6.00	12.00
RCA Music Service edition						

Label, Number		Title	Year	VG	VG+	NM
Paisley Park R 140234		Parade	1986	3.00	6.00	12.00
RCA Music Service edition						
Paisley Park R 154087		Lovesexy	1988	3.50	7.00	14.00
BMG Direct Marketing edition						
Paisley Park R 234107	(2)	Graffiti Bridge	1990	4.50	9.00	18.00
Also includes The Time, Tevin Campbell; BMG Direct Marketing edition						
Paisley Park R 261991	(2)	Sign "O" The Times	1987	4.50	9.00	18.00
BMG Direct Marketing edition						
Warner Bros. BSK 3150		For You	1978	5.00	10.00	20.00
First edition on Burbank "palm trees" label						
Warner Bros. BSK 3150		For You	1978	3.00	6.00	12.00
White WB label						
Warner Bros. BSK 3366		Prince	1979	3.00	6.00	12.00
Warner Bros. BSK 3478		Dirty Mind	1980	3.00	6.00	12.00
Warner Bros. BSK 3601		Controversy	1981	3.00	6.00	12.00
Warner Bros. PRO-A-7270	(2) DJ	Come	1994	8.75	17.50	35.00
Promo-only release of CD/cassette of the same name						
Warner Bros. PRO-A-7330	DJ	The Black Album	1994	12.50	25.00	50.00
Promo-only release of CD/cassette of the same name						
Warner Bros. PRO-A-7835	(2) DJ	The Gold Experience	1995	25.00	50.00	100.00
Promo-only release of CD/cassette of the same name, on two gold vinyl LPs with numbered gold foil jacket.						
Warner Bros. 23720	(2)	1999	1982	3.75	7.50	15.00
Warner Bros. 25110		Purple Rain	1984	12.50	25.00	50.00
Purple vinyl; comes with poster						
Warner Bros. 25110		Purple Rain	1984	2.50	5.00	10.00
With poster						
Warner Bros. 25936		Batman (Soundtrack)	1989	2.50	5.00	10.00
Warner Bros. R 160175		Purple Rain	1984	3.00	6.00	12.00
RCA Music Service edition; includes poster						
Warner Bros. R 160344		Batman (Soundtrack)	1989	3.00	6.00	12.00
BMG Direct Marketing edition						
Warner Bros. R 252483	(2)	1999	1982	4.50	9.00	18.00
RCA Music Service edition						

45s

Label, Number		Title	Year	VG	VG+	NM
NPG 72514		The Most Beautiful Girl in the World				
			1994			*Cassette only*
Paisley Park GWB 0528		Purple Rain/Raspberry Beret	1986			3.00
"Back to Back Hits" reissue						
Paisley Park GWB 0529		Pop Life/America	1986			3.00
"Back to Back Hits" reissue						
Paisley Park PRO-S-3371		I Wish U Heaven (Radio Edit of Remix)/				
		I Wish U Heaven (Single Edit of Remix)				
			1988	3.75	7.50	15.00
Paisley Park 18583		The Morning Papers/Live 4 Love	1993			3.00
Paisley Park 18700		Damn U/2 Whom It May Concern	1993			3.00
Paisley Park 18707		My Name Is Prince/Sexy Mutha	1992			3.00
Paisley Park 18817		Sexy M.F./Strollin'	1992			3.00
Paisley Park 18824		7/7 (Acoustic Version)	1992			3.00
Paisley Park 19020		Money Don't Matter 2 Night/Call the Law				
			1992			3.00
Paisley Park 19083		Diamonds and Pearls/X-Cerpts	1991			3.00
Paisley Park 19090		Insatiable/I Love U in Me	1991			3.00
Paisley Park 19175		Cream/Horny Pony	1991			3.00
Paisley Park 19225		Gett Off/Horny Pony	1991			3.00
Paisley Park 19525		New Power Generation/New Power Generation				
			1990			3.00
Paisley Park 19751		Thieves in the Temple/Thieves in the Temple				
			1990			3.00
Paisley Park 27745		I Wish U Heaven/Scarlet Pussy	1988			3.00
Paisley Park 27745	PS	I Wish U Heaven/Scarlet Pussy	1988			3.00
Paisley Park 27806		Glam Slam/Escape	1988			3.00
Paisley Park 27806	PS	Glam Slam/Escape	1988			3.00
Heavy plastic sleeve with title sticker						

Prince's pre-*1999* output, from the years 1978-82, remains highly collectible. The 45 is "So Blue," the B-side of the first Prince single, "Soft and Wet." This is much scarcer than double-sided promos of the A-side. Also shown is a copy of the LP *Dirty Mind* meant for radio stations. It promotes the "hit" single "Uptown" and warns programmers to listen before arbitrarily playing anything off the album.

Label, Number		Title	Year	VG	VG+	NM
Paisley Park 27900		Alphabet St./Alphabet St. Part 2	1988			3.00
Paisley Park 27900	PS	Alphabet St./Alphabet St. Part 2	1988			3.00
Heavy plastic sleeve with title sticker						
Paisley Park 28288		I Could Never Take the Place of Your Man/Hot Thing				
			1987			3.00
Paisley Park 28288	PS	I Could Never Take the Place of Your Man/Hot Thing				
			1987			3.00
Paisley Park 28289		U Got the Look/Housequake	1987			3.00
Paisley Park 28289	PS	U Got the Look/Housequake	1987			3.00
Paisley Park 28334		If I Was Your Girlfriend/Shockadelica				
			1987			3.00
Paisley Park 28334	PS	If I Was Your Girlfriend/Shockadelica				
			1987			3.00
Paisley Park 28399		Sign "O" the Times/La, La, La, He, He, Hee				
			1987			3.00
Paisley Park 28399	PS	Sign "O" the Times/La, La, La, He, He, Hee				
			1987			3.00
Paisley Park 28620		Anotherloverholenyohead/Girls and Boys				
			1986			3.00
Paisley Park 28620	PS	Anotherloverholenyohead/Girls and Boys				
			1986			3.00
Paisley Park 28711		Mountains/Alexa de Paris	1986			3.00
Paisley Park 28711	PS	Mountains/Alexa de Paris	1986			3.00
Paisley Park 28751		Kiss/Love or $	1986			3.00
Paisley Park 28751	PS	Kiss/Love or $	1986			3.00
Paisley Park 28972		Raspberry Beret/She's Always In My Hair				
			1985			3.00
Paisley Park 28972	PS	Raspberry Beret/She's Always In My Hair				
			1985			3.00
Paisley Park 28998		Pop Life/Hello	1985			3.00
Paisley Park 28998	PS	Pop Life/Hello	1985			3.00
Paisley Park 28999		America/Girl	1985			3.00
Paisley Park 28999	PS	America/Girl	1985			3.00
Paisley Park 29052		Paisley Park/She's Always In My Hair				
			1985			*Unreleased*
Paisley Park 29052	PS	Paisley Park/She's Always In My Hair				
			1985	125.00	250.00	500.00
Warner Bros. GWB 0392		I Wanna Be Your Lover/Why You Wanna Treat Me So Bad?				
			1982		2.00	4.00
"Back to Back Hits" reissue						
Warner Bros. GWB 0468		1999/Little Red Corvette	1984			3.00
"Back to Back Hits" reissue						
Warner Bros. GWB 0476		Delirious/Let's Pretend We're Married				
			1984			3.00
"Back to Back Hits" reissue						
Warner Bros. GWB 0516		When Doves Cry/Let's Go Crazy	1985			3.00
"Back to Back Hits" reissue						
Warner Bros. GWB 0517		I Would Die 4 U/Take Me With U	1985			3.00
"Back to Back Hits" reissue						
Warner Bros. 8619		Soft and Wet/So Blue	1978	7.50	15.00	30.00
Warner Bros. 8619	DJ	Soft and Wet (mono/stereo)	1978	3.75	7.50	15.00
Warner Bros. 8713		Just As Long As We're Together/In Love				
			1978	7.50	15.00	30.00
Warner Bros. 8713	DJ	Just As Long As We're Together (mono/stereo)				
			1978	3.75	7.50	15.00
Warner Bros. 17715		Gold/Rock 'N' Roll Is Alive! (and it lives in Minneapolis)				
			1995			3.00
Warner Bros. 17811		I Hate U/I Hate U	1995			3.00
Warner Bros. 17903		Purple Medley/Kirk J's B Sides Remix				
			1995			3.00
Warner Bros. 18012		Space (Radio Remix)/Space (Album Version)				
			1994			3.00

Label, Number		Title	Year	VG	VG+	NM
Warner Bros. 18074		Letitgo/Solo	1994			3.00
Warner Bros. 18371		Pink Cashmere/Soft and Wet	1993			3.00
Warner Bros. 18372		Peach/Nothing Compares 2 U (Live)				
			1993			3.00
Warner Bros. 21858		I Could Never Take the Place of Your Man/Alphabet St.				
			1989			3.00
"Back to Back Hits" series						
Warner Bros. 21859		Batdance/Partyman	1989			3.00
"Back to Back Hits" series						
Warner Bros. 21938		Sign "O" the Times/U Got the Look				
			1988			3.00
"Back to Back Hits" series						
Warner Bros. 21980		Anotherloverholenyohead/Mountains				
			1987			3.00
"Back to Back Hits" series						
Warner Bros. 21981		Uptown/Controversy	1987			3.00
"Back to Back Hits" series						
Warner Bros. 21982		Kiss/Soft and Wet	1987			3.00
"Back to Back Hits" series						
Warner Bros. 22757		The Arms of Orion/I Love U in Me				
			1989			3.00
Warner Bros. 22757	PS	The Arms of Orion/I Love U in Me				
			1989			3.00
With Sheena Easton						
Warner Bros. 22814		Partyman/Feel U Up	1989			3.00
Warner Bros. 22814	PS	Partyman/Feel U Up	1989			3.00
Warner Bros. 22824		Scandalous/When 2 R In Love	1989			3.00
Warner Bros. 22824	PS	Scandalous/When 2 R In Love	1989			3.00
Warner Bros. 22924		Batdance/200 Balloons	1989			3.00
Warner Bros. 22924	PS	Batdance/200 Balloons	1989			3.00
Warner Bros. 29079		Take Me With U/Baby I'm a Star	1985		2.00	4.00
Warner Bros. 29079	PS	Take Me With U/Baby I'm a Star	1985		2.00	4.00
Warner Bros. 29121		I Would Die 4 U/Another Lonely Christmas				
			1984		2.00	4.00
Warner Bros. 29121	PS	I Would Die 4 U/Another Lonely Christmas				
			1984		2.00	4.00
Warner Bros. 29174		Purple Rain/God	1984		2.00	4.00
Purple vinyl						
Warner Bros. 29174		Purple Rain/God	1984	2.00	4.00	8.00
Black vinyl						
Warner Bros. 29174	PS	Purple Rain/God	1984	2.00	4.00	8.00
Plastic semi-transparent sleeve						
Warner Bros. 29216		Let's Go Crazy/Erotic City	1984		2.00	4.00
Warner Bros. 29216	PS	Let's Go Crazy/Erotic City	1984	2.00	4.00	8.00
Warner Bros. 29286		When Doves Cry/17 Days	1984			3.00
Black vinyl						
Warner Bros. 29286	DJ	When Doves Cry/17 Days	1984	2.50	5.00	10.00
Purple vinyl						
Warner Bros. 29286	PS	When Doves Cry/17 Days	1984			3.00
Warner Bros. 29503		Delirious/Horny Toad	1983		3.00	6.00
Label erroneously lists A-side time at 3:56						
Warner Bros. 29503		Delirious/Horny Toad	1983			3.00
Label lists correct A-side time of 2:37						
Warner Bros. 29503	PS	Delirious/Horny Toad	1983	12.50	25.00	50.00
Fold-out poster sleeve						
Warner Bros. 29548		Let's Pretend We're Married/Irresistible Bitch				
			1983		2.50	5.00
Warner Bros. 29548	PS	Let's Pretend We're Married/Irresistible Bitch				
			1983	2.50	5.00	10.00
Warner Bros. 29746		Little Red Corvette/All the Critics Love U in New York				
			1983		2.50	5.00
Not issued with picture sleeve in U.S.						

Label, Number		Title	Year	VG	VG+	NM
Warner Bros. 29896		1999/How Come U Don't Call Me Anymore?				
			1982		2.50	5.00
Warner Bros. 29896	PS	1999/How Come U Don't Call Me Anymore?				
			1982	2.50	5.00	10.00
Warner Bros. 29942		Do Me, Baby/Private Joy	1982	3.75	7.50	15.00
Warner Bros. 29942	DJ	Do Me, Baby (same on both sides)				
			1982		3.75	7.50
Warner Bros. 49050	DJ	My Love Is Forever (mono/stereo)				
			1979	3.75	7.50	15.00
Warner Bros. 49050	PS	My Love Is Forever	1979	18.75	37.50	75.00
		Promo-only sleeve; withdrawn when "I Wanna Be Your Lover" was pushed as the A-side				
Warner Bros. 49050		I Wanna Be Your Lover/My Love Is Forever				
			1979	2.50	5.00	10.00
Warner Bros. 49050	DJ	I Wanna Be Your Lover (mono/stereo)				
			1979	3.75	7.50	15.00
Warner Bros. 49178		Why You Wanna Treat Me So Bad/Baby				
			1980	7.50	15.00	30.00
Warner Bros. 49178	DJ	Why You Wanna Treat Me So Bad (mono/stereo)				
			1980	3.75	7.50	15.00
Warner Bros. 49226		Still Waiting/Bambi	1980	3.75	7.50	15.00
Warner Bros. 49226	DJ	Still Waiting (mono/stereo)	1980		3.75	7.50
Warner Bros. 49559		Uptown/Crazy You	1980	3.75	7.50	15.00
Warner Bros. 49559	DJ	Uptown (mono/stereo)	1980		3.75	7.50
Warner Bros. 49559	PS	Uptown/Crazy You	1980	3.75	7.50	15.00
Warner Bros. 49638		Dirty Mind/When We're Dancing Close and Slow				
			1980	3.75	7.50	15.00
Warner Bros. 49638	DJ	Dirty Mind (same on both sides)	1980		3.75	7.50
Warner Bros. 49808		Controversy/When You Were Mine				
			1981	3.75	7.50	15.00
Warner Bros. 49808	DJ	Controversy (same on both sides)	1981		3.75	7.50
Warner Bros. 50002		Let's Work/Ronnie Talk to Russia				
			1982	3.75	7.50	15.00
Warner Bros. 50002	DJ	Let's Work (same on both sides)	1982		3.75	7.50

12-Inch Singles

Label, Number		Title	Year	VG	VG+	NM
Paisley Park PRO-A-2300	DJ	America (same on both sides)	1985	3.75	7.50	15.00
Paisley Park PRO-A-2313	DJ	Raspberry Beret (same on both sides)				
			1985	3.75	7.50	15.00
Paisley Park PRO-A-2331	DJ	Pop Life (same on both sides)	1985	3.75	7.50	15.00
Paisley Park PRO-A-2458	DJ	Kiss (Extended Version) (same on both sides)				
			1986	3.75	7.50	15.00
Paisley Park PRO-A-2476	DJ	Mountains/Mountains (10:03)	1986	4.50	9.00	18.00
Paisley Park PRO-A-2687	DJ	Sign "O" the Times/Sign "O" the Times (Edit)				
			1987	2.50	5.00	10.00
Paisley Park PRO-A-2758	DJ	If I Was Your Girlfriend (same on both sides)				
			1987	3.00	6.00	12.00
Paisley Park PRO-A-2770	DJ	I Could Never Take the Place of Your Man/				
		I Could Never Take the Place of Your Man (Fade)				
			1987	4.50	9.00	18.00
Paisley Park PRO-A-2771	DJ	U Got the Look (same on both sides)				
			1987	3.75	7.50	15.00
Paisley Park PRO-A-3283	DJ	I Wish U Heaven (same on both sides)				
			1988	3.00	6.00	12.00
Paisley Park PRO-A-4345	DJ	Thieves in the Temple (same on both sides)				
			1990	2.50	5.00	10.00
Paisley Park PRO-A-4515	DJ	New Power Generation (same on both sides)				
			1990	2.50	5.00	10.00
Paisley Park PRO-A-4578	DJ	New Power Generation (Funky Weapon Remix)				
		(same on both sides)	1990	2.50	5.00	10.00
Paisley Park PRO-A-4977	DJ	Gett Off (6 versions)	1991	3.00	6.00	12.00
Paisley Park PRO-A-5141	DJ	Insatiable/Insatiable (Edit)	1991	3.75	7.50	15.00

Label, Number		Title	Year	VG	VG+	NM
Paisley Park PRO-A-5148	DJ	Diamonds and Pearls/Diamonds and Pearls (Edit)				
			1991	3.75	7.50	15.00
Paisley Park PRO-A-5298	DJ	Money Don't Matter 2 Night/Money Don't Matter 2 Night (Edit)				
			1992	3.75	7.50	15.00
Paisley Park PRO-A-5570	DJ	Sexy MF (same on both sides)	1992	3.00	6.00	12.00
Paisley Park PRO-A-5770	DJ	My Name Is Prince/My Name Is Prince (Edit)				
			1992	3.75	7.50	15.00
Paisley Park PRO-A-5890	DJ	Damn U (same on both sides)	1992	3.00	6.00	12.00
Paisley Park PRO-A-5993	DJ	Pink Cashmere (3 versions)	1993	6.25	12.50	25.00
With picture cover (deduct 40% if missing)						
Paisley Park PRO-A-5994	DJ	Nothing Compares 2 U/Nothing Compares 2 U (Edit)				
			1993	3.00	6.00	12.00
Paisley Park 20355		Raspberry Beret (Remix)/She's Always in My Hair (Remix)				
			1985	3.75	7.50	15.00
Paisley Park 20357		Pop Life/Hello	1985	2.50	5.00	10.00
Paisley Park 20389		America/Girl	1985	2.50	5.00	10.00
Paisley Park 20442		Kiss/Love or $	1986	3.00	6.00	12.00
Paisley Park 20465		Mountains/Alexa de Paris	1986	3.00	6.00	12.00
Paisley Park 20516		Anotherloverholenyohead/Girls and Boys				
			1986	2.00	4.00	8.00
Paisley Park 20648		Sign "O" the Times/La, La, La, He, He, Hee				
			1987	2.50	5.00	10.00
Paisley Park 20697		If I Was Your Girlfriend/Shockadelica				
			1987	2.50	5.00	10.00
Paisley Park 20727		U Got the Look (2 versions)/Housequake (2 versions)				
			1987	3.75	7.50	15.00
Paisley Park 20728		I Could Never Take the Place of Your Man/Hot Thing (3 versions)				
			1987	2.50	5.00	10.00
Paisley Park 20930		Alphabet St./Alphabet St. "This is not music, this is a trip"				
			1988	2.50	5.00	10.00
Paisley Park 21005		Glam Slam/Escape	1988	2.00	4.00	8.00
Paisley Park 21074		I Wish U Heaven/Scarlet Pussy	1988	2.50	5.00	10.00
Paisley Park 21598		Thieves in the Temple (3 versions)				
			1990	2.00	4.00	8.00
Paisley Park 21783		New Power Generation/T.C.'s Rap/Brother with a Purpose/Gett Off/ The Lubricated Lady/Loveleft, Loveright				
			1990	2.00	4.00	8.00
Paisley Park 40138		Gett Off (3 versions)/Violet the Organ Grinder/Gangster				
			1991	2.50	5.00	10.00
Paisley Park 40197		Cream (2 mixes)/Things Have Gotta Change/2 the Wire/ Get Some Solo//Do Your Dance/Housebangers/Q in Doubt/ Ethereal Mix				
			1991	2.50	5.00	10.00
Warner Bros. PRO-A-781	DJ	Soft and Wet (same on both sides)				
			1978	20.00	40.00	80.00
Warner Bros. PRO-A-832	DJ	I Wanna Be Your Lover (same on both sides)				
			1979	18.75	37.50	75.00
Warner Bros. PRO-A-848	DJ	Why You Wanna Treat Me So Bad?/Bambi				
			1979	18.75	37.50	75.00
Warner Bros. PRO-A-870	DJ	Still Waiting (same on both sides)				
			1980	15.00	30.00	60.00
Warner Bros. PRO-A-904	DJ	Uptown (4:09)/Uptown (5:29)	1980	15.00	30.00	60.00
Warner Bros. PRO-A-915	DJ	Head/Sister/Party Up	1980	20.00	40.00	80.00
Warner Bros. PRO-A-916	DJ	When You Were Mine (same on both sides)				
			1980	15.00	30.00	60.00
Warner Bros. PRO-A-929	DJ	Dirty Mind (same on both sides)	1980	15.00	30.00	60.00
Warner Bros. PRO-A-937	DJ	Head/When U Were Mine/Uptown//Gotta Stop (Messin' About) + 1				
			1981	20.00	40.00	80.00
Warner Bros. PRO-A-938	DJ	Gotta Stop (Messin' About) (same on both sides)				
			1981	15.00	30.00	60.00
Warner Bros. PRO-A-980	DJ	Controversy (2 versions)	1981	12.50	25.00	50.00
Warner Bros. PRO-A-1002	DJ	Let's Work (Dance Remix)/Let's Work (7" Version)				
			1982	18.75	37.50	75.00

Label, Number		Title	Year	VG	VG+	NM
Warner Bros. PRO-A-1035	DJ	Do Me, Baby/Private Joy	1982	18.75	37.50	75.00
Warner Bros. PRO-A-1070	DJ	1999 (Edit)/1999 (LP Version)	1982	15.00	30.00	60.00
Warner Bros. PRO-A-1082	DJ	Let's Pretend We're Married/D.M.S.R./Automatic				
			1982	12.50	25.00	50.00
Warner Bros. PRO-A-2001	DJ	Little Red Corvette (Dance Mix)/Little Red Corvette (LP Version)				
			1983	10.00	20.00	40.00
Warner Bros. PRO-A-2042	DJ	1999/Free/Automatic	1983	12.50	25.00	50.00
Warner Bros. PRO-A-2080	DJ	Delirious (2 versions)	1983	7.50	15.00	30.00
Warner Bros. PRO-A-2139	DJ	When Doves Cry (Long)/When Doves Cry (Short)				
			1984	6.25	12.50	25.00
Warner Bros. PRO-A-2173	DJ	Let's Go Crazy (LP version)/Let's Go Crazy (Edit)				
			1984	7.50	15.00	30.00
Warner Bros. PRO-A-2182	DJ	Let's Go Crazy (7:35)/Let's Go Crazy (4:40)				
			1984	10.00	20.00	40.00
Warner Bros. PRO-A-2192	DJ	Purple Rain (LP version)/Purple Rain (Edit)				
			1984	10.00	20.00	40.00
Purple vinyl						
Warner Bros. PRO-A-2233	DJ	I Would Die 4 U (same on both sides)				
			1984	5.00	10.00	20.00
Warner Bros. PRO-A-2263	DJ	Take Me With U (same on both sides)				
			1985	7.50	15.00	30.00
Warner Bros. PRO-A-3579	DJ	Batdance (LP Version)/Batdance (edit)				
			1989	2.50	5.00	10.00
Warner Bros. PRO-A-3702	DJ	Batdance (4 versions)	1989	2.50	5.00	10.00
Warner Bros. PRO-A-3705	DJ	Partyman (same on both sides)	1989	2.00	4.00	8.00
Warner Bros. PRO-A-7000	DJ	Letitgo/Letitgo (Edit)	1994	3.75	7.50	15.00
Warner Bros. PRO-A-7481	DJ	Purple Medley (3:34)/Purple Medley (11:03)				
			1995	6.25	12.50	25.00
Warner Bros. PRO-A-7594	DJ	I Hate U/I Hate U (Edit)	1995	3.75	7.50	15.00
Warner Bros. PRO-A-7941	DJ	Gold (3 mixes)/Rock 'N' Roll Is Alive! (and it lives in Minneapolis)				
			1995	5.00	10.00	20.00
Gold vinyl						
Warner Bros. 20120		1999/Little Red Corvette	1983	5.00	10.00	20.00
Warner Bros. 20129	PD	Little Red Corvette/1999	1983	10.00	20.00	40.00
Picture disc with custom sticker						
Warner Bros. 20170		Let's Pretend We're Married/Irresistible Bitch				
			1983	5.00	10.00	20.00
Warner Bros. 20228		When Doves Cry/17 Days	1984	2.50	5.00	10.00
Warner Bros. 20246		Let's Go Crazy/Erotic City	1984	2.50	5.00	10.00
Warner Bros. 20267		Purple Rain/God	1984	6.25	12.50	25.00
Purple vinyl						
Warner Bros. 20267		Purple Rain/God	1984	3.75	7.50	15.00
Black vinyl						
Warner Bros. 20291		I Would Die 4 U/Another Lonely Christmas				
			1984	3.75	7.50	15.00
Oversized picture label with die-cut picture cover						
Warner Bros. 21257		Batdance (2 mixes)/200 Balloons	1989	2.50	5.00	10.00
Warner Bros. 21370		The Purple Party Mix/Partyman Music Mix/Partyman/Feel U Up				
			1989	2.00	4.00	8.00
Warner Bros. 21422		The Scandalous Sex Suite/When 2 R in Love				
			1989	2.00	4.00	8.00
Warner Bros. 41745		Letitgo (8 versions)	1994	2.00	4.00	8.00
Warner Bros. 41833		Space (5 versions)	1994	2.00	4.00	8.00
Warner Bros. 50028		Let's Work/Gotta Stop (Messin' About)				
			1982	15.00	30.00	60.00

Proclaimers, The

Scottish duo.

Vinyl Albums

Chrysalis F1-21668		Sunshine on Leith	1989	3.00	6.00	12.00
Chrysalis FV 41602		This Is the Story	1988	3.00	6.00	12.00

Nationally, Pretty Poison is best known for its dance-pop hit "Catch Me (I'm Falling)." But in the Philadelphia-New Jersey area, the group had been making new-wave-style records for several years. This was a four-song 12-inch EP that came out in 1983.

"I'm Gonna Be (500 Miles)" became a hit thanks to its inclusion in the 1993 film *Benny and Joon*. But this American picture sleeve (with the lyrics on the other side) had come out in 1988 with the song's original release. Try to find this now.

Label, Number		Title	Year	VG	VG+	NM
Chrysalis R 152320		Sunshine on Leith	1989	3.50	7.00	14.00
BMG Music Service edition						

45s

Chrysalis S7-17493		I'm Gonna Be (500 Miles)/Better Days				
			1993		2.00	4.00
Green vinyl						
Chrysalis S7-17800		Let's Get Married/Letter from America				
			1994			3.00
Chrysalis 43283		I'm Gonna Be (500 Miles)/Better Days				
			1988		2.50	5.00
Chrysalis 43283	PS	I'm Gonna Be (500 Miles)/Better Days				
			1988		2.50	5.00

Producers, The

New-wave act from Atlanta, Georgia.

Vinyl Albums

	Title	Year	VG	VG+	NM
Marathon MR 111	Run For Your Life	198?	4.50	9.00	18.00
Portrait NJR 37097	The Producers	1981	3.00	6.00	12.00
Portrait ARR 38060	You Make the Heat	1982	3.00	6.00	12.00

45s

	Title	Year	VG	VG+	NM
Portrait 02092	What She Does to Me (The Diana Song)/Here's to You				
		1981		2.00	4.00
Portrait 02445	What's He Got/Boys Say When -- Girls Say Why				
		1981		2.00	4.00
Portrait 03255	Chinatown/She Sheila	1982			3.00

Pseudo Echo

Australian techno-synth-rock group.

Vinyl Albums

	Title	Year	VG	VG+	NM
EMI America ST-17130	Pseudo Echo	1985	2.50	5.00	10.00
RCA 5730-1-R	Love An Adventure	1987	3.00	6.00	12.00
Without "Funkytown"					
RCA 5730-1-RX	Love An Adventure	1987	2.00	4.00	8.00
With "Funkytown"					
RCA 8503-1-R	Race	1989	2.50	5.00	10.00

45s

	Title	Year	VG	VG+	NM
EMI America 8232	Listening/In Their Time	1984		2.00	4.00
EMI America 8256	Beat for You/Walk Away	1984		2.00	4.00
RCA 5125-7-R	Living in a Dream/Don't Go	1987			3.00
RCA 5217-7-R	Funky Town/Lies or Nothing	1987		2.00	4.00
First pressing has A-side title as two words					
RCA 5217-7-R	Funkytown/Lies or Nothing	1987			3.00
Second pressing correctly has A-side title as one word					
RCA 5272-7-R	Listening/Lonely Without You	1987			3.00
RCA 5323-7-R	A Beat for You/Try	1987			3.00

12-Inch Singles

		Title	Year	VG	VG+	NM
EMI America 7856		A Beat for You (Vocal Dance)/A Beat for You (Echo Dub)				
			1984	2.00	4.00	8.00
RCA 5799	DJ	Living in a Dream (same on both sides)				
			1986		3.00	6.00
RCA 6302		Living in a Dream (3 versions)	1986		3.00	6.00
RCA 6431		Funkytown (2 versions)/Lies Are Nothing				
			1987		3.00	6.00
RCA 6507		Funkytown (4 versions)	1987		3.50	7.00
RCA 6619		Listening (4 versions)	1987		3.00	6.00
RCA 6763		A Beat for You (4 versions)	1987		3.50	7.00

Label, Number		Title	Year	VG	VG+	NM

Psychedelic Furs

British new-wave group, moved to U.S. and became a cult favorite.

Vinyl Albums

Label, Number		Title	Year	VG	VG+	NM
Columbia AS 1296	DJ	Interchords	1981	6.25	12.50	25.00
Columbia CAS 01310	DJ	Interchords with Richard Butler	1988	5.00	10.00	20.00
Columbia CAS 2719	DJ	Richard Butler Interview	1987	3.75	7.50	15.00
Columbia NFC 36791		Psychedelic Furs	1980	3.00	6.00	12.00
Columbia PC 36791		Psychedelic Furs	198?	2.00	4.00	8.00
Budget-line reissue						
Columbia NFC 37339		Talk Talk Talk	1981	2.50	5.00	10.00
Columbia PC 37339		Talk Talk Talk	1983	2.00	4.00	8.00
Budget-line reissue						
Columbia ARC 38261		Forever Now	1982	2.50	5.00	10.00
Columbia PC 38261		Forever Now	198?	2.00	4.00	8.00
Budget-line reissue						
Columbia BFC 39278		Mirror Moves	1984	2.50	5.00	10.00
Columbia PC 39278		Mirror Moves	198?	2.00	4.00	8.00
Budget-line reissue						
Columbia FC 40466		Midnight to Midnight	1987	2.50	5.00	10.00
Columbia FC 44377		All of This and Nothing	1988	2.50	5.00	10.00
Columbia FC 45412		Book of Days	1989	2.50	5.00	10.00

45s

Label, Number		Title	Year	VG	VG+	NM
A&M 2826		Pretty in Pink (Long)/Pretty in Pink (Short)				
			1986			3.00
A&M 2826	PS	Pretty in Pink (Long)/Pretty in Pink (Short)				
			1986	6.25	12.50	25.00
Columbia 03340		Love My Way/I Don't Want to Be Your Shadow				
			1982		2.00	4.00
Columbia 03930		Run and Run/President Gas	1983			3.00
Columbia 04416		The Ghost in You/Heartbeat (Remix)				
			1984			3.00
Columbia 04416	PS	The Ghost in You/Heartbeat (Remix)				
			1984			3.00
Columbia 04577		Here Come Cowboys/Another Edge				
			1984			3.00
Columbia 04627		Heaven/Alice's House	1984			3.00
Columbia 06420		Heartbreak Beat/New Dream	1986			3.00
Columbia 06420	PS	Heartbreak Beat/New Dream	1986			3.00
Columbia 07224		Shock/President Gas (Live)	1987			3.00
Columbia 07440		Angels Don't Cry/Mack the Knife				
			1987			3.00
Columbia 07974		All That Money Wants/Birdland	1988			3.00
Columbia 07974	PS	All That Money Wants/Birdland	1988			3.00
Columbia 08499		Heaven/India	1988			3.00
Columbia 74055		Until She Comes/Sometimes	1991			*Cassette only*

12-Inch Singles

Label, Number		Title	Year	VG	VG+	NM
A&M 17367	DJ	Pretty in Pink/If You Leave	1986	2.50	5.00	10.00
B-side by Orchestral Manoeuvres in the Dark; promo from movie "Pretty in Pink"						
Columbia AS 879	DJ	We Love You/Sister Europe	1980	2.00	4.00	8.00
Columbia AS 1538	DJ	Love My Way/Forever Now/President Gas/Angels				
			1980	5.00	10.00	20.00
Columbia AS 1839	DJ	The Ghost in You (Edit)/The Ghost in You (LP Version)				
			1984	2.00	4.00	8.00
Columbia CAS 1877	DJ	Should God Forget/Badman	1989	2.00	4.00	8.00
Columbia AS 1908	DJ	Here Comes Cowboy (Remix Edit)/				
		Here Comes Cowboy (LP Version)	1984	2.00	4.00	8.00
Columbia CAS 2538	DJ	Heartbreak Beat (LP version)/Heartbreak Beat (7" version)				
			1986		3.00	6.00
Columbia CAS 02829	DJ	Angels Don't Cry (LP version)/Angels Don't Cry (7" Remix)				
			1987		3.00	6.00

Label, Number		Title	Year	VG	VG+	NM
Columbia 03197		Love My Way/Goodbye/Aeroplane				
			1982		3.00	6.00
Columbia 04984		The Ghost in You/Heartbeat (New York Mix)				
			1984		3.00	6.00
Columbia 05696		Heartbreak Beat (Extended)/Heartbreak Beat (Dub)/New Dream				
			1987		3.00	6.00
Columbia 06862		Shock (3 versions)	1987		3.00	6.00
Columbia 07862		All That Money Wants (Special Version)				
			1988		3.00	6.00

Psychotic Pineapple, The
Punk band from Richmond, California.

Vinyl Albums

Richmond 6026		Where's the Party	1980	6.25	12.50	25.00

45s

Pynotic (no #)		I Want Her So Bad/Say That You Wil				
			1978	5.00	10.00	20.00
Pynotic (no #)	PS	I Want Her So Bad/Say That You Will				
			1978	5.00	10.00	20.00
Richmond 1		I Wanna Wanna Wanna Wanna Wanna Wanna Wanna Get Rid of				
		You/Ahead of My Time	1979		3.75	7.50
Richmond 1	PS	I Wanna Wanna Wanna Wanna Wanna Wanna Wanna Get Rid of				
		You/Ahead of My Time	1979		3.75	7.50

Public Enemy
Rap group, often as (in)famous for its politics as for its raps.

Vinyl Albums

Def Jam BFC 40658		Yo! Bum Rush the Show	1987	3.00	6.00	12.00
Def Jam BFW 44303		It Takes a Nation of Millions to Hold Us Back				
			1988	3.00	6.00	12.00
Def Jam C 45413		Fear of a Black Planet	1990	3.00	6.00	12.00
Def Jam C2 47374	(2)	Apocalypse 91... The Enemy Strikes Black				
			1991	3.75	7.50	15.00
Def Jam C2 53014	(2)	Greatest Misses	1993	3.75	7.50	15.00
Def Jam 523 362-1	(2)	Muse Sick-N-Hour Mess Age	1994	2.50	5.00	10.00

45s

Def Jam 06670		Public Enemy #1/(B-side unknown)				
			1987			3.00
Def Jam 07222		You're Gonna Get Yours/Miuzi Weighs a Ton				
			1987			3.00
Def Jam 07934		Don't Believe the Hype/Prophets of Rage				
			1988			3.00
Def Jam 08072		Night of the Living Baseheads/Cold Lampin' With Flavor				
			1988			3.00
Def Jam 08072	PS	Night of the Living Baseheads/Cold Lampin' With Flavor				
			1988			3.00
Def Jam 68613		Black Steel in the House of Chaos/Caught, Can We Get a Witness				
			1989			3.00
Def Jam 73086		Welcome to the Terrordome/(instrumental)				
			1989		*May be cassette-only*	
Def Jam 73309		911 Is a Joke/Revolutionary Generation				
			1990		*Cassette only*	
Def Jam 73390		Brother's Gonna Work It Out/Anti-Nigger Machine				
			1990		*Cassette only*	
Def Jam 73612		Can't Do Nuttin' For Ya Man/Burn Hollywood Burn				
			1990		*Cassette only*	
Def Jam 73870		Can't Truss It/Can't Truss It	1991		*Cassette only*	

Label, Number		Title	Year	VG	VG+	NM
Def Jam 74269		Shut 'Em Down/By the Time I Get to Arizona				
			1992		*Cassette only*	
Def Jam 74272		Nighttrain/Nighttrain (Instrumental)				
			1992		*Cassette only*	
Motown 1972		Fight the Power/Flavor Flav Meets Spike Lee				
			1989			3.00

12-Inch Singles

Label, Number		Title	Year	VG	VG+	NM
Def Jam SE-2	DJ	Give It Up (3 versions)/Bedlam (Clean)/Bedlam (Instrumental)				
			1994	3.75	7.50	15.00
Def Jam CAS 2082	DJ	Brothers Gonna Work It Out (4 mixes)/				
		Anti-Nigger Machine (censored)	1990	3.00	6.00	12.00
Def Jam 06861		You're Gonna Get Yours (2 versions)/Miuzi Weighs a Ton/				
		Rebel Without a Pause	1987	3.00	6.00	12.00
Def Jam 73179		911 Is a Joke (vocal & instrumental)/Revolutionary Generation				
		(vocal & instrumental)	1990	2.00	4.00	8.00
Def Jam 73391		Brother's Gonna Work It Out (2 mixes)/Anti-Nigger Machine/				
		Powersex/Power to the People	1990	2.00	4.00	8.00
Def Jam 73613		Can't Do Nuttin' For Ya Man (2 mixes)/Get the F___ Outta Dodge				
		(2 mixes)/Burn Hollywood Burn	1990	2.00	4.00	8.00
Def Jam 73869		Can't Truss It (3 mixes)/Move!	1991	2.00	4.00	8.00
Def Jam 74165		Shut 'Em Down (4 mixes)/By the Time I Get to Arizona				
			1992	2.00	4.00	8.00
Def Jam 74254		Nighttrain (4 mixes)/More News at 11				
			1992	2.00	4.00	8.00
Def Jam 74487		Hazy Shade of Criminal (3 mixes)/Tie Goes to the Runner (2 mixes)				
			1992	2.00	4.00	8.00
Def Jam 853 317-1		Give It Up (3 versions)/Live and Undrugged Pt. 2/Bedlam				
		(Vocal)/Bedlam (Instrumental)	1994	2.00	4.00	8.00
MCA 2586	DJ	Livin' in a Zoo (4 versions)	1992	2.50	5.00	10.00
Perspective 28968 1723 1		Get Off My Back (4 versions)	1992	3.00	6.00	12.00

Public Image Ltd.

*John Lydon, formerly Johnny Rotten, in his post-**Sex Pistols** group.*

Vinyl Albums

Label, Number		Title	Year	VG	VG+	NM
Elektra 60365		This Is What You Want... This Is What You'll Get				
			1984	2.50	5.00	10.00
Elektra 60438		Public Image Ltd. Album	1986	2.50	5.00	10.00
Elektra 60491		Live in Tokyo	1985	2.50	5.00	10.00
Island 2WX 3288	(2)	Second Edition	1980	4.50	9.00	18.00
Virgin 90642		Happy	1987	2.50	5.00	10.00
Virgin 91062		9	1989	2.50	5.00	10.00
Warner Bros. 2WX 3288	(2)	Second Edition	198?	3.00	6.00	12.00
Reissue						
Warner Bros. BSK 3536		Flowers of Romance	1981	3.00	6.00	12.00

12-Inch Singles

Label, Number		Title	Year	VG	VG+	NM
Elektra ED 5129	DJ	Rise (3 versions)	1986	2.00	4.00	8.00
Virgin 1120	DJ	Seattle (12" Mix)/Body (12" Mix)				
			1987	2.00	4.00	8.00
Virgin 1406	DJ	Happy (3 versions)	1989		3.00	6.00
Virgin 2247	DJ	Body (Remix)/Body (7" version)	1988	2.00	4.00	8.00
Virgin 2709	DJ	Disappointed (3 versions)	1989	2.50	5.00	10.00
Virgin 96519		Warriors (2 versions)/Happy (2 versions)				
			1989	2.00	4.00	8.00
Virgin 96729		Seattle (12" Mix)/Body (12" Mix)				
			1987		3.00	6.00

Label, Number		Title	Year	VG	VG+	NM

Pussy Galore

Punk group.

Vinyl Albums

Label, Number		Title	Year	VG	VG+	NM
Buy Our Records 10	EP	Pussy Gold 5000	1986	12.50	25.00	50.00
Caroline 1337		Right Now!	1987	5.00	10.00	20.00
Caroline CAROL 1369		Dial "M"	1989	5.00	10.00	20.00
Shove 2		Groovy Hate Fuck	1986	12.50	25.00	50.00

7-Inch Extended Play Singles

Label, Number		Title	Year	VG	VG+	NM
Adult Contemporary 004		Feel Good About Your Body	1985	12.50	25.00	50.00
Adult Contemporary 004	PS	Feel Good About Your Body	1985	12.50	25.00	50.00
Lo-Fi (# unknown)		Love You Live	199?		2.50	5.00
Lo-Fi (# unknown)	PS	Love You Live	199?		2.50	5.00

45s

Label, Number		Title	Year	VG	VG+	NM
Sub Pop 37		Damaged 2/Damaged 1	1989	3.75	7.50	15.00
B-side by Tad						
Sub Pop 37	PS	Damaged 2/Damaged 1	1989	3.75	7.50	15.00
B-side by Tad; #8 in Sub Pop Singles Club series						
Supernatural AGN 2		Penetration in the Centerfold/One Shot World	198?	3.00	6.25	12.50
B-side by Black Snakes						
Supernatural AGN 2	PS	Penetration in the Centerfold/One Shot World	198?	3.00	6.25	12.50

Q

Queen and David Bowie

45s

Label, Number		Title	Year	VG	VG+	NM
Elektra 47230		Under Pressure/Soul Brother	1981		2.00	4.00
B-side by Queen						
Elektra 47230	PS	Under Pressure/Soul Brother	1981		3.00	6.00

Queer Pills, The

See Angry Samoans

Queers, The

New Hampshire-based punk rock band.

Vinyl Albums

Label, Number		Title	Year	VG	VG+	NM
Selfless (# unknown)		Rocket to Russia	1994	3.50	7.00	14.00
Shakin' Street 010		Grow Up	198?	50.00	100.00	200.00
Only 100-150 copies exist of a planned pressing of 500 (others were destroyed at the plant)						

7-Inch Extended Play Singles

Label, Number		Title	Year	VG	VG+	NM
Doheny (no #)		The Queers	1982	30.00	60.00	120.00
Doheny (no #)	PS	The Queers	1982	10.00	20.00	40.00
Handwritten sleeve						
Doheny (no #)		Kicked Out of the Weeblos	1983	30.00	60.00	120.00
This record has been bootlegged. If in doubt, ask an expert.						
Doheny (no #)	PS	Kicked Out of the Weeblos	1983	7.50	15.00	30.00
Also known with some handwritten sleeves						

Label, Number		Title	Year	VG	VG+	NM

R

R.E.M.
Athens, Georgia-based jangle-pop group. Enormously popular since late-1980s. Side projects: **Hindu Love Gods, Backbeat Band.**

Vinyl Albums

Label, Number		Title	Year	VG	VG+	NM
I.R.S. 5592		Fables of the Reconstruction	1985	3.00	6.00	12.00
I.R.S. 5783		Life's Rich Pageant	1986	3.00	6.00	12.00
I.R.S. 6262		Eponymous	1988	2.50	5.00	10.00
I.R.S. 42059		Document	1987	2.50	5.00	10.00
I.R.S. SP-70014		Murmur	1983	3.75	7.50	15.00
Original number?						
I.R.S. SP-70044		Reckoning	1984	3.00	6.00	12.00
I.R.S. SP-70054		Dead Letter Office	1987	3.00	6.00	12.00
I.R.S. SP-70502	EP	Chronic Town	1982	3.00	6.00	12.00
Original pressings have a custom gargoyle label						
I.R.S. SP-70502	EP	Chronic Town	1982		3.00	6.00
Later pressings have a standard I.R.S. label						
I.R.S. SP-70604		Murmur	1983	3.00	6.00	12.00
Reissue?						
I.R.S. R 100701		Eponymous	1988	3.00	6.00	12.00
BMG Direct Marketing edition						
I.R.S. R 163503		Document	1987	3.00	6.00	12.00
BMG Direct Marketing edition						
I.R.S. R 173669		Life's Rich Pageant	1986	3.50	7.00	14.00
RCA Music Service edition						
Mobile Fidelity 1-231		Murmur	1995	5.00	10.00	20.00
Original Master Recording						
Warner Bros. PRO-A-3377	(2) DJ	Should We Talk About the Weather?				
			1988	10.00	20.00	40.00
Promo-only interviews and music						
Warner Bros. 25795		Green	1988	3.00	6.00	12.00
Warner Bros. W1-25795		Green	1988	3.75	7.50	15.00
Columbia House edition						
Warner Bros. 26496		Out of Time	1991	2.50	5.00	10.00
Warner Bros. 45055		Automatic for the People	1992	2.50	5.00	10.00
Warner Bros. 45740		Monster	1994	2.50	5.00	10.00
Warner Bros. R 100715		Green	1988	3.00	6.00	12.00
BMG Direct Marketing edition						
Warner Bros. R 124762		Out of Time	1991	4.00	8.00	16.00
BMG Direct Marketing edition; one of the last BMG vinyl releases						

45s

Label, Number		Title	Year	VG	VG+	NM
Evatone 105900-15		Dark Globe (one-sided)	1989		3.00	6.00
5-inch black flexi-disc included in issue of Sassy magazine (double value if record is still attached to magazine)						
Fan Club REM 92		Where's Captain Kirk?/Toyland	1992	3.75	7.50	15.00
Fan Club REM 92	PS	Where's Captain Kirk?/Toyland	1992	3.75	7.50	15.00
Any of three variations of a gray sleeve						
Fan Club REM 92	PS	Where's Captain Kirk?/Toyland	1992	3.75	7.50	15.00
White sleeve						
Fan Club REM 94		Sex Bomb/Christmas in Tunisia	1994	2.50	5.00	10.00
Fan Club REM 94	PS	Sex Bomb/Christmas in Tunisia	1994	3.75	7.50	15.00
Picture sleeve also included a magnet, stamps and sticker						
Fan Club REM 95		Wicked Game/Java	1995	2.50	5.00	10.00
Fan Club REM 95	PS	Wicked Game/Java	1995	2.50	5.00	10.00
Fan Club REM 1993		Silver Bells/Christmas Time Is Here				
			1993	3.75	7.50	15.00
Fan Club REM 1993	PS	Silver Bells/Christmas Time Is Here				
			1993	3.75	7.50	15.00

Label, Number		Title	Year	VG	VG+	NM
Fan Club U-23518M		Parade of the Wooden Soldiers/See No Evil				
			1988	12.50	25.00	50.00
Green vinyl						
Fan Club U-23518M	PS	Parade of the Wooden Soldiers/See No Evil				
			1988	12.50	25.00	50.00
Fan Club 122589		Good King Wenceslas/Academy Fight Song				
			1989	12.50	25.00	50.00
Fan Club 122589	PS	Good King Wenceslas/Academy Fight Song				
			1989	12.50	25.00	50.00
Fold-out poster sleeve						
Fan Club 122590		Ghost Reindeer in the Sky/Summertime				
			1990	7.50	15.00	30.00
Fan Club 122590	PS	Ghost Reindeer in the Sky/Summertime				
			1990	7.50	15.00	30.00
Fan Club 122591		Baby Baby/Christmas Griping	1991	7.50	15.00	30.00
Fan Club 122591	PS	Baby Baby/Christmas Griping	1991	7.50	15.00	30.00
Hib-Tone HT-0001		Radio Free Europe/Sitting Still	1981	18.75	37.50	75.00
First pressing, with no address for Hib-Tone Records on label						
Hib-Tone HT-0001		Radio Free Europe/Sitting Still	1981	12.50	25.00	50.00
Hib-Tone HT-0001	PS	Radio Free Europe/Sitting Still	1981	18.75	37.50	75.00
I.R.S. 9916		Radio Free Europe/There She Goes Again				
			1983	2.50	5.00	10.00
I.R.S. 9916	PS	Radio Free Europe/There She Goes Again				
			1983	7.50	15.00	30.00
I.R.S. 9927		So. Central Rain (I'm Sorry)/King of the Road				
			1984		2.00	4.00
I.R.S. 9927	PS	So. Central Rain (I'm Sorry)/King of the Road				
			1984	2.50	5.00	10.00
I.R.S. 9931		(Don't Go Back to) Rockville/Catapult (Live)				
			1984	2.50	5.00	10.00
I.R.S. 9931	PS	(Don't Go Back to) Rockville/Catapult (Live)				
			1984	2.50	5.00	10.00
I.R.S. 52642		Can't Get There from Here/Bandwagon				
			1985		3.00	6.00
I.R.S. 52642	PS	Can't Get There from Here/Bandwagon				
			1985		3.00	6.00
I.R.S. 52678		Driver 8/Crazy	1985		3.00	6.00
I.R.S. 52678	PS	Driver 8/Crazy	1985		3.00	6.00
I.R.S. 52883		Fall on Me/Rotary Ten	1986		2.50	5.00
I.R.S. 52883	PS	Fall on Me/Rotary Ten	1986		2.50	5.00
I.R.S. 52971		Superman/White Tornado	1986		2.50	5.00
I.R.S. 52971	PS	Superman/White Tornado	1986		2.50	5.00
I.R.S. 53171		The One I Love/Maps and Legends				
			1987			3.00
I.R.S. 53171	PS	The One I Love/Maps and Legends				
			1987			3.00
I.R.S. 53220		It's the End of the World As We Know It (And I Feel Fine)/				
		Last Date	1987			3.00
I.R.S. 53220	PS	It's the End of the World As We Know It (And I Feel Fine)/				
		Last Date	1987			3.00
The Bob 5		Tighten Up (one-sided)	198?	4.50	9.00	18.00
Flexi-disc included with The Bob magazine						
The Bob 20		Femme Fatale (one-sided)	1986	3.75	7.50	15.00
Flexi-disc included with The Bob magazine; red						
The Bob 20		Femme Fatale (one-sided)	1986	3.75	7.50	15.00
Flexi-disc included with The Bob magazine; black						
The Bob 20	PS	Femme Fatale (one-sided)	1986	10.00	20.00	40.00
Picture sleeve sent to The Bob subscribers only						
Warner Bros. 17737		Tongue/Tongue (Live)	1995			3.00
Warner Bros. 17900		Strange Currencies/(Instrumental)				
			1995			3.00
Warner Bros. 17994		Bang and Blame/(Instrumental)	1995			3.00

Label, Number		Title	Year	VG	VG+	NM
Warner Bros. 18050		What's the Frequency, Kenneth?/(Instrumental)				
			1994			3.00
Warner Bros. 18523		The Sidewinder Sleeps Tonite/The Lion Sleeps Tonight				
			1993			3.00
Warner Bros. 18638		Everybody Hurts/Mandolin Strum				
			1993			3.00
Warner Bros. 18642		Man on the Moon/New Orleans Instrumental #2				
			1992			3.00
Warner Bros. 18729		Drive/Winged Mammal Theme	1992			3.00
Warner Bros. 19242		Shiny Happy People/Forty Second Song				
			1991			3.00
Warner Bros. 19246		Radio Song/Love Is All Around	1991			3.00
Warner Bros. 19392		Losing My Religion/Rotary Eleven				
			1991			3.00
Warner Bros. 21864		Stand/Pop Song 89	1989			3.00
"Back to Back Hits" series						
Warner Bros. 22780		Singleactiongreen	1989	6.25	12.50	25.00

Box set of 4 7-inch 45s (WB 27688, 927 652, 27640 and 22791), each with picture sleeve, plus poster. Sticker on box claims the set contains "Orange Crush" b/w "Ghost Rider" but it actually contains "Orange Crush" b/w "Memphis Train Blues."

Warner Bros. 22791		Get Up/Funtime	1989			3.00
Warner Bros. 22791	PS	Get Up/Funtime	1989			3.00
Warner Bros. 27640		Pop Song 89/Pop Song 89 (Acoustic Version)				
			1989			3.00
Warner Bros. 27640	PS	Pop Song 89/Pop Song 89 (Acoustic Version)				
			1989			

Only issued as part of Warner Bros. 22780; not available otherwise

Warner Bros. 27688		Stand/Memphis Train Blues	1988			3.00
Warner Bros. 27688	PS	Stand/Memphis Train Blues	1988			3.00
Warner Bros. 927 652		Orange Crush/Memphis Train Blues				
			1989			

Import with large hole, issued in U.S. as part of Warner Bros. 22780

Warner Bros. 927 652	PS	Orange Crush/Memphis Train Blues				
			1989			

Import, issued in U.S. as part of Warner Bros. 22780

12-Inch Singles

I.R.S. L33-17034	DJ	Driver 8/Driver 8 (Live)	1985	6.25	12.50	25.00
I.R.S. L33-17060	DJ	Life and How to Live It/Bandwagon/Crazy				
			1985	6.25	12.50	25.00
I.R.S. L33-17159	DJ	Fall on Me (same on both sides)	1986	6.25	12.50	25.00
I.R.S. L33-17199	DJ	I Believe/Toys in the Attic	1986	4.50	9.00	18.00
I.R.S. L33-17200	DJ	Superman (same on both sides)	1986	3.75	7.50	15.00
I.R.S. L33-17384	DJ	The One I Love (same on both sides)				
			1987	5.00	10.00	20.00
I.R.S. L33-17430	DJ	It's the End of the World As We Know It (And I Feel Fine)/				
		Disturbance Heroin House (Live)	1987	5.00	10.00	20.00
I.R.S. L33-17510	DJ	Finest Worksong (same on both sides)				
			1988	3.75	7.50	15.00
I.R.S. 23792		The One I Love/The One I Love (Live)/Maps and Legends				
			1987	3.00	6.00	12.00
I.R.S. 23850		Finest Worksong (Dub)/Finest Worksong (Other)/				
		Time After Time (Live)	1988	3.75	7.50	15.00
I.R.S. 70416	DJ	Ages of You (same on both sides)	1987	2.00	4.00	8.00
I.R.S. 70982	DJ	(Don't Go Back to) Rockville (Edit)/Catapult (Live)				
			1984	6.25	12.50	25.00
Warner Bros. PRO-A-3306	DJ	Orange Crush (same on both sides)				
			1988	5.00	10.00	20.00
Orange vinyl, custom labels						
Warner Bros. PRO-A-5263	DJ	Radio Song (Tower of Luv Bug Mix)/Radio Song (Monster Remix)				
			1991	6.25	12.50	25.00
Warner Bros. 40229		Radio Song (Tower of Luv Bug Mix)/Love Is All Around/				
		Belong (Live)	1991	2.00	4.00	8.00

Label, Number		Title	Year	VG	VG+	NM
Warner Bros. 41857		Bang and Blame/Losing My Religion (Live)/ Country Feedback (Live)/Begin the Begin (Live)				
			1994	2.00	4.00	8.00

Radio Birdman
Australian punk band.

Vinyl Albums						
Sire SRK 6050		Radio Appears	1978	3.75	7.50	15.00
45s						
Sire 1014		Murder City Nights/What Gives	1978		3.00	6.00

Radio Heart
*With **Gary Numan**.*

45s						
Critique 99454		Radio Heart/Mistasax Version #2				
			1987			3.00
Critique 99454	PS	Radio Heart/Mistasax Version #2				
			1987			3.00
12-Inch Singles						
Critique 1068	DJ	Radio Heart (3 versions)	1987		2.50	5.00

Radiohead
Oxford, England, rock group.

45s						
Capitol S7-17591		Creep/Anyone Can Play Guitar	1993		2.50	5.00
Green vinyl						
Capitol S7-18728		Fake Plastic Trees/The Bends	1995			3.00
Capitol S7-19017		High and Dry/Black Star	1996			3.00

Rage Against The Machine
*From Los Angeles, loud punkers were formerly known as **Inside Out**.*

Vinyl Albums						
Epic E 52959		Rage Against The Machine	1996	2.50	5.00	10.00
CD and cassette released in 1992						
Epic E 57523		Evil Empire	1996	2.50	5.00	10.00
45s						
Epic 74927		Bullet in the Head/Darkness	1993		2.50	5.00
Epic 74927	PS	Bullet in the Head/Darkness	1993		2.50	5.00

Raincoats, The
British all-female new wave band.

Vinyl Albums						
Rough Trade ROUGH US 13		Odyshape	1981	6.25	12.50	25.00
Sounds Like 12	EP	The Raincoats	1994	2.00	4.00	8.00

Ramone, Dee Dee
*Member of **The Ramones**.*

Vinyl Albums						
Sire 25884		Standing in the Spotlight	1988	2.50	5.00	10.00
12-Inch Singles						
Rock Hotel 7159		Funky Man	1987	2.50	5.00	10.00

Label, Number		Title	Year	VG	VG+	NM

Ramones, The

*New York punk/pop group, one of the original new wave bands from the mid-1970s. Still recording as of 1995. Also see **Ramone, Dee Dee**.*

Vinyl Albums

Label, Number		Title	Year	VG	VG+	NM
Radioactive 10615		Mondo Bizarro	1992	2.50	5.00	10.00
Radioactive 11273		Adios Amigos!	1995	2.50	5.00	10.00
Sire PRO-A-605	DJ	Rock 'n' Roll High School Radio Sampler				
			1979	6.25	12.50	25.00
Sire PRO-A-756	DJ	Road to Ruin Radio Sampler	1978	6.25	12.50	25.00
Sire PRO-A-996	DJ	Pleasant Dreams Radio Sampler	1980	6.25	12.50	25.00
Sire SRK 3571		Pleasant Dreams	1981	3.75	7.50	15.00
Sire SR 6020		Ramones	1978	4.50	9.00	18.00
Reissue, distributed by Warner Bros.; originals have no bar code						
Sire SR 6031		Ramones Leave Home	1978	4.50	9.00	18.00
Third issue, distributed by Warner Bros., tracks as on second issue; originals have no bar code						
Sire SRK 6042		Rocket to Russia	1978	3.75	7.50	15.00
Sire SRK 6063		Road to Ruin	1979	3.75	7.50	15.00
Sire SRK 6077		End of the Century	1980	3.75	7.50	15.00
Sire SASD-7520		Ramones	1976	6.25	12.50	25.00
First issue, distributed by ABC						
Sire SASD-7528		Ramones Leave Home	1977	12.50	25.00	50.00
First issue, distributed by ABC, with "Carbona Not Glue"						
Sire SASD-7528		Ramones Leave Home	1977	6.25	12.50	25.00
Second issue, distributed by ABC, with "Sheena Is a Punk Rocker" replacing "Carbona Not Glue"						
Sire 23800		Subterranean Jungle	1983	3.75	7.50	15.00
Sire 25187		Too Tough to Die	1984	3.00	6.00	12.00
Sire 25433		Animal Boy	1986	3.00	6.00	12.00
Sire 25641		Halfway to Sanity	1987	3.00	6.00	12.00
Sire 25709	(2)	RamonesMania	1988	3.75	7.50	15.00
Sire 25905		Brain Drain	1989	3.00	6.00	12.00

45s

Label, Number		Title	Year	VG	VG+	NM
RSO 1055		I Wanna Be Sedated/The Return of Jackie and Judy				
			1980		2.50	5.00
Sire 725		Blitzkrieg Bop/Havana Affair	1976	10.00	20.00	40.00
Promo copies worth slightly less						
Sire 734		I Wanna Be Your Boyfriend//California Sun/ I Don't Wanna Walk Around with You				
			1976		3.00	6.00
Sire 734	PS	I Wanna Be Your Boyfriend//California Sun/ I Don't Wanna Walk Around with You				
			1976	3.50	7.00	14.00
Sire 738		Swallow My Pride/Pinhead	1977		3.00	6.00
Sire 738	PS	Swallow My Pride/Pinhead	1977	3.00	6.00	12.00
Sire 746		Sheena Is a Punk Rocker/I Don't Care				
			1977		3.00	6.00
Sire 746	PS	Sheena Is a Punk Rocker/I Don't Care				
			1977	3.00	6.00	12.00
Sire 1006		Sheena Is a Punk Rocker/I Don't Care				
			1977		2.00	4.00
Sire 1006	PS	Sheena Is a Punk Rocker/I Don't Care				
			1977	2.00	4.00	8.00
Sire 1008		Rockaway Beach/Locket Love	1977		2.00	4.00
Sire 1008	PS	Rockaway Beach/Locket Love	1977	2.00	4.00	8.00
Sire 1017		Do You Wanna Dance?/Baby Sitter				
			1978	2.50	5.00	10.00
Sire 1017	PS	Do You Wanna Dance?/Baby Sitter				
			1978	7.50	15.00	30.00
Sire 1025		Don't Come Close/I Don't Want You				
			1978		3.00	6.00

One of the rarest American R.E.M. picture sleeves is this one from "Pop Song 89." It was not issued with regular copies of the 45, but only with those included in the singles box set *Singleactiongreen.*

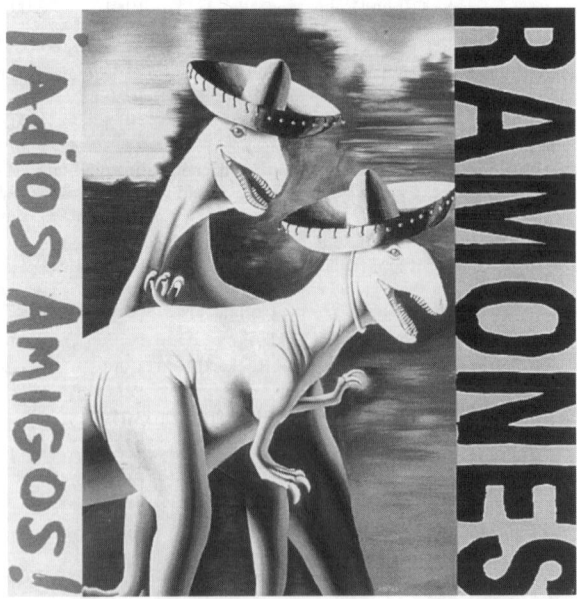

The Ramones LP *Adios Amigos!* ($10) is rumored to be their last in the studio, but the band hasn't officially broken up as of the time this is being written.

Label, Number		Title	Year	VG	VG+	NM
Sire 1045		Needles and Pins/I Wanted Everything				
			1979		2.50	5.00
Sire 1051		Rock 'N' Roll High School/Do You Wanna Dance				
			1979		2.00	4.00
Sire 1051	PS	Rock 'N' Roll High School/Do You Wanna Dance				
			1979	2.00	4.00	8.00
Sire 22911		Pet Sematary/Sheena Is a Punk Rocker				
			1989		2.50	5.00
Sire 22911	PS	Pet Sematary/Sheena Is a Punk Rocker				
			1989		2.50	5.00
Sire 27663		I Wanna Be Sedated/I Wanna Be Sedated				
		(Ramones On 45 Mega-Mix)	1988		2.00	4.00
Sire 27663	PS	I Wanna Be Sedated/I Wanna Be Sedated				
		(Ramones On 45 Mega-Mix)	1988		3.00	6.00
Sire 28599		Something to Believe In/Animal Boy				
			1986	2.00	4.00	8.00
Sire 29107		Howling at the Moon (Sha La La)/Wart Hog				
			1985	2.00	4.00	8.00
Sire 29606		The Time Has Come Today/Psycho Therapy				
			1983		3.00	6.00
Sire 49182		Baby I Love You/High Risk Insurance				
			1980		2.50	5.00
Sire 49261		Do You Remember Rock & Roll Radio/Let's Go				
			1980	2.00	4.00	8.00
Sire 49812		We Want the Airwaves/All's Quiet on the Western Front				
			1981	2.00	4.00	8.00

12-Inch Singles

Label, Number		Title	Year	VG	VG+	NM
Sire PRO-A-2219	DJ	Howling at the Moon/Chasing the Night				
			1984	2.50	5.00	10.00
Sire PRO-A-2816	DJ	I Wanna Live (same on both sides)				
			1987		3.00	6.00
Sire PRO-A-3193	DJ	I Wanna Be Sedated/Sedated (Ramones On 45 Mega-Mix)/				
		Indian Giver	1988	5.00	10.00	20.00

Rancid

Berkeley, California punk band. Its three LPs on Epitaph are still in print and bring $10 NM.

7-Inch Extended Play Singles

Label, Number		Title	Year	VG	VG+	NM
Lookout 59		I'm Not the Only One/Battering Ram//The Sentence/				
		Media Controller/Idle Hands	1993			2.00
Lookout 59	PS	I'm Not the Only One/Battering Ram//The Sentence/				
		Media Controller/Idle Hands	1993			2.00

45s

Label, Number		Title	Year	VG	VG+	NM
Epitaph 86455		Time Bomb//The Wars End/Blast 'Em				
			1995			3.00
Small center hole						
Epitaph 86455	PS	Time Bomb//The Wars End/Blast 'Em				
			1995			3.00
Epitaph 86464		Ruby Soho//That's Entertainment/Disorder and Disarray				
			1995			3.00
Small center hole						
Epitaph 86464	PS	Ruby Soho//That's Entertainment/Disorder and Disarray				
			1995			3.00

Randoms, The

Los Angeles punk band, with John Doe (later of X) on lead guitar.

45s

Label, Number		Title	Year	VG	VG+	NM
Dangerhouse PT 1		ABCD/Let's Get Rid of New York				
			1977	3.00	6.25	12.50

Label, Number		Title	Year	VG	VG+	NM
Dangerhouse PT 1	PS	ABCD/Let's Get Rid of New York				
			1977	3.00	6.25	12.50

Rank And File

Vinyl Albums

Rhino RNLP 70830		Rank and File	1987	2.50	5.00	10.00
Slash SR 114		Sundown	1982	3.00	6.00	12.00
Slash 23833		Sundown	1983	2.50	5.00	10.00
Slash 25087		Long Gone Dead	1984	3.00	6.00	12.00

45s

Slash 29297		Sound of the Rain/Long Gone Road				
			1984		2.00	4.00
Slash 29591		Amanda Ruth/Lucky Day	1983		2.00	4.00

Rapeman

Vinyl Albums

Touch & Go 19		Budd	1988	3.00	6.00	12.00
Touch & Go 36		Two Nuns and a Pack Mule	1989	3.00	6.00	12.00

45s

Ruthless (# unknown)		Marmoset/Hated Chinee	1989	9.25	18.75	37.50
Ruthless (# unknown)	PS	Marmoset/Hated Chinee	1989	9.25	18.75	37.50
Sub Pop 40		Inki's Butt Crack/Song Number One				
			1989	8.00	16.25	32.50

First 1,000 on clear vinyl

Sub Pop 40		Inki's Butt Crack/Song Number One				
			1989	4.25	8.75	17.50

Black vinyl

Sub Pop 40	PS	Inki's Butt Crack/Song Number One				
			1989	4.25	8.75	17.50

#10 in Sub Pop Singles Club series

Ravers, The

45s

Zombie/Ariola 7683		It's Gonna Be a Punk Rock Christmas/Silent Night				
			1977		2.50	5.00
Zombie/Ariola 7683	PS	It's Gonna Be a Punk Rock Christmas/Silent Night				
			1977		2.50	5.00

Re-Flex

Techno-rock group from England.

Vinyl Albums

Capitol ST-12314		The Politics of Dancing	1983	2.50	5.00	10.00
Capitol ST-12314	DJ	The Politics of Dancing	1983	3.75	7.50	15.00

High-grade vinyl edition (sticker on cover)

45s

Capitol 5301		The Politics of Dancing/Flex It	1983			3.00
Capitol 5301	PS	The Politics of Dancing/Flex It	1983		2.00	4.00
Capitol 5348		Hurt/Cruel World	1984			3.00
Capitol 5348	PS	Hurt/Cruel World	1984		2.00	4.00
Capitol S7-18904		The Politics of Dancing/She Blinded Me with Science				
			1996			3.00

B-side by Thomas Dolby

12-Inch Singles

Capitol 8574		The Politics of Dancing/Flex It	1983	3.00	6.00	12.00

Label, Number		Title	Year	VG	VG+	NM
Capitol 8588		Hurt (2 mixes)	1984	2.00	4.00	8.00
Capitol SPRO 9033/4	DJ	The Politics of Dancing (single)/The Politics of Dancing (LP)				
			1983	5.00	10.00	20.00
Capitol SPRO 9083	DJ	Praying to the Beat (same on both sides)				
			1983	2.00	4.00	8.00
Capitol SPRO 9120/1	DJ	Hurt (6:45)/Hurt (9:30)	1983	2.00	4.00	8.00
Capitol SPRO 9122	DJ	Hurt (same on both sides)	1983	2.00	4.00	8.00
Capitol SPRO 9127/8	DJ	Hurt (5:35)/Hurt (6:45)	1983	2.00	4.00	8.00

Real Life
Australian synth-pop band.

Vinyl Albums

Label, Number		Title	Year	VG	VG+	NM
Curb 10624		Let's Fall in Love	1989	2.50	5.00	10.00
Curb 77271		Lifetime	1990	2.50	5.00	10.00
Curb/MCA 1443		Heart Land	1985	2.00	4.00	8.00
Budget-line reissue						
Curb/MCA 5469		Heart Land	1983	2.50	5.00	10.00
Curb/MCA 5639		Flame	1986	2.50	5.00	10.00

45s

Label, Number		Title	Year	VG	VG+	NM
Curb 10531		Send Me An Angel '89/(B-side unknown)				
			1989			3.00
Curb/MCA 52287		Send Me An Angel/Like a Gun	1983			3.00
Curb/MCA 52362		Catch Me I'm Falling/Exploding Bullets				
			1984			3.00
Curb/MCA 52362	PS	Catch Me I'm Falling/Exploding Bullets				
			1984			3.00
Curb/MCA 52712		Face to Face/Flame	1985			3.00

12-Inch Singles

Label, Number		Title	Year	VG	VG+	NM
Curb 10308		Let's Fall in Love (6 mixes)/Bleeding Babies				
			1989	2.50	5.00	10.00
Curb 77070		Kiss the Ground (6 versions)	1990		3.00	6.00
Curb/MCA L33-1166	DJ	Catch Me I'm Falling/Openhearted/Heartland				
			1984	2.00	4.00	8.00
Curb/MCA L33-1169	DJ	Send Me An Angel/Catch Me I'm Falling				
			1984	2.50	5.00	10.00
Curb/MCA 13977		Send Me An Angel (2 versions)/Like a Gun				
			1983	2.00	4.00	8.00
Curb/MCA 17058	DJ	Face to Face (Rock Edit)/Face to Face (Dance Mix)				
			1985		3.50	7.00
Curb/MCA 17176	DJ	Babies (3 versions)	1986	2.00	4.00	8.00
Curb/MCA 23661		Babies (Rock Mix)/Babies (Club Mix)				
			1986		2.50	5.00

Really Red
Houston punk band.

Vinyl Albums

Label, Number		Title	Year	VG	VG+	NM
C.I.A. 006		Teaching You the Fear	1981	6.25	12.50	25.00

7-Inch Extended Play Singles

Label, Number		Title	Year	VG	VG+	NM
C.I.A. 003		Despise Moral Majority	1981	2.50	5.00	10.00
Recorded live in Texas in 1980						
C.I.A. 003	PS	Despise Moral Majority	1981	2.50	5.00	10.00

45s

Label, Number		Title	Year	VG	VG+	NM
C.I.A. 001		Crowd Control/Corporate Settings				
			1979	2.50	5.00	10.00
C.I.A. 001	PS	Crowd Control/Corporate Settings				
			1979	2.50	5.00	10.00

Label, Number		Title	Year	VG	VG+	NM
C.I.A. 002		Modern Needs/White Lies	1980	2.50	5.00	10.00
C.I.A. 002	PS	Modern Needs/White Lies	1980	2.50	5.00	10.00

Records, The
British pop-rock group.

Vinyl Albums

Virgin International VI 2206		Music on Both Sides	1982	2.50	5.00	10.00
Virgin VA 13130		The Records	1979	3.75	7.50	15.00
With bonus 4-song EP "Abracadabra" (deduct 33% if missing)						
Virgin VA 13140		Crashes	1980	3.00	6.00	12.00

7-Inch Extended Play Singles

Virgin PR 338		Abracadabra/See My Friends/1984/ Have You Seen Your Mother, Baby 1979				3.00
Virgin PR 338	PS	Abracadabra/See My Friends/1984/ Have You Seen Your Mother, Baby 1979				3.00
Came with their Virgin LP						

45s

Virgin 67000		Starry Eyes/Paint Her Face	1979		2.00	4.00
Virgin 67000	PS	Starry Eyes/Paint Her Face	1979		2.00	4.00
Virgin 67002		Teenarama/Held Up High	1979		2.00	4.00
Virgin 67002	PS	Teenarama/Held Up High	1979		2.00	4.00
Virgin 67008		Hearts in Her Eyes/So Sorry	1980		2.00	4.00
Virgin 67008	PS	Hearts in Her Eyes/So Sorry	1980		2.50	5.00

12-Inch Singles

Virgin PR 337	DJ	Starry Eyes/Paint Her Face/Another Star 1989		3.75	7.50	15.00
Virgin PR 365	DJ	Rumour Sets the Woods Alight/Hearts in Her Eyes 1980		2.00	4.00	8.00

Red Hot Chili Peppers
Los Angeles punk/alternative band.

Vinyl Albums

EMI America ST-17128		Red Hot Chili Peppers	1984	2.50	5.00	10.00
EMI America ST-17168		Freaky Styley	1985	2.50	5.00	10.00
EMI America E1-48036		The Uplift Mofo Party Plan	1987	2.50	5.00	10.00
EMI Manhattan E1-90869	EP	The Abbey Road E.P.	1988	2.00	4.00	8.00
EMI E1-29665		Out in L.A.	1994	2.50	5.00	10.00
EMI E1-92152		Mother's Milk	1989	3.00	6.00	12.00
Warner Bros. PRO-A-5170	(2) DJ	Blood Sugar Sex Magik	1991	10.00	20.00	40.00
"Radio-ready" version of LP, this is the only U.S. vinyl release of this band's biggest album.						

45s

		Title	Year	VG	VG+	NM
EMI S7-56949		Behind the Sun/Fire	1993		2.00	4.00
EMI S7-57992		Higher Ground/If You Want Me to Stay 1992			2.00	4.00
Warner Bros. 15993		Under the Bridge/Give It Away	1992			3.00
Reissue; first release of B-side on U.S. 45						
Warner Bros. 18401		Soul to Squeeze/Nobody Weird Like Me 1993				3.00
Warner Bros. 18978		Under the Bridge/The Righteous and the Wicked 1992			2.00	4.00
Warner Bros. 18988		Breaking the Girl	1992		*Cassette only*	
Warner Bros. 19147		Give It Away	1992		*Cassette only*	
WTG 68678		Taste the Rain/All for Love	1989		2.00	4.00
B-side by Nancy Wilson (of Heart)						

Label, Number		Title	Year	VG	VG+	NM
12-Inch Singles						
EMI SPRO 04385	DJ	Stone Cold Bush/Fire/Nobody Weird Like Me + 1				
			1989	3.75	7.50	15.00
EMI SPRO 04387	DJ	Higher Ground (2 versions)	1989	2.50	5.00	10.00
EMI SPRO 04504	DJ	Taste the Pain/Castles (Live)/Special Secret Sauce (Live)/				
		F.U. (Live)	1989	5.00	10.00	20.00
EMI SPRO 04542	DJ	Show Me Your Soul (same on both sides)				
			1990	2.50	5.00	10.00
EMI SPRO 04896	DJ	Higher Ground (3 mixes)/If You Want Me to Stay (2 versions)				
			1992	3.75	7.50	15.00
EMI America SPRO 04002	DJ	Behind the Sun/Special Secret Song				
			1987	2.00	4.00	8.00
EMI America SPRO 9466	DJ	Jungle Man/Nevermind/Stranded				
			1986	2.00	4.00	8.00
EMI America 7839		Get Up and Jump/Baby Appeal	1984	3.00	6.00	12.00
EMI America 7862		Hollywood (Extended)/Hollywood (Dub)/Never Mind				
			1985	2.50	5.00	10.00
EMI Manhattan SPRO 79147	DJ	Fight Like a Brave (same on both sides)				
			1988		3.50	7.00
Warner Bros. PRO-A-5182	DJ	Give It Away (3 versions)	1991	3.00	6.00	12.00

Redd Kross

Los Angeles trash-rock band. Also recorded as Red Cross.

Label, Number		Title	Year	VG	VG+	NM
Vinyl Albums						
Atlantic 82148		Third Eye	1990	2.50	5.00	10.00
Big Time 6034-1		Neurotica	1987	3.00	6.00	12.00
Frontier FLP 1018		Born Innocent	1986	3.00	6.00	12.00
Reissue						
Frontier 4609-1-L		Born Innocent	1991	2.50	5.00	10.00
Reissue						
Gasatanka E 1170		Teen Babies from Monsanto	1984	3.00	6.00	12.00
Posh Boy 1010	EP	Red Cross	1980	3.75	7.50	15.00
Posh Boy 1010	EP	Annette's Got the Hits	1987	2.50	5.00	10.00
Reissue						
Smoke SMK7-103		Born Innocent	1982	3.75	7.50	15.00
Sympathy For The Record	10	2,500 Redd Kross Fans Can't Be Wrong				
Industry 260			1993	2.50	5.00	10.00

Reed, Francine (Featuring Lyle Lovett)

Also see Lyle Lovett.

Label, Number	Title	Year	VG	VG+	NM
45s					
Ichiban 95-339	Why I Don't Know/Wild Women				
		1995			3.00
B-side by Francine Reed solo					

Reed, Lou

Former member of The Velvet Underground; a solo performer for over 20 years.

Label, Number		Title	Year	VG	VG+	NM
Vinyl Albums						
Arista AL 4100		Rock and Roll Heart	1976	3.75	7.50	15.00
Originals on light blue labels						
Arista AL 4169		Street Hassle	1978	3.75	7.50	15.00
Arista AL 4229		The Bells	1979	3.00	6.00	12.00
Arista ALB6-8390		City Lights -- Classic Performances by Lou Reed				
			1985	2.50	5.00	10.00
Arista AL11 8434	(2)	Rock and Roll Diary 1967-1980	198?	4.00	8.00	16.00
Reissue						
Arista AL 8502	(2)	Live! Take No Prisoners	1978	4.50	9.00	18.00
Arista A2L 8603	(2)	Rock and Roll Diary 1967-1980	1980	4.50	9.00	18.00

Label, Number		Title	Year	VG	VG+	NM
Arista AL 9522		Growing Up in Public	1980	3.00	6.00	12.00
Arista R 252506	(2)	Rock and Roll Diary 1967-1980	1980	4.50	9.00	18.00
RCA Music Service edition						
Direct Disk	DJ	Blue Mask	1982	37.50	75.00	150.00
Only exists on test pressings; no stock copies made						
RCA Victor APL1-0207		Berlin	1973	3.00	6.00	12.00
RCA Victor APL1-0472		Rock & Roll Animal	1974	3.00	6.00	12.00
RCA Victor AFL1-0472		Rock & Roll Animal	1977	2.00	4.00	8.00
Reissue						
RCA Victor CPL1-0611		Sally Can't Dance	1974	5.00	10.00	20.00
RCA Victor AFL1-0611		Sally Can't Dance	1977	2.00	4.00	8.00
Reissue						
RCA Victor APL1-0915		Coney Island Baby	1976	4.00	8.00	16.00
RCA Victor APL1-0959		Lou Reed Live	1975	3.75	7.50	15.00
RCA Victor AFL1-0959		Lou Reed Live	1977	2.00	4.00	8.00
Reissue						
RCA Victor CPL2-1101	(2)	Metal Machine Music	1975	12.50	25.00	50.00
Orange or brown label.						
RCA Victor APD2-1101	(2) Q	Metal Machine Music	1975	37.50	75.00	150.00
RCA Victor APL1-2001		Walk on the Wild Side	1977	3.00	6.00	12.00
RCA Victor AFL1-2001		Walk on the Wild Side	1978	2.00	4.00	8.00
Reissue						
RCA Victor ANL1-2480		Coney Island Baby	1977	2.00	4.00	8.00
Reissue						
RCA Victor AYL1-3664		Rock & Roll Animal	1980	2.00	4.00	8.00
Best Buy Series reissue						
RCA Victor AYL1-3752		Lou Reed Live	1980	2.00	4.00	8.00
Best Buy Series reissue						
RCA Victor AYL1-3753		Walk on the Wild Side	1980	2.00	4.00	8.00
Best Buy Series reissue						
RCA Victor AYL1-3806		Transformer	1980	2.00	4.00	8.00
Best Buy Series reissue						
RCA Victor AYL1-3807		Coney Island Baby	1980	2.00	4.00	8.00
Best Buy Series reissue						
RCA Victor AFL1-4221		Blue Mask	1982	2.50	5.00	10.00
RCA Victor DJL1-4266	DJ	Special Radio Series, Vol. XVII	1980	6.25	12.50	25.00
Promo-only with insert						
RCA Victor DJL1-4267		Blue Mask Interview Album	1982	10.00	20.00	40.00
RCA Victor DJL1-4345	DJ	Blue Mask Sampler	1982	3.00	6.00	12.00
Three-song EP released to radio						
RCA Victor AYL1-4388		Berlin	1983	2.00	4.00	8.00
Best Buy Series reissue						
RCA Victor AYL1-4555		Sally Can't Dance	1983	2.00	4.00	8.00
Best Buy Series reissue						
RCA Victor AFL1-4568		Legendary Hearts	1983	2.50	5.00	10.00
RCA Victor LSP-4701		Lou Reed	1972	5.00	10.00	20.00
RCA Victor AYL1-4780		Blue Mask	1984	2.00	4.00	8.00
Best Buy Series reissue						
RCA Victor LSP-4807		Transformer	1972	5.00	10.00	20.00
RCA Victor AFL1-4807		Transformer	1977	2.00	4.00	8.00
Reissue						
RCA Victor AFL1-4998		New Sensations	1984	2.00	4.00	8.00
RCA Victor AFL1-7190		Mistrial	1986	3.00	6.00	12.00
Sire 25829		New York	1989	2.50	5.00	10.00
Sire R 101058		New York	1989	3.00	6.00	12.00
BMG Music Service edition						

45s

Label, Number	Title	Year	VG	VG+	NM
A&M 2781	September Song/Oh Heavenly Salvation				
		1985		2.00	4.00
B-side by Mark Bingham/Johnny Adams/Aaron Neville					
Arista 0215	I Believe in Love/Senselessly Cruel				
		1976		2.00	4.00

Lou Reed, a pioneer in alternative music as a member of the Velvet Underground, recorded *Transformer* in 1972. It features his only big hit single, "Walk on the Wild Side." Original RCA orange-label pressings are getting harder to find.

The Washington, D.C. area was a hotbed for the hardcore scene. Some of the all-stars of the area collaborated in this one-off Christmas single under the name "The Re-ind Dears." This lo-fi, Phil-Spector-meets-the-Ramones-before-he-did-in-real-life record gets $15.

Label, Number			Title	Year	VG	VG+	NM
Arista 0431			City Lights/I Want to Boogie with You				
				1979		2.00	4.00
Arista 0535			Growing Up in Public/The Power of Positive Drinking				
				1980		2.00	4.00
Atlantic 89468			My Love Is Chemical/(B-side unknown)				
				1985			3.00
Atlantic 89468	PS		My Love Is Chemical/(B-side unknown)				
				1985			3.00
RCA Victor APBO-0054			Vicious/Good Night Ladies	1973		2.50	5.00
RCA Victor APBO-0172			Lady Day/How Do You Think It Feels				
				1973		2.50	5.00
RCA Victor APBO-0238			Sweet Jane/Lady Day	1974	7.50	15.00	30.00
Part of U.S. numbering system, but pressed for export.							
RCA Victor 74-0727			I Can't Stand It/Going Down	1972		3.00	6.00
RCA Victor 74-0784			Walk and Talk It/Wild Child	1972		3.00	6.00
RCA Victor 74-0887			Walk on the Wild Side/Perfect Day				
				1973		3.00	6.00
RCA Victor 74-0964			Satellite of Love/Walk and Talk It				
				1973		3.00	6.00
RCA Victor GB-10162			Walk on the Wild Side/Vicious	1975			3.00
Gold Standard Series reissue							
RCA Victor PB-10053			Sally Can't Dance/Vicious	1974		2.00	4.00
RCA Victor PB-10081			Sally Can't Dance/Ennui	1974		2.00	4.00
RCA Victor PB-10573			Charley's Girl/Nowhere At All	1976		2.00	4.00
RCA Victor PB-10648			Crazy Feeling/Nowhere At All	1976		2.00	4.00
RCA JB-13558			Martial Law/Don't Talk to Me About Work				
				1983			3.00
RCA PB-14368			No Money Down/Don't Hurt a Woman				
				1986			3.00
Sire 18959			What's Good/The Room	1992		*Cassette only?*	
Sire 22876			Romeo Had Juliette/Busload of Faith				
				1989			3.00
Sire 22876	PS		Romeo Had Juliette/Busload of Faith				
				1989			3.00

12-Inch Singles

Label, Number			Title	Year	VG	VG+	NM
A&M 17352	DJ		September Song/September Song (7" Version)				
				1986		3.00	6.00
Arista SP-14	DJ		Street Hassle (stereo)/Street Hassle (mono)				
				1978	2.50	5.00	10.00
Arista SP-36	DJ		Walk on the Wild Side/Coney Island Baby/Satellite of Love				
				1978	2.50	5.00	10.00
Arista SP-56	DJ		Disco Mystic/I Wanna Boogie with You				
				1979	2.50	5.00	10.00
Arista SP-84	DJ		How Do You Speak to An Angel/Keep Away/				
			The Power of Positive Drinking/Standing on Ceremony				
				1980	3.75	7.50	15.00
Arista 9375	DJ		Hot Hips (same on both sides)	1985	2.50	5.00	10.00
Atlantic 819	DJ		My Love Is Chemical (same on both sides)				
				1985		3.50	7.00
RCA 5711-1			Original Wrapper (2 versions)/Video Violence (2 versions)				
				198?	2.00	4.00	8.00
RCA JR-13849	DJ		I Love You, Suzanne (same on both sides)				
				1984		3.50	7.00
RCA PD-13928			My Red Joystick (remix) (instrumental)/I Love You Suzanne				
				1984	2.50	5.00	10.00
RCA Victor JR-14343	DJ		No Money Down (same on both sides)				
				1986	3.00	6.00	12.00
Green vinyl							
RCA PD-14388			No Money Down (Extended)/No Money Down (Dub)/				
			Don't Hurt a Woman	1986	2.00	4.00	8.00

Label, Number		Title	Year	VG	VG+	NM
RCA Victor JR-14420	DJ	Video Violence (same on both sides)				
			1986	2.00	4.00	8.00
RCA PD-14427		The Original Wrapper (3 mixes)/Video Violence				
			1986	2.00	4.00	8.00
Sire PRO-A-3359	DJ	Dirty Blvd. (Radio Edit)/Dirty Blvd. (LP Version)				
			1988	2.00	4.00	8.00

Reed, Lou, and John Cale

Vinyl Albums

Sire 26140		Songs for Drella	1990	2.50	5.00	10.00

Reed, Lou, and Sam Moore

45s

A&M 2883		Soul Man/Sweet Sarah	1986			3.00

12-Inch Singles

A&M 17434	DJ	Soul Man (same on both sides)	1986		3.00	6.00

Reind Dears, The

Washington, D.C.-area ad hoc punkish group.

45s

Limp 013		Xmas (Is Going to Bring Me...)/White Christmas				
			1978	2.00	4.00	8.00
Limp 013	PS	Xmas (Is Going to Bring Me...)/White Christmas				
			1978	2.00	4.00	8.00

Rembrandts, The

*Pop band from California. Former members of **Great Buildings**.*

45s

EastWest 64429		I'll Be There for You/Snippets	1995			3.00

Rentals, The

45s

Maverick 17720		Friends of P./So Soon	1995			3.00

Replacements, The

*Minneapolis indie-rock legends. Also see **Westerberg, Paul**.*

Vinyl Albums

Sire PRO-A-4632	DJ	Don't Sell Or Buy...It's Crap	1991	7.50	15.00	30.00
Promo-only 5-track sampler						
Sire 25330		Tim	1985	2.50	5.00	10.00
Sire 25557		Pleased to Meet Me	1987	2.50	5.00	10.00
Sire 25831		Don't Tell a Soul	1989	2.50	5.00	10.00
Sire R 101024		Don't Tell a Soul	1989	3.00	6.00	12.00
BMG Music Service edition						
Twin/Tone TTR 8123		Sorry, Ma, Forgot to Take Out the Trash				
			1981	3.75	7.50	15.00
Twin/Tone TTR 8228	EP	The Replacements Stink	1982	3.00	6.00	12.00
Twin/Tone TTR 8332		Hootenanny	1983	3.75	7.50	15.00
Twin/Tone TTR 8441		Let It Be	1984	3.75	7.50	15.00
Warner Bros. WBMS-148	DJ	The Warner Bros. Music Show: An Interview with Paul Westerberg				
			1987	10.00	20.00	40.00

Label, Number		Title	Year	VG	VG+	NM
45s						
Sire 22992		I'll Be You/Date to Church	1989			3.00
Sire 22992	PS	I'll Be You/Date to Church	1989			3.00
Sire 28151		Can't Hardly Wait/Cool Water	1987			3.00
Twin/Tone 8120		I'm in Trouble/If Only You Were Lonely				
			1981	3.00	6.00	12.00
Twin/Tone 8120	PS	I'm in Trouble/If Only You Were Lonely				
			1981	3.00	6.00	12.00
12-Inch Singles						
Sire PRO-A-2412	DJ	Kiss Me on the Bus (same on both sides)				
			1985	3.00	6.00	12.00
Sire PRO-A-2727	DJ	The Ledge (same on both sides)	1987		3.00	6.00
Sire PRO-A-2761	DJ	Alex Chilton (same on both sides)				
			1987	3.00	6.00	12.00
Sire PRO-A-2863	DJ	Can't Hardly Wait (Remix)/Can't Hardly Wait (LP Version)				
			1987	2.00	4.00	8.00
Sire PRO-A-3419	DJ	I'll Be You (same on both sides)	1989	2.50	5.00	10.00
Twin/Tone TTR 8440		I Will Dare/20th Century Boy/Hey Good Lookin' (Live)				
			1984	5.00	10.00	20.00

Residents, The

Anonymous San Francisco-based band known for wearing giant eyeball masks when it performs.

Label, Number		Title	Year	VG	VG+	NM
Vinyl Albums						
Cryptic S-18335 SP-2		For Elsie	1987	18.75	37.50	75.00
Green vinyl one-sided LP						
Enigma 73547		The King & Eye	1989	2.50	5.00	10.00
Episode ED 21		The Census Taker (Soundtrack)	1985	6.25	12.50	25.00
Red vinyl						
Episode ED 21		The Census Taker (Soundtrack)	1985	5.00	10.00	20.00
OP 011	DJ	Freak Show	1991	12.50	25.00	50.00
Promo-only black vinyl pressing; 400 made						
OP 011	PD	Freak Show	1991	3.00	6.00	12.00
Picture disc						
Ralph Mole Show 001		The Mole Show (The Roxy)	1983	7.50	15.00	30.00
Ralph RR 0274		Meet the Residents	1974	50.00	100.00	200.00
First version: "Meet the Beatles" LP parody cover and "First Edition" on back cover						
Ralph RR 0278		Duck Stab	1978	3.00	6.00	12.00
First version: Green titles box on back						
Ralph RR 0278		Duck Stab	1978	2.50	5.00	10.00
Second version: Yellow titles box on back						
Ralph RR 0677		Meet the Residents	1977	5.00	10.00	20.00
Second version: "She Loves You" picture sleeve parody cover, split "a" Ralph logo						
Ralph RR 0677		Meet the Residents	1977	3.75	7.50	15.00
Third version: same cover as second version, black "a" Ralph logo						
Ralph RR 0677		Meet the Residents	1977	2.50	5.00	10.00
Fourth version: same cover as second version, modified and orange back cover						
Ralph RR 1075		The Third Reich 'N' Roll	1976	12.50	25.00	50.00
First version of 1,000: Liner notes inside, orange carrot						
Ralph RR 1075		The Third Reich 'N' Roll	1976	3.75	7.50	15.00
Second version: Gray carrot, split "a" Ralph logo						
Ralph RR 1075		The Third Reich 'N' Roll	1976	3.00	6.00	12.00
Third version: Orange carrot, black "a" Ralph logo						
Ralph RR 1075		The Third Reich 'N' Roll	1976	2.50	5.00	10.00
Fourth version: Gray carrot, black "a" Ralph logo						
Ralph RR 1075		The Third Reich 'N' Roll	1976	12.50	25.00	50.00
Censored cover with swastikas obscured, pressed in U.S. for export to Germany						
Ralph RR 1075		The Third Reich 'N' Roll	1976	375.00	750.00	1,500.00
Numbered box set on marbled vinyl, silkscreened cover and lithographs inside						
Ralph RR 1174		Not Available	1978	6.25	12.50	25.00
Purple label, mis-mastered, "Re-1" in trail-off vinyl						
Ralph RR 1174		Not Available	1978	3.75	7.50	15.00
Orange label, remastered, "Re-3" in trail-off vinyl						

Label, Number		Title	Year	VG	VG+	NM
Ralph RR 1174		Not Available	1978	3.00	6.00	12.00
Green label, address is "444 Grove"						
Ralph RR 1174		Not Available	1978	2.50	5.00	10.00
Green label, address is "109 Minna"						
Ralph RR 1276		Fingerprince	1977	18.75	37.50	75.00
First version: Dark brown cover, "First Pressing" written on back cover						
Ralph RR 1276		Fingerprince	1977	5.00	10.00	20.00
Second version: Lighter brown cover						
Ralph RR 1276		Fingerprince	1977	2.50	5.00	10.00
Third version: Color cover						
Ralph RZ 7707	PD	Meet the Residents	1986	6.25	12.50	25.00
Picture disc, with original cover on one side, replacement cover on other						
Ralph DJ 7901	DJ	Please Do Not Steal It!	1979	6.25	12.50	25.00
Promo-only sampler						
Ralph ESK 7906		Eskimo	1979	6.25	12.50	25.00
First version: White vinyl, gatefold cover						
Ralph ESK 7906		Eskimo	1979	3.75	7.50	15.00
Second version: Black vinyl, gatefold						
Ralph ESK 7906		Eskimo	1979	2.50	5.00	10.00
Third version: Black vinyl, standard cover						
Ralph RZ 7906	PD	Eskimo	1979	7.50	15.00	30.00
Picture disc						
Ralph RZ 8052		The Residents Commercial Album	1980	5.00	10.00	20.00
First version: Purple Ralph logo, songs listed in wrong order						
Ralph RZ 8052		The Residents Commercial Album	1980	3.75	7.50	15.00
Second version: Corrected song order, green logo						
Ralph RZ 8052		The Residents Commercial Album	1980	3.00	6.00	12.00
Third version: Green vinyl						
Ralph RZ 8152		Mark of the Mole	1981	12.50	25.00	50.00
Signed brown vinyl edition with lyrics						
Ralph RZ 8152		Mark of the Mole	1981	2.50	5.00	10.00
Ralph RZ 8202		The Tunes of Two Cities	1982	3.00	6.00	12.00
First edition: "444 Grove Street" address						
Ralph RZ 8202		The Tunes of Two Cities	1982	2.50	5.00	10.00
Second edition: "109 Minna Street" address						
Ralph RZ 8252		Intermission	1982	3.50	7.00	14.00
Red vinyl						
Ralph RZ 8252		Intermission	1982	3.00	6.00	12.00
Ralph RR 8315		Title in Limbo	1983	3.00	6.00	12.00
With Renaldo and The Loaf						
Ralph RZ 8402		George & James	1984	7.50	15.00	30.00
First edition: Rejected mix with "Re-1" in trail-off						
Ralph RZ 8402		George & James	1984	2.50	5.00	10.00
Second edition: Approved mix with "Re-5" in trail-off						
Ralph RZ 8452		Whatever Happened to Vileness Fats?	1984	12.50	25.00	50.00
Red vinyl						
Ralph RZ 8452		Whatever Happened to Vileness Fats?	1984	3.00	6.00	12.00
Ralph RZ 8552		The Big Bubble	1985	12.50	25.00	50.00
Pink vinyl						
Ralph RZ 8552		The Big Bubble	1985	3.00	6.00	12.00
Ralph RZ 8602		The Eyeball Show (The 13th Anniversary Show) Live in Japan	1986	5.00	10.00	20.00
White vinyl						
Ralph RZ 8602		The Eyeball Show (The 13th Anniversary Show) Live in Japan	1986	2.50	5.00	10.00
Ralph RZ 8652		Stars & Hank Forever	1986	5.00	10.00	20.00
Blue vinyl						
Ralph RZ 8652		Stars & Hank Forever	1986	2.50	5.00	10.00
Ralph RR 82761		Fingerprince	1988	3.00	6.00	12.00
New number, purple vinyl						

Label, Number		Title	Year	VG	VG+	NM
Ralph RR 82761		Fingerprince	1988	2.50	5.00	10.00
New number, black vinyl						
Ralph RR 87521		Duck Stab	1988	3.00	6.00	12.00
New number, red vinyl						
Ralph RR 87521		Duck Stab	1988	2.50	5.00	10.00
New number, black vinyl						
Ralph RR 88521		Meet the Residents	1988	3.75	7.50	15.00
Original "Meet the Beatles" parody cover restored, white vinyl						
Ralph RR 88521		Meet the Residents	1988	3.00	6.00	12.00
Original "Meet the Beatles" parody cover restored, black vinyl						
Ryko Analogue RALP-0044-2		God in Three Persons	1988	2.50	5.00	10.00
2-LP set on clear vinyl						
Ryko Analogue RALP-0045-2		God in Three Persons Instrumental				
			1988	2.50	5.00	10.00
Clear vinyl						

7-Inch Extended Play Singles

Label, Number		Title	Year	VG	VG+	NM
Ralph RR 0377		Babyfingers	1979	18.75	37.50	75.00
Ralph RR 0377	PS	Babyfingers	1979	18.75	37.50	75.00
Ralph RR 1177		Duck Stab	1978		2.50	5.00
Red label						
Ralph RR 1177	PS	Duck Stab	1978	11.25	22.50	45.00
Shiny cover						
Ralph RR 1177	PS	Duck Stab	1978		2.50	5.00
Matte cover						
Ralph WEIRD 1		Babyfingers	1981	5.00	10.00	20.00
Pink vinyl on labels left over from fan club issue						
Ralph WEIRD 1	PS	Babyfingers	1981	5.00	10.00	20.00
W.E.I.R.D. WEIRD 1		Babyfingers	1981	5.00	10.00	20.00
Fan club reissue						
W.E.I.R.D. WEIRD 1	PS	Babyfingers	1981	5.00	10.00	20.00

45s

Label, Number		Title	Year	VG	VG+	NM
Cryptic RZ-SP-1SP 1		Earth Vs. the Flying Saucers	1986	5.00	10.00	20.00
Green vinyl, one-sided, bonus with collector's edition of book "The Cryptic Guide to the Residents"						
Eva-tone 10371900-1		Diskomo (Live)	1988		2.50	5.00
Flexi-disc included with April 1988 issue of Reflex						
Ralph RR 0577		Beyond the Valley of A Day in the Life/Flying				
			1977	37.50	75.00	150.00
Ralph RR 0577	PS	Beyond the Valley of A Day in the Life/Flying				
			1977	37.50	75.00	150.00
Also known as "The Residents Meet the Beatles and The Beatles Meet the Residents"						
Ralph RR 0776		Satisfaction/Loser Is Congruent to Weed				
			1976	37.50	75.00	150.00
Ralph RR 0776	PS	Satisfaction/Loser Is Congruent to Weed				
			1976	37.50	75.00	150.00
Ralph RR 1272		Fire/Aircraft Damage	1972	25.00	50.00	100.00
Part of "Santa Dog" two-7" single set						
Ralph RR 1272		Lightning/Explosion	1972	25.00	50.00	100.00
Part of "Santa Dog" two-7" single set						
Ralph RR 1272	PS	Santa Dog: Fire/Aircraft Damage; Lightning/Explosion				
			1972	100.00	200.00	400.00
Signed, intentionally misnumbered sleeve for above two records						
Ralph RR 7803		Satisfaction/Loser Is Congruent to Weed				
			1978		2.00	4.00
Ralph RR 7803	PS	Satisfaction/Loser Is Congruent to Weed				
			1978		2.00	4.00
Ralph RR 7812		Santa Dog '78/Fire	1978	5.00	10.00	20.00
Ralph RR 7812	PS	Santa Dog '78/Fire	1978	5.00	10.00	20.00
Ralph RR 8722		Hit the Road Jack/For Elsie (Excerpt)				
			1987			3.00
Ralph RR 8722	PD	Hit the Road Jack/For Elsie (Excerpt)				
			1987	2.50	5.00	10.00
Picture disc						

Label, Number		Title	Year	VG	VG+	NM
Ralph RR 8722	PS	Hit the Road Jack/For Elsie (Excerpt)				
			1987			3.00
Ralph RZ 8422		It's a Man's Man's Man's World/Safety Is a Cootie Wootie				
			1984	3.75	7.50	15.00
White vinyl picture disc; first pressing was mislabeled						
Ralph RZ 8422		It's a Man's Man's Man's World/Safety Is a Cootie Wootie				
			1984	2.50	5.00	10.00
White vinyl picture disc						
Ralph RZ 8422		It's a Man's Man's Man's World/Safety Is a Cootie Wootie				
			1984			3.00
Ralph RZ 8422	PS	It's a Man's Man's Man's World/Safety Is a Cootie Wootie				
			1984			3.00
Ralph RZ 8621	PD	Kaw-Liga/Stars and Stripes Forever				
			1986	2.50	5.00	10.00
Ralph RZ 8622		Kaw-Liga/Stars and Stripes Forever				
			1986			3.00
Ralph RZ 8622		Kaw-Liga/Stars and Stripes Forever				
			1986	2.00	4.00	8.00
White vinyl						
Ralph RZ 8622	PS	Kaw-Liga/Stars and Stripes Forever				
			1986			3.00

12-Inch Singles

Label, Number	Title	Year	VG	VG+	NM
Ralph RR 8721	Hit the Road Jack (Dance Mix)/Jambalaya-Firefly-The Big Bubble-Cry for the Fire	1987	2.00	4.00	8.00
Ralph RZ 8006-D	Diskomo/Goosebump	1980	5.00	10.00	20.00
Green vinyl					
Ralph RZ 8006-D	Diskomo/Goosebump	1980	2.50	5.00	10.00

Reverend Horton Heat

Vinyl Albums

Label, Number		Title	Year	VG	VG+	NM
Sub Pop 96	10	Smoke 'Em If You Got 'Em	1991	3.00	6.00	12.00
Sub Pop 202		The Full Custom Gospel Sounds of Reverend Horton Heat				
			1993	2.50	5.00	10.00
Sub Pop 250		Liquor in the Front	1994	2.50	5.00	10.00

45s

Label, Number		Title	Year	VG	VG+	NM
Sub Pop 96		Psychobilly Freakout/Baby You Know Who				
			1990	2.25	4.50	9.00
First 4,000 on blue vinyl						
Sub Pop 96		Psychobilly Freakout/Baby You Know Who				
			1990		3.00	6.00
2,500 on black vinyl						
Sub Pop 96	PS	Psychobilly Freakout/Baby You Know Who				
			1990		3.00	6.00

#26 in Sub Pop Singles Club series; yes, this and 10-inch LP have the same number!

Revolting Cocks

*Side project of Al Jourgensen of **Ministry**.*

Vinyl Albums

Label, Number	Title	Year	VG	VG+	NM
Wax Trax! 017	Big Sexy Land	1986	3.00	6.00	12.00
Wax Trax! 037	You Goddamned Son of a Bitch	1988	3.00	6.00	12.00
Wax Trax! 7063	Beers Steers and Queers	1990	3.00	6.00	12.00

12-Inch Singles

Label, Number	Title	Year	VG	VG+	NM
Sire 41088	Do Ya Think I'm Sexy/Sergio Guitar/Wrong Sexy Mix				
		1993		3.00	6.00
Sire 41383	Crackin' Up (2 mixes)/Gila Copter (Version 2)				
		1994	2.00	4.00	8.00
Wax Trax! 011	No Devotion/Attack Ships/On Fire				
		1985	2.50	5.00	10.00

Label, Number		Title	Year	VG	VG+	NM
Wax Trax! 022		You Often Forget (Benign Mix)/You Often Forget (Malignant Mix)				
			1986	2.50	5.00	10.00
Wax Trax! 042		Stainless Steel Providers/At the Top/TV Mind				
			1988	2.00	4.00	8.00
Wax Trax! 9086		(Let's Get) Physical/(Let's Talk) Physical				
			1989	2.00	4.00	8.00
Wax Trax! 9149		Beers Steers and Queers (2 mixes)/Stainless Steel Provider/				
		Public Image (Live)	1990	2.00	4.00	8.00

Rezillos, The

Scottish new wave group.

Vinyl Albums

Sire SR 6057		Can't Stand the Rezillos	1978	3.00	6.00	12.00

Rhino 39

Los Angeles punk band.

45s

Dangerhouse RH 39		Prolixin Stomp/Xerox/No Compromise				
			1979	5.00	10.00	20.00
Dangerhouse RH 39	PS	Prolixin Stomp/Xerox/No Compromise				
			1979	5.00	10.00	20.00

Richman, Jonathan, and the Modern Lovers

*Pioneer power-popper whose band featured **Jerry Harrison** (of **Talking Heads**) and a member of **The Cars** at various times.*

Vinyl Albums

Beserkley BZ-0048	Jonathan Richman and the Modern Lovers				
		1976	7.50	15.00	30.00
Distributed by GRT					
Beserkley JBZ 0048	Jonathan Richman and the Modern Lovers				
		1976	6.25	12.50	25.00
Distributed by Playboy/CBS					
Beserkley BZ-0050	The Modern Lovers	1976	7.50	15.00	30.00
Distributed by GRT					
Beserkley JBZ 0050	The Modern Lovers	1978	6.25	12.50	25.00
Distributed by Playboy/CBS					
Beserkley BZ-0053	Rock 'N' Roll with the Modern Lovers				
		1977	4.50	9.00	18.00
Distributed by Janus/GRT					
Beserkley JBZ 0055	Modern Lovers "Live"	1978	3.50	7.00	14.00
Distributed by Playboy/CBS					
Beserkley JBZ 0060	Back in Your Life	1979	2.50	5.00	10.00
Distributed by Playboy/CBS					
Beserkley 10060	Back in Your Life	1980	3.00	6.00	12.00
Reissue -- change in distributing label to Elektra					
Beserkley PZ 34800	Rock 'N' Roll with the Modern Lovers				
		1977	3.50	7.00	14.00
Distributed by Playboy/CBS					
Bomp! 4021	The Original Modern Lovers	1981	5.00	10.00	20.00
Same album as Mohawk release					
Home of the Hits HH-1910	The Modern Lovers	1975	12.50	25.00	50.00
Mohawk SCALP 0002	The Original Modern Lovers	1981	6.25	12.50	25.00
Rhino RNLP 70091	The Modern Lovers	1986	3.00	6.00	12.00
Reissue					
Rhino RNLP 70092	Jonathan Richman and the Modern Lovers				
		1986	3.00	6.00	12.00
Reissue					

Label, Number		Title	Year	VG	VG+	NM
Rhino RNLP 70093		Rock 'N' Roll with the Modern Lovers				
			1986	3.00	6.00	12.00
Reissue						
Rhino RNLP 70094		Modern Lovers "Live"	1986	3.00	6.00	12.00
Reissue						
Rhino RNLP 70095		Back in Your Life	1986	3.00	6.00	12.00
Reissue						
Rounder 9014		Modern Lovers '88	1988	3.00	6.00	12.00
Rounder 9021		Jonathan Richman	1989	3.00	6.00	12.00
Rounder 9024		Jonathan Goes Country	1990	3.00	6.00	12.00
Sire 23939		Jonathan Sings!	1983	3.00	6.00	12.00
45s						
Beserkley 5701		Roadrunner/Friday on My Mind	1975	2.50	5.00	10.00
B-side by Earth Quake						
Beserkley 5701	PS	Roadrunner/Friday on My Mind	1975	2.50	5.00	10.00
Beserkley 5743		New England/Here Come the Martians				
			1976	2.50	5.00	10.00
Beserkley 5743	PS	New England/Here Come the Martians				
			1976	2.50	5.00	10.00

Right Said Fred

British pop group.

45s						
Charisma 98595		Don't Talk Just Kiss/Don't Talk Just Kiss (Dance Mix)				
			1992			3.00
Charisma 98671		I'm Too Sexy/I'm Too Sexy (Spanish Version)				
			1992		2.00	4.00
12-Inch Singles						
Charisma 1743	DJ	I'm Too Sexy (6 versions)	1991	3.75	7.50	15.00

Robinson, Tom, Band

British new-wave act. Also had a band called Sector 27 (included below). One of the first openly gay rockers.

Vinyl Albums						
Geffen GHS 24053		Hope and Glory	1984	2.50	5.00	10.00
Harvest STBB-11778	(2)	Power in the Darkness	1978	3.00	6.00	12.00
Harvest ST-11930		TRB 2	1979	3.00	6.00	12.00
I.R.S. SP-70013		Tom Robinson's Sector 27	1980	3.00	6.00	12.00
45s						
Geffen 29130		War Baby/Hell Yes	1984			3.00
Harvest 4533		2-4-6-8 Motorway/I Shall Be Released				
			1978			3.00
Harvest 4568		Glad to Be Gay/Right On Sister	1978			3.00
Harvest 4726		Our People/Bully for You	1979			3.00
I.R.S. 9503		Can't Keep Away//Mary Lynn/Dungannon				
			1981			3.00
I.R.S. 9503	PS	Can't Keep Away//Mary Lynn/Dungannon				
			1981			3.00
12-Inch Singles						
Geffen PRO-A-2209	DJ	War Baby/Atmospherics/Listen to the Radio/				
		Rikki Don't Lose That Number	1984		3.00	6.00
I.R.S. 70960		Now Martin's Gone (2 versions)/Bonfire				
			1982		2.50	5.00

Label, Number		Title	Year	VG	VG+	NM

Rocket from the Crypt

45s

Sub Pop 154		Normal Carpet Ride/Where Are the Fuckers/Slumber				
			1992		3.00	6.00
Azure blue vinyl						
Sub Pop 154	PS	Normal Carpet Ride/Where Are the Fuckers/Slumber				
			1992		3.00	6.00
#44 in Sub Pop Singles Club series						

Rockets, The
Detroit rock group. Features former members of Mitch Ryder's band, The Detroit Wheels.

45s

Capitol 5262		Turn Up the Radio/Can't Sleep	1983			3.00
Capitol 5262	PS	Turn Up the Radio/Can't Sleep	1983			3.00
Elektra 47212		Lift You Up/Tired of Wearing Black				
			1981			3.00
Elektra 69985		Rollin' By the Record Machine	1982			3.00
RSO 926		Can't Sleep/Something Ain't Right				
			1979		2.00	4.00
RSO 935		Oh Well/Love Me Once More	1979		2.00	4.00
RSO 1022		Desire/Troublemaker	1980		2.00	4.00
RSO 1028		Sad Song/Takin' It Back	1980		2.00	4.00
Tortoise Int'l. TB-11207		She's a Pretty One/I've Got to Move				
			1978		2.00	4.00

Vinyl Albums

Elektra 6E-351		Back Talk	1981	2.50	5.00	10.00
Elektra 60143		Rocket Roll	1982	2.50	5.00	10.00
RSO RS1-3047		The Rockets	1979	3.00	6.00	12.00
RSO RS1-3071		No Ballads	1980	3.00	6.00	12.00
Tortoise Int'l. BYL1-2572		Love Transfusion	1977	3.00	6.00	12.00

Rockpile
*English pop band featuring **Nick Lowe** and **Dave Edmunds**.*

Vinyl Albums

Columbia JC 36886		Seconds of Pleasure	1980	3.75	7.50	15.00
Includes bonus EP, "Nick Lowe and Dave Edmunds Sing the Everly Brothers."						

45s

Columbia 11388		Teacher Teacher/Fool Too Long	1980		2.00	4.00
Columbia 11388	PS	Teacher Teacher/Fool Too Long	1980	2.50	5.00	10.00
Promo-only sleeve detailing the history of Rockpile						
Columbia 60503		Heart/Take a Message to Mary	1981		2.00	4.00
B-side by Dave Edmunds and Nick Lowe						

Rodney and the Brunettes
Rodney Bingenheimer, KROQ-Los Angeles disc jockey, with Blondie as his backing band.

45s

Bomp! 127		Little G.T.O./Holocaust on Sunset Blvd.				
			1980	25.00	50.00	100.00
First pressing, issued by mistake in Europe, is a demo with Deborah Harry of Blondie on vocals instead of Rodney. These were quickly recalled and destroyed.						
Bomp! 127		Little G.T.O./Holocaust on Sunset Blvd.				
			1980		2.00	4.00
Bomp! 127	PS	Little G.T.O./Holocaust on Sunset Blvd.				
			1980		2.00	4.00

Label, Number		Title	Year	VG	VG+	NM

Rollins Band, The
*Henry Rollins, formerly of **Black Flag**.*

Vinyl Albums

Label, Number		Title	Year	VG	VG+	NM
1/4 Stick 0002		Turned On	1990	3.00	6.00	12.00
Imago 21034		Weight	1994	3.00	6.00	12.00

45s

Label, Number		Title	Year	VG	VG+	NM
Sub Pop 72		Earache My Eye/You Know Me	1990	3.75	7.50	15.00
Black vinyl pressing of 2,000						
Sub Pop 72		Earache My Eye/You Know Me	1990	6.25	12.50	25.00
Pink and red vinyl pressing of 2,000						
Sub Pop 72	PS	Earache My Eye/You Know Me	1990	3.75	7.50	15.00
#21 in Sub Pop Singles Club series						

Romantics, The
Detroit power-pop band.

Vinyl Albums

Label, Number		Title	Year	VG	VG+	NM
Nemperor JZ 36273		The Romantics	1980	2.50	5.00	10.00
Nemperor JZ 36881		National Breakout	1980	2.50	5.00	10.00
Nemperor ARZ 37435		Strictly Personal	1981	2.50	5.00	10.00
Nemperor BFZ 38880		In Heat	1983	2.50	5.00	10.00
Nemperor FZ 40106		Rhythm Romance	1985	2.50	5.00	10.00

45s

Label, Number		Title	Year	VG	VG+	NM
Bomp! 120		Tell It to Carrie/First in Line	1978			3.00
Bomp! 120	PS	Tell It to Carrie/First in Line	1978			3.00
Columbia 06445		Talking in Your Sleep/Mystified	198?			3.00
Reissue						
Columbia 07527		What I Like About You/First in Line	198?			3.00
Reissue						
Nemperor 02581		No One Like You/She's Hot	1981		2.00	4.00
Nemperor 04135		Talking in Your Sleep/I'm Hip	1983			3.00
Nemperor 04373		One in a Million/Do Me Anyway You Wanna	1984			3.00
Nemperor 04373	PS	One in a Million/Do Me Anyway You Wanna	1984			3.00
Nemperor 05587		Test of Time/Better Make a Move	1985			3.00
Nemperor 05587	PS	Test of Time	1985		2.50	5.00
"Demonstration -- Not for Sale" on back						
Nemperor 05587	PS	Test of Time/Better Make a Move	1985			3.00
Nemperor 05684		Mystified/Make It Last	1985			3.00
Nemperor 7527		What I Like About You/First in Line	1979		2.50	5.00
Nemperor 7527	PS	What I Like About You/First in Line	1979	2.50	5.00	10.00
Nemperor 7530		When I Look in Your Eyes/Little White Lies	1980			3.00
Nemperor 7531		Tell It to Carrie/Hung on You	1980			3.00
Nemperor 7537		Forever Yours/New Cover Story	1981		2.00	4.00
Nemperor 70063		A Night Like This/I Ain't Got You	1981		2.00	4.00
Spider SPDR-101		Little White Lies/I Can't Tell You Anything	1977		2.00	4.00
Spider SPDR-101	PS	Little White Lies/I Can't Tell You Anything	1977		2.00	4.00

12-Inch Singles

Label, Number		Title	Year	VG	VG+	NM
Nemperor AS 870	DJ	National Breakout/21 and Over	1980	2.50	5.00	10.00

Label, Number		Title	Year	VG	VG+	NM
Nemperor AS 1330	DJ	She's Hot/Bop/Look at Her/Can't Get Over You				
			1981	2.50	5.00	10.00
Nemperor AS 1814	DJ	One in a Million/Open Up Your Door/Rock You Up				
			1983	2.50	5.00	10.00
Nemperor AS 2168	DJ	Test of Time (same on both sides)				
			1985		2.50	5.00
Nemperor 04203		Talking in Your Sleep/(instrumental)				
			1983	2.50	5.00	10.00
Nemperor 05312		Mystified (3 versions)	1985		3.00	6.00

Romeo Void

San Francisco new wave band.

Vinyl Albums

415 Records A-0004		It's a Condition	1981	3.75	7.50	15.00
415 Records A-0007	EP	Never Say Never	1981	7.50	15.00	30.00
Columbia PC 38178	EP	Never Say Never	1982	3.00	6.00	12.00
Reissue						
Columbia ARC 38182		Benefactor	1982	2.50	5.00	10.00
Columbia PC 38182		Benefactor	198?	2.00	4.00	8.00
Reissue						
Columbia BFC 39155		Instincts	1984	2.50	5.00	10.00
Columbia PC 39155		Instincts	1985	2.00	4.00	8.00
Reissue						

45s

415 Records 0012		White Sweater/Apache	1982			3.00
415 Records 0012	PS	White Sweater/Apache	1982			3.00
Columbia 03378		Never Say Never/Guards	1982			3.00
Columbia 04534		A Girl in Trouble (Is a Temporary Thing)/Going to Be Neon				
			1984			3.00
Columbia 04704		Say No/Six Days and One	1984			3.00
Columbia 04704	PS	Say No/Six Days and One	1984			3.00
Columbia 04704	PS	Say No	1984		2.50	5.00
"Demonstration -- Not for Sale" on back						

12-Inch Singles

Columbia 05103		A Girl in Trouble (Is a Temporary Thing)/Six Days and One				
			1984		3.00	6.00
Columbia 05135		Say No/Out on My Own	1984		3.50	7.00

Rotters, The

Los Angeles punk group.

45s

Rotten TR 002		Sit on My Face Stevie Nicks/Amputee				
			1978	3.75	7.50	15.00
Rotten TR 002	PS	Sit on My Face Stevie Nicks/Amputee				
			1978	6.25	12.50	25.00
Rotten TR 003		Sink the Whales (Buy Japanese Goods)/Disco Queen				
			1979	6.25	12.50	25.00

Roxy Music

*English band, influenced much of the new wave/new romantic scene of the 1980s. **Brian Eno** was an early member. Also see **Ferry, Bryan.***

Vinyl Albums

Atco SD 7045		Stranded	1974	3.00	6.00	12.00
Atco SD 32-102		Flesh + Blood	1980	2.50	5.00	10.00
Atco SD 36-106		Country Life	1975	3.75	7.50	15.00
Original cover shows two semi-naked women on a grassy background						

Label, Number		Title	Year	VG	VG+	NM
Atco SD 36-106A		Country Life	1975	2.50	5.00	10.00
Revised cover deletes women, leaves only the grassy background						
Atco SD 36-127		Siren	1975	2.50	5.00	10.00
Originals have yellow labels						
Atco SD 36-133		The First Roxy Music Album	1975	3.00	6.00	12.00
Reissue of Reprise MS 2114; originals have yellow labels						
Atco SD 36-134		For Your Pleasure	1975	3.00	6.00	12.00
Reissue of Warner Bros. BS 2696; originals have yellow labels						
Atco SD 36-139		Viva! Roxy Music (Live)	1976	2.50	5.00	10.00
Originals have yellow labels						
Atco SD 38-103		Greatest Hits	1977	2.50	5.00	10.00
Atco SD 38-114		Manifesto	1979	2.50	5.00	10.00
Atco SD 38-114	PD	Manifesto	1979	5.00	10.00	20.00
Picture disc						
Atco 90122		The Atlantic Years (1973-80)	1983	2.50	5.00	10.00
Reprise MS 2114		Roxy Music	1972	7.50	15.00	30.00
Reprise 25857	(2)	Street Life: 20 Greatest Hits	1989	3.75	7.50	15.00
By "Bryan Ferry & Roxy Music"						
Warner Bros. BS 2696		For Your Pleasure	1973	3.75	7.50	15.00
Warner Bros. 23686		Avalon	1982	2.50	5.00	10.00
Warner Bros. 23808	EP	Musique -- The High Road	1983	2.00	4.00	8.00

45s

Label, Number		Title	Year	VG	VG+	NM
Atco 7018		The Thrill of It All/The Application Failed				
			1975		2.00	4.00
Atco 7042		Love Is the Drug/Both Ends Burning				
			1975		2.00	4.00
Atco 7100		Dance Away/Trash 2	1979		2.00	4.00
Atco 7204		Angel Eyes/My Little Girl	1979		2.00	4.00
Atco 7301		Over You/My Only Love	1980		2.00	4.00
Atco 7310		Oh Yeah (On the Radio)/Rain, Rain, Rain				
			1980		2.00	4.00
Atco 7315		In the Midnight Hour/(B-side unknown)				
			1980		2.00	4.00
Atco 7329		Jealous Guy/To Turn You On	1981		2.00	4.00
Atco 7329	PS	Jealous Guy/To Turn You On	1981		2.00	4.00
Atlantic 13269		Love Is the Drug/Dance Away	198?			3.00
Oldies Series reissue						
Reprise 1124		Virginia Plan/The Numberer	1972		2.50	5.00
Warner Bros. GWB 0316		Do the Strand/Virginia Plain	197?			3.00
"Back to Back Hits" series						
Warner Bros. 7719		Do the Strand/Editions of You	1973		2.50	5.00
Warner Bros. 29912		More Than This/Always Unknowing				
			1982			3.00
Warner Bros. 29978		Take a Chance with Me/India	1982			3.00
Warner Bros. 29978	PS	Take a Chance with Me/India	1982			3.00

12-Inch Singles

Label, Number		Title	Year	VG	VG+	NM
Warner Bros. PRO-A-1056	DJ	Take a Chance with Me (2 versions)/More Than This/Avalon				
			1982	3.00	6.00	12.00
Warner Bros. PRO-A-2033	DJ	More Than This/Avalon	1982	2.50	5.00	10.00

Royal Trux

45s

Label, Number		Title	Year	VG	VG+	NM
Sub Pop 203		Steal Your Face/Get Off	1993		2.50	5.00
Sub Pop 203	PS	Steal Your Face/Get Off	1993		2.50	5.00
#54 in Sub Pop Singles Club series						

Label, Number		Title	Year	VG	VG+	NM

Ruby

10-Inch Singles

Work 30S 7512	DJ	Paraffin (4 mixes)	1996		3.00	6.00
On red vinyl in plastic sleeve						

Rumour, The

*Backing band for **Graham Parker**, and also recorded without him.*

Vinyl Albums

Arista AL 4235	Frogs, Sprouts, Clogs & Krauts	1979	3.00	6.00	12.00
Hannibal 1305	Purity of Essence	1981	3.75	7.50	15.00
Mercury SRM-1-1174	Max	1977	3.75	7.50	15.00

45s

Arista 0451	Emotional Traffic/Hard Enough to Show				
		1979		2.00	4.00
Mercury 73949	I'm So Glad/This Town	1977		2.00	4.00
Also see Graham Parker					

Run-D.M.C.

Rap duo. The first to gain massive MTV airplay, they singlehandedly revived the moribund career of Aerosmith.

Vinyl Albums

Profile PRO-1202		Run-D.M.C.	1984	3.00	6.00	12.00
Profile PRO-1205		King of Rock	1985	3.00	6.00	12.00
Profile PRO-1217		Raising Hell	1986	3.00	6.00	12.00
Profile PRO-1265		Tougher Than Leather	1988	3.00	6.00	12.00
Profile PRO-1401		Back from Hell	1990	3.00	6.00	12.00
Profile PRO-1419	(2)	Together Forever: Greatest Hits 1983-1991				
			1991	3.75	7.50	15.00

45s

MCA 53680		Ghost Busters/Ghost Busters (Ghost Power Instrumental)				
			1989		3.50	7.00
Profile 5019		It's Like That/It's Like That (instrumental)				
			1983		2.50	5.00
Profile 5036		Hard Times-Jam Master Jay/	1983		2.50	5.00
		Hard Times-Jam Master Jay (instrumental)				
Profile 5045		Rock Box/Rock Box (Dub Version)				
			1984		2.50	5.00
Profile 5051		30 Days/30 Days (instrumental)	1984		2.50	5.00
Profile 5058		Hollis Crew/Hollis Crew (instrumental)				
			1984		2.50	5.00
Profile 5064		King of Rock/King of Rock (instrumental)				
			1985		2.50	5.00
Profile 5069		You Talk Too Much/Daryll and Joe (Krush Groove)				
			1985		2.50	5.00
Profile 5080		Jam-Master Jammin'/Jam-Master Jammin' (instrumental)				
			1985		2.50	5.00
Profile 5088		Can You Rock Like This/Together Forever				
			1986		2.50	5.00
Profile 5102		My Adidas/Peter Piper	1986		2.00	4.00
Profile 5102	PS	My Adidas/Peter Piper	1986		2.00	4.00
Profile 5112		Walk This Way/King of Rock	1986		2.00	4.00
A-side: With Steven Tyler and Joe Perry of Aerosmith						
Profile 5112	PS	Walk This Way/King of Rock	1986		2.00	4.00
Profile 5119		You Be Illin'/Hit It Run	1986		2.00	4.00
Profile 5119	PS	You Be Illin'/Hit It Run	1986		2.00	4.00
Profile 5131		It's Tricky/Proud to Be Black	1987		2.00	4.00
Profile 5131	PS	It's Tricky/Proud to Be Black	1987		2.00	4.00

Label, Number		Title	Year	VG	VG+	NM
Profile 5202		Run's House/Beats to the Rhyme	1988		2.00	4.00
Profile 5202	PS	Run's House/Beats to the Rhyme	1988		2.00	4.00
Profile 5211		Mary, Mary/Rock Box	1988		2.00	4.00
Profile 5211	PS	Mary, Mary/Rock Box	1988		2.00	4.00
Profile 5224		I'm Not Going Out Like That/How'd Ya Do It Dee				
			1988		2.00	4.00
Profile 5224	PS	I'm Not Going Out Like That/How'd Ya Do It Dee				
			1988		2.00	4.00

12-Inch Singles

Label, Number		Title	Year	VG	VG+	NM
Profile 7036		Hard Times (vocal & instrumental)/Jam Master				
		(vocal & instrumental)	1983	2.00	4.00	8.00
Profile 7045		Rock Box (3 versions)	1984	2.00	4.00	8.00
Profile 7051		30 Days (2 versions)	1984	2.00	4.00	8.00
Profile 7069		You Talk Too Much/(Instrumental)/Daryll & Joe (Krush Groove3)				
			1985	3.00	6.00	12.00
Profile 7080		Jam Master Jammin' (3 versions)	1985	2.00	4.00	8.00
Profile 7112		Walk This Way (vocal)/(instrumental)				
			1986	3.00	6.00	12.00

With Steve Tyler and Joe Perry of Aerosmith

Label, Number	Title	Year	VG	VG+	NM
Profile 7131	It's Tricky (4 versions)/Proud to Be Black				
		1987	3.00	6.00	12.00
Profile 7202	Run's House (vocal & instrumental)/				
	Beats to the Rhyme (vocal & Instrumental)				
		1988	3.00	6.00	12.00
Profile 7211	Mary, Mary (vocal) (instrumental)/Rock Box				
		1988	2.50	5.00	10.00
Profile 7224	I'm Not Going Out Like That (2 versions)/How'd Ya Do It Dee				
		1988		3.50	7.00
Profile 7234	Papa Crazy (2 versions)/Tougher Than Leather (2 versions)				
		1988		3.50	7.00
Profile 7262	Pause/Ghostbusters	1989	2.00	4.00	8.00

Runaways, The

*Ahead-of-its-time all-female pop-punk band, assembled by Kim Fowley. **Joan Jett** became prominent as a solo act whose stature has grown through the years; Lita Ford hit it big as a heavy-metal pinup; Cherie Currie recorded an LP with her sister Marie (see **Currie, Cherie and Marie**); Micki Steele, under her full name, Michael Steele, became one-fourth of the **Bangles**.*

Vinyl Albums

Label, Number		Title	Year	VG	VG+	NM
Marilyn USM 1004		Born to Be Bad	1991	2.00	4.00	8.00
Mercury SRM-1-1090		The Runaways	1976	5.00	10.00	20.00
Mercury SRM-1-1126		Queens of Noise	1977	5.00	10.00	20.00
Mercury SRM-1-3705		Waiting for the Night	1977	5.00	10.00	20.00
Mercury SRM-1-3740		Live in Japan	1978	5.00	10.00	20.00
Rhino RNDF-250	PD	Little Lost Girls	1982	3.75	7.50	15.00
Rhino RNEP-602	EP	Mama Weer All Crazee Now	1983	3.75	7.50	15.00
Rhino RNLP-70861		Little Lost Girls	1987	3.00	6.00	12.00

Reissue of Rhino 250 on regular vinyl

45s

Label, Number	Title	Year	VG	VG+	NM
Mercury 73819	Cherry Bomb/Blackmail	1976	2.50	5.00	10.00
Mercury 73890	Heartbeat/Neon Angels on the Road to Ruin				
		1977	2.50	5.00	10.00

Label, Number		Title	Year	VG	VG+	NM

S

S.F. Seals

45s

Sub Pop 204		Nowhereica/Being Cheated	1993		2.50	5.00
All copies on clear pink vinyl						
Sub Pop 204	PS	Nowhereica/Being Cheated	1993		2.50	5.00
#55 in Sub Pop Singles Club series						

S.O.A. (State Of Alert)
Washington, D.C. hardcore band.

7-Inch Extended Play Singles

Dischord 2		No Policy	1981	10.00	20.00	40.00
First pressing of 1,000 on green vinyl						
Dischord 2		No Policy	1981	7.50	15.00	30.00
Second pressing of 1,000 on black vinyl with no band name on label						
Dischord 2		No Policy	1981	7.50	15.00	30.00
Third pressing of 1,000 on black vinyl with band name on label						
Dischord 2	PS	No Policy	1981	7.50	15.00	30.00

Saad, Sue, and the Next
British new-wave band.

Vinyl Albums

Planet 4		Sue Saad and the Next	1979	3.00	6.00	12.00

45s

Planet 45912		Won't Give It Up/Kamonbaybeh				
			1980		2.00	4.00
Planet 45912	PS	Won't Give It Up/Kamonbaybeh				
			1980		2.00	4.00
Planet 45913		Gimme Love-Gimme Pain	1980		2.00	4.00
Planet 45915		Next Prisoner/I Want Him	1980		2.00	4.00
Warner Bros. 49851		Looker/Looker	1981		2.00	4.00
B-side by Barry DeVorzon and Michael Towers						

Sade
Exotic Nigerian mellow soul singer.

Vinyl Albums

Epic OE 44210		Stronger Than Pride	1988	2.50	5.00	10.00
Epic E2 66686	(2)	The Best of Sade	1994	3.75	7.50	15.00
Portrait BFR 39581		Diamond Life	1984	3.00	6.00	12.00
Portrait BFR 40263		Promise	1985	2.50	5.00	10.00

45s

Epic 07904		Paradise/Super Bien Total	1988			3.00
Epic 07904	PS	Paradise/Super Bien Total	1988			3.00
Epic 07977		Nothing Can Come Between Us/Make Some Room				
			1988			3.00
Epic 08465		Smooth Operator/Hang On to Your Love				
			1988			3.00
Reissue						
Epic 08466		Your Love Is King/Cherry Pie	1988			3.00
Reissue						
Epic 08467		The Sweetest Taboo/Never As Good As the First Time				
			1988			3.00
Reissue						

Label, Number		Title	Year	VG	VG+	NM
Epic 08503		Turn My Back on You/Keep Looking				
			1988			3.00
Epic 68595		Love Is Stronger Than Pride/Make Some Room				
			1989			3.00
Epic 74734		No Ordinary Love/Paradise (Remix)				
			1992			3.00
Epic 74848		Kiss of Life/Room 55	1993			3.00
Epic 74903		Feel No Pain/Love Is Stronger Than Pride				
			1993			3.00
Epic 74980		Cherish the Day (Sade Remix Short Version)/				
		Cherish the Day (Ronin Remix) 1993				3.00
Portrait 04664		Hang On to Your Love/Cherry Pie				
			1984			3.00
Portrait 04664	PS	Hang On to Your Love/Cherry Pie				
			1984			3.00
Portrait 04664	PS	Hang On to Your Love	1984		2.50	5.00
"Demonstration -- Not for Sale" on rear						
Portrait 04807		Smooth Operator/Spirit	1985			3.00
Portrait 04807	PS	Smooth Operator/Spirit	1985			3.00
Portrait 04807	PS	Smooth Operator	1985		2.50	5.00
"Demonstration -- Not for Sale" on rear						
Portrait 05408		Your Love Is King/Love Affair with Life				
			1985			3.00
Portrait 05408	PS	Your Love Is King/Love Affair with Life				
			1985			3.00
Portrait 05437		Your Love Is King/Love Affair with Life				
			1985			3.00
Portrait 05437	PS	Your Love Is King/Love Affair with Life				
			1985			3.00
Portrait 05713		The Sweetest Taboo/You're Not the Man				
			1985			3.00
Portrait 05713	PS	The Sweetest Taboo/You're Not the Man				
			1985			3.00
Portrait 05846		Never As Good As the First Time/Keep Hangin' On				
			1986			3.00
Portrait 05846	PS	Never As Good As the First Time/Keep Hangin' On				
			1986			3.00
Portrait 06121		Is It a Crime/Punch Drunk	1986			3.00
Portrait 06121	PS	Is It a Crime/Punch Drunk	1986			3.00

12-Inch Singles

Label, Number		Title	Year	VG	VG+	NM
Epic EAS 01121	DJ	Paradise (extended)/Paradise (7" Mix)				
			1988	2.00	4.00	8.00
Epic EAS 01499	DJ	Love Is Stronger Than Pride (same on both sides)				
			1988	2.00	4.00	8.00
Epic EAS 04876	DJ	No Ordinary Love (3 versions)/Paradise (Remix)				
			1992	3.75	7.50	15.00
Epic 77117		Cherish the Day (3 mixes)/Feel No Pain/No Ordinary Love				
			1993	2.00	4.00	8.00
Portrait AS 2293	DJ	Never As Good As the First Time (2 mixes)/Keep Hangin' On				
			1986	2.00	4.00	8.00
Portrait 05122		Hang On to Your Love (2 versions)				
			1984	2.00	4.00	8.00
Portrait 05375		Never As Good As the First Time (extended)/				
		Keep Hangin' On (Live Instrumental)				
			1986	2.00	4.00	8.00

Label, Number		Title	Year	VG	VG+	NM

Saints, The
British punk band.

Vinyl Albums

Label, Number		Title	Year	VG	VG+	NM
Sire SR 6039		(I'm) Stranded	1977	3.75	7.50	15.00
Sire SRK 6055		Eternally Yours	1978	3.75	7.50	15.00
TVT 2111		All Fools Day	1987	2.50	5.00	10.00
TVT 2121		Prodigal Son	1988	2.50	5.00	10.00

45s

Label, Number		Title	Year	VG	VG+	NM
Sire 1005		(I'm) Stranded/No Time	1977	3.75	7.50	15.00
Promo copy worth 50% less						
Sire 1005	PS	(I'm) Stranded/No Time	1977		3.50	7.00

12-Inch Singles

Label, Number		Title	Year	VG	VG+	NM
TVT 2111	DJ	Just Like Fire Would (same on both sides)				
			1987	2.50	5.00	10.00
TVT 2123		The Music Goes 'Round My Head/Stay				
			1988	2.50	5.00	10.00

Salt-N-Pepa
Female rappers.

Vinyl Albums

Label, Number		Title	Year	VG	VG+	NM
London 828 392-1		Very Necessary	1993	3.00	6.00	12.00
Next Plateau PL 1011		A Salt with a Deadly Pepa	1988	3.00	6.00	12.00
Next Plateau PL 1019		Blacks' Magic	1989	3.00	6.00	12.00

45s

Label, Number		Title	Year	VG	VG+	NM
London 850 346-7		Ain't Nuthin' But a She Thing (Album Version)/(Remix)				
			1995			3.00
London 857 356-7		Shoop/Whatta Man	1994			3.00
Next Plateau KF 315		Push It (Remix) (same on both sides)				
			1987		2.00	4.00
Next Plateau KF 319		Shake Your Thang/Spinderella's Not a Fella (But a Girl D.J.)				
			1988			3.00
Next Plateau KF 319	PS	Shake Your Thang/Spinderella's Not a Fella (But a Girl D.J.)				
			1988			3.00
Next Plateau KF 321		Twist and Shout/Get Up Everybody (Get Up)				
			1988			3.00
Next Plateau KF 321	PS	Twist and Shout/Get Up Everybody (Get Up)				
			1988			3.00
Next Plateau KF 329		Expression (Half-step)/Expression (Brixton Radio Remix)				
			1989		2.00	4.00

12-Inch Singles

Label, Number		Title	Year	VG	VG+	NM
Next Plateau 50043		I'll Take Your Man/(Instrumental)				
			1986		3.00	6.00
Next Plateau 50053		Beauty and the Beat (5 mixes)	1986	2.50	5.00	10.00
Next Plateau 50055		My Mike Sounds Nice/(Instrumental)/It's All Right				
			1987	2.00	4.00	8.00
Next Plateau 50063		Tramp (3 mixes)/Push It (2 mixes)/Idle Chatter				
			1987	2.50	5.00	10.00
Next Plateau 50071		I Am Down (3 versions)/Chick on the Side (2 versions)/				
		Pass the Salt N Pepa (Medley)	1987	2.50	5.00	10.00
Next Plateau 50077		Spinderella's Not a Fella (3 mixes)/Shake Your Thang (4 mixes				
			1988	2.50	5.00	10.00
Next Plateau 50083		Get Up Everybody (5 versions)	1988	2.50	5.00	10.00
Next Plateau 50083		Twist and Shout (3 versions)	1988	2.00	4.00	8.00
Next Plateau 50101		Expression (5 versions)/Clubhouse/Clubhouse (Instrumental)				
			1989	2.00	4.00	8.00
Next Plateau 50137		Do You Want Me (3 versions)/Gotcha (Once Again)				
			1990	2.00	4.00	8.00

Label, Number		Title	Year	VG	VG+	NM
Next Plateau 50157		Let's Talk About Sex (3 versions)/Swift				
			1991	2.50	5.00	10.00
Next Plateau 50165		You Showed Me (4 mixes)	1992	2.50	5.00	10.00
Next Plateau 50185		Do You Want Me '92 (4 versions)				
			1992	2.00	4.00	8.00
Next Plateau 857 315-1		Shoop (4 versions)/Emphatically No/AIDS P.S.A.				
			1993	2.00	4.00	8.00
Next Plateau 857 391-1		Whatta Man (4 versions)	1993	2.00	4.00	8.00
Next Plateau 857 715-1		None of Your Business (3 versions)/Shoop/				
		Heaven 'N' Hell (Carron Hall Mix)				
			1994	2.00	4.00	8.00
Next Plateau 869 863-1		Start Me Up (4 versions)	1992	2.00	4.00	8.00
Soul 2127	DJ	He's Gamin' On Ya (3 versions)				
			1991		3.00	6.00

Samhain

*Post-**Misfits** and pre-**Danzig** band for **Glenn Danzig**.*

Vinyl Albums

Plan 9 PL9-04		Initium	1984	12.50	25.00	50.00
No more than 100 on marbled black and white vinyl						
Plan 9 PL9-04		Initium	1984	6.25	12.50	25.00
500 on red vinyl						
Plan 9 PL9-04		Initium	1984	3.00	6.00	12.00
Regular issue on black vinyl						
Plan 9 PL9-07		November Coming Fire	1986	6.25	12.50	25.00
200 on orange vinyl						
Plan 9 PL9-07		November Coming Fire	1986	3.00	6.00	12.00
Regular issue on black vinyl						

7-Inch Extended Play Singles

Plan 9 PL9-05		Unholy Passion	1985	15.00	30.00	60.00
White vinyl						
Plan 9 PL9-05		Unholy Passion	1985	12.50	25.00	50.00
Red vinyl						
Plan 9 PL9-05	PS	Unholy Passion	1985	12.50	25.00	50.00
Maroon cover						
Plan 9 PL9-05	PS	Unholy Passion	1985	15.00	30.00	60.00
Tan cover						

Schilling, Peter

German techno-pop singer.

Vinyl Albums

Elektra 60265		Error in the System	1983	2.50	5.00	10.00
Elektra 60404		Things to Come	1985	2.50	5.00	10.00
Elektra 60863		The Different Story	1989	2.50	5.00	10.00

45s

Elektra 65986		Major Tom (Coming Home)/Major Tom (German Version)				
			198?			3.00
"Spun Gold" reissue						
Elektra 69307		The Different Story (World of Lust and Crime)/(Instrumental)				
			1989			3.00
Elektra 69307	PS	The Different Story (World of Lust and Crime)/(Instrumental)				
			1989		3.00	6.00
A scarce picture sleeve						
Elektra 69641		Chill of the Night/The Hurricane (Hammers on the Shore)				
			1985			3.00
Elektra 69811		Major Tom (Coming Home)/Major Tom (Bollig Losgelost)				
			1983			3.00

Label, Number		Title	Year	VG	VG+	NM
12-Inch Singles						
Elektra ED 4951	DJ	The Noah Plan/Die Wuste Lebt	1983	2.00	4.00	8.00
Elektra ED 5054	DJ	Chill of the Night (same on both sides)				
			1985		3.50	7.00
Elektra 66709		The Different Story (3 versions)	1989		3.50	7.00
Elektra 66995		Major Tom (4 versions)	1983	2.00	4.00	8.00

Schneider, Fred
Of The B-52's.

Label, Number		Title	Year	VG	VG+	NM
Vinyl Albums						
Warner Bros. 25158		Fred Schneider and the Shake Society				
			1984	3.00	6.00	12.00
12-Inch Singles						
Warner Bros. PRO-A-2224	DJ	Monster/Boonga	1984	2.50	5.00	10.00

Scott, Robin/Ryuichi Sakamoto
Robin Scott also recorded as M.

Label, Number	Title	Year	VG	VG+	NM
12-Inch Singles					
Epic 03341	Once in a Lifetime/Just About Enough				
		1982	3.75	7.50	15.00

Screaming Blue Messiahs

Label, Number		Title	Year	VG	VG+	NM
Vinyl Albums						
Elektra 60488		Gun-Shy	1985	3.75	7.50	15.00
Elektra 60755		Bikini Red	1987	2.50	5.00	10.00
Elektra 60755	DJ	Bikini Red	1987	3.00	6.00	12.00
Promo-only pressing on audiophile vinyl						
Elektra 60859		Totally Religious	1989	2.50	5.00	10.00
Elektra 60859	DJ	Totally Religious	1989	3.00	6.00	12.00
Promo-only pressing on audiophile vinyl						
45s						
Elektra 69433		I Wanna Be a Flintstone/(B-side unknown)				
			1987		2.50	5.00
Elektra 69433	PS	I Wanna Be a Flintstone/(B-side unknown)				
			1987		2.50	5.00
12-Inch Singles						
Elektra ED 5150	DJ	Wild Blue Yonder (Short)/Wild Blue Yonder (Long)				
			1986		3.00	6.00
Elektra ED 5173	DJ	Smash the Market Place (same on both sides)				
			1986		3.00	6.00
Elektra ED 5262	DJ	I Wanna Be a Flintstone (same on both sides)				
			1987		3.00	6.00
Elektra ED 5282	DJ	Bikini Red (same on both sides)	1987		3.00	6.00
Red vinyl						

Screaming Trees
Alterna-rock band from Ellensburg, Washington.

Label, Number		Title	Year	VG	VG+	NM
Vinyl Albums						
Epic E 46800		Uncle Anesthesia	1991	3.00	6.00	12.00
Epic E 48996		Sweet Oblivion	1992	3.00	6.00	12.00
SST 105	EP	Other Worlds	1986	2.50	5.00	10.00
Reissue of Velvetone cassette-only release						
SST 132		Even If and Especially When	1987	2.50	5.00	10.00
SST 188		Invisible Lantern	1988	2.50	5.00	10.00

Label, Number		Title	Year	VG	VG+	NM
SST 248		Buzz Factory	1989	2.50	5.00	10.00
SST 260	(2)	Anthology	1991	3.00	6.00	12.00

7-Inch Extended Play Singles

Label, Number		Title	Year	VG	VG+	NM
Sub Pop 48		Change Has Come	1989	3.75	7.50	15.00
Two 7-inch 45s, one black vinyl, one white						
Sub Pop 48		Change Has Come	1989	15.00	30.00	60.00
Second pressing of above: red vinyl						
Sub Pop 48	PS	Change Has Come	1989	3.75	7.50	15.00
Poster sleeve						

45s

Label, Number		Title	Year	VG	VG+	NM
Epic Soundtrax 74419		Nearly Lost You/Dyslexic Heart	1992		2.50	5.00
B-side by Paul Westerberg						

12-Inch Singles

Label, Number		Title	Year	VG	VG+	NM
Epic EAS 3092	DJ	Something About Today/This Perfect Day/New Day Yesterday	1991	2.00	4.00	8.00
Epic 73539		Uncle Anesthesia/Who Lies in Darkness/Ocean of Confusion/ Something About Today	1990	2.00	4.00	8.00

Scritti Politti

British synth-pop band.

Vinyl Albums

Label, Number		Title	Year	VG	VG+	NM
Warner Bros. 25302		Cupid & Psyche '85	1985	2.50	5.00	10.00
Warner Bros. 25686		Provision	1988	2.50	5.00	10.00
Warner Bros. R 100460		Provision	1988	3.00	6.00	12.00
BMG Direct Marketing edition						
Warner Bros. R 144294		Cupid & Psyche '85	1985	3.00	6.00	12.00
RCA Music Service edition						

45s

Label, Number		Title	Year	VG	VG+	NM
Sire 28949	DJ	Perfect Way/Perfect Way	1985	3.00	6.00	12.00
Independent Project limited edition promo						
Sire 28949	PS	Perfect Way/Perfect Way	1985	3.00	6.00	12.00
Letterpress cardboard sleeve with sheet of stamps						
Warner Bros. 21978		Perfect Way/Wood Beez (pray like aretha franklin)	198?			3.00
"Back to Back Hits" reissue						
Warner Bros. 27710		Oh Patti (Don't Feel Sorry for Loverboy)/Best Thing Ever	1988			3.00
With Miles Davis						
Warner Bros. 27976		Boom! There She Was/A World Come Back to Life	1988			3.00
A-side: With Roger						
Warner Bros. 27976	PS	Boom! There She Was/A World Come Back to Life	1988			3.00
Warner Bros. 28811		Wood Beez (pray like aretha franklin)/ Wood Beez (pray like aretha franklin)	1986			3.00
Warner Bros. 28811	PS	Wood Beez (pray like aretha franklin)/ Wood Beez (pray like aretha franklin)	1986			3.00
Warner Bros. 28949		Perfect Way/Perfect Way	1985			3.00
Warner Bros. 28949	PS	Perfect Way/Perfect Way	1985			3.00
Warner Bros. 29152		Wood Beez (pray like aretha franklin)/ Wood Beez (pray like arethe franklin)	1984		2.50	5.00

12-Inch Singles

Label, Number		Title	Year	VG	VG+	NM
Warner Bros. 20225		Wood Beez (pray like aretha franklin) (2 versions)/ Absolute (2 versions)	1984		3.00	6.00

Label, Number		Title	Year	VG	VG+	NM
Warner Bros. 20292		Hypnotize (3 versions)	1984		2.50	5.00
Warner Bros. 20362		Perfect Way (2 mixes)	1985		3.00	6.00
Warner Bros. 20417		Wood Beez (pray like aretha franklin) (Version)/				
		Wood Beez (pray like aretha franklin) (Remix)				
			1986		3.00	6.00
Warner Bros. 20870		Boom! There She Was (3 versions)/A World Come Back to Life				
			1988		2.50	5.00
Warner Bros. PRO-A-2397	DJ	Perfect Way (Remix)/Perfect Way (7")				
			1985		3.50	7.00

Seal

*British (of Nigerian and Brazilian ancestry) soul/pop singer. Also sang with **Adamski**.*

45s

Sire 17896		I'm Alive/Kiss from a Rose	1995			3.00
Sire 18053		Newborn Friend/Blues in "E"	1994			3.00
Sire 18138		Prayer for the Dying/Dreaming in Metaphors				
			1994			3.00
Sire 19119		Killer	1992			*Cassette only*
Sire 19298		Crazy/Sparkle	1991			3.00
Warner Bros. 17708		Don't Cry/Fast Changes	1996			3.00

12-Inch Singles

Sire PRO-A-5065	(2) DJ	The Beginning (10 versions)	1991	2.50	5.00	10.00
Two-record promo-only release						
Sire PRO-A-7057	DJ	Prayer for the Dying (3 versions)				
			1994	5.00	10.00	20.00
Sire 40200		The Beginning (5 versions)/Deep Water				
			1991		3.00	6.00

Searchers, The

Original British Invasion band that stuck around long enough to put out two highly-acclaimed new-wave albums in the early 1980s.

Vinyl Albums

Kapp KL-1363	M	Meet the Searchers	1964	10.00	20.00	40.00
With black and blue label						
Kapp KL-1363	M	Meet the Searchers	1964	6.25	12.50	25.00
With black label						
Kapp KL-1409	M	This Is Us	1964	6.25	12.50	25.00
Version 1: No sticker on front cover						
Kapp KL-1409	M	This Is Us	1964	6.25	12.50	25.00
Version 2: With sticker on front cover referring to "Love Potion No. 9"						
Kapp KL-1412	M	The New Searchers LP	1965	6.25	12.50	25.00
Kapp KL-1449	M	The Searchers No. 4	1965	6.25	12.50	25.00
Kapp KL-1477	M	Take Me for What I'm Worth	1966	6.25	12.50	25.00
Kapp KS-3363	S	Meet the Searchers	1964	12.50	25.00	50.00
With black and blue label						
Kapp KS-3363	S	Meet the Searchers	1964	7.50	15.00	30.00
With black label						
Kapp KS-3409	S	This Is Us	1964	7.50	15.00	30.00
Version 1: No sticker on front cover						
Kapp KS-3409	S	This Is Us	1964	7.50	15.00	30.00
Version 2: With sticker on front cover referring to "Love Potion No. 9"						
Kapp KS-3412	S	The New Searchers LP	1965	7.50	15.00	30.00
Kapp KS-3419	S	The Searchers No. 4	1965	7.50	15.00	30.00
Kapp KS-3477	S	Take Me for What I'm Worth	1966	7.50	15.00	30.00
Mercury MG-20914	M	Hear! Hear!	1964	12.50	25.00	50.00
Version 1: With only the title on the front cover						
Mercury MG-20914	M	Hear! Hear!	1964	10.00	20.00	40.00
Version 2: With sticker "Live from the Star Club" on cover						

The Searchers' "comeback" album ($10) was a staple of college radio in 1980 and on many critics' Top 10 lists for the year, but it was hard for the general public to believe that an original British Invasion band could still make good music. (After all, 1980 saw the release of one of the Rolling Stones' worst albums, *Emotional Rescue*.)

For all the hype and publicity surrounding the Sex Pistols, only one of their 45s was ever released here. It's scarce on stock copies; here is the record's B-side, "Sub-Mission."

Label, Number		Title	Year	VG	VG+	NM
Mercury MG-20914	M	Hear! Hear!	1964	7.50	15.00	30.00
Version 3: With "Live from the Star Club" imprinted on cover						
Mercury MG-20914	M/DJ	Hear! Hear!	1964	12.50	25.00	50.00
White label promo						
Mercury MG-20994	M	The Searchers Meet the Rattles	1965	18.75	37.50	75.00
Mercury SR-60914	S	Hear! Hear!	1964	10.00	20.00	40.00
Version 1: With only the title on the front cover						
Mercury SR-60914	S	Hear! Hear!	1964	7.50	15.00	30.00
Version 2: With sticker "Live from the Star Club" on cover						
Mercury SR-60914	S	Hear! Hear!	1964	6.25	12.50	25.00
Version 3: With "Live from the Star Club" imprinted on cover						
Mercury SR-60994	S	The Searchers Meet the Rattles	1965	12.50	25.00	50.00
Pye 501		The Searchers	197?	3.75	7.50	15.00
Reissue of Kapp hits						
Pye 508		The Searchers, Vol. 2	1976	3.75	7.50	15.00
Rhino RNLP 162		Greatest Hits	1985	2.50	5.00	10.00
Rhino R1-70162		Greatest Hits	1988	2.00	4.00	8.00
Reissue of RNLP 162						
Sire SRK 3523		Love's Melodies	1981	2.50	5.00	10.00
Sire SRK 6082		The Searchers	1980	2.50	5.00	10.00

45s

Label, Number		Title	Year	VG	VG+	NM
Kapp KCS-27		Love Potion Number Nine/Hi-Heel Sneakers	1964	2.50	5.00	10.00
Orange label "Winners Circle Series"; no black label counterpart						
Kapp KCS-29		Bumble Bee/Everything You Do	1964	2.50	5.00	10.00
Orange label "Winners Circle Series"; no black label counterpart						
Kapp KCS-49		Bumble Bee/A Tear Fell	1965	2.50	5.00	10.00
Orange label "Winners Circle Series"; no black label counterpart						
Kapp 577		Needles and Pins/Ain't That Just Like Me	1964	2.50	5.00	10.00
Kapp 577	PS	Needles and Pins (promo-only version)	1964	12.50	25.00	50.00
Kapp 577	PS	Needles and Pins/Ain't That Just Like Me	1964	7.50	15.00	30.00
Kapp 584		Ain't That Just Like Me/Ain't Gonna Kiss You	1964	2.50	5.00	10.00
Kapp 584	PS	Ain't That Just Like Me (special promo sleeve)	1964	12.50	25.00	50.00
Kapp 593		Don't Throw Your Love Away/I'll Pretend I'm with You	1964	2.50	5.00	10.00
Kapp 609		Someday We're Gonna Love Again/No One Else Could Love Me	1964	2.50	5.00	10.00
Kapp 609	PS	Someday We're Gonna Love Again/No One Else Could Love Me	1964	7.50	15.00	30.00
Kapp 618		When You Walk in the Room/I'll Be Missing You	1964	2.50	5.00	10.00
Kapp 644		What Have They Done to the Rain/This Feeling Inside	1965	2.50	5.00	10.00
Kapp 658		Goodbye My Lover Goodbye/'Til I Met You	1965	2.50	5.00	10.00
Kapp 686		He's Got No Love/So Far Away	1965	2.50	5.00	10.00
Kapp 706		Don't You Know Why/You Can't Lie to a Liar	1965	2.50	5.00	10.00
Kapp 729		Take Me for What I'm Worth/Too Many Miles	1966	2.50	5.00	10.00
Kapp 783		Have You Ever Loved Somebody/It's Just the Way	1966	2.50	5.00	10.00
Kapp 811		Lovers/Popcorn Double Feature	1966	2.50	5.00	10.00
Liberty 55646		Sugar and Spice/Saints and Sinners	1963	6.25	12.50	25.00
Liberty 55689		Sugar and Spice/Saints and Sinners	1964	3.75	7.50	15.00
Mercury 72172		Sweets for My Sweet/It's All Been a Dream	1963	6.25	12.50	25.00

Label, Number		Title	Year	VG	VG+	NM
Mercury 72390		(Ain't That) Just Like Me/I Can Tell				
			1964	3.75	7.50	15.00
RCA Victor 74-0484		Desdemona/The World Is Waiting for Tomorrow				
			1971		3.00	6.00
RCA Victor 74-0652		Love Is Everywhere/And the Button				
			1972		3.00	6.00
Sire 49175		It's Too Late/Don't Hang On	1980		2.00	4.00
Sire 49665		Love's Melody/Little Bit of Heaven				
			1981		2.00	4.00

Seaweed
Punk band from Washington state.

7-Inch Extended Play Singles

Label, Number		Title	Year	VG	VG+	NM
Leopard Gecko LG 007		Inside	1989	10.50	21.25	42.50
Blue/green vinyl						
Leopard Gecko LG 007		Inside	1989	4.25	8.75	17.50
Leopard Gecko LG 007	PS	Inside	1989	4.25	8.75	17.50

45s

Label, Number		Title	Year	VG	VG+	NM
K # XVI		Deertrap/Carousel	1990		2.50	5.00
K # XVI	PS	Deertrap/Carousel	1990		2.50	5.00
Leopard Gecko LG 009		Just a Smirk/Installing	1990	3.75	7.50	15.00
1,000 copies on green vinyl						
Leopard Gecko LG 009	PS	Just a Smirk/Installing	1990	3.75	7.50	15.00
Sub Pop 141		Bill/Pumpkin	1992		3.75	7.50
Green vinyl						
Sub Pop 141	PS	Bill/Pumpkin	1992		3.75	7.50

Seizure
Early Seattle punk band.

45s

Label, Number	Title	Year	VG	VG+	NM
Regressive 53667	Cutie's Wrong Now/Frontline	1978	4.50	9.00	18.00
Not issued with picture sleeve					

Selecter, The
British ska band.

Vinyl Albums

Label, Number	Title	Year	VG	VG+	NM
Chrysalis CHR 1274	Too Much Pressure	1980	2.50	5.00	10.00
Chrysalis CHR 1306	Celebrate the Bullet	1981	2.50	5.00	10.00
Chrysalis PV 41274	Too Much Pressure	1983	2.00	4.00	8.00
Reissue					
Chrysalis PV 41306	Celebrate the Bullet	198?	2.00	4.00	8.00
Reissue					

45s

Label, Number	Title	Year	VG	VG+	NM
Chrysalis/2 Tone 2374	The Selecter/Gangsters	1979		2.00	4.00
*B-side by **The Specials***					
Chrysalis 2376	On My Radio/Too Much Pressure				
		1979		2.50	5.00

Setzer, Brian
*Of **Stray Cats.***

Vinyl Albums

Label, Number	Title	Year	VG	VG+	NM
EMI America ST-17178	The Knife Feels Like Justice	1986	2.50	5.00	10.00
EMI America ST-517178	The Knife Feels Like Justice	1986	3.75	7.50	15.00
Columbia House edition					
EMI Manhattan E1-46963	Live Nude Guitars	1988	2.50	5.00	10.00

Label, Number		Title	Year	VG	VG+	NM
12-Inch Singles						
EMI America SPRO 9865	DJ	Boulevard of Broken Dreams (same on both sides)				
			1986	3.00	6.00	12.00
EMI America SPRO-9576	DJ	The Knife Feels Like Justice (same on both sides)				
			1985	4.00	8.00	16.00
EMI Manhattan 04109	DJ	Rebelene (same on both sides)	1988	3.00	6.00	12.00
EMI Manhattan 56097		When the Sky Comes Tumblin' Down (4 versions)/Cross of Love				
			1988	3.00	6.00	12.00

Severin

Label, Number		Title	Year	VG	VG+	NM
45s						
Sub Pop 213		Waste of Time/Powerplay	1993		2.50	5.00
All copies on clear green vinyl						
Sub Pop 213	PS	Waste of Time/Powerplay	1993		2.50	5.00

Sex Clark Five

Punkish alternative band from Alabama.

Label, Number		Title	Year	VG	VG+	NM
Vinyl Albums						
Blood Money ERATO 59		Battle of Sex Clark Five	1989	4.50	9.00	18.00
Records to Russia RTR-LP 408		Strum & Drum!	1986	12.50	25.00	50.00
Rare test pressing with 24 tracks						
Records to Russia RTR-LP 408		Strum & Drum!	1987	3.75	7.50	15.00
First pressing: 20 tracks						
Records to Russia RTR-LP 408		Strum & Drum!	1987	2.50	5.00	10.00
Second pressing: 20 tracks, no halftones, different back photo						
Skyclad (NOT) BM 131		Antedium	1992	3.00	6.00	12.00
7-Inch Extended Play Singles						
Records to Russia RTR 916-59		Ketchup If You Can	1991			3.00
All copies on red vinyl						
Records to Russia RTR 916-59	PS	Ketchup If You Can	1991			3.00
Records to Russia RTR-01211		Neita Grew Up Last Night	1986		3.00	6.00
Records to Russia RTR-01211	PS	Neita Grew Up Last Night	1986		3.00	6.00
Wernher Bros. WBEP-001		Martinlutherkinks Hit Parade	1994		2.00	4.00
Brown vinyl						
Wernher Bros. WBEP-001		Martinlutherkinks Hit Parade	1994			3.00
Clear vinyl						
Wernher Bros. WBEP-001	PS	Martinlutherkinks Hit Parade	1994			3.00
Three different covers exist, each of equal value.						

Sex Pistols

Notorious British band that was among the first to be called "punk rock." Johnny Rotten (John Lydon) joined **Public Image Ltd.** *after the breakup.*

Label, Number		Title	Year	VG	VG+	NM
Vinyl Albums						
Restless 72255		Better Live Than Dead	1988	3.00	6.00	12.00
Restless 72256	EP	The Mini-Album	1988	2.00	4.00	8.00
Restless 72257		The Ex-Pistols: The Swindle Continues				
			1988	3.00	6.00	12.00
Restless 72511		Live at Chelmsford Top Security Prison				
			1990	2.50	5.00	10.00
Skyclad SEX 6		We've Cum For Your Children	1988	3.00	6.00	12.00
Warner Bros. BSK 3147		Never Mind the Bollocks Here's the Sex Pistols				
			1978	7.50	15.00	30.00
With sticker "Contains Sub-Mission"						
Warner Bros. BSK 3147		Never Mind the Bollocks Here's the Sex Pistols				
			1978	6.25	12.50	25.00
Any other version with custom label						

Label, Number		Title	Year	VG	VG+	NM
Warner Bros. BSK 3147		Never Mind the Bollocks Here's the Sex Pistols				
			1978	2.50	5.00	10.00
With white WB label						
45s						
Warner Bros. 8516		Pretty Vacant/Sub-Mission	1978	5.00	10.00	20.00
Warner Bros. 8516	DJ	Pretty Vacant (mono/stereo)	1978	2.50	5.00	10.00
Warner Bros. 8516	PS	Pretty Vacant/Sub-Mission	1978	2.50	5.00	10.00

Shaggs, The

Legendary New Hampshire do-it-yourself sisters whose total lack of musical ability inspired many others to give music a try.

Vinyl Albums					
Rounder 3032	Philosophy of the World	1980	6.25	12.50	25.00
Rounder 3056	Shaggs' Own Thing	1982	6.25	12.50	25.00
Third World 3001	Philosophy of the World	1969	500.00	1,000.00	2,000.00

Shakespears Sister

*Siobhan Fabey Stewart of **Bananarama** with Marcella Detroit, the former **Marcy Levy**.*

12-Inch Singles				
FFRR 886 583-1	Heroine (3 versions)/Dirty Mind (2 versions)			
	1989	2.00	4.00	8.00
FFRR 886 951-1	Break My Heart (4 versions)/Run Silent			
	1988	2.00	4.00	8.00

Sham 69

British punk band.

Vinyl Albums					
Sire SRK-6060	Tell Us the Truth	1978	3.75	7.50	15.00

Sharkey, Feargal

*Irish rocker, formerly a member of **The Undertones**.*

Vinyl Albums					
A&M SP6-5108	Feargal Sharkey	1985	2.50	5.00	10.00
Virgin 90895	Wish	1988	2.50	5.00	10.00
45s					
A&M 2804	A Good Heart/Anger Is Holy	1985			3.00
12-Inch Singles					
Virgin 2260	DJ	If This Is Love (same on both sides)			
		1988		2.50	5.00

Sheer Smegma

*See **Teddy and the Frat Girls***

Shirkers, The

Washington, D.C. punk band.

45s					
Limp 003	Drunk and Disorderly/Suicide	1978	3.75	7.50	15.00

Label, Number		Title	Year	VG	VG+	NM
Limp 003	PS	Drunk and Disorderly/Suicide	1978	3.75	7.50	15.00
"Broken bottle" sleeve						
Limp 003	PS	Drunk and Disorderly/Suicide	1978	3.00	6.00	12.00
Gray live photo sleeve						

Shirts, The

New York new-wave group. Played its first gig at CBGB's in 1975.

Vinyl Albums

Capitol SW-11791		The Shirts	1978	3.50	7.00	14.00
Capitol ST-11944		Street Light Shine	1979	3.50	7.00	14.00
Capitol SW-12085		Inner Sleeve	1980	3.00	6.00	12.00

45s

Capitol 4750		Can't Cry Anymore/I'm in Love Again				
			1979			3.00
Capitol 4750	PS	Can't Cry Anymore/I'm in Love Again				
			1979			3.00
Capitol 4783		Don't You Hesitate/Ground Zero				
			1979			3.00
Capitol 4783	PS	Don't You Hesitate/Ground Zero				
			1979			3.00

Shit Dogs

New Orleans punk group.

7-Inch Extended Play Singles

Pangolin Productions		Present the History of Cheese	1980	18.75	37.50	75.00
(# unknown)						
Pangolin Productions	PS	Present the History of Cheese	1980	18.75	37.50	75.00
(# unknown)						
Pangolin Productions		You Bet!	1981	6.25	12.50	25.00
(# unknown)						
Pangolin Productions	PS	You Bet!	1981	6.25	12.50	25.00
(# unknown)						

Shocked, Michelle

Ex-American singer-songwriter.

Vinyl Albums

Mercury PRO 797	DJ	Live	1990	5.00	10.00	20.00
Five-song mini-LP for radio stations with custom jacket						
Mercury 834 581-1		The Texas Campfire Tapes	1988	3.00	6.00	12.00
Mercury 834 924-1		Short Sharp Shocked	1988	2.50	5.00	10.00
Mercury 838 878-1		Captain Swing	1989	2.50	5.00	10.00

45s

Mercury 870 611-7		Anchorage/Anchorage (Live Video Version)				
			1988			3.00
Mercury 870 611-7	PS	Anchorage/Anchorage (Live Video Version)				
			1988			3.00
Mercury 872 590-7		When I Grow Up/Fogtown	1989			3.00
Mercury 872 590-7	PS	When I Grow Up/Fogtown	1989			3.00

12-Inch Singles

Mercury 618	DJ	Anchorage (same on both sides)				
			1988		3.00	6.00
Mercury PRO 701	DJ	When I Grow Up/Memories of East Texas/Yamboree Queen/				
		Strawberry Jam	1988	3.75	7.50	15.00
Mercury 757	DJ	On the Greener Side/Must Be Luff				
			1989	2.50	5.00	10.00

Label, Number		Title	Year	VG	VG+	NM

Shoes

Power pop band from Zion, Illinois.

Vinyl Albums

Label, Number		Title	Year	VG	VG+	NM
Black Vinyl 51477		Black Vinyl Shoes	1977	7.50	15.00	30.00
Elektra 6E-244		Present Tense	1979	2.50	5.00	10.00
Elektra 6E-303		Tongue Twister	1980	2.50	5.00	10.00
Elektra AS 11570	DJ	Shoes on Ice -- Live	1982	10.00	20.00	40.00
Promo-only 7-song live record; issued in generic jacket						
Elektra 60146		Boomerang	1982	2.50	5.00	10.00
PVC 7904		Black Vinyl Shoes	1979	4.00	8.00	16.00

45s

Label, Number		Title	Year	VG	VG+	NM
Bomp! 116		Okay/Tomorrow Night	1978		2.00	4.00
Bomp! 116	PS	Okay/Tomorrow Night	1978		2.00	4.00
Elektra 46557		Too Late/Now and Then	1979		2.00	4.00
Elektra 46557	PS	Too Late/Now and Then	1979		2.00	4.00
Elektra 46571		Tomorrow Night/Now and Then	1979		2.00	4.00
Elektra 46598		I Don't Miss You/In My Arms Again	1980		2.00	4.00
Elektra 47130		Karen/She Satisfies	1981		2.00	4.00

12-Inch Singles

Label, Number		Title	Year	VG	VG+	NM
Elektra 11440	DJ	I Don't Wanna Hear It/Now and Then	1979	3.75	7.50	15.00

Shonen Knife

Japanese girl group.

45s

Label, Number		Title	Year	VG	VG+	NM
Rockville 6056		Lazybone/Blue Oyster Cult	1991	2.50	5.00	10.00
Rockville 6056	PS	Lazybone/Blue Oyster Cult	1991	2.50	5.00	10.00
Sub Pop 108		Neon Zebra/Bear Up Bison (Live)	1991	3.00	6.25	12.50
#30 in Sub Pop Singles Club series						
Sub Pop 108	PS	Neon Zebra/Bear Up Bison (Live)	1991	3.00	6.25	12.50

Shooting Star

Kansas City-based pop-rock group.

Vinyl Albums

Label, Number		Title	Year	VG	VG+	NM
Epic NFE 37407		Hang On for Your Life	1981	2.50	5.00	10.00
Epic PE 37720		Shooting Star	1982	2.00	4.00	8.00
Reissue of Virgin VA 13133						
Epic FE 38020		3 Wishes	1982	2.50	5.00	10.00
Epic BFE 38683		Burning	1983	2.50	5.00	10.00
Geffen GHS 24056		Silent Scream	1985	2.50	5.00	10.00
Virgin VA 13133		Shooting Star	1979	2.50	5.00	10.00

45s

Label, Number		Title	Year	VG	VG+	NM
Epic 02516		Flesh and Blood/You've Got Love	1981			3.00
Epic 04025		Straight Ahead/Taken Enough	1983			3.00
Geffen 28994		Summer Sun/Time	1985			3.00
Geffen 28994	PS	Summer Sun/Time	1985			3.00
Virgin 02755		Hang On for Your Life/Hollywood	1982			3.00
Virgin 03028		Do You Feel Alright/Where You Gonna Run	1982			3.00

Label, Number		Title	Year	VG	VG+	NM
Virgin 03285		Heartache/Let It Out	1982			3.00
Virgin 67005		You've Got What I Need/Wild in the Streets	1980			3.00
Virgin 67005	PS	You've Got What I Need/Wild in the Streets	1980			3.00
Virgin 67010		Bring It On/(B-side unknown)	1980			3.00
12-Inch Singles						
Epic AS 1739	DJ	Winner/Train Rolls On	1983	2.00	4.00	8.00
Geffen PRO-A-2335	DJ	Summer Sun (same on both sides)	1985	2.00	4.00	8.00
Geffen PRO-A-2351	DJ	Heat of the Night (same on both sides)	1985	2.00	4.00	8.00
Pasha AS 1877	DJ	Take It/Get Ready Boy	1984	2.00	4.00	8.00

Sigue Sigue Sputnik

British band that actually put commercials on its first album.

Label, Number		Title	Year	VG	VG+	NM
Vinyl Albums						
EMI E1-48700		Dress for Excess	1989	2.50	5.00	10.00
Manhattan ST-53033		Flaunt It	1986	2.50	5.00	10.00
45s						
Manhattan 50035		Love Missile F 1-11/Hack Attack	1986		2.00	4.00
Manhattan 50051		Massive Retaliation/Teenage Thunder	1986		2.00	4.00
12-Inch Singles						
EMI Manhattan 56130		Success (6 versions)	1988		3.00	6.00
Manhattan SPRO 9677/8	DJ	Love Missile F 1-11 (single version)/ Love Missile F 1-11 (extended version)	1986	3.00	6.00	12.00
Manhattan 56037		Massive Retaliation (3 versions)/Teenage Thunder	1986	2.00	4.00	8.00

Silly Killers

*With Duff McKagan (later of **Guns N' Roses**).*

Label, Number		Title	Year	VG	VG+	NM
7-Inch Extended Play Singles						
No Threes 007		Not That Time Again/Knife Manual/Social Bitch/Sissy Faggots	1982	6.25	12.50	25.00
No Threes 007	PS	Not That Time Again/Knife Manual/Social Bitch/Sissy Faggots	1982	6.25	12.50	25.00

Silver Chalice

Los Angeles punk band.

Label, Number		Title	Year	VG	VG+	NM
45s						
Final Gear 000		Wasted/Hot Tears	1979	5.00	10.00	20.00
Final Gear 000	PS	Wasted/Hot Tears	1979	7.50	15.00	30.00

Simple Minds

British synth-pop group fronted by Jim Kerr.

Label, Number		Title	Year	VG	VG+	NM
Vinyl Albums						
A&M SP-3927		Street Fighting Years	1989	2.50	5.00	10.00
A&M SP-6-4928		New Gold Dream (81-82-83-84)	1982	3.00	6.00	12.00
Originals have gold and purple marbled vinyl						
A&M SP-6-4981		Sparkle in the Rain	1984	3.00	6.00	12.00

Label, Number		Title	Year	VG	VG+	NM
A&M SP-5092		Once Upon a Time	1985	2.50	5.00	10.00
A&M SP-6850	(2)	Live in the City of Light	1987	4.50	9.00	18.00
A&M R 101142		Street Fighting Years	1989	3.75	7.50	15.00
BMG Direct Marketing edition						
A&M R 142320		Once Upon a Time	1985	3.75	7.50	15.00
RCA Music Service edition; has front and back covers reversed						
A&M R 209526	(2)	Live in the City of Light	1987	5.00	10.00	20.00
BMG Direct Marketing edition						
PVC 7910		Life in a Day	1979	3.75	7.50	15.00
Stiff TEES-102		Themes for Great Cities	1982	3.75	7.50	15.00
Virgin 90610		Sister Feelings Call	1987	2.50	5.00	10.00
Virgin 90858		Life in a Day	1988	2.50	5.00	10.00
Reissue						
Virgin 90859		Real to Real Cacophony	1988	2.50	5.00	10.00

45s

Label, Number		Title	Year	VG	VG+	NM
A&M 1413		This Is Your Land/Saturday Girl	1989		2.00	4.00
A&M 2523		Promised You a Miracle/The American				
			1983		2.00	4.00
A&M 2556	DJ	Someone, Somewhere in Summertime (same on both sides)				
			1983		2.00	4.00
No stock copy was issued						
A&M 2629		Speed Your Love to Me/Bass Line				
			1984		2.00	4.00
A&M 2703		Don't You (Forget About Me)/A Brass Bed in Africa				
			1984			3.00
A&M 2703	PS	Don't You (Forget About Me)/A Brass Bed in Africa				
			1984			3.00
A&M 2783		Alive & Kicking/Up on the Catwalk (Live)				
			1985			2.00
A&M 2783	PS	Alive & Kicking/Up on the Catwalk (Live)				
			1985			2.00
A&M 2810		Sanctify Yourself/Sanctify Yourself (Dub Version)				
			1986			2.00
A&M 2810	PS	Sanctify Yourself/Sanctify Yourself (Dub Version)				
			1986			2.00
A&M 2828		All the Things She Said/Don't You (Forget About Me) (Live)				
			1986			2.00
A&M 2828	PS	All the Things She Said/Don't You (Forget About Me) (Live)				
			1986	2.00	4.00	8.00
A&M 2954		Promised You a Miracle/Book of Brilliant Things				
			1987			2.00
A&M 2954	PS	Promised You a Miracle/Book of Brilliant Things				
			1987			2.00
A&M 8662		Alive and Kicking/Don't You (Forget About Me)				
			198?			3.00
Reissue						
Virgin S7-18402		She's a River (Single Edit)/Celtic Strings				
			1995		2.00	4.00
Blue vinyl						
Virgin S7-18558		Hypnotised/And the Band Played On				
			1995			3.00

12-Inch Singles

Label, Number	Title	Year	VG	VG+	NM
A&M 12057	Promised You a Miracle (Extended)/Promised You a Miracle (Dub)/				
	The American	1982	3.75	7.50	15.00
A&M 12125	Don't You (Forget About Me) (long)/A Brass Band in Africa				
		1985	3.00	6.00	12.00
A&M 12172	Sanctify Yourself (extended)/Sanctify Yourself (dub)				
		1985	2.00	4.00	8.00
A&M 12177	All the Things She Said (Extended)/				
	Don't You (Forget About Me) (Live)				
		1986	2.50	5.00	10.00

Label, Number		Title	Year	VG	VG+	NM
A&M 12244		Promised You a Miracle/Book of Brilliant Things/Glittering Prize/				
		Celebrate (all live)	1987	2.00	4.00	8.00
A&M 17223	DJ	Promised You a Miracle (Long)/Promised You a Miracle (Short)				
			1982	2.50	5.00	10.00
A&M 17277	DJ	Speed Your Love to Me/Waterfront				
			1984	2.50	5.00	10.00
A&M 17363	DJ	Sanctify Yourself (same on both sides)				
			1985	2.00	4.00	8.00
A&M 17371	DJ	All the Things She Said (same on both sides)				
			1986	2.00	4.00	8.00
A&M 17480	DJ	Alive & Kicking (Live)/Don't You (Forget About Me) (Live)/				
		Promised You a Miracle (Live)	1988	2.00	4.00	8.00
A&M 17728	DJ	This Is Your Land (Edit)/This Is Your Land (LP)/Saturday Girl/				
		Year of the Dragon	1989	2.00	4.00	8.00
Virgin 12726	DJ	Hypnotised (4 versions)	1995	2.00	4.00	8.00

Simply Red

British pop group led by soulster Mick Hucknall.

Vinyl Albums

Label, Number		Title	Year	VG	VG+	NM
Elektra ED 5236	DJ	Simply Red Interview	1989	7.50	15.00	30.00
Nelson George interviews Mick Hucknall and Lamont Dozier; promo-only						
Elektra 60452		Picture Book	1985	3.00	6.00	12.00
Elektra 60727		Men and Women	1987	2.50	5.00	10.00
Elektra 60828		A New Flame	1989	2.50	5.00	10.00
Elektra R 101012		A New Flame	1989	3.00	6.00	12.00
BMG Direct Marketing edition						
Elektra R 152858		Men and Women	1987	3.00	6.00	12.00
RCA Music Service edition						
Elektra R 153936		Picture Book	1985	3.50	7.00	14.00
RCA Music Service edition						

45s

Label, Number		Title	Year	VG	VG+	NM
Elektra 65939		If You Don't Know Me By Now/You've Got It				
			199?			3.00
"Spun Gold" reissue						
Elektra 65979		Holding Back the Years/Money$ Too Tight (To Mention)				
			198?			3.00
"Spun Gold" reissue						
Elektra 69269		You've Got It/She'll Have to Go	1989			3.00
Elektra 69297		If You Don't Know Me By Now/Move On Out				
			1989			3.00
Elektra 69297	PS	If You Don't Know Me By Now/Move On Out				
			1989			3.00
Elektra 69317		It's Only Love/Turn It Up	1989			3.00
Elektra 69317	PS	It's Only Love/Turn It Up	1989			3.00
Elektra 69428		Supper/Let Me Have It All	1987			3.00
Elektra 69448		Maybe Someday.../Broken Man	1987			3.00
Elektra 69448	PS	Maybe Someday.../Broken Man	1987			3.00
Elektra 69468		Infidelity/Lady Godiva's Room	1987			3.00
Elektra 69468	PS	Infidelity/Lady Godiva's Room	1987			3.00
Elektra 69487		The Right Thing/There's a Light	1987			3.00
Elektra 69487	PS	The Right Thing/There's a Light				
			1987			3.00
Elektra 69528		Money$ Too Tight (To Mention)/Picture Book (Dub)				
			1986			3.00
Elektra 69528	PS	Money$ Too Tight (To Mention)/Picture Book (Dub)				
			1986			3.00
Elektra 69564		Holding Back the Years/I Won't Feel Bad				
			1986			3.00

Not issued with picture sleeve in U.S.

Label, Number		Title	Year	VG	VG+	NM
Elektra 69574		Come to My Aid (Remix)/Look At You Now				
			1986		2.00	4.00
Elektra 69607		Money$ Too Tight (To Mention)/(B-side unknown)				
			1985		2.00	4.00

12-Inch Singles

Label, Number		Title	Year	VG	VG+	NM
EastWest 1738	DJ	Something Got Me Started (3 mixes)				
			1991	2.50	5.00	10.00
Elektra 5088	DJ	Money$ Too Tight (To Mention) (3 versions)				
			1985	2.50	5.00	10.00
Elektra ED 5112	DJ	Come to My Aid (2 mixes)/Granma's Hands				
			1985	2.00	4.00	8.00
Elektra 5210	DJ	The Right Thing (3 versions)	1987		3.00	6.00
Elektra 5227	DJ	Infidelity/Infidelity (Stretch Mix)				
			1987		2.50	5.00
Elektra 5247	DJ	Maybe Someday ... (same on both sides)				
			1987		2.50	5.00
Elektra 5268	DJ	Suffer (Edit) (same on both sides)				
			1987		3.00	6.00
Elektra 5358	DJ	It's Only Love (Valentine Mix)/It's Only Love (Edit of Mix)				
			1989		2.50	5.00
Elektra ED 5378	DJ	If You Don't Know Me By Now (same on both sides)				
			1989	2.00	4.00	8.00
Elektra 5407	DJ	You've Got It (same on both sides)				
			1989		3.50	7.00
Elektra 66703		If You Don't Know Me By Now/Move On Out (Live)/Shine (Live)				
			1989	2.00	4.00	8.00
Elektra 66883		Money$ Too Tight (To Mention) (3 versions)				
			1985	2.00	4.00	8.00

Sinceros, The

British new-wave group.

Vinyl Albums

Label, Number		Title	Year	VG	VG+	NM
Columbia JC 36134		The Sound of Sunbathing	1979	3.00	6.00	12.00
Columbia NFC 37349		Pet Rock	1980	2.50	5.00	10.00

45s

Label, Number		Title	Year	VG	VG+	NM
Columbia 02121		Disappearing/Torture Myself	1981		2.00	4.00
Columbia 11115		Take Me to Your Leader/Good Luck (To You)				
			1979		2.00	4.00
Columbia 11178		Worlds Apart/Hanging On Too Long				
			1980		2.00	4.00

12-Inch Singles

Label, Number		Title	Year	VG	VG+	NM
Columbia AS 970	DJ	Disappearing/Memory Lane/Barcelona				
			1981		3.00	6.00

Single Bullet Theory

From Norfolk, Virginia.

Vinyl Albums

Label, Number		Title	Year	VG	VG+	NM
Nemperor ARZ 38368		Single Bullet Theory	1983	2.50	5.00	10.00

45s

Label, Number		Title	Year	VG	VG+	NM
Artifacts (# unknown)		Peggy Got Her Eyes Full/There Is the Boy				
			1981		2.50	5.00
Artifacts (# unknown)	PS	Peggy Got Her Eyes Full/There Is the Boy				
			1981		2.50	5.00
Nemperor 03300		Keep It Tight/A Blink of An Eye				
			1983			3.00

Label, Number		Title	Year	VG	VG+	NM
Nemperor 03300	PS	Keep It Tight/A Blink of An Eye				
			1983			3.00
Nemperor 03890		Too Hot to Handle/Hang On to Your Heart				
			1983			3.00

12-Inch Singles

Artifacts 112263		Rocker's Night Out/Rock Around the Apocalypse/Lies/				
		Les Bonnes Chansons	1977	3.75	7.50	15.00

Siouxsie and the Banshees

British punk/new wave group.

Vinyl Albums

Label, Number		Title	Year	VG	VG+	NM
Geffen GEF 24387		Superstition	1991	3.00	6.00	12.00
Geffen GEF 24630		The Rapture	1995	3.00	6.00	12.00
Geffen GHS 24030		Hyaena	1984	2.50	5.00	10.00
Geffen GHS 24046		The Scream	1984	2.50	5.00	10.00
Reissue of Polydor PD1-6207						
Geffen GHS 24047		Join Hands	1984	2.50	5.00	10.00
Apparently, this 1979 album's first U.S. release						
Geffen GHS 24048		Kaleidoscope	1984	2.50	5.00	10.00
Reissue of PVC 7921						
Geffen GHS 24049		A Kiss in the Dream House	1984	2.50	5.00	10.00
Apparently, this 1982 album's first U.S. release						
Geffen GHS 24050		Juju	1984	2.50	5.00	10.00
Reissue of PVC 8903						
Geffen GHS 24051		Once Upon a Time: The Singles				
			1984	2.50	5.00	10.00
Reissue of PVC 8906						
Geffen GHS 24052	(2)	Nocturne	1984	2.50	5.00	10.00
Geffen GHS 24092		Tinderbox	1986	2.50	5.00	10.00
Geffen GHS 24134		Through the Looking Glass	1987	2.50	5.00	10.00
Geffen GHS 24205		Peepshow	1988	2.50	5.00	10.00
Polydor PD1-6207		The Scream	1978	7.50	15.00	30.00
PVC 7921		Kaleidoscope	1980	5.00	10.00	20.00
PVC 8903		Juju	1981	5.00	10.00	20.00
Original copies include bonus single "Israel"/"Red Over White"						
PVC 8906		Once Upon a Time: The Singles	1981	3.75	7.50	15.00
With poster and inner sleeve						

45s

Geffen 19031		Kiss Them for Me	1991			*Cassette only*
Geffen 19111		Fear (Of the Unknown)	1991			*Cassette only*
Geffen 27760		Peek-A-Boo/False Face	1988			3.00
Geffen 28813		Cities in Dust/An Execution	1986			3.00
Geffen 28813	PS	Cities in Dust/An Execution	1986			3.00
Geffen 29358		Dear Prudence/Tattoo	1984			3.00
Geffen 29358	PS	Dear Prudence/Tattoo	1984			3.00
Polydor 14561		Hong Kong Garden/Overground	1979	10.00	20.00	40.00
PVC 1001		Israel/Red Over White	1980		2.50	5.00
PVC 1001	PS	Israel/Red Over White	1980		2.50	5.00
Warner Bros. 18825		Face to Face	1993			*Cassette only*

12-Inch Singles

Geffen PRO-A-2114	DJ	Dear Prudence/Dazzle	1984	5.00	10.00	20.00
Geffen PRO-A-2478	DJ	Cities in Dust (Remix)/Cities in Dust (LP Version)				
			1986	5.00	10.00	20.00
Geffen PRO-A-2648	DJ	This Wheel's on Fire (7")/This Wheel's on Fire (LP Version)				
			1987	2.00	4.00	8.00
Geffen PRO-A-2731	DJ	The Passenger (3 versions)	1987	3.75	7.50	15.00

Label, Number		Title	Year	VG	VG+	NM
Geffen PRO-A-3195	DJ	Peek-a-Boo (3 versions)	1988	2.50	5.00	10.00
Geffen 4281	DJ	Kiss Them for Me (4 versions)	1991	2.50	5.00	10.00
Geffen 4361	DJ	Fear (Of the Unknown) (6 versions)				
			1991	3.00	6.00	12.00
Geffen 4368	DJ	Fear (Of the Unknown) (Techno-Vertigo Mix)/				
		Fear (Of the Unknown) (Dub)	1991	2.50	5.00	10.00
Geffen 20399		Cities in Dust (2 versions)/An Execution/				
		Quarter Drawing of the Dog	1986	3.00	6.00	12.00
Geffen 20609		Wheels on Fire (Remix)/Shooting Sun/Sleepwalking				
			1987		3.00	6.00
Geffen 20977		Peek-a-Boo (2 versions)/False Face/Catwalk				
			1988	2.00	4.00	8.00
Geffen 21100		The Killing Jar (3 mixes)/Something Wicked/				
		Are You Still Dying, Darling?	1988	3.00	6.00	12.00
Geffen 21383		Standing There (2 mixes)/Divided/Solar Choir				
			1989	3.00	6.00	12.00
PVC 4902		Arabian Knights/Supernatural Thing//Conga Conga/Slap Dash Snap				
			1981	3.75	7.50	15.00

Sister Double Happiness

Vinyl Albums

Reprise PRO-A-5010	DJ	Heart and Mind	1991	10.00	20.00	40.00
Available as stock copy on cassette and CD only						
SST 162		Sister Double Happiness	1988	2.50	5.00	10.00

45s

Sub Pop 77		Don't Worry/Wheels a-Spinnin'	1990		3.00	6.00
First 2,000 on green vinyl						
Sub Pop 77		Don't Worry/Wheels a-Spinnin'	1990			2.00
Sub Pop 77	PS	Don't Worry/Wheels a-Spinnin'	1990			2.00
Still in print as of the end of 1995						

Sister Ray

Grungy band from Youngstown, Ohio.

7-Inch Extended Play Singles

Sad (# unknown)		Coming to Terms	1985	15.00	30.00	60.00
Sad (# unknown)	PS	Coming to Terms	1985	15.00	30.00	60.00

45s

Ajax 004		Psycho Sis/Bathroom Blues	198?		2.00	4.00
Red vinyl						
Ajax 004	PS	Psycho Sis/Bathroom Blues	198?		2.00	4.00
Forced Exposure 016		Purgatory/Hillside	198?		2.00	4.00
Forced Exposure 016	PS	Purgatory/Hillside	198?		2.00	4.00
Sad (# unknown)		Feel Like This/Invasion of the Pussy Music				
			198?		3.00	6.00
Sad (# unknown)	PS	Feel Like This/Invasion of the Pussy Music				
			198?		3.00	6.00
Sad (# unknown)		Yellow with Black Lace/This Girl				
			1986	15.00	30.00	60.00
Sad (# unknown)	PS	Yellow with Black Lace/This Girl				
			1986	15.00	30.00	60.00
Sad (# unknown)		Survivors/Your Every Word/Black (Live)				
			1987	6.25	12.50	25.00
Sad (# unknown)	PS	Survivors/Your Every Word/Black (Live)				
			1987	6.25	12.50	25.00
Sub Pop 75		The King/Push Me	1990	3.75	7.50	15.00
First 2,500 on yellow vinyl						
Sub Pop 75		The King/Push Me	1990		2.50	5.00
Last 1,500 on black vinyl						

Label, Number		Title	Year	VG	VG+	NM
Sub Pop 75	PS	The King/Push Me	1990		2.50	5.00
#22 in Sub Pop Singles Club series						

Sisters of Mercy
British post-punk band.

Vinyl Albums
Elektra 60405		First and Last and Always	1985	3.00	6.00	12.00
Elektra 60762		Floodland	1987	3.00	6.00	12.00

45s
Elektra 69378		Lucretia My Reflection/Long Train	1988			3.00
Elektra 69378	PS	Lucretia My Reflection/Long Train	1988			3.00
Elektra 69434		This Corrosion/Torch	1987			3.00
Elektra 69434	PS	This Corrosion/Torch	1987			3.00

12-Inch Singles
Elektra ED 5263	DJ	This Corrosion (2 mixes)	1987	2.50	5.00	10.00
Elektra 5294	DJ	Dominion/Dominion Mother Russia	1987	2.00	4.00	8.00
Elektra ED 5321	DJ	Lucretia My Reflection (3 versions)	1987	2.50	5.00	10.00
Elektra 66790		This Corrosion/Torch/Colours	1987	2.50	5.00	10.00

Sleepers
*San Francisco punk band. With former members of **Tuxedomoon**.*

Vinyl Albums
Adolescent ARTT 007		Painless Nights	1981	3.00	6.00	12.00

7-Inch Extended Play Singles
Win 7777777		Sleepers	1978	7.50	15.00	30.00
Win 7777777	PS	Sleepers	1978	15.00	30.00	60.00
Numbered outer sleeve						
Win 7777777	PS	Sleepers	1978	7.50	15.00	30.00
Numbered inner sleeve						
Win 7777777	PS	Sleepers	1978	7.50	15.00	30.00
Un-numbered sleeve						

45s
Adolescent (no #)		Mirror/Theory	1980		2.00	4.00
Adolescent (no #)	PS	Mirror/Theory	1980		2.00	4.00
Mediumistic 200		Holding Back/B-Side	1994			3.00
Mediumistic 200	PS	Holding Back/B-Side	1994			3.00
Search & Destroy (#unknown)		Mirror/Theory	1980		2.50	5.00
Search & Destroy (#unknown)	PS	Mirror/Theory	1980	3.75	7.50	15.00
White bordered paper sleeve						
Search & Destroy (#unknown)	PS	Mirror/Theory	1980		2.50	5.00
Cardboard borderless black sleeve						

Slickee Boys
Washington, D.C. garage band, one of America's first "new wave" bands.

Vinyl Albums
Dacoit 1001		Separated Vegetables	1977	18.75	37.50	75.00
Limited edition of 100 copies						
Giant GR 16037-1		Live at Last	1989	2.50	5.00	10.00
Limp 1003		Separated Vegetables	1980	6.25	12.50	25.00
Limited edition of 300 copies; reissue with new cover						
Twin/Tone TTR 8337		Cybernetic Dreams of Pi	1983	3.75	7.50	15.00
Twin/Tone TTR 8544		Uh Oh, No Breaks	1985	3.00	6.00	12.00

Label, Number		Title	Year	VG	VG+	NM
7-Inch Extended Play Singles						
Dacoit 001		Hot and Cool	1976	2.00	4.00	8.00
Dacoit 001	PS	Hot and Cool	1976	4.00	8.00	16.00
Gatefold full-color picture sleeve (not every copy of this EP has a picture sleeve)						
DSI 8		10th Anniversary EP	1988		2.50	5.00
First pressing of 500 on black vinyl						
DSI 8		10th Anniversary EP	1988		2.50	5.00
Second pressing of 500 on white vinyl						
DSI 8	PS	10th Anniversary EP	1988		2.50	5.00
First pressing of sleeve is beige						
DSI 8	PS	10th Anniversary EP	1988		2.50	5.00
Second pressing of sleeve is green						
Limp 001		Mersey Mersey Me	1978	3.00	6.00	12.00
Yellow labels						
Limp 001		Mersey Mersey Me	1978	2.00	4.00	8.00
Blue labels						
Limp 001	PS	Mersey Mersey Me	1978	3.00	6.00	12.00
Blue sleeve						
Limp 001	PS	Mersey Mersey Me	1978	2.00	4.00	8.00
Pink sleeve						
Limp 005		3rd EP	1979	2.50	5.00	10.00
Limp 005	PS	3rd EP	1979	2.50	5.00	10.00
Includes decal, lyrics and fan club insert						
45s						
Dacoit 004		The Brain That Refused to Die/Love In	1980		3.00	6.00
Dacoit 004	PS	The Brain That Refused to Die/Love In	1980		3.00	6.00
Dacoit 005		Here to Stay/Porcelain Butter Kitchen	1981		3.00	6.00
Dacoit 005	PS	Here to Stay/Porcelain Butter Kitchen	1981		3.00	6.00
Dacoit 011		When I Go to the Beach/Invisible People	1983	2.00	4.00	8.00
3,000 copies were pressed						
Dacoit 011	PS	When I Go to the Beach/Invisible People	1983	2.00	4.00	8.00
Deceased 005		Long Way to Go/Control (Live)	1995			3.00
Limited edition of 500						
Deceased 005	PS	Long Way to Go/Control (Live)	1995			3.00
Twin/Tone TTR 8336		When I Go to the Beach/Invisible People	1984			3.00
3,000 copies were pressed						
Twin/Tone TTR 8336	PS	When I Go to the Beach/Invisible People	1984			3.00

Slits, The

All-female punk band from England. Their LP cover is a classic.

Label, Number		Title	Year	VG	VG+	NM
Vinyl Albums						
Antilles AN-7077		Cut	1979	10.00	20.00	40.00
45s						
Antilles ANS-102		Typical Girls/I Heard It Through the Grapevine	1980		3.75	7.50
Antilles ANS-102	PS	Typical Girls/I Heard It Through the Grapevine	1980		3.75	7.50
Fold-out poster sleeve						
12-Inch Singles						
Epic 02576		Earthbeat & Earthdub//Or What Is It	1981	2.00	4.00	8.00

Label, Number		Title	Year	VG	VG+	NM

Sly Fox
New York synth-pop/dance-pop duo.

Vinyl Albums
Capitol ST-12367		Let's Go All the Way	1985	2.00	4.00	8.00
Capitol ST-512367		Let's Go All the Way	1985	2.50	5.00	10.00
Columbia House edition						

45s
Capitol 5463		Let's Go All the Way/Let's Go All the Way (Bonus Beats)				
			1985		2.50	5.00
Capitol 5505		Como Tu Te Llama (What Is Your Name)/Won't Let You Go				
			1985		2.50	5.00
Capitol 5552		Let's Go All the Way/Como Tu Te Llama (What Is Your Name)				
			1986			3.00
Capitol 5581		Stay True/If Push Comes to Shove				
			1986			3.00
Capitol 5581	PS	Stay True/If Push Comes to Shove				
			1986			3.00

12-Inch Singles
Capitol 8639		Let's Go All the Way (extended)/Bonus Beats				
			1985		3.00	6.00
Capitol SPRO 9643/4	DJ	Let's Go All the Way (3 versions)				
			1985		3.00	6.00

Smashing Pumpkins
Chicago alterna-rock band.

Vinyl Albums
Caroline 1705		Gish	1991	3.00	6.00	12.00
Caroline 1740	(2)	Siamese Dream	1993	5.00	10.00	20.00
Caroline 1767		Pisces Iscariot	1994	3.00	6.00	12.00

45s
Sub Pop 90		Tristessa/La Dolly Vita	1991	13.75	27.50	55.00
Pink vinyl						
Sub Pop 90		Tristessa/La Dolly Vita	1991		2.50	5.00
Black vinyl						
Sub Pop 90	PS	Tristessa/La Dolly Vita	1991		2.50	5.00

Smegma
Portland, Oregon industrial/psych band.

45s
Pigface 002		Can't Look Straight/Flashcards	1979	8.75	17.50	35.00
Pigface 002	PS	Can't Look Straight/Flashcards	1979	8.75	17.50	35.00

Smith, Patti, Group
Chicago-born, New Jersey-bred poet and singer. Her androgynous look influenced a generation of females, as did her music.

Vinyl Albums
Arista AL 4066	Horses	1975	3.75	7.50	15.00
With the word "Horses" in black letters on the front cover					
Arista AL 4066	Horses	1975	3.00	6.00	12.00
With the word "Horses" in white letters on the front cover					
Arista AL 4097	Radio Ethiopia	1977	3.00	6.00	12.00
Arista AB 4171	Easter	1978	3.00	6.00	12.00
Arista AB 4221	Wave	1979	2.50	5.00	10.00
Arista ALB6-8349	Easter	198?	2.00	4.00	8.00
Reissue					

The first pressing of Patti Smith's debut album had both her name and the title in all-black letters (upper right). Later pressings had the title in one color, the artist in another.

The Smiths' *Louder Than Bombs* was their first American compilation (and the only one on vinyl). While most of the band's LPs are relatively common, its singles are not (the Smiths never had an American hit) and are highly collectible.

Label, Number		Title	Year	VG	VG+	NM
Arista ALB6-8362		Horses	198?	2.00	4.00	8.00
Reissue						
Arista ALB6-8379		Radio Ethiopia	198?	2.00	4.00	8.00
Reissue						
Arista AL 8453		Dreams of Life	1988	2.50	5.00	10.00
Arista AL 8546		Wave	1990	2.00	4.00	8.00
Reissue						
Arista R 100469		Dreams of Life	1988	3.00	6.00	12.00
BMG Music Service edition						
45s						
Arista SP-2	DJ	Pissing in the River (Stereo)/Pissing in the River (Mono)				
			1976	6.25	12.50	25.00
Arista SP-4	DJ	Ask the Angels (mono/stereo)	1977	6.25	12.50	25.00
With lyric insert (deduct 20% if missing)						
Arista 0171		Gloria/My Generation	1976	2.50	5.00	10.00
Arista 0171	PS	Gloria/My Generation	1976	2.50	5.00	10.00
Arista 0318		Because the Night/God Speed	1978		2.00	4.00
A-side co-written by Bruce Springsteen						
Arista 0318	PS	Because the Night/God Speed	1978	2.00	4.00	8.00
Arista 0427		Frederick/Frederick (Live)	1979		2.00	4.00
Arista 0427	PS	Frederick/Frederick (Live)	1979	2.00	4.00	8.00
Arista 0453		So You Want to Be a Rock and Roll Star//5-4-3-2-1/				
		A Fire of Unknown Origin	1979		2.00	4.00
Arista 0453	PS	So You Want to Be a Rock and Roll Star//5-4-3-2-1/				
		A Fire of Unknown Origin	1979	5.00	10.00	20.00
Arista 9173		Because the Night/So You Want to Be a Rock 'n' Roll Star				
			198?			3.00
"Flashback" reissue						
Arista 9689		People Have the Power/Wild Leaves				
			1988			3.00
Arista 9689	PS	People Have the Power/Wild Leaves				
			1988			3.00
Arista 9762		I Was (Looking for You)/Up There Down There				
			1988			3.00
Mer 601		Hey Joe/Piss Factory	1974	15.00	35.00	75.00
Sire 1009		Hey Joe/Piss Factory	1977	2.00	4.00	8.00
Sire 1009		Hey Joe/Piss Factory	1977	2.00	4.00	8.00
12-Inch Singles						
Arista SP-62	DJ	Frederick (Studio)/Frederick (Live)				
			1977	3.75	7.50	15.00
Arista 9688		People Have the Power/Where Duty Calls/Wild Leaves				
			1988		3.00	6.00

Smithereens, The

New Jersey pop-rock group.

Label, Number		Title	Year	VG	VG+	NM
Vinyl Albums						
Capitol C1-91194		11	1989	3.00	6.00	12.00
Capitol/Enigma C1-48375		Green Thoughts	1988	2.50	5.00	10.00
Capitol/Enigma R 130120		Green Thoughts	1988	3.00	6.00	12.00
BMG Direct Marketing edition						
Enigma (no #)	DJ	Live at the Roxy -- Special Forces Radio Concert				
			1986	10.00	20.00	40.00
Enigma ST-73208		Especially for You	1986	2.50	5.00	10.00
Enigma 73220	EP	Beauty and Sadness	1988	2.00	4.00	8.00
Remixed version of Little Ricky 103 with one track deleted						
Enigma SEAX-73258	PD	Especially for You	1986	5.00	10.00	20.00
Picture disc in plastic sleeve, sticker on sleeve						
Enigma R 164050		Especially for You	1987	3.00	6.00	12.00
BMG Direct Marketing edition						
Little Ricky 103	EP	Beauty and Sadness	1983	10.00	20.00	40.00

Label, Number		Title	Year	VG	VG+	NM
7-Inch Extended Play Singles						
D-Tone DT 150		Girls About Town/Girl Don't Tell Me//Got Me a Girl/				
		Girls Are Like That	1980	12.50	25.00	50.00
D-Tone DT 150	PS	Girls About Town	1980	12.50	25.00	50.00
45s						
Capitol S7-18206		Rudolph, the Red Nosed Reindeer/A Girl Like You				
			1994		2.00	4.00
Red vinyl						
Capitol S7-18871		One After 909/It Don't Come Easy				
			1995			3.00
Capitol 44480		A Girl Like You/Like Someone in Love				
			1989		*Cassette only*	
Capitol 7PRO-79842	DJ	A Girl Like You (same on both sides)				
			1989	3.75	7.50	15.00
Capitol/Enigma 44150		Only a Memory/The Seeker	1988		2.50	5.00
Add 100% to values for promo copy						
Capitol/Enigma 44150	PS	Only a Memory/The Seeker	1988		2.50	5.00
Capitol/Enigma 44174		House We Used to Live In/Only a Memory				
			1988		*Unreleased*	
Capitol/Enigma 44174	DJ	House We Used to Live In (same on both sides)				
			1988	2.50	5.00	10.00
Capitol/Enigma 44174	PS	House We Used to Live In/Only a Memory				
			1988	125.00	250.00	500.00

Was supposed to accompany this single's commercial release; when that was canceled, a handful of the sleeves escaped. This sleeve has been called "(their) 'Street Fighting Man'." No sales have been documented. Value is estimated and may be much lower or muuch higher.

Label, Number		Title	Year	VG	VG+	NM
Capitol/Enigma 44238		Drown in My Own Tears/House We Used to Live In				
			1988		3.00	6.00
Enigma 75002		Behind the Wall of Sleep/Blood and Roses				
			1986	2.50	5.00	10.00
Enigma 75002	PS	Behind the Wall of Sleep/Blood and Roses				
			1986		2.50	5.00
Enigma 75003		In a Lonely Place/Blood and Roses (Live)				
			1986	2.50	5.00	10.00
Enigma 75003	PS	In a Lonely Place/Blood and Roses (Live)				
			1986		2.50	5.00
RCA 62803	DJ	Sick of Seattle + 2	1993		3.75	7.50
RCA 62803	PS	Sick of Seattle + 2	1993		3.75	7.50
RCA Victor 62807	(4)	A Date with the Smithereens	1994	5.00	10.00	20.00

Boxed set of 4 EPs with 4 picture sleeves, comprising 12 remixed tracks from the CD of the same name plus three bonus tracks. Price is for entire package

Label, Number		Title	Year	VG	VG+	NM
12-Inch Singles						
Capitol SPRO-79276	DJ	Only a Memory (same on both sides)				
			1988	2.00	4.00	8.00
Capitol/Enigma SPRO-79335	DJ	House We Used to Live In (same on both sides)				
			1988		3.00	6.00
Enigma EPRO 5	DJ	Blood and Roses (same on both sides)				
			1986	2.50	5.00	10.00
Enigma EPRO 14	DJ	Behind the Wall of Sleep (same on both sides)				
			1986	2.00	4.00	8.00
Enigma EPRO 21	DJ	Behind the Wall of Sleep/(two more songs)				
			1986	2.00	4.00	8.00
Enigma EPRO 22	DJ	In a Lonely Place (same on both sides)				
			1986		3.50	7.00
Enigma EPRO 26	DJ	Time and Time Again (same on both sides)				
			1986		3.00	6.00
Enigma 75501		In a Lonely Place//Behind the Wall of Sleep (Live)/				
		Beauty and Sadness (Live)	1986	2.50	5.00	10.00

Label, Number		Title	Year	VG	VG+	NM

Smiths, The

*British gloom-rockers. Johnny Marr later was with **Electronic**. Lead singer **Morrissey went solo.***

Vinyl Albums

Label, Number		Title	Year	VG	VG+	NM
Sire 25065		The Smiths	1984	2.50	5.00	10.00
Sire 25269		Meat Is Murder	1985	2.50	5.00	10.00
Sire 25426		The Queen Is Dead	1986	2.50	5.00	10.00
Sire 25649		Strangeways, Here We Come	1987	2.50	5.00	10.00
Sire 25669	(2)	Louder Than Bombs	1987	3.75	7.50	15.00
Sire 25786		"Rank"	1988	2.50	5.00	10.00
Warner Bros. WBMS-130	DJ	The Warner Bros. Music Show	1985	3.50	7.00	14.00

One side: The Smiths; the other side: The Blasters

45s

Label, Number		Title	Year	VG	VG+	NM
Sire 28136		Stop Me If You Think You've Heard This One Before/ I Keep Mine Hidden	1987		2.50	5.00
Sire 28136	PS	Stop Me If You Think You've Heard This One Before/ I Keep Mine Hidden	1987	2.50	5.00	10.00
Sire 29007		How Soon Is Now?/Shakespear's Sister/Headmaster Ritual	1985	3.75	7.50	15.00
Sire 29007	PS	How Soon Is Now?/Shakespear's Sister/Headmaster Ritual	1985	5.00	10.00	20.00
Sire 29239		What Difference Does It Make/Back to the Old Home	1984	2.50	5.00	10.00
Sire 29239	PS	What Difference Does It Make/Back to the Old Home	1984	5.00	10.00	20.00

12-Inch Singles

Label, Number		Title	Year	VG	VG+	NM
Sire PRO-A-2843	DJ	Girlfriend in a Coma (same on both sides)	1987	5.00	10.00	20.00
Sire PRO-A-2893	DJ	Stop Me If You've Heard This One Before (same on both sides)	1987	3.75	7.50	15.00
Sire 20284		How Soon Is Now? (long 6:43) (edit)/Girl Afraid	1984	3.00	6.00	12.00
Sire 20392		The Boy with the Thorn in His Side/Rubber Ring/Asleep	1986	3.00	6.00	12.00
Sire 20544		Panic/Vicar in a Tutu/The Draize Train	1986	3.75	7.50	15.00
Sire 20591		Ask/Cemetery Gates/Golden Lights	1986	2.50	5.00	10.00
Sire 40583		This Charming Man (7 versions)/Wonderful Woman	1990	4.50	9.00	18.00

Smoking Popes

Crystal Lake, Illinois' contribution to modern rock.

45s

Label, Number	Title	Year	VG	VG+	NM
Capitol S7-18841	Need You Around/Supermodel	1995			3.00

*B-side by **Jill Sobule***

Sniff 'N' The Tears

British pop-rock group.

Vinyl Albums

Label, Number	Title	Year	VG	VG+	NM
Atlantic SD 19242	Fickle Heart	1979	2.50	5.00	10.00

Some pressings erroneously contain an edit of "Driver's Seat" with the entire first verse missing

Label, Number	Title	Year	VG	VG+	NM
Atlantic SD 19242	Fickle Heart	1979	3.50	7.00	14.00

With full version of "Driver's Seat"

Label, Number	Title	Year	VG	VG+	NM
Atlantic SD 19272	The Game's Up	1980	2.50	5.00	10.00
MCA 821	Love Action	1983	2.00	4.00	8.00

Budget-line reissue

Label, Number	Title	Year	VG	VG+	NM
MCA 5242	Love Action	1981	2.50	5.00	10.00

Label, Number		Title	Year	VG	VG+	NM

45s

Atlantic 3604		Driver's Seat/Slide Away	1979		2.00	4.00
Atlantic 3626		New Lines on Love/Fight for Love				
			1979		2.00	4.00

Snowbud

45s

Sub Pop 219		Killer Bud/3rd Shelf	1993		2.50	5.00
Sub Pop 219	PS	Killer Bud/3rd Shelf	1993		2.50	5.00
#58 in Sub Pop Singles Club series						

Sobule, Jill

Alterna-rocker from Denver by way of Nashville. Best known for "I Kissed a Girl" (unavailable on vinyl).

Vinyl Albums

MCA 6375		Things Here Are Different	1990	4.00	8.00	16.00

45s

Capitol S7-18841		Supermodel/Need You Around	1995			3.00
*B-side by **Smoking Popes***						

Social Distortion

Los Angeles-based punk/grunge/noise band.

Vinyl Albums

Epic E 46055		Social Distortion	1990	3.00	6.00	12.00
Epic E 47948		Somewhere Between Heaven and Hell				
			1992	3.00	6.00	12.00
Restless 72251		Prison Bound	1988	3.00	6.00	12.00
Triple X 51019		Mommy's Little Monster	1989	3.00	6.00	12.00
Clear vinyl						

45s

(No label or number)		Ball & Chain (Skeletal Mix) (same on both sides)				
			1990	2.00	4.00	8.00
KROQ (Los Angeles)-related promo dated 12-21-90						
Epic ES7 4568	DJ	Cold Feelings/Bad Luck (Live Acoustic)				
			1992		2.00	4.00
Epic 74229		Bad Luck/Bye Bye Baby	1992			3.00
Posh Boy PBS 11		Mainliner/Playpen	1981	3.00	6.25	12.50
Posh Boy PBS 11	PS	Mainliner/Playpen	1981	3.00	6.25	12.50
Social Distortion (# unknown)		1945/Under My Thumb/Playpen				
			1982	7.50	15.00	30.00
Social Distortion (# unknown)	PS	1945/Under My Thumb/Playpen				
			1982	7.50	15.00	30.00
Sleeve notes distribution by Faulty Products						
Social Distortion 4502		Mommy's Little Monster/Another State of Mind				
			1983	4.00	8.00	16.00
Social Distortion 4502	PS	Mommy's Little Monster/Another State of Mind				
			1983	4.00	8.00	16.00
Triple X 51023-7		Another State of Mind/Mommy's Little Monster				
			1989		2.50	5.00
Clear vinyl						
Triple X 51023-7	PS	Another State of Mind/Mommy's Little Monster				
			1989		2.50	5.00

12-Inch Singles

13th Story SD 4501		1945/Under My Thumb/Playpen	1985	3.75	7.50	15.00
Epic EAS 2120	DJ	Ring of Fire/Lonesome Train	1990	3.75	7.50	15.00
Epic EAS 4348	DJ	Bad Luck (same on both sides)	1992	3.75	7.50	15.00

Label, Number		Title	Year	VG	VG+	NM

Social Unrest
Northern California punk band.

Vinyl Albums
Libertine LSU 1	EP	Rat in a Maze	1982	6.25	12.50	25.00
Libertine LSU 2461		SU-2000	1985	5.00	10.00	20.00

45s
Infa Red 001		Making Room for Youth/Rush Hour				
			1981	6.25	12.50	25.00
Infa Red 001	PS	Making Room for Youth/Rush Hour				
			1981	6.25	12.50	25.00

Soft Cell
British synth-pop duo.

Vinyl Albums
Sire BSK 3647		Non-Stop Erotic Cabaret	1981	3.00	6.00	12.00
Sire 23694	EP	Non-Stop Ecstatic Dancing	1982	2.50	5.00	10.00
Sire 23769		The Art of Falling Apart	1983	3.00	6.00	12.00
With limited 12-inch EP						
Sire 23989	EP	Soul Inside	1983	2.50	5.00	10.00
Sire 25096		This Last Night	1984	2.50	5.00	10.00

45s
Sire GSRE 0435		Tainted Love/Where Did Our Love Go//What				
			1983		2.00	4.00
Back to Back Hits series; First release of medley on U.S. stock 45						
Sire PRO-S-1028	DJ	Tainted Love/Where Did Our Love Go (Long)//Tainted Love/ Where Did Our Love Go (Short)				
			1982	2.50	5.00	10.00
Sire 29641		Heat/It's a Mugs Game	1983		2.00	4.00
Sire 29812		Loving You Hating Me/It's a Mugs Game				
			1983	2.25	4.50	9.00
Sire 29812	DJ	Loving You Hating Me (mono/stereo)				
			1983			3.00
Sire 29812	PS	Loving You Hating Me/It's a Mugs Game				
			1983			3.00
Sire 29976		What!/A Man Could Get Lost	1982		2.00	4.00
Sire 49855		Tainted Love/Memorabilia	1981			3.00
Sire 49855	PS	Tainted Love/Memorabilia	1981		3.00	6.00

12-Inch Singles
Amnesia 62201		It's a Mugs Game (7" and 12" mixes)/Sex Dwarf				
			1981	5.00	10.00	20.00
Sire PRO-A-1037	DJ	What!/Insecure Me	1982	3.75	7.50	15.00
Sire PRO-A-1096	DJ	Loving You, Hating Me (2 versions)/Heat				
			1983	3.00	6.00	12.00
Sire 49856		Tainted Love-Where Did Our Love Go/Memorabilia/Tainted Dub				
			1981	2.00	4.00	8.00

Soho
London pop-rock trio. Their hit "Hippychick" samples **The Smiths'** *"How Soon is Now?".*

Vinyl Albums
Atco 91585		Goddess	1990	3.00	6.00	12.00

45s
Atco 98908		Hippychick/Taxi	1990		2.00	4.00

12-Inch Singles
Atco 1637	DJ	Freaky (6 mixes)	1990		3.50	7.00
Atco 1842	DJ	Ride (6 versions)	1991	2.00	4.00	8.00

Label, Number		Title	Year	VG	VG+	NM
Atco 1896	DJ	Radio Soul Groove (4 versions) 1991			3.00	6.00

Sonic Youth

*Punk legends. Also see **Moore, Thurston; Ciccone Youth**.*

Vinyl Albums

Label, Number		Title	Year	VG	VG+	NM
DGC 24297		Goo	1990	5.00	10.00	20.00
DGC 24485		Dirty	1992	5.00	10.00	20.00
DGC 24632		Experimental Jet Set, Trash and No Star				
			1994	2.50	5.00	10.00
DGC 24825	(2)	Washing Machine	1995	3.75	7.50	15.00
Enigma 75403	(2)	Daydream Nation	1988	5.00	10.00	20.00
Homestead HMS 016		Bad Moon Rising	1985	5.00	10.00	20.00
Homestead HMS 021	EP	Death Valley '69	1985	5.00	10.00	20.00
*With **Lydia Lunch***						
Mobile Fidelity 1-257		Goo	1996	5.00	10.00	20.00
Original Master Recording						
Neutral N-1	EP	Sonic Youth	1982	12.50	25.00	50.00
Neutral 001	EP	Sonic Youth	1982	12.50	25.00	50.00
Neutral 9		Confusion Is Sex	1983	10.00	20.00	40.00
Rhino R1 71591		Made in U.S.A. (Soundtrack)	1995	2.50	5.00	10.00
Clear vinyl record and sleeve; music recorded in 1986						
SST 059		Evol	1986	3.75	7.50	15.00
SST 080	EP	Starpower	1986	3.75	7.50	15.00
SST 096		Confusion Is Sex	1987	3.75	7.50	15.00
Reissue of Neutral 9						
SST 097	EP	Sonic Youth	1987	3.00	6.00	12.00
SST 134		Sister	1987	3.75	7.50	15.00
SST 155	EP	Master Dik	1988	3.00	6.00	12.00

45s

Label, Number		Title	Year	VG	VG+	NM
DGC 106610	DJ	Goo	1990	2.50	5.00	10.00
Promo flexi-disc with backing card						
DGC 19664		Personality Crisis/Dirty Boots	1990	3.75	7.50	15.00
Given away with copies of Sassy magazine						
Forced Exposure 001		Making the Nature Scene/ I Killed Christgau with				
		My Big Fuckin' Dick	1984	30.00	60.00	120.00
Test pressing (25 made with special sleeve)						
Forced Exposure 001	PS	Making the Nature Scene/I Killed Christgau with				
		My Big Fuckin' Dick	1984	30.00	60.00	120.00
Special multi-color sleeve with live band shot on rear; only released with test pressings (25 made)						
Forced Exposure 001		Making the Nature Scene/I Killed Christgau with				
		My Big Fuckin' Dick	1984	12.50	25.00	50.00
Forced Exposure 001	PS	Making the Nature Scene/I Killed Christgau with				
		My Big Fuckin' Dick	1984	12.50	25.00	50.00
Black and white sleeve						
Forced Exposure 012		Silver Rocket/You Pose You Lose/Non-Metal Dude				
		Wearing Metal Tee	1988	6.25	12.50	25.00
Forced Exposure 012	PS	Silver Rocket/You Pose You Lose/Non-Metal Dude				
		Wearing Metal Tee	1988	6.25	12.50	25.00
Iridescence 12		Death Valley 69/Brave Men Run				
			1984	3.00	6.25	12.50
*With **Lydia Lunch***						
Iridescence 12	PS	Death Valley 69/Brave Men Run				
			1984	3.00	6.25	12.50
Sub Pop 26		Touch Me I'm Sick/Halloween	1988	7.50	15.00	30.00
*B-side by **Mudhoney**; clear vinyl*						
Sub Pop 26		Touch Me I'm Sick/Halloween	1988	3.75	7.50	15.00
*B-side by **Mudhoney**; black vinyl*						
Sub Pop 26	PS	Touch Me I'm Sick/Halloween	1988	5.00	10.00	20.00
#2 in Sub Pop Singles Club series						

Label, Number		Title	Year	VG	VG+	NM
12-Inch Singles						
Blast First BFUS 34		Teenage Riot (edit)/Silver Rocket/Kissability				
			1988	2.50	5.00	10.00
DGC 4123	DJ	Kool Thing/Kool Thing (8-track demo)				
			1990	3.00	6.00	12.00
DGC 4172	DJ	Disappear (3 versions)	1991	2.00	4.00	8.00
Enigma EPRO 182	DJ	Candle (Edit)/Hey Joni (Live)/Flower (Live)/Ghost Bitch (Live)				
			1989	6.25	12.50	25.00
Homestead HMS 047		Flower/Halloween	1986	6.25	12.50	25.00

Soul Asylum

Minneapolis-based alterna-rockers.

Label, Number		Title	Year	VG	VG+	NM
Vinyl Albums						
A&M SP-5197		Hang Time	1988	3.00	6.00	12.00
A&M SP-5318		...And the Horse They Rode In On				
			1990	3.00	6.00	12.00
Columbia C 48898		Grave Dancers Union	1993	3.00	6.00	12.00
Columbia C 57616		Let Your Dim Light Shine	1995	2.50	5.00	10.00
Twin/Tone TTR 8439		Say What You Will, Clarence...Karl Sold the Truck				
			1984	3.00	6.00	12.00
Twin/Tone TTR 8666		Made to Be Broken	1986	3.00	6.00	12.00
Twin/Tone TTR 8691		While You Were Out	1986	3.00	6.00	12.00
Twin/Tone TTR 88144	EP	Clam Dip & Other Delights	1988	2.00	4.00	8.00
45s						
Columbia 74966		Runaway Train/Never Really Been (Live)				
			1993			*Cassette only*
Columbia 77959		Misery/Hope	1995			3.00
Columbia 77959	PS	Misery/Hope	1995			3.00
Columbia 78215		Promises Broken/Can't Even Tell (Live)				
			1996			2.00
Columbia 78215	PS	Promises Broken/Can't Even Tell (Live)				
			1996			2.00
Twin/Tone TTR 8560		Tied to the Tracks/Long Way Home				
			1985	3.00	6.25	12.50
Twin/Tone TTR 8560	PS	Tied to the Tracks/Long Way Home				
			1985	3.00	6.25	12.50
12-Inch Singles						
A&M 17552	DJ	Sometime to Return (same on both sides)				
			1988		3.00	6.00
A&M 17610	DJ	Standing in the Doorway/James at 16 medley				
			1988	2.00	4.00	8.00
A&M 75021 7401 1	DJ	Spinning/All the King's Friends	1990		3.00	6.00
A&M 75021 7410 1	DJ	Easy Street/One Way Conversation				
			1991	2.50	5.00	10.00
A&M 75021 7503 1	DJ	Something Out of Nothing/Freaks (Live)/To Sir with Love (Live)/				
		Marionette (Live)	1990	5.00	10.00	20.00

Soundgarden

Seattle band, both grungy and heavy.

Label, Number		Title	Year	VG	VG+	NM
Vinyl Albums						
A&M SP-5252		Louder Than Love	1989	12.50	25.00	60.00
Green vinyl						
A&M SP-5252		Louder Than Love	1989	10.00	20.00	40.00
Red vinyl						
A&M SP-5252		Louder Than Love	1989	5.00	10.00	20.00
A&M SP-17951	DJ	Louder Than Live	1990	12.50	25.00	50.00
Promo-only live album on blue vinyl						

This is the rear cover of *Beauty and Sadness,* the Smithereens' 12-inch EP on Little Ricky Records ($40). A remixed and shortened version of this later came out on Enigma.

As if to make up for the lack of American vinyl singles from their breakthrough album *Grave Dancers Union* (even "Runaway Train" is available on 45 only on import), Soul Asylum's recent American singles have had attractive picture sleeves, such as this from the 1996 "Promises Broken" ($2 now, but it'll go up).

Label, Number		Title	Year	VG	VG+	NM
A&M 31454 0198 1	(2)	Superunknown	1994	3.75	7.50	15.00
Gold vinyl						
A&M 31454 0198 1	(2)	Superunknown	1994	3.75	7.50	15.00
Blue vinyl						
A&M 31454 0198 1	(2)	Superunknown	1994	3.75	7.50	15.00
Clear vinyl						
A&M 31454 0526 1	(2)	Down on the Upside	1996	3.00	6.00	12.00
Colored vinyl						
A&M 75021 5374 1		Badmotorfinger	1991	5.00	10.00	20.00
Limited edition on yellow vinyl						
SST 201		Ultramega OK	1988	3.75	7.50	15.00
SST 231	EP	Flower	1988	3.75	7.50	15.00
SST 911	10	Flower	1988	2.50	5.00	10.00
Sub Pop 12	EP	Screaming Life	1987	37.50	75.00	150.00
First 500 copies on orange vinyl						
Sub Pop 12	EP	Screaming Life	1987	10.00	20.00	40.00
Sub Pop 12	EP	Screaming Life	1987	2.50	5.00	10.00
Recent reissue on colored vinyl (not the same as the orange one)						
Sub Pop 17	EP	Fopp	1988	15.00	30.00	60.00

45s

Label, Number		Title	Year	VG	VG+	NM
A&M 31458 0766 7		Black Hole Sun/Spoonman	1994			3.00
A&M 31458 0974 7		Fell On Black Days/My Wave	1995			3.00
Sub Pop 12a		Hunted Down/Nothing to Say	1987	16.25	32.50	65.00
500 copies pressed, all on blue vinyl						
Sub Pop 12a	PS	Hunted Down/Nothing to Say	1987	16.25	32.50	65.00
Special blue sleeve (not a PS) with above						
Sub Pop 83		Room a Thousand Years Wide/H.I.V. Baby				
			1990	3.75	7.50	15.00
Black vinyl; bonus in Sub Pop Singles Club series						
Sub Pop 83		Room a Thousand Years Wide/H.I.V. Baby				
			1990	7.50	15.00	30.00
Grape vinyl						
Sub Pop 83	PS	Room a Thousand Years Wide/H.I.V. Baby				
			1990	5.00	10.00	20.00

12-Inch Singles

Label, Number		Title	Year	VG	VG+	NM
A&M 75021 7290 1	DJ	Jesus Christ Pose/Drawing Flies	1992	2.00	4.00	8.00
A&M 75021 7338 1	DJ	Rusty Cage (2 versions)/Girl U Want/Show Me/Into the Void				
			1991	3.75	7.50	15.00
A&M SP-17896	DJ	Hands All Over (same on both sides)				
			1989	5.00	10.00	20.00
A&M SP-17933	DJ	Loud Love (same on both sides)	1989	5.00	10.00	20.00

Soup Dragons

Glasgow, Scotland-based pop-rock group.

Vinyl Albums

Label, Number		Title	Year	VG	VG+	NM
Big Life/Mercury 842 985-1		Lovegod	1990	3.00	6.00	12.00
Mercury 522 732-1	(2)	Hydrophonic	1994	3.00	6.00	12.00
Clear vinyl						
Sire 25666		Hang Ten!	1987	2.00	4.00	8.00
Sire 25702		This Is Our Art	1988	2.00	4.00	8.00

45s

Label, Number		Title	Year	VG	VG+	NM
Fontana 865 604-7		Divine Thing/Driving	1992		2.00	4.00

12-Inch Singles

Label, Number		Title	Year	VG	VG+	NM
Big Life 897	DJ	Backwards Dog (3 versions)	1989	2.00	4.00	8.00
Big Life PRO 1010		Pleasure (2 remixes)	1990	2.50	5.00	10.00
Big Life 877 843-1		I'm Free (3 versions)/Lovegod (Dub)				
			1990	2.00	4.00	8.00
Big Life 879 545-1		Mother Universe (2 versions)/Sweetheart/Softly (Live)				
			1991		3.00	6.00

Label, Number		Title	Year	VG	VG+	NM
Sire PRO-A-2965	DJ	Majestic Head (same on both sides)				
			1988	3.00	6.00	12.00

Southern Culture on the Skids
Country-punk band from North Carolina.

Vinyl Albums

Telstar 20		Dirt Track Date	1995	3.00	6.00	12.00

7-Inch Extended Play Singles

S.C.O.T.S. (no #)		Live to 2 Tracks	198?		3.00	6.00
S.C.O.T.S. (no #)	PS	Live to 2 Tracks	198?		3.00	6.00
Four-photo folder sleeve with 7x7 art, "low-fi" inserts and Lewis address						
S.C.O.T.S. (no #)	PS	Live to 2 Tracks	198?	2.25	4.50	9.00
Larger folder sleeve, different insert and Lloyd St. address with extra spray-paint art						
S.C.O.T.S. (no #)	PS	Live to 2 Tracks	198?		3.00	6.00
Larger folder sleeve, different insert and Lloyd St. address						

45s

DGC Geffen 19392		Soul City/Voodoo Cadillac	1995			3.00
Moist (# unknown)		Clyde's Lament/CW James/Double-O Spy				
			1990			3.00
Moist (# unknown)	PS	Clyde's Lament/CW James/Double-O Spy				
			1990			3.00

Spacemen 3

45s

Forced Exposure 017		Transparent Radiation/Honey	1989	18.75	37.50	75.00
Test pressing (25 made)						
Forced Exposure 017	PS	Transparent Radiation/Honey	1989	18.75	37.50	75.00
Full-color pasted-on art; accompanied test pressing (25 made)						
Forced Exposure 017		Transparent Radiation/Honey	1989	6.25	12.50	25.00
Forced Exposure 017	PS	Transparent Radiation/Honey	1989	6.25	12.50	25.00

Spandau Ballet
English synth-pop group.

Vinyl Albums

Chrysalis CHR 1331		Journeys to Glory	1981	3.00	6.00	12.00
Chrysalis CHR 1353		Diamond	1982	2.50	5.00	10.00
Chrysalis FV 41331		Journeys to Glory	198?	2.00	4.00	8.00
Reissue						
Chrysalis FV 41353		Diamond	1983	2.00	4.00	8.00
Reissue						
Chrysalis PV 41353		Diamond	1986	2.00	4.00	8.00
Reissue						
Chrysalis B6V 41403		True	1983	3.00	6.00	12.00
Chrysalis FV 41403		True	1983	2.00	4.00	8.00
Reissue						
Chrysalis FV 41473		Parade	1984	2.50	5.00	10.00
Chrysalis FV 41498		The Singles Collection	1985	2.50	5.00	10.00
Epic FE 40642		Through the Barricades	1987	3.00	6.00	12.00
Mobile Fidelity 1-152		True	1984	6.25	12.50	25.00
Original Master Recording						

45s

Chrysalis 2473		To Cut a Long Story Short/(B-side unknown)				
			1981		2.50	5.00
Chrysalis 2528		Chant No. 1/Feel the Chant	1981		2.50	5.00
Chrysalis 42686		Lifeline/(B-side unknown)	1983		2.00	4.00
Chrysalis 42720		True/Gently	1983			3.00
Chrysalis 42720	PS	True/Gently	1983			3.00

Label, Number		Title	Year	VG	VG+	NM
Chrysalis 42743		Gold/Gold (Live)	1983			3.00
Chrysalis 42743	PS	Gold/Gold (Live)	1983			3.00
Chrysalis 42770		Communication/Code of Love	1984			3.00
Chrysalis 42792		Only When You Leave/Paint Me Down				
			1984			3.00
Chrysalis 42792	PS	Only When You Leave/Paint Me Down				
			1984			3.00
Chrysalis 42950		Chant No. 1/Lifeline	1985			3.00
Silver label reissue						
Chrysalis 42951		True/Gold	1985			3.00
Silver label reissue						
Chrysalis 42952		Communication/Only When You Leave				
			1985			3.00
Silver label reissue						
Epic 06664		How Man Lies/Snakes and Lovers				
			1987			3.00
Epic 07190		Through the Barricades/Snakes and Lovers				
			1987			3.00
12-Inch Singles						
Chrysalis AS 1630	DJ	Lifeline (same on both sides)	1983		3.00	6.00
Chrysalis CDS-2528		Chant No. 1/Feel the Chant//To Cut a Long Story Short				
			1981		3.00	6.00
Chrysalis CDS-2598		Instinction/Glow	1982		3.00	6.00
Chrysalis 42740		Gold (Extended)/(Instrumental)	1983	2.00	4.00	8.00
Chrysalis 42805		Only When You Leave (2 versions)/Paint Me Down (Live)				
			1984		3.00	6.00
Epic EAS 02664	DJ	How Many Lies (same on both sides)				
			1986		3.50	7.00

Specials, The

Leader of the ska revival in England in the late-1970s. Formed own label, 2-Tone. Also known as "The Special AKA". Ex- members created **Fun Boy Three**.

Vinyl Albums						
Chrysalis CHR 1265		The Specials	1979	3.75	7.50	15.00
Chrysalis CHR 1303		More Specials	1980	3.00	6.00	12.00
Chrysalis PV 41265		The Specials	1986	2.50	5.00	10.00
Reissue						
Chrysalis PV 41303		More Specials	1983	2.00	4.00	8.00
Reissue						
45s						
Chrysalis/2 Tone 2374		Gangsters/The Selecter	1979		2.00	4.00
B-side by **The Selecter**						
Chrysalis/2 Tone 2374	PS	Gangsters/The Selecter	1979	2.00	4.00	8.00
Sleeve says "The Specials," theoretically for use with any Specials single						
Chrysalis 42794		Free Nelson Mandela/Break Down the Door				
			1984	2.50	5.00	10.00
12-Inch Singles						
Chrysalis/2 Tone CDS-2525		Ghost Town/Why/Friday Night, Saturday Morning				
			1981	2.50	5.00	10.00
Chrysalis 42793		Free Nelson Mandela (3 mixes)	1984	2.50	5.00	10.00

Speech

Former rapper with **Arrested Development**.

45s						
Chrysalis S7-18947		Like Marvin Gaye Said (What's Going On)/ Impregnated Tidbits of Dope Hits				
			1995			3.00

Label, Number	Title	Year	VG	VG+	NM

Spencer, Jon, Blues Explosion

Vinyl Albums

Caroline 1719	Jon Spencer Blues Explosion	1992	2.50	5.00	10.00
Crypt 29	Crypt Style	1991	3.75	7.50	15.00
Matador OLE 52-1	Extra Width	1993	3.00	6.00	12.00
Matador OLE 105-1	Orange	1994	2.50	5.00	10.00

45s

In The Red ITR 007	Shirt Jac/Latch On	1992	3.75	7.50	15.00
In The Red ITR 011	Son of Sam/Bent	1992	3.75	7.50	15.00
In The Red ITR 019	Train #3/Train #1	1993	3.00	6.00	12.00
Sub Pop 180	Big Yule Log Boogie/My Christmas Wish	1992	5.00	10.00	20.00
Green vinyl					
Sub Pop 180	Big Yule Log Boogie/My Christmas Wish	1992	12.50	25.00	50.00

Mispress on clear lilac vinyl; labels claim this is "Max Gomez Love"/"Assassin" by Wolverton Bros.

Sub Pop 180 PS	Big Yule Log Boogie/My Christmas Wish	1992	5.00	10.00	20.00

#51 in Sub Pop Singles Club series

Spin Doctors

New York alterna-rockers.

Vinyl Albums

Epic E 52907	Turn It Upside Down	1994	2.50	5.00	10.00

45s

Epic 74910	How Could You Want Him/Hard to Exist	1993		3.00
Epic 74929	Jimmy Olsen's Blues/Yo Mamas A Pajama	1993		3.00
Epic 77525	Cleopatra's Cat/Uranium Century	1994		3.00
Epic 77600	You Let Your Heart Go Too Fast/Cleopatra's Cat	1994		3.00
Epic 77714	Mary Jane/Hungry Hamed's	1994		3.00
Epic Associated 74473	Little Miss Can't Be Wrong/Two Princes	1992	2.00	4.00

Split Enz

*Australian pop band. Founding member Neil Finn later founded **Crowded House. Tim Finn** recorded mostly solo.*

Vinyl Albums

A&M SP-3153	Frenzy	1981	3.00	6.00	12.00
First U.S. issue of 1979 recording					
A&M SP-3235	True Colours	198?	2.00	4.00	8.00
Reissue					
A&M SP-3255	Waiata	198?	2.00	4.00	8.00
Reissue					
A&M SP-3256	Time & Tide	198?	2.00	4.00	8.00
Reissue					
A&M SP-3289	History Never Repeats: The Best of Split Enz	1987	2.50	5.00	10.00
A&M SP-4822	True Colors	1980	2.50	5.00	10.00
Album jacket exists with many different color backgrounds (red, yellow, green, etc.) All are worth about the same.					
A&M SP-4848	Waiata	1981	2.50	5.00	10.00
A&M SP-4894	Time & Tide	1982	3.00	6.00	12.00
A&M SP-4963	Conflicting Emotions	1984	2.50	5.00	10.00
Chrysalis CHR 1131	Mental Notes	1976	3.00	6.00	12.00

Label, Number		Title	Year	VG	VG+	NM
Chrysalis CHR 1145		Disrythmia	1977	3.00	6.00	12.00
Chrysalis PV 41131		Mental Notes	198?	2.00	4.00	8.00
Budget-line reissue						
Chrysalis PV 41145		Disrythmia	198?	2.00	4.00	8.00
Budget-line reissue						

45s

Label, Number		Title	Year	VG	VG+	NM
A&M 2252		I Got You/Double Happy	1980		2.00	4.00
A&M 2252	PS	I Got You/Double Happy	1980	2.00	4.00	8.00
A&M 2285		I Hope I Never/Choral Sea	1980		3.00	6.00
A&M 2285	PS	I Hope I Never/Choral Sea	1980		2.00	4.00
A&M 2293		What's the Matter with Me/Nobody Takes Me Seriously				
			1980		2.00	4.00
A&M 2339		One Step Ahead/In the Wars	1981		2.50	5.00
First pressing: Laser-etched design on record						
A&M 2339		One Step Ahead/In the Wars	1981		2.00	4.00
Regular release						
A&M 2339	PS	One Step Ahead/In the Wars	1981		2.50	5.00
Special picture sleeve for laser-etched single						
A&M 2339	PS	One Step Ahead/In the Wars	1981		2.00	4.00
No reference to laser-etched single on sleeve						
A&M 2351		Iris/Clumsy	1981			3.00
A&M 2411		Six Months in a Leaky Boat/Make Sense of It				
			1982			3.00
A&M 2411	PS	Six Months in a Leaky Boat/Make Sense of It				
			1982			3.00
A&M 2430	DJ	Dirty Creature (same on both sides)				
			1982		2.50	5.00
A&M 2430		Dirty Creature/Make Sense of It	1982			*Unreleased*
A&M 2652		Message to My Girl/Kia Kaha	1984			3.00
A&M 2958		I Got You/(B-side unknown)	1987		2.50	5.00
Fan Club (no #)	DJ	Merry Christmas from Split Enz	1982	2.50	5.00	10.00
Green vinyl for members of fan club						

12-Inch Singles

Label, Number		Title	Year	VG	VG+	NM
A&M 17157	PD	I Don't Wanna Dance/Hard Act to Follow/History Never Repeats				
			1981	5.00	10.00	20.00
Promo-only picture disc						
A&M 17192	DJ	Six Months in a Leaky Boat/Hello Sandy Allen/				
		Never Ceases to Amaze	1982	2.00	4.00	8.00
A&M 17483	DJ	Message to My Girl/I Got You	1987	2.00	4.00	8.00

Squeeze

*British new-wave/pop band. During a hiatus, the band's chief writers recorded as **Difford and Tilbrook**.*

Vinyl Albums

Label, Number		Title	Year	VG	VG+	NM
A&M SP-3185		U.K. Squeeze	198?	2.00	4.00	8.00
Reissue						
A&M SP-3231		Cool for Cats	198?	2.00	4.00	8.00
Reissue						
A&M SP-3232		Argybargy	198?	2.00	4.00	8.00
Reissue						
A&M SP-3253		East Side Story	198?	2.00	4.00	8.00
Reissue						
A&M SP-3253		Sweets from a Stranger	198?	2.00	4.00	8.00
Reissue; none of these have 2-inch flap						
A&M SP-3413	EP	Six Squeeze Songs Crammed Into One 10-Inch Record				
			1979	2.50	5.00	10.00
10-inch EP in 12-inch "squeezed" jacket						
A&M SP-4687		U.K. Squeeze	1978	5.00	10.00	20.00
First pressing on red vinyl						
A&M SP-4687		U.K. Squeeze	1978	3.00	6.00	12.00
Later pressings on black vinyl						
A&M SP-4759		Cool for Cats	1979	3.00	6.00	12.00

Label, Number		Title	Year	VG	VG+	NM
A&M SP-4802		Argybargy	1980	3.00	6.00	12.00
A&M SP-4854		East Side Story	1981	2.50	5.00	10.00
A&M SP-4899		Sweets from a Stranger	1982	3.00	6.00	12.00
Original pressings have a 2-inch flap on the right side of the front cover with critics' raves						
A&M SP-4899		Sweets from a Stranger	1982	2.50	5.00	10.00
With flap removed or never there						
A&M SP-4922		Singles 45's and Under	1983	2.50	5.00	10.00
A&M SP-5085		Cosi Fan Tutti Frutti	1985	2.50	5.00	10.00
A&M SP-5161		Babylon and On	1987	2.50	5.00	10.00
A&M SP-5278		Frank	1989	2.50	5.00	10.00
A&M R 124200		Frank	1989	3.00	6.00	12.00
BMG Music Service edition						

45s

Label, Number		Title	Year	VG	VG+	NM
A&M 1457		If It's Love/Frank's Bag	1989		*May be cassette-only*	
A&M 1616		If I Didn't Love You/Another Nail in My Heart				
			1980	2.50	5.00	10.00
5-inch single with small hole, plays at 33 1/3 RPM						
A&M 1616	PS	If I Didn't Love You/Another Nail in My Heart				
			1980	2.50	5.00	10.00
Special "Tiny Collector's Edition" sleeve with above single						
A&M 2033	DJ	Take Me, I'm Yours (mono)/Take Me, I'm Yours (stereo)				
			1978		2.00	4.00
Label credit: U.K. Squeeze						
A&M 2033		Take Me, I'm Yours/Night Nurse				
			1978			
Label credit: U.K. Squeeze; the existence of this record as a stock copy has not been confirmed						
A&M 2146		Cool for Cats/Model	1979		2.00	4.00
A&M 2146	PS	Cool for Cats/Model	1979		2.00	4.00
A&M 2168		Goodbye Girl/Slightly Drunk	1979		2.00	4.00
A&M 2168	PS	Goodbye Girl/Slightly Drunk	1979		2.00	4.00
A&M 2229		If I Didn't Love You/Pretty One	1980		2.00	4.00
A&M 2229	PS	If I Didn't Love You/Pretty One	1980		3.00	6.00
A&M 2247		Pulling Mussels (From the Shell)/Pretty One				
			1980		2.00	4.00
A&M 2247	PS	Pulling Mussels (From the Shell)/Pretty One				
			1980		2.00	4.00
A&M 2263		Another Nail in My Heart//Going Crazy/What the Butler Saw				
			1980		2.00	4.00
A&M 2263	PS	Another Nail in My Heart//Going Crazy/What the Butler Saw				
			1980	2.00	4.00	8.00
A&M 2345		Tempted/Trust	1981			3.00
A&M 2345	PS	Tempted/Trust	1981		3.00	6.00
A&M 2377		Messed Around/Yap, Yap, Yap	1981			3.00
A&M 2413		I've Returned/When the Hangover Strikes				
			1982			3.00
A&M 2424		Black Coffee in Bed/The Hunt	1982			3.00
A&M 2424	PS	Black Coffee in Bed/The Hunt	1982	2.50	5.00	10.00
A tough sleeve to find						
A&M 2518		Annie Get Your Gun/Spanish Guitar				
			1983			3.00
A&M 2534		Another Nail in My Heart//Going Crazy/What the Butler Saw				
			1983			3.00
A&M 2776		Hits of the Year/Fortnight Saga	1985			3.00
A&M 2776	PS	Hits of the Year/Fortnight Saga	1985			3.00
A&M 2967		Hourglass/Wedding Bells	1987			3.00
A&M 2967	PS	Hourglass/Wedding Bells	1987			3.00
A&M 2994		853-5937/Take Me I'm Yours (Live)				
			1987			3.00
A&M 2994	PS	853-5937/Take Me I'm Yours (Live)				
			1987	2.00	4.00	8.00
A tough sleeve to find						

   In the minds of many who listened to college radio in the early 1980s, Split Enz and Squeeze are linked: They're both from abroad (though from different countries), they're close in the alphabet, they both recorded for A&M here, and neither got the acclaim it deserved. "I Got You" was Split Enz's first American single, and its sleeve is somewhat tough to find. Squeeze's sleeve for "If I Didn't Love You" is sought-after worldwide because it is unique to America.

Label, Number		Title	Year	VG	VG+	NM
A&M 3021		Footprints/Black Coffee in Bed (Live)				
			1988			3.00
A&M 8683		Tempted/Black Coffee in Bed	198?			3.00
Reissue						
RCA 62800		Tempted/My Sharona	1994		2.00	4.00
B-side by **The Knack**						
RCA 62800	PS	Tempted/My Sharona	1994		2.00	4.00
B-side by **The Knack**						
12-Inch Singles						
A&M 17158	DJ	Tempted/Is That Love/Messed Around				
			1981	2.00	4.00	8.00
A&M 17349	DJ	Hits of the Year/By Your Time/Last Time Forever				
			1985	2.00	4.00	8.00
A&M 17489	DJ	Hourglass (same on both sides)	1987	2.00	4.00	8.00

Stains, The

Hardcore band from Portland, Maine.

7-Inch Extended Play Singles						
Gutterworst 001		Feel Guilty/Give Ireland Back to the Snakes/Sick of Being Sick/				
		Submission	1980	5.00	10.00	20.00
Gutterworst 001	PS	Feel Guilty/Give Ireland Back to the Snakes/Sick of Being Sick/				
		Submission	1980	5.00	10.00	20.00
45s						
Radical (no #)		John Wayne Was a Nazi/Born to Die				
			1980	7.50	15.00	30.00
Radical (no #)	PS	John Wayne Was a Nazi/Born to Die				
			1980	7.50	15.00	30.00

Stamey, Chris

Later a member of **The dB's.**

45s						
Car 7		I Thought You Wanted to Know/If and When				
			1978	3.00	6.00	12.00
Car 7	PS	I Thought You Wanted to Know/If and When				
			1978	3.00	6.00	12.00
Car/Ork 2/81982		The Summer Sun/Where the Fun Is				
			1977		3.00	6.00
Car/Ork 2/81982	PS	The Summer Sun/Where the Fun Is				
			1977	3.75	7.50	15.00
Orange and black sleeve						
Car/Ork 2/81982	PS	The Summer Sun/Where the Fun Is				
			1977		3.00	6.00
Black and white sleeve						
Coyote (# unknown)		Christmas Time/Occasional Shivers				
			197?		2.50	5.00
Green vinyl						
Coyote (# unknown)	PS	Christmas Time/Occasional Shivers				
			197?		2.50	5.00
Actually a plain white sleeve with gold sticker						

Stansfield, Lisa

British soul singer. Also see **Coldcut.**

Vinyl Albums						
Arista AL9-8554		Affection	1990	2.50	5.00	10.00
Arista R 134198		Affection	1990	3.00	6.00	12.00
BMG Music Service edition						

Label, Number		Title	Year	VG	VG+	NM
45s						
Arista 2024		You Can't Deny It/Lay Me Down				
			1990			3.00
Arista 2049		This Is the Right Time/Apple Heart				
			1990			3.00
Arista 9928		All Around the World/Affection				
			1989			3.00
Arista 9928	PS	All Around the World/Affection				
			1989			3.00
Arista 12362		Change/It's Got to Be Real	1991			3.00
Arista 12398		All Woman/Everything Will Get Better				
			1991			3.00
Arista 12439		Time to Make You Mine/All Around the World				
			1992			*Cassette only*
B-side guest vocal: Barry White						
Arista 12449		A Little More Love/Set Your Loving Free				
			1992			*Cassette only*
12-Inch Singles						
Arista 2025		You Can't Deny It (3 mixes)/Lay Me Down				
			1990	2.00	4.00	8.00
Arista 2038		You Can't Deny It (4 versions)	1990		3.00	6.00
Arista 9929		All Around the World (2 mixes)/Affection				
			1989	2.00	4.00	8.00
Arista 12363		Change (3 mixes)/A Little More Love				
			1991	2.00	4.00	8.00
Arista 12399		Everything Will Get Better (3 mixes)/All Woman				
			1991	2.00	4.00	8.00
Arista 12451		A Little More Love (4 mixes)	1992	2.00	4.00	8.00
Giant PRO-A-7240	DJ	Make It Right (4 versions)	1994	2.00	4.00	8.00

Stereolab

Label, Number		Title	Year	VG	VG+	NM
45s						
Elektra 64615	DJ	Jenny Onioline Pt. 1/Golden Ball				
			1993	5.00	10.00	20.00
Clear vinyl in Elektra sleeve						
Teen Beat 121		Mountain/Where Are All Those Puerto Rican Boys?				
			1993	3.75	7.50	15.00
B-side by Unrest; special record sold on tour						
Teen Beat 121	PS	Mountain/Where Are All Those Puerto Rican Boys?				
			1993	3.75	7.50	15.00

Stevens, Shakin'

From Wales, a neo-rockabilly singer-songwriter.

Label, Number		Title	Year	VG	VG+	NM
Vinyl Albums						
Epic 3E 36924	10	Shakin' Stevens	1981	2.00	4.00	8.00
Epic FE 37415		Get Shakin'	1981	3.50	7.00	14.00
Epic ARE 38022		You Drive Me Crazy	1982	2.50	5.00	10.00
Epic BFE 38449		Give Me Your Heart Tonight	1983	2.50	5.00	10.00
Epic BFE 39286		The Bop Won't Stop	1983	2.50	5.00	10.00
45s						
Epic 02072		The Ole House/Let Me Show You How				
			1981			3.00
Epic 02217		You Drive Me Crazy/Let Me Show You How				
			1981			3.00
Epic 02865		Baby You're a Child/You Drive Me Crazy				
			1982			3.00
Epic 03508		I'll Be Satisfied/Boppity Bop	1983			3.00

Label, Number		Title	Year	VG	VG+	NM
Epic 04338		I Cry Just a Little Bit/Love Me Tonight				
			1984			3.00
Epic 04558		A Love Worth Waiting For/Why Do You Treat Me This Way				
			1984			3.00
12-Inch Singles						
Epic AS 1863	DJ	I Cry Just a Little Bit/(Instrumental)				
			1983	2.50	5.00	10.00

Stewart, Dave
The male half of Eurythmics.

Vinyl Albums						
Arista AL9-8626		Dave Stewart and the Spiritual Cowboys				
			1990	2.50	5.00	10.00
45s						
Arista 2112		Love Shines/Instant Karma	1990			3.00
Dave Stewart and the Spiritual Cowboys						
Arista 2187		Lily Was Here/Lily Was Here (DNA 7" Remix)				
			1991			3.00
David A. Stewart, Introducing Candy Dulfer						
12-Inch Singles						
Arista 2046		Party Town (Party On Down)/Party Town (Party Politico Mix)				
			1990		3.00	6.00
Dave Stewart and the Spiritual Cowboys						
Arista 2188		Lily Was Here (4 versions)	1991		3.50	7.00
David A. Stewart, Introducing Candy Dulfer						

Stiff Little Fingers
New-wave band from Belfast, Northern Ireland.

	Title	Year	VG	VG+	NM
Vinyl Albums					
Caroline 1377	See You Up There	1990	3.00	6.00	12.00
Chrysalis CHR 1270	Nobody's Heroes	1980	5.00	10.00	20.00
Chrysalis CHR 1300	Hanx	1980	5.00	10.00	20.00
Chrysalis CHR 1339	Go For It	1981	5.00	10.00	20.00
Rough Trade ROUGH US 5	Inflammable Material	1980	6.25	12.50	25.00
Released in U.K. in 1979					

Stimulators, The
New York City new-wave band.

		Title	Year	VG	VG+	NM
45s						
CB (# unknown)		Loud Fast Rules!/Run Run Run	1979	10.00	20.00	40.00
CB (# unknown)	PS	Loud Fast Rules!/Run Run Run	1979	10.00	20.00	40.00
A very difficult sleeve to find in near-mint, as the top inch or so of the oversized sleeve is usually mangled						

Sting
Formerly of The Police.

		Title	Year	VG	VG+	NM
Vinyl Albums						
A&M SP-3295	EP	...Nada Como El Sol	1988	2.50	5.00	10.00
Spanish versions of songs from "...Nothing Like the Sun"						
A&M SP-3750		The Dream of the Blue Turtles	1985	2.50	5.00	10.00
A&M SP-6402	(2)	...Nothing Like the Sun	1987	3.00	6.00	12.00
A&M R 150266		The Dream of the Blue Turtles	1985	3.00	6.00	12.00
RCA Music Service edition						
A&M R 273965	(2)	...Nothing Like the Sun	1987	3.50	7.00	14.00
BMG Direct Marketing edition						
A&M 75021 6405-1		The Soul Cages	1991	3.00	6.00	12.00

Label, Number		Title	Year	VG	VG+	NM
Mobile Fidelity 1-185 *Original Master Recording*		The Dream of the Blue Turtles	1985	7.50	15.00	30.00
45s						
A&M 1200		Englishman in New York/If You're There 1988				3.00
A&M 1200	PS	Englishman in New York/If You're There 1988				3.00
A&M 1211		Fragile/Gragilidad	1988			3.00
A&M 1242		They Dance Alone (Gueca Solo)/They Dance Alone (Gueca Solo) 1988				3.00
A&M 1541		All This Time/I Miss You Kate	1991		2.00	4.00
A&M 2501		Spread a Little Happiness/Only You 1982			2.00	4.00
A&M 2738		If You Love Somebody Set Them Free/Another Day 1985				3.00
Normal red and black label A&M 2738		If You Love Somebody Set Them Free/Another Day 1985			2.00	4.00
Blue custom label A&M 2738	PS	If You Love Somebody Set Them Free/Another Day 1985				3.00
A&M 2765		If You Love Somebody Set Them Free/Another Day 1985			2.50	5.00
A&M 2765	PS	If You Love Somebody Set Them Free/Another Day 1985			2.50	5.00
A&M 2767		Fortress Around Your Heart/Consider Me Gone 1985				3.00
A&M 2767	PS	Fortress Around Your Heart/Consider Me Gone 1985				3.00
A&M 2787		Love Is the Seventh Wave/The Dream of the Blue Turtles 1985				3.00
A&M 2787	PS	Love Is the Seventh Wave/The Dream of the Blue Turtles 1985				3.00
A&M 2799		Russians/Gabriel's Message	1985			3.00
A&M 2799	PS	Russians/Gabriel's Message	1985			3.00
A&M 2983		We'll Be Together/Conversation with a Dog 1987				3.00
A&M 2983	PS	We'll Be Together/Conversation with a Dog 1987				3.00
A&M 2992		Be Still My Beating Heart/Ghost in the Strand 1987				3.00
A&M 2992	PS	Be Still My Beating Heart/Ghost in the Strand 1987				3.00
A&M 8655		If You Love Somebody Set Them Free/Fortress Around Your Heart 198?				3.00
Reissue A&M 8656		Love Is the Seventh Wave/Russians 198?				3.00
Reissue A&M 8722		All This Time/Be Still My Beating Heart 199?				3.00
Reissue A&M 8723		The Soul Cages/Why Should I Cry for You? 199?				3.00
Reissue series; first appearance on U.S. 45 for both sides A&M 8740		Shape of My Heart/If I Ever Lose My Faith in You 1996				3.00
Reissue A&M 31458 0530 7		Shape of My Heart/If I Ever Lose My Faith in You 1994				3.00
A&M 31458 0838 7		When We Dance/Fields of Gold	1994			3.00

Label, Number		Title	Year	VG	VG+	NM
A&M 31458 1582 7		You Still Touch Me/Let Your Soul Be Your Pilot				
			1996			2.00
A&M 31458 1582 7	PS	You Still Touch Me/Let Your Soul Be Your Pilot				
			1996			2.00
12-Inch Singles						
A&M 12132		If You Love Somebody Set Them Free (3 versions)/Another Day				
			1985	2.00	4.00	8.00
Original copies have an insert						
A&M 12153		Love Is the Seventh Wave (2 versions)				
			1985		3.00	6.00
A&M 12164		Russians/Gabriel's Message/I Burn for You (Live)				
			1985		3.00	6.00
A&M 12251		We'll Be Together (4 versions)/Conversation with a Dog				
			1987	2.00	4.00	8.00
A&M 17216	DJ	I Burn for You/Only You	1982	2.50	5.00	10.00
A&M 17324	DJ	If You Love Somebody Set Them Free (same on both sides)				
			1985		3.00	6.00
A&M 17339	DJ	Fortress Around Your Heart/Consider Me Gone (Live)				
			1985		3.00	6.00
A&M 17526	DJ	Be Still My Beating Heart (2 versions)				
			1987		3.00	6.00
A&M 31458 0465 1		Demolition Man (6 versions)	1993	2.00	4.00	8.00
A&M 31458 8380 1	(2) DJ	When We Dance (3 versions)/If You Love Somebody Set Them Free (8 versions)/Demolition Man	1994	6.25	12.50	25.00

Stone Roses, The

Manchester, England pop band.

Vinyl Albums						
Silvertone 1184-1-J		The Stone Roses	1989	3.00	6.00	12.00
12-Inch Singles						
Silvertone 1301		I Wanna Be Adored (2 versions)/Going Down/Simeone				
			1989	2.00	4.00	8.00
Silvertone 1315-1		Fool's Gold (9:53)/Fool's Gold (4:15)/				
		What the World Is Waiting For	1990	2.50	5.00	10.00
Gold vinyl						
Silvertone 1399-1		One Love (7:45)/One Love (3:35)/Something's Burning				
			1990	2.00	4.00	8.00

Stone Temple Pilots

San Diego-based pop-rock-alternative band.

Vinyl Albums						
Atlantic 82607		Purple	1994	2.50	5.00	10.00
Atlantic 82871		Tiny Music -- Music from the Vatican Gift Shop				
			1996	2.50	5.00	10.00

STP

No relation to Stone Temple Pilots.

7-Inch Extended Play Singles						
Circuit 7004		Smoke 'Em	1990	12.50	25.00	50.00
Gold vinyl (100 made)						
Circuit 7004		Smoke 'Em	1990	6.25	12.50	25.00
Black vinyl (900 made)						
Circuit 7004	PS	Smoke 'Em	1990	6.25	12.50	25.00

Label, Number		Title	Year	VG	VG+	NM

Stranglers, The

British proto-punk band.

Vinyl Albums

Label, Number		Title	Year	VG	VG+	NM
A&M SP-4648		Rattus Norvegicus	1977	3.75	7.50	15.00
A&M SP-4659		No More Heroes	1977	3.00	6.00	12.00
A&M SP-4706		Black and White	1978	3.75	7.50	15.00
Grey marbled vinyl						
A&M SP-4706		Black and White	1978	3.00	6.00	12.00
Black vinyl						
EMI America ST-17189		The Men in Black	1986	3.75	7.50	15.00
Reissue						
EMI America SQ-17207		La Folie	1986	3.75	7.50	15.00
U.S. issue of 1981 U.K. release						
Epic BFE 38542		Feline	1983	2.50	5.00	10.00
Epic BFE 39959		Aural Sculpture	1985	3.00	6.00	12.00
Epic BFE 40607		Dreamtime	1986	2.50	5.00	10.00
Epic FE 44209		All Live and All of the Night	1988	2.50	5.00	10.00
Epic E 46120		Stranglers 10	1990	2.50	5.00	10.00
Epic E 47081		The Stranglers Greatest Hits 1977-1990				
			1990	3.00	6.00	12.00
I.R.S. SP-70011		Stranglers IV	1980	3.75	7.50	15.00
First pressings with bonus 7-inch EP (SP-70952)						
Stiff America USE-10		The Men in Black	1981	3.75	7.50	15.00

7-Inch Extended Play Singles

Label, Number		Title	Year	VG	VG+	NM
I.R.S. SP-70952		White Room/Straighten Out//Do the European/Choosey Suzie				
			1980		3.00	6.00
Bonus with early copies of LP "Stranglers IV"; no picture sleeve						

45s

Label, Number		Title	Year	VG	VG+	NM
A&M 1973		Hanging Around/Grip (Get a Grip on Yourself)/ Something Better Change/Straighten Out				
			1977		2.50	5.00
With pink and white marbled vinyl						
A&M 1973	DJ	Hanging Around/Grip (Get a Grip on Yourself)/ Something Better Change/Straighten Out				
			1977		2.00	4.00
With pink and white marbled vinyl; "totally safe" promo versions						
A&M 1973	PS	Hanging Around/Grip (Get a Grip on Yourself)/ Something Better Change/Straighten Out				
			1977		2.50	5.00
A&M 1973	PS	Hanging Around/Grip (Get a Grip on Yourself)/ Something Better Change/Straighten Out				
			1977		2.00	4.00
Sleeve accompanying "totally safe" promo versions						
A&M 2054		Nice 'N' Sleazy/Shut Up	1978		2.00	4.00
Epic 06990		Always the Sun/Mayan Skies	1987			3.00
Epic 07205		Dreamtime/Ghost Train	1987			3.00
I.R.S. 9018		The Raven/Duchess	1980		2.00	4.00
I.R.S. 9018	PS	The Raven/Duchess	1980		2.00	4.00

12-Inch Singles

Label, Number		Title	Year	VG	VG+	NM
Epic EAS 1022	DJ	All Day and All of the Night (short)/ All Day and All of the Night (Long)				
			1988		3.00	6.00
Epic EAS 2067	DJ	Sweet Smell of Success (4 versions)/Instead of This/Poisonality				
			1990	3.00	6.00	12.00
Epic EAS 2160	DJ	Someone Like You/Motorbike/Something				
			1990	2.50	5.00	10.00
Epic EAS 02573	DJ	Always the Sun (3 mixes)	1986		3.00	6.00
Epic EAS 02711	DJ	Dreamtime/Shakin' Like a Leaf (Jelly Mix)				
			1986		3.00	6.00

Label, Number		Title	Year	VG	VG+	NM
Epic 03564		Midnight Summer Dream/Paradise				
			1983	2.00	4.00	8.00
Epic 05144		Skin Deep/Here and There/Vladimir and the Beast				
			1985	2.00	4.00	8.00

Stray Cats

*American neo-rockabilly band that had to go to England to get a break. Backed up **Dave Edmunds** for awhile. Also see **Setzer, Brian**.*

Vinyl Albums

Label, Number		Title	Year	VG	VG+	NM
EMI America SN-16354		Rant 'n' Rave with the Stray Cats				
			1985	2.00	4.00	8.00
Budget-line reissue						
EMI America ST-17070		Built for Speed	1982	3.00	6.00	12.00
EMI America SO-17102		Rant 'n' Rave with the Stray Cats				
			1983	2.50	5.00	10.00
EMI R 101178		Blast Off	1989	3.00	6.00	12.00
BMG Music Service edition						
Mobile Fidelity 1-125		Built for Speed	1983			
Apparently released only on cassette (if at all)						

45s

Label, Number		Title	Year	VG	VG+	NM
EMI America 8122		Stray Cat Strut/You Don't Believe Me				
			1982			3.00
EMI America 8122	PS	Stray Cat Strut/You Don't Believe Me				
			1982		3.00	6.00
Somewhat tough sleeve to find						
EMI America 8132		Rock This Town/You Can't Hurry Love				
			1982			3.00
EMI America 8132	PS	Rock This Town/You Can't Hurry Love				
			1982			3.00
EMI America 8168		(She's) Sexy + 17/Lookin' Better Every Beer				
			1983			3.00
EMI America 8168	PS	(She's) Sexy + 17/Lookin' Better Every Beer				
			1983			3.00
EMI America 8169-1		(She's) Sexy + 17/Lookin' Better Every Beer				
			1983		2.50	5.00
Paired with 8169-2						
EMI America 8169-2		Cruisin'/Lucky Charm	1983		2.50	5.00
Paired with 8169-1						
EMI America 8169-1/2	PS	(She's) Sexy + 17/Lookin' Better Every Beer/Cruisin'/Lucky Charm				
			1983		2.50	5.00
Gatefold sleeve for two-record set						
EMI America 8185		I Won't Stand In Your Way/I Won't Stand In Your Way				
		(Acapella Version)	1983			3.00
EMI America 8194		Look at That Cadillac/Lucky Charm				
			1984			3.00
EMI America 8194	PS	Look at That Cadillac/Lucky Charm				
			1984			3.00

12-Inch Singles

Label, Number		Title	Year	VG	VG+	NM
EMI America SPRO-9868	DJ	Reckless (same on both sides)	1986	3.00	6.00	12.00
EMI America SPRO-9959/65	DJ	(She's) Sexy + 17 (3:13)/(She's) Sexy + 17 (3:28)				
			1983	3.00	6.00	12.00

Strummer, Joe

*Formerly of **The Clash**.*

Vinyl Albums

Label, Number	Title	Year	VG	VG+	NM
Epic E 45372	Earthquake Weather	1989	3.00	6.00	12.00

45s

Label, Number	Title	Year	VG	VG+	NM
Virgin 99381	Filibustero/Straight Shooter	1988		2.00	4.00

Label, Number		Title	Year	VG	VG+	NM
12-Inch Singles						
Epic EAS 01103	DJ	Trash City (same on both sides)	1988		2.50	5.00
MCA 23655		Love Kills (3 versions)	1986	2.00	4.00	8.00
Virgin 1125	DJ	Filibustero (3 versions)	1987		3.00	6.00
Virgin 96725		Filibustero (2 versions)/Brooding Six	1987		3.00	6.00

Style Council, The

*Paul Weller's pop group after **The Jam** broke up.*

Label, Number		Title	Year	VG	VG+	NM
Vinyl Albums						
Geffen GHS 24061		Internationalists	1985	2.50	5.00	10.00
Geffen GHS 24103		Home and Abroad	1986	2.50	5.00	10.00
Geffen GHS 4029		My Ever Changing Moods	1984	2.50	5.00	10.00
Polydor 815 277-1	EP	Introducing the Style Council	1983	2.00	4.00	8.00
Polydor 831 443-1		The Cost of Loving	1987	3.00	6.00	12.00
Polydor 835 785-1		Confessions of a Pop Group	1988	3.00	6.00	12.00
45s						
Geffen 28674		(When You) Call Me/Internationalists	1986			3.00
Geffen 28674	PS	(When You) Call Me/Internationalists	1986			3.00
Geffen 28941		The Boy Who Cried Wolf/Our Favourite Shop	1985			3.00
Geffen 28941	PS	The Boy Who Cried Wolf/Our Favourite Shop	1985			3.00
Geffen 29248		You're the Best Thing/Big Boss Groove	1984			3.00
Geffen 29248	PS	You're the Best Thing/Big Boss Groove	1984			3.00
Geffen 29359		My Ever Changing Moods/Mixed Company	1984			3.00
Geffen 29359	PS	My Ever Changing Moods/Mixed Company	1984			3.00
Polydor 815 276-7		Long Hot Summer/Le Depart	1983		2.00	4.00
Polydor 885 707-7		Heaven's Above/It Didn't Matter	1987			3.00
Polydor 887 753-7		How She Threw It All Away/Long Hot Summer	1988			2.00
Polydor 887 753-7	PS	How She Threw It All Away/Long Hot Summer	1988			2.00
Polydor PRO 617-7	DJ	How She Threw It All Away (Edit) (same on both sides)	1988		2.00	4.00
12-Inch Singles						
EMI America SPRO-9690	DJ	Have You Ever Had It Blue (2 mixes)	1986		3.00	6.00
Geffen PRO-A-2319	DJ	Internationalists/Walls Come Tumbling	1984		3.00	6.00
Geffen PRO-A-2490	DJ	(When You) Call Me (same on both sides)	1986		3.00	6.00
Geffen 20366		The Boy Who Cried Wolf/Lodgers (Remix)	1985		3.00	6.00
Polydor 241	DJ	Long Hot Summer (same on both sides)	1983		3.00	6.00
Polydor 889 147-1		Promised Land (2 versions)/Can You Still Love Me? (2 dub mixes)	1989		3.50	7.00

Label, Number		Title	Year	VG	VG+	NM

Suede

British pop group. Recently changed its name to London Suede.

45s

Nude/Columbia 77275		The Singles	1993	6.25	12.50	25.00

Box set of four 45s with small center holes, non-LP B-sides and picture sleeves. Individual records are listed (but not priced) below.

Nude/Columbia 77276		The Drowners/To the Birds	1993			
Nude/Columbia 77276	PS	The Drowners/To the Birds	1993			
Nude/Columbia 77277		Metal Mickey/He's Dead	1993			
Nude/Columbia 77277	PS	Metal Mickey/He's Dead	1993			
Nude/Columbia 77278		Animal Nitrate/The Big Time	1993			
Nude/Columbia 77278	PS	Animal Nitrate/The Big Time	1993			
Nude/Columbia 77279		So Young/High Rising	1993			
Nude/Columbia 77279	PS	So Young/High Rising	1993			

Sugar

*Featuring **Bob Mould**, formerly of **Husker Du.***

Vinyl Albums

Ryko Analogue RALP 10300		File Under: Easy Listening	1994	3.00	6.00	12.00

Sugar Hill Gang

Studio rap group, the first to make an impact beyond the streets.

Vinyl Albums

Sugar Hill 245		Sugar Hill Gang	1980	3.00	6.00	12.00
Sugar Hill 249		8th Wonder	1981	2.50	5.00	10.00
Sugar Hill 9206		Livin' in the Fast Lane	1984	2.50	5.00	10.00

45s

Sugar Hill 752	DJ	Rapper's Delight (4:55)/Rapper's Delight (6:30)				
			1979	5.00	10.00	20.00

12-Inch Singles

Diamond Head (no #)		Boyz from Da Hill (2 versions)/Here We Go (3 versions)				
			1994	2.00	4.00	8.00
Sugar Hill 459		Kickin' It Live from 9 to 5/(Instrumental)				
			1983	2.00	4.00	8.00
Sugar Hill 524		Rapper's Delight (Hip Hop Remix 4:00 and 7:00)/ Hot Hot Summer Day	198?	3.00	6.00	12.00
Sugar Hill 542		Rapper's Delight (Long)/Rapper's Delight (Short)				
			1979	7.50	15.00	30.00
Sugar Hill 553		8th Wonder/Sugar Hill Groove	1980	2.00	4.00	8.00
Sugar Hill 567		Apache/(instrumental)	1981	2.00	4.00	8.00
Sugar Hill 578		Funk Box/(instrumental)	1982	3.75	7.50	15.00
Sugar Hill 581		The Lover in You/(Instrumental)				
			1982	2.50	5.00	10.00
Sugar Hill 597		The Word Is Out/(Instrumental)				
			1983	2.00	4.00	8.00
Sugar Hill 32021		Livin' in the Fast Lane/(Instrumental)				
			1984	2.00	4.00	8.00
Sugar Hill 32030		Troy/Girls	1985	2.00	4.00	8.00
Sugar Hill 32037		Work, Work the Body/(Instrumental)				
			1985	2.00	4.00	8.00
Sugar Hill 32051		The Down Beat/(Instrumental)	1985	2.00	4.00	8.00

Label, Number		Title	Year	VG	VG+	NM

Sugarcubes, The

Pop group from Iceland. Lead singer Bjork went solo.

Vinyl Albums

Label, Number		Title	Year	VG	VG+	NM
Elektra 60801		Life's Too Good	1988	3.00	6.00	12.00
Elektra 60801	DJ	Life's Too Good	1988	3.75	7.50	15.00
White label promo on audiophile vinyl						
Elektra 60860		Here Today, Tomorrow, Next Week!				
			1989	3.00	6.00	12.00
Elektra 60860	DJ	Here Today, Tomorrow, Next Week!				
			1989	3.75	7.50	15.00
White label promo on audiophile vinyl						

45s

Label, Number		Title	Year	VG	VG+	NM
Elektra 64999		Planet/Planeta	1990		2.50	5.00
Elektra 69270		Regina/Regina (Icelandic)	1989		2.50	5.00
Elektra 69355		Motorcrash/Blue Eyed Pop	1988		2.50	5.00
Elektra 69355	PS	Motorcrash/Blue Eyed Pop	1988		2.50	5.00
Elektra 69377		Cold Sweat/Birthday	1988		2.50	5.00

12-Inch Singles

Label, Number		Title	Year	VG	VG+	NM
Elektra 5306	DJ	Birthday/Birthday (Icelandic Version)				
			1988		3.00	6.00
Elektra ED 5322	DJ	Cold Sweat (remix)/Cold Sweat (edit)				
			1988		3.00	6.00
Elektra ED 5337	DJ	Motorcrash (same on both sides)				
			1989	2.00	4.00	8.00
Elektra 5341	DJ	Motorcrash (same on both sides)				
			1988		3.00	6.00
Elektra 5406	DJ	Regina (same on both sides)	1989		3.00	6.00
Elektra ED 5433	DJ	Planet (LP)/Planet (Somersault Version)/Planet (Icelandic Version)				
			1989	2.00	4.00	8.00
Elektra 5627	DJ	Leash Called Love (3 versions)	199?	2.50	5.00	10.00
Elektra 66746		Cold Sweat (Meat Mix)/Birthday (Icelandic)/Delicious Demon				
			1988	2.00	4.00	8.00

Suicidal Tendencies

Venice, California punk band.

Vinyl Albums

Label, Number		Title	Year	VG	VG+	NM
Caroline CAROL 1336		Join the Army	198?	3.00	6.00	12.00
Epic FE 44288		How Will I Laugh Tomorrow When I Can't Even Smile Today				
			1988	3.00	6.00	12.00
Epic 6E 45244		Controlled by Hatred/Feel Like Shit...Deja Vu				
			1989	2.50	5.00	10.00
Epic E 45389		Lights...Camera...Revolution	1990	3.00	6.00	12.00
Frontier 4604-1-L		Suicidal Tendencies	198?	3.75	7.50	15.00

45s

Label, Number		Title	Year	VG	VG+	NM
Epic 74868		I'll Hate You Better/Mandatory Love Songs// Just Another Love Song/Won't Fall in Love Today				
			1993	2.00	4.00	8.00
Heart-shaped purple vinyl in plastic sleeve						

12-Inch Singles

Label, Number		Title	Year	VG	VG+	NM
Caroline 1453		Possessed to Skate/Human Guinea Pig/ + 1				
			198?	3.00	6.00	12.00
Epic AS 1386	DJ	Surf and Slam/Pledge Your Allegiance				
			1988	3.00	6.00	12.00
Epic 07873		Trip at the Brain/Sulcyco Mania	1988	3.00	6.00	12.00

Label, Number	Title	Year	VG	VG+	NM

Suicide
New York City synth-pop duo, long before synth-pop duos became popular.

Vinyl Albums

Antilles AN-7080	Alan Vega-Martin Rev	1980	3.00	6.00	12.00
Red Star RS-1	Suicide	1977	3.75	7.50	15.00
Red Star RED-800	Suicide	1980	3.00	6.00	12.00
Reissue of RS-1					
Wax Trax! 7072	A Way of Life	1989	2.50	5.00	10.00

Suicide Commandos
Minneapolis new-wave/punk band.

Vinyl Albums

Blank 002	The Suicide Commandos Make a Record				
		1977	6.25	12.50	25.00
Twin/Tone TTR 7906	The Commandos Commit Suicide Dance Concert				
		1979	18.75	37.50	75.00
Limited edition of 1,000 copies					

45s

P.S. (# unknown)		Emisson Control/Cliche Ole/Monster Au Go Go				
			1976	3.75	7.50	15.00
P.S. (# unknown)	PS	Emisson Control/Cliche Ole/Monster Au Go Go				
			1976	3.75	7.50	15.00
P.S. (# unknown)		Match Mismatch/Mark He's a Terror				
			1977		2.50	5.00
P.S. (# unknown)	PS	Match Mismatch/Mark He's a Terror				
			1977		2.50	5.00

Summers, Andy
*Formerly of **The Police**.*

Vinyl Albums

MCA 42007	XYZ	1987	2.50	5.00	10.00
Private Music 2039-1-P	Mysterious Barricades	1988	2.50	5.00	10.00

45s

A&M 2704		2010/To Hal and Back	1984			3.00
A&M 2704	PS	2010/To Hal and Back	1984			3.00
MCA 53112		Love Is the Strangest Way/XYZ	1987			3.00

12-Inch Singles

A&M 12119	2010/To Hal and Back	1984	2.00	4.00	8.00

Summers, Andy, and Robert Fripp

Vinyl Albums

A&M SP-4913		I Advance Masked	1982	2.50	5.00	10.00
A&M SP9-5011		Bewitched	1984	2.50	5.00	10.00
A&M SP-17299	DJ	Speak Out Interview	1982	6.25	12.50	25.00
Issued in generic cover with sticker						

45s

A&M 2513	DJ	I Advance Masked (same on both sides)				
			1982		2.00	4.00
No stock copy was issued						
A&M 2699		Parade/Train	1984			3.00

12-Inch Singles

A&M 17219	DJ	I Advance Masked (same on both sides)				
			1982	2.50	5.00	10.00

Label, Number		Title	Year	VG	VG+	NM

Sundays, The
British alterna-pop band.

Vinyl Albums
DGC 24277		Reading, Writing and Arithmetic				
			1990	3.00	6.00	12.00

45s
Geffen 19144		Love	1992		*Cassette only*	
Geffen 19691		Here's Where the Story Ends/Skin and Bones				
			1990		*Cassette only?*	

Superchunk
Punk-pop band from Chapel Hill, North Carolina.

7-Inch Extended Play Singles
Merge MRG 018		The Freed Seed	1991	2.50	5.00	10.00
Merge MRG 018	PS	The Freed Seed	1991	2.50	5.00	10.00

45s
Merge MR 004		What Do I/My Noise/Train from Atlantic City				
			1989	12.50	25.00	50.00
As "Chunk"; gold vinyl						
Merge MR 004		What Do I/My Noise/Train from Atlantic City				
			1989	6.25	12.50	25.00
As "Chunk"; black vinyl						
Merge MR 004	PS	What Do I/My Noise/Train from Atlantic City				
			1989	6.25	12.50	25.00
As "Chunk"						
Merge MR 004		What Do I/My Noise/Train from Atlantic City				
			1990	7.50	15.00	30.00
As "Superchunk"; red vinyl; enclosed with mail-order copies of their first album						
Merge MR 004	PS	What Do I/My Noise/Train from Atlantic City				
			1990	7.50	15.00	30.00
Merge MRG 007		Slack Motherfucker/Night Creatures				
			1990	6.75	13.75	27.50
Blue vinyl (300 made)						
Merge MRG 007		Slack Motherfucker/Night Creatures				
			1990	3.00	6.25	12.50
Black vinyl (700 made)						
Merge MRG 007	PS	Slack Motherfucker/Night Creatures				
			1990	3.00	6.25	12.50

Surf Punks
Their name kinda says it all.

45s
Columbia 07301		My Beach/Surfin' Bird	1987			3.00
B-side by **Pee Wee Herman**						
Columbia 07301	PS	My Beach/Surfin' Bird	1987			3.00
Soul City SC 0011		Surf's Up Medley	197?	3.00	6.00	12.00

Sweet, Matthew
Power-pop maestro from Lincoln, Nebraska.

Vinyl Albums
A&M SP-5233		Earth	1989	3.00	6.00	12.00
Columbia BFC 40417		Inside	1986	3.75	7.50	15.00
Zoo/Classic 11015		Girlfriend	1995	4.50	9.00	18.00
Audiophile vinyl pressing; released on CD in 1991						
Zoo/Classic 11050		Altered Beast	1995	4.50	9.00	18.00
Audiophile vinyl pressing; released on CD in 1993						

Label, Number		Title	Year	VG	VG+	NM
Zoo/Classic 11081		100% Fun	1995	2.50	5.00	10.00
45s						
Columbia 06286		Save Time for Me/Watch You Walking				
			1986			3.00
Columbia 06640		Blue Fools/Anyone Would Say You're Wrong				
			1987			3.00
12-Inch Singles						
A&M 17691	DJ	Vertigo (2 versions)/You Gotta/Silent City				
			1989		3.00	6.00
Columbia CAS 2484	DJ	Save Time for Me (same on both sides)				
			1986		2.50	5.00

Sweet, Rachel

From Akron, Ohio.

Vinyl Albums						
Columbia FC 38342		Blame It on Love	1982	2.50	5.00	10.00
Stiff/Columbia JC 36101		Fool Around	1979	3.00	6.00	12.00
Stiff/Columbia NJC 36337		Protect the Innocent	1980	2.50	5.00	10.00
Stiff/Columbia ARC 37077		...And Then He Kissed Me	1981	2.50	5.00	10.00
45s						
Columbia 03411		Voo Doo/American Girl	1982			3.00
Columbia 11100		B-A-B-Y/Stranger in the House	1979		2.00	4.00
Columbia 11245		Lover's Lane/Take Good Care of Me				
			1980		2.00	4.00
Columbia 68580		Life Ain't Worth Living (When You're Dead)/ Romance (Love Theme from "Sing")				
			1989			3.00
MCA 53303		(Theme from) Hairspray/Hairspray (Instrumental)				
			1988			3.00
Stiff/Columbia 02537		Then He Kissed Me/Be My Baby//Streetheart				
			1981			3.00
Stiff/Columbia 11052		I Go to Pieces/Suspended Animation				
			1979			3.00
Stiff/Columbia 11272		Spellbound/Tonight	1980			3.00
Stiff/Columbia 11314		Lover's Lane/Tonight Ricky	1980			3.00
12-Inch Singles						
MCA 17513	DJ	(Theme from) Hairspray (same on both sides)				
			1988		3.00	6.00

Sweet, Rachel, and Rex Allen

45s						
Stiff/Columbia 02169		Everlasting Love//Still Thinking of You/Billy and the Gun				
			1981			3.00

B-side features one song each by Rex Allen and Rachel Sweet

Stiff/Columbia 02169	PS	Everlasting Love//Still Thinking of You/Billy and the Gun				
			1981			3.00
Stiff/Columbia 02169	PS	Everlasting Love	1981		3.00	6.00

"Demonstration -- Not for Sale" on rear

Swimming Pool Q's, The

Athens, Georgia pop-rock band.

Vinyl Albums						
A&M SP-5107		Blue Tomorrow	1986	2.50	5.00	10.00
Capitol C1-91068		World War Two Point Five	1989	3.00	6.00	12.00
DB 55		The Deep End	1981	3.75	7.50	15.00

Label, Number		Title	Year	VG	VG+	NM
DB 87	EP	Firing Squad for God	1985	2.00	4.00	8.00

45s

Chlorinated 079		Rat Bait/The A-Bomb Woke Me Up				
			1979		2.00	4.00
Chlorinated 079	PS	Rat Bait/The A-Bomb Woke Me Up				
			1979		2.50	5.00
Orange sleeve						
Chlorinated 079	PS	Rat Bait/The A-Bomb Woke Me Up				
			1979		2.00	4.00
Gray sleeve						
DB 64		Little Misfit/Stingray	1979			3.00
DB 64	PS	Little Misfit/Stingray	1979			3.00

12-Inch Singles

A&M 17369	DJ	Now I'm Talking About Now (same on both sides)				
			1986		2.50	5.00
A&M 17399	DJ	More Than One Heaven (Remix) (same on both sides)				
			1986		2.50	5.00
Capitol SPRO-79552	DJ	The Common Years (same on both sides)				
			1989		2.50	5.00

Swing Out Sister

British pop group with jazz overtones.

Vinyl Albums

Fontana 838 293-1		Kaleidoscope World	1989	2.50	5.00	10.00
Mercury 832 213-1		It's Better to Travel	1987	2.50	5.00	10.00

45s

Collectables 4856		Breakout/In a Big Country	199?			3.00
Reissue; B-side by Big Country						
Fontana 874 190-7		Waiting Game/Coney Island Man				
			1989			3.00
Fontana 874 190-7	PS	Waiting Game/Coney Island Man				
			1989			3.00
Mercury 888 016-7		Breakout/Dirty Money	1987			3.00
Mercury 888 016-7		Breakout/Dirty Money	1987			3.00
Mercury 888 243-7		Surrender/Who's to Blame	1987			3.00
Mercury 888 484-7		Twilight World/Another Lost Weekend				
			1987			3.00
Mercury 888 484-7	PS	Twilight World/Another Lost Weekend				
			1987			3.00

12-Inch Singles

Fontana 866 855-1		Not Gonna Change (4 versions)	1992	2.00	4.00	8.00
Mercury PRO 560	DJ	Twilight World (4 versions)	1986		3.00	6.00
Mercury PRO 588	DJ	Surrender (Stuffed Gun Mix)/Surrender (Popstand Mix)				
			1986		3.00	6.00
Mercury 870 015-1		Twilight World (3 versions)/Another Lost Weekend				
			1987		2.50	5.00	10.00

Sylvain Sylvain

*Syl Sylvain, formerly of the **New York Dolls**.*

Vinyl Albums

RCA Victor AFL1-3475		Sylvain Sylvain	1980	3.00	6.00	12.00
RCA Victor AFL1-3913		Syl Sylvain and the Teardrops	1982	3.00	6.00	12.00
RCA Victor DJL1-4062	DJ	RCA Special Radio Series XII	1981	3.75	7.50	15.00
Promo-only interviews and music						

Label, Number		Title	Year	VG	VG+	NM
45s						
RCA PB-11937		Every Boy and Every Girl/Deeper and Deeper				
			1980		2.50	5.00
RCA PB-11937	PS	Every Boy and Every Girl/Deeper and Deeper				
			1980		2.50	5.00
RCA JJ-12010		14th Street Beat/Tonight	1980			*Unreleased*

Sylvian, David

*Formerly of the group **Japan**.*

Vinyl Albums						
Virgin 2167	DJ	Ink in the Well -- A Conversation				
			1987	5.00	10.00	20.00
Promo-only interview album						
Virgin 90677		Secrets of the Beehive	1987	2.50	5.00	10.00
Virgin 90904		Plight and Premonition	1988	2.50	5.00	10.00
With Holger Czukay						

Sylvian, David, and Robert Fripp

12-Inch Singles						
Virgin 14125	DJ	Darshan (3 versions)	1994	3.00	6.00	12.00

T

T'Pau

Pop-rock group from Shrewsbury, England.

Vinyl Albums						
Virgin 90595		Bridge of Spies	1987	2.50	5.00	10.00
Virgin R 133568		Bridge of Spies	1987	3.00	6.00	12.00
BMG Direct Marketing edition						
45s						
Virgin 99369		Friends Like These/China in Your Hands				
			1988			3.00
Virgin 99417		Bridge of Spies/No Sense of Pride				
			1987			3.00
Virgin 99417	PS	Bridge of Spies/No Sense of Pride				
			1987			3.00
Virgin 99466		Heart and Soul/On the Wing	1987			3.00
Virgin 99466	PS	Heart and Soul/On the Wing	1987			3.00
12-Inch Singles						
Virgin 1046	DJ	Heart and Soul (2 versions)/On the Wing				
			1987	2.50	5.00	10.00
Virgin PR 2001	DJ	Heart and Soul (Edit) (same on both sides)				
			1987	2.50	5.00	10.00
Virgin 2092	DJ	Bridge of Sighs (AOR Remix) (same on both sides)				
			1987	2.00	4.00	8.00

Tad

Seattle alterna-rock band.

Vinyl Albums						
Sub Pop 27		God's Balls	1989	5.00	10.00	20.00
First 2,000 with gatefold cover						
Sub Pop 27		God's Balls	1989	3.75	7.50	15.00
Next 500 with "Manzine"						

Label, Number		Title	Year	VG	VG+	NM
Sub Pop 27		God's Balls	1989	2.50	5.00	10.00
Others in standard cover						
Sub Pop 49	EP	Salt Lick	1990	2.00	4.00	8.00
Sub Pop 89		8-Way Santa	1991	2.50	5.00	10.00
45s						
Sub Pop 19		Ritual Device/Daisy	1988	15.50	31.25	62.50
70 on gold vinyl						
Sub Pop 19		Ritual Device/Daisy	1988	9.25	18.75	37.50
964 on clear vinyl						
Sub Pop 19	PS	Ritual Device/Daisy	1988	9.25	18.75	37.50
Plastic sleeve						
Sub Pop 37		Damaged 1/Damaged 2	1989	3.75	7.50	15.00
B-side by Pussy Galore						
Sub Pop 37	PS	Damaged 1/Damaged 2	1989	3.75	7.50	15.00
B-side by Pussy Galore; #8 in Sub Pop Singles Club series						
Sub Pop 55		Loser/Cooking with Gas	1990	5.50	11.25	22.50
First 3,000 on green vinyl						
Sub Pop 55		Loser/Cooking with Gas	1990		3.75	7.50
Sub Pop 55	PS	Loser/Cooking with Gas	1990		3.75	7.50
Sub Pop 80		Jinx/Pig Iron	1990	7.50	15.00	30.00
Some on "glacial white vinyl"						
Sub Pop 80		Jinx/Pig Iron	1990	5.00	10.00	20.00
2,000 on yellow vinyl						
Sub Pop 80		Jinx/Pig Iron	1990		2.50	5.00
Black vinyl						
Sub Pop 80	PS	Jinx/Pig Iron	1990		2.50	5.00
Sub Pop 182		Salem/Welt	1993			2.00
Sub Pop 182	PS	Salem/Welt	1993			2.00
Sub Pop 1000		Jack Pepsi/Plague Years	1991	6.25	12.50	25.00
No picture sleeve; bonus in Sub Pop Singles Club series						

Talk Talk

British new wave band.

Vinyl Albums						
EMI America ST-17083		The Party's Over	1982	3.00	6.00	12.00
EMI America ST-17113		It's My Life	1983	2.50	5.00	10.00
EMI America ST-17179		The Colour of Spring	1986	2.50	5.00	10.00
EMI America MLP-19001	EP	Talk Talk	1982	2.00	4.00	8.00
45s						
EMI America 8136		Talk Talk/Mirror Man	1982			3.00
EMI America 8195		It's My Life/Again A Game, Again				
			1984			3.00
EMI America 8195	PS	It's My Life/Again A Game, Again				
			1984			3.00
EMI America 8215		Such a Shame/Call In the Night Boy				
			1984			3.00
EMI America 8244		Why Is It So Hard/It's My Life	1984			3.00
EMI S7-18919		It's My Life/Turning Japanese	1995			3.00
*Reissue; B-side by **The Vapors***						
12-Inch Singles						
EMI SPRO 04735/51	DJ	Living in Another World (4 versions)/Talk Talk (Remix)				
			1991	2.50	5.00	10.00
EMI America 7821		It's My Life (2 versions)/Again, A Game...Again				
			1984	3.00	6.00	12.00
EMI America 7828		Such a Shame/Call in the Night Boy				
			1984	2.50	5.00	10.00
EMI America SPRO 9155/6	DJ	Such a Shame (extended)/Such a Shame (single)/				
		Such a Shame (dub)	1984	2.00	4.00	8.00
EMI America SPRO 9580	DJ	Life's What You Make It (same on both sides)				
			1985	2.00	4.00	8.00

Label, Number		Title	Year	VG	VG+	NM
EMI America SPRO 9651/2	DJ	Living in Another World (Edit)/Living in Another World (LP)				
			1986		3.50	7.00
EMI America 19203		Life's What You Make It (3 versions)				
			1986	2.50	5.00	10.00
EMI Manhattan SPRO 04172		The Rainbow (edit)/Eden (edit)/Desire (edit)/I Believe in You (edit)				
			1988	3.75	7.50	15.00

Talking Heads

*Seminal New York new-wave band. Also see **Byrne, David; Harrison, Jerry; Tom Tom Club.***

Label, Number		Title	Year	VG	VG+	NM
Vinyl Albums						
Sire PRO-A-930	DJ	Talking Heads	1980	3.75	7.50	15.00
Promo-only 4-song sampler from "Remain in Light"						
Sire PRO-A-1033	DJ	Psycho Killer/Life During Wartime/Take Me to the River/				
		Houses in Motion (all live)	1982	3.75	7.50	15.00
Sire 2SR 3590	(2)	The Name of This Band Is Talking Heads				
			1982	5.00	10.00	20.00
Sire SR 6036		Talking Heads '77	1977	3.00	6.00	12.00
Sire SR 6058		More Songs About Buildings and Food				
			1978	3.00	6.00	12.00
Sire SRK 6058		More Songs About Buildings and Food				
			1979	2.00	4.00	8.00
Reissue with new prefix						
Sire SRK 6076		Fear of Music	1979	2.50	5.00	10.00
Sire SRK 6095		Remain in Light	1981	2.50	5.00	10.00
Sire 23771		Speaking in Tongues	1983	3.75	7.50	15.00
Clear vinyl in oversize plastic container with Robert Rauschenberg artwork						
Sire 23883		Speaking in Tongues	1983	2.50	5.00	10.00
Standard issue						
Sire 25121		Stop Making Sense (Soundtrack)				
			1984	3.75	7.50	15.00
First issue with booklet and black & white cover						
Sire 25186		Stop Making Sense (Soundtrack)				
			1984	2.50	5.00	10.00
Second issue: No booklet, color cover						
Sire 25305		Little Creatures	1985	2.50	5.00	10.00
Sire 25512		True Stories	1986	2.50	5.00	10.00
Sire 25654		Naked	1988	2.50	5.00	10.00
Sire R 124560		Stop Making Sense	1984	3.00	6.00	12.00
RCA Music Service edition						
Sire R 150102		Speaking in Tongues	1983	3.00	6.00	12.00
BMG Direct Marketing edition						
Sire R 153810		Naked	1988	3.00	6.00	12.00
BMG Direct Marketing edition						
Sire R 153839		Little Creatures	1985	3.00	6.00	12.00
RCA Music Service edition						
Warner Bros. WBMS-104	DJ	The Warner Bros. Music Show -- Talking Heads Live on Tour				
			1979	6.25	12.50	25.00
Promo-only radio show (has been counterfeited)						
45s						
Sire GSRE 0452		Take Me to the River/Life During Wartime				
			198?			3.00
"Back to Back Hits" reissue						
Sire GSRE 0479		Burning Down the House/This Must Be the Place				
			198?			3.00
"Back to Back Hits" reissue						
Sire 737		Love Goes to Building on Fire/New Feeling				
			1977	2.00	4.00	8.00
Sire 737	PS	Love ----> Building on Fire/New Feeling				
			1977	2.00	4.00	8.00
Sire 1002		Uh-Oh, Love Comes to Town/I Wish You Wouldn't Say That				
			1977		3.00	6.00

Label, Number		Title	Year	VG	VG+	NM
Sire 1002	PS	Uh-Oh, Love Comes to Town/I Wish You Wouldn't Say That				
			1977		3.00	6.00
Sire 1013		Psycho Killer/Psycho Killer (Acoustic)				
			1978	2.00	4.00	8.00
Sire 1013	PS	Psycho Killer/Psycho Killer (Acoustic)				
			1978	2.00	4.00	8.00
Sire 1032		Take Me to the River/Thank You for Sending Me an Angel				
		(Version)	1978		2.00	4.00
Sire 1032	PS	Take Me to the River/Thank You for Sending Me an Angel				
		(Version)	1978		2.00	4.00
Sire 21975		Wild Wild Life/And She Was	198?			3.00
"Back to Back Hits" reissue						
Sire 27948		Blind/Still	1988			2.00
Sire 27948	PS	Blind/Still	1988			2.00
Sire 27992		(Nothing But) Flowers/Ruby Dear				
			1988			2.00
Sire 27992	PS	(Nothing But) Flowers/Ruby Dear				
			1988			2.00
Sire 28497		Love for Sale/Hey Now	1987			2.00
Sire 28497	PS	Love for Sale/Hey Now	1987			2.00
Sire 28629		Wild Wild Life/People Like Us (Movie Version)				
			1986			2.00
Sire 28629	PS	Wild Wild Life/People Like Us (Movie Version)				
			1986			2.00
Sire 28917		And She Was/And She Was (Dub)				
			1985			2.00
Sire 28917	PS	And She Was/And She Was (Dub)				
			1985			2.00
Sire 28987		Road to Nowhere/Give Me Back My Name				
			1985			3.00
Sire 28987	PS	Road to Nowhere/Give Me Back My Name				
			1985			3.00
Sire 29080		Stop Making Sense (Girlfriend Is Better)/Heaven				
			1985			3.00
Sire 29163		Once in a Lifetime/This Must Be the Place (Naive Melody)				
			1984			3.00
Sire 29163	PS	Once in a Lifetime/This Must Be the Place (Naive Melody)				
			1984			3.00
Sire 29451		This Must Be the Place (Naive Melody)/Moon Rocks				
			1983			3.00
Sire 29451	PS	This Must Be the Place (Naive Melody)/Moon Rocks				
			1983			3.00
Sire 29565		Burning Down the House/I Get Wild-Wild Gravity				
			1983			3.00
Sire 29565	PS	Burning Down the House/I Get Wild-Wild Gravity				
			1983			3.00
Sire 49075		Life During Wartime (This Ain't No Party...This Ain't No				
		Disco...This Ain't No Foolin' Around)/Electric Guitar				
			1979		2.00	4.00
Sire 49649		Once in a Lifetime/Seen and Not Seen				
			1981		2.00	4.00
Sire 49734		Houses in Motion/The Overload	1981		2.00	4.00

12-Inch Singles

Label, Number		Title	Year	VG	VG+	NM
Sire PRO-A-846	DJ	Life During Wartime/I Zimbra/Air				
			1979	4.00	8.00	16.00
Sire PRO-A-903	DJ	Crosseyed and Painless (long)/Crosseyed and Painless (Short)				
			1980	4.00	8.00	16.00
Sire PRO-A-2046	DJ	Burning Down the House/Pull Up the Roots/Slippery People				
		(Cassette Version)	1983	2.00	4.00	8.00
Sire PRO-A-2057	DJ	Burning Down the House (same on both sides)				
			1983	2.00	4.00	8.00

Label, Number		Title	Year	VG	VG+	NM
Sire PRO-A-2101	DJ	This Must Be the Place (Naive Melody)/ This Must Be the Place (Naive Melody) (Edit) 1983		2.00	4.00	8.00
Sire PRO-A-2207	DJ	Once in a Lifetime (Edit) (same on both sides) 1984			3.00	6.00
Sire PRO-A-2305	DJ	Road to Nowhere (LP version)/Road to Nowhere (Edit) 1985			3.00	6.00
Sire PRO-A-2348	DJ	And She Was (same on both sides) 1985			3.00	6.00
Sire PRO-A-2376	DJ	Stay Up Late (same on both sides) 1985			3.00	6.00
Sire PRO-A-2556	DJ	Wild Wild Life (same on both sides) 1986			3.00	6.00
Sire PRO-A-2593	DJ	Puzzlin' Evidence (same on both sides) 1986		2.00	4.00	8.00
Sire PRO-A-2638	DJ	Love for Sale (same on both sides) 1986			2.50	5.00
Sire PRO-A-2947	DJ	(Nothing But) Flowers (Radio Edit)/(Nothing But) Flowers (LP Version) 1988			2.50	5.00
Sire PRO-A-3182	DJ	Blind (Extended Remix) (same on both sides) 1988			2.50	5.00
Sire 20143		Slippery People/Making Flippy Floppy 1983			3.50	7.00
Sire 20171		Swamp (2 mixes)/Slippery People 1983			3.50	7.00
Sire 20378		And She Was (Extended)/Television Man (Remix) 1985			3.00	6.00
Sire 20593		Wild Wild Life (2 mixes)/People Like Us (Movie Version) 1986		2.50	5.00	10.00
Sire 20620		Love for Sale (3 mixes)/Hey Now (Kids Mix) 1987		2.50	5.00	10.00
Sire 20732		Radio Head (2 versions)/Hey Now (2 versions) 1988			3.00	6.00
Sire 20892		Blind (4 mixes)/Bill	1988		3.00	6.00

Tami Show

Chicago pop group.

45s

Chrysalis 43146		She's Only Twenty/Don't Say No 1987				3.00
Chrysalis 43146	PS	She's Only Twenty/Don't Say No 1987				3.00
Chrysalis 43264		Cupid's Soldier/Stranger	1988			3.00

Taylor, Andy

Of Duran Duran. Also see Power Station, The.

Vinyl Albums

MCA 5837		Thunder	1987	2.50	5.00	10.00
MCA R 153322		Thunder	1987	3.00	6.00	12.00
BMG Direct Marketing edition						

45s

Atlantic 89414		Take It Easy/Angel Eyes	1986			3.00
Atlantic 89414	PS	Take It Easy/Angel Eyes	1986			3.00
MCA 52946		When the Rain Comes Down/Broken Windows 1986				3.00
MCA 52946	PS	When the Rain Comes Down/Broken Windows 1986				3.00

Label, Number		Title	Year	VG	VG+	NM
MCA 52999		Life Goes On/Broken Window	1987			3.00
MCA 53085		Don't Let Me Die Young/Broken Window				
			1987			3.00
12-Inch Singles						
Atlantic PR 896	DJ	Take It Easy (same on both sides)				
			1986	2.00	4.00	8.00
Capitol SPRO-79463	DJ	Dead on the Money (same on both sides)				
			1988	2.00	4.00	8.00

Taylor, John

Member of Duran Duran. Also see Power Station, The.

45s						
Capitol 5551		I Do What I Do...(Theme for 9 1/2 Weeks)/Jazz				
			1986			3.00
Capitol 5551	PS	I Do What I Do...(Theme for 9 1/2 Weeks)/Jazz				
			1986			3.00
12-Inch Singles						
Capitol SPRO-9653	DJ	I Do What I Do... (same on both sides)				
			1986	2.50	5.00	10.00
Capitol 15223		I Do What I Do...(4 versions)/The Final Cut				
			1986	3.00	6.00	12.00

Tchaikovsky, Bram

Lead singer of a British rock/new wave band that had the same name that he did.

Vinyl Albums						
Arista AB 4292		Funland	1981	2.50	5.00	10.00
Polydor PD1-6211		Strange Man, Changed Man	1979	3.00	6.00	12.00
Polydor PD1-6273		Pressure	1980	2.50	5.00	10.00
45s						
Arista 0601		Shall We Dance	1981			3.00
Arista 0621		Together My Love/Stand and Deliver				
			1981			3.00
Polydor 2016		Lady from the U.S.A./Turn On the Light				
			1979			3.00
Polydor 2101		Let's Dance/Hollywood Nightmare				
			1980			3.00
Polydor 14575		Girl of My Dreams/Sarah Smiles				
			1979			3.00
12-Inch Singles						
Arista SP-104	DJ	Shall We Dance/Miracle Cure	1981	2.00	4.00	8.00
Polydor PRO 109	DJ	Lady from the USA (same on both sides)				
			1979		2.50	5.00

Teardrop Explodes, The

British new-wave band from Liverpool. Leader Julian Cope went solo.

Vinyl Albums						
Mercury SRM-1-4016		Kilimanjaro	1981	3.00	6.00	12.00
Mercury SRM-1-4035		Wilder	1981	3.00	6.00	12.00
12-Inch Singles						
Mercury 172	DJ	When I Dream/Ha Ha I'm Drowning/Reward				
			1980	5.00	10.00	20.00

Label, Number		Title	Year	VG	VG+	NM

Tears For Fears

British synth-pop duo. Extremely popular in the mid-1980s.

Vinyl Albums

Label, Number		Title	Year	VG	VG+	NM
Fontana 838 730-1		The Seeds of Love	1989	2.50	5.00	10.00
Fontana R 133653		The Seeds of Love	1989	3.00	6.00	12.00
BMG Direct Marketing edition						
Mercury 811 039-1		The Hurting	1983	3.75	7.50	15.00
Mercury 824 300-1		Songs from the Big Chair	1985	2.50	5.00	10.00
Mercury R 143666		Songs from the Big Chair	1985	3.00	6.00	12.00
BMG Direct Marketing edition						

45s

Label, Number		Title	Year	VG	VG+	NM
Fontana 874 710-7		Sowing the Seeds of Love/Tears Roll Down				
			1989			3.00
Fontana 874 710-7	PS	Sowing the Seeds of Love/Tears Roll Down				
			1989			3.00
Fontana 876 248-7		Woman in Chains/Always in the Past				
			1990			3.00
Fontana 876 248-7	PS	Woman in Chains/Always in the Past				
			1990			3.00
Mercury PRO 392-7	DJ	Head Over Heels (Live) (same on both sides)				
			1985	2.50	5.00	10.00
Mercury 812 677-7		Change/The Conflict	1983		2.00	4.00
Mercury 862 240-7		Break It Down Again/Bloodletting Go				
			1993			3.00
Mercury 862 804-7		Goodnight Song/New Star	1993			3.00
Mercury 880 294-7		Shout/The Big Chair	1985			3.00
Mercury 880 294-7	PS	Shout/The Big Chair	1985			3.00
Mercury 880 659-7		Everybody Wants to Rule the World/Pharaohs				
			1985			3.00
Mercury 880 899-7		Head Over Heels/When in Love with a Blind Man				
			1985			3.00
Mercury 880 899-7	PS	Head Over Heels/When in Love with a Blind Man				
			1985			3.00
Mercury 884 636-7		Mothers Talk/(B-side unknown)	1986			3.00
Mercury 884 636-7	PS	Mothers Talk/(B-side unknown)	1986			3.00

12-Inch Singles

Label, Number		Title	Year	VG	VG+	NM
Mercury 234	DJ	Pale Shelter (same on both sides)				
			1983	2.00	4.00	8.00
Mercury 238	DJ	Mad World (same on both sides)				
			1983	3.00	6.00	12.00
Mercury PRO 340-1	DJ	Everybody Wants to Rule the World (same on both sides)				
			1985	2.00	4.00	8.00
Mercury PRO 363-1	DJ	Shout (Edit)/Shout (LP version)	1985	3.00	6.00	12.00
Mercury 374	DJ	Head Over Heels (Remix 45 Version)/ Broken-Head Over Heels-Broken				
			1985	2.00	4.00	8.00
Mercury PRO 393-1	DJ	Head Over Heels (Live)/Broken-Head Over Heels-Broken (Live)				
			1985	3.75	7.50	15.00
Mercury 410	DJ	Mothers Talk (same on both sides)				
			1986		3.00	6.00
Mercury 880 659-1		Everybody Wants to Rule the World (remix) (LP version)/Pharaohs				
			1985	2.50	5.00	10.00
Mercury 880 890-1		Head Over Heels (2 versions)/When in Love with a Blind Man				
			1985	3.00	6.00	12.00
Mercury 880 929-1		Shout (2 remixes)/The Big Chair				
			1985	3.00	6.00	12.00
Mercury 884 638-1		Mothers Talk (3 versions)	1986	2.00	4.00	8.00

Label, Number	Title	Year	VG	VG+	NM

Teddy and the Frat Girls
Raunch-rock band from West Palm Beach, Florida.

7-Inch Extended Play Singles

FFD (# unknown)	Audio Suicide	1980	7.50	15.00	30.00
Label calls them "Sheer Smegma"					
FFD (# unknown) PS	Audio Suicide	1980	7.50	15.00	30.00
Original had a rubber-stamped plain sleeve					
FFD (# unknown) PS	Audio Suicide	1980	17.50	35.00	70.00
Sleeve with "Teddy and the Frat Girls" on it, added later					

Teen Idles
*Washington, D.C. hardcore band. Members later joined **Minor Threat**.*

7-Inch Extended Play Singles

Dischord 1	Minor Disturbance	1980	8.75	17.50	35.00
Dischord 1 PS	Minor Disturbance	1980	10.00	20.00	40.00
Heavy stock					
Dischord 1 PS	Minor Disturbance	1980	8.75	17.50	35.00
Thin paper stock. Both versions include poster and lyric insert.					

Teenage Jesus and the Jerks
*Original band of **Lydia Lunch**.*

Vinyl Albums

Migraine/Lust Unlust CC-336 EP	Teenage Jesus and the Jerks	1979	5.00	10.00	20.00
Pink vinyl					
Migraine/Lust Unlust CC-336 EP	Teenage Jesus and the Jerks	1979	3.75	7.50	15.00

45s

Migraine/Lust Unlust CC-333	Orphans/Less of Me	1978	3.00	6.25	12.50
Migraine/Lust Unlust CC-333 PS	Orphans/Less of Me	1978	3.00	6.25	12.50
Migraine/Lust Unlust CC-334	Baby Doll/Freud in Flop/Race Mixing	1979	3.00	6.25	12.50
Migraine/Lust Unlust CC-334 PS	Baby Doll/Freud in Flop/Race Mixing	1979	3.00	6.25	12.50

Television
*Early New York City punk/new-wave band. Broke up in late 1970s, reunited (most of them) in 1992. Also see **Verlaine, Tom; Hell, Richard, and the Voidoids**.*

Vinyl Albums

Capitol SPRO-79456 DJ	Television	1992	5.00	10.00	20.00
Promo-only vinyl release (stock copies on CD and cassette only)					
Elektra 6E-133	Adventure	1978	2.50	5.00	10.00
Elektra 7E-1098	Marquee Moon	1977	3.00	7.50	15.00

45s

Elektra 45516	Ain't That Nothin'/Glory	1978		2.50	5.00
Elektra 45516 DJ	Ain't That Nothin' (mono/stereo)	1978	6.25	12.50	25.00
Radically different recording than on LP; unknown whether this also appears on stock copy					
Ork 81975	Little Johnny Jewel Pt. 1/Little Johnny Jewel Pt. 2	1975	6.25	12.50	25.00

Temple of the Dog
*Ad-hoc group of **Pearl Jam** and **Soundgarden** members, formed in tribute to Andrew Wood, deceased singer of **Mother Love Bone**.*

12-Inch Singles

A&M 75021 7533 1 DJ	Pushin' Forward Back/Hunger Strike/Your Savior	1991	3.75	7.50	15.00

The front cover of the picture sleeve for the Talking Heads' first single, "Love Goes to Building on Fire," reflects the makeup of the band at the time -- three members. Jerry Harrison was not yet in the group, but would join by the time its first album was released.

"Trouble Me" was the only 10,000 Maniacs song to make significant inroads on the pop charts until "Because the Night" was released from its MTV Unplugged concert. This neat sleeve from 1989, with the lyrics in prose, rather than verse, form on the back, is obscure but not especially rare (yet).

Label, Number		Title	Year	VG	VG+	NM

10,000 Maniacs

Jamestown, New York, new wave band. Featuring Natalie Merchant as lead singer.

Vinyl Albums

Label, Number		Title	Year	VG	VG+	NM
Christian Burial P-2010	EP	Human Conflict #5	1983	18.75	37.50	75.00
Christian Burial P-3001		Secrets of the I Ching	1984	31.25	62.50	125.00
Elektra 5270	DJ	Interview	1987	6.25	12.50	25.00
Lenny Kaye interviews Natalie Merchant; promo only						
Elektra 60428		The Wishing Chair	1985	3.00	6.00	12.00
Elektra 60738		In My Tribe	1987	2.50	5.00	10.00
Elektra 60738	DJ	In My Tribe	1987	3.00	6.00	12.00
Promo-only audiophile pressing						
Elektra 60815		Blind Man's Zoo	1989	3.00	6.00	12.00
Elektra 60815	DJ	Blind Man's Zoo	1989	3.75	7.50	15.00
Promo-only audiophile pressing (promo labels)						
Elektra R 100481		In My Tribe	1987	3.00	6.00	12.00
BMG Direct Marketing edition						
Elektra R 130236		Blind Man's Zoo	1989	3.75	7.50	15.00
BMG Direct Marketing edition						

45s

Label, Number		Title	Year	VG	VG+	NM
Elektra 64595		Because the Night/Eat for Two	1993			3.00
Elektra 65962		Like the Weather/Peace Train	198?			3.00
"Spun Gold" reissue						
Elektra 69253		You Happy Puppet/Gunshy	1989		2.00	4.00
Elektra 69298		Trouble Me/The Lion's Share	1989		2.00	4.00
Elektra 69298	PS	Trouble Me/The Lion's Share	1989		2.00	4.00
Elektra 69388		What's the Matter Here?/Cherry Tree	1988		2.00	4.00
Elektra 69388	PS	What's the Matter Here?/Cherry Tree	1988		2.00	4.00
Elektra 69418		Like the Weather/A Campfire Song	1988		2.00	4.00
Elektra 69418	PS	Like the Weather/A Campfire Song	1988		2.00	4.00
Elektra 69439		Don't Talk/City of Angels	1987		2.00	4.00
Elektra 69439	PS	Don't Talk/City of Angels	1987		2.00	4.00
Elektra 69457		Peace Train/Painted Desert	1987		2.00	4.00
Elektra 69457	PS	Peace Train/Painted Desert	1987		2.00	4.00

12-Inch Singles

Label, Number		Title	Year	VG	VG+	NM
Elektra ED 5239	DJ	Peace Train (same on both sides)	1987		2.50	5.00
Elektra ED 5258	DJ	Don't Talk (LP)/Don't Talk (Edit)	1987		3.00	6.00
Elektra ED 5278	DJ	Like the Weather (same on both sides)	1987		3.00	6.00
Elektra ED 5312	DJ	What's the Matter Here (LP version)/What's the Matter Here (Edit)	1987		2.50	5.00
Elektra ED 5376	DJ	Trouble Me (same on both sides)	1989	2.00	4.00	8.00
Elektra ED 5399	DJ	Eat for Two (same on both sides)	1989		2.50	5.00
Elektra ED 5416	DJ	You Happy Puppet (same on both sides)	1989		2.50	5.00
Elektra ED 5499	DJ	My Mother the War (same on both sides)	1990		3.00	6.00

Label, Number		Title	Year	VG	VG+	NM

That Petrol Emotion
Irish pop-rock group.

Vinyl Albums

Polydor 833 132-1		Babble	1987	2.50	5.00	10.00
Virgin 91019		End of the Millennium Psychosis Blues				
			1988	2.50	5.00	10.00
Virgin 91354		Chemicrazy	1990	2.50	5.00	10.00

45s

Virgin 99238		Groove Check/Smooth	1989			3.00

12-Inch Singles

Polydor 514	DJ	Big Decision (Extended)/Big Decision (Edit)				
			1987		2.50	5.00
Polydor 528	DJ	Big Decision (3 versions)	1987		2.50	5.00
Virgin 1290	DJ	Groove Check (same on both sides)				
			1988		2.50	5.00
Virgin 1516	DJ	Abandon/Hey Venus/Sensitize/Groove Check				
			1989	2.00	4.00	8.00
Virgin 96580		Groove Check (12" Version)/Groove Check (Dub)				
			1989		3.00	6.00

The The
*British new wave/punk/electropop band that's been around since 1979. Johnny Marr, ex-member of **The Smiths,** has played guitar in recent years.*

Vinyl Albums

Epic BFE 39266		Soul Mining	1985	3.00	6.00	12.00
Epic BFE 40471		Infected	1987	3.00	6.00	12.00
Epic FE 45241		Mindbomb	1989	3.00	6.00	12.00

45s

Epic ES7 02718	DJ	Heartland/Slow Train to Dawn	1987		3.75	7.50
Epic ES7 02718	PS	Heartland/Slow Train to Dawn	1987		3.75	7.50
Promo item for Record World chain						
Epic 04478		This Is the Day/The Sinking Feeling				
			1984	2.00	4.00	8.00
Epic 68883		The Beat(en) Generation/Angel				
			1989		2.50	5.00
Epic 74990		Love Is Stronger Than Death/Infected (Live)				
			1993		2.50	5.00

12-Inch Singles

Epic AS 1873	DJ	This Is the Day (Long)/This Is the Day (Short)				
			1983	3.75	7.50	15.00
Epic EAS 01895	DJ	Kingdom of Rain/Flesh & Bones/Nature of Virtue/				
		Waitin' for the Upturn	1989	3.00	6.00	12.00
Epic EAS 01958	DJ	Jealous of Youth (2 versions)/Beyond Love				
			1990	2.50	5.00	10.00
Epic EAS 2567	DJ	Infected/Infected (Remix)	1986	3.00	6.00	12.00
Epic EAS 2690	DJ	Heartland (2 versions)/Slow Train to Dawn (2 versions)				
			1986	3.00	6.00	12.00
Epic 04315		This Is the Day/I've Been Waitin' for Tomorrow (All of My Life)				
			1984	4.50	9.00	18.00
Epic 05982		Infected (3 mixes)	1986	2.00	4.00	8.00
Epic 06810		Slow Train to Dawn/Harbour Lights/Heartland/				
		Born in the New S.A.	1986	3.00	6.00	12.00
Epic 68774		The Beat(en) Generation (3 versions)/Angel				
			1989	2.00	4.00	8.00

Label, Number		Title	Year	VG	VG+	NM
Sire PRO-A-1005	DJ	Uncertain Smile (Long Version Edit)/Uncertain Smile				
		(Short Version Edit)	1982	6.25	12.50	25.00
Sire 29878		Uncertain Smile/Three Orange Kisses From Kazan/				
		Waitin' for the Upturn	1983	3.75	7.50	15.00

Thee Headcoats

45s

Sub Pop 71		Davey Crockett (Gabba Hey)/Time Will Tell				
			1990		2.00	4.00
Black vinyl pressing of 2,000						
Sub Pop 71		Davey Crockett (Gabba Hey)/Time Will Tell				
			1990	2.00	4.00	8.00
Blue vinyl pressing of 2,000						
Sub Pop 71	PS	Davey Crockett (Gabba Hey)/Time Will Tell				
			1990		2.00	4.00
#20 in Sub Pop Singles Club series						

They Might Be Giants

Boston satirical alterna-rock duo, now based in Brooklyn.

Vinyl Albums

Bar None A-HAON 002		They Might Be Giants	1986	3.75	7.50	15.00
Bar None A-HAON 004	EP	Don't Let's Start	1987	3.75	7.50	15.00
Bar None 72600		Lincoln	1988	2.50	5.00	10.00
Bar None/Restless 72611	EP	They'll Need a Crane	1989	2.50	5.00	10.00
Elektra 60907		Flood	1990	2.50	5.00	10.00
Elektra E1-60907		Flood	1990	3.00	6.00	12.00
Columbia House edition						
Elektra R 114772		Flood	1990	3.00	6.00	12.00
BMG Music Service edition						

45s

Elektra 64578		O Tannenbaum/Christmas Cards				
			1993			2.00
Green vinyl						
Elektra 64578	PS	O Tannenbaum/Christmas Cards				
			1993			2.00
Elektra 64602		Why Does the Sun Shine? (The Sun Is a Mass of Incandescent Gas)/				
		Jessica	1993			2.00
Elektra 64602	PS	Why Does the Sun Shine? (The Sun Is a Mass of Incandescent Gas)/				
		Jessica	1993			2.00
Elektra 64998		Birdhouse in Your Soul/Hot Cha				
			1990		2.50	5.00
Wiggle Diskette (#unknown)		Everything Right Is Wrong/You'll Miss Me				
			1985	2.00	4.00	8.00
Flexidisc						
Wiggle Diskette (#unknown)	PS	Everything Right Is Wrong/You'll Miss Me				
			1985	2.00	4.00	8.00

12-Inch Singles

Bar None 130	DJ	Ana Ng (same on both sides)	1988	2.00	4.00	8.00
Bar None 167	DJ	They'll Need a Crane (same on both sides)				
			1989	2.00	4.00	8.00
Elektra 5427	DJ	Birdhouse in Your Soul (same on both sides)				
			1989		3.00	6.00
Elektra 5453	DJ	Twisting (same on both sides)	1990		3.00	6.00
Elektra 5458	DJ	Twisting/James K. Polk/Ant	1990	2.00	4.00	8.00
Elektra ED 5496	DJ	Your Racist Friend (same on both sides)				
			1990	2.00	4.00	8.00

Label, Number		Title	Year	VG	VG+	NM

Thomas, Marlo, and Friends
*Includes a track by **Soul Asylum**.*

Vinyl Albums

A&M SP-5196		Free to Be...A Family	1988	3.00	6.00	12.00

Thompson Twins
British synth-pop group. No one in the band was either named Thompson or a twin.

Vinyl Albums

Label, Number		Title	Year	VG	VG+	NM
Arista SP-137	EP	Identical and Fraternal	1982	3.75	7.50	15.00
Promo-only remixes of early tracks						
Arista AL 6601		In the Name of Love	1982	3.00	6.00	12.00
Arista AL 6607		Side Kicks	1983	3.00	6.00	12.00
Arista AL8-8200		Into the Gap	1984	2.50	5.00	10.00
Arista AL8-8276		Here's to Future Days	1985	2.50	5.00	10.00
Arista AL6-8309		Side Kicks	1985	2.00	4.00	8.00
Reissue						
Arista AL6-8310		In the Name of Love	1985	2.00	4.00	8.00
Reissue						
Arista AL8-8449		Close to the Bone	1987	2.50	5.00	10.00
Arista AL 8542		Best of the Thompson Twins: Greatest Mixes				
			1988	2.50	5.00	10.00
Arista ADP 9586	DJ	Interview Sampler	1987	5.00	10.00	20.00
One side of interviews, the other of music; promo only						
Arista R 124567		Into the Gap	1984	3.00	6.00	12.00
RCA Music Service edition						
Arista R 144367		Here's to Future Days	1985	3.00	6.00	12.00
RCA Music Service edition						
Arista R 154307		Close to the Bone	1987	3.00	6.00	12.00
BMG Direct Marketing edition						
Arista R 154479		Best of the Thompson Twins: Greatest Mixes				
BMG Direct Marketing edition			1988	3.00	6.00	12.00
Warner Bros. 25921		Big Trash	1989	2.50	5.00	10.00

45s

Label, Number		Title	Year	VG	VG+	NM
Arista 0671		In the Name of Love/Coastline	1982		2.00	4.00
Arista 1024		Lies/Beach Culture	1982		2.00	4.00
Arista 1056		Love On Your Side/Love On Your Back				
			1983		2.00	4.00
Arista 1056	PS	Love On Your Side/Love On Your Back				
			1983		2.00	4.00
Arista 9013		Love On Your Side/Love On Your Back				
			1983			3.00
Arista 9013	PS	Love On Your Side/Love On Your Back				
			1983			3.00
Arista 9164		Hold Me Now/Let Loving Start	1984			3.00
Arista 9164	PS	Hold Me Now/Let Loving Start	1984			3.00
Arista 9209		Doctor! Doctor!/Nurse Shark	1984			3.00
Arista 9209	PS	Doctor! Doctor!/Nurse Shark	1984			3.00
Arista 9237		Lies/Love on Your Side	1984			3.00
"Flashback" reissue						
Arista 9238		In the Name of Love/Coastline	1984			3.00
"Flashback" reissue						
Arista 9244		You Take Me Up/Passion Planet	1984			3.00
Arista 9244	PS	You Take Me Up/Passion Planet	1984			3.00
Arista 9290		The Gap/Out of the Gap	1984			3.00
Arista 9347		Hold Me Now/Doctor! Doctor!	1985			3.00
Reissue						
Arista 9396		Lay Your Hands on Me/The Lewis Carol				
		(Adventures in Wonderland)	1985			3.00
Arista 9396	PS	Lay Your Hands on Me/The Lewis Carol				
		(Adventures in Wonderland)	1985			3.00

Label, Number		Title	Year	VG	VG+	NM
Arista 9450		King for a Day/Rollunder	1985			3.00
Arista 9450	PS	King for a Day/Rollunder	1985			3.00
Arista 9485		Lay Your Hands on Me/King for a Day				
			1986			3.00
Reissue						
Arista 9511		Nothing in Common/Nothing to Lose				
			1986			3.00
Arista 9511	PS	Nothing in Common/Nothing to Lose				
			1986			3.00
Arista 9577		Get That Love/Perfect Day	1987			3.00
Arista 9577	PS	Get That Love/Perfect Day	1987			3.00
Arista 9609		Long Goodbye/Dancin' in Your Shoes				
			1987			3.00
Arista 9622		Follow Your Heart/Bush Baby	1987			3.00
EMI America 8227		You Take Me Up/Letters from the Road				
			1984			3.00
Warner Bros. 22819		Sugar Daddy/Monkey Man	1989			3.00
Warner Bros. 22819	PS	Sugar Daddy/Monkey Man	1989			3.00

12-Inch Singles

Label, Number		Title	Year	VG	VG+	NM
Arista 712		In the Name of Love/In the Beginning/Coastline				
			1982		2.50	5.00
Arista 9158		Hold Me Now (2 versions)/Let Loving Start				
			1984	2.50	5.00	10.00
Arista 9201		Hold Me Now (Remix)/Let Loving Start				
			1984		3.00	6.00
Arista 9211		Doctor! Doctor! (2 versions)/Nurse Shark				
			1984	2.50	5.00	10.00
Arista 9245	DJ	You Take Me Up (same on both sides)				
			1984	2.00	4.00	8.00
Arista 9289		The Gap/Out of the Gap	1984		3.00	6.00
Arista 9397		Lay Your Hands on Me/The Lewis Carol				
		(Adventures in Wonderland)	1985	2.50	5.00	10.00
Arista 9442		King for a Day (edit)/King for a Day (LP)/Rollover				
			1985		3.50	7.00
Arista 9519		Nothing in Common (4 versions)/Revolution (Extended)				
			1986		3.00	6.00
Arista 9578		Get That Love (3 versions)/Perfect Day				
			1987		2.50	5.00
Arista 9731		In the Name of Love '88 (5 mixes)				
			1988		3.00	6.00
Warner Bros. PRO-A-3901	DJ	Bombers in the Sky (4 versions)	1989		3.00	6.00
Warner Bros. PRO-A-4941	(2) DJ	Come Inside (8 versions)	1991	3.00	6.00	12.00
Two 12-inch singles in promo-only gatefold sleeve						
Warner Bros. PRO-A-5207	DJ	Groove On (5 versions)	1991	2.00	4.00	8.00
Warner Bros. 21320		Sugar Daddy (5 versions)/Monkey Man				
			1989		3.00	6.00
Warner Bros. 40071		Come Inside (3 versions)/The Saint (3 versions)				
			1991		3.00	6.00
Warner Bros. 40309		Groove On (5 versions)/Queer	1991		3.00	6.00
Warner Bros. 40607		Play With Me (Jane) (3 versions)/The Saint (3 versions)				
			1991	2.50	5.00	10.00

Three Fish

*Side project of Jeff Ament of **Pearl Jam.***

Vinyl Albums

Label, Number		Title	Year	VG	VG+	NM
Epic E 67652	(2)	Three Fish	1996	3.00	6.00	12.00

Label, Number		Title	Year	VG	VG+	NM

Throwing Muses

*Boston alterna-rock band. Former member Tanya Donnelly also is in **Belly** and was with **The Breeders**. Also see **Hersh, Kristin.***

Vinyl Albums

Label, Number		Title	Year	VG	VG+	NM
Sire 25640		The Fat Skier	1987	2.50	5.00	10.00
Sire 25710		House Tornado	1988	2.50	5.00	10.00
Sire 25855		Hunkpapa	1989	2.50	5.00	10.00
Sire 26489		The Real Ramona	1991	3.00	6.00	12.00

7-Inch Extended Play Singles

Label, Number		Title	Year	VG	VG+	NM
Spewing Mouses (# unknown)		Stand Up/Dirt Is On the Floor/The Party + 1				
			1984	15.00	30.00	60.00
Spewing Mouses (# unknown)PS		Stand Up/Dirt Is On the Floor/The Party + 1				
			1984	15.00	30.00	60.00
Oversized 9-inch sleeve						

45s

Label, Number		Title	Year	VG	VG+	NM
Sire 17937		Bright Yellow Gun/Like a Dog	1995			3.00

12-Inch Singles

Label, Number		Title	Year	VG	VG+	NM
Sire PRO-A-3070	DJ	The River (same on both sides)	1988		3.00	6.00
Sire PRO-A-3157	DJ	Saving Grace/Kristin Hersh Interview				
			1988	2.00	4.00	8.00
Sire PRO-A-3395	DJ	Dizzy (Too Many Words Mix)/Dizzy (Too Many Notes Mix)				
			1989		3.00	6.00

Thrown-Ups, The

*With Steve Turner, later of **Mudhoney**.*

7-Inch Extended Play Singles

Label, Number		Title	Year	VG	VG+	NM
Amphetamine Reptile SCALE 4		Felch	1986	11.50	21.25	42.50
Amphetamine Reptile SCALE 4PS		Felch	1986	11.50	21.25	42.50
500 made						
Amphetamine Reptile SCALE 7		Smiling Panties	1987	9.25	18.75	37.50
Amphetamine Reptile SCALE 7 PS		Smiling Panties	1987	9.25	18.75	37.50
600 made						
Amphetamine Reptile SCALE 10		Eat My Dump	1988	7.50	15.00	30.00
Amphetamine Reptile SCALE 10	PS	Eat My Dump	1988	7.50	15.00	30.00

'Til Tuesday

Boston pop-rock group with lead singer Aimee Mann, who has gone solo.

Vinyl Albums

Label, Number		Title	Year	VG	VG+	NM
Epic EAS 1350	EP	Crash and Burn + 3	1988	3.00	6.00	12.00
Promo-only sampler from Everything's Different Now LP						
Epic BFE 39458		Voices Carry	1985	3.00	6.00	12.00
Epic FE 40314		Welcome Home	1986	2.50	5.00	10.00
Epic OE 44041		Everything's Different Now	1988	2.50	5.00	10.00

45s

Label, Number		Title	Year	VG	VG+	NM
Epic 04795		Voices Carry/Are You Serious	1985			3.00
Epic 04795	PS	Voices Carry/Are You Serious	1985			3.00
Epic 04795	PS	Voices Carry	1985		2.50	5.00
"Demonstration -- Not for Sale" on back						
Epic 04935		Looking Over My Shoulder (Single Mix)/Don't Watch Me Bleed				
			1985			3.00
Epic 04935	PS	Looking Over My Shoulder (Single Mix)/Don't Watch Me Bleed				
			1985			3.00

Label, Number		Title	Year	VG	VG+	NM
Epic 05673		Love in a Vacuum/No More Crying				
			1985			3.00
Epic 06289		What About Love/Will She Just Fall Down				
			1986			3.00
Epic 06289	PS	What About Love/Will She Just Fall Down				
			1986			3.00
Epic 06450		Voices Carry/Love in a Vacuum	1986			3.00
Reissue						
Epic 06571		Coming Up Close/Angels Never Call				
			1986			3.00
Epic 06571	PS	Coming Up Close/Angels Never Call				
			1986		3.00	6.00
A somewhat scarce sleeve						
Epic 08059		(Believed You Were) Lucky/Limits to Love				
			1988			3.00
Epic 08059	PS	(Believed You Were) Lucky/Limits to Love				
			1988			3.00
Epic 68622		Rip in Heaven/How Can You Give Up				
			1989			3.00

12-Inch Singles

Label, Number		Title	Year	VG	VG+	NM
Epic EAS 01492	DJ	Rip in Heaven (same on both sides)				
			1989		2.50	5.00
Epic AS 2104	DJ	Looking Over My Shoulder (long) (short)				
			1985	2.00	4.00	8.00
Epic EAS 2210	DJ	Love in a Vacuum (Long)/Love in a Vacuum (Remix)				
			1985	2.00	4.00	8.00
Epic AS 2470	DJ	What About Love (one-sided)	1986		2.50	5.00
Epic AS 2577	DJ	Coming Up Close (Long)/Coming Up Close (Short)				
			1986		3.00	6.00

Timbuk 3
Husband-and-wife synth-pop duo based in Austin, Texas by way of Wisconsin.

Vinyl Albums

Label, Number	Title	Year	VG	VG+	NM
I.R.S. 5739	Greetings from Timbuk 3	1986	3.50	7.00	14.00
I.R.S. 42124	Eden Alley	1987	2.50	5.00	10.00
I.R.S. 82015	Edge of Allegiance	1989	3.00	6.00	12.00
I.R.S. R 143810	Greetings from Timbuk 3	1986	4.00	8.00	16.00
RCA Music Service edition					

45s

Label, Number		Title	Year	VG	VG+	NM
I.R.S. 52940		The Future's So Bright, I Gotta Wear Shades/I'll Do All Right				
			1986			3.00
I.R.S. 52940	PS	The Future's So Bright, I Gotta Wear Shades/I'll Do All Right				
			1986		2.50	5.00
Title in small print						
I.R.S. 52940	PS	The Future's So Bright, I Gotta Wear Shades/I'll Do All Right				
			1986			3.00
Title in larger print						
I.R.S. 53017		Life Is Hard/I Love You in the Strangest Way				
			1987			3.00
I.R.S. 53054		Hairstyles and Attitudes/I Just Want to Make Love to You				
			1987			3.00
I.R.S. 53221		All I Want for Christmas/Medley: Blue Christmas-I Love You x 3				
			1987		2.50	5.00
I.R.S. 53221	PS	All I Want for Christmas/Medley: Blue Christmas-I Love You x 3				
			1987		2.50	5.00
I.R.S. 53338		Easy/I Love You in the Strangest Way				
			1988			3.00
I.R.S. 53338	PS	Easy/I Love You in the Strangest Way				
			1988			3.00

Label, Number		Title	Year	VG	VG+	NM
12-Inch Singles						
I.R.S. 17183	DJ	The Future's So Bright, I Gotta Wear Shades (same on both sides)				
			1986	2.00	4.00	8.00
I.R.S. 17236	DJ	Life Is Hard (same on both sides)				
			1986		2.50	5.00
I.R.S. 17285	DJ	Hairstyles and Attitudes (same on both sides)				
			1985		2.50	5.00
I.R.S. 17427	DJ	All I Want for Christmas/Medley: Blue Christmas-I Want You x 3				
			1987	3.75	7.50	15.00
I.R.S. 17540	DJ	Rev. Jack and His Roamin' Cadillac Church (same on both sides)				
			1988		2.50	5.00
I.R.S. 17631	DJ	Reckless Driver (same on both sides)				
			1988		3.00	6.00

Timelords, The

*Originally known as The JAMs, the members of this group became **The KLF**.*

45s						
TVT 4025		Doctorin' the Tardis/Gary in the Tardis Remix				
			1988			3.00
TVT 4025		Doctorin' the Tardis/Gary in the Tardis Remix				
			1988			3.00
12-Inch Singles						
TVT 4020		Doctorin' the Tardis (3 versions)	1989	2.50	5.00	10.00
TVT 14041		Burn the Beat (4 mixes)	1988	3.00	6.00	12.00
As "The JAMS, AKA The Timelords"						

Tin Huey

Cleveland-area new wave band.

Vinyl Albums						
Warner Bros. BSK 3297		Contents Dislodged During Shipment				
			1979	3.00	6.00	12.00
7-Inch Extended Play Singles						
Clone CL-002		Puppet Wipes/Cuyahoga Creeping Bent// Poor Alphonso/The Tin Huey Story				
			1977		2.00	4.00
Clone CL-002	PS	Puppet Wipes/Cuyahoga Creeping Bent// Poor Alphonso/The Tin Huey Story				
			1977		2.00	4.00
Clone CL-004		Breakfast with the Hueys	1978			3.00
Clone CL-004	PS	Breakfast with the Hueys	1978			3.00
45s						
Clone CL-011		English Kids/Sister Rose	1980		2.00	4.00
Clone CL-011	PS	English Kids/Sister Rose	1980		2.00	4.00
Warner Bros. 49001		I'm a Believer/New York's Finest Dining Experience				
			1979		2.00	4.00
12-Inch Singles						
Warner Bros. PRO 806	DJ	I'm a Believer/Hump Day	1979	2.00	4.00	8.00

Tin Machine

*Featuring **David Bowie**.*

Vinyl Albums						
EMI E1-91990		Tin Machine	1989	3.00	6.00	12.00
EMI R 164054		Tin Machine	1989	3.50	7.00	14.00
BMG Direct Marketing edition						

Label, Number		Title	Year	VG	VG+	NM
12-Inch Singles						
EMI SPRO 04282	DJ	Under the God (same on both sides)				
			1989	3.75	7.50	15.00
EMI SPRO 04374	DJ	Heaven's In Here/Heaven's In Here (Edit)				
			1989	3.75	7.50	15.00

Toad The Wet Sprocket

Santa Barbara, California alterna-pop band.

Label, Number		Title	Year	VG	VG+	NM
Vinyl Albums						
Columbia FC 45326		Bread and Circus	1989	3.00	6.00	12.00
Columbia C 46060		Pale	1990	3.00	6.00	12.00
Columbia C 47309		Fear	1991	3.75	7.50	15.00
45s						
Columbia 74706		All I Want/Walk on the Ocean	1992			3.00
Columbia 74892		I Will Not Take These/So Alive	1993			*Cassette only*
Columbia 77474		Fall Down/All Right	1994			3.00

Tom Tom Club

*Splinter group from **Talking Heads** featuring Chris Frantz and Tina Weymouth.*

Label, Number		Title	Year	VG	VG+	NM
Vinyl Albums						
Sire SRK 3628		Tom Tom Club	1981	2.50	5.00	10.00
Sire 23916		Close to the Bone	1983	2.50	5.00	10.00
Sire 25888		Boom Boom Chi Boom Boom	1989	2.50	5.00	10.00
Warner Bros. WBMS-120	DJ	Wordy Rapping with the Tom Tom Club				
			1986	6.25	12.50	25.00
Part of "The Warner Bros. Music Show"; promo only						
45s						
Sire GSRE 0430		Genius of Love/Wordy Rappinghood				
			198?			3.00
"Back to Back Hits" reissue						
Sire 18695		You Sexy Thing	1993			*Cassette only*
Sire 18862		Sunshine and Ecstasy	1992			*Cassette only*
Sire 22998		Suborceana/Devil Does Your Dog Bite				
			1989			3.00
Sire 29437		Pleasure of Love/Never Took a Penny				
			1983			3.00
Sire 29549		The Man with the 4-Way Hips/The Man with the 4-Way Hips (Dub)				
			1983			3.00
Sire 29549	PS	The Man with the 4-Way Hips/The Man with the 4-Way Hips (Dub)				
			1983			3.00
Sire 49813		Wordy Rappinghood (edit)/(You Don't Stop) Wordy Rappinghood				
			1981		2.00	4.00
Sire 49882		Genius of Love/Lorelei	1981			3.00
Sire 50067		Wordy Rappinghood (edit)/(You Don't Stop) Wordy Rappinghood				
			1982			3.00
12-Inch Singles						
Sire PRO-A-996	DJ	Genius of Love/Lorelei	1981	2.50	5.00	10.00
Sire PRO-A-2096	DJ	Pleasure of Love/(Instrumental)	1983		3.50	7.00
Sire 20132		The Man with the 4-Way Hips (3 versions)				
			1983		3.00	6.00
Sire 20164		Pleasure of Love/(Instrumental)	1983		3.00	6.00
Sire 21198		Suboceana (4 mixes)/Devil Does Your Dog Bite				
			1989		3.00	6.00
Sire 21285		Call of the Wild (2 mixes)/Genius of Love (Live)/				
			1989		3.00	6.00

Label, Number		Title	Year	VG	VG+	NM
Sire 29930		Under the Boardwalk/On, On, On, On/Lorelei				
		Wordy Rappinghood (Live)	1982		3.50	7.00
Sire 40444		Sunshine and Ecstasy (6 versions)/As the Disco Ball Turns				
			1992	2.50	5.00	10.00
Sire 40600		You Sexy Thing (5 mixes)/Who Wants an Ugly Girl?				
			1992	2.50	5.00	10.00
Sire 49817		Wordy Rappinghood/Spooks	1981	2.50	5.00	10.00
Sire 50057		Wordy Rappinghood	1982	2.50	5.00	10.00

Tommy Tutone

San Francisco rock group.

Vinyl Albums

Columbia AS 1461	DJ	Tommy Tutone	1982	4.50	9.00	18.00
Three tracks from "Tommy Tutone-2" and the same three tracks live; promo-only						
Columbia JC 36372		Tommy Tutone	1980	3.00	6.00	12.00
Columbia ARC 37401		Tommy Tutone-2	1981	3.00	6.00	12.00
Columbia PC 37401		Tommy Tutone-2	198?	2.00	4.00	8.00
Budget-line reissue						
Columbia FC 38425		National Emotion	1983	2.50	5.00	10.00

45s

Columbia 02646		867-5309/Jenny//Not Say Goodbye				
			1981		2.00	4.00
Columbia 03002		Which Man Are You/Only One	1982			3.00
Columbia 04235		Get Around Girl/Imaginary Heart				
			1983			3.00
Columbia 05473		867-5309/Jenny//Not Say Goodbye				
			198?			3.00
Reissue						
Columbia 11278		Angel Say No/The Blame	1980			3.00
Columbia 11333		Cheap Date/Dancing Girl	1980			3.00
Columbia 11353		Girl on the Back Seat/Am I Supposed to Live				
			1980			3.00

Too Much Joy

Scarsdale, New York alterna-pop group.

Vinyl Albums

Alias A-003		Son of Sam I Am	1988	2.50	5.00	10.00
Giant PRO-A-5054	EP	Besides	1991	3.00	6.00	12.00
Promo-only collection						
Stonegarden SGN-901		Green Eggs and Crack	1987	50.00	100.00	200.00

7-Inch Extended Play Singles

JoyBuzzer JB-001		Dr. Seuss Is Dead	1994	3.75	7.50	15.00
Giveaway for people who join Too Much Joy's fan club						
Warner Bros. PRO-S-5034	DJ	Rap Like Mine/G.I. Jesus//No Good for You (Live)/				
		Lucifer Chicken	1991	3.75	7.50	15.00
"Soil X Samples 5"; clear yellow vinyl, purple label; B-side by Sister Double Happiness						

45s

Discovery 74526		The Kids Don't Understand/Get Me Out of Here				
			1996			2.00
Pink marbled vinyl						
Discovery 74526	PS	The Kids Don't Understand/Get Me Out of Here				
			1996			2.00

12-Inch Singles

Giant PRO-A-4352	DJ	That's a Lie (Remix)/Seasons in the Sun/If I Was a Mekon				
			1990	2.00	4.00	8.00

Label, Number		Title	Year	VG	VG+	NM

Total Coelo

British all-girl new-wavish group. Known in the U.K. as Toto Coelo, the name was changed here to prevent confusion with American group Toto.

45s

Label, Number		Title	Year	VG	VG+	NM
Chrysalis 42669		I Eat Cannibals/Mucho Macho	1983			3.00
Chrysalis 42669	PS	I Eat Cannibals/Mucho Macho	1983			3.00

12-Inch Singles

Label, Number		Title	Year	VG	VG+	NM
Chrysalis 03545		I Eat Cannibals (Long)/I Eat Cannibals (Short) 1983			3.00	6.00
Chrysalis 42709		Milk from the Coconut Part 1/Milk from the Coconut Part 2 1983			2.50	5.00

Tourists, The

*British band. Members **Annie Lennox** and **Dave Stewart** left to form **Eurythmics**.*

Vinyl Albums

Label, Number		Title	Year	VG	VG+	NM
Epic JE 36386		Reality Effect	1980	3.75	7.50	15.00
Epic NJE 36757		Luminous Basement	1980	3.75	7.50	15.00
Epic PC 39318		Should Have Been Greatest Hits	1984	3.00	6.00	12.00

45s

Label, Number		Title	Year	VG	VG+	NM
Epic 50850		I Only Want to Be with You/In My Mind (There's Sorrow) 1980		2.00	4.00	8.00

Toxic Reasons

Dayton, Ohio punk group.

45s

Label, Number		Title	Year	VG	VG+	NM
Benit 4057		War Hero/Somebody Help Me	1980	12.50	25.00	50.00
Benit 4057	PS	War Hero/Somebody Help Me	1980	12.50	25.00	50.00
Risky (# unknown)		Ghost Town/Killer/Noise Boys	198?	6.25	12.50	25.00
Risky (# unknown)	PS	Ghost Town/Killer/Noise Boys	198?	6.25	12.50	25.00

Transvision Vamp

British pop-rock group.

Vinyl Albums

Label, Number		Title	Year	VG	VG+	NM
Uni 5		Pop Art	1988	3.00	6.00	12.00
Uni 605		Velveteen	1989	3.00	6.00	12.00

45s

Label, Number		Title	Year	VG	VG+	NM
MCA 53786		Baby I Don't Care/Strings in My Heart 1990				3.00
Uni 50001		Tell That Girl to Shut Up/God Save the Royalties 1988				3.00
Uni 50001	PS	Tell That Girl to Shut Up/God Save the Royalties 1988				3.00
Uni 50009		I Want Your Love/Evolution Evie 1988				3.00

12-Inch Singles

Label, Number		Title	Year	VG	VG+	NM
MCA 1523	DJ	(I Just Wanna) Be With U (4 versions) 1991			3.50	7.00
MCA 2051	DJ	If Looks Could Kill (4 versions)	1991		3.50	7.00
MCA 54113		(I Just Wanna) Be with You (2 versions)/Trash City/ Tell That Girl to Shut Up/Sex Kick/I Want Your Love 1991			3.50	7.00

Label, Number		Title	Year	VG	VG+	NM
MCA 54233		(I Just Wanna) Be with You (2 versions)/Trash City/				
		Tell That Girl to Shut Up/Sex Kick/I Want Your Love				
			1991		3.50	7.00
MCA 54273		If Looks Could Kill (2 mixes)/Twangy Wig Out/My Friend the				
			1991		3.00	6.00
		Tom Cat/Puppy Dog Tails				
Uni 8004		Tell That Girl to Shut Up (2 remixes)/God Save the				
			1988	2.00	4.00	8.00
		Royalties				
Uni 8010		I Want Your Love/Sweet Thing/Evolution Evie				
			1988	3.00	6.00	12.00
Uni 10009	DJ	I Want Your Love (extended) (7" version)				
			1988	3.00	6.00	12.00

Triplets, The

Girl group -- and yes, they really are triplets! Their Elektra recordings were the result of winning a contest on MTV.

Vinyl Albums

Elektra 60455	EP	Break the Silence	1986	2.00	4.00	8.00

45s

Elektra 69542		Boys/Message of Love	1986			3.00
Elektra 69556		Translate/(B-side unknown)	1986			3.00
Mercury 878 864-7		You Don't Have to Go Home Tonight/Pyramids of Pleasure				
			1990			3.00

Tsunami

45s

Sub Pop 137		Left Behind//Warm/Crawl	1992		3.75	7.50
All copies on strawberry-red vinyl; B-side by **Velocity Girl**						
Sub Pop 137	PS	Left Behind//Warm/Crawl	1992		3.75	7.50
#39 in Sub Pop Singles Club series						

Tubes, The

San Francisco-based group, usually considered among the first new wave acts, though they were far more pop than most. Also see **Waybill, Fee.**

Vinyl Albums

A&M SP-3161		The Tubes	198?	2.00	4.00	8.00
Reissue						
A&M SP-3222		Young and Rich	198?	2.00	4.00	8.00
Reissue						
A&M SP-3242		Remote Control	198?	2.00	4.00	8.00
Reissue						
A&M SP-3243		Now	198?	2.00	4.00	8.00
Reissue						
A&M SP-3244		T.R.A.S.H. (Tubes Rarities And Smash Hits)				
			198?	2.00	4.00	8.00
Reissue						
A&M SP-4535		The Tubes	1975	3.75	7.50	15.00
A&M SP-4580		Young and Rich	1976	3.75	7.50	15.00
A&M SP-4632		Now	1977	3.75	7.50	15.00
A&M SP-4751		Remote Control	1979	3.75	7.50	15.00
A&M SP-4870		T.R.A.S.H. (Tubes Rarities And Smash Hits)				
			1981	3.00	6.00	12.00
A&M SP-6003	(2)	What Do You Want From Live!				
			1978	3.75	7.50	15.00

Label, Number		Title	Year	VG	VG+	NM
A&M SP-17012	DJ	Tubes Live/Edited for Trouble-Free Airplay				
			1978	6.25	12.50	25.00
Generic cover with sticker; promo only						
Capitol SOO-12151		The Completion Backward Principle				
			1981	3.00	6.00	12.00
Capitol ST-12260		Outside/Inside	1983	2.50	5.00	10.00
Capitol ST-12381		Love Bomb	1985	2.50	5.00	10.00
Capitol SN-16360		Outside/Inside	1985	2.00	4.00	8.00
Reissue						
Capitol SN-16378		The Completion Backward Principle				
			1986	2.00	4.00	8.00
Reissue						
Capitol SN-16446		Love Bomb	1987	2.00	4.00	8.00
Reissue						

45s

Label, Number		Title	Year	VG	VG+	NM
A&M 1733		White Punks on Dope/White Punks on Dope				
			1975		2.50	5.00
A&M 1755		What Do You Want from Life/Space Baby				
			1975		2.50	5.00
A&M 1826		Don't Touch Me There/Proud to Be an American				
			1976		2.50	5.00
A&M 1956		This Town/I'm Just a Mess	1977		2.50	5.00
A&M 2037		Show Me a Reason/I Saw Her Standing There				
			1978		2.50	5.00
A&M 2120		Prime Time/No Way Out	1979		2.50	5.00
A&M 2149		Love's a Mystery (I Don't Understand)/Telecide				
			1979		2.50	5.00
A&M 8591		White Punks on Dope/What Do You Want from Life?				
			198?			3.00
Reissue						
Capitol 5007		Don't Want to Wait Anymore/Think About Me				
			1981			3.00
Capitol 5007	PS	Don't Want to Wait Anymore/Think About Me				
			1981			3.00
Capitol 5016		Talk To Ya Later/Power Tools	1981		2.00	4.00
Capitol 5091		Gonna Get It Next Time/Sports Fans				
			1982		2.00	4.00
Capitol 5217		She's a Beauty/When You're Ready to Come				
			1983		2.00	4.00
First pressing: Purple label						
Capitol 5217	PS	She's a Beauty/When You're Ready to Come				
			1983		2.00	4.00
Sleeve only came with first pressing, and then not with all of them						
Capitol 5217		She's a Beauty/When You're Ready to Come				
			1983			3.00
Second pressing: Black label with multi-colored ring						
Capitol 5254		The Monkey Time/Sports Fans	1983			3.00
Capitol 5254	PS	The Monkey Time/Sports Fans	1983			3.00
Capitol 5258		Tip of My Tongue/Keyboard Kids				
			1983			3.00
Capitol 5443		Piece by Piece/The Right People	1985			3.00
Capitol SPRO-9740	DJ	Sports Fans (same on both sides)				
			1982		2.50	5.00

12-Inch Singles

Label, Number		Title	Year	VG	VG+	NM
A&M 17068	DJ	Prime Time/No Way Out	1979	2.00	4.00	8.00
Capitol SPRO 9332	DJ	Piece by Piece (same on both sides)				
			198?		3.00	6.00
Capitol SPRO 9728	DJ	Gonna Get It Next Time (same on both sides)				
			1982		3.00	6.00

Label, Number		Title	Year	VG	VG+	NM

Tubeway Army
See Numan, Gary.

Tucker, Maureen
Former member of The Velvet Underground.

Vinyl Albums

Label, Number		Title	Year	VG	VG+	NM
50 Skidillion Watts MOE 1	EP	Moejadkatebarry	1987	3.50	7.00	14.00
50 Skidillion Watts MOE 7		Life in Exile After Abdication	1989	3.00	6.00	12.00

Tuff Darts
Featuring Robert Gordon before he went solo.

Vinyl Albums

Label, Number		Title	Year	VG	VG+	NM
Sire SRK 6048		Tuff Darts!	1978	3.00	6.00	12.00

45s

Label, Number		Title	Year	VG	VG+	NM
Sire 1015		(I Wanna Know) Who's Been Sleeping Here?/Rats				
			1978		2.00	4.00
Sire 1015	PS	(I Wanna Know) Who's Been Sleeping Here?/Rats				
			1978		2.00	4.00

Tuxedomoon
San Francisco synth-electronic band, later relocating to Europe.

Vinyl Albums

Label, Number		Title	Year	VG	VG+	NM
Ralph TX 8004-L		Half-Mute	1980	3.00	6.00	12.00
Ralph TX 8104		Desire	1981	3.00	6.00	12.00
Ralph TX 8354		A Thousand Lives by Picture	1983	3.00	6.00	12.00
Tuxedomoon EP 45	EP	New Machine/Litebulb Overkill/Night and Day/No Tears				
			1978	5.00	10.00	20.00
Tuxedomoon EP 79	EP	Scream with a View	1979	5.00	10.00	20.00

45s

Label, Number		Title	Year	VG	VG+	NM
Ralph TX 8003		What Use?/Crash	1980		2.00	4.00
Ralph TX 8003	PS	What Use?/Crash	1980		2.00	4.00
Ralph TX 8054		Dark Companion/59 to 1 Remix				
			1980		2.00	4.00
Ralph TX 8054	PS	Dark Companion/59 to 1 Remix				
			1980		2.00	4.00
Tidal Wave TWR 101		Joeboy (The Electronic Ghost)/Pinheads on the Move				
			1978	3.75	7.50	15.00
Tidal Wave TWR 101	PS	Joeboy (The Electronic Ghost)/Pinheads on the Move				
			1978	3.75	7.50	15.00
Time Release TRR 101		Joeboy (The Electronic Ghost)/Pinheads on the Move				
			1979		3.75	7.50
Time Release TRR 101	PS	Joeboy (The Electronic Ghost)/Pinheads on the Move				
			1979		3.75	7.50
Time Release TRR 102		Stranger/Love/No Hope	1979		3.75	7.50
Time Release TRR 102	PS	Stranger/Love/No Hope	1979		3.75	7.50

12-Inch Singles

Label, Number		Title	Year	VG	VG+	NM
Ralph TX 8204		What Use? (Remix)/Crash!	1982	5.50	11.00	22.00

Label, Number		Title	Year	VG	VG+	NM

U

U-Men
Seattle grunge-rockers.

45s

Label, Number		Title	Year	VG	VG+	NM
Amphetamine Reptile SCALE 8		Freezebomb/That's Wild About Jack				
			1988	6.25	12.50	25.00
Amphetamine Reptile SCALE 8PS		Freezebomb/That's Wild About Jack				
			1988	6.25	12.50	25.00
First sleeve has gray heavy paper						
Amphetamine Reptile SCALE 8PS		Freezebomb/That's Wild About Jack				
			1988	5.00	10.00	20.00
Second sleeve has white heavy paper						
Black Label (# unknown)		Solid Action/Dig It a Hole	1987		3.75	7.50
Black Label (# unknown)	PS	Solid Action/Dig It a Hole	1987	4.25	8.75	17.50
First sleeve has silver title						
Black Label (# unknown)	PS	Solid Action/Dig It a Hole	1987		3.75	7.50
Second sleeve has black title						

UB40
British reggae band.

Vinyl Albums

Label, Number		Title	Year	VG	VG+	NM
A&M SP-4955		UB40 1980-1983	1983	3.00	6.00	12.00
A&M SP6-4980		Labour of Love	1983	3.00	6.00	12.00
A&M SP-5033		Geffery Morgan	1984	2.50	5.00	10.00
A&M SP6-5090	EP	Little Baggariddim	1985	3.00	6.00	12.00
Original copies are in a clear plastic sleeve						
A&M SP-5090	EP	Little Baggariddim	1985	2.00	4.00	8.00
Second printings are in standard album cover						
A&M SP-5137		Rat in the Kitchen	1986	2.50	5.00	10.00
A&M SP-5168		CCCP/Live in Moscow	1987	2.50	5.00	10.00
A&M SP-5213		UB40	1988	2.50	5.00	10.00
A&M R 100479		UB40	1988	3.00	6.00	12.00
BMG Direct Marketing edition						
A&M R 100677		Labour of Love	1986	3.50	7.00	14.00
BMG Direct Marketing edition						
A&M R 134092		Rat in the Kitchen	1986	3.00	6.00	12.00
RCA Music Service edition						
A&M R 144329		CCCP/Live in Moscow	1987	3.00	6.00	12.00
BMG Direct Marketing edition						
Virgin 91324		Labour of Love II	1989	3.75	7.50	15.00

45s

Label, Number		Title	Year	VG	VG+	NM
A&M 1236		Breakfast in Bed/(instrumental)	1988			3.00
A&M 1244		Red Red Wine/Sufferin'	1988		2.00	4.00
A&M 1270		Where Did I Go Wrong/Dance with the Devil				
			1989			3.00
A&M 2600		Red Red Wine/Sufferin'	1983		2.00	4.00
A&M 2630		Please Don't Make Me Cry/Food for Thought (Live)				
			1984			3.00
A&M 2630	PS	Please Don't Make Me Cry/Food for Thought (Live)				
			1984			3.00
A&M 2649		Cherry Oh Baby/Food for Thought				
			1984			3.00
A&M 2681		If It Happens Again/Nkomo A Go Go				
			1984			3.00
A&M 2758		I Got You Babe/Nkomo A Go Go				
			1985			3.00
A-side: UB40/Chrissie Hynde						

Label, Number		Title	Year	VG	VG+	NM
A&M 2758	PS	I Got You Babe/Nkomo A Go Go				
			1985			3.00
Green sleeve						
A&M 2758	PS	I Got You Babe/Nkomo A Go Go				
			1985			3.00
Brown sleeve						
A&M 2792		Don't Break My Heart/Mek Ya Rok				
			1985			3.00
A&M 2858		Sing Our Own Song/(instrumental)				
			1986			3.00
A&M 2858	PS	Sing Our Own Song/(instrumental)				
			1986			3.00
A&M 2898		Rat in My Kitchen (Long)/Rat in My Kitchen (Short)				
			1986			3.00
A&M 2961		Cherry Oh Baby	1987			3.00
A&M 8664		Red Red Wine/I Got You Babe	198?			3.00
Reissue; first pressing has short version of A-side						
A&M 8664		Red Red Wine/I Got You Babe	199?			3.00
Reissue; second pressing has long version of A-side						
Virgin S7-17402		Can't Help Falling in Love/Jungle Love				
			1993		2.00	4.00
Virgin S7-17448		The Way You Do the Things You Do/Here I Am				
		(Come and Take Me)	1993		2.00	4.00
First U.S. 45 release of 1991-92 hits						
Virgin S7-17596		Higher Ground/Chronic	1993		2.00	4.00
Clear vinyl						
Virgin S7-17909		C'est La Vie/Bad Ekko	1994			3.00
Virgin 99141		Here I Am (Come and Take Me)/Gator				
			1990		*May be cassette-only*	

12-Inch Singles						
A&M 12090		Red Red Wine/She Caught the Train				
			1983		3.00	6.00
A&M 12112		If It Happens Again (Long)/If It Happens Again (Short)/				
		Nkomo A Go Go	1984		2.50	5.00
A&M 12194		Sing Our Own Song (8.5 minute version)/Sing Our Own Song				
		(Dep Mix)	1986		3.50	7.00
A&M 12703		I've Got Mine (Edit)/I've Got Mine (Extended)/Dubmobile/				
		One in Ten	1983		2.50	5.00
A&M 17350	DJ	Don't Break My Heart/Don't Break My Heart (Remix)				
			1985	2.00	4.00	8.00
A&M 17424	DJ	Sing Our Own Song (Long)/Sing Our Own Song (Short)				
			1986	2.00	4.00	8.00
A&M 17440	DJ	Rat in the Kitchen/Rat in the Kitchen (Single)				
			1986	2.00	4.00	8.00
A&M 17487	DJ	Cherry Oh Baby (Live in Moscow) (same on both sides)				
			1986	2.00	4.00	8.00

Ultravox

*British new-wave band. Best-known member was **Midge Ure**.*

Vinyl Albums		Title	Year	VG	VG+	NM
Antilles AN 7069		Systems of Romance	1978	3.75	7.50	15.00
Antilles AN 7079		Three Into One	1980	3.75	7.50	15.00
Chrysalis CHR 1296		Vienna	1980	2.50	5.00	10.00
Chrysalis CHR 1338		Rage in Eden	1981	2.50	5.00	10.00
Chrysalis FV 41394		Quartet	1983	2.50	5.00	10.00
Chrysalis FV 41459		Lament	1984	3.00	6.00	12.00
Chrysalis FV 41490		The Collection	1984	3.00	6.00	12.00

45s						
Chrysalis 2515		Vienna/Passing Strangers	1981		2.00	4.00

Label, Number		Title	Year	VG	VG+	NM
Chrysalis 42682		Reap the Wild Wind/(B-side unknown)				
			1983		2.00	4.00
Chrysalis 42781		Dancing with Tears in My Eyes/Building				
			1984		2.00	4.00
12-Inch Singles						
Chrysalis CHS-22-PDJ	DJ	Sleepwalk (same on both sides)	1980	2.50	5.00	10.00
Chrysalis CHS 35 PDJ	DJ	The Voice (same on both sides)	1981	2.00	4.00	8.00
Chrysalis CHS 51 PDJ	DJ	Reap the Wild Wind/Hosanna	1982	3.75	7.50	15.00
Chrysalis AS 1662	DJ	Hymn (2 versions)/Reap the Wild Wind				
			1983	2.00	4.00	8.00
Chrysalis VAS 1840	DJ	One Small Day (same on both sides)				
			1984		3.00	6.00
Chrysalis VAS 2028	DJ	Love's Great Adventure/One Small Day (Edit)				
			1985		3.50	7.00
Chrysalis 2522		All Stood Still (Remix)/Alles Klar-Keep Talking				
			1981	2.50	5.00	10.00
Chrysalis 42783		Dancing with Tears in My Eyes/One Small Day				
			1984	2.00	4.00	8.00

Undead

*Band formed by Bobby Steele after the breakup of **The Misfits**.*

7-Inch Extended Play Singles						
Post Mortem 1001		Nine Toes Later	1982	2.75	5.50	11.00
Post Mortem 1001	PS	Nine Toes Later	1982	2.75	5.50	11.00
Stiff TEES-7-14		Nine Toes Later	1982	3.75	7.50	15.00
Stiff TEES-7-14	PS	Nine Toes Later	1982	3.75	7.50	15.00
45s						
Post Mortem 1003		Never Say Die/In Eighty-Four	1985	3.75	7.50	15.00
Post Mortem 1003	PS	Never Say Die/In Eighty-Four	1985	3.75	7.50	15.00

Undertones, The

*British new-wave band. Member **Feargal Sharkey** had solo records released in the U.S.*

		Title	Year	VG	VG+	NM
Vinyl Albums						
Capitol ST-12358		All Wrapped Up	1983	2.50	5.00	10.00
Harvest ST-12159		Positive Touch	1981	2.50	5.00	10.00
Sire SRK 6081		The Undertones	1979	3.00	6.00	12.00
Sire SRK 6088		Hypnotised	1980	3.00	6.00	12.00
45s						
Harvest 5027		It's Going to Happen/Fairly in the Money Now				
			1981		2.50	5.00
Sire 49		195Teenage Kicks/Smarter Than U				
			1980		2.50	5.00
Sire 49283		Wednesday Week/Told You So				
			1980		2.50	5.00

Unholy Swill

With Jim Gibson, head of Noiseville Records and a record dealer as well.

		Title	Year	VG	VG+	NM
45s						
Noiseville 2		Wanna Be God/Where's That Damn Cat?				
			1989	12.50	25.00	50.00
Yellow vinyl (90 made)						
Noiseville 2		Wanna Be God/Where's That Damn Cat?				
			1989	6.25	12.50	25.00
Black vinyl (210 made)						

Label, Number		Title	Year	VG	VG+	NM
Noiseville 2		Wanna Be God/Where's That Damn Cat?				
			1989		3.75	7.50
Burgundy vinyl						
Noiseville 2	PS	Wanna Be God/Where's That Damn Cat?				
			1989	6.25	12.50	25.00
Hand-painted sleeve (with either yellow or black vinyl version)						
Noiseville 2	PS	Wanna Be God/Where's That Damn Cat?				
			1989		3.75	7.50
Printed cover						
Noiseville 10		Satan Swill Santa/Armless Legless				
			1989	12.50	25.00	50.00
Noiseville 10	PS	Satan Swill Santa/Armless Legless				
			1989	12.50	25.00	50.00
Box set, numbered edition of 100						
Noiseville 13		Tapeworm in My Head/Basketcase				
			1990	2.50	5.00	10.00
First pressing on black vinyl (500 made)						
Noiseville 13		Tapeworm in My Head/Basketcase				
			1990	5.00	10.00	20.00
Second pressing on yellow vinyl (100 made)						
Noiseville 13		Tapeworm in My Head/Basketcase				
			1990	2.50	5.00	10.00
Continued second pressing on red vinyl (900 made)						
Noiseville 13		Tapeworm in My Head/Basketcase				
			1990		2.50	5.00
Third pressing on burgundy vinyl						
Noiseville 13	PS	Tapeworm in My Head/Basketcase				
			1990		2.50	5.00
Noiseville 17		War Pigs/War Pigs	1990	9.25	18.75	37.50
Test pressing (record recalled before release)						
Noiseville 17	PS	War Pigs/War Pigs	1990	9.25	18.75	37.50
With skulls pasted over photos of Black Sabbath; exactly 40 were made						

Unnatural Axe

Boston punk band.

7-Inch Extended Play Singles

Varulven 87-66		They Saved Hitler's Brain/The Creeper/The Plug/Summertime				
			1978	10.00	20.00	40.00
Varulven 87-66	PS	They Saved Hitler's Brain/The Creeper/The Plug/Summertime				
			1978	10.00	20.00	40.00

45s

Ver 16		The Man I Don't Wanna Be/They Saved Hitler's Brain				
			1982	5.00	10.00	20.00
Ver/Taang! 16		The Man I Don't Wanna Be/They Saved Hitler's Brain				
			1982	5.00	10.00	20.00
Roughly 100 have a "Taang!" rubberstamp on them						
Ver/Taang! 16	PS	The Man I Don't Wanna Be/They Saved Hitler's Brain				
			1982	5.00	10.00	20.00

Unrest

Washington, D.C. industrial/hardcore group.

7-Inch Extended Play Singles

Teen Beat 28		Catchpellet	1989	6.25	12.50	25.00
Teen Beat 28	PS	Catchpellet	1989	6.25	12.50	25.00
Limited edition of 399						

45s

Sub Pop 103		A Factory Record	1991	6.50	12.50	25.00
First 4,000 on lilac vinyl						

Label, Number		Title	Year	VG	VG+	NM
Sub Pop 103		A Factory Record	1991	2.50	5.00	10.00
Last 3,000 on black vinyl						
Sub Pop 103	PS	A Factory Record	1991	2.50	5.00	10.00
#29 in Sub Pop Singles Club series						
Teen Beat (# unknown)		So You Wanna Be a Rock 'N' Roll Star	198?	9.25	18.75	37.50
Teen Beat (# unknown)	PS	So You Wanna Be a Rock 'N' Roll Star	198?	9.25	18.75	37.50
Limited edition of 300						
Teen Beat IPU 17		Yes She Is My Skinhead Girl/Hydroplane	1990		3.75	7.50
Teen Beat IPU 17	PS	Yes She Is My Skinhead Girl/Hydroplane	1990		3.75	7.50
Teen Beat 105		Cath Carroll/So So Sick/Capezio d.	1993		3.75	7.50
Teen Beat 105	PS	Cath Carroll/So So Sick/Capezio d.	1993		3.75	7.50
Teen Beat 121		Where Are All Those Puerto Rican Boys?/Mountain	1993	3.75	7.50	15.00
B-side by Stereolab; special record sold on tour						
Teen Beat 121	PS	Where Are All Those Puerto Rican Boys?/Mountain	1993	3.75	7.50	15.00

Unsane
New York grunge-style band.

45s

Label, Number		Title	Year	VG	VG+	NM
PCP Entertainment (# unknown)		Jungle Music/Blood Boy//My Right	1991	9.25	18.75	37.50
Red vinyl (100 made)						
PCP Entertainment (# unknown)		Jungle Music/Blood Boy//My Right	1991	3.00	6.25	12.50
Black vinyl (900 made)						
PCP Entertainment (# unknown)	PS	Jungle Music/Blood Boy//My Right	1991	3.00	6.25	12.50
PCP Entertainment 003		Breaththing Out/Streetsweeper	1990	9.25	18.75	37.50
Clear vinyl (100 made)						
PCP Entertainment 003		Breaththing Out/Streetsweeper	1990	3.00	6.25	12.50
Black vinyl (900 made)						
PCP Entertainment 003	PS	Breaththing Out/Streetsweeper	1990	3.00	6.25	12.50
B-side by Slug						
Sub Pop 76		Vandal-X/Street Sweeper	1990	5.50	11.25	22.50
First 2,500 on green vinyl						
Sub Pop 76		Vandal-X/Street Sweeper	1990		3.75	7.50
Last 1,500 on black vinyl						
Sub Pop 76	PS	Vandal-X/Street Sweeper	1990		3.75	7.50
#23 in Sub Pop Singles Club series						
Treehouse TR 020		This Town/Urge to Kill	1989	3.75	7.50	15.00
Black vinyl						
Treehouse TR 020		This Town/Urge to Kill	1989	8.75	17.50	35.00
Yellow vinyl						
Treehouse TR 020	PS	This Town/Urge to Kill	1989	3.75	7.50	15.00

Untamed Youth, The
Neo-surf group.

45s

Label, Number	Title	Year	VG	VG+	NM
Norton 45-004	Santa's Gonna Shut 'Em Down/Santa's Midnight Run	1989			2.00

Label, Number		Title	Year	VG	VG+	NM
Norton 45-004	PS	Santa's Gonna Shut 'Em Down/Santa's Midnight Run				
			1989			2.00

Ure, Midge
Formerly of Ultravox.

Vinyl Albums
Chrysalis BFV 41508		The Gift	1985	2.50	5.00	10.00
Chrysalis FV 41649		Answer to Nothing	1988	2.50	5.00	10.00

45s
Chrysalis 42905		If I Was/(B-side unknown)	1985			3.00
Chrysalis 43319		Dear God/Music #1	1988			3.00
Chrysalis 43319	PS	Dear God/Music #1	1988			3.00

12-Inch Singles
Chrysalis VAS 2257	DJ	If I Was (Edit)/If I Was (LP version)				
			1985		3.50	7.00
Chrysalis SPRO 23387	DJ	Just For You (same on both sides)				
			1989		3.00	6.00

Urge Overkill
Chicago alterna-rock band.

Vinyl Albums
Geffen GEF 24529		Saturation	1993	3.00	6.00	12.00
Geffen GEF-24818		Exit the Dragon	1995	3.00	6.00	12.00
Touch & Go 37		Jesus Urge Superstar	1989	2.50	5.00	10.00
Touch & Go 52		Americruiser	1990	2.50	5.00	10.00
Touch & Go 70		The Supersonic Storybook	1991	2.50	5.00	10.00
Touch & Go 86	10	Stull	1992	6.25	12.50	25.00
Whitish vinyl original						

45s
Sub Pop 109		Now That's the Barclords/What's This Generation Coming To				
			1991	3.00	6.25	12.50
Sub Pop 109	PS	Now That's the Barclords/What's This Generation Coming To				
			1991	3.00	6.25	12.50
#31 in Sub Pop Singles Club series						
Touch N Go 27		Wichita Lineman/Head On	1987	3.00	6.25	12.50
Touch N Go 27	PS	Wichita Lineman/Head On	1987	3.00	6.25	12.50
Touch N Go 55		Ticket to L.A./(I'm on a) Drunk	1990		2.50	5.00
Touch N Go 55	PS	Ticket to L.A./(I'm on a) Drunk	1990		2.50	5.00
Touch N Go 55	PS	Ticket to L.A./(I'm on a) Drunk	1990	3.75	7.50	15.00
With hand-stamped autograph on back of sleeve						

Urinals, The
Los Angeles punk band.

7-Inch Extended Play Singles
Happy Squid 001		The Urinals E.P.	1978	7.50	15.00	30.00
Happy Squid 001	PS	The Urinals E.P.	1978	7.50	15.00	30.00
Happy Squid 002		Another E.P.	1979	7.50	15.00	30.00
Happy Squid 002	PS	Another E.P.	1979	7.50	15.00	30.00

45s
Happy Squid 003		Sex/Go Away Girl	1980	6.25	12.50	25.00
Happy Squid 003	PS	Sex/Go Away Girl	1980	6.25	12.50	25.00

Label, Number		Title	Year	VG	VG+	NM

US3
Hip-hop group known for rapping over jazz samples, mostly from the Blue Note Records archives.

Vinyl Albums

Label, Number		Title	Year	VG	VG+	NM
Blue Note B1-80883		Hand on the Torch	1993	3.00	6.00	12.00

12-Inch Singles

Blue Note 58139		Tukka Yoot's Riddim (5 versions)				
			1994		3.00	6.00
Capitol 15892		Cantaloop (4 versions)	1993	2.00	4.00	8.00

USA For Africa
*Charity all-star group, inspired by **Band Aid,** organized by Harry Belafonte. Not many alternative artists appeared, although **Cyndi Lauper** had a solo line and **Prince** has a song on the album.*

Vinyl Albums

Columbia USA 40043		We Are the World	1985	3.75	7.50	15.00

45s

Columbia US7-04839		We Are the World/Grace	1985		2.00	4.00
B-side by Quincy Jones						
Columbia US7-04839	PS	We Are the World/Grace	1985		2.00	4.00

12-Inch Singles

Columbia US2-05179		We Are the World/Grace	1985	2.50	5.00	10.00
B-side by Quincy Jones						

U2
*Irish rock-pop band. Also see **Passengers.***

Vinyl Albums

Island PR 2049	DJ	The Joshua Tree Interview...Their Words and Music				
			1987	6.25	12.50	25.00
Island ILPS 9646		Boy	1980	3.75	7.50	15.00
Island ILPS 9680		October	1981	4.50	9.00	18.00
Back cover is blank (no engineering credits, etc.) in upper left						
Island ILPS 9680		October	1981	3.75	7.50	15.00
Back cover has engineering credits, etc., in upper left						
Island 90040		Boy	1983	3.00	6.00	12.00
Reissue; first pressings have dark purple labels						
Island 90040		Boy	1983	2.50	5.00	10.00
Second pressings have light blue labels						
Island 90040		Boy	1983	2.00	4.00	8.00
Third pressings have black labels						
Island 90067		War	1983	3.00	6.00	12.00
Original pressings have dark purple labels						
Island 90067		War	1983	2.50	5.00	10.00
Second pressings have light blue labels						
Island 90067		War	1983	2.00	4.00	8.00
Third pressings have black labels						
Island 90092		October	1983	3.00	6.00	12.00
Reissue; first pressings have dark purple labels						
Island 90092		October	1983	2.50	5.00	10.00
Second pressings have light blue labels						
Island 90092		October	1983	2.00	4.00	8.00
Third pressings have black labels						
Island 90127-1-B		Under a Blood Red Sky	1983	5.00	10.00	20.00
White labels with "Mini LP" logo; with version of "The Electric Co." in which Bono sings snippets of "A-Me-Ri-Ca" from West Side Story and "Send In The Clowns" during the instrumental break.						
Island 90127-1-B	EP	Under a Blood Red Sky	1983	2.50	5.00	10.00
White labels with "Mini LP" logo; edited version of "The Electric Co."						
Island 90279-1-A	EP	Wide Awake in America	1985	2.50	5.00	10.00

Label, Number		Title	Year	VG	VG+	NM
Island 90581		The Joshua Tree	1987	3.00	6.00	12.00
With lyric sheet						
Island 91003	(2)	Rattle and Hum	1988	3.75	7.50	15.00
Island R 114632		October	1983	3.00	6.00	12.00
RCA Music Service edition						
Island R 124619		War	1983	3.00	6.00	12.00
BMG Direct Marketing edition						
Island R 140642	EP	Wide Awake in America	1985	3.00	6.00	12.00
RCA Music Service edition						
Island R 144636		Boy	1983	3.00	6.00	12.00
RCA Music Service edition						
Island R 153501		The Joshua Tree	1987	3.00	6.00	12.00
RCA Music Service edition; no lyric sheet						
Island R 153598	EP	Under a Blood Red Sky	1983	3.00	6.00	12.00
BMG Direct Marketing edition						
Island R 154515		The Unforgettable Fire	1985	3.00	6.00	12.00
RCA Music Service edition						
Island R 200596	(2)	Rattle and Hum	1988	4.50	9.00	18.00
BMG Direct Marketing edition						
Island 510 347-1		Achtung Baby	1991	5.00	10.00	20.00
Island 518 047-1		Zooropa	1993	3.00	6.00	12.00
All "U.S." copies actually are British imports						
Island 811 148-1		War	1990	2.00	4.00	8.00
Reissue; new sticker placed on leftover Island/Atco pressings						
Island 818 008-1		Under a Blood Red Sky	1990		3.00	6.00
Reissue; new sticker placed on leftover Island/Atco pressings						
Island 822 898-1		The Unforgettable Fire	1990	2.00	4.00	8.00
Reissue; new sticker placed on leftover Island/Atco pressings						
Island 842 296-1		Boy	1990	2.00	4.00	8.00
Reissue; new sticker placed on leftover Island/Atco pressings						
Island 842 297-1		October	1990	2.00	4.00	8.00
Reissue; new sticker placed on leftover Island/Atco pressings						
Island 842 298-1		The Joshua Tree	1990	2.00	4.00	8.00
Reissue; new sticker placed on leftover Island/Atco pressings						
Island 842 299-1	(2)	Rattle and Hum	1990	3.00	6.00	12.00
Reissue; new sticker placed on leftover Island/Atco pressings						
Island 842 479-1	EP	Wide Awake in America	1990		2.50	5.00
Reissue; new sticker placed on leftover Island/Atco pressings						
Mobile Fidelity 1-207		The Unforgettable Fire	1994	5.00	10.00	20.00
Original Master Recording						

45s

Island PR 564	DJ	I Will Follow (Mini LP Version)/I Will Follow (Radio Remix)				
			1983	7.50	15.00	30.00
Island 49716		I Will Follow/Boy-Girl	1980			

The existence of a U.S. version of this single with this B-side has not been confirmed. This was the A/B combination in England and elsewhere, though.

Island 49716	PS	I Will Follow/Boy-Girl	1980			

The existence of a U.S. version of this sleeve with this B-side has not been confirmed.

Island 49716		I Will Follow/Out of Control (Live)				
			1980	2.50	5.00	10.00
Island 49716	PS	I Will Follow/Out of Control (Live)				
			1980	2.50	5.00	10.00
Island 49716	PS	I Will Follow/Out of Control (Live)				
			1980	6.25	12.50	25.00

Promo-only poster sleeve with tour dates

Island 94961		With or Without You/In God's Country				
			1988		2.00	4.00

Gold label "Revival of the Fittest" series

Island 94974		Gloria/Sunday Bloody Sunday				
			1987		2.50	5.00

Gold label "Revival of the Fittest" series; first U.S. 45 release for either

Island 94975		New Year's Day/Two Hearts Beat As One				
			1987		2.00	4.00

Gold label "Revival of the Fittest" series

U2's most difficult American stock picture sleeves to find were based on album covers. "I Will Follow" ($20 for sleeve with stock copy of 45) was the group's first single here; "Two Hearts Beat as One" ($10 for sleeve with stock 45) came from the album *War.*

Label, Number		Title	Year	VG	VG+	NM
Island 94976		I Will Follow/Pride (In the Name of Love)	1987		2.00	4.00
Gold label "Revival of the Fittest" series						
Island 99199		All I Want Is You/Unchained Melody	1989			3.00
Island 99199	PS	All I Want Is You/Unchained Melody	1989			3.00
Island 99225		When Love Comes to Town/Dancing Barefoot	1989			3.00
A-side: With B.B. King						
Island 99225	PS	When Love Comes to Town/Dancing Barefoot	1989			3.00
Island 99250		Desire/Hallelujah Here She Comes	1988			3.00
Island 99250	PS	Desire/Hallelujah Here She Comes	1988		3.00	6.00
Cardboard gatefold sleeve						
Island 99250	PS	Desire/Hallelujah Here She Comes	1988			3.00
Standard paper sleeve						
Island 99254		Angel of Harlem/A Room at the Heartbreak Hotel	1988			3.00
Island 99254	PS	Angel of Harlem/A Room at the Heartbreak Hotel	1988			3.00
Island 99384		In God's Country/Bullet the Blue Sky	1988			3.00
Black label jukebox pressing; both sides play at 45 rpm						
Island 99385		In God's Country//Bullet the Blue Sky/Running to Stand Still	1988		2.00	4.00
A-side plays at 45 rpm, B-side at 33 1/3 rpm						
Island 99385	PS	In God's Country//Bullet the Blue Sky/Running to Stand Still	1988		2.00	4.00
Cardboard sleeve						
Island 99385	PS	In God's Country//Bullet the Blue Sky/Running to Stand Still	1988		2.00	4.00
Paper sleeve						
Island 99407		Where the Streets Have No Name/Silver and Gold	1987		2.00	4.00
Black label jukebox pressing; both sides play at 45 rpm						
Island 99408		Where the Streets Have No Name//Silver and Gold/Sweetest Thing	1987			3.00
A-side plays at 45 rpm, B-side at 33 1/3 rpm						
Island 99408	PS	Where the Streets Have No Name//Silver and Gold/Sweetest Thing	1987		2.00	4.00
Cardboard sleeve						
Island 99408	PS	Where the Streets Have No Name//Silver and Gold/Sweetest Thing	1987			3.00
Paper sleeve						
Island 99430		I Still Haven't Found What I'm Looking For//Spanish Eyes/ Deep in the Heart	1987			3.00
Island 99430	PS	I Still Haven't Found What I'm Looking For//Spanish Eyes/ Deep in the Heart	1987		2.00	4.00
Cardboard sleeve						
Island 99430	PS	I Still Haven't Found What I'm Looking For// Spanish Eyes/Deep in the Heart	1987			3.00
Paper sleeve						
Island 99431		I Still Haven't Found What I'm Looking For/Spanish Eyes	1987	2.50	5.00	10.00
Black label jukebox pressing; both sides play at 45 rpm						
Island 99453		With or Without You/Walk on the Water	1987	2.50	5.00	10.00
White label jukebox pressing, both sides play at 45 rpm						

Label, Number		Title	Year	VG	VG+	NM
Island 99469		With or Without You//Luminous Times (Hold On to Love)/ Walk on the Water	1987			3.00
Island 99469	PS	With or Without You//Luminous Times (Hold On to Love)/ Walk on the Water	1987		2.00	4.00
Cardboard sleeve						
Island 99469	PS	With or Without You//Luminous Times (Hold On to Love)/ Walk on the Water	1987			3.00
Paper sleeve						
Island 99704		Pride (In the Name of Love)/Boomerang	1984		2.00	4.00
Island 99704	PS	Pride (In the Name of Love)/Boomerang	1984		2.00	4.00
Island 99789		I Will Follow (Live)/Two Hearts Beat as One (Live)	1983		2.50	5.00
Island 99861		Two Hearts Beat as One/Endless Deep	1983		2.50	5.00
Island 99861	PS	Two Hearts Beat as One/Endless Deep	1983		2.50	5.00
Island 99915		New Year's Day/Treasure (Whatever Happened to Pete the Chop?)	1983		2.50	5.00
Island/Capitol 858 076-7		Stay (Faraway, So Close!)/I've Got You Under My Skin	1994		2.00	4.00
B-side: Frank Sinatra and Bono						
Island/Capitol 858 076-7	PS	Stay (Faraway, So Close!)/I've Got You Under My Skin	1994		2.00	4.00
B-side: Frank Sinatra and Bono						

12-Inch Singles

Label, Number		Title	Year	VG	VG+	NM
Island DMD 604	DJ	New Year's Day (same on both sides)	1983	3.75	7.50	15.00
Contains a slightly longer version than on LP						
Island PR 635	DJ	(Pride) In the Name of Love (same on both sides)	1984	3.75	7.50	15.00
With title parentheses in the wrong place as above						
Island DMD 643	DJ	Two Hearts Beat As One (5:57)//(Album Version) (Edit)	1983	6.25	12.50	25.00
Island PR 675	DJ	Wire (same on both sides)	1984	3.75	7.50	15.00
Island PR 701	DJ	A Sort of Homecoming (same on both sides)	1984	3.75	7.50	15.00
Island PR 774	DJ	Bad (Live) (same on both sides)	1985	18.75	37.50	75.00
Island PRO-A2-940 RE-1	DJ	I Will Follow/Night Train	1980	17.75	35.00	70.00
B-side by Steve Winwood						
Island PR 1021	DJ	With or Without You (same on both sides)	1987	2.50	5.00	10.00
Island DMD 1258	DJ	Desire (2:59) (5:58)/Hallelujah Here She Comes	1988	3.75	7.50	15.00
Island PR 1269	DJ	Angel of Harlem/A Room at the Heartbreak Hotel/ Love Rescue Me (Live)	1988	2.50	5.00	10.00
Island DMD 1310	DJ	When Love Comes to Town (7:30) (3:30)/God Part II/ Dancing Barefoot	1989	3.75	7.50	15.00
Island 1324	DJ	When Love Comes to Town (same on both sides)	1989	3.75	7.50	15.00
Island DMD 1349	DJ	All I Want Is You/Unchained Melody/Everlasting Love	1989	3.00	6.00	12.00
Island 2499	DJ	Desire (same on both sides)	1988	2.50	5.00	10.00
Island PR12 6715	PD	Zoo Station/Lady with the Spinning Head (2 versions)	1992	18.75	37.50	75.00
Promo-only picture disc						
Island PR12 6784	DJ	Numb (same on both sides)	1993	10.00	20.00	40.00
No label name on label						
Island 96550		All I Want Is You//Unchained Melody/Everlasting Love	1988	2.50	5.00	10.00

Label, Number		Title	Year	VG	VG+	NM
Island 96590		Angel of Harlem/A Room at the Heartbreak Hotel/Love Rescue Me				
		(Live)	1988	2.50	5.00	10.00
Island 96600		Desire (2:59) (5:58)/Hallelujah Here She Comes				
			1988	2.50	5.00	10.00
Island 862 957-1		Lemon (5 versions)	1993	2.00	4.00	8.00
Island 866 189-1		Mysterious Ways (5 versions)	1991	2.00	4.00	8.00
Island 866 977-1		Even Better Than the Real Thing/Salome/				
		Where Did It All Go Wrong/Lady with the Spinning Head				
			1992	2.00	4.00	8.00
Island 868 885-1		The Fly/Alex Descends Into Hell for a Glass of Milk/				
		The Lounge Fly Mix	1991	2.00	4.00	8.00

10-Inch Singles

Label, Number		Title	Year	VG	VG+	NM
Island PR12 6804	DJ	Lemon (Bad Yard Dub)/Lemon (Serious Def Dub)				
			1993	12.50	25.00	50.00

Promo-only 10-inch single on yellow vinyl

V

Vains, The

*Seattle hardcore/punk band, with Duff McKagan (future **Guns N' Roses**) as Andy Freeze.*

7-Inch Extended Play Singles

Label, Number		Title	Year	VG	VG+	NM
No Threes 004		You Cannot Deny Terror	1980	7.50	15.00	30.00
No Threes 004	PS	You Cannot Deny Terror	1980	7.50	15.00	30.00

Vapors, The

British new-wave/pop band.

Vinyl Albums

Label, Number	Title	Year	VG	VG+	NM
Liberty LT-1049	New Clear Days	1981	2.50	5.00	10.00
Reissue					
Liberty LT-1090	Magnets	1981	2.50	5.00	10.00
United Artists LT-1049	New Clear Days	1980	3.75	7.50	15.00

45s

Label, Number	Title	Year	VG	VG+	NM
EMI S7-18919	Turning Japanese/It's My Life	1995			3.00
*Reissue; B-side by **Talk Talk***					
Liberty 1364	Turning Japanese/Talk Talk	1980			3.00
Liberty 1411	Jimmie Jones/Silver Machine	1981			3.00
United Artists 1364	Turning Japanese/Talk Talk	1980		2.00	4.00

10-Inch Singles

Label, Number	Title	Year	VG	VG+	NM
United Artists 1364	Turning Japanese	1980	3.75	7.50	15.00

Oblong white vinyl with custom sleeve

Velocity Girl

45s

Label, Number		Title	Year	VG	VG+	NM
Slumberland DRYL 004		I Don't Care If You Go/Always	1990	12.50	25.00	50.00
Yellow vinyl (100 made)						
Slumberland DRYL 004		I Don't Care If You Go/Always	1990	6.25	12.50	25.00
Black vinyl (900 made)						
Slumberland DRYL 004	PS	I Don't Care If You Go/Always	1990	6.25	12.50	25.00
Slumberland DRYL 010		My Forgotten Favorite/Why Should I Be Nice to You?				
			1991	3.00	6.25	12.50
Red vinyl						
Slumberland DRYL 010	PS	My Forgotten Favorite/Why Should I Be Nice to You?				
			1991	3.00	6.25	12.50

Label, Number		Title	Year	VG	VG+	NM
Sub Pop 137		Warm/Crawl//Left Behind	1992	3.00	6.25	12.50
All copies on strawberry-red vinyl; B-side by **Tsunami**						
Sub Pop 137	PS	Warm/Crawl//Left Behind	1992	3.00	6.25	12.50
#39 in Sub Pop Singles Club series						
Sub Pop 179		Crazy Town/Creepy	1992	5.00	10.00	20.00
First pressing (2,000) on green vinyl						
Sub Pop 179		Crazy Town/Creepy	1992		2.50	5.00
Sub Pop 179	PS	Crazy Town/Creepy	1992		2.50	5.00

Velvet Elvis

Vinyl Albums

Enigma 73300		Velvet Elvis	1988	2.50	5.00	10.00

Velvet Monkeys

All-star band includes **Thurston Moore (Sonic Youth)**, *J Mascis (**Dinosaur Jr**), etc.*

Vinyl Albums

Rough Trade RUS 102		Rake	1990	3.00	6.00	12.00

7-Inch Extended Play Singles

Ecstatic Peace E 8	(2)	Band Sounds Like Car Crash	1990		3.75	7.50
Ecstatic Peace E 8	PS	Band Sounds Like Car Crash	1990		3.75	7.50

45s

Bona Fide 7002		Colors Part 1/Colors Part 2	1985		3.00	6.00
Bona Fide 7002	PS	Colors Part 1/Colors Part 2	1985		3.00	6.00
Sub Pop 102		Rock the Nation/Why Don't We Do It In the Road?				
			1991	5.00	10.00	20.00
First 4,000 on clear vinyl						
Sub Pop 102		Rock the Nation/Why Don't We Do It In the Road?				
			1991		2.50	5.00
Last 3,000 on black vinyl						
Sub Pop 102	PS	Rock the Nation/Why Don't We Do It In the Road?				
			1991		2.50	5.00
#28 in Sub Pop Singles Club series						

Velvet Underground, The

An influence far beyond its record sales. Also see ex-members **Cale, John; Reed, Lou; Tucker, Maureen.**

Vinyl Albums

Cotillion SD 9034	DJ	Loaded	1970	18.75	37.50	75.00
White label promo						
Cotillion SD 9034		Loaded	1970	5.00	10.00	20.00
Original pressing has a light blue label						
Cotillion SD 9034		Loaded	197?	3.75	7.50	15.00
Reissue with purplish label						
Cotillion SD 9034		Loaded	198?	3.00	6.00	12.00
Reissue with purplish label and bar code on back cover						
Cotillion SD 9500	DJ	Live at Max's Kansas City	1972	18.75	37.50	75.00
White label promo						
Cotillion SD 9500		Live at Max's Kansas City	1972	5.00	10.00	20.00
Original pressing has a light blue label						
Cotillion SD 9500		Live at Max's Kansas City	197?	3.75	7.50	15.00
Reissue with purplish label						
Cotillion SD 9500		Live at Max's Kansas City	198?	3.00	6.00	12.00
Reissue with purplish label and bar code on back cover						
Mercury SRM-2-7504	(2)	1969 (Live)	1974	12.50	25.00	50.00
Originals with red labels						
Mercury SRM-2-7504	(2)	1969 (Live)	1974	3.75	7.50	15.00
Reissues with Chicago skyline or black labels						
MGM GAS-131		The Velvet Underground (Golden Archive Series)				
			1970	10.00	20.00	40.00

Label, Number		Title	Year	VG	VG+	NM
MGM SE-4617	DJ	The Velvet Underground	1969	75.00	125.00	250.00
Yellow label promo						
MGM SE-4617		The Velvet Underground	1969	12.50	25.00	50.00
MGM M3G 4950		Archetypes	1974	5.00	10.00	20.00
Pride 0022		Lou Reed and the Velvet Underground				
			1973	3.75	7.50	15.00
Verve V-5008	M	The Velvet Underground and Nico				
			1967	75.00	150.00	300.00
Version 1: With peel-off banana peel, photo of band framed by a male torso (deduct 50% if banana sticker is gone)						
Verve V-5008	M	The Velvet Underground and Nico				
			1967	75.00	150.00	300.00
Version 2: With peel-off banana peel, photo of torso obscured by a sticker (deduct 50% if both stickers are gone)						
Verve V-5008	M	The Velvet Underground and Nico				
			1967	50.00	100.00	200.00
Version 3: With peel-off banana peel, torso is airbrushed off the cover (deduct 50% if banana sticker is gone)						
Verve V6-5008	S	The Velvet Underground and Nico				
			1967	50.00	100.00	200.00
Version 1: With peel-off banana peel, photo of band framed by a male torso (deduct 50% if banana sticker is gone)						
Verve V6-5008	S	The Velvet Underground and Nico				
			1967	50.00	100.00	200.00
Version 2: With peel-off banana peel, photo of torso obscured by a sticker (deduct 50% if stickers removed)						
Verve V6-5008	S	The Velvet Underground and Nico				
			1967	37.50	75.00	150.00
Version 3: With peel-off banana peel, torso is airbrushed off the cover (deduct 50% if banana sticker removed)						
Verve V6-5008	S	The Velvet Underground and Nico				
			1968	25.00	50.00	100.00
Version 4: With unpeelable banana						
Verve V-5046	M/DJ	White Light/White Heat	1967	75.00	150.00	300.00
White label promo						
Verve V-5046	M	White Light/White Heat	1967	25.00	50.00	100.00
Version 1: "Skeleton" cover -- a black-on-black skeleton is visible when cover is viewed at an angle						
Verve V-5046	M	White Light/White Heat	1967	12.50	25.00	50.00
Version 2: No "skeleton" on cover						
Verve V6-5046	S/DJ	White Light/White Heat	1967	62.50	125.00	250.00
Yellow label promo						
Verve V6-5046	S	White Light/White Heat	1967	12.50	25.00	50.00
Version 1: "Skeleton" cover -- a black-on-black skeleton is visible when cover is viewed at an angle						
Verve V6-5046	S	White Light/White Heat	1967	6.25	12.50	25.00
Version 2: No "skeleton" on cover						
Verve/Polydor 815 454-1		The Velvet Underground	1985	3.00	6.00	12.00
Reissue of MGM SE-4617						
Verve/Polydor 823 290-1		The Velvet Underground and Nico				
			1985	3.00	6.00	12.00
Reissue of Verve V6-5008						
Verve/Polydor 823 721-1		VU	1985	3.00	6.00	12.00
Verve/Polydor 825 119-1		White Light/White Heat	1985	3.00	6.00	12.00
Reissue of Verve V6-5046						
Verve/Polydor 826 284-1	(2)	1969 (Live)	1985	3.00	6.00	12.00
Reissue of Mercury SRM-2-7504						
Verve/Polydor 829 405-1		Another View	1986	3.00	6.00	12.00

45s

Label, Number		Title	Year	VG	VG+	NM
Cotillion 44107		Who Loves the Sun/Oh, Sweet Nothin'				
			1971	75.00	150.00	300.00
Cotillion 44107	DJ	Who Loves the Sun (mono/stereo)				
			1971	25.00	50.00	100.00
MGM 14057		What Goes On/Jesus	1969	75.00	150.00	300.00
Existence of a stock copy of this record has been questioned.						
MGM 14057	DJ	What Goes On/Jesus	1969	50.00	100.00	200.00
Verve 10427		All Tomorrow's Parties/I'll Be Your Mirror				
			1966	100.00	200.00	400.00
Verve 10427	DJ	All Tomorrow's Parties/I'll Be Your Mirror				
			1966	75.00	150.00	300.00

Label, Number		Title	Year	VG	VG+	NM
Verve 10427	PS	All Tomorrow's Parties/I'll Be Your Mirror				
			1966	1,250.00	2,500.00	5,000.00

Only one known copy, it sold for $4,000 NM in 1992.

Verve 10466		Femme Fatale/Sunday Morning	1966	75.00	150.00	300.00
Verve 10466	DJ	Femme Fatale/Sunday Morning	1966	50.00	100.00	200.00
Verve 10560		White Light/White Heat//Here She Comes Now				
			1967	75.00	150.00	300.00
Verve 10560	DJ	White Light/White Heat//I Heard Her Call My Name				
			1967	75.00	150.00	300.00

12-Inch Singles

| Polydor PRO 349 | DJ | Foggy Notion (same on both sides) | | | | |
| | | | 1985 | 3.75 | 7.50 | 15.00 |

Verlaine, Tom
Member of Television.

Vinyl Albums

Elektra 6E-216		Tom Verlaine	1979	3.75	7.50	15.00
I.R.S. 42050		Flash Light	1987	2.50	5.00	10.00
Warner Bros. BSK 3539		Dreamtime	1981	2.50	5.00	10.00
Warner Bros. BSK 3685		Words from the Front	1982	2.50	5.00	10.00
Warner Bros. 25144		Cover	1984	2.50	5.00	10.00

12-Inch Singles

| I.R.S. 17369 | DJ | A Town Called Walker/Marquee Moon (Live) | | | | |
| | | | 1987 | 2.50 | 5.00 | 10.00 |

Vertigo
Minneapolis punk/grunge group.

45s

Amphetamine Reptile SCALE 21		Bad Syd/Going to Pieces	1989	3.75	7.50	15.00
Amphetamine Reptile SCALE 21	PS	Bad Syd/Going to Pieces	1989	3.75	7.50	15.00
Skid Mark SMT 004		Two Lives//Front End Loader/Phil 105				
			1988	3.75	7.50	15.00
Skid Mark SMT 004	PS	Two Lives//Front End Loader/Phil 105				
			1988	12.50	25.00	50.00

First sleeve is a numbered edition of 300 -- all numbered #1!

| Skid Mark SMT 004 | PS | Two Lives//Front End Loader/Phil 105 | | | | |
| | | | 1988 | 3.75 | 7.50 | 15.00 |

Second sleeve is unnumbered

Veruca Salt
Chicago alterna-rock band.

Vinyl Albums

Minty Fresh MF-7		American Thighs	1994	2.50	5.00	10.00
Minty Fresh MF-9	10	Nunber One Blind	1995		3.00	6.00
Pink vinyl						

45s

Minty Fresh MF-6		Seether/All Hail Me	1994	6.25	12.50	25.00
First pressing: See-through orange vinyl, numbered edition (100 made)						
Minty Fresh MF-6		Seether/All Hail Me	1994	3.75	7.50	15.00
Second pressing: See-through orange vinyl, un-numbered edition (2,000 made)						
Minty Fresh MF-6		Seether/All Hail Me	1994	2.50	5.00	10.00
Third pressing: Opaque orange vinyl						
Minty Fresh MF-6	PS	Seether/All Hail Me	1994	2.50	5.00	10.00

Label, Number		Title	Year	VG	VG+	NM

Victims, The
New York City punk band.

45s

Label, Number		Title	Year	VG	VG+	NM
BRG 101		You Got the Magic/Destination Undecided/Don't Come Knockin'/				
		Help Me Baby/	1977	8.75	17.50	35.00
BRG 101	PS	You Got the Magic/Destination Undecided/Don't Come Knockin'/				
		Help Me Baby	1977	8.75	17.50	35.00
Plan 9 PL 1005		Annette/I Want Head/Behind the Times/Nervous				
			1978	17.50	35.00	70.00
Plan 9 PL 1005	PS	Annette/I Want Head/Behind the Times/Nervous				
			1978	17.50	35.00	70.00
Red and white sleeve						
Plan 9 PL 1005	PS	Annette/I Want Head/Behind the Times/Nervous				
			1978	15.00	30.00	60.00
Black and white sleeve						

Violent Femmes
Punk band from Milwaukee, Wisconsin.

Vinyl Albums

Label, Number		Title	Year	VG	VG+	NM
Slash 23845		Violent Femmes	1983	3.75	7.50	15.00
Slash 25094		Hallowed Ground	1984	3.00	6.00	12.00
Slash 25340		The Blind Leading the Naked	1986	2.50	5.00	10.00
Slash 25819		3	1988	2.50	5.00	10.00
Warner Bros. PRO-A-3519	DJ	3 On 3	1989	6.25	12.50	25.00
Promo-only interviews and music						

45s

Label, Number		Title	Year	VG	VG+	NM
Slash 28683		Children of the Revolution/World Without Mercy				
			1986		2.00	4.00
Slash 29521		Gone Daddy Gone/Good Feeling				
			1983		2.00	4.00

12-Inch Singles

Label, Number		Title	Year	VG	VG+	NM
Slash PRO-A-2422	DJ	Children of the Revolution/Children of the Revolution (Edit)				
			1986		3.00	6.00
Slash PRO-A-3411	DJ	Nightmares/World We're Living In				
			1989	2.50	5.00	10.00
Warner Bros. PRO-A-2422	DJ	Children of the Revolution (edit) (LP)				
			1986	5.00	10.00	20.00

Visage
*Loose confederation of former and future members of many British groups, including **Magazine** and **Ultravox.***

Vinyl Albums

Label, Number		Title	Year	VG	VG+	NM
Polydor PX1-501	EP	Visage	1981	3.00	6.00	12.00
Polydor PD1-6304		Visage	1981	3.00	6.00	12.00
Polydor PD1-6350		The Anvil	1982	3.00	6.00	12.00
Polydor 815 347-1		Fade to Grey -- The Singles Collection				
			1983	3.00	6.00	12.00
Polydor 823 052-1		Beat Boy	1984	3.00	6.00	12.00

45s

Label, Number		Title	Year	VG	VG+	NM
Polydor 2158		Fade to Grey/Malpaso Man	1981		2.00	4.00
Polydor 2183		Fade to Grey/Tar	1981			*Cancelled*

12-Inch Singles

Label, Number		Title	Year	VG	VG+	NM
Polydor 178	DJ	Damned Don't Cry/Horseman/Night Train				
			1982	2.50	5.00	10.00

Label, Number		Title	Year	VG	VG+	NM
Polydor 521	DJ	Night Train (2 versions)/I'm Still Searching				
			1982	2.50	5.00	10.00
Polydor 881 032-1		Love Glove (2 versions)/She's a Machine				
			1984	2.00	4.00	8.00

Vktms
San Francisco punk group badly in need of buying a vowel.

7-Inch Extended Play Singles
Emergency Room ERR-OR2		Vktms E.P.	1979	7.50	15.00	30.00
Emergency Room ERR-OR2	PS	Vktms E.P.	1979	7.50	15.00	30.00

45s
415 Records S-0010		100% White Girl/No Long Goodbyes				
			1980	2.50	5.00	10.00
415 Records S-0010	PS	100% White Girl/No Long Goodbyes				
			1980	2.50	5.00	10.00

Voice of the Beehive
Poppish band formed in London by California expatriates.

Vinyl Albums
London 828 100-1		Let It Bee	1988	5.00	10.00	20.00

45s
London 886 334-7		I Say Nothing/Things You See When You Don't Have Your Gun				
			1988			3.00
London 886 334-7	PS	I Say Nothing/Things You See When You Don't Have Your Gun				
			1988			3.00
London 886 500-7		Don't Call Me Baby	1989			3.00

12-Inch Singles
London 886 370-1		I Say Nothing/The Things You See... (Live)/In the Flesh				
			1987	2.50	5.00	10.00

Vomit Pigs, The
Dallas punk group.

7-Inch Extended Play Singles
Bad Wrecors (# unknown)		Take One	1979	37.50	75.00	150.00
Bad Wrecors (# unknown)	PS	Take One	1979	37.50	75.00	150.00

W

Waitresses, The
New-wave band from Akron, Ohio.

Vinyl Albums
Polydor PX1-507	EP	I Could Rule the World If...	1982	2.50	5.00	10.00
Polydor PD1-6348		Wasn't Tomorrow Wonderful?	1982	2.50	5.00	10.00
Polydor 810 980-1		Bruiseology	1983	2.50	5.00	10.00
Polydor 810 980-1	DJ	Bruiseology	1983	6.25	12.50	25.00
Promo only on purplish vinyl						

45s
Antilles ANS-105		I Know What Boys Like/No Guilt				
			1980		2.50	5.00
Small center hole						
Antilles ANS-105	PS	I Know What Boys Like/No Guilt				
			1980		2.50	5.00

"Christmas Wrapping" has become the Waitresses' best-known song, though its first American single release wasn't until this 1994 issue on Collectables ($3). It was available on at least two Christmas collections here, plus on a British 45 in edited form.

"Wake Me Up Before You Go-Go" was Wham!'s first American hit and also has the hardest picture sleeve to find among its hit singles.

Label, Number		Title	Year	VG	VG+	NM
Antilles ANS-4504		I Know What Boys Like/No Guilt				
			1980		2.50	5.00
Collectables 4949		Christmas Wrapping/I Know What Boys Like				
			1994			3.00
First U.S. single release of this holiday classic						
Polydor 2196		I Know What Boys Like/It's My Car				
			1982		2.00	4.00
Polydor 2214		No Guilt/Go On	1982		2.00	4.00
Polydor 2225		Square Pegs/The Smartest Person I Know				
			1982		2.00	4.00
Polydor 813 394-7		Pleasure/Make the Weather	1983		2.00	4.00
12-Inch Singles						
Polydor PRO 179	DJ	I Know What Boys Like/No Guilt				
			1982	2.00	4.00	8.00
Polydor PRO 196	DJ	Bread and Butter (Remix)/Bread and Butter (Dub)				
			1983		3.50	7.00
Polydor 203	DJ	Bruiseology/Make the Weather	1983		3.50	7.00

Wall of Voodoo

*Los Angeles snyth-pop group led by Stanard Ridgway. See also **Copeland, Stewart/Stanard Ridgway**.*

Vinyl Albums						
I.R.S. 5662		Seven Days in Sammystown	1985	3.00	6.00	12.00
I.R.S. 5997		Happy Planet	1987	2.50	5.00	10.00
I.R.S. 42140		The Ugly American in Australia	1988	2.50	5.00	10.00
I.R.S. SP-70022		Dark Continent	1981	3.00	6.00	12.00
I.R.S. SP-70026		Call of the West	1982	3.00	6.00	12.00
Index/I.R.S. SP-70401	EP	Wall of Voodoo	1980	3.00	6.00	12.00
45s						
I.R.S. 9912		Mexican Radio/Call of the West	1983			3.00
I.R.S. 9912	PS	Mexican Radio/Call of the West	1983			3.00
I.R.S. 53136		Do It Again/Back to the Laundromat				
			1987			3.00
I.R.S. 53136	PS	Do It Again/Back to the Laundromat				
			1987			3.00
I.R.S. 70963	DJ	Mexican Radio (Stereo)/Mexican Radio (Mono)				
			1982		2.00	4.00
Promo-only number						
I.R.S. 70963	PS	Mexican Radio (Stereo)/Mexican Radio (Mono)				
			1982		2.00	4.00
Promo-only number						
12-Inch Singles						
I.R.S. 17051	DJ	Far Side of Crazy (same on both sides)				
			1985		3.00	6.00
I.R.S. 23694		Do It Again (4 versions)	1987	2.50	5.00	10.00
I.R.S. SP-70407		Mexican Radio/There's Nothing on This Side				
			1982	3.00	6.00	12.00
Index 12.001		Ring of Fire (Remix)/Morricone Themes (Live)				
			1982	3.00	6.00	12.00

Wang Chung

British pop-rock band. Originally recorded as Huang Chung; those releases are noted below.

Vinyl Albums						
Arista AL 6603		Huang Chung	1982	3.75	7.50	15.00
As "Huang Chung"						
Geffen GHS 4004		Points on the Curve	1983	2.50	5.00	10.00
Geffen GHS 24115		Mosaic	1986	2.50	5.00	10.00
Geffen GHS 24222		The Warmer Side of Cool	1989	2.50	5.00	10.00

Label, Number		Title	Year	VG	VG+	NM
Geffen R 101063		The Warmer Side of Cool	1989	3.00	6.00	12.00
BMG Direct Marketing edition						
Geffen R 144369		Points on the Curve	1983	3.00	6.00	12.00
RCA Music Service edition						
Geffen R 163751		Mosaic	1986	3.00	6.00	12.00
RCA Music Service edition						

45s

A&M 2728		Fire in the Twilight/The Reggae (Instrumental)				
			1985		2.50	5.00
Arista 1012	DJ	Hold Back the Tears (same on both sides)				
			1983	2.00	4.00	8.00
As "Huang Chung"; stock copy appears not to exist						
Geffen 22969		Praying to a New God/Tall Trees in a Blue Sky				
			1989			2.00
Geffen 22969	PS	Praying to a New God/Tall Trees in a Blue Sky				
			1989			2.00
Geffen 28359		Hypnotise Me/Lullabye	1987			2.00
Geffen 28359	PS	Hypnotise Me/Lullabye	1987			2.00
Geffen 28531		Let's Go!/The World In Which You Live				
			1986			2.00
Geffen 28531	PS	Let's Go!/The World In Which You Live				
			1986			2.00
Geffen 28562		Everybody Have Fun Tonight/Fun Tonight: The Early Years				
			1986			2.00
Geffen 28562	PS	Everybody Have Fun Tonight/Fun Tonight: The Early Years				
			1986			2.00
Geffen 28891		To Live and Die in L.A./Black-Blue-White				
			1985			2.00
Geffen 28891	PS	To Live and Die in L.A./Black-Blue-White				
			1985			2.00
Geffen 29193		Don't Be My Enemy/Wait				
			1984			3.00
Geffen 29310		Dance Hall Days/Ornamental Elephant				
			1984			3.00
Geffen 29310	PS	Dance Hall Days/Ornamental Elephant				
			1984			3.00
Geffen 29377		Don't Let Go/There Is a Nation	1984			3.00
Geffen 29377	PS	Don't Let Go/There Is a Nation	1984			3.00

12-Inch Singles

A&M 12131		Fire in the Twilight/Heart Too Hot to Hold				
			1985		3.00	6.00
Arista SP-143	DJ	China/Ti Na Na	1982	2.50	5.00	10.00
As "Huang Chung"						
Geffen PRO-A-2108	DJ	Don't Let Go/Wait/Dance Hall Days				
			1983		3.00	6.00
Geffen PRO-A-2152	DJ	Wait/Wait (Edit)	1984	2.50	5.00	10.00
Geffen PRO-A-2205	DJ	Don't Be My Enemy/Don't Be My Enemy (Edit Remix)				
			1984		3.00	6.00
Geffen PRO-A-2581	DJ	Everybody Have Fun Tonight (2 mixes)				
			1986	2.50	5.00	10.00
Geffen PRO-A-2582	DJ	Dance Hall Days/To Live and Die in L.A. (edit)/				
		Everybody Have Fun Tonight (edit)				
			1986	3.00	6.00	12.00
Geffen PRO-A-2589	DJ	Everybody Have Fun Tonight (4 mixes)				
			1986	2.00	4.00	8.00
Geffen PRO-A-2630	DJ	Eyes on the Girl (same on both sides)				
			1986		2.50	5.00
Geffen 20194		Dance Hall Days/Don't Let Go	1984	3.00	6.00	12.00
Geffen 20252		Don't Be My Enemy/Wait	1983		2.50	5.00
Geffen 20602		Let's Go (3 mixes)/Betrayal	1986		2.50	5.00

Label, Number		Title	Year	VG	VG+	NM

Was (Not Was)

Detroit new-wave/funk/pop group. Don Was has gained fame as a producer in the 1990s.

Vinyl Albums

Label, Number		Title	Year	VG	VG+	NM
Chrysalis FV 41664		What's Up Dog?	1988	2.50	5.00	10.00
Chrysalis R 100615		What's Up Dog?	1988	3.00	6.00	12.00
BMG Direct Marketing edition						
Geffen PRO-A-2079	DJ	Shake Your Head + 3	1983	3.00	6.00	12.00
Promo-only sampler from Born to Laugh at Tornadoes						
Geffen GHS 4016		Born to Laugh at Tornadoes	1983	2.50	5.00	10.00
Island ILPS 9666		Was (Not Was)	1981	3.00	6.00	12.00

45s

Label, Number		Title	Year	VG	VG+	NM
Chrysalis 23350		Papa Was a Rollin' Stone/Ballad of You	1989			3.00
Chrysalis 43266		Spy in the House of Love/Dad, I'm in Jail	1988			2.00
Chrysalis 43266	PS	Spy in the House of Love/Dad, I'm in Jail	1988			2.00
Chrysalis 43331		Walk the Dinosaur/Wedding Vows in Vegas	1988			2.00
Chrysalis 43331	PS	Walk the Dinosaur/Wedding Vows in Vegas	1988			2.00
Chrysalis 43365		Anything Can Happen (Pop)/Anything Can Happen (R&B)	1989			2.00
Chrysalis 43365	PS	Anything Can Happen (Pop)/Anything Can Happen (R&B)	1989			2.00
Geffen 29407		Knocked Down Made Small (Treated Like a Rubber Ball)/ Man Vs. the Empire Brain Building	1983		2.00	4.00
Geffen 29477		Smile/The Party Broke Up	1983		2.00	4.00
Island 49756		Out Come the Freaks/Out Come the Freaks (Dub Version)	1981		2.50	5.00

12-Inch Singles

Label, Number		Title	Year	VG	VG+	NM
4th & B'Way PRO 493	DJ	White People Can't Dance (same on both sides)	1989	2.00	4.00	8.00
Chrysalis 23411		Boy's Gone Crazy (3 versions)/The Death of Mr. Ping Pong	1990		3.00	6.00
Chrysalis 23540		Papa Was a Rollin' Stone (3 versions)	1990		3.00	6.00
Chrysalis 23541		Papa Was a Rollin' Stone/You, You, You and Syd Straw/ Elvis Rolls Royce Was Leonard Cohen	1990	2.50	5.00	10.00
Chrysalis 23641		How the Heart Behaves (4 mixes)	1991		3.00	6.00
Chrysalis 43262		Spy in the House of Love (4 mixes)	1988		2.50	5.00
Chrysalis 43332		Walk the Dinosaur (4 mixes)	1988		2.50	5.00
Chrysalis 43378		Anything Can Happen (4 versions)/The Death of Mr. Pong	1989		2.50	5.00
Island PRO 961	DJ	Out Come the Freaks (Extended)/Out Come the Freaks (Dub)	1981	2.00	4.00	8.00
Island PRO 1000	DJ	Tell Me That I'm Dreaming (2 versions)	1981		3.00	6.00
Island 50011		Out Come the Freaks/Tell Me That I'm Dreaming	1982		3.00	6.00

Label, Number		Title	Year	VG	VG+	NM

Waterboys, The

London band. Early member Karl Wallinger left to become **World Party.**

Vinyl Albums

Label, Number		Title	Year	VG	VG+	NM
Chrysalis PV 41541		The Waterboys	1986	2.00	4.00	8.00
Reissue of first U.K. LP						
Chrysalis PV 41542		A Pagan Place	1986	2.00	4.00	8.00
Reissue						
Chrysalis FV 41543		This Is the Sea	1986	2.50	5.00	10.00
Reissue						
Chrysalis FV 41589		Fisherman's Blues	1988	2.50	5.00	10.00
Island 90147	EP	The Waterboys	1983	2.50	5.00	10.00
Island 90190		A Pagan Place	1984	3.75	7.50	15.00
Island 90457		This Is the Sea	1985	3.00	6.00	12.00

45s

Label, Number		Title	Year	VG	VG+	NM
Chrysalis S7-17527		Fisherman's Blues/Sweet Thing	1993			3.00
Chrysalis S7-18398		The Whole of the Moon/Medicine Bow	1995			3.00

12-Inch Singles

Label, Number		Title	Year	VG	VG+	NM
Ensign 201		December (long) (edit)	1983	3.75	7.50	15.00
Island 661	DJ	Church Not Made with Hands (Edit) (same on both sides)	1984	2.00	4.00	8.00
Island 840	DJ	Don't Bang the Drum (same on both sides)	1985		3.00	6.00

Waters, Roger

Ex-member of Pink Floyd (not in this book). The below is listed because of its guest stars, who include **The Hooters** *and* **Cyndi Lauper.**

Vinyl Albums

Label, Number		Title	Year	VG	VG+	NM
Mercury 846 611-1	(2)	The Wall -- Live in Berlin	1990	3.75	7.50	15.00
Mercury R 209833	(2)	The Wall -- Live in Berlin	1990	5.00	10.00	20.00
BMG Direct Marketing edition						

Watt, Mike

Formerly of **The Minutemen** *and* **fIREHOSE.**

Vinyl Albums

Label, Number		Title	Year	VG	VG+	NM
Columbia C 66464		Ball-Hog Or Tugboat?	1995	3.00	6.00	12.00

45s

Label, Number		Title	Year	VG	VG+	NM
Columbia 77898		Big Train/Amnesty Report	1995			2.00
Columbia 77898	PS	Big Train/Amnesty Report	1995			2.00

Waybill, Fee

Formerly of **The Tubes.**

Vinyl Albums

Label, Number		Title	Year	VG	VG+	NM
Capitol ST-12369		Read My Lips	1984	2.50	5.00	10.00

45s

Label, Number		Title	Year	VG	VG+	NM
Capitol 5399		Who Said Life Would Be Pretty/You're Still Laughing	1984			3.00
Capitol 5441		I Don't Even Know Your Name (Passion Play)/Star of the Show	1985			3.00

Label, Number		Title	Year	VG	VG+	NM

Weasels, The
Los Angeles trashy punk group.

45s

Siamese 002		Beat Her with a Rake/I'm the Commander				
			1978	3.75	7.50	15.00
Siamese 002	PS	Beat Her with a Rake/I'm the Commander				
			1978	3.75	7.50	15.00

Ween
Alterna-rock duo from Lambertville, New Jersey (across the Delaware from New Hope, Pennsylvania).

Vinyl Albums

Grand Royal GR 010		Chocolate and Cheese	1994	3.00	6.00	12.00
Cassette and CD on Elektra 61639						

45s

Sub Pop 214		Skycruiser/Cruise Control	1993	2.50	5.00	10.00
Clear pink vinyl						
Sub Pop 214	PS	Skycruiser/Cruise Control	1993	2.50	5.00	10.00
#57 in Sub Pop Singles Club series						

Weirdos
Los Angeles new-wave group.

Vinyl Albums

Bomp! 4007	EP	Who? What? When? Where? Why?				
			1979	3.75	7.50	15.00
Frontier 4623-1-L		Condor	1990	3.00	6.00	12.00
Frontier 4630-1-L		Weird World	1991	3.00	6.00	12.00
Out of Darkness OTD 001	DJ	Message from the Underworld	198?	10.00	20.00	40.00
Promo-only release						
Rhino RNEP 508	EP	Action Design	1980	5.00	10.00	20.00

45s

(No label, no number)		Skateboards to Hell/Adult Hood	1979	3.00	6.25	12.50
(No label, no number)	PS	Skateboards to Hell/Adult Hood	1979	3.00	6.25	12.50
Bomp! 112		Destroy All Music/Why Do You Exist?/A Life of Crime				
			1977	10.00	20.00	40.00
Black label, pressed on styrene						
Bomp! 112		Destroy All Music/Why Do You Exist?/A Life of Crime				
			1977	5.00	10.00	20.00
White label, pressed on styrene						
Bomp! 112		Destroy All Music/Why Do You Exist?/A Life of Crime				
			1977	2.25	4.50	9.00
White label, pressed on vinyl						
Bomp! 112	PS	Destroy All Music/Why Do You Exist?/A Life of Crime				
			1977	2.25	4.50	9.00
Dangerhouse 1063		We Got the Neutron Bomb/Solitary Confinement				
			1978	5.00	10.00	20.00
Dangerhouse 1063	PS	We Got the Neutron Bomb/Solitary Confinement				
			1978	5.00	10.00	20.00

Westerberg, Paul
*Formerly of **The Replacements**.*

45s

Epic Soundtrax 74419		Dyslexic Heart/Nearly Lost You				
			1992		2.00	4.00
*B-side by **Screaming Trees***						

Label, Number		Title	Year	VG	VG+	NM

Wet Wet Wet
Pop-rock group from Glasgow, Scotland.

45s

Label, Number		Title	Year	VG	VG+	NM
London 856 194-7		Love Is All Around/Goodnight Girl				
			1994			3.00
Uni 50000		Wishing I Was Lucky/(B-side unknown)				
			1987			3.00
Uni 50000	PS	Wishing I Was Lucky/(B-side unknown)				
			1987			3.00
Uni 50006		Angel Eyes/(B-side unknown)	1988			3.00
Uni 50006	PS	Angel Eyes/(B-side unknown)	1988			3.00

12-Inch Singles

Label, Number		Title	Year	VG	VG+	NM
Uni 8000		Wishing I Was Lucky (3 versions)				
			1988		3.00	6.00
Uni 8005		Sweet Little Mystery (3 versions)				
			1988		3.00	6.00
Uni L33-10000	DJ	Wishing I Was Lucky (same on both sides)				
			1987		2.50	5.00

Wham!
*British pop-rock duo of **George Michael** and Andrew Ridgeley. Records originally released in the U.S. under the name "Wham! U.K."*

Vinyl Albums

Label, Number		Title	Year	VG	VG+	NM
Columbia BFC 38911		Fantastic	1983	3.75	7.50	15.00
Cover and label list artist as "Wham! U.K."						
Columbia FC 38911		Fantastic	1985	2.50	5.00	10.00
Reissue; cover and label list artist as "Wham!"						
Columbia FC 39595		Make It Big	1984	2.50	5.00	10.00
Columbia 9C9 40062	PD	Make It Big	1985	6.25	12.50	25.00
Picture disc						
Columbia OC 40285		Music from the Edge of Heaven	1986	2.50	5.00	10.00
With "removable sticker" list of song titles still on front cover						

45s

Label, Number		Title	Year	VG	VG+	NM
Columbia CS7 2591	DJ	Last Christmas (6:43)/Last Christmas (4:24)				
			1986	2.50	5.00	10.00
Columbia 03611		Young Guns (Go For It)/Going For It				
			1983		2.50	5.00
As "Wham! U.K."						
Columbia 03611	PS	Young Guns (Go For It)/Going For It				
			1983		2.50	5.00
As "Wham! U.K."						
Columbia 03611	PS	Young Guns (Go For It)	1983	2.00	4.00	8.00
As "Wham! U.K."; "Demonstration -- Not for Sale" on rear						
Columbia 03932		Bad Boys/Bad Boys (Instrumental)				
			1983		2.50	5.00
As "Wham! U.K."						
Columbia 04552		Wake Me Up Before You Go-Go/(instrumental)				
			1984			3.00
Columbia 04552	PS	Wake Me Up Before You Go-Go/(instrumental)				
			1984	2.00	4.00	8.00
Columbia 04691		Careless Whisper/(instrumental)	1984			3.00
As "Wham! featuring George Michael"						
Columbia 04691	PS	Careless Whisper/(instrumental)	1984	2.00	4.00	8.00
As "Wham! featuring George Michael"; color sleeve						
Columbia 04691	PS	Careless Whisper	1984	2.50	5.00	10.00
As "Wham! featuring George Michael"; color sleeve; "Demonstration -- Not for Sale" on rear						
Columbia 04691	PS	Careless Whisper/(instrumental)	1984		2.50	5.00
As "Wham! featuring George Michael"; black & white sleeve						

Label, Number		Title	Year	VG	VG+	NM
Columbia 04840		Everything She Wants/Like a Baby				
			1985			3.00
Columbia 04840	PS	Everything She Wants/Like a Baby				
			1985			3.00
Columbia 05409		Freedom/Heartbeat	1985			3.00
Columbia 05409	PS	Freedom/Heartbeat	1985			3.00
Columbia 05721		I'm Your Man/Do It Right	1985			3.00
Columbia 05721	PS	I'm Your Man/Do It Right	1985			3.00
Columbia 06182		The Edge of Heaven/Blue (Live in China)				
			1986			3.00
Columbia 06182	PS	The Edge of Heaven/Blue (Live in China)				
			1986			3.00
Columbia 06294		Where Did Your Heart Go?/Wham! Rap '86				
			1986			3.00
Columbia 06294	PS	Where Did Your Heart Go?/Wham! Rap '86				
			1986			3.00
Columbia 68712		Wake Me Up Before You Go-Go/(Instrumental)				
			1988			3.00
Reissue						
Columbia 68713		Careless Whisper/(Instrumental)	1988			3.00
Reissue						
Columbia 68715		Everything She Wants/Like a Baby				
			1988			3.00
Reissue						

12-Inch Singles

Label, Number		Title	Year	VG	VG+	NM
Columbia AS 1980	DJ	Careless Whisper (same on both sides)				
			1984	3.75	7.50	15.00
As "Wham! featuring George Michael"						
Columbia CAS 2122	DJ	Freedom/Freedom (Single Remix)				
			1985	6.25	12.50	25.00
Columbia 03177		Enjoy What You Do (Wham Rap)/(instrumental)				
			1982	5.00	10.00	20.00
As "Wham! U.K."						
Columbia 03501		Young Guns (Go For It)/Going For It				
			1983	3.00	6.00	12.00
As "Wham! U.K."						
Columbia 03933		Bad Boys/Bad Boys (Instrumental)				
			1983	5.00	10.00	20.00
As "Wham! U.K."						
Columbia 05049		Wake Me Up Before You Go-Go/(Instrumental)				
			1984	2.50	5.00	10.00
Columbia 05170		Careless Whisper (extended)/(instrumental)				
			1984	5.00	10.00	20.00
As "Wham! featuring George Michael"						
Columbia 05180		Everything She Wants/Like a Baby				
			1985	2.00	4.00	8.00
Columbia 05238		Freedom (extended)/Freedom (Instrumental)/Heartbeat				
			1985		3.00	6.00
Columbia 05322		I'm Your Man (2 mixes)/Do It Right				
			1985	2.00	4.00	8.00

What Is This

Pop-rock group with lead singer Alain Johannes, who sounds uncannily like **Boy George,** _at least on the almost-hit "I'll Be Around."_

Vinyl Albums

Label, Number		Title	Year	VG	VG+	NM
MCA L33-1174	EP	What Is This	1985	3.75	7.50	15.00
Promo-only version with custom labels and sleeve						
MCA 5598		What Is This	1985	2.50	5.00	10.00
MCA 39041		3 Out of 5 Live	1985		3.00	6.00

Label, Number		Title	Year	VG	VG+	NM
45s						
MCA 52593		I'll Be Around/Whisper	1985			3.00
12-Inch Singles						
MCA 23573		I'll Be Around (2 versions)	1985		2.50	5.00

When In Rome
British synth-pop trio.

Label, Number		Title	Year	VG	VG+	NM
Vinyl Albums						
Virgin 90994		When In Rome	1988	2.50	5.00	10.00
45s						
Virgin 99253		Heaven Knows/Whatever the Weather				
			1989			2.00
Virgin 99253	PS	Heaven Knows/Whatever the Weather				
			1989			2.00
Virgin 99323		The Promise/The Promise (Dub)	1988			3.00
12-Inch Singles						
Virgin 1270	DJ	Heaven Knows (8:00)/Heaven Knows (Dub)/Whatever the Weather				
			1988		3.00	6.00
Virgin 96560		Sight of Your Tears (5 versions)	1988		3.50	7.00
Virgin 96589		Heaven Knows (8:00)/Heaven Knows (Dub)/Whatever the Weather				
			1988	2.00	4.00	8.00
Virgin DMD 1319	DJ	Sight of Your Tears (5 mixes)	1988		3.00	6.00

Wiedlin, Jane
*Formerly of the **Go-Go's**.*

Label, Number		Title	Year	VG	VG+	NM
Vinyl Albums						
EMI Manhattan E1-48683		Fur	1988	2.50	5.00	10.00
EMI Manhattan R 152262		Fur	1988	3.00	6.00	12.00
BMG Direct Marketing edition						
I.R.S. 5638		Jane Wiedlin	1985	2.50	5.00	10.00
45s						
EMI Manhattan 50118		Rush Hour/The End of Love	1988			2.00
EMI Manhattan 50118	PS	Rush Hour/The End of Love	1988		2.00	4.00
EMI Manhattan 50145		Inside a Dream/Song of the Factory				
			1988			2.00
EMI Manhattan 50145	PS	Inside a Dream/Song of the Factory				
			1988			2.00
I.R.S. 52674		Blue Kiss/My Traveling Heart	1985			3.00
I.R.S. 52674	PS	Blue Kiss/My Traveling Heart	1985			3.00
12-Inch Singles						
EMI 56179		World on Fire (4 versions)/Flowers on the Battlefield				
			1990		3.00	6.00
EMI Manhattan 56085		Rush Hour (4 versions)/End of Love				
			1988	2.00	4.00	8.00
EMI Manhattan 56105		Inside a Dream (5 mixes)/Song of the Factory				
			1988	2.00	4.00	8.00
I.R.S. 23585		Blue Kiss (3 versions)	1985	2.00	4.00	8.00

Wilco
Alterna-country group created from the ashes of cult favorites Uncle Tupelo.

Label, Number		Title	Year	VG	VG+	NM
Vinyl Albums						
Sire 45857		A.M.	1995	2.50	5.00	10.00
Red vinyl in generic plastic sleeve with sticker in upper left corner						

Label, Number		Title	Year	VG	VG+	NM

45s

Warner Bros. PRO-S-????	DJ	Childlike and Evergreen/Someone Else's Song//He's My Star				
			1995		3.50	7.00

"Soil Samples #19" promo on white vinyl; B-side by Poster Children

Wilde, Kim

Pop-rock/new wave singer from England.

Vinyl Albums

	Title	Year	VG	VG+	NM
EMI America SN-16351	Kids in America	198?	2.00	4.00	8.00
Budget-line reissue of first LP					
EMI America ST-17065	Kim Wilde	1981	2.50	5.00	10.00
MCA 5550	Teases and Dares	1985	3.00	6.00	12.00
MCA 5903	Another Step	1987	3.00	6.00	12.00
MCA 42230	Close	1988	2.50	5.00	10.00

45s

		Title	Year	VG	VG+	NM
EMI America 8110		Kids in America/You'll Never Be So Wrong				
			1982		2.00	4.00
EMI America 8110	PS	Kids in America/You'll Never Be So Wrong				
			1982		2.00	4.00
EMI America 8139		Chequered Love/Everything We Know				
			1982		2.00	4.00
MCA 52513		Go For It/Lovers on a Beach	1984			3.00
MCA 52513	PS	Go For It/Lovers on a Beach	1984		3.00	6.00
Fold-out poster sleeve						
MCA 52925		Say You Really Want Me/(Instrumental)				
			1986		2.00	4.00
MCA 52952		Say You Really Want Me/Say You Really Want Me (Radio Edit)				
			1986			3.00
MCA 53024		You Keep Me Hangin' On/Loving You				
			1987			3.00
MCA 53024	PS	You Keep Me Hangin' On/Loving You				
			1987			3.00
MCA 53130		Say You Really Want Me/She Hasn't Got Time for You				
			1987			3.00
MCA 53130	PS	Say You Really Want Me/She Hasn't Got Time for You				
			1987			3.00
MCA 53192		Another Step (Closer to You)/Hold Back				
			1987			3.00
MCA 53370		You Came/Tell Me Where You Are				
			1988			3.00
MCA 53370	PS	You Came/Tell Me Where You Are				
			1988			3.00
MCA 53480		Four Letter Word/She Hasn't Got Time for You				
			1988			3.00

12-Inch Singles

	Title	Year	VG	VG+	NM
MCA 23533	Go For It (Remix)/Go For It (Dub)				
		1985		2.50	5.00
MCA 23678	Say You Really Want Me (3 mixes)				
		1986	2.00	4.00	8.00
MCA 23717	You Keep Me Hangin' On (Extended)/You Keep Me Hangin' On (7")/				
	Loving You	1986	2.50	5.00	10.00
MCA 23884	You Came (3 versions)	1988	2.50	5.00	10.00
MCA 54737	If I Can't Have You (3 versions)	1993	2.50	5.00	10.00

Label, Number		Title	Year	VG	VG+	NM

Williams, Lucinda

*Unclassifiable female singer. She's done folk and rock, and countryish **Mary Chapin Carpenter** had her biggest pop hit with her "Passionate Kisses."*

Vinyl Albums

Folkways 31066		Ramblin' On My Mind	1979	5.00	10.00	20.00
As "Lucinda"						
Folkways 31067		Happy Woman Blues	1980	5.00	10.00	20.00
As "Lucinda"						
Rough Trade 66	EP	Passionate Kisses	1989	2.50	5.00	10.00
Smithsonian/Folkways 40003		Happy Woman Blues	1990	3.00	6.00	12.00
Reissue						

Williams, Wendy O.

*Formerly with **The Plasmatics**.*

Vinyl Albums

Passport PB-6034	W.O.W.	1984	3.00	6.00	12.00
Profile PAL 1230	Maggots: The Record	1987	3.75	7.50	15.00

Wipers, The

Portland, Oregon punk band. Grunge before it was called grunge.

Vinyl Albums

Park Ave. (# unknown)	Is This Real?	1980	5.00	10.00	20.00
Park Ave. 82802	Youth of America	1981	5.00	10.00	20.00
Restless 72026	Wipers Live	1985	3.00	6.00	12.00
Restless 72094	Land of the Lost	1986	3.00	6.00	12.00
Restless 72187	Over the Edge	1987	3.00	6.00	12.00
Reissue					
Restless 72194	Follow Blind	1987	3.00	6.00	12.00
Tim/Kerr 31	Silver Sail	1993	3.00	6.00	12.00

45s

Park Ave. PA-10		Alien Boy//Image of Man/Telepathic Love/Voices in the Rain				
			1980	3.00	6.25	12.50
Park Ave. PA-10	PS	Alien Boy//Image of Man/Telepathic Love/Voices in the Rain				
			1980	3.00	6.25	12.50
Tim/Kerr 7064		Silver Sail/Never Win	1993			2.00
Tim/Kerr 7064	PS	Silver Sail/Never Win	1993			2.00
Trap 008		Romeo/No Solution	1982	3.00	6.00	12.00
Trap 008	PS	Romeo/No Solution	1982	3.00	6.00	12.00
Trap 810x44		Better Off Dead//Up in Flames/Does It Hurt?				
			1978	3.75	7.50	15.00
Trap 810x44	PS	Better Off Dead//Up in Flames/Does It Hurt?				
			1978	6.25	12.50	25.00
Red and black on yellow sleeve, printed on both sides						
Trap 810x44	PS	Better Off Dead//Up in Flames/Does It Hurt?				
			1978	3.75	7.50	15.00
Black on orange sleeve, printed on one side, address on rear						

Wire

British new-wave band.

Vinyl Albums

Harvest ST-11757		Pink Flag	1977	3.75	7.50	15.00
Mute/Enigma SWAO-73270		The Ideal Copy	1987	3.00	6.00	12.00
Mute/Enigma MLP-73273	EP	Snakedrill	1987	3.00	6.00	12.00
Mute/Enigma D1-73314		A Bell Is a Cup Until It Is Struck				
			1988	3.00	6.00	12.00

Label, Number		Title	Year	VG	VG+	NM
Mute/Enigma D1-73516		It's Beginning To and Back Again				
			1989	2.50	5.00	10.00
Warner Bros. BSK 3398		154	1979	3.00	6.00	12.00
12-Inch Singles						
Enigma EPRO 215	DJ	In Vivo (3 versions)	1989	2.50	5.00	10.00
Enigma 75528		In Vivo (3 versions)/Illuminated (Remix)/Finest Drops (Live)				
			1989	2.50	5.00	10.00
Mute/Enigma 75520		Eardrum Buzz (LP)/Eardrum Buzz (Edit)/The Offer/It's a Boy				
			1986		3.00	6.00
Restless 72245		Kidney Bingos/Pieta (2 versions)/Over Theirs (Live)/Drill (Live)				
			1987	3.75	7.50	15.00
Restless 72299		Silk Skin Paws/German Shepherds/Ambitious (Remix)/				
		Come Back in Two Halves	1988	2.50	5.00	10.00

Wolfgang Press, The

British synth-pop group.

Label, Number		Title	Year	VG	VG+	NM
45s						
4AD 17914		Going South/She's So Soft	1995			3.00
12-Inch Singles						
Warner Bros. PRO-A-7174	DJ	Going South (2 versions)/11 Years/Executioner				
			1994	2.00	4.00	8.00

Wolverton Bros.

Label, Number		Title	Year	VG	VG+	NM
45s						
Sub Pop 181		Max Gomez Love/Assassin	1993		2.50	5.00
White vinyl						
Sub Pop 181		Max Gomez Love/Assassin	1993	12.50	25.00	50.00
Clear lilac vinyl with these labels actually plays two songs by Jon Spencer Blues Explosion						
Sub Pop 181	PS	Max Gomez Love/Assassin	1993		2.50	5.00
#51 in Sub Pop Singles Club series (this sleeve accompanies both correct and incorrect pressings)						

Woolley, Bruce, and the Camera Club

*A member of **The Buggles** before they recorded their first album, Bruce's own band included future solo star **Thomas Dolby**.*

Label, Number		Title	Year	VG	VG+	NM
Vinyl Albums						
Columbia NJC 36301		Bruce Woolley and the Camera Club				
			1980	3.75	7.50	15.00
45s						
Columbia 11226		English Garden/Flying Man	1980		2.00	4.00
Columbia 11264		Video Killed the Radio Star/Clean Clean//				
		Trouble Is/Only Babies Can Fly	1980		2.50	5.00
Columbia 11264	PS	Video Killed the Radio Star/Clean Clean//				
		Trouble Is/Only Babies Can Fly	1980		2.50	5.00

World Party

*One-man band of Karl Wallinger, formerly of **The Waterboys**.*

Label, Number		Title	Year	VG	VG+	NM
Vinyl Albums						
Chrysalis BFV 41552		Private Revolution	1986	2.50	5.00	10.00
Chrysalis F1-21654		Goodbye Jumbo	1990	2.50	5.00	10.00
Chrysalis R 134261		Private Revolution	1987	3.00	6.00	12.00
RCA Music Service edition						

Label, Number		Title	Year	VG	VG+	NM
45s						
Chrysalis 43052		Ship of Fools (Save Me From Tomorrow)/Holy Water				
			1987			3.00
Chrysalis 43052	PS	Ship of Fools (Save Me From Tomorrow)/Holy Water				
			1987			3.00
Chrysalis 43132		All Come True	1987			3.00
12-Inch Singles						
Chrysalis VAS 2482	DJ	Ship of Fools (same on both sides)				
			1986		2.50	5.00
Chrysalis VAS 2657	DJ	Private Revolution (same on both sides)				
			1987		2.50	5.00
Chrysalis VAS 2708	DJ	All Come True (same on both sides)				
			1987		2.50	5.00

Wreckless Eric

British new-waver.

Label, Number		Title	Year	VG	VG+	NM
Vinyl Albums						
Stiff USE 1		Whole Wide World	1979	3.75	7.50	15.00
Stiff/Epic AS 785	EP	Wreckless Eric	1980	3.75	7.50	15.00
Promo-only 5-song sample from E2 36463						
Stiff/Epic E2 36463	(2)	Big Smash	1980	4.50	9.00	18.00
45s						
Stiff/Epic 50870		Broken Doll/A Little Bit More	1980		2.00	4.00

X

X

Legendary Los Angeles punk band.

Label, Number		Title	Year	VG	VG+	NM
Vinyl Albums						
Elektra 60150		Under the Big Black Sun	1982	3.00	6.00	12.00
Elektra 60283		More Fun in the New World	1983	2.50	5.00	10.00
Elektra 60430		Ain't Love Grand	1985	2.50	5.00	10.00
Elektra 60492		See How We Are	1987	2.50	5.00	10.00
Elektra 60788	(2)	Live at the Whiskey A-Go-Go on the Fabulous Sunset Strip				
			1988	3.00	6.00	12.00
Slash SR-104		Los Angeles	1980	3.75	7.50	15.00
Slash SR-107		Wild Gift	1981	3.00	6.00	12.00
Slash 23930		Los Angeles	1983	2.50	5.00	10.00
Reissue of Slash 104						
Slash 23931		Wild Gift	1983	2.50	5.00	10.00
Reissue of Slash 107						
45s						
Curb 10538	DJ	Wild Thing/Wild Thing, Part 2	1988	7.50	15.00	30.00
Does not exist as stock copy						
Dangerhouse D-88		Adult Books/We're Desperate	1978	10.00	20.00	40.00
Dangerhouse D-88	PS	Adult Books/We're Desperate	1978	10.00	20.00	40.00
Folded picture sleeve in plastic bag						
Elektra 69462		Fourth of July/Positively Fourth Street				
			1987		2.00	4.00
Elektra 69462	PS	Fourth of July/Positively Fourth Street				
			1987		2.00	4.00
Elektra 69626		Burning House of Love/Love Shack				
			1985	2.00	4.00	8.00
Elektra 69626	DJ	Burning House of Love (edit) (same on both sides)				
			1985		2.00	4.00

Label, Number		Title	Year	VG	VG+	NM
Elektra 69626	PS	Burning House of Love/Love Shack				
			1985		2.00	4.00
Elektra 69709		Wild Thing/Devil Doll	1984		2.00	4.00
Elektra 69825		Breathless/Riding with Mary	1983		2.00	4.00
Elektra 69825	PS	Breathless/Riding with Mary	1983		2.00	4.00
Elektra 69885		Blue Spark/Dancing with Tears in My Eyes				
			1982	3.00	6.00	12.00
Elektra 69885	PS	Blue Spark/Dancing with Tears in My Eyes				
			1982	3.00	6.00	12.00
Slash 106		White Girl/Your Phone's Off the Hook				
			1980		3.75	7.50
Slash 106	PS	White Girl/Your Phone's Off the Hook				
			1980		3.75	7.50
Green sleeve						
Slash 106	PS	White Girl/Your Phone's Off the Hook				
			1980		3.75	7.50
Blue sleeve						

12-Inch Singles

Label, Number		Title	Year	VG	VG+	NM
Elektra 4912	DJ	Breathless/Riding with Mary	1983	2.50	5.00	10.00
Elektra 4943	DJ	True Love Part II (3 versions)	1983	2.00	4.00	8.00
Elektra 5068	DJ	Burning House of Love (same on both sides)				
			1985	2.00	4.00	8.00
Elektra ED 5106	DJ	Around My Heart (Edit)/Around My Heart (LP)				
			1985		3.00	6.00
Elektra ED 5232	DJ	4th of July (same on both sides)	1987	2.00	4.00	8.00
Elektra 5248	DJ	See How We Are (same on both sides)				
			1987		3.00	6.00
Elektra ED 5305	DJ	Devil Doll/New World/Burning House of Love				
			1988		3.00	6.00
Elektra 66966		Wild Thing (long)/True Love Pt. 2 (Club Remix)				
			1984	3.75	7.50	15.00

X-Ray Spex

British new-wave group.

Vinyl Albums

Label, Number	Title	Year	VG	VG+	NM
Blue Plate CAROL-1813-1	Germ Free Adolescents	1992	3.75	7.50	15.00
Recorded in 1978, this is this classic new wave LP's first American issue					
EMI INS-3023	Germ Free Adolescents	1978	7.50	15.00	30.00
British release only, no U.S. version until 1992					

X-Terminators

California punk band.

45s

Label, Number	Title	Year	VG	VG+	NM
Radio Active 1	Microwave Radiation/Occasional Lay				
		1978	15.00	30.00	60.00

XTC

British new-wave band that has never received the respect or the popularity it deserves Stateside.

Vinyl Albums

Label, Number	Title	Year	VG	VG+	NM
Geffen GHS 4027	Mummer	1983	2.50	5.00	10.00
Geffen GHS 4032	White Music	1984	2.50	5.00	10.00
Reissue of Virgin/Epic 38153					
Geffen GHS 4033	Go2	1984	2.50	5.00	10.00
Reissue of Virgin/Epic 38152					
Geffen GHS 4034	Drums and Wires	1984	2.50	5.00	10.00
Reissue of Virgin/Epic 38151					
Geffen GHS 4035	Black Sea	1984	2.50	5.00	10.00
Reissue of Virgin/Epic 38150					

Label, Number		Title	Year	VG	VG+	NM
Geffen GHS 4036	(2)	English Settlement	1984	3.75	7.50	15.00
First release of British version of this album in U.S.						
Geffen GHS 4037		Waxworks (Some Singles, 1977-82)				
			1984	3.00	6.00	12.00
Geffen GHS 24054		The Big Express	1984	2.50	5.00	10.00
Geffen GHS 24117		Skylarking	1986	3.75	7.50	15.00
First pressing, without "Dear God"						
Geffen GHS 24117		Skylarking	1986	2.50	5.00	10.00
Second pressing, with "Dear God"						
Geffen GHS 24218	(2)	Oranges and Lemons	1989	3.75	7.50	15.00
Geffen R 201086	(2)	Oranges and Lemons	1989	3.75	7.50	15.00
BMG Music Service edition						
Virgin International VI-2095		White Music	1979	3.75	7.50	15.00
Virgin International VI-2108		Go2	1979	3.75	7.50	15.00
Virgin VA 13134		Drums and Wires	1979	3.00	6.00	12.00
Originals have a bonus 7-inch record (PR 344) enclosed; priced separately in 45 section						
Virgin VA 13147		Black Sea	1980	5.00	10.00	20.00
Original issue, distributed by Atlantic; with green bag (deduct 20% if missing)						
Virgin/Epic ARE 37943		English Settlement	1982	2.50	5.00	10.00
Drastically edited version of U.K. original, which was a 2-record set						
Virgin/Epic PE 38150		Black Sea	1982	2.50	5.00	10.00
Reissue of Virgin/RSO VR-1-1000						
Virgin/Epic PE 38151		Drums and Wires	1982	2.50	5.00	10.00
Reissue of Virgin 13134						
Virgin/Epic PE 38152		Go2	1982	2.50	5.00	10.00
Reissue of Virgin International VI-2108						
Virgin/Epic PE 38153		White Music	1982	2.50	5.00	10.00
Reissue of Virgin International VI-2095						
Virgin/RSO VR-1-1000		Black Sea	1980	3.75	7.50	15.00
With green bag (deduct 20% if missing)						

45s

Label, Number		Title	Year	VG	VG+	NM
Epic 02875		Senses Working Overtime/English Roundabout				
			1982		2.50	5.00
Geffen 19124		The Ballad of Peter Pumpkinhead				
			1992		*Cassette only*	
Geffen 22953		King for a Day/Toys	1989			2.00
Geffen 22953	PS	King for a Day/Toys	1989			2.00
Geffen 27552		The Mayor of Simpleton/One of the Millions				
			1989			2.00
Geffen 27552	PS	The Mayor of Simpleton/One of the Millions				
			1989			2.00
Geffen 28394		Dear God/Mermaid Smiled	1987			3.00
Geffen 29351		Wonderland/Jump	1984		2.00	4.00
Virgin PR 344	DJ	Limelight//Day In Day Out/Chain of Command				
			1979		3.00	6.00
7-inch 33 1/3 record with small center hole; included in first 15,000 copies of album VA 13134						
Virgin 67004		Ten Feet Tall//Helicopter/Somnambulist				
			1980		3.50	7.00
Virgin 67004	DJ	Ten Feet Tall (mono/stereo)	1980			3.00
Virgin 67004	PS	Ten Feet Tall//Helicopter/Somnambulist				
			1980			3.00
Virgin 67009		Making Plans for Nigel//This Is Pop/Meccanik Dancing				
			1980		3.50	7.00
Virgin 67009	DJ	Making Plans for Nigel (mono/stereo)				
			1980			3.00
Virgin 67009	PS	Making Plans for Nigel//This Is Pop/Meccanik Dancing				
			1980			3.00
Virgin/RSO 300		Generals and Majors/Living Through Another Cuba				
			1981		2.50	5.00
Virgin/RSO 301		Love at First Sight/Rocket from a Bottle				
			1981		2.50	5.00

Label, Number		Title	Year	VG	VG+	NM
12-Inch Singles						
Epic AS 1405	DJ	Ball & Chain/Senses Working Overtime				
			1982	3.00	6.00	12.00
Geffen PRO-A-2117	DJ	Great Fire/Love on a Farmboy's Wages/Funk Pop a Roll				
			1983	3.00	6.00	12.00
Geffen PRO-A-2214	DJ	All You Pretty Girls/Wake Up/Shake You Donkey Up				
			1984	3.75	7.50	15.00
Geffen PRO-A-3522	DJ	King for a Day (3 mixes)/Toys/Desert Island				
			1989	2.00	4.00	8.00
Geffen 20630		Grass/Earn Enough for Us/Extrovert/Dear God				
			1986	2.00	4.00	8.00
Geffen 21160		The Mayor of Simpleton/One of the Millions/Ella Guru/				
		Living in a Haunted Heart/The Good Things				
			1989	2.00	4.00	8.00

Y

Y Kant Tori Read

*Attempted hair-metal music with lead vocals by **Tori Amos**.*

Label, Number		Title	Year	VG	VG+	NM
Vinyl Albums						
Atlantic 81845		Y Kant Tori Read	1989	31.25	62.50	125.00
Deduct 20% for albums with a gold promo stamp and cut-out mark						
45s						
Atlantic 89021		Cool on Your Island/Heart Attack at 23				
			1988			
May not exist						
Atlantic 89021	DJ	Cool on Your Island (same on both sides)				
			1988	6.25	12.50	25.00
Atlantic 89021	PS	Cool on Your Island	1988	12.50	25.00	50.00
Atlantic 89086		The Big Picture/You Go to My Head				
			1988			
May not exist						
Atlantic 89086	DJ	The Big Picture (same on both sides)				
			1988	6.25	12.50	25.00

Yankovic, "Weird Al"

The king of recent musical parody. Many of his best parodies have been of new wave, punk, grunge and other alternative music.

Label, Number		Title	Year	VG	VG+	NM
Vinyl Albums						
Rock N Roll BFZ 38679		Weird Al	1983	2.50	5.00	10.00
Rock N Roll PZ 38679		Weird Al	1985	2.00	4.00	8.00
Budget-line reissue						
Rock N Roll FZ 39221		In 3-D	1984	2.50	5.00	10.00
Rock N Roll FZ 40033		Dare to Be Stupid	1985	2.50	5.00	10.00
Rock N Roll FZ 44149		Even Worse	1988	2.50	5.00	10.00
45s						
Capitol 4816		My Bologna/School Cafeteria	1980	5.00	10.00	20.00
Placebo 3626		Another One Rides the Bus (Live)/Happy Birthday/ + 2				
			1980	2.50	5.00	10.00
Placebo 3626	PS	Another One Rides the Bus (Live)/Happy Birthday/ + 2				
			1980	2.50	5.00	10.00
Rock N Roll 03849		Ricky/Buckingham Blues	1983		2.50	5.00
Rock N Roll 03849	PS	Ricky/Buckingham Blues	1983		2.50	5.00
Rock N Roll 03998		I Love Rocky Road/Happy Birthday				
			1983		2.50	5.00
Rock N Roll 04374		Eat It/That Boy Could Dance	1984			3.00
Rock N Roll 04374	PS	Eat It/That Boy Could Dance	1984			3.00

Label, Number		Title	Year	VG	VG+	NM
Rock N Roll 04451		King of Suede/Nature Trail to Hell				
			1984			3.00
Rock N Roll 04451	PS	King of Suede/Nature Trail to Hell				
			1984			3.00
Rock N Roll 04469		I Lost on Jeopardy/I'll Be Mellow When I'm Dead				
			1984			3.00
Rock N Roll 04469	PS	I Lost on Jeopardy/I'll Be Mellow When I'm Dead				
			1984			3.00
Rock N Roll 04708		This Is the Life (Theme from Johnny Dangerously)/				
		Buy Me a Condo	1984			3.00
Rock N Roll 04708	PS	This Is the Life (Theme from Johnny Dangerously)/				
		Buy Me a Condo	1984			3.00
Rock N Roll 04937		Like a Surgeon/Slime Creatures from Outer Space				
			1985			3.00
Rock N Roll 04937	PS	Like a Surgeon/Slime Creatures from Outer Space				
			1985			3.00
Rock N Roll 04937	PS	Like a Surgeon	1985		3.00	6.00
"Demonstration Only -- Not for Sale" on rear						
Rock N Roll 05483		Eat It/I Lost on Jeopardy	1985			3.00
Reissue						
Rock N Roll 05578		I Want a New Duck/Cable TV	1985			3.00
Rock N Roll 05578	PS	I Want a New Duck/Cable TV				
			1985			3.00
Rock N Roll 05606		One More Minute/Midnight Star				
			1985			3.00
Rock N Roll 05606	PS	One More Minute/Midnight Star				
			1985			3.00
Rock N Roll 06207		Dare to Be Stupid/The Touch	1986			3.00
Rock N Roll 06400		Living with a Hernia/Don't Wear Those Shoes				
			1986			3.00
Rock N Roll 06400	PS	Living with a Hernia/Don't Wear Those Shoes				
			1986			3.00
Rock N Roll 06435		Like a Surgeon/King of Suede	1986			3.00
Reissue						
Rock N Roll 06588		Christmas At Ground Zero/One of Those Days				
			1986		2.50	5.00
Rock N Roll 06588	PS	Christmas At Ground Zero/One of Those Days				
			1986		2.50	5.00
Rock N Roll 07769		Fat/You Make Me	1988			3.00
Rock N Roll 07769	PS	Fat/You Make Me	1988			3.00
Rock N Roll 07961		Lasagna/(B-side unknown)	1988			3.00
Rock N Roll 07961	PS	Lasagna/(B-side unknown)	1988			3.00
Rock N Roll 08046		I Think I'm a Clone Now/(This Song's Just) Six Words Long				
			1988			3.00
Rock N Roll 68992		UHF/Attack of the Radioactive Hamsters from a Planet Near Mars				
			1989			3.00
Rock N Roll 69019		Money for Nothing-Beverly Hillbillies/Generic Blues				
			1989			3.00
Scotti Bros. 866 956-7 (PO 219)		Smells Like Nirvana/Waffle King				
			1992		2.50	5.00
Europe-only release; no U.S. vinyl						
Scotti Bros. 866 956-7 (PO 219)PS		Smells Like Nirvana/Waffle King				
			1992		2.50	5.00
Europe-only release						
TK 1043		Another One Rides the Bus/Gotta Boogie				
			1981	5.00	10.00	20.00

12-Inch Singles

Label, Number		Title	Year	VG	VG+	NM
Rock N Roll 1830	DJ	Eat It (same on both sides)	1984	2.50	5.00	10.00
Rock N Roll 1887	DJ	I Lost on Jeopardy/Mr. Popeil	1985	2.50	5.00	10.00
Rock N Roll 2536	DJ	Living with a Hernia (same on both sides)				
			1986	2.50	5.00	10.00
Rock N Roll 05154		This Is the Life/Buy Me a Condo				
			1984	2.50	5.00	10.00

Label, Number		Title	Year	VG	VG+	NM

Yaz

*British synth-pop duo: **Alison Moyet** and Vince Clarke, formerly of **Depeche Mode** and later of **Erasure**. Early U.S. records were released by "Yazoo," but for unknown reasons (probably legal) the band's name was shortened (but remained unchanged in England). American "Yazoo" records are highly collectible.*

Vinyl Albums

Label, Number		Title	Year	VG	VG+	NM
Sire 23737		Upstairs at Eric's	1982	5.00	10.00	20.00
First pressing: Band called "Yazoo"						
Sire 23737		Upstairs at Eric's	1982	2.50	5.00	10.00
Sire 23903		You and Me Both	1983	2.50	5.00	10.00

45s

Label, Number		Title	Year	VG	VG+	NM
Sire GSRE 0508		Situation/Only You	198?			3.00
"Back to Back Hits" reissue						
Sire 29569		Nobody's Diary/State Farm	1983		2.00	4.00
Sire 29844		Only You/Winter Kills	1982		2.00	4.00
Sire 29953		Situation/Situation (Dub)	1982	3.75	7.50	15.00
First pressing: Band called "Yazoo"						
Sire 29953	PS	Situation/Situation (Dub)	1982	3.75	7.50	15.00
First pressing: Band called "Yazoo"						
Sire 29953		Situation/Situation (Dub)	1982	2.00	4.00	8.00
Sire 29953	PS	Situation/Situation (Dub)	1982	2.50	5.00	10.00

12-Inch Singles

Label, Number		Title	Year	VG	VG+	NM
Sire 20121		Nobody's Diary/State Farm	1983	3.00	6.00	12.00
Sire 29886		Winter Kills (2 mixes)/Don't Go (2 mixes)				
			1982	2.50	5.00	10.00
Sire 29950		Situation/Situation (Dub)	1982	5.00	10.00	20.00
First pressing: Band called "Yazoo"						
Sire 29950		Situation/Situation (Dub)	1982	2.50	5.00	10.00

Yello

Synthesizer group from Zurich, Switzerland.

Vinyl Albums

Label, Number		Title	Year	VG	VG+	NM
Elektra 60271		You Gotta Say Yes to Another Excess				
			1983	3.00	6.00	12.00
Elektra 60401		Stella	1985	3.00	6.00	12.00
Mercury 812 166-1		You Gotta Say Yes to Another Excess				
			1988	2.00	4.00	8.00
Reissue						
Mercury 818 339-1		Solid Pleasure	1988	2.00	4.00	8.00
Reissue						
Mercury 818 340-1		Claro Que Si	1988	2.00	4.00	8.00
Reissue						
Mercury 822 820-1		Stella	1988	2.00	4.00	8.00
Reissue						
Mercury 832 675-1		One Second	1987	3.00	6.00	12.00
Mercury 836 426-1		Flag	1989	3.00	6.00	12.00
Ralph YL 8059-L		Solid Pleasure	1980	4.00	8.00	16.00
Ralph YL 8159		Claro Que Si	1981	4.00	8.00	16.00

45s

Label, Number		Title	Year	VG	VG+	NM
Elektra 69656		Vicious Games/Blue Nabou	1985			3.00
Elektra 69824		I Love You/Rubber Vest	1983			3.00
Mercury 884 935-7		Oh Yeah/Oh Yeah (Indian Summer Music)				
			1986			3.00
Mercury 884 935-7	PS	Oh Yeah/Oh Yeah (Indian Summer Music)				
			1986		2.00	4.00
Yellow sleeve with reference to movie "Ferris Bueller's Day Off"						
Mercury 884 935-7	PS	Oh Yeah/Oh Yeah (Indian Summer Music)				
			1987			3.00
Multicolored sleeve						

A scarce U.S. picture sleeve, this comes from the original 45 release of "Situation," before the group became Yaz.

One of the easier Ralph Records sleeves to find, this comes from synthesizer band Yello's recording of "Bimbo."

Label, Number		Title	Year	VG	VG+	NM
Mercury 888 311-7		Call It Love/L'Hotel	1987			3.00
Mercury 888 311-7	PS	Call It Love/L'Hotel	1987			3.00
Ralph YL 8058		Bimbo/I.T. Splash	1980		2.00	4.00
Ralph YL 8058	PS	Bimbo/I.T. Splash	1980		2.00	4.00
12-Inch Singles						
4th & B'Way PR12 607	DJ	Tremendous Pain (4 mixes)	1995	2.50	5.00	10.00
Black vinyl						
4th & B'Way PR12 609	DJ	Tremendous Pain (4 versions)	1995	2.50	5.00	10.00
Yellow vinyl						
4th & B'Way 445 604-1		How How (6 versions)	1994	2.50	5.00	10.00
Elektra EAOR 4920	DJ	I Love You (3 versions)	1983	2.50	5.00	10.00
Elektra 4941	DJ	Pumping Velvet/No More Words/Lost Again/Bostich				
			1983	2.50	5.00	10.00
Elektra ED 5039	DJ	Vicious Games (3 versions)	1985	2.50	5.00	10.00
Elektra 5487	DJ	Unbelievable (6 versions)	1990	2.00	4.00	8.00
Elektra 67917		I Love You/Heavy Whispers	1983	2.00	4.00	8.00
FFRR 350 005-1		Bostich (6 versions)	1992	3.75	7.50	15.00
Yellow vinyl						
Mercury PRO 744-1	DJ	The Race (4 versions)/I Love You				
			1989	3.00	6.00	12.00
Mercury PRO 768-1	DJ	Tied Up (4 versions)	1988	2.00	4.00	8.00
Mercury 872 761-1		Tied Up (4 versions)/Oh Yeah	1989		3.00	6.00
Mercury 874 939-1		The Race (3 mixes)/Blazing Saddles (2 mixes)				
			1989	2.00	4.00	8.00
Mercury 884 930-1		Oh Yeah (3 mixes)	1985	2.00	4.00	8.00
Mercury 888 994-1		Call It Love (4 versions)	1987	2.00	4.00	8.00
Ralph YL 8209		Bimbo/Smile on You	1982	3.75	7.50	15.00
Smash 440 812-1		Vicious Games (4 new versions)	199?	2.50	5.00	10.00
Smash 445 815-1	(2)	Do It (8 versions)	1994	3.00	6.00	12.00
Two-record set, stock or promo						
Smash 880 003-1		Jungle Bill (4 versions)	1992	2.50	5.00	10.00
Stiff TEES 12-12		You Gotta Say Yes/Heavy Whispers				
			1982	3.75	7.50	15.00

Yo La Tengo

Alterna-rock band from Hoboken, New Jersey.

45s						
Coyote 87104		For Turnstiles/Asparagus Song	1987	2.00	4.00	8.00
Coyote 87104	PS	For Turnstiles/Asparagus Song	1987	2.00	4.00	8.00
Egon 03		River of Water/A House Is Not a Motel				
			1985	2.00	4.00	8.00
Egon 03	PS	River of Water/A House Is Not a Motel				
			1985	2.00	4.00	8.00

Yoakam, Dwight

Country singer steeped in the old traditions, but heavily influenced by pre-Beatles rock 'n' roll.

Vinyl Albums						
Oak OR 2356	EP	Guitars, Cadillacs, Etc.	1984	137.50	375.00	750.00
Reprise 25372		Guitars, Cadillacs, Etc., Etc.	1986	2.50	5.00	10.00
Reprise W1-25372		Guitars, Cadillacs, Etc., Etc.	1986	3.00	6.00	12.00
Columbia House edition						
Reprise 25567		Hillbilly Deluxe	1987	2.50	5.00	10.00
Reprise W1-25567		Hillbilly Deluxe	1987	3.00	6.00	12.00
Columbia House edition						
Reprise 25749		Buenas Noches from a Lonely Room				
			1988	2.50	5.00	10.00
Reprise W1-25749		Buenas Noches from a Lonely Room				
			1988	3.00	6.00	12.00
Columbia House edition						

Label, Number		Title	Year	VG	VG+	NM
Reprise 25989		Just Lookin' for a Hit	1989	2.50	5.00	10.00
Reprise W1-25989		Just Lookin' for a Hit	1989	3.00	6.00	12.00
Columbia House edition						
Reprise R 100009		Buenas Noches from a Lonely Room				
			1988	3.00	6.00	12.00
BMG Direct Marketing edition						
Reprise R 150223		Guitars, Cadillacs, Etc., Etc.	1986	3.00	6.00	12.00
RCA Music Service edition						
Reprise R 164146		Hillbilly Deluxe	1987	3.00	6.00	12.00
BMG Direct Marketing edition						
Reprise R 164310		If There Was a Way	1990	3.75	7.50	15.00
BMG Direct Marketing edition; only U.S. vinyl version						
Reprise R 174052		Just Lookin' for a Hit	1989	3.00	6.00	12.00
BMG Direct Marketing edition						
45s						
Epic 74753		Suspicious Minds/Burning Love	1992			3.00
B-side by Travis Tritt						
Reprise 17734		Nothing/Gone (That'll Be Me)	1995			3.00
Reprise 18239		Try Not to Look So Pretty/Wild Ride				
			1994			3.00
Reprise 18341		Fast As You/Home for Sale	1993			3.00
Reprise 18528		A Thousand Miles from Nowhere/Ain't That Lonely Yet				
			1993			3.00
Reprise 18590		Ain't That Lonely Yet/Lonesome Roads				
			1993			3.00
Reprise 18846		Send a Message to My Heart/Takes a Lot to Rock You				
			1992			3.00
With Patti Loveless						
Reprise 18966		The Heart That You Own/Dangerous Man				
			1992			3.00
Reprise 19148		It Only Hurts When I Cry/Let's Work Together				
			1991			3.00
Reprise 19256		Nothing's Changed Here/Sad, Sad Music				
			1991			3.00
Reprise 19405		You're the One/If There Was a Way				
			1991			3.00
Reprise 19543		Turn It On, Turn It Up, Turn Me Loose/				
		Since I Started Drinkin' Again	1990			3.00
Reprise 21868		I Sang Dixie/Long White Cadillac				
			1989			3.00
"Back to Back Hits" reissue						
Reprise 21898		Streets of Bakersfield/Please Please Baby				
			198?			3.00
"Back to Back Hits" reissue						
Reprise 21947		Little Sister/Little Ways	198?			3.00
"Back to Back Hits" reissue						
Reprise 21957		Honky Tonk Man/Guitars, Cadillacs				
			198?			3.00
"Back to Back Hits" reissue						
Reprise 22799		Long White Cadillac/Little Ways				
			1989			3.00
Reprise 22944		Buenos Noches from a Lonely Room/Why I Don't Know				
			1989			3.00
Reprise 27567		I Got You/South of Cincinnati	1989			3.00
Reprise 27715		I Sang Dixie/Floyd County	1988			3.00
Reprise 27715	PS	I Sang Dixie/Floyd County	1988		2.00	4.00
Reprise 27964		Streets of Bakersfield/One More Name				
			1988			3.00
Reprise 27964	PS	Streets of Bakersfield/One More Name				
			1988		2.00	4.00
With Buck Owens						

Label, Number		Title	Year	VG	VG+	NM
Reprise 27994		Always Late with Your Kisses/1,000 Miles				
			1988			3.00
Reprise 27994	PS	Always Late with Your Kisses/1,000 Miles				
			1988			3.00
Reprise 28156		Santa Claus Is Back in Town/Jingle Bells				
			1987		2.50	5.00
Reprise 28156	PS	Santa Claus Is Back in Town/Jingle Bells				
			1987		2.50	5.00
Reprise 28174		Please, Please Baby/Throughout All Time				
			1987			3.00
Reprise 28310		Little Ways/Readin', Rightin', Rt. 23				
			1987			3.00
Reprise 28432		Little Sister/This Drinkin' Will Kill Me				
			1987			3.00
Reprise 28565		It Won't Hurt/Bury Me (Duet with Maria McKee)				
			1986			3.00
Reprise 28688		Guitars, Cadillacs/I'll Be Gone	1986			3.00
Reprise 28688	PS	Guitars, Cadillacs/I'll Be Gone	1986	2.00	4.00	8.00
Reprise 28793		Honky Tonk Man/Miner's Prayer				
			1986			3.00
Warner Bros. PRO-S-2424	DJ	This Drinkin' Will Kill Me (Live)/Miner's Prayer (Live)				
			1985	2.00	4.00	8.00
12-Inch Singles						
Reprise PRO-A-3799	DJ	Long White Cadillac (Edit)/Long White Cadillac (FM)				
			1989	2.00	4.00	8.00

Young and the Useless, The

*With Adam O of the **Beastie Boys**.*

7-Inch Extended Play Singles

Rat Cage MOTR 24		Real Men Don't Floss	1982	3.75	7.50	15.00
Rat Cage MOTR 24	PS	Real Men Don't Floss	1982	3.75	7.50	15.00

Young, Neil

All over the place musically, from proto-grunge to hillbilly country, he made vital records in the 1960s, 1970s, 1980s and 1990s. Who else did the same?

Vinyl Albums

Geffen GHS 2018		Trans	1982	3.00	6.00	12.00
First pressings have a sticker on rear cover explaining the absence of "If You've Got Love"						
Geffen GHS 2018		Trans	1982	2.50	5.00	10.00
Later pressings have neither sticker nor title of absent song						
Geffen GHS 2018	DJ	Trans	1982	3.75	7.50	15.00
Promo on Quiex II audiophile vinyl						
Geffen GHS 4013		Everybody's Rockin'	1983	2.50	5.00	10.00
Geffen GHS 4013	DJ	Everybody's Rockin'	1983	3.75	7.50	15.00
Promo on Quiex II audiophile vinyl						
Geffen GHS 24068		Old Ways	1985	3.00	6.00	12.00
Geffen GHS 24109		Landing on Water	1986	3.00	6.00	12.00
Geffen GHS 24154		Life	1987	3.00	6.00	12.00
Geffen R 134125		Landing on Water	1986	3.75	7.50	15.00
RCA Music Service edition						
Geffen R 144439		Life	1987	3.75	7.50	15.00
BMG Direct Marketing edition						
Geffen R 163233		Old Ways	1985	3.75	7.50	15.00
RCA Music Service edition						
Mobile Fidelity 1-252		Old Ways	1996	5.00	10.00	20.00
Original Master Recording						
Nautilus NR-44		Harvest	1982	31.25	62.50	125.00
Half-speed master						

Label, Number		Title	Year	VG	VG+	NM
Reprise MS 2032		Harvest	1972	3.75	7.50	15.00
First pressings have textured cover and lyric insert						
Reprise MS 2032		Harvest	1972	2.50	5.00	10.00
Reprise M 2151	M/DJ	Time Fades Away	1973	25.00	50.00	100.00
Special mono pressing for radio stations						
Reprise MS 2151		Time Fades Away	1973	50.00	100.00	200.00
With a cardboard inner sleeve, withdrawn after the earliest pressing.						
Reprise MS 2151		Time Fades Away	1973	2.50	5.00	10.00
Reprise MS 2180		On the Beach	1974	2.50	5.00	10.00
Reprise MS 2221		Tonight's the Night	1975	2.50	5.00	10.00
Reprise MS 2242		Zuma	1975	2.50	5.00	10.00
Reprise 3RS 2257	(3) DJ	Decade	1977	125.00	250.00	500.00
Test pressing; "Campaigner" contains extra verse deleted from the final version						
Reprise 3RS 2257	(3)	Decade	1977	10.00	20.00	40.00
Reprise MSK 2261		American Stars 'N' Bars	1977	2.50	5.00	10.00
Reprise MSK 2266	DJ	Ode to the Wind	1978	250.00	500.00	1,000.00
Test pressing; plain white jacket with inserts. Title changed to "Comes A Time" for commercial release.						
Reprise MSK 2266		Comes A Time	1978	18.75	37.50	75.00
With "Lotta Love" listed and playing as the last song on side 1						
Reprise MSK 2266		Comes A Time	1978	2.50	5.00	10.00
With "Peace of Mind" as the last song on side 1. Covers can list either "Lotta Love" or "Peace of Mind."						
Reprise MSK 2277		Harvest	1978	2.00	4.00	8.00
Brown "Reprise" label; new number						
Reprise MSK 2282		Everybody Knows This Is Nowhere				
			1978	2.00	4.00	8.00
Brown "Reprise" label; new number						
Reprise MSK 2283		After the Gold Rush	1978	10.00	20.00	40.00
Contains remixed extended version of "When You Dance I Can Really Love." Title on cover in red, "RE 2" in trail-off vinyl						
Reprise HS 2295		Rust Never Sleeps	1979	2.50	5.00	10.00
Reprise 2RX 2296	(2)	Live Rust	1979	3.75	7.50	15.00
Reprise HS 2297		Hawks & Doves	1980	2.50	5.00	10.00
Reprise HS 2304		Re-Ac-Tor	1981	2.50	5.00	10.00
Reprise RS 6317		Neil Young	1968	37.50	75.00	150.00
Brown and orange "Reprise/W7" label, no name on front cover						
Reprise RS 6317		Neil Young	1969	18.75	37.50	75.00
Re-release: Brown and orange "Reprise/W7" label, no name on front cover, four tracks remixed ("RE 1" etched in trail-off vinyl)						
Reprise RS 6317		Neil Young	1970	3.75	7.50	15.00
Reissue: Brown "Reprise" label, Neil Young's name is now on front cover						
Reprise RS 6349	DJ	Everybody Knows This Is Nowhere				
			1969	18.75	37.50	75.00
White label promo						
Reprise RS 6349		Everybody Knows This Is Nowhere				
			1969	7.50	15.00	30.00
Brown and orange "Reprise/W7" label						
Reprise RS 6349		Everybody Knows This Is Nowhere				
			1970	3.75	7.50	15.00
Brown "Reprise" label						
Reprise RS 6383		After the Gold Rush	1970	10.00	20.00	40.00
Brown and orange label; photo of Marc Bolan (of T. Rex) appears erroneously in gatefold						
Reprise RS 6383		After the Gold Rush	1970	8.75	17.50	35.00
Brown and orange label; photo of Neil Young appears erroneously printed upside down in gatefold						
Reprise RS 6383		After the Gold Rush	1970	3.75	7.50	15.00
Brown and orange label; all photos correct						
Reprise RS 6383		After the Gold Rush	1970	2.50	5.00	10.00
Brown "Reprise" label						
Reprise 2XS 6480	(2)	Journey Through the Past (Soundtrack)				
			1972	5.00	10.00	20.00
Reprise 25719		This Note's for You	1988	3.00	6.00	12.00
Reprise 25899		Freedom	1989	3.00	6.00	12.00
Reprise 26315		Ragged Glory	1990	3.00	6.00	12.00
Reprise 45749	(2)	Sleeps with Angels	1994	3.75	7.50	15.00

Label, Number		Title	Year	VG	VG+	NM
Reprise 45934	(2)	Mirror Ball	1995	3.75	7.50	15.00
With Pearl Jam (uncredited)						
Reprise R 113998		Harvest	1972	3.00	6.00	12.00
RCA Music Service edition						
Reprise R 154182		This Note's for You	1987	3.00	6.00	12.00
BMG Direct Marketing edition						
Vapor 46171	(2)	Dead Man (Soundtrack)	1996	3.00	6.00	12.00
Warner Bros. WBMS-107	DJ	The Warner Bros. Music Show	1979	12.50	25.00	50.00
Promo-only interview album						

45s

Label, Number		Title	Year	VG	VG+	NM
Columbia 05566		Are There Any More Real Cowboys/I'm a Memory				
			1985			3.00
A-side: Willie Nelson and Neil Young. B-side: Willie Nelson						
Geffen 28196		Mideast Vacation/Long Walk Home				
			1987			3.00
Geffen 28623		Weight of the World/Pressure	1986			3.00
Geffen 28623	PS	Weight of the World/Pressure	1986			3.00
Geffen 28753		Old Ways/Once an Angel	1986			3.00
Geffen 28883		Get Back to the Country/Misfits	1985			3.00
Geffen 29433		Cry, Cry, Cry/Payola Blues	1983		2.00	4.00
Geffen 29574		Wonderin'/Payola Blues	1983		2.00	4.00
Geffen 29574	PS	Wonderin'/Payola Blues	1983		2.00	4.00
Geffen 29707		Mr. Soul/Mr. Soul	1983		2.00	4.00
Geffen 29887		Little Thing Called Love/We Are In Control				
			1982		2.00	4.00
Geffen 29887	PS	Little Thing Called Love/We Are In Control				
			1982		2.00	4.00
Reprise 0746		Only Love Can Break Your Heart/Cinnamon Girl				
			1971			3.00
"Back to Back Hits" release						
Reprise 0785		The Loner/Sugar Mountain	1968	12.50	25.00	50.00
Reprise 0819		Everyone Knows This Is Nowhere/The Emperor of Wyoming				
			1969	12.50	25.00	50.00
Reprise 0819	DJ	Everyone Knows This Is Nowhere/The Emperor of Wyoming				
			1969	75.00	150.00	300.00
Alternate acoustic version of A-side						
Reprise 0819	DJ	Everyone Knows This Is Nowhere/The Emperor of Wyoming				
			1969	5.00	10.00	20.00
Standard version of A-side, with "RE-1" in trail-off wax						
Reprise 0836		Down By the River/(When You're On the) Losing End				
			1969	12.50	25.00	50.00
Reprise 0861		Oh, Lonesome Me/Sugar Mountain				
			1969	12.50	25.00	50.00
Reprise 0898		I've Been Waiting for You/Oh, Lonesome Me				
			1970	12.50	25.00	50.00
Reprise 0911		Cinnamon Girl/Sugar Mountain	1970		2.50	5.00
Reprise 0958		Only Love Can Break Your Heart/Birds				
			1970		2.50	5.00
Reprise 0996		When You Dance I Can Really Love/Sugar Mountain				
			1971		2.50	5.00
Reprise 1023		Brave Belt/Rock and Roll Band	1971		2.50	5.00
With Graham Nash						
Reprise 1065		Heart of Gold/Sugar Mountain	1971		2.50	5.00
Without reference to "Harvest" LP on label						
Reprise 1065		Heart of Gold/Sugar Mountain	1971		2.00	4.00
With reference to "Harvest" LP on label						
Reprise 1084		Old Man/The Needle and the Damage Done				
			1972		2.00	4.00
Reprise 1099		War Song/The Needle and the Damage Done				
			1972		2.00	4.00
With Graham Nash						

Label, Number		Title	Year	VG	VG+	NM
Reprise 1152		Heart of Gold/Old Man	1972			3.00
"Back to Back Hits" release						
Reprise 1184		Time Fades Away/The Last Train to Tulsa (Live)				
			1973	2.50	5.00	10.00
Reprise 1209		Walk On/For the Turnstiles	1974		2.00	4.00
Reprise 1209	DJ	Walk On (same on both sides)	1974	3.75	7.50	15.00
Small hole						
Reprise 1209	DJ	Walk On (same on both sides)	1974	2.50	5.00	10.00
Large hole						
Reprise 1344		Lookin' for a Love/Sugar Mountain				
			1976		2.00	4.00
Reprise 1350		Drive Back/Stupid Girl	1976		2.00	4.00
Reprise 1390		Hey Baby/Homegrown	1977		2.00	4.00
Reprise 1391		Like a Hurricane/Hold Back the Tears				
			1978		2.00	4.00
Reprise 1393		Sugar Mountain/The Needle and the Damage Done				
			1978		2.00	4.00
Reprise 1395		Comes a Time/Motorcycle Mama				
			1978		2.00	4.00
Reprise 1395	PS	Comes a Time/Motorcycle Mama				
			1978		2.00	4.00
Reprise 1396		Four Strong Winds/Human Highway				
			1979		2.00	4.00
Reprise 18685		Harvest Moon/Old King	1992		2.00	4.00
Reprise 19483		Over and Over	1990			*Cassette only*
Reprise 22776		Rockin' in the Free World/Rockin' in the Free World (Live)				
			1989		2.00	4.00
Reprise 22776	DJ	Rockin' in the Free World (same on both sides)				
			1989	2.50	5.00	10.00
Reprise 22776	PS	Rockin' in the Free World/Rockin' in the Free World (Live)				
			1989		2.00	4.00
Reprise 27848		This Note's For You (LP Version)/				
		This Note's For You (Edited Live Version)				
			1988		2.00	4.00
Reprise 27848	PS	This Note's For You (LP Version)/				
		This Note's For You (Edited Live Version)				
			1988		2.00	4.00
Reprise 27908		Ten Men Workin'/I'm Goin'	1988			3.00
Reprise 27908	PS	Ten Men Workin'/I'm Goin'	1988	2.00	4.00	8.00
A scarce picture sleeve						
Reprise 49031		Rust Never Sleeps (Hey Hey, My My [Into the Black])/				
		Rust Never Sleeps (My My, Hey Hey [Out of the Blue])				
			1979		2.00	4.00
Reprise 49031	PS	Rust Never Sleeps (Hey Hey, My My [Into the Black])/				
		Rust Never Sleeps (My My, Hey Hey [Out of the Blue])				
			1979	2.50	5.00	10.00
Reprise 49189		The Loner/Cinnamon Girl	1980		2.00	4.00
Reprise 49555		Hawks and Doves/Union Man	1980			3.00
Reprise 49555	PS	Hawks and Doves/Union Man	1980			3.00
Reprise 49641		Stayin' Power/Captain America	1980			3.00
Reprise 49870		Southern Pacific/Motor City	1981			3.00
Reprise 50014		Opera Star/Surfer Joe and Moe the Sleaze				
			1982			3.00

12-Inch Singles

Label, Number		Title	Year	VG	VG+	NM
Geffen PRO-A-2373	DJ	Get Back to the Country (Long)/Get Back to the Country (Short)				
			1985	2.50	5.00	10.00
Geffen PRO-A-2528	DJ	Weight of the World (same on both sides)				
			1986	2.50	5.00	10.00
Geffen PRO-A-2623	DJ	People on the Street (same on both sides)				
			1986	2.50	5.00	10.00

Label, Number		Title	Year	VG	VG+	NM
Geffen PRO-A-2811	DJ	Too Lonely (Remix Edit) (same on both sides)				
			1987	2.50	5.00	10.00
Reprise PRO2-901	DJ	Hawks & Doves/Union Man	1980	2.50	5.00	10.00
Blue vinyl						
Reprise 49895		Southern Pacific/Motor City	1982	75.00	150.00	300.00
Picture disc, triangle-shaped						
Reprise 49895		Southern Pacific/Motor City	1982	50.00	100.00	200.00
Green vinyl, triangle-shaped						
Reprise 49895		Southern Pacific/Motor City	1982	2.50	5.00	10.00
Red vinyl, triangle-shaped						
Reprise 49895		Southern Pacific/Motor City	1982	2.50	5.00	10.00
Black vinyl, triangle-shaped						

Youth Brigade

Washington-D.C. area hardcore band.

7-Inch Extended Play Singles

Dischord 6		Youth Brigade	1981	8.75	17.50	35.00
Dischord 6	PS	Youth Brigade	1981	8.75	17.50	35.00

45s

BYO 006		What Price Happiness/Where Are We Going/				
		Who Can You Believe In	1984	16.25	32.50	65.00
Yellow vinyl						
BYO 006		What Price Happiness/Where Are We Going/				
		Who Can You Believe In	1984	8.75	17.50	35.00
Red vinyl (fewer than 200 made)						
BYO 006		What Price Happiness/Where Are We Going/				
		Who Can You Believe In	1984	2.25	4.50	9.00
Black vinyl						
BYO 006	PS	What Price Happiness/Where Are We Going/				
		Who Can You Believe In	1984	2.25	4.50	9.00

Z

Zappa, Frank

Pioneer iconoclastic musician. Albums below include those he recorded with the Mothers of Invention. 45s have the label credit listed if it's not "Frank Zappa."

Vinyl Albums

Angel DS-38170		Boulez Conducts Zappa: The Perfect Stranger				
			1983	3.00	6.00	12.00
Barking Pumpkin 7X4-1		The Old Masters Sampler	1984	6.25	12.50	25.00
Barking Pumpkin AS 995	DJ	Tinsel Town Rebellion	1981	5.00	10.00	20.00
Promo-only sampler						
Barking Pumpkin BPR-1111		Shut Up 'N' Play Yer Guitar	1981	5.00	10.00	20.00
Mail-order item only						
Barking Pumpkin BPR-1112		Shut Up 'N' Play Yer Guitar Some More				
			1981	5.00	10.00	20.00
Mail-order item only						
Barking Pumpkin BPR-1113		Return of the Son of Shut Up 'N' Play Yer Guitar				
			1981	5.00	10.00	20.00
Mail-order item only						
Barking Pumpkin BPRP-1114 PD		Zappa	1982	3.75	7.50	15.00
Picture disc with two songs						
Barking Pumpkin BPRP-1115 PD		Baby Snakes	1983	3.75	7.50	15.00
Picture disc						
Barking Pumpkin AS 1294	DJ	You Are What You Is Special Clean Cuts Edition				
			1981	5.00	10.00	20.00
Barking Pumpkin 7777	(8)	The Old Masters, Box 1	1984	15.00	30.00	60.00
Boxed set						

Label, Number		Title	Year	VG	VG+	NM
Barking Pumpkin 8888	(8)	The Old Masters, Box 2	1986	15.00	30.00	60.00
Another boxed set						
Barking Pumpkin 8888X		The Old Masters Sampler 2	1986	6.25	12.50	25.00
Barking Pumpkin 9999	(8)	The Old Masters, Box 3	1987	15.00	30.00	60.00
Still another boxed set						
Barking Pumpkin PW2 37336	(2)	Tinsel Town Rebellion	1981	5.00	10.00	20.00
Barking Pumpkin PW2 37537	(2)	You Are What You Is	1981	5.00	10.00	20.00
Barking Pumpkin FW 38066		Ship Arriving Too Late to Save a Drowning Witch				
			1982	3.00	6.00	12.00
Barking Pumpkin W3X-38290	(3)	Shut Up 'N' Play Yer Guitar	1982	6.25	12.50	25.00
Box set containing all three "Shut Up 'N' Play Yer Guitar" albums						
Barking Pumpkin FW 38403		Man from Utopia	1983	3.00	6.00	12.00
Barking Pumpkin FW 38820		London Symphony Orchestra	1983	3.00	6.00	12.00
Barking Pumpkin SVBO-74200	(2)	Them Or Us	1984	3.75	7.50	15.00
Barking Pumpkin SWCO-74201	(3)	Thing-Fish	1984	5.00	10.00	20.00
Barking Pumpkin ST-74202		Francesco Zappa	1985	2.50	5.00	10.00
Barking Pumpkin ST-74203		Frank Zappa Meets the Mothers of Prevention				
			1985	2.50	5.00	10.00
Barking Pumpkin ST-74205		Jazz from Hell	1986	2.50	5.00	10.00
Barking Pumpkin 74206	(3)	Joe's Garage, Acts 1, 2 and 3	1986	12.50	25.00	50.00
Box set, two gatefolds, with insert						
Barking Pumpkin SJ-74207		London Symphony Orchestra, Volume 2				
			1987	2.50	5.00	10.00
Barking Pumpkin D1-74212	(2)	Guitar	1988	2.50	5.00	10.00
Barking Pumpkin D1-74213	(3)	You Can't Do That On Stage Anymore				
			1988	5.00	10.00	20.00
Barking Pumpkin R1 74213		You Can't Do That On Stage Anymore Sampler				
			1988	3.00	6.00	12.00
Barking Pumpkin D1-74217	(3)	You Can't Do That On Stage Anymore Vol. 2				
			1988	5.00	10.00	20.00
Barking Pumpkin D1-74218		Broadway the Hard Way	1988	2.50	5.00	10.00
Bizarre MS 2024	(2)	Uncle Meat	1969	8.75	17.50	35.00
Originals come with a booklet; blue label						
Bizarre MS 2024	(2)	Uncle Meat	1973	5.00	10.00	20.00
Reissue with brown Reprise label						
Bizarre MS 2028		Weasels Ripped My Flesh	1970	6.25	12.50	25.00
Blue label original						
Bizarre MS 2028		Weasels Ripped My Flesh	1973	3.75	7.50	15.00
Reissue with brown Reprise label						
Bizarre MS 2030		Chunga's Revenge	1970	12.50	25.00	50.00
White label promo						
Bizarre MS 2030		Chunga's Revenge	1970	6.25	12.50	25.00
Blue label original						
Bizarre MS 2030		Chunga's Revenge	1973	3.75	7.50	15.00
Reissue with brown Reprise label						
Bizarre MS 2042		Fillmore East, June 1971	1971	6.25	12.50	25.00
Blue label original						
Bizarre MS 2042		Fillmore East, June 1971	1973	2.75	7.50	15.00
Reissue with brown Reprise label						
Bizarre MS 2075		Just Another Band from L.A.	1972	6.25	12.50	25.00
Blue label original						
Bizarre MS 2075		Just Another Band from L.A.	1973	3.75	7.50	15.00
Reissue with brown Reprise label						
Bizarre MS 2093		The Grand Wazoo	1972	6.25	12.50	25.00
Blue label original						
Bizarre MS 2093		The Grand Wazoo	1973	3.75	7.50	15.00
Reissue with brown Reprise label						
Bizarre MS 2094		Waka/Jawaka	1972	6.25	12.50	25.00
Blue label original						
Bizarre MS 2094		Waka/Jawaka	1973	3.75	7.50	15.00
Reissue with brown Reprise label						
Bizarre RS-6356		Hot Rats	1969	12.50	25.00	50.00
Blue label original						

Label, Number		Title	Year	VG	VG+	NM
Bizarre RS-6356		Hot Rats	1973	3.75	7.50	15.00
Reissue with brown Reprise label						
Bizarre RS-6370		Burnt Weenie Sandwich	1970	6.25	12.50	25.00
Blue label original; with booklet						
Bizarre RS-6370		Burnt Weenie Sandwich	1973	3.75	7.50	15.00
Reissue with brown Reprise label						
Columbia (no #)	(4) DJ	Lather	1977	187.50	375.00	750.00
Test pressing only, made during dispute with Warner Bros.; parts of this LP are on DSK 2291, 2292 and 2294						
DiscReet MS 2149		Over-Nite Sensation	1973	5.00	10.00	20.00
DiscReet MS4 2149	Q	Over-Nite Sensation	1973	10.00	20.00	40.00
DiscReet DS 2175		Apostrophe (')	1974	12.50	25.00	50.00
White label promo						
DiscReet DS 2175		Apostrophe (')	1974	3.75	7.50	15.00
DiscReet DS4 2175	Q	Apostrophe (')	1974	8.75	17.50	35.00
DiscReet 2DS 2202	(2)	Roxy & Elsewhere	1974	6.25	12.50	25.00
DiscReet DS 2216		One Size Fits All	1975	3.75	7.50	15.00
DiscReet DS 2234		Bongo Fury	1975	3.75	7.50	15.00
DiscReet DSK 2288		Over-Nite Sensation	1977	3.00	6.00	12.00
Reissue of DiscReet 2149 with new number						
DiscReet DSK 2289		Apostrophe (')	1977	3.00	6.00	12.00
Reissue with new number						
DiscReet 2D 2290	(2)	Zappa in New York	1978	62.50	125.00	250.00
Stock copy with "Punky's Whips" erroneously listed on jacket						
DiscReet 2D 2290	(2)	Zappa in New York	1978	5.00	10.00	20.00
DiscReet 2D 2290	(2) DJ	Zappa in New York	1978	100.00	200.00	400.00
Test pressing with "Punky's Whips"						
DiscReet DSK 2291		Studio Tan	1978	3.75	7.50	15.00
DiscReet DSK 2292		Sleep Dirt	1978	3.75	7.50	15.00
DiscReet DSK 2294		Orchestral Favorites	1978	3.75	7.50	15.00
Foo-eee R1-70372	(11)	Beat the Boots #2	1992	25.00	50.00	100.00
Legitimate box-set release by Rhino of 11 bootlegged concerts						
Foo-eee R1-70907	(10)	Beat the Boots	1991	25.00	50.00	100.00
Legitimate box-set release by Rhino of eight bootlegged concerts						
MCA 4183	(2)	200 Motels (movie soundtrack)	1986	3.75	7.50	15.00
Reissue						
MGM GAS-112	DJ	The Mothers of Invention	1970	25.00	50.00	100.00
Yellow label promo						
MGM GAS-112		The Mothers of Invention	1970	12.50	25.00	50.00
MGM SE-4754	DJ	The Worst of the Mothers	1971	37.50	75.00	150.00
Yellow label promo						
MGM SE-4754		The Worst of the Mothers	1971	12.50	25.00	50.00
Rhino/Del-Fi RNEP-604		Rare Meat: The Early Productions of Frank Zappa				
			1984	10.00	20.00	40.00
With original cover						
Ryko Analogue RALP 10503		We're Only In It for the Money	1995	3.00	6.00	12.00
Vinyl reissue						
Ryko Analogue RALP 40500	(2)	Strictly Commercial: The Best of Frank Zappa				
			1995	5.00	10.00	20.00
Issued with obi						
United Artists UAS-9956	(2)	200 Motels (movie soundtrack)	1971	12.50	25.00	50.00
Verve V-5005-2	(2) M	Freak Out!	1966	100.00	200.00	400.00
White label promo						
Verve V-5005-2	(2) M	Freak Out!	1966	50.00	100.00	200.00
Cover version 1: Has blurb on inside gatefold on how to get a map of "freak-out hot spots" in L.A.						
Verve V-5005-2	(2) M	Freak Out!	1966	37.50	75.00	150.00
Cover version 2: Has no blurb inside on getting a map of "freak-out hot spots"						
Verve V6-5005-2	(2) S	Freak Out!	1966	75.00	150.00	300.00
Yellow label promo						
Verve V6-5005-2	(2) S	Freak Out!	1966	25.00	50.00	100.00
Cover version 1: Has blurb on inside gatefold on how to get a map of "freak-out hot spots" in L.A.						
Verve V6-5005-2	(2) S	Freak Out!	1966	18.75	37.50	75.00
Cover version 2: Has no blurb inside on getting a map of "freak-out hot spots"						
Verve V-5013	M	Absolutely Free	1967	75.00	150.00	300.00
White label promo						

Label, Number		Title	Year	VG	VG+	NM
Verve V-5013	M	Absolutely Free	1967	37.50	75.00	150.00
Verve V6-5013	S	Absolutely Free	1967	18.75	37.50	75.00
Verve V-5045	M	We're Only In It for the Money	1968	75.00	150.00	300.00
White label promo						
Verve V-5045	M	We're Only In It for the Money	1968	37.50	75.00	150.00
With sheet of cut-outs a la "Sgt. Pepper's Lonely Hearts Club Band"						
Verve V6-5045	S	We're Only In It for the Money	1968	18.75	37.50	75.00
Un-censored version, with cut-outs						
Verve V6-5045	S	We're Only In It for the Money	1968	50.00	100.00	200.00
Censored version: the songs "Who Needs the Peace Corps?" and "Let's Make the Water Turn Black" have lines deleted						
Verve V6-5055		Cruising with Ruben and the Jets	1968	50.00	100.00	200.00
Yellow label promo						
Verve V6-5055		Cruising with Ruben and the Jets	1968	18.75	37.50	75.00
Verve V6-5068		Mothermania -- The Best of the Mothers	1969	37.50	75.00	150.00
Yellow label promo						
Verve V6-5068		Mothermania -- The Best of the Mothers	1969	18.75	37.50	75.00
Verve V6-5074		The XXXX of the Mothers	1969	37.50	75.00	150.00
Yellow label promo						
Verve V6-5074		The XXXX of the Mothers	1969	12.50	25.00	50.00
Verve V6-8741		Lumpy Gravy	1968	50.00	100.00	200.00
Yellow label promo						
Verve V6-8741		Lumpy Gravy	1968	12.50	25.00	50.00
Warner Bros. BS-2970		Zoot Allures	1976	3.75	7.50	15.00
Zappa MK-78	DJ	Sheik Yerbouti Clean Cuts	1979	8.75	17.50	35.00
Zappa MK-129	DJ	Joe's Garage Acts I, II and III Sampler	1980	8.75	17.50	35.00
Zappa SRZ-2-1501	(2)	Sheik Yerbouti	1979	5.00	10.00	20.00
Zappa SRZ-2-1502	(2)	Joe's Garage, Acts II and III	1980	5.00	10.00	20.00
Zappa SRZ-1-1603		Joe's Garage, Act I	1979	3.75	7.50	15.00

45s

Label, Number		Title	Year	VG	VG+	NM
Barking Pumpkin 02972		Valley Girl/You Are What You Is	1982			3.00
A-side: Frank and Moon Zappa						
Barking Pumpkin 02972	PS	Valley Girl/You Are What You Is	1982		3.50	7.00
A-side: Frank and Moon Zappa						
Bizarre 0840		My Guitar/Dog Breath	1969	12.50	25.00	50.00
The Mothers of Invention						
Bizarre 0889		Peaches En Regalia/Little Umbrellas	1970	12.50	25.00	50.00
Bizarre 0892		WPLJ/My Guitar	1970	12.50	25.00	50.00
The Mothers of Invention						
Bizarre 0967		Tell Me You Love Me/Would You Go All the Way for the U.S.A.?	1970	12.50	25.00	50.00
Bizarre 1027		Tears Began to Fall/Junior Mintz Boogie	1971	12.50	25.00	50.00
Junior Mintz						
Bizarre 1052		Tears Began to Fall/Junior Mintz Boogie	1971	12.50	25.00	50.00
Frank Zappa and The Mothers of Invention						
Bizarre 1127		Cletus Awreetus-Awrightus/Eat That Question	1972	8.75	17.50	35.00
The Mothers of Invention						
DiscReet 1180		I'm the Slime/Montana	1973	6.25		12.50	25.00
The Mothers						
DiscReet 1312		Don't Eat the Yellow Snow/Cosmic Debris	1974	3.75	7.50	15.00
United Artists 50857		Magic Fingers/Daddy, Daddy, Daddy	1971	12.50	25.00	50.00

Label, Number		Title	Year	VG	VG+	NM
Verve 10418		How Could I Be Such a Fool/				
		Help I'm a Rock (3rd Movement: It Can't Happen Here)				
			1966	50.00	100.00	200.00
Verve 10418	DJ	How Could I Be Such a Fool/				
		Help I'm a Rock (3rd Movement: It Can't Happen Here)				
			1966	25.00	50.00	100.00
Verve 10458		Who Are the Brain Police/Trouble Comin' Every Day				
			1966	50.00	100.00	200.00
The Mothers of Invention; the existence of this stock copy has been questioned						
Verve 10458	DJ	Who Are the Brain Police/Trouble Comin' Every Day				
			1966	25.00	50.00	100.00
The Mothers of Invention						
Verve 10513		Why Don't You Do Me Right/Big Leg Emma				
			1967	50.00	100.00	200.00
The Mothers of Invention						
Verve 10513	DJ	Why Don't You Do Me Right/Big Leg Emma				
			1967	25.00	50.00	100.00
The Mothers of Invention						
Verve 10570		Mother People/Lonely Little Girl				
			1967	50.00	100.00	200.00
The Mothers of Invention						
Verve 10570	DJ	Mother People/Lonely Little Girl				
			1967	25.00	50.00	100.00
The Mothers of Invention						
Verve 10632		Jelly Roll Gum Drop/Any Way the Wind Blows				
			1968	37.50	75.00	150.00
Ruben & The Jets						
Verve 10632	DJ	Jelly Roll Gum Drop/Any Way the Wind Blows				
			1968	18.75	37.50	75.00
Ruben & The Jets						
Verve 10632		Jelly Roll Gum Drop/Deseri	1968	37.50	75.00	150.00
Ruben & The Jets						
Verve 10632	DJ	Jelly Roll Gum Drop/Deseri	1968	18.75	37.50	75.00
Ruben & The Jets						
Warner Bros. 8296		Find Her Finer/Zoot Allures	1976	6.25	12.50	25.00
Warner Bros. 8342		Disco Boy/Miss Pinky	1977	6.25	12.50	25.00
Zappa Z-10		Dancin' Fool/Baby Snakes	1979	2.50	5.00	10.00
Zappa ZR 1001		I Don't Wanna Get Drafted/Ancient Armaments (Live)				
			1980		2.00	4.00

12-Inch Singles

Label, Number		Title	Year	VG	VG+	NM
Zappa MK 107	DJ	Joe's Garage/Central Scrutinizer				
			1979	10.00	20.00	40.00
Barking Pumpkin 02616		Goblin Girl/Pink Napkins	1982	7.50	15.00	30.00
Picture disc						
Barking Pumpkin 03069		Valley Girl/You Are What You Is				
			1982	3.75	7.50	15.00
A-side: Frank and Moon Zappa						

Zero Boys

Indianapolis punk band.

Vinyl Albums

Label, Number		Title	Year	VG	VG+	NM
Nimrod (# unknown)		Vicious Circle	1982	5.00	10.00	20.00
Toxic Shock TXLP 11		Vicious Circle	1987	3.00	6.00	12.00
Reissue of Nimrod release						

7-Inch Extended Play Singles

Label, Number		Title	Year	VG	VG+	NM
Z-Disk (# unknown)		Livin' in the 80's	1980	18.75	37.50	75.00
Z-Disk (# unknown)	PS	Livin' in the 80's	1980	18.75	37.50	75.00
Value is an average; an unusually wide range of values was reported						

Label, Number		Title	Year	VG	VG+	NM

Zeros
Los Angeles poppy punk group.

Vinyl Albums

Label, Number		Title	Year	VG	VG+	NM
Bomp! 4035		Don't Push Me Around	1991	3.00	6.00	12.00

45s

Label, Number		Title	Year	VG	VG+	NM
Bomp! 110		Don't Push Me Around/Wimp	1977	3.75	7.50	15.00
Bomp! 110	PS	Don't Push Me Around/Wimp	1977	3.75	7.50	15.00
Bomp! 118		Wild Weekend/Beat Your Heart Out	1978	3.75	7.50	15.00
Bomp! 118	PS	Wild Weekend/Beat Your Heart Out	1978	3.75	7.50	15.00
Sympathy For The Record Industry 166		I Don't Wanna/Little Latin Lupe Lu	1993			2.50
Sympathy For The Record Industry 166	PS	I Don't Wanna/Little Latin Lupe Lu	1993			2.50
Test Tube 003		They Say That Everything's Alright/Getting Nowhere Fast	1980	3.75	7.50	15.00
Test Tube 003	PS	They Say That Everything's Alright/Getting Nowhere Fast	1980	3.75	7.50	15.00

Two of alternative music's biggest influences, directly or indirectly, are Neil Young and Frank Zappa/The Mothers of Invention. Young's last American picture sleeve, for "Rockin' in the Free World," is a bargain at $4. Also here is the front cover of the Ryko reissue of the classic Mothers album *We're Only In It for the Money*, still available at retail for about $12.

Title	Label, Number	Year	VG	VG+	NM

Soundtracks

Vinyl Albums

Title	Label, Number	Year	VG	VG+	NM
1969	Polydor R 100724	1988	2.50	5.00	10.00
Includes Pretenders ("Windows of the World")					
9 1/2 Weeks	Capitol SV-12470	1986	2.50	5.00	10.00
Includes John Taylor, Devo ("Bread and Butter"), Eurythmics, Stewart Copeland					
9 1/2 Weeks	Capitol SV-512470	1986	3.75	7.50	15.00
Includes John Taylor, Devo ("Bread and Butter"), Eurythmics, Stewart Copeland; Columbia House edition					
About Last Night...	EMI America SV-17210	1986	2.50	5.00	10.00
Includes The Del-Lords					
Absolute Beginners	EMI America SV-17182	1986	3.00	6.00	12.00
Includes David Bowie (2), Sade, The Style Council, Jerry Dammers					
All This and World War II	(2) 20th Century T2-522	1976	5.00	10.00	20.00
Includes Peter Gabriel					
Allnighter, The	PD Chameleon CHPD 9601	1987	7.50	15.00	30.00
Includes Redd Kross; picture disc					
Allnighter, The	Chameleon CHST 9601	1987	3.75	7.50	15.00
Includes Redd Kross					
Always	MCA 8036	1990	3.00	6.00	12.00
Includes Lyle Lovett					
Amateur	Matador OLE 098-1	1995	3.00	6.00	12.00
Includes Liz Phair, My Bloody Valentine, P.J. Harvey, Yo La Tengo, etc.					
American Anthem	Atlantic 81661	1986	2.50	5.00	10.00
Includes Andy Taylor (2), INXS					
American Flyers	GRP 2001	1985	3.00	6.00	12.00
Includes Chris Isaak					
American Gigolo	Polydor PD1-6259	1980	3.00	6.00	12.00
Includes Blondie					
Americathon	Lorimar JS 36174	1979	3.00	6.00	12.00
Includes Elvis Costello (2), Nick Lowe					
Armed and Dangerous	Manhattan SJ-53041	1986	2.50	5.00	10.00
Includes Sigue Sigue Sputnik					
Arthur 2: On the Rocks	A&M SP-3916	1988	2.50	5.00	10.00
Includes Orchestral Manoeuvres in the Dark					
Athens, Ga. -- Inside/Out	I.R.S. 6185	1987	2.50	5.00	10.00
Includes R.E.M. (2), Dreams So Real					
Bachelor Party	I.R.S. SP-70047	1984	3.00	6.00	12.00
Includes R.E.M., Oingo Boingo (2), The Fleshtones, The Alarm					
Back to School	MCA 6175	1986	2.50	5.00	10.00
Includes Oingo Boingo					
Back to the Beach	Columbia SC 40892	1987	2.50	5.00	10.00
Includes Aimee Mann, Dave Edmunds, Fishbone, Pee-wee Herman					
Band of the Hand	MCA 6187	1986	3.00	6.00	12.00
Includes Andy Summers					
Batman	Warner Bros. 25977	1989	3.00	6.00	12.00
Music composed and conducted by Danny Elfman					
Batman Forever	(2) Atlantic PR 6339	1995	5.00	10.00	20.00
Promo only generic white cover with sticker; includes Seal, U2, P.J. Harvey, Mazzy Star, The Flaming Lips, etc.					
Beat Street	Atlantic 80154	1984	2.50	5.00	10.00
Includes Grandmaster Melle Mel, others					
Beetlejuice	Geffen GHS 24204	1988	2.50	5.00	10.00
Music composed and conducted by Danny Elfman					
Beetlejuice	Geffen R 174166	1988	3.00	6.00	12.00
Music composed and conducted by Danny Elfman; BMG Direct Marketing edition					
Beverly Hills Cop	MCA 5553	1984	2.50	5.00	10.00
Includes Danny Elfman					
Beverly Hills Cop II	MCA 6207	1987	2.00	4.00	8.00
Includes George Michael					

Title	Label, Number	Year	VG	VG+	NM
Beverly Hills Cop II	MCA R 123346	1987	2.50	5.00	10.00
Includes George Michael ("I Want Your Sex")					
Black Rain	Virgin 91292	1989	2.50	5.00	10.00
Includes UB40, Iggy Pop					
Bodyguard, The	Arista 18699	1992	3.00	6.00	12.00
Includes Lisa Stansfield					
Border Radio	Enigma ST-73221	1987	3.00	6.00	12.00
Includes John Doe					
Born on the Fourth of July	MCA 6340	1989	3.00	6.00	12.00
Includes Edie Brickell and New Bohemians					
Boyz 'n the Hood	DJ Warner Bros. PRO-A-4996	1991	5.00	10.00	20.00
Includes Ice Cube					
Breakin'	Polydor 821 919-1	1984	2.50	5.00	10.00
Includes Re-Flex					
Bright Lights, Big City	Warner Bros. 25688	1988	2.50	5.00	10.00
Includes M/A/R/R/S, Depeche Mode, New Order, Prince					
Bright Lights, Big City	Warner Bros. R 100483	1988	3.00	6.00	12.00
Includes M/A/R/R/S, Depeche Mode, New Order, Prince; BMG Direct Marketing edition					
Brimstone & Treacle	A&M SP-4915	1982	2.50	5.00	10.00
Includes Sting, The Police, Go-Go's, Squeeze					
Bull Durham	Capitol C1-90586	1988	2.50	5.00	10.00
Includes Los Lobos, The Blasters, House of Schock					
Burglar	MCA 6201	1987	2.50	5.00	10.00
Includes Belinda Carlisle, The Belle Stars, The Smithereens					
Buster	Atlantic 81905	1988	2.50	5.00	10.00
Includes The Searchers ("Sweets for My Sweet")					
Captive	Virgin 90609	1987	3.75	7.50	15.00
Music by The Edge and Larry Mullen of U2					
Cat People	Backstreet BSR 6107	1982	2.50	5.00	10.00
Includes David Bowie ("Cat People")					
Catherine Wheel, The	Sire SRK 3645	1981	3.00	6.00	12.00
Includes David Byrne, who also composed all the music					
China Beach (Music and Memories)	SBK K1-93744	1990	3.00	6.00	12.00
Includes Katrina and the Waves					
Christiane F.	RCA ABL1-4239	1981	3.75	7.50	15.00
Includes David Bowie ("Helgen [Heroes]")					
Clockers	MCA 11304	1995	2.50	5.00	10.00
Includes Seal					
Colors	Sire R 154136	1988	3.00	6.00	12.00
Includes Ice-T ("Colors")					
Colors	Warner Bros. 25713	1988	2.50	5.00	10.00
Includes Ice-T, Salt-N-Pepa					
Courier	Virgin 90954	1989	3.00	6.00	12.00
Includes U2, Elvis Costello (as Declan MacManus), Hothouse Flowers					
Cruising	Columbia JS 36410	1980	3.00	6.00	12.00
Includes The Germs, others					
Dance Craze	Chrysalis CHR 1299	1981	4.50	9.00	18.00
Includes The Specials, The Selecter, Bad Manners, Madness, The English Beat, The Bodysnatchers; a great introduction to 2-Tone ska					
Dangerously Close	Enigma SJ-73204	1986	2.50	5.00	10.00
Includes The Smithereens, Lords of the New Church					
Darkman	MCA 10094	1990	3.00	6.00	12.00
Composed and conducted by Danny Elfman					
Days of Thunder	DGC 24294	1990	3.75	7.50	15.00
Includes Guns N' Roses, Joan Jett and the Blackhearts					
Decline of Western Civilization, The	Slash 105	1981	5.00	10.00	20.00
Includes Black Flag, X, The Germs, Fear, others					
Do the Right Thing	Motown 6272	1989	2.50	5.00	10.00
Includes Public Enemy					
Doctor Detroit	Backstreet 6120	1983	2.50	5.00	10.00
Includes Devo (2)					

Title	Label, Number	Year	VG	VG+	NM
Dogs in Space	Atlantic 81789	1987	3.00	6.00	12.00

Includes Iggy Pop, Michael Hutchense (of INXS), Brian Eno, etc.

Title	Label, Number	Year	VG	VG+	NM
Doors, The	Elektra E1-61047	1991	5.00	10.00	20.00

Includes The Velvet Underground; Columbia House edition (only U.S. pressing)

Title	Label, Number	Year	VG	VG+	NM
Down and Out in Beverly Hills	MCA 6160	1986	2.50	5.00	10.00

Includes Andy Summers (6)

Title	Label, Number	Year	VG	VG+	NM
Dragnet	MCA 6210	1987	2.50	5.00	10.00

Includes Art of Noise

Title	Label, Number	Year	VG	VG+	NM
Dudes	MCA 6212	1987	2.50	5.00	10.00

Includes Jane's Addiction

Title	Label, Number	Year	VG	VG+	NM
Earth Girls Are Easy	Sire 25835	1989	2.50	5.00	10.00

Includes The B-52's, Depeche Mode, The Jesus and Mary Chain, Julie Brown (2), Stewart Copeland

Title	Label, Number	Year	VG	VG+	NM
Easy Money	Columbia JS 38968	1983	2.50	5.00	10.00

Includes Nick Lowe

Title	Label, Number	Year	VG	VG+	NM
Eating Raoul	Varese Sarabande STV 81164	1982	3.00	6.00	12.00
Falcon and the Snowman, The	EMI America SV-17150	1985	2.50	5.00	10.00

Includes David Bowie ("This Is Not America")

Title	Label, Number	Year	VG	VG+	NM
Fast Times at Ridgemont High	(2)Full Moon/Asylum 60158	1982	3.75	7.50	15.00

Includes Go-Go's, Oingo Boingo

Title	Label, Number	Year	VG	VG+	NM
Fine Mess, A	Motown 6180	1986	2.50	5.00	10.00

Includes Los Lobos

Title	Label, Number	Year	VG	VG+	NM
Firstborn	EMI America ST-17144	1984	2.50	5.00	10.00

Includes Wang Chung, Talk Talk, Re-Flex

Title	Label, Number	Year	VG	VG+	NM
Firstborn	EMI America ST-517144	1984	3.00	6.00	12.00

Includes Wang Chung, Talk Talk, Re-Flex; Columbia House edition

Title	Label, Number	Year	VG	VG+	NM
Fletch	MCA 6142	1985	2.50	5.00	10.00

Includes The Fixx, Kim Wilde

Title	Label, Number	Year	VG	VG+	NM
Footloose	PD Columbia 9C9 39404	1984	5.00	10.00	20.00

Includes Moving Pictures; picture disc

Title	Label, Number	Year	VG	VG+	NM
Footloose	Columbia JS 39242	1984	2.50	5.00	10.00

Includes Moving Pictures

Title	Label, Number	Year	VG	VG+	NM
Forbidden Zone	Varese Sarabande STV 81170	1983	3.00	6.00	12.00
Friday	(2) Priority P1-53959	1995	3.75	7.50	15.00

Includes Ice Cube, Dr. Dre, other gangsta rappers

Title	Label, Number	Year	VG	VG+	NM
Fright Night	Private I SZ 40087	1985	3.00	6.00	12.00

Includes Devo ("Let's Talk")

Title	Label, Number	Year	VG	VG+	NM
Get Crazy	Morocco 6065	1983	3.50	7.00	14.00

Includes Ramones, Marshall Crenshaw, Lou Reed, Fear

Title	Label, Number	Year	VG	VG+	NM
Ghostbusters	Arista AL8-8246	1984	3.75	7.50	15.00

Includes The Bus Boys, Thompson Twins; first pressing has smaller print on front and eight photos on back

Title	Label, Number	Year	VG	VG+	NM
Ghostbusters	Arista AL8-8246	1984	2.50	5.00	10.00

Includes The Bus Boys, Thompson Twins; later pressings have large print on front and seven photos on back

Title	Label, Number	Year	VG	VG+	NM
Ghostbusters II	MCA R 151964	1989	2.50	5.00	10.00

Includes Run-D.M.C. ("Ghostbusters"), Oingo Boingo

Title	Label, Number	Year	VG	VG+	NM
Girls Just Want to Have Fun	Mercury 824 510-1	1985	2.50	5.00	10.00

Includes Animotion

Title	Label, Number	Year	VG	VG+	NM
Golden Child, The	Capitol SJ-12544	1986	2.50	5.00	10.00

Includes Martha Davis

Title	Label, Number	Year	VG	VG+	NM
Good Morning, Vietnam	A&M R 154001	1987	3.00	6.00	12.00

Includes The Searchers; BMG Direct Marketing edition

Title	Label, Number	Year	VG	VG+	NM
Goonies, The	Epic SE 40067	1985	2.50	5.00	10.00

Includes Cyndi Lauper (2), Bangles

Title	Label, Number	Year	VG	VG+	NM
Gotcha!	MCA Curb 5596	1985	3.00	6.00	12.00

Includes Joan Jett and the Blackhearts, Bronski Beat

Title	Label, Number	Year	VG	VG+	NM
Great Outdoors, The	Atlantic 81859	1988	2.50	5.00	10.00

Includes Pop Will Eat Itself

Title	Label, Number	Year	VG	VG+	NM
Gremlins	EP Geffen GHSP 24044	1984	2.50	5.00	10.00

Includes Peter Gabriel

Title	Label, Number	Year	VG	VG+	NM
Hard Country	Epic SE 37367	1981	2.50	5.00	10.00
Includes Joe Ely					
Heavenly Bodies	Private I SZ 39930	1985	2.50	5.00	10.00
Includes The Tubes					
Heavenly Bodies Sampler	DJ Private I AS 1965	1984	2.00	4.00	8.00
Includes The Tubes; promo-only 4-song sampler					
Heavy Metal	(2) Full Moon/Asylum DP-90004	1981	3.75	7.50	15.00
Includes Devo					
Hiding Out	Virgin 90661	1987	2.00	4.00	8.00
Includes Pretty Poison ("Catch Me I'm Falling"), Boy George ("Live My Life"); Public Image Ltd. ("Seattle")					
Hiding Out	Virgin R 163706	1987	2.50	5.00	10.00
Includes Pretty Poison ("Catch Me I'm Falling"), Boy George ("Live My Life"); Public Image Ltd. ("Seattle")					
House Party	Motown 9296	1990	3.00	6.00	12.00
Includes L.L. Cool J, Flavor Flav (of Public Enemy)					
Howard the Duck	MCA 6173	1986	2.50	5.00	10.00
Includes Dolby's Cube (Thomas Dolby)					
Hunger, The	Varese Sarabande STV-81184	1984	2.50	5.00	10.00
I Was a Teenage Zombie	Enigma SJ-73296	1987	3.00	6.00	12.00
Includes The Fleshtones, The Del Fuegos, the dB's, The Dream Syndicate, Violent Femmes, The Waitresses, The Smithereens, Los Lobos					
I'm Gonna Git You Sucka	Arista AL-8574	1988	2.50	5.00	10.00
Includes Fishbone (with Curtis Mayfield)					
Innerspace	Geffen GHS 24161	1987	2.50	5.00	10.00
Includes Wang Chung, Berlin					
Juice	MCA 10577	1992	2.50	5.00	10.00
Includes Naughty By Nature, others; issued in generic sleeve with sticker					
Jumpin' Jack Flash	Mercury 830 545-1	1986	2.50	5.00	10.00
Includes Bananarama					
Just One of the Guys	Elektra 60426	1985	2.50	5.00	10.00
Includes Berlin					
Karate Kid, The	Casablanca 822 213-1	1984	3.00	6.00	12.00
Includes The Flirts (with Jan & Dean), Gang of Four					
King of Comedy, The	Warner Bros. 23765	1983	2.50	5.00	10.00
Includes The Pretenders ("Back on the Chain Gang"), Talking Heads, Ric Ocasek					
Krush Groove	Warner Bros. 25295	1985	2.50	5.00	10.00
Includes Beastie Boys, L.L. Cool J, Krush Groove All-Stars, Debbie Harry					
La Bamba	Slash/Warner Bros. 25605	1987	2.50	5.00	10.00
Includes Los Lobos (8 tracks), Marshall Crenshaw ("Crying, Waiting, Hoping"), Brian Setzer ("Summertime Blues")					
La Bamba	Slash/Warner Bros. R 120062	1987	3.00	6.00	12.00
Includes Los Lobos (8 tracks), Marshall Crenshaw ("Crying, Waiting, Hoping"), Brian Setzer ("Summertime Blues")					
Labyrinth	EMI America SV-17206	1986	2.50	5.00	10.00
Includes David Bowie					
Last American Virgin, The	Columbia JS 38279	1982	10.00	20.00	40.00
Includes Devo, Tommy Tutone, U2, The Cars, Oingo Boingo, The Police					
Last Emperor, The	Virgin 90690	1987	2.50	5.00	10.00
One side of music by David Byrne					
Lean On Me	Warner Bros. 25843	1987	2.50	5.00	10.00
Includes Guns N' Roses ("Welcome to the Jungle")					
Less Than Zero	Def Jam SC 44042	1987	2.50	5.00	10.00
Includes Bangles, Joan Jett and the Blackhearts, Glenn Danzig, Public Enemy, L.L. Cool J, Oran "Juice" Jones					
Lethal Weapon	Warner Bros. 25561	1987	2.50	5.00	10.00
Includes Honeymoon Suite					
Letter to Brezhnev	MCA/London 6162	1985	2.50	5.00	10.00
Includes Fine Young Cannibals, Bronski Beat					
Light of Day	Blackheart SZ 40654	1986	3.00	6.00	12.00
Includes The Barbusters (Joan Jett and the Blackhearts), Dave Edmunds					
Lost Angels	A&M SP-3926	1989	3.00	6.00	12.00
Includes The Cure, Soundgarden, The Pogues, Soul Asylum, Happy Mondays					
Lost Boys, The	Atlantic 81767	1987	2.50	5.00	10.00
Includes INXS and Jimmy Barnes, Echo and the Bunnymen					

Title	Label, Number	Year	VG	VG+	NM
Made in USA	Chrysalis OV 41566	1987	2.50	5.00	10.00
Includes Timbuk 3, World Party, Sonic Youth, Mojo Nixon & Skid Roper					
Major League	Curb 10402	1989	3.00	6.00	12.00
Includes X, Beat Farmers, Lyle Lovett					
Mallrats	MCA 11294	1995	2.50	5.00	10.00
Includes Weezer, Elastica, Belly, etc.					
Married to the Mob	Reprise 25763	1988	3.00	6.00	12.00
Includes New Order, Sinead O'Connor, Chris Isaak, Debbie Harry, Brian Eno, The Feelies, Tom Tom Club					
Mask, The	DJ Chaos 6455	1994	3.75	7.50	15.00
Includes Fishbone, Buster Poindexter; generic cover; no other U.S. vinyl					
Merry Christmas, Mr. Lawrence	MCA 6125	1983	3.00	6.00	12.00
Includes David Sylvian					
Metropolis	Columbia JS 39526	1984	2.50	5.00	10.00
Includes Adam Ant					
Miami Vice	MCA 6150	1985	2.50	5.00	10.00
Includes Grandmaster Melle Mel					
Miami Vice II	MCA 6192	1986	2.50	5.00	10.00
Includes The Damned, Andy Taylor, Roxy Music					
Miami Vice II	MCA R 154220	1987	3.00	6.00	12.00
Includes The Damned, Andy Taylor, Roxy Music; BMG Direct Marketing edition					
Mighty Quinn, The	A&M SP-3924	1989	2.50	5.00	10.00
Includes UB40, Yello					
Modern Girls	Warner Bros. 25526	1986	2.50	5.00	10.00
Includes Depeche Mode, Toni Basil, Icehouse, The Jesus and Mary Chain					
My Stepmother Is an Alien	Polydor 837 798-1	1988	2.50	5.00	10.00
Includes Animotion, M/A/R/R/S					
National Lampoon's Vacation	Warner Bros. 23909	1983	2.50	5.00	10.00
Includes Ramones					
Never Ending Story, The	EMI America ST-17139	1984	3.00	6.00	12.00
Includes Limahl					
New Jack City	Giant 24409	1991	3.00	6.00	12.00
Includes Ice-T					
New York Stories	Elektra Musician 60857	1988	3.00	6.00	12.00
Includes Kid Creole and the Coconuts, Transvision Vamp					
Night in Heaven, A	A&M SP-4966	1983	3.00	6.00	12.00
Includes The English Beat					
Nightmare on Elm Street 4: The Dream Master	Chrysalis R 100504	198?	3.00	6.00	12.00
Includes Blondie ("Rip Her to Shreds")					
Over the Edge	Warner Bros. HS 3335	1979	2.50	5.00	10.00
Includes The Ramones, The Cars					
Party Party	A&M SP 3212	1982	3.75	7.50	15.00
Includes Elvis Costello, Dave Edmunds ("Run Rudolph Run"), Bananarama, Midge Ure, Bad Manners, etc.					
Perfect	Arista AL9 8278	1985	2.50	5.00	10.00
Includes Wham! ("Wham Rap")					
Perfect	Arista R 163614	1985	3.00	6.00	12.00
Includes Wham! ("Wham Rap")					
Permanent Record	Epic E 40879	198?	3.00	6.00	12.00
Includes Joe Strummer (5 tracks), Lou Reed, The Stranglers					
Playing for Keeps	Atlantic 81678	1986	2.50	5.00	10.00
Includes Arcadia					
Porky's Revenge	DJ Columbia CAS 2034	1985	3.00	6.00	12.00
Promo-only sampler; includes Dave Edmunds, Jeff Beck and George Harrison					
Porky's Revenge	Columbia JS 39983	1985	3.00	6.00	12.00
Includes Dave Edmunds					
Pretty in Pink	A&M R 144487	1986	2.50	5.00	10.00
Includes Orchestral Manoeuvres in the Dark ("If You Leave"); Psychedelic Furs ("Pretty in Pink"); etc.					

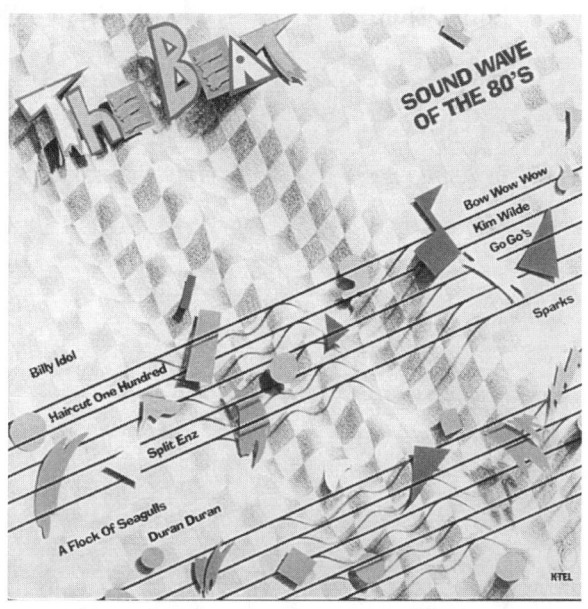

In retrospect, these two albums are among the best collections of late 1970s-early 1980s new-wave material. *The Beat,* an unusually inspired 1982 collection, was put together by K-Tel, of all companies, and features singles by Depeche Mode and Duran Duran released before most of America had heard of either. *Times Square* was going to do for new wave what earlier RSO soundtracks had done for disco and 1950s nostalgia, but the movie stiffed and so did the album. It's worth getting, though.

Title	Label, Number	Year	VG	VG+	NM
Pretty Woman	EMI E1-93492	1990	3.00	6.00	12.00
Includes David Bowie, Go West, Red Hot Chili Peppers, Jane Wiedlin					
Return of Superfly	Capitol C1-94244	1990	3.00	6.00	12.00
Includes Ice-T					
Rikki and Pete	DRG SBL-12593	1988	3.00	6.00	12.00
Includes Crowded House					
Roadie	(2) Warner Bros. 2HS 3441	1980	3.75	7.50	15.00
Includes Blondie					
Rock 'n' Roll High School	Sire QSR-6070	1980	3.75	7.50	15.00
Includes The Ramones (title song), Devo					
Rumble Fish	A&M SP-6-4983	1983	2.50	5.00	10.00
Includes Stewart Copeland (ex-Police)					
Salvation	Giant GR-16002	1988	3.00	6.00	12.00
Includes New Order, Cabaret Voltaire					
Scarface	MCA 6126	1983	2.50	5.00	10.00
Includes Debbie Harry					
Shag	Sire 25800	1989	2.50	5.00	10.00
Includes k.d. lang, Chris Isaak					
She's Out of Control	MCA 6281	1989	2.50	5.00	10.00
Includes Oingo Boingo					
Show, The	(2) Def Jam 529 021-1	1995	3.00	6.00	12.00
Includes L.L. Cool J, etc.					
Sid & Nancy	MCA 6181	1986	2.50	5.00	10.00
Includes Joe Strummer (ex-Clash), John Cale, The Pogues, Steve Jones (ex-Pistols)					
Something Wild	MCA 6194	1986	2.50	5.00	10.00
Includes New Order					
Soul Man	A&M SP-3903	1986	2.00	4.00	8.00
Includes Lou Reed, Martha Davis					
Spaceballs	Atlantic 81770	1987	2.50	5.00	10.00
Includes Berlin					
Streets of Fire	MCA 5492	1984	2.50	5.00	10.00
Includes The Fixx, The Blasters					
Strictly Business	MCA 10428	1991	2.50	5.00	10.00
Includes L.L. Cool J					
Tapeheads	Island 91030	1988	2.50	5.00	10.00
Includes Devo ("Baby Doll" sung in Swedish!), Fishbone					
Teenage Cruisers	Rhino RNLP-016	197?	3.75	7.50	15.00
Includes The Blasters, many others					
Tequila Sunrise	Capitol C1-91185	1988	3.00	6.00	12.00
Includes Crowded House, Duran Duran					
They Call It An Accident	Island ILPS 9757	1982	2.50	5.00	10.00
Includes U2 (two versions of "October")					
Times Square	(2) RSO RS-2-4203	1980	3.75	7.50	15.00
Includes The Ramones ("I Wanna Be Sedated"), Talking Heads ("Life During Wartime"), XTC, Patti Smith, The Cure, etc.					
Times Square Sampler	DJ RSO RPO 1026	1980	3.00	6.00	12.00
Includes Talking Heads, Roxy Music, Pretenders, two others					
To Wong Foo, Thanks for Listening! Julie Newmar	MCA 11231	1995	3.00	6.00	12.00
Includes Cyndi Lauper, Salt-N-Pepa					
Trouble in Mind	Island 90501	1986	2.50	5.00	10.00
Includes Marianne Faithfull					
True Stories, Sounds from	Sire 25515	1986	2.50	5.00	10.00
Includes individual members of Talking Heads...not to be confused with the Talking Heads album True Stories.					
Urgh! A Music War	(2) A&M SP 6019	1981	3.00	6.00	12.00
Includes live tracks by The Police, Joan Jett and the Blackhearts, Wall of Voodoo, XTC, Go-Go's, Orchestral Manoeuvres in the Dark, Pere Ubu, Devo, Gary Numan, X, Gang of Four, The Cramps, etc.					
Vision Quest	Geffen R 153920	1985	2.50	5.00	10.00
Includes Madonna ("Crazy for You," "Gambler")					
When the Wind Blows	Virgin 90599	1987	2.50	5.00	10.00
Includes David Bowie, Squeeze					

Title	Label, Number	Year	VG	VG+	NM
Where the Buffalo Roam	Backstreet 5126	1980	3.00	6.00	12.00
Includes Neil Young					
Who's That Girl	Sire R 100761	1987	2.50	5.00	10.00

Includes Madonna ("Who's That Girl," "Causing a Commotion," "The Look of Love," "Can't Stop"); Scritti Politti ("Best Thing Ever")

Wonder Years, The	Atlantic 82032	1989	2.50	5.00	10.00
Includes Indigo Girls					
Wraith, The	Scotti Bros. SZ 40429	1986	2.50	5.00	10.00
Includes Honeymoon Suite					
Young Einstein	A&M SP 3929	1988	2.50	5.00	10.00

Includes Mental As Anything, The Saints, Icehouse, Models

Title	Label, Number	Year	VG	VG+	NM

Various Artists Collections

7-Inch Extended Play Singles

Title	Label, Number	Year	VG	VG+	NM
1981 New Musicr Seminar Tour Sample	PS Stiff BE-4	1981		2.50	5.00
Picture sleeve plus insert for the above					
1981 New Music Seminar Tour Sampler	DJ Stiff BE-4	1981		2.50	5.00
Includes Men Without Hats, several others; promo-only 7-inch record					
Alice Cooper Tribute	Sub Pop 121	1991	2.50	5.00	10.00
Same as above, but black vinyl for club members					
Alice Cooper Tribute	PS Sub Pop 121	1991	2.50	5.00	10.00
#32 and #33 in Sub Pop Singles Club series (club sleeves have letter and order form)					
Alice Cooper Tribute	Sub Pop 121	1991	6.25	12.50	25.00
Includes Sonic Youth, 3 others; two 7-inch singles in one package; blue-gray vinyl					
Dope Guns 'N' Fucking in the Streets, Vol. 1	Amphetamine Reptile SCALE 12	198?	25.00	50.00	100.00
Includes Mudhoney, Halo of Flies, U-Men, Thrown-Ups; 250 on red vinyl					
Dope Guns 'N' Fucking in the Streets, Vol. 1	Amphetamine Reptile SCALE 12	198?	12.50	25.00	50.00
Includes Mudhoney, Halo of Flies, U-Men, Thrown-Ups; 250 on black vinyl					
Dope Guns 'N' Fucking in the Streets, Vol. 1	PS Amphetamine Reptile SCALE 12	198?	12.50	25.00	50.00
Dope Guns 'N' Fucking in the Streets, Vol. 2	(2) Amphetamine Reptile SCALE 16	198?	7.50	15.00	30.00
Includes Lonely Moans, Helios Creed, Tar, God Bullies; one record is black, the other yellow; price is for both records together					
Dope Guns 'N' Fucking in the Streets, Vol. 2	PS Amphetamine Reptile SCALE 16	198?	7.50	15.00	30.00
Dope Guns 'N' Fucking in the Streets, Vol. 3	Amphetamine Reptile 18	198?	12.50	25.00	50.00
100 copies on clear vinyl					
Dope Guns 'N' Fucking in the Streets, Vol. 3	Amphetamine Reptile 18	198?	6.25	12.50	25.00
900 copies on black vinyl					
Dope Guns 'N' Fucking in the Streets, Vol. 3	PS Amphetamine Reptile 18	198?	6.25	12.50	25.00
Dope Guns 'N' Fucking in the Streets, Vol. 4	Amphetamine Reptile 23	198?	6.75	13.75	27.50
500 on red vinyl					
Dope Guns 'N' Fucking in the Streets, Vol. 4	Amphetamine Reptile 23	198?	3.00	6.25	12.50
1,500 on black vinyl					
Dope Guns 'N' Fucking in the Streets, Vol. 4	PS Amphetamine Reptile 23	198?	3.00	6.25	12.50
Dope Guns 'N' Fucking in the Streets, Vol. 5	Amphetamine Reptile SCALE 28	198?	6.75	13.75	27.50
500 on yellow vinyl					
Dope Guns 'N' Fucking in the Streets, Vol. 5	Amphetamine Reptile SCALE 28	198?	3.00	6.25	12.50
1,500 on black vinyl					
Dope Guns 'N' Fucking in the Streets, Vol. 5	PS Amphetamine Reptile SCALE 28	198?	3.00	6.25	12.50

Title	Label, Number	Year	VG	VG+	NM
Dope Guns 'N' Fucking in the Streets, Vol. 6 *500 on red vinyl*	Amphetamine Reptile SCALE 37	199?	4.25	8.75	17.50
Dope Guns 'N' Fucking in the Streets, Vol. 6 *1,500 on black vinyl*	Amphetamine Reptile SCALE 37	199?		3.75	7.50
Dope Guns 'N' Fucking in the Streets, Vol. 6	PS Amphetamine Reptile SCALE 37	199?		3.75	7.50
Dope Guns 'N' Fucking in the Streets, Vol. 7 *500 on yellow vinyl*	Amphetamine Reptile SCALE 43	199?	6.75	13.75	27.50
Dope Guns 'N' Fucking in the Streets, Vol. 7 *1,500 on black vinyl*	Amphetamine Reptile SCALE 43	199?	3.00	6.25	12.50
Dope Guns 'N' Fucking in the Streets, Vol. 7	PS Amphetamine Reptile SCALE 43	199?	3.00	6.25	12.50
Dope Guns 'N' Fucking in the Streets, Vol. 8 *2,000 (all copies) on purple marbled vinyl*	Amphetamine Reptile 64	199?	2.50	5.00	10.00
Dope Guns 'N' Fucking in the Streets, Vol. 8	PS Amphetamine Reptile 64	199?	2.50	5.00	10.00
Dope Guns 'N' Fucking in the Streets, Vol. 9 *Price for both records together*	(2) Amphetamine Reptile 68	199?		3.75	7.50
Dope Guns 'N' Fucking in the Streets, Vol. 9	PS Amphetamine Reptile 68	199?		3.75	7.50
Dope Guns 'N' Fucking in the Streets, Vol. 10 *500 on purple vinyl*	Amphetamine Reptile 73	199?		3.50	7.00
Dope Guns 'N' Fucking in the Streets, Vol. 10 *2,500 on black vinyl*	Amphetamine Reptile 73	199?			3.00
Dope Guns 'N' Fucking in the Streets, Vol. 10	PS Amphetamine Reptile 73	199?			3.00
New Wave Rock 'n' Roll... *Includes Dead Boys, Talking Heads, The Saints, Richard Hell and the Voidoids; two 7" EPs*	(2) Sire PRO 696	1977	2.50	5.00	10.00
New Wave Rock 'n' Roll... *Gatefold sleeve for above*	PS Sire PRO 696	1977	2.50	5.00	10.00
Newslines Vol. 2 *Includes Slickee Boys*	DJ Line LS 1060	1981	3.75	7.50	15.00
Now Wave Sampler, The *Promo-only 4-song sampler*	DJ Columbia AE7 1187	1979	2.50	5.00	10.00
Teriyaki Asthma Vol. 1	PS C/Z CZ 009	1988	6.25	12.50	25.00
Teriyaki Asthma Vol. 1 *Includes Nirvana; 7-inch, 4-song sampler*	C/Z CZ 009	1988	6.25	12.50	25.00
What Kind of Heaven Do You Want?	PS Slumberland DRYL 001	1989	6.25	12.50	25.00
What Kind of Heaven Do You Want? *Includes Velocity Girl*	Slumberland DRYL 001	1989	6.25	12.50	25.00

516

Title	Label, Number	Year	VG	VG+	NM

Vinyl Albums

Title	Label, Number	Year	VG	VG+	NM
1969 Warner-Reprise Record Show, The	DJ Warner Bros./7 Arts PRO 336	1969	5.00	10.00	20.00
Includes The Mothers of Invention, Neil Young					
1984 on the Dance Floor	DJ EMI America SPRO 9077/8	1984	3.00	6.00	12.00
Includes Kate Bush					
2 X 5	Red Star RED-100	1980	3.75	7.50	15.00
Includes The Fleshtones, etc.					
30 Seconds Over D.C.	Limp 1001	1978	3.75	7.50	15.00
Includes Slickee Boys; issued on orange vinyl					
A La Carte	DJ Warner Bros. PRO 794	1979	3.75	7.50	15.00
Includes B-52's, etc.					
All Singing -- All Talking...	DJ Warner Bros. PRO 573	1973	4.50	9.00	18.00
Includes Frank Zappa					
Alternatives	Warner Bros. BS 1873	1970	3.00	6.00	12.00
Includes Neil Young, The Mothers of Invention					
Alternatives, The	DJ Epic AS 710	1979	3.00	6.00	12.00
Includes Ian Dury, The Clash					
Animal Liberation	Wax Trax! 025	1987	3.00	6.00	12.00
Includes Lene Lovich & Nina Hagen, Howard Jones, etc.					
Anthology of British Rock (2)	Compleat 672011	1985	3.75	7.50	15.00
Includes David Bowie (6), The Searchers (2)					
Appetizers (2)	DJ Warner Bros. PRO 56919			733.757.5015.00		
Includes John Cale					
Arista AOR Sampler	(2) DJ Arista ALS 06	1978	5.00	10.00	20.00
Includes Patti Smith (2), Ian Dury (2), Lou Reed (2)					
Arista Records Fall Sampler, The	DJ Arista ALS 01	1976	3.00	6.00	12.00
Includes Patti Smith, Lou Reed					
Arista's Greatest Hits: Portrait of a Decade 1975-1985	(3) Arista/Silver Eagle SE 10383	1985	5.00	10.00	20.00
Includes Lou Reed, Patti Smith Group, Graham Parker, Haircut One Hundred, A Flock of Seagulls, Thompson Twins					
Arista: A 15-Year History of Hits	Arista AL 8655	1991	3.00	6.00	12.00
Includes Lisa Stansfield, Aretha Franklin and George Michael					
Attack of the Killer B's	Warner Bros. 23837	1983	3.00	6.00	12.00
Includes The Blasters, Marshall Crenshaw, Gang of Four, Peter Gabriel, The Ramones, Pretenders, Talking Heads, Laurie Anderson					
Back to School	DJ Epic AS 1279	1981	3.00	6.00	12.00
Includes Adam and the Ants, Orchestral Manoeuvres in the Dark, Lene Lovich, others; promo sent to college radio stations					
Back to School with a Beat	DJ A&M SP-17204	1982	2.50	5.00	10.00
Includes Joe Jackson, Oingo Boingo					
Battle of the Garages	Voxx 200.006	1981	3.00	6.00	12.00
Includes Slickee Boys, others					
Beat The Retreat: Songs by Richard Thompson	Capitol C1 95929	1994	2.50	5.00	10.00
Includes X, R.E.M., Bob Mould, Los Lobos, Graham Parker, David Byrne					
Beat, The: Sound Wave of the 80's	K-Tel TU 5040	1982	5.00	10.00	20.00
Includes A Flock of Seagulls, Kim Wilde, Haircut One Hundred, Split Enz, Graham Parker, The Waitresses, Go-Go's, Bow Wow Wow, Duran Duran, Thompson Twins, Depeche Mode, Orchestral Manoeuvres in the Dark, Billy Idol					
Beserkley's Back	Beserkley 0067	1978	3.75	7.50	15.00
Includes Jonathan Richman and the Modern Lovers					
Best for '89 from the Entire Capitol Family, The	DJ Capitol SPRO 79471	1988	3.75	7.50	15.00
Includes Crowded House, dozens of others; personal seasons' greetings					

Title	Label, Number	Year	VG	VG+	NM
Best of Bomp! Volume One, The	Bomp! 4002	1978	5.00	10.00	20.00

Includes Iggy and the Stooges, Shoes, etc. First pressings on white vinyl.

Title	Label, Number	Year	VG	VG+	NM
Best of British Rock, The	Vee Jay VJS 1209	198?	3.00	6.00	12.00

Includes Marianne Faithfull

Best of Cotillion, The	DJ Atlantic PR 505	1983	3.75	7.50	15.00

Includes Neil Young (snippets)

Best of Limp, Limp 1004		1980	10.00	20.00	40.00
Rest of Limp					

Includes Slickee Boys (3), Bad Brains, Nurses; numbered edition of 1,000

Best of Ralph	(2) Ralph RR 8251-2	1982	5.00	10.00	20.00

Includes The Residents, Yello, Tuxedomoon, Art Bears, etc.

Best of the King Biscuit Flower Hour, The	(3) Silver Eagle SE 10674	1988	6.25	12.50	25.00

Includes The Tubes

Big Ball, The	(2) Warner Bros. PRO 358	1970	3.75	7.50	15.00

Includes Neil Young, The Mothers of Invention

Big Hits of Mid-America Volume Three	(2) Twin/Tone TTTR 7907/8	1979	5.00	10.00	20.00

Includes Suicide Commandos, other Minneapolis-area bands

Big Red Music	DJ Columbia AS 536	1978	3.75	7.50	15.00

Includes Boomtown Rats; red vinyl

Big Time Syndrome, The	Big Time 6050-1-B	1987	2.50	5.00	10.00

Includes Love and Rockets, Redd Kross, Dream Syndicate

Bill Hard Sampler	DJ Epic AS 725	1979	2.50	5.00	10.00

Includes The Clash, Lene Lovich, The Romantics

Blasting Concept, The, Vol. II	SST 043	1986	3.00	6.00	12.00

Includes Black Flag, Husker Du, Meat Puppets, Minutemen, etc.

Bowling Balls from Hell	Clone CL-010	1980	3.75	7.50	15.00

Includes The Waitresses; compilation of Akron, Ohio bands

Bowling Balls II	Clone CL-013	1981	3.75	7.50	15.00

Includes The Waitresses, Tin Huey, more Akron bands

Breakers	DJ A&M SP-17271	1984	3.00	6.00	12.00

Includes UB40, Simple Minds, The Alarm

Breaking the Rules	(2) DJ Columbia A2S 881	1980	5.00	10.00	20.00

Includes Elvis Costello, Rachel Sweet, Nina Hagen, Rockpile, Psychedelic Furs

British Invasion -- The History of British Rock, Vol. 2	Rhino R1-70321	1988	2.50	5.00	10.00

Includes The Searchers

British Invasion -- The History of British Rock, Vol. 3	Rhino R1-70322	1988	2.50	5.00	10.00

Includes The Searchers

Can You Hear Me? Music from the Deaf Club	Optional/Walking Dead 001	1980	6.25	12.50	25.00

Includes Dead Kennedys, Tuxedomoon, etc.

Can You Hear Me? Music from the Deaf Club	PVC 7920	1980	5.00	10.00	20.00

Includes Dead Kennedys, Tuxedomoon, etc.; reissue

Capitol Hits Sampler	DJ Capitol SPRO-9481	1985	3.75	7.50	15.00

Includes The Power Station, The Motels, etc.

Capitol In-Store Sampler	DJ Capitol SPRO 9867/8	1982	3.75	7.50	15.00

Includes Missing Persons (2), Duran Duran -- also includes "Love Me Do" by the Beatles

CBS Records Nashville Super Hitline '88	DJ Columbia AS 1424	1988	3.00	6.00	12.00

Includes Roseanne Cash (snippet)

Chartbusters: the Best of Beserkley Records 1975-1978	Rhino RNLP 70096	1986	2.50	5.00	10.00

Includes Jonathan Richman and the Modern Lovers (3)

Title	Label, Number	Year	VG	VG+	NM
Christmas Record, A Ze/Passport	PB 6020	1982	5.00	10.00	20.00

Includes The Waitresses ("Christmas Wrapping"), Was (Not Was), August Darnell

Christmas Rock Album, The	Priority SL 9465	1986	3.75	7.50	15.00

Includes The Waitresses, Dave Edmunds (and while it's not alternative, the first U.S. appearance of "Thank God It's Christmas" by Queen was on this album)

Christmas Tradition, A, Volume II	Warner Bros. 25762	1988	2.50	5.00	10.00

Includes Dwight Yoakam

Chrysalis 65 Hits	DJ Chrysalis VAS 2677	1987	3.75	7.50	15.00

Includes edits of songs by David Bowie, Billy Idol, Icehouse, Blondie, many others

Chrysalistener, The	DJ Chrysalis AS 1602	1982	3.00	6.00	12.00

Includes Divinyls, Ultravox

Chunks	New Alliance 003	1981	3.75	7.50	15.00

Includes Minutemen, etc.

Classic Rock 1964	(2) Time-Life SCLR-03	1987	3.75	7.50	15.00

Includes The Searchers

Classic Rock 1964: Shakin' All Over	(2) Time-Life SCLR-16	1989	3.75	7.50	15.00

Includes The Searchers

Classic Rock 1964: The Beat Goes On	(2) Time-Life SCLR-09	1988	3.75	7.50	15.00

Includes The Searchers

Classic Rock -- Rock Renaissance	(2) Time-Life SCLR-17	1989	3.75	7.50	15.00

Includes MC5

Classic Rock -- Rock Renaissance II	(2) Time-Life SCLR-21	1990	3.75	7.50	15.00

Includes The Velvet Underground

Classic Rock -- Rock Renaissance III	(2) Time-Life SCLR-26	1990	3.75	7.50	15.00

Includes The Searchers

Classic Rock -- Rock Renaissance IV	(2) Time-Life SCLR-30	1991	3.75	7.50	15.00

Includes MC5, The Velvet Underground and Nico

Club MTV Party to Go	Tommy Boy TB 1037	1991	3.00	6.00	12.00

Includes Digital Underground, Depeche Mode

Collector's Series Sampler Record	DJ London LCX 1004	1977	5.00	10.00	20.00

Includes David Bowie

Collectus Interruptus	(2) DJ Warner Bros. PRO-A-726	1978	4.50	9.00	18.00

Includes Prince, Sex Pistols, The Ramones

Columbia Fall '82 New Artists Sampler	DJ Columbia AS 1563	1982	3.00	6.00	12.00

Includes Men At Work, Romeo Void, Psychedelic Furs

Columbia Pictures Music Group	DJ Columbia Pictures (#unknown)	1987	3.00	6.00	12.00

Includes Peter Gabriel, Kid Creole, etc.

Columbia Slow Jams II	DJ Columbia CAS 5640	1993	2.50	5.00	10.00

Includes Terence Trent D'Arby

Columbia's 24 Hits in the Top 20 for 1982	! (2) DJ Columbia A2S 1588	1982	6.25	12.50	25.00

Includes Men At Work, Tommy Tutone

Concerts for the People of Kampuchea	(2) Atlantic SD 2-7005	1981	5.00	10.00	20.00

Includes Pretenders, Elvis Costello, Rockpile, The Clash, Ian Dury and the Blockheads, The Specials

Connected	Limp 1005	1981	5.00	10.00	20.00

Includes Slickee Boys (2)

Conspiracy of Hope	Mercury 830 617-1	1986	3.00	6.00	12.00

Includes Peter Gabriel, Tears for Fears, Howard Jones, Sting, Simple Minds

Title	Label, Number	Year	VG	VG+	NM
Country Christmas	(3) Time-Life STL-109	1988	5.00	10.00	20.00
3-LP box set; Includes Dwight Yoakam					
Cracks in the Sidewalk	New Alliance 001	1980	3.75	7.50	15.00
Includes Minutemen, Black Flag, others					
Crawling from Within	77 Records (# unknown)	1987	3.00	6.00	12.00
Includes Lemonheads					
Crink Chronicles, The	DJ CBS Associated AS 1120	1988	3.00	6.00	12.00
Includes Midnight Oil, Prefab Sprout, Terence Trent D'Arby					
Current Events	DJ Arista SP-150	1983	3.75	7.50	15.00
Includes Ministry, Heaven 17, Thompson Twins, etc.					
D.I.Y. Album, The	D.I.Y./JW Productions DIY-0001	1982	12.50	25.00	50.00
Includes Slickee Boys, Black Flag, others; band copies on black vinyl					
D.I.Y. Album, The	D.I.Y./JW Productions DIY-0001A	1982	7.50	15.00	30.00
Includes Slickee Boys, Black Flag, others; store copies on clear vinyl (3-D pressing was planned but never done)					
Dance II It, Volume 1	A&M SP-4970	1983	2.50	5.00	10.00
Includes Simple Minds, The Police, The Cure, etc.					
Dance Rhythm 'N' Rock New Music Seminar Mixer	DJ Warner Bros. PRO-A-2061	1983	18.75	37.50	75.00
Includes Madonna, Prince, Talking Heads, Depeche Mode, Echo and the Bunnymen, etc. (all mixed up)					
Dance Traxx	(2) Atlantic R 263754	198?	3.00	6.00	12.00
Includes INXS					
Dangerhouse Volume One	Frontier 4629-1-L	1991	3.00	6.00	12.00
Includes X, Weirdos, many others					
Days of Wine and Vinyl	DJ Warner Bros. PRO-450	1972	4.50	9.00	18.00
Loss-leader sampler includes David Bowie					
Deep Six	C/Z CZ 001	1985	12.50	25.00	50.00
Includes Soundgarden, Green River, etc.					
Def Jam Recordings -- Retail Tracks	DJ Def Jam CAS 2715	1987	5.00	10.00	20.00
Includes L.L. Cool J, Beastie Boys, Public Enemy, Oran "Juice" Jones					
Devotees Album, The	Rhino RNSP-301	1980	3.00	6.00	12.00
Includes Devo sound-alike contest winners...sort of a tribute to Devo?					
Diamond Hidden in the Mouth of a Corpse, A	Giomo Poetry Systems 035	1985	7.50	15.00	30.00
Includes Husker Du, David Johansen, Cabaret Voltaire, Sonic Youth					
Doctor Death's Volume 1	C'est La Mort 001	1986	7.50	15.00	30.00
Includes Throwing Muses					
Elektrock -- the Sixties	(3) Elektra 60503	1985	10.00	20.00	40.00
Includes MC5, The Stooges; 3-LP box set					
EMI America Holiday Sampler	DJ EMI America SPRO 9883/4	1986	3.75	7.50	15.00
Includes Pet Shop Boys, Stray Cats					
Enigma Variations, The	(2) Enigma 72001	1985	4.50	9.00	18.00
Includes Redd Kross, many more					
Enigma Variations 2, The	(2) Enigma SQBB-73247	1987	3.75	7.50	15.00
Every Day Is a Holly Day	Emergo EM 9465	1989	3.00	6.00	12.00
Includes Slickee Boys					
Every Man Has a Woman	Polydor 823 490-1	1984	2.50	5.00	10.00
Includes Elvis Costello, Roseanne Cash; tribute album to Yoko Ono					
Exposed: A Cheap Peek at Today's Provocative New Rock	(2) CBS X2 37124	1981	2.50	5.00	10.00
Includes Adam and the Ants, Ian Gomm, Roseanne Cash, The Romantics, The Boomtown Rats, Garland Jeffreys					
Exposed II	(2) CBS X2 37601	1981	2.50	5.00	10.00
Includes Tommy Tutone, Gary Myrick and the Figures, Psychedelic Furs, Orchestral Manoeuvres in the Dark, Jo Jo Zep and the Falcons, etc.					
Fast Mutant Pop	PVC 7912	1980	4.00	8.00	16.00
Includes Human League, Gang of Four, Mekons, others					

Title	Label, Number	Year	VG	VG+	NM
Fire & Ice	Realistic/Warner 51-3000 (OP 1525)	1982	3.00	6.00	12.00
Includes Blondie, Pretenders					
First Decade	(3) DJ WEA 10	1981	37.50	75.00	150.00
Includes Neil Young, Prince, many others; only 1,000 were made paying tribute to WEA's 10th anniversary					
Flashback! Rock Classics of the '70s	Realm 1P 8075	1991	3.75	7.50	15.00
Includes The Cars					
Flex Your Head	Dischord 7	1982	12.50	25.00	50.00
Includes Teen Idles, Untouchables, Minor Threat, Government Issue, Youth Brigade, etc.					
Folkways: A Vision Shared	Columbia OC 44034	1988	3.00	6.00	12.00
Includes U2 ("Jesus Christ"), Little Richard with Fishbone					
Follow Our Tracks	DJ Warner Bros. PRO-A-3503	1989	3.00	6.00	12.00
Includes Elvis Costello, New Order, Ramones, Violent Femmes, R.E.M., Lou Reed, etc.					
Follow Our Trax, Vol. 2	DJ Reprise PRO-A-3655	1989	3.00	6.00	12.00
Includes Morrissey, The B-52's, Tom Tom Club, Chris Isaak, others					
Force, The	DJ Warner Bros. PRO 593	1974	3.00	6.00	12.00
Includes Frank Zappa					
Force, The	(2) DJ Warner Bros. PRO 596	1974	3.00	6.00	12.00
Includes Frank Zappa					
Foreplay	DJ A&M SP-17000	1978	3.00	6.00	12.00
Includes The Tubes					
Foreplay	DJ A&M SP-17018	1978	3.75	7.50	15.00
Includes U.K. Squeeze, The Stranglers; with booklet					
Foreplay #16	DJ A&M SP-17071	1979	3.00	6.00	12.00
Includes The Dickies, The Tubes					
Foreplay #17	DJ A&M SP-17074	1979	2.50	5.00	10.00
Includes U.K. Squeeze					
Foreplay #26	DJ A&M SP-17102	1979	3.75	7.50	15.00
Includes The Police, Joe Jackson; one-sided, with booklet					
Foreplay #27	DJ A&M SP-17107	1979	3.75	7.50	15.00
Includes Squeeze; with booklet					
Foreplay	DJ A&M SP-17146	1981	2.50	5.00	10.00
Includes The Cramps, John Cale					
Foreplay #42	DJ A&M SP-17150	1981	2.50	5.00	10.00
Includes Magazine, Split Enz					
Foreplay #43	DJ A&M SP-17154	1981	3.00	6.00	12.00
Includes Oingo Boingo, Squeeze					
Foreplay #44	DJ A&M SP-17159	1981	3.00	6.00	12.00
Includes Oingo Boingo, Magazine					
Foreplay #45	DJ A&M SP-17162	1981	6.25	12.50	25.00
Includes Joe Jackson, Go-Go's, The Tubes, 20 minute collage of music from "Urgh! A Music War"					
Foreplay #46	DJ A&M SP-17166	1981	2.50	5.00	10.00
Includes Wall of Voodoo					
Foreplay #47	DJ A&M SP-17174	1981	3.00	6.00	12.00
Includes The Police, The Cure					
Foreplay #48	DJ A&M SP-17177	1981	2.50	5.00	10.00
Includes Split Enz, The Fleshtones, Humans					
Four Old 7" on a 12"	Dischord 14	1985	3.00	6.00	12.00
Includes Teen Idles, S.O.A., Government Issue, Youth Brigade					
Frank Johnson's Favorites	Ralph 8110	1981	5.00	10.00	20.00
Includes The Residents, Tuxedomoon, Yello, Art Bears, more					
Frankenstein and Other Rock Monsters!	CBS Associated FZ 39257	1984	2.50	5.00	10.00
Includes The Romantics, David Johansen					
Full Tilt	K-Tel TU 2770	1981	2.50	5.00	10.00
Includes Blondie, Devo					
Future Looks Bright, The	DJ SST/Posh Boy PBS 120	1981	7.50	15.00	30.00
Includes Black Flag, Minutemen, Social Distortion, Descendents, others; vinyl is promo-only					
Gold & Platinum	Realm 1P 7679	1985	2.50	5.00	10.00
Includes Cyndi Lauper, The Police, Men At Work, The Cars, Nena					

Title	Label, Number	Year	VG	VG+	NM
Gold & Platinum, Volume Two	Realm 1P 7726	1986	2.50	5.00	10.00

Includes Wham! ("Careless Whisper"); Cyndi Lauper, Tears For Fears, Sade, 'Til Tuesday

Title	Label, Number	Year	VG	VG+	NM
Gold & Platinum, Volume Three	Realm 1P 7765	1987	2.50	5.00	10.00

Includes Bangles ("If She Knew What She Wants"), Belinda Carlisle ("Mad About You"), Hooters, The Outfield

Title	Label, Number	Year	VG	VG+	NM
Gold & Platinum, Volume Four	(2) Realm 2P 7826	1988	3.75	7.50	15.00

Includes Beastie Boys ("Fight for Your Right"); Billy Idol ("Mony Mony")

Title	Label, Number	Year	VG	VG+	NM
Gold & Platinum, Volume Five	Realm 1P 7898	1989	2.50	5.00	10.00

Includes Midnight Oil, U2, INXS, Bangles

Title	Label, Number	Year	VG	VG+	NM
Gold & Platinum, Volume Six	Realm 1P 7899	1989	2.50	5.00	10.00

Includes Terence Trent D'Arby, George Michael, Icehouse

Title	Label, Number	Year	VG	VG+	NM
Gold Medal	DJ Warner Bros. PRO-A-841	1980	3.00	6.00	12.00

Includes Pearl Harbour and the Explosions, The Undertones, Pretenders

Title	Label, Number	Year	VG	VG+	NM
Greatest Rap Hits, Vol. 1	Sugar Hill 9132	1984	5.00	10.00	20.00

Includes Sugar Hill Gang, other early rappers

Title	Label, Number	Year	VG	VG+	NM
Greatest Rap Hits, Vol. 2	Sugar Hill 9133	1984	3.00	6.00	12.00

Includes Grandmaster Flash, Sugar Hill Gang

Title	Label, Number	Year	VG	VG+	NM
Greenpeace	A&M SP-5091	1985	3.00	6.00	12.00

Includes Peter Gabriel, Kate Bush, Thomas Dolby, Pretenders, Depeche Mode, etc.

Title	Label, Number	Year	VG	VG+	NM
Greenpeace Rainbow Warriors	(2) Geffen GHS 24236	1989	3.00	6.00	12.00

Includes U2, Belinda Carlisle, Sting, Terence Trent D'Arby, World Party, Lou Reed, Eurythmics, Pretenders, INXS, Thompson Twins, Talking Heads, Simple Minds, The Waterboys, R.E.M., Peter Gabriel, Sade, etc.

Title	Label, Number	Year	VG	VG+	NM
Hard Goods	DJ Warner Bros. PRO 583	1974	4.50	9.00	18.00

Includes Frank Zappa, Neil Young

Title	Label, Number	Year	VG	VG+	NM
Hard to Believe -- A Kiss Covers Compilation	C/Z CZ 024	1990	7.50	15.00	30.00

Includes Nirvana, etc.

Title	Label, Number	Year	VG	VG+	NM
Hearts of Gold: The Pop Collection	Foundation K1-96427	1991	3.75	7.50	15.00

Includes George Michael, Bangles, Sinead O'Connor; only U.S. vinyl release through Columbia House

Title	Label, Number	Year	VG	VG+	NM
Heavy Metal (Superstars of the 70s, Volume 2)	Warner Special Products SP-2001	1974	5.00	10.00	20.00

Includes MC5.

Title	Label, Number	Year	VG	VG+	NM
Hell Comes to Your House	Bemis Brain 123/124	1981	3.75	7.50	15.00

Includes Social Distortion, Red Cross (Redd Kross), etc.

Title	Label, Number	Year	VG	VG+	NM
Hell Comes to Your House, Vol. 2	Bemis Brain E 1049	1982	3.00	6.00	12.00

Includes Minutemen, etc.

Title	Label, Number	Year	VG	VG+	NM
History of British Rock, Volume Three	(2) Sire SASH-3712-2	1975	5.00	10.00	20.00

Includes David Bowie, The Searchers

Title	Label, Number	Year	VG	VG+	NM
Hitchhiker College Radio Hour, The	DJ Columbia CAS 1598	1989	6.25	12.50	25.00

Includes Roseanne Cash, Mary Chapin Carpenter

Title	Label, Number	Year	VG	VG+	NM
Hitchhiker 2	DJ Columbia CAS 1826	1989	6.25	12.50	25.00

Includes music and interviews: Indigo Girls, Mary Chapin Carpenter, Rosanne Cash

Title	Label, Number	Year	VG	VG+	NM
Hitchhiker Exampler	DJ Columbia CAS 2011	1990	3.75	7.50	15.00

Includes Mary Chapin Carpenter, Indigo Girls, Roseanne Cash

Title	Label, Number	Year	VG	VG+	NM
Holiday Greetings from EPA	DJ CBS CAS 2664	1987	3.00	6.00	12.00

Includes holiday greetings from Aimee Mann and "Weird Al" Yankovic, among others

Title	Label, Number	Year	VG	VG+	NM
Hollywood Confidential	GNP Crescendo 2132	1980	3.00	6.00	12.00

Includes The Runaways; a collection of Kim Fowley productions

522

Title	Label, Number	Year	VG	VG+	NM
Hot Hits to Warm Your Winter	DJ Polygram SA 054	1985	3.75	7.50	15.00
Includes Big Country					
Hot No. 1 Hits!	Realm 1P 8195	1992	3.75	7.50	15.00
Includes George Michael (with Elton John)					
Hot Ones	DJ EMI America SPRO 9865/6	1982	2.50	5.00	10.00
Includes Stray Cats					
Hot Tracks from Arista	DJ Arista SP-127	1982	3.00	6.00	12.00
Includes Thompson Twins, Haircut One Hundred, A Flock of Seagulls					
I Love the Smell of Napalm	Creation 001	1986	3.75	7.50	15.00
Includes early Primal Scream, among others					
I.R.S. Greatest Hits Volume 1	I.R.S. SP-70950	1980	3.00	6.00	12.00
Includes Berlin, Buzzcocks, Oingo Boingo, Klark Kent, The Stranglers					
I.R.S. Greatest Hits Volumes 2 & 3	(2) I.R.S. SP-70800	1981	3.75	7.50	15.00
Includes Buzzcocks, John Cale, The Cramps, The Damned, The Fall, The Fleshtones, Klark Kent, The Humans, Oingo Boingo, The Police, Tom Robinson, Squeeze, The Stranglers					
If You Can't Please Yourself, You Can't Please Anyone Else	Capitol ST-12439	1985	3.00	6.00	12.00
Includes The The, Yello, etc.					
In a Mellow Mood	DJ Elektra 5188	1986	3.00	6.00	12.00
Includes Simply Red					
In From the Storm: The Music of Jimi Hendrix	PD RCA Victor 68233-1	1995	3.00	6.00	12.00
Includes Sting (with many jazz and rock musicians); limited edition picture disc (no regular U.S. vinyl exists)					
In-Store Sampler Vol. 2	DJ EMI America SPRO-9842	1982	3.75	7.50	15.00
Includes Stray Cats (2), Kim Wilde, etc.					
Incredible Collection, The -- Dr. Knew's Music	DJ RCA Victor DJL1-4860	1983	3.00	6.00	12.00
Includes Hayzi Fantayzee, Eurythmics, etc.					
Island Story, The	(2) Island 90684	1988	4.50	9.00	18.00
Includes U2 ("With Or Without You"), Frankie Goes to Hollywood ("Relax"); The Buggles ("Video Killed the Radio Star"); Marianne Faithfull ("Broken English")					
Island Story, The	(2) Island R 243395	1988	5.00	10.00	20.00
Same as Island 90684; BMG Direct Marketing edition					
It Came from Hollywood!	DJ Capitol SPRO 79199	1987	3.75	7.50	15.00
Includes Flesh For Lulu					
Keats Rides a Harley	Happy Squid HS 002	1981	5.00	10.00	20.00
Includes Meat Puppets					
Kill Rock Stars	Kill Rock Stars KRS 201	1991	3.00	6.00	12.00
Includes Nirvana, etc.					
Kiss My Ass -- Classic Kiss Regrooved	Mercury 522 123-1	1994	3.00	6.00	12.00
Includes Lenny Kravitz, Gin Blossoms, Toad The Wet Sprocket, The Lemonheads, The Mighty Mighty Bosstones; all copies on red vinyl					
Knebworth	(2) Polydor 847 042-1	1990	3.75	7.50	15.00
Includes Tears For Fears					
L.A. In	Rhino RNLP 009	1979	3.75	7.50	15.00
Includes The Knack, Motels, Oingo Boingo, others					
Last Compilation Album, The	Stiff USE-3	1980	3.75	7.50	15.00
Includes The Cure, The Damned, Dexy's Midnight Runners, Madness, Wreckless Eric, etc.					
Last Record Album, The	A&M (# unknown)	1989	10.00	20.00	40.00
Includes Sting, Joe Jackson, Iggy Pop					
Laughtour, The	EP Sire PRO-A-3931	1990	5.00	10.00	20.00
Includes Mighty Lemon Drops, The Ocean Blue, John Wesley Harding; promo-only					
Let Them Eat Jellybeans	Alternative Tentacles VIRUS 4	1982	6.25	12.50	25.00
Includes Dead Kennedys, Black Flag, lots of other bands					

Title	Label, Number	Year	VG	VG+	NM
Life in the European Theater	Elektra 60179	1982	3.75	7.50	15.00

Includes The Clash, The Jam, The [English] Beat, The Specials, XTC, Peter Gabriel, Madness, Bad Manners, The Stranglers, The Undertones, Echo & The Bunnymen, The Au Pairs

Title	Label, Number	Year	VG	VG+	NM
Life Is Beautiful, So Why Not Eat Health Food?	New Underground 44	1981	5.00	10.00	20.00

Includes The Germs, Minutemen, etc.

Title	Label, Number	Year	VG	VG+	NM
Life Is Ugly, So Why Not Kill Yourself?	New Underground 11	1981	5.00	10.00	20.00

Includes Red Cross, Minutemen, etc.

Title	Label, Number	Year	VG	VG+	NM
Live at CBGB's	(2) CBGB/Omfug 315	1976	7.50	15.00	30.00

Includes Tuff Darts, The Shirts, Mink DeVille, etc.

Title	Label, Number	Year	VG	VG+	NM
Live at CBGB's	(2) Atlantic SD2-508	1976	5.00	10.00	20.00

Includes Tuff Darts, The Shirts, Mink DeVille, etc. Same album as CBGB/Omfug release

Title	Label, Number	Year	VG	VG+	NM
Live at Target	Subterranean 3	1980	6.25	12.50	25.00

Includes Flipper

Title	Label, Number	Year	VG	VG+	NM
Live for Ireland	MCA 42113	1987	2.50	5.00	10.00

Includes U2, The Boomtown Rats, Elvis Costello, The Pogues

Title	Label, Number	Year	VG	VG+	NM
Live! For Life	I.R.S. 5731	1986	2.50	5.00	10.00

Includes Stewart Copeland, R.E.M., The Alarm, General Public, Sting, Bangles, Oingo Boingo, Go-Go's, Squeeze

Title	Label, Number	Year	VG	VG+	NM
Long Hit Summer, The	DJ Epic AS 2118	1985	3.00	6.00	12.00

Includes Dead Or Alive, Sade

Title	Label, Number	Year	VG	VG+	NM
Lost in the Stars	A&M SP-9-5104	1985	3.00	6.00	12.00

Includes Marianne Faithfull, Sting, Lou Reed

Title	Label, Number	Year	VG	VG+	NM
Maiden Australia	A&M SP-4952	1983	2.50	5.00	10.00

Includes Split Enz, Mental As Anything, Jo Jo Zep, etc.

Title	Label, Number	Year	VG	VG+	NM
March '84 In-Store Sampler	DJ Capitol SPRO 9089	1984	2.50	5.00	10.00

Includes Duran Duran, Thomas Dolby, Missing Persons

Title	Label, Number	Year	VG	VG+	NM
Max's Kansas City 1976	Ram 1213	1976	5.00	10.00	20.00

Includes Pere Ubu, Suicide, others

Title	Label, Number	Year	VG	VG+	NM
Max's Kansas City Presents New Wave Hits for the '80s	Max's Kansas City 19801	1981	5.00	10.00	20.00

Includes Pere Ubu, Suicide, others; compilation of first two Max's Kansas City albums plus new tracks

Title	Label, Number	Year	VG	VG+	NM
Max's Kansas City Vol. 2, 1977	Ram 2213	1977	3.00	6.00	12.00
Mega Hits 1986	MCA 5985	1987	2.50	5.00	10.00

Includes Belinda Carlisle, The Outfield

Title	Label, Number	Year	VG	VG+	NM
Melting Pot, The	SST 249	198?	3.00	6.00	12.00

Includes Sonic Youth

Title	Label, Number	Year	VG	VG+	NM
Michigan Rocks	(2) Seeds and Stems 77001	1977	6.25	12.50	25.00

Includes MC5

Title	Label, Number	Year	VG	VG+	NM
MTV High Priority	RCA Victor 6396-1-R	1987	2.50	5.00	10.00

Includes Bangles ("Manic Monday"), Cyndi Lauper ("Time After Time"), Belinda Carlisle ("I Feel the Magic"), Bananarama ("More Than Physical")

Title	Label, Number	Year	VG	VG+	NM
MTV's Rock 'N Roll to Go	Elektra 60399	1985	2.50	5.00	10.00

Includes The Cars, The Fixx, Billy Idol, Cyndi Lauper, Madonna, The Police, Thompson Twins, Wang Chung

Title	Label, Number	Year	VG	VG+	NM
MTV, BET, VH-1 Power Players	EMI R 100737	1988	2.50	5.00	10.00

Includes L.L. Cool J ("I Need Love"), Cutting Crew ("I Just Died in Your Arms"); BMG Direct Marketing edition

Title	Label, Number	Year	VG	VG+	NM
Music and Rhythm Sampler	DJ PVC EP 2	1982	6.25	12.50	25.00

Includes XTC, Peter Gabriel, David Byrne, The (English) Beat; one-LP sampler of two-record set

Title	Label, Number	Year	VG	VG+	NM
Mutant Pop	PVC 7912	1980	3.00	6.00	12.00

Includes Gang of Four, Human League, several others

Title	Label, Number	Year	VG	VG+	NM
Neighborhood Rhythms	(2) Freeway 213	1984	10.00	20.00	40.00

Includes Henry Rollins, Exene Cervenka, Mike Watt, many others on mostly spoken-word collection

Title	Label, Number	Year	VG	VG+	NM
New Music Seminar '84	DJ Capitol SPRO 9216	1984	2.50	5.00	10.00

Includes Duran Duran, Thomas Dolby, etc.

Title	Label, Number	Year	VG	VG+	NM
New Music Seminar Sampler	(2) DJ Columbia AS 1521	198?	3.00	6.00	12.00

Includes Boomtown Rats, Dave Edmunds, Nina Hagen, Romeo Void, many more

Live! For Life is pretty self-explanatory. It's one of many places you can find otherwise obscure tracks by R.E.M., the Bangles and many others.

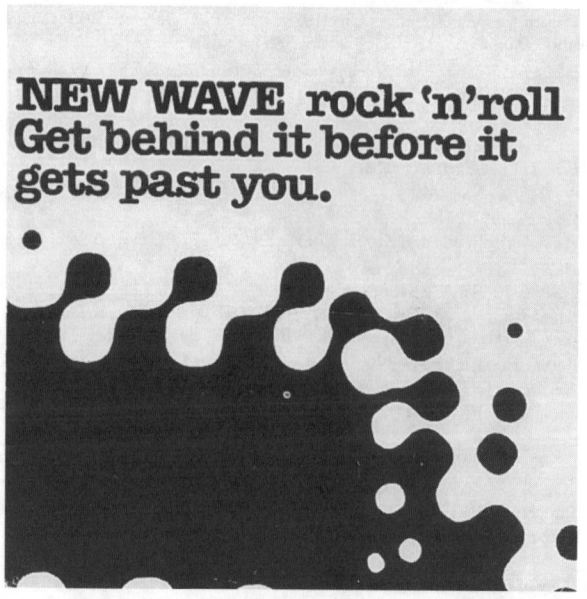

For a long time, the 1977 Sire two-record 7-inch sampler *New Wave Rock 'n' Roll* was easy to find, but it has all but vanished in recent years. Its two seven-inch small-holed records contain two tracks each by Talking Heads, Dead Boys, Richard Hell and the Voidoids, and the Saints.

Title	Label, Number	Year	VG	VG+	NM
New Tradition Sings the Old Tradition, The	Warner Bros. R 124450	1989	3.00	6.00	12.00

Includes Dwight Yoakam, k.d. lang; BMG Direct Marketing edition

No Age	SST 102	198?	2.50	5.00	10.00

Includes Black Flag, etc.

No New York	Antilles AN-7067	1978	3.00	6.00	12.00

Includes Teenage Jesus and the Jerks, etc.

No Wave	DJ A&M PR 4738	1978	6.25	12.50	25.00

Includes Squeeze, The Dickies, The Police, The Stranglers, Joe Jackson, etc.; white label promo on watercolor blue vinyl; numbered sticker on generic cover

No Wave	A&M SP 4738	1978	3.75	7.50	15.00

Includes Squeeze, The Dickies, The Police, The Stranglers, Joe Jackson, etc.; first pressing on watercolor blue vinyl

No Wave	A&M SP 4738	1978	2.00	4.00	8.00

Same as above, on black vinyl

Not So Quiet on the Western Front	(2) Alternative Tentacles VIRUS 14	1982	6.25	12.50	25.00

Includes Dead Kennedys, Flipper, lots of others

Plenty Good Music	DJ Capitol SPRO 9937	1983	3.00	6.00	12.00

Includes The Tubes, Duran Duran

Polydor Dance Classics -- British Edition	Polydor 885 004-1	1986	3.75	7.50	15.00

Includes Level 42, Visage

Polygram Radio Instore Sampler	DJ Polygram 051	1983	3.00	6.00	12.00

Includes Big Country, The Style Council

Posse, The, Chapter 2	Macola 1080	1988	3.00	6.00	12.00

Includes Ice-T, Digital Underground

Prince's Trust 10th Anniversary Birthday Party, The	A&M SP-3906	1987	2.50	5.00	10.00

Includes Howard Jones ("No One Is to Blame"), Midge Ure, Big Country, Level 42

Prince's Trust 10th Anniversary Birthday Party, The	A&M R 144451	1987	3.75	7.50	15.00

Same as SP-3906; BMG Direct Marketing edition

Propaganda	A&M SP 4786	1979	5.00	10.00	20.00

Includes Joe Jackson (live), The Police (live), Squeeze, etc. Includes poster.

Punk and Disorderly	Posh Boy PBS-131	1982	3.75	7.50	15.00

Includes Dead Kennedys, more

Radio Radio/Soul Twist/ You've Gotta Be Cruel to Be Kind	DJ Columbia AS 443	1979	8.75	17.50	35.00

Includes Elvis Costello, Mink DeVille, Nick Lowe; promo-only 3-song sampler on orange vinyl

Radio Tokyo Tapes, Vol. 2	Enigma E 1086	1984	3.00	6.00	12.00
Radio Tokyo Tapes, Vol. 3	PVC 8931	1985	3.00	6.00	12.00

Includes Minutemen, Henry Rollins

Radio U.	DJ Epic AS 1742	1983	3.00	6.00	12.00

Includes Cyndi Lauper, Altered Images, Nena, etc.

Rainy Day	Enigma E 1024	1983	3.00	6.00	12.00

Includes Susanna Hoffs (early solo track)

Rat Music for Rat People	Go 003	1982	5.00	10.00	20.00

Includes Dead Kennedys, Bad Brains, Black Flag, Flipper, etc.

Red Hot & Bothered 1	10 Kinetic/Reprise 45954	1995	2.50	5.00	10.00

With booklet "The Indie Rock Guide to Dating"; limited edition of 5,000

Red Hot & Bothered 2	10 Kinetic/Reprise 45982	1995	2.50	5.00	10.00

With booklet "The Indie Rock Guide to Dating 2"; limited edition of 5,000

Restless Variations	Restless 72101	1985	3.00	6.00	12.00

Includes The Dead Milkmen, Mojo Nixon and Skid Roper, etc.

Retail In-Store Sampler	DJ Columbia AS 1912	1984	2.50	5.00	10.00

Includes Elvis Costello, Bangles, Dave Edmunds

Revenge of the Killer B's	Warner Bros. 25068	1984	2.50	5.00	10.00

Includes Madonna ("Ain't No Big Deal"), The B-52's, The Pretenders, Marshall Crenshaw, Aztec Camera, Echo and the Bunnymen

Title	Label, Number	Year	VG	VG+	NM
Rock 80	K-Tel TU 2780	1980	2.50	5.00	10.00

Includes Gary Numan, Pretenders, Sniff 'N' The Tears, Nick Lowe, Joe Jackson, Blondie, The Ramones, The Knack, Ian Gomm, M

Rock at the Edge	Arista AL 8436	1986	2.50	5.00	10.00

Includes Patti Smith Group, Iggy Pop, Blondie, Lou Reed., Television, Ian Dury, Richard Hell, Graham Parker

Rock at the Edge	Arista R 114791	1986	3.00	6.00	12.00

Same as above; RCA Music Service edition.

Rocking Christmas Stocking, A	(2) DJCapitol SPRO 9303/4/5/6	1984	5.00	10.00	20.00

Includes David Bowie, Duran Duran, etc.

Rodney on the 'ROQ	Posh Boy PBA-106	1980	3.00	6.00	12.00

Includes Black Flag, lots of others; with special edition of Flipside, a fanzine (add 50% if magazine is included)

Rodney on the 'ROQ, Vol. 2	Posh Boy PBS-123	1981	3.75	7.50	15.00

Includes Black Flag, Minutemen, Red Cross (Redd Kross), etc.; with special edition of Flipside (#28) (add 50%)

Romantics and Friends: Midwest Pop Explosion	Quark CATCH 3	1981	3.75	7.50	15.00

Includes The Romantics, Stiv Bators

Saturday Morning -- Cartoons' Greatest Hits	(2) MCA 11348	1995	3.00	6.00	12.00

Includes Liz Phair, Matthew Sweet, Collective Soul, Butthole Surfers, The Ramones, Reverend Horton Heat, Violent Femmes, etc.

Saturday Night Pogo	Rhino RNLP 003	1978	3.75	7.50	15.00

Includes Motels, other L.A. bands

Secret Policeman's Other Ball, The	Island ILPS 9698	1982	3.00	6.00	12.00

Includes Sting ("Message in a Bottle"), Bob Geldof ("I Don't Like Mondays")

Secret Policeman's Third Ball, The	Virgin 90643	1987	3.00	6.00	12.00

Includes Kate Bush, Duran Duran, Lou Reed, Bob Geldof, Erasure, Peter Gabriel (live recordings)

Seize the Beat	Ze ILPS-9667	1981	3.00	6.00	12.00

Includes Kid Creole and the Coconuts (i.e., Don Armando's 2nd Avenue Rumba Band), Was (Not Was)

Selections from Urgh! A Music War	DJ A&M SP-17169	1981	3.75	7.50	15.00

Promo-only sampler; Includes Devo, Echo and the Bunnymen, Go-Go's, Oingo Boingo, The Police, XTC

Sharp Cuts	Planet P-6	1980	2.50	5.00	10.00

Includes Suburban Lawns, Single Bullet Theory, The dB's, etc.

Siren, The	Posh Boy PBS-103	1980	5.00	10.00	20.00

Includes Red Cross (Redd Kross)

Songs of John Lennon and Paul McCartney, The	(2) 20th Century T2-540	1977	3.75	7.50	15.00

Includes Peter Gabriel; reissue of soundtrack of "All This and World War II"

Sound of Hollywood, The	Mystic MLP 33124	1983	3.75	7.50	15.00

Includes Bad Religion, a lot more

Sound of Hollywood, The	Mystic MLP 33128	198?	3.75	7.50	15.00

Includes Black Flag, Government Issue, more

Sound Waves	K-Tel TU 2690	1980	2.50	5.00	10.00

Includes Prince

Soundtrack Smashes	MCA 6435	1990	2.50	5.00	10.00

Includes Oingo Boingo

Squares Blot Out the Sun	DB 72	1990	2.50	5.00	10.00

Includes Swimming Pool Q's, Pylon, The Brains

Start Swimming	Stiff SINK 1	1981	5.00	10.00	20.00

Includes live tracks by the dB's, Fleshtones, and other similar acts

Start the Party Vol. 1	(2) Big Beat/Atlantic 92425	1994	3.75	7.50	15.00

Includes Simply Red

Stay Awake	A&M SP 3918	1988	3.00	6.00	12.00

Includes Bonnie Raitt and Was (Not Was); Natalie Merchant, Michael Stipe, Mark Bingham and The Roches; Sinead O'Connor; Buster Poindexter; The Replacements, etc.

Stay Awake	A&M R 100600	1988	3.75	7.50	15.00

Same as A&M SP-3918; BMG Direct Marketing edition

Title	Label, Number	Year	VG	VG+	NM
Stiffs Live	Stiff/Arista STF-0001	1978	2.50	5.00	10.00

Includes Elvis Costello, Ian Dury and the Blockheads, Nick Lowe, Wreckless Eric

Title	Label, Number	Year	VG	VG+	NM
Street Beat	(2) Sugar Hill 9228	1984	6.25	12.50	25.00

Includes Sugar Hill Gang, Grandmaster Flash and Melle Mel, other early rap acts

Title	Label, Number	Year	VG	VG+	NM
Sub Pop 100	Sub Pop 10	1986	12.50	25.00	50.00
Sub Pop 200	(3) EP Sub Pop 25	1988	12.50	25.00	50.00

White vinyl; includes Nirvana, Soundgarden, Mudhoney, many others

Title	Label, Number	Year	VG	VG+	NM
Summer Coolers	DJ EMI America SPRO 9448/9	1985	2.50	5.00	10.00

Includes Limahl, Red Hot Chili Peppers

Title	Label, Number	Year	VG	VG+	NM
Summer's Best Music (In-Store Sampler)	DJ Columbia CAS 2089	1985	2.50	5.00	10.00

Includes Hooters, Alison Moyet, Cock Robin

Title	Label, Number	Year	VG	VG+	NM
Superstar In-Store Sampler	DJ Epic EAS 2495	1986	3.75	7.50	15.00

Includes Joan Jett and the Blackhearts, 'Til Tuesday, Cyndi Lauper

Title	Label, Number	Year	VG	VG+	NM
Survival Sampler	DJ Warner Bros. PRO-A-2161	1984	2.00	4.00	8.00

Includes The Church, Scritti Politti

Title	Label, Number	Year	VG	VG+	NM
Tame Yourself	Rhino 90082	1991	6.25	12.50	25.00

Includes Howard Jones, Jane Wiedlin, Erasure, Nina Hagen and Lena Lovich, etc.

Title	Label, Number	Year	VG	VG+	NM
Taste of MCA, A	DJ MCA L33-1803	1979	3.75	7.50	15.00

Includes Joe Ely

Title	Label, Number	Year	VG	VG+	NM
Taste Test #1 -- Live from Brain Cookies	(2) New Alliance 045	1990	6.25	12.50	25.00

Includes fIREHOSE, Screaming Trees and many others

Title	Label, Number	Year	VG	VG+	NM
That's the Way I Feel Now	(2) A&M SP 6600	1984	3.75	7.50	15.00

Includes Joe Jackson

Title	Label, Number	Year	VG	VG+	NM
This Is Fort Apache	MCA 11179	1995	3.00	6.00	12.00

Includes Belly, The Lemonheads, Throwing Muses, Radiohead, Juliana Hatfield

Title	Label, Number	Year	VG	VG+	NM
This Is Your Country	Realm 1P 8126	1992	3.00	6.00	12.00

Includes Mary Chapin Carpenter; only available on vinyl through Columbia House

Title	Label, Number	Year	VG	VG+	NM
Town South of Bakersfield, A	Enigma 72059-1	1985	3.00	6.00	12.00

Includes Dwight Yoakam

Title	Label, Number	Year	VG	VG+	NM
Troublemakers	(2) DJ Warner Bros. PRO-A-857	1978	5.00	10.00	20.00

Includes Sex Pistols, John Cale, Devo, The Modern Lovers, etc.

Title	Label, Number	Year	VG	VG+	NM
Two Rooms: Celebrating the Songs of Elton John & Bernie Taupin	(2) Polydor P1-47570	1990	6.25	12.50	25.00

Includes Kate Bush, George Michael, Sinead O'Connor, Sting; U.S. vinyl available only through Columbia House

Title	Label, Number	Year	VG	VG+	NM
Unscene, The	Big Green Laugh (no #)	1985	3.75	7.50	15.00

Includes an early Faith No More track

Title	Label, Number	Year	VG	VG+	NM
Up Another Octave Transmission, The	Up Another Octave (no #)	1981	6.25	12.50	25.00

Includes early Berlin

Title	Label, Number	Year	VG	VG+	NM
Urban Exposure	K-Tel NU 1990	1986	3.00	6.00	12.00

Includes Run-D.M.C.

Title	Label, Number	Year	VG	VG+	NM
Very Special Christmas, A	A&M SP 3911	1987	3.75	7.50	15.00

Includes U2, Eurythmics, The Pretenders, Alison Moyet, Sting, Madonna, Run-D.M.C.

Title	Label, Number	Year	VG	VG+	NM
View from Here, The	Medical MR 2707	1987	2.50	5.00	10.00

Includes Camper Van Beethoven

Title	Label, Number	Year	VG	VG+	NM
Wanna Buy a Bridge?	Rough Trade ROUGH US 3	1980	4.50	9.00	18.00

Same as above; green cover

Title	Label, Number	Year	VG	VG+	NM
Wanna Buy a Bridge?	Rough Trade ROUGH US 3	1980	4.50	9.00	18.00

Includes Scritti Politti, The Slits, Cabaret Voltaire, Stiff Little Fingers, many others; blue cover

Title	Label, Number	Year	VG	VG+	NM
Warner Bros. 20th Anniversary LP	DJ Warner Bros. PRO 775	1979	3.00	6.00	12.00

Includes Neil Young

Title	Label, Number	Year	VG	VG+	NM
Water Music Compilation Album, The	Water Music WMR 88121	1988	2.50	5.00	10.00

Includes the dB's, others

Title	Label, Number	Year	VG	VG+	NM
Waves	Bomp! 4003	1979	6.25	12.50	25.00

Includes The Romantics; originals on blue vinyl

Title	Label, Number	Year	VG	VG+	NM
We Killed McKinley	Maxwell MXC 3630	1988	2.50	5.00	10.00
Includes an early Goo Goo Dolls track					
We've Got Your Music					
(2) DJ Atlantic PR 273		1977	3.75	7.50	15.00
Includes Peter Gabriel					
Where the Action Is Bomp!	DJ Bomp! 3001	1980	3.75	7.50	15.00
Includes Romantics, Stiv Bators, Weirdos, others					
Why Study?	DJ Columbia AS 1765	1983	3.00	6.00	12.00
Includes Elvis Costello, Wham! U.K., Midnight Oil; comes in plain black sleeve					
Winter Warnerland (2) DJ	Warner Bros. PRO-A-3328	1988	10.00	20.00	40.00
Includes R.E.M., Los Lobos, Lou Reed, Throwing Muses, Honeymoon Suite, Julie Brown, Pee-wee Herman, etc.; one record red vinyl, the other green					
Wish It Were September DJ	Columbia CAS 2087	1985	3.00	6.00	12.00
Includes Fishbone, The Boomtown Rats, Nina Hagen					
WMMR Breakout	WMMR 93.3	1979	3.00	6.00	12.00
Compilation of unsigned Philadelphia bands; Includes Cats, Hot Property (with three members who became 3/5 of the original Hooters)					
Working Class Hero --	DJ Hollywood ED-62015-1	1995	3.75	7.50	15.00
A Tribute to John Lennon					
Promo only on white vinyl; includes Red Hot Chili Peppers, Candlebox, Blues Traveler, Screaming Trees, The Flaming Lips, Collective Soul, Toad The Wet Sprocket, Mary Chapin Carpenter, etc.					
Works, The (2) DJ	Warner Bros. PRO 610	1975	4.50	9.00	18.00
Includes Frank Zappa					
WRCA Plays the Hits for DJ	RCA DJL1-1785	1976	5.00	10.00	20.00
Your Customers					
Includes David Bowie					
Year of the Ear	DJ Elektra/Asylum 277	1977	3.00	6.00	12.00
Includes Television					
Yes L.A.	PD Dangerhouse EW 79	1979	20.00	40.00	80.00
Includes X, The Germs, etc.; one-sided clear picture disc					
You Can't Resist It	DJ MCA L33-1005	1986	3.00	6.00	12.00
Includes Steve Earle, Lyle Lovett					
You'll Hate This Record	The Only Label LP 001	1983	4.50	9.00	18.00
Record, The					
Includes GG Allin, etc.					
Yulesville (2) DJ	Warner Bros. PRO-A-2896	1988	6.25	12.50	25.00
Includes Madonna, The Ramones; red vinyl, promo-only					
Zig Zag Festival	DJ Mercury SRD-2-29	1970	6.25	12.50	25.00
Includes David Bowie					
Zoo's Next -- WMMR	Comedy Spotlight (no #)	1986	5.00	10.00	20.00
Morning Zoo					
Includes Beat Farmers (and other goofy music)					